ANDREW JOHNSON

Courtesy of D. Appleton & Co.

ANDREW JOHNSON

PLEBEIAN AND PATRIOT

BY

ROBERT W. WINSTON

BARNES & NOBLE, Inc.
NEW YORK
PUBLISHERS & BOOKSELLERS SINCE 1873

Printed in the United States of America

PREFATORY NOTE

First of all I wish to acknowledge my obligation to Andrew Johnson Patterson, grandson of Andrew Johnson. Mr. Patterson has given me free access to President Johnson's old home and to his heirlooms, entrusting me with scrap books, newspaper files, letters and other material. During the years 1926 and 1927 I visited Tennessee, where many of the older people remembered their former countryman. From them I gathered numerous anecdotes and other incidents. But for the atmosphere of Johnson's home and of glorious East Tennessee I could not, I am sure, have discovered the real flesh and blood Andrew Johnson. The Congressional Library, especially the manuscript and newspaper rooms, and the libraries of the University of North Carolina, of Duke University, and of Williams College, have been generous in the use of material. The North Carolina Historical Society, the Tennessee Historical Society, and the Carnegie Library at Nashville have likewise furnished me with newspaper files and records shedding additional light on Johnson. With this and other material in hand, I have been enabled to follow the tailor-President from birth to death,—a task, I may add, not heretofore undertaken. Citations in the footnotes are generally abbreviated after the first reference; the bibliography supplements the notes, giving dates and places of publication and authors' names. In the notes I refer both to Johnson Mss. and to Johnson Mss. at Greeneville; in the former case, the manuscripts are in the Congressional Library.

ROBERT W. WINSTON.

Williamstown, Mass.
February 12, 1928.

CONTENTS

PART I: ODDS
1808-1860

PART II: ALONE
1860-1865

PART III: UNBOWED
1865 and After

CONTENTS

ILLUSTRATIONS

INTRODUCTION

I would not venture to say when I first became interested in Andrew Johnson, but it must have been as early as 1865, when I was a mere child. A thousand times I have passed Casso's Inn and the little cabin in the rear, where "Andy" was born. When a barefoot boy I waded in the old swimming holes around Raleigh, where Andy and his brother Bill and Selby's other "bound" boys, fifty years before, had dived and ducked each other. I tramped the same woods and caught suckers and goggle-eyed perch from the same streams. Well do I remember a famous watch and chain President Johnson presented my elder brother, valedictorian of his class, spouting an oration on the Constitution and the Union in June 1867, when thousands crowded the University campus, at Chapel Hill, to get a look at the tailor-President.

I can hear Andrew Johnson's rich mellow voice, as he tells the students of his cramped childhood and of a long journey afoot in 1826, when he was making his way through the village and out to his future home, in far-away Tennessee. Nor shall I forget the crowds that gathered in Raleigh to meet the President, once an orphan boy apprenticed to Selby the tailor; or the solemn words he spoke and the ludicrous turn an old woman in the crowd, who had known Andy in his tailor-shop days, gave one of the President's figures of speech. "I have no other ambition in life," President Johnson declared, "but to mend and repair the *breaches* in the torn and tattered Constitution of my country." "Bless his dear heart," said the old lady, "Andy's going to come back home and open up his tailor shop again."

I also remember the thousand and one lies people were telling on him, not maliciously, I think, but—well, it seems to be permissible to manufacture stories about those in high place. His birth and origin puzzled the wiseacres. Surely old Jacob

xi

Johnson's son, the stocky little black-haired, black-eyed Andy, who used to be Selby's "bound boy," could not have risen, step by step, to the Presidency. Some other than Jacob must have been the boy's daddy. Was it Chief Justice Ruffin or was it Banker Haywood? It must have been Haywood, for as Andrew Johnson, the President, and Dallas Haywood, the Mayor, sat side by side that June day, was there ever a more striking likeness? They were "the very spit and image" of each other!

These were childish fancies and memories. In later years, however, I became interested in Andrew Johnson for deeper reasons, and went out to Tennessee to study him at first hand. In Greeneville I loved to wander down to the far end of the town to the Johnson residence, to drink from the Gum spring, in the garden, and to stroll up Water Street and by the old ruined mill, with its overshot wheel; to the A. Johnson tailor-shop and there to take in my hands the very thimble and shears and goose with which Johnson earned a livelihood up to the day he became a Congressman. There, too, I saw his coat and vest, made with his own hands, blue and starchy, just the same Clay and Calhoun and Benton used to wear. James Park, son of Johnson's abolition and Union friend, and Dick Self, son of Squire Lewis Self, Andy Johnson's old foreman, pointed out Depot Street where in days of Civil War a Confederate banner was stretched branding Andrew Johnson as a traitor, and where a few years later another streamer hailed him as the patriot, and bade him welcome home.

Under the shaded and leafy scuppernong vine, away back in the garden of Dr. Alex Williams, I crept and there I stood on the spot where Morgan, the noted Confederate raider, was shot. Shot dead by the Andrew Johnson Guards. I climbed the Daniel Boone trail also, and from the top of Pinnacle, near the Cumberland Gap, looked over the valley of the Watauga and the Nolichucky, over Greeneville and the Dan Stover place miles away, so dear to Andrew Johnson, until I could hear the patriotic man, in the dark months of 1861 and 1862, though a fugitive from home and hunted like a beast through the fast-nesses of the mountains, "exhorting the Tennessee Unionists to die on the mountain top and make the everlasting hills their sole monument rather than give up those lovely valleys to the unresisted march of armed bands of traitors." [1]

Surely, I thought, the human side of Andrew Johnson should be brought to light, the events of his checkered career should be collected, sifted and analyzed. No doubt Johnson's bulldog courage, and the malignity with which he had been pursued, urged me to undertake the job of writing his life. Anyway, I set about the task. In the Congressional library, where I first went, I found nothing about him collected or grouped, there being little substantial or permanent to collect or arrange. The card index pointed to seven biographies, five of these thrown together in 1866 to catch the popular breeze, setting Johnson's way, and Jones's *Life*, a local compilation, published more than twenty-five years ago. In magazines and newspaper files I found an abundance of material, though fugitive and generally on questionable authority, and apparently scribbled to deepen unfavorable impressions. And yet from these hostile sources one could see that Andrew Johnson was not altogether bad. I then began a study of the Johnson manuscripts, purchased by Congress and made available about 1910, and of Welles's *Diary* published in 1911, unavailable, I will add, to the fair-minded historian, James Ford Rhodes, when he wrote the history of Johnson's administration. Unless I am greatly mistaken, these publications, and an analysis of them by modern writers, are beginning to shed a new light on Andrew Johnson.

Undoubtedly the recent decision of the Supreme Court that Johnson was right and Congress dead wrong, in the matters in controversy between them on which the Impeachment was founded, is making the fair-minded public prick up their ears and ask, "What sort of a fellow did President Lincoln pick as a running mate anyhow; was he what Lincoln said he was, a man 'to whom the country owes a debt of gratitude it can never repay;' [2] or was he merely 'that drunken tailor at the other end of the avenue,' as old Thad Stevens sized him up?"

The story of Andrew Johnson's life is difficult of approach.

---

[1] Bacon's *Life of Johnson*, Chap. I.
[2] *Life and Services of Andrew Johnson*, p. 209.

The approach, however, is of importance. Unless Johnson's motives are understood one is sure to miss the man. In approaching the subject it must be borne in mind that Johnson lived in a rough, uncouth time. A century ago, democracy being new and untried, philosophers had a way of reminding us that "the genius of America is not in executives or legislatures, not in colleges or churches or parlors, but in the common people." In that early day our public men were on their knees to the masses—Webster, our greatest orator and justly known as "the divine Daniel," publicly lamenting he had not been born in a log cabin. And yet is not all this the merest bunk? In this land of the free are not class distinctions as sharply drawn as elsewhere? Is it not recorded that Jefferson, the apostle of American democracy, lived so elegantly at Monticello that Patrick Henry, the stern old Virginia patriot, refused to vote for him. "Why, the fellow eats French victuals," he protested. And even "Old Hickory" Jackson kept up an establishment at the Hermitage in regal style.

Now Jefferson and Jackson are great men, of a quite different order from Johnson, and yet I cannot but feel that this obstinate, narrow-minded defender of lost causes must be regarded as the only President who practiced what he preached, drawing no distinction between rich and poor, or high and low. No doubt Johnson's combativeness, and a certain plebeian appeal, have blinded us to the fact that he was sincere and not merely acting a part. It seems ironical that the most democratic of presidents should have happened to be a man who had these weaknesses, one who was so tactless that he often threw obstacles in his own way and ran against snags that might have been avoided. These handicaps rendered Johnson an easy mark for ridicule, and to-day, more than half a century after his death, it is charged, and no doubt generally believed, that he was "a dirty, drunken fellow with squinting, blinking eyes and a coarse, thick voice;" that he had "the manners of a demagogue" and "entertained decided objections to gentlemen." [3]

[3] The phrase "decided objections to gentlemen" may illustrate the tendency to belittle Johnson; Oberholtzer quotes it from Moore's *Life*, but quotes only

When I first began a study of Johnson I cherished the hope that the charges of boorishness and uncouthness were true, that he was what Carlyle calls a savage Baresark. Such a character would fit in well with the tough, impossible job he tackled. But I was doomed to disappointment. The charge was untrue. Johnson's private secretary assures us he wore well-fitting boots, a broadcloth coat, silk vest, stock cravat and a tall hat. Alas, he also indulged in a daily bath. But there was a graver charge against him. He was an ambitious, cheap-john politician, and his acts were based on a general falsity of life. This theory of his falsity is one that has been incredible to me. For myself I cannot understand how one may act a part while he devotes his life to a great cause; or how he may be "a prince of lies and no lies spoken by him."

Some day the psychologist may delve into Johnson's childhood and there find what has puzzled the historian and biographer. No doubt it will be discovered that Johnson's neglected and impoverished infancy developed a complex, perhaps an under-dog and a plebeian complex. Would this not explain Henry Watterson's remark that poverty in rags always appealed to Andrew Johnson? Explain also why he was everlastingly telling the world he was a plebeian, and humble born, and that hunger, gaunt and haggard monster, had driven him from his native state; why, even after he was President, he could hardly pass a tailor shop without going in and exchanging compliments with the knights of the goose and needle? This complex, call it "under-dog" or what one likes, appears again and again in Johnson's life. Therefore I might explain more fully that his childhood was, in fact, as rasping as Oliver Twist's. After being left an orphan of three years, he was bound to a tailor. He then ran away, married at nineteen, and was taught to read and write by his wife. Until thirty-five years of age he was bending over the tailor's bench for a livelihood. And yet, during this cramped and scant period, his indomitable will was not broken for an instant.

a part of the sentence. What the biographer Moore wrote was, Johnson "had decided objections to gentlemen reared in affluence and idleness, arrogating to themselves the right to all knowledge in the world."

Do not these facts furnish an explanation of Johnson's life? Do they not show why he had the courage to go up against caste and cheap aristocracy, why he dared to stand for the under-dog, whether Catholic, Hebrew, foreigner, mechanic, or child; and to cling like death to the old flag and the Union? In a word do they not explain Johnson's apparent egotism, his obstinacy and his bull-headedness? He was but expressing himself, he was under an impulse to fight. He had been oppressed, he had had no free school, the wolf had been at his door, on him the laws had borne hard, because of class distinctions and unequal laws. Hence he lunged at these monsters, vainly seeking to build up an ideal Democracy where "there would be a rich people and a poor government," equal laws, and no class distinctions. This impulse also drove him out of the slave autocracy and into a country of free land and free men. "In the secession movement he saw only an agency that would widen the interval between the laborer and the employer, and reduce non slave-holding whites to the level of the African slave." [4]

On the whole, therefore, I must conclude that Andrew Johnson has not had a fair deal, that his life, though angular and old-fashioned, was honest and a real contribution to our civilization. Though he was often rough and unconventional, it must be remembered he had a rough job. He was a leader of the labor forces, but he was not a socialist or a destructionist. Thrice daily, with Eastern devotion, he bowed to the Constitution, to the laws, and to the three departments of government, but to a fourth department he rendered a peculiar homage— to him the people were above Presidents, Congresses, or Courts.

R. W. W.

[4] Bacon's *Life of Johnson*, Chap. I.

PART I: ODDS
1808-1860

CHAPTER I

RUNAWAY APPRENTICE

At the beginning of the last century, there stood in the town of Raleigh, North Carolina, a spacious, ramshackled building called Casso's Inn. Within the hotel yard a small cottage for the use of employees of the establishment had been provided, and there, on December 29, 1808, Andrew, second son of Jacob Johnson and Mary McDonough his wife, was born.[1]

This inn was a noted place in its day. Located on two highways, one running north and south and the other east and west, and just across the street from the State House, it boasted of "a stable equal to any on the continent, sufficient to contain from thirty to forty head of horses," and of a bar unexcelled for its brands of foreign and domestic liquors. During festive occasions the townspeople would come together at Casso's and celebrate with round dances and the cotillion, with bountiful feasts, and with the ever-flowing bowl. And Peter Casso, the landlord, was well fitted for the position of host. Having been a soldier in the Revolutionary War, he was a man of the world; his wife was received into the best circles, and their daughter, "pretty Peggy," as Colonel William Polk once named her in a gracious toast, was a general favorite. But the popularity of the inn was not more due to the Casso family than to their porter, Jacob Johnson, and to "Polly," his faithful wife.[2]

Now the occasion of Andy Johnson's birth is well remembered. That particular night, it being Christmas week, with seven days of frolic and merrymaking, a ball was going on at the inn. Soon after the ball, it became known that a son had

[1] R. H. Battle, *Library Southern Literature*, Vol. VI, p. 2719.
[2] David L. Swain, *Early Times in Raleigh*, 1867; *Memorial Address on Jacob Johnson*, by the same.

been born to the Johnson family, and pretty Peggy tripped
down to the cottage to lend a hand. "What are you going to
name the boy?" she asked. Mrs. Johnson invited suggestions.
"Andrew Jackson Johnson," was the reply. And so, with the
middle name omitted for the sake of brevity, Andrew Johnson
set out on his earthly pilgrimage.[3]

The community into which this young chap was thus un-
ceremoniously ushered was typically southern. Though the
little town, of less than a thousand souls, could not claim to be
as aristocratic as Richmond and Charleston, it was not without
a slave-holding aristocracy.[4] During the hunting season, Governor Turner, Treasurer Haywood, General Beverly Daniel
and other notables, "mounted on well-bred horses, accoutered
with shot-pouch and horn and followed by a pack of yelping
hounds, could be seen driving the deer or chasing the fox."
Evening teas at the homes of the Devereaux, the Mordecais,
Hoggs, Hills, Camerons, and Polks were presided over by Mrs.
Gales, mother of the editor of the *National Intelligencer*, and
"other intellectual ladies, who graciously mingled with the
young and the beautiful of the village." Fishing parties on
Crab Tree Creek were frequent, "winding up with a dance at
the paper mills"; and, on the first of May, "beautiful ceremonies honored the Queen" of that historic day.

Jacob Johnson's relationship to the aristocratic people of
Raleigh was a peculiar one. Socially, he had no recognition
at all—he was simply "a poor white." Yet in the position of
a dependent, with the requisites of "vigor, docility and fidelity," he was the best-loved person in town. Belonging to that
class which Hammond, the scholarly Senator from South Carolina, dubbed the "mud-sills of society and political government," he could not, without great effort, have risen in the
social or political scale; but he did not wish to rise; the likeable
fellow craved no more than he had. His cottage, situated on
Main Street only a few steps from the Capitol, was in the
heart of things, and there was work a plenty, menial though

---

[3] President K. P. Battle, *Centennial Address*, "Early History of Raleigh."
Johnson's relatives think he was named for his mother's brother, but Dr.
Battle gives the account in the text.

[4] S. A. Ashe, *Biographical History of North Carolina*, Vol. IV, pp. 228-241.

it might be.[5] "Mud-sills," the Johnsons were born, and mud-sills they died. As their son in after-days rather proudly declared, they belonged to that class called "plebeians." In fact, so little impression did Jacob and his wife make on the community, no one has taken the pains to remember or record the parentage of either. Their pedigree, lost in obscurity as Mr. Lincoln said of his, was short and sweet like the annals of the poor. This much however is known of Jacob Johnson, no man in the community "bore a more blameless character," and no woman was more deserving of respect than Mary McDonough, his Scotch wife.

And it would be a mistake to conclude that Jacob Johnson was a person of no consequence. In the cardinal virtues, such as honesty and bravery, no one stood higher than Jacob. When Colonel Polk, cousin of President James K. Polk, opened the first state bank at Raleigh he appointed Jacob Johnson its porter. At one time he was captain of Muster Division No. 20 of the Town of Raleigh, with sundry citizen-soldiers under him. Occasionally he filled the position of sexton to the Presbyterian Church and had the privilege of ringing the only bell in town. As this bell hung at Casso's corner, the inn had a great advantage over the rival hotel called the Eagle which had no such distinguishing appurtenance.[6]

Standing under the spreading oaks which give the name of "The City of Oaks" to Raleigh, Jacob Johnson would pull away at the bell-rope, ringing for weddings, for fires or for funerals. And Jacob had other accomplishments; he was an excellent caterer, and could barbecue and baste the young pig to a nicety; he was also a huntsman, a fisherman, and an all-round good fellow. In a word, no man of his class was more esteemed than Jacob Johnson. Mrs. Polly Johnson, too, was indispensable, not only serving Mrs. Casso but being her friend. Such Fourth of July dinners they spread—roasting ears, Brunswick stew, barbecued pig, and hard cider, while the noisy

[5] W. H. Wheeler, *Reminiscences*, p. 435. The cottage is now located in Raleigh's public park; it then stood about 200 feet north of the present Masonic Temple.
[6] Governor Swain, *Address*.

patriots, crowding the four-acre square across the street, drank "as many standing toasts as there were states in the Union."

In the midst of rich and powerful friends one might think Jacob would have accumulated property, but he did not. The acquisitive instinct he did not possess. Though Dr. William G. Hill, the town physician, Colonel Thomas Henderson, editor of the Raleigh *Star*, Colonel William Polk, and other influential men were his friends, nothing came of their friendship. At birth as at death, poverty was Jacob's portion, and how could it have been otherwise? In the southern life of that day, based on pedigree and slavery and looking down on manual labor, it must be said there was no influential middle class. A race had been developed unsurpassed for elegance of manner, for bravery, for loyalty, and for other attributes of manhood, but of a substantial yeomanry there was none—from master to slave there was no half-way ground. The caste system forbade it.

With these conditions Jacob Johnson and his wife were not dissatisfied. One looks in vain for traces of that galling of the spirit, which marked their second-born son. Since there was no work Jacob Johnson could engage in but menial labor, he cheerfully went about his daily task. Uneducated and without family connections, he could not, had he desired, have entered a learned profession. Poor, he could not purchase a farm or operate a mercantile business. Raleigh being a rural village, without factories or other industries, and the uplands of that section well-nigh exhausted by unscientific agriculture, opportunities for making a living were few and far between.

As Jacob's patrons and friends were the owners of rich river bottoms on the Cape Fear, the Neuse, the Roanoke and the Tar, he might have been an overseer and lived on one of these plantations; but a life in town he preferred to a life in the country. His genial, social disposition craved the companionship of the city, where the legislature met, State and United States courts sat, where there were occasional circuses and minstrel shows, and where Peter Casso's fine bar was in easy reach. Not that he drank to excess, for he did not; Colonel Polk, his employer, would not have stood for that. But country life to such a happy-go-lucky fellow would have been simply unbearable. The days of "come-easy go-easy" were soon to end. Fate had something sterner in store than barbecues and fish-frys for the little family.

One December day in 1811, a merry party had gathered at Hunter's Mill, on Walnut Creek, a few miles from town. In the midst of the revelry, no doubt dancing, cock-fighting, gander-pulling, and general carousal, Colonel Tom Henderson and two other hilarious individuals pushed off from the shore in a canoe and were soon amid stream and in ten-foot water. One of the number rocked the boat and over it turned. There were loud cries for help. The Colonel and one of the men, who could not swim, were sinking beneath the waves for the third and last time, when, rushing to the gunwale, and "heedless of his own life," Jacob Johnson sprang into the icy stream. Diving and struggling, he succeeded, "with great effort," in fishing up his friend the Colonel, to whose coat the other drowning man was clinging. In a word, he saved the lives of two human beings, but lost his own. Exposure and exhaustion proved too much for him. Shortly afterwards Jacob Johnson, father of the seventeenth President of the United States, died a martyr and a hero.

The Raleigh *Star* of January 12, 1912, announcing his death, called attention to his useful life, to his "honesty, sobriety, industry and humane friendly disposition." "No one laments his death more than the editor of this paper," Colonel Henderson wrote; "for he owes his life to the boldness and humanity of Johnson." Fifty years after this heroic act a monument was erected to the memory of Jacob Johnson, as a testimonial of his courage and self-sacrifice and as the appreciation of a grateful community. On this tablet one may read:

"In memory of Jacob Johnson. An honest man, loved and respected by all who knew him."

Little Andy was now three years old, and William, his older brother, afterwards turning out to be a ne'er-do-well, was eight. The mother left penniless, with two small children dependent upon her, was almost an object of charity. But with brave heart she secured a hand-loom and set up the business of weaving and spinning cloth. By industry and enterprise, she soon acquired such a reputation she was known as "Polly, the Weaver." The burden of supporting the family was too heavy for her, however, and on August 14, 1814, she disposed of Bill by apprenticing him to Colonel Thomas Henderson, her husband's friend. About this time, Mrs. Johnson entered upon a second matrimonial venture. This second husband, a fellow named Turner Dougherty, was more impecunious, if possible, than herself and bad matters were made worse.

In a year or so, Colonel Henderson died and Bill's apprenticeship came to an end. He was then bound to J. J. Selby, the town tailor. Andy had grown to be fourteen years old at that time and he too was apprenticed to the same tailor. By the terms of the indenture, the boys were to serve Selby till they arrived at age. The master bound himself to furnish them with victuals and clothes and "to instruct them in the trade of a tailor." At this point historians have gone somewhat astray as to a certain date; they assert that Andy was ten years old when he became a "bound-boy," whereas, he was fourteen years of age. As witness the following record:

State of North Carolina ⎱
Wake County ⎰

At a court of Pleas and Quarterly Sessions begun and held at the Court House in Raleigh on the 3rd Monday of February, 1822 being the forty-sixth year of American Independence (and the 18th day of February).

The Worshipful ⎫ CHARLES L. HINTON
Present   ⎬ NATHANIEL RAND
      ⎭ MERRITT DILLARD

Ordered that A. Johnson, an orphan boy and the son of Jacob Johnson, deceased, 14 years of age, be bound to Jas. J. Selby till he arrive at lawful age to learn the trade of a Tailor.

Andy, only three years old when his father died, could have remembered little or nothing of him or of his cordial intercourse with the men who ran the town. But as the child grew and looked about and saw other children at play or at school, living in comfortable homes with gardens of roses, honeysuckle, and bamboo, or watched the well-to-do people as they rode here and there "in coaches drawn by dapple grays" and driven by negro coachmen, while he, a bound-boy, was penned indoors or after the day's grind trudged afoot, could he do less than contrast his lot with theirs? Who, indeed, can say how much those days at Selby's shop, and before, fixed the child's mind, making him resentful of any reflection on the laboring man, and the champion of his rights.

However this may be, at Selby's the sturdy chap never flinched or repined. Among the lads of the town he "always led the crowd." "Somehow or other Andy would have things his own way." "If he said 'go a-hunting,' the boys went hunting; if he said 'let's go swimming,' they went swimming." A small piercing black eye, a will to do or die, a spirit that never quailed—these set the lad above his surroundings.[7] And he was always courteous and attentive to business. When a rich patron on horseback would come to the shop Andy would run out and hold his mount, graciously accepting the tip and listening to many a word of cheer and advice.

At this time the foreman of the tailor shop was an educated man named Litchford, who took a fancy to the chap. As Litchford describes Andy, he was "a wild, harum-scarum boy with no unhonorable traits, however."[8] On holidays, or during summer afternoons, the apprentice boy, with his playmates, would roam the forests, climb the trees for bird nests, go seining in the creeks, and often return home with clothing dripping wet or torn to shreds. The exasperated Mrs. Selby scolded in vain; finally she made a coarse, heavy, homespun shirt, and, stripping Andy to the skin, clothed him in this nontearable "whole undergarment."

It was Mr. Litchford and Dr. Hill who taught the boy his A B C's. As there was no public school in Raleigh at that time, and his mother could not read or write, the only education the lad received was at the hands of these two men, who occasionally would drop into Selby's tailor shop and instruct him, or, while he was plying his needle and shoving his hot goose, read

[7] John Savage, *Life of Johnson*, Chap. I.
[8] *Ibid.*

from Enfield's *Speaker*, or from the newspapers of the day.[9]
Once Dr. Hill read a paragraph ˙from an essay on elocu-
tion. This essay gives the rules for successful oratory. First
and most important one must speak slowly. "Almost all persons who have not studied the art of speaking," so the book
runs, "have a habit of uttering their words so rapidly that the
exercise of reading aloud, slowly and deliberately, ought to be
made use of for a considerable time. Aim at nothing higher,
till you can read distinctly and deliberately.

> " 'Learn to speak slow, all other graces
> Will follow in their proper places.' " [10]

By following these directions—speaking slowly and deliberately—Andrew Johnson's voice was well trained; it would
"carry further than a city block." As an encouragement to
the little fellow and a reward for his desire to educate himself, Dr. Hill presented him with the collection of speeches and
essays. Unfortunately, when Johnson's home at Greeneville,
Tennessee, was seized by the Confederate Government, the little
keep-sake, dog-eared and well-worn, was destroyed.[11]

And so the days of Andy Johnson's apprenticeship grew into
weeks, the weeks into months. Many hours a day, shut out
from fresh air, crouched down over needle and thread, deprived
of the joys of childhood, the lad bent to his task; the inside
of a schoolhouse he never saw. Finally, after two years of apprenticeship, an incident happened that changed the course
of his life—he ran away from his master. One account of this
event is that Selby insulted the lad "and was soundly
thrashed"; but Litchford gives another account. At that time
in Raleigh there was living an old woman named Wells, and
Andy Johnson and three other bound-boys "rocked" this old
lady's house,—precisely why is not recorded. Any way, she
threatened to "persecute" the boys and off they skipped.

---

[9] Jacob Johnson, not being able to write, made his cross mark to the bond
he was required to give at marriage.

[10] This book is referred to as the *United States Speaker;* the *Standard
Speaker;* the *Columbia Speaker.* I have chosen *Enfield's Speaker* because
copies of it are at the University of North Carolina, near Johnson's native
place. Cf. *Harper's Young People,* September 30, 1890.

[11] Savage, p. 22.

However this may be, on June 24, 1824, the citizens of Raleigh read in the Raleigh *Gazette* the following notice:

TEN DOLLARS REWARD

Ran away from the Subscriber, on the night of the 15th instant, two apprentice boys, legally bound, named WILLIAM and ANDREW JOHNSON. The former is of a dark complexion, black hair, eyes, and habits. They are much of a height, about 5 feet 4 or 5 inches. The latter is very fleshy, freckled face, light hair, and fair complexion. They went off with two other apprentices, advertised by Messrs. Wm. & Chas. Fowler. When they went away, they were well clad—blue cloth coats, light colored homespun coats, and new hats, the maker's name in the crown of the hats, is Theodore Clark. I will pay the above Reward to any person who will deliver said apprentices to me in Raleigh, or I will give the above Reward for Andrew Johnson alone.

All persons are cautioned against harboring or employing said apprentices on pain of being prosecuted.

JAMES J. SELBY, *Tailor.*

Raleigh, N. C. June 24, 1824.

Now Selby was in such a dudgeon when he wrote this notice he described Bill for Andy and Andy for Bill, Andy having the black hair and black eyes and Bill the light hair and freckled face. At all events the reward brought no tangible results.

After a flight of several days, the run-aways hauled up at the town of Carthage, about seventy-five miles from Raleigh; and there they made a halt and remained several months. Renting a shack, Andy opened a tailor shop of his own and advertised for business. Business came pouring in. Specimens of Andy's handicraft are still preserved in that section, and a monument commemorates the occasion of his residence in Carthage.

But Carthage was too near Raleigh. Memories of Selby still haunting Andy, he took to his heels again, arriving at Laurens, South Carolina, sometime during the winter of 1824. At Laurens the usual love affair of a youngster of sixteen took place. Andy fell in love with a "beautiful" young woman named Sarah Word, by whom the tender passion was reciprocated. Unhappily for the course of true love, the parents

objected.   A boy with no equipment but a kit of tailor's tools
was surely no match for a promising South Carolina beauty.
The dutiful maiden, therefore, "sighing like a lover but obeying like a child," broke the affair up and the romance ended.
Andy's connection with this love scrape and his failure to
press his suit and marry Sarah, over the heads of her parents,
added to the esteem in which he was held by the people of
Laurens.[12]

After a year or so in South Carolina, Andy and his brother
Bill worked their way back to Raleigh.   Andy was determined
to serve out his apprenticeship with Selby.   But Selby had
given up his shop in Raleigh and moved twenty miles away in
the country.   On the boy trudged to make apology and take up
his dog's life again.   Selby wanted security, however.   This
Andy would not give and master and servant parted company
forever.

As Andrew Johnson, penniless and out of a job, walked the
streets of Raleigh or hung around Casso's inn during those dis-
mal days of 1826, the game of life seemed blocked against him.
Though his old friend Litchford had opened a shop of his own,
he was afraid to employ an advertised run-away.   And then
there was Selby—at any moment he might "put the law" to
Andy for jumping his contract of indenture.   In fact, the jails
were full of debtors, who could not pay their debts.   The up-
shot of the business was that Andy resolved to leave North
Carolina and to go west where there were fertile, unappropri-
ated lands, and where he thought the laws were respecters of
persons as well as of property.   Why not Tennessee?   Tennessee had already enticed from North Carolina her ablest sons,
James Robertson, "the father of Tennessee," John Haywood,
her greatest judge, Andrew Jackson, Hugh L. White and
James K. Polk.

The little Johnson family, therefore, put their heads together, resolving that matters might be improved by a move.
They certainly could not be made worse.   One August day
in 1826, dumping their earthly belongings into a two-wheeled
cart, without cover against rain or shine, they set out for

12 Greeneville *Sentinel*, February 10, 1910; *National Magazine* 6:63.

their new home. No covered wagon, no barking, prancing dog, no romance. One hour Turner Dougherty and Polly would ride and the boys would walk; then, turn and turn about, the boys would ride and the old folks walk. "Ride and tie," this arrangement is called by the poorer southern country folk when making a long journey with an over-crowded vehicle. At the end of the first day the little caravan had made nearly thirty miles, hauling up at Chapel Hill, the seat of the University of North Carolina. Here a family named Craig gave them shelter for the night.[13] Leaving Chapel Hill, they moved westward, fording rivers, climbing mountains, camping by the wayside. The Eno, the Haw, the Yadkin, the Catawba, the Swannanoa, the French Broad, the Pigeon, the Nolichucky, and their tributaries, many of these streams without bridges, all lay between them and their journey's end. Following the Daniel Boone trail, they scaled the Blue Ridge where Andrew Jackson crossed half a century before and—tradition says— met "old Hickory" on horseback.[14] Here they camped for the night and Bill and Andy went forth and killed a mountain bear. Next day, they passed down the French Broad River and along the Allen Stand road, until they came into the Nolichucky country.[15]

A wonderful sight now caught their eye. To the west lay the Cumberland Mountains, to the north and east the Blue Ridge, between, a fertile valley. Here their journey ended, and on a certain Saturday evening in September 1826 the weary little band pitched their tent for the last time, camping at the "Gum Spring" in the town of Greeneville, Tennessee. Unharnessing the weary pony, Andy walked up the hillside and got a bundle of fodder while his mother was busy with supper. W. R. Brown, an old resident, let him have the provender, and took such a fancy to the boy that a long friendship began. Next day Andy visited the tailor shop and procured work. In a short time, however, he moved on to Rutledge in the adjoining

[13] Forty years after, President Johnson and Secretary Seward arrived in this village to be invested with academic honors and fêted as befitted their station.

[14] Thompson, *Southern Hero Tales*, p. 66.

[15] Johnson MS. at Greeneville.

county, resolved to possess and run a shop in his own name. At Rutledge, and at other places in Tennessee, he worked at his trade for several months.   But in March 1827, when he heard that the Greeneville tailor had quit business, he rejoined his mother and opened up a shop of his own—the "A. Johnson Tailor Shop," renowned in song and story.

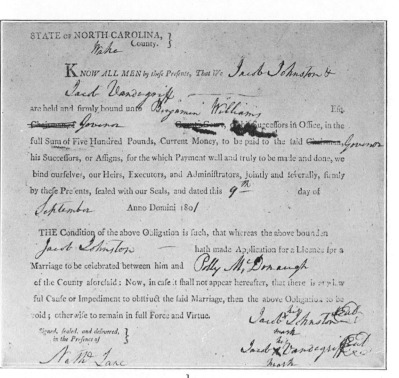

1. Jacob Johns(t)on's Marriage Bond.
2. Andrew Johnson's Birthplace, Raleigh, N. C.

CHAPTER II

A. JOHNSON, TAILOR

When the Johnson family set out from Raleigh they were bound for the Sequatchie Valley, some distance southwest of Greeneville, where a sister of Mrs. Johnson lived. So far as we know, therefore, the selection of Greeneville was a mere accident, the Johnsons not having a friend or an acquaintance in the place. Doubtless, when they struck Greeneville they had exhausted their patience; certainly they had exhausted their funds and could go no farther. Anyway, no better location for a tailor to start business could have been found.

In that early day much of the soil of East Tennessee was untouched by the plowshare, and the population which had drifted in from Free States as well as Slave was more cosmopolitan and better suited to Andrew Johnson's simple notions than that of the more conservative State of North Carolina. There was also another advantage, the people of East Tennessee were less than ten per cent. negro. Slavery did not count for much, nor was manual labor considered beneath one's dignity. In fact, much of the State was still occupied by Indians. In 1826 the East Tennessean owned his farm, generally less than a hundred acres, and raised enough corn, cattle and home supplies for his family's needs. Tobacco was the chief money crop, and the housewife increased the income by the sale of eggs and poultry, butter, fruit, vegetables and honey.[1] Tennessee, being a grass-growing country, sheep and cattle were also raised and horses and mules bred for the market.

Two hundred dollars a year in cash, a Tennessee historian assures us, were enough to supply a mountain family with coffee, sugar and other necessaries not raised on the farm. These thrifty people would not think of going to stores and

[1] Garrett and Goodpasture, *History of Tennessee*, p. 74.

squandering their money on clothing, hats and shoes.   The
shoemaker, or the cobbler as he was politely called, and the
saddler, traveling from section to section, would make shoes
and harness from hides tanned in the local vats, and the tailor
would make clothes from cotton and woolen cloth woven by the
women.   The men were usually hunters and trappers, did their
own thinking, and voted to suit themselves. Many were fathers
of boys who in after days served in the Union ranks under
Sherman, Thomas and Rosecrans.   Not a few of them were
Abolitionists, though generally each family owned at least one
domestic servant.   In 1821, Ben Lundy, the Ohio Abolitionist,
established the first Abolition paper in the South at Greeneville, Tennessee.   He called his paper *The Genius of Universal
Emancipation*, and finally moved it to the city of Baltimore.[2]
From such surroundings sprang Dave Crockett and Admiral
Farragut, Sergeant York, and many another typical Tennessee mountain boy, clothed in homespun, shod with raw-hide
boots, and with wool hat on his head.

It was this picture of an independent, ideal, country community Andrew Johnson had in mind when he said, "If you
wish to make a useful citizen, take a worthy laborer, though
he may have no property, no trade, no work, and transplant
him to the West; give such a man one hundred and sixty acres
of fat virgin soil and soon he will clear up a few acres around
him, get a horse, a mule or two, and some fat, thrifty hogs
grunting around his log cabin, a few milch cows lowing at the
barnyard, and when his country calls him, he will unhitch his
horse, leave the plow standing idle in the furrow, shoulder
his musket, and march to the front."   And it was just this
kind of a country community Andrew Johnson delighted to
find in the mountain sections of East Tennessee.[3]

But it must not be concluded that the town of Greeneville
was an Arcadia or social Paradise, or anything of that sort.
Like other places, Greeneville had its classes and its masses, its
aristocrats and its democrats.   Just before Tennessee became
a State, Greeneville, in fact, had been a capital city, the capital

2 *Magazine American History*, Vol. XX, p. 43.
3 Garrett and Goodpasture, *History of Tennessee*, p. 230.

of the state of Franklin. Among its citizens were men of wealth and distinction: Col. Thomas Arnold, handsome and aristocratic, long a Congressman from the First District; Dr. Alex Williams, the Whig boss of that entire section; the Dixons and others. These old families, before Andrew Johnson's arrival, had selected the best sites in town and built commodious mansion houses. Connected with "the great house," as the plain people deferentially called such establishments, were slave quarters and extensive gardens; usually an orchard, a scuppernong vine, sometimes covering a quarter of an acre of ground, and groves of oak, elms and hickory. The head of the Dixon family numbered his slaves by the score; while "Alexander the Great," for such Andy Johnson dubbed Dr. Alex Williams, his fierce political antagonist, was the owner of no less than sixty fox hounds.

It did not take Andy Johnson long, after arriving in Greeneville, to decide in which crowd he belonged. He was a laborer, it was true, and dependent upon the well-to-do for custom, yet he did not fawn on the rich or turn himself to those who purchased his merchandise. It was to the man by his side he went, to the plasterer and the carpenter, the brick-layer and the shoemaker, the stock-raiser and the farmer. In one of these laborers, a stern, tough-fibered fellow named Blackstone McDaniel, he found a man of congenial tastes, democratic, hard to sweep off his feet, and with a head full of brains. "Old Mac," as Andy called Blackstone McDaniel, was the village plasterer, and from first to last, as every one in Greeneville well knew, was "Andy Johnson's only intimate."

To be sure there were others with whom Andrew Johnson ran. For instance, there were Squire Mordecai Lincoln, the village magistrate, and perhaps an uncle of Abraham Lincoln, who dispensed justice and tied the marriage knot, and Bill Lowery, the best scribe of the bunch, and John Jones, a peculiar fellow, a recluse and a college graduate living a few miles in the country. Besides these, there were a likeable lawyer named Russell, a poor young Scotchman named Brown, whose widow afterwards married General Ewell, of Confederate fame, and last but not least, Lewis Self, a man of vast stores

of homely wisdom and mother wit. But there was only one
"dear Old Mac." To Blackstone McDaniel, Andrew Johnson
went with his secrets and his troubles, and between the two,
with many a bloody oath, plans were laid to build up a real
democracy in Greeneville and to put the slave-holding oligarchy to rout. The headquarters of this gang of village
philosophers was Andy Johnson's tailor shop, located at first
near the present Opera House and not far from the Court
House. Busy as the young tailor was, he never got too busy
to welcome his fellow-toiler to the unwashed, democratic salon
which he had established.

Soon after Andy and McDaniel struck up an acquaintance,
they engaged in a public discussion on the subject of the Indian
tribes living in Tennessee. The query was, "Shall the criminal laws of Tennessee be extended to the Tennessee Indians?"
On the appointed evening a large crowd gathered at the town
academy to hear the debate between the young village Demos-
theneses. Mac opened the discussion and Andy replied, then
there was a fifteen minute rejoinder by each. When the vote
was taken, Andy won the debate, but soon afterward lost the
championship to John Park. Park was the crack debater of the
town; an independent, unique character, he despised the institution of slavery and advocated its immediate abolition. This
overthrow of Andy created a stir in the community, which we
of the present day cannot fully appreciate. It must be remembered, however, that a hundred years ago debating clubs
were the most exciting forms of diversion. Andy's defeat only
spurred him on to greater efforts; he was determined to fit
himself to vanquish the best debater in town. About four
miles from Greeneville there was, at that time, a small college
called Greeneville College, where public debates were indulged
in every Friday night. Andy got permission to join this club
and once every week for several years, four miles out and
four miles in, he walked, through hot and through cold, taking
part in the college debates. Finally the college suspended and
Andy transferred his membership to Tusculum College, about
four miles from Greeneville in an opposite direction.

Every Saturday when the boys would come to town they

would gather in Andy Johnson's tailor shop and fight the debates over again. With them Andy grew to be a prime favorite, and being much older than they were, he was heralded forth as a mighty debater. In his relation to these young college students, who like himself were poor and many dependent upon their own labors to pay their way through college, he developed a trait which aided him through life,—the rare gift of making and retaining friends among the people of his own class.

At Greeneville College Andy Johnson fell in with a man who influenced and largely shaped his life. This tall mountaineer, democratic to the core and standing firm in his shoes, was plain and modest, "and of respectable parentage." As Blackstone McDaniel was Johnson's personal friend, so Sam Milligan became his political and legal adviser. Milligan was a graduate of William and Mary College in Virginia and was teaching at Greeneville College when Andy was taking part in the debates. Very soon Milligan was attracted to the prodigy of the tailor shop and loaned him books from the library and assisted him in picking up useful information. While Sam Milligan was no speaker, he was a man of poise and good judgment. He also had a sense of duty, an inflexible honesty and a broad national point of view.[4]

But Andrew Johnson was interested in other things besides his tailor shop during the fine spring days of 1827. In fact, almost from the very first day he landed in Greeneville, the gossips were saying that his fancy had been turning to thoughts of love. Alas for the fickleness of the sterner sex, his love affair with Sarah Word, the South Carolina maiden, so dainty and coy looking, in her lace gown and bonnet, had passed out of mind. Forgotten was the cotton quilt of many colors he and Sarah had created with joint needle and thread; forgotten too the familiar chair on which they had carved in imperishable characters the sweet words, "S. W. 1820."[5]

Eliza McCardle, for she it was who had supplanted Sarah

[4] Johnson MS. at Greeneville.
[5] "A President's Love Affairs." *National Magazine*, Vol. VI, p. 63, with portraits of Sarah Word, snug as a Puritan maiden, also with pictures of the quilt and chair.

in Andy's affections, was an orphan, seventeen years of age, when she first encountered her future husband. Her father, a Scotchman and a shoemaker, had died a few years before and Eliza, the only child, was living with her widowed mother. A typical Scotch lassie, her nut-brown hair played around an ample forehead, her eyes were soft hazel, and her unusually long Greek nose Phidias would undoubtedly have envied; add to these attractions a generous mouth and a tall shapely figure and we have Eliza McCardle, when Andy Johnson ran into her on a certain September morning in 1826. As every one in Greeneville will tell you even to this day, on the occasion in question Eliza McCardle and a bevy of school girls from Rhea Academy were standing on the sidewalk of Greeneville when Andy Johnson, penniless and friendless, passed along to the tailor shop looking for a job. The instant Eliza's eyes fell upon the sturdy chap, moving with firm step and resolute manner, she shyly whispered to a girl friend by her side, "There goes my beau." The courtship and engagement were of short duration. In a few days, as we have seen, Andy moved off to Rutledge but soon returned to Greeneville, and, on May 17th following, the marriage took place. At the bride's home the brave young couple, with stout hearts and empty purses were joined together by Mordecai Lincoln, one of Andy's best friends.[6]

From this time, the education of Andrew Johnson began in dead earnest. Though he could spell just a little, and read simple words, at the time of his marriage he was unable to write. The task of teaching him to read and to write was undertaken by his girl-wife with a loving heart, and so well did she succeed that in ten years her husband was writing a legible, though an unformed, hand, was a fair speller, as spelling went in those days, and was reading everything he could get his hands upon. But the toil of the young couple is shown not only in the education of Andy but also in the accumulation of property and the increase of their influence. Almost

6 J. H. Barrett, *Abe Lincoln and His Presidency*, Vol. I, p. 7 note: "Married at Greeneville, Tennessee, on May 17, 1827, Andrew Johnson to Eliza McCardle, by Mordecai Lincoln, Esq., probably a son of Abraham Lincoln's grandfather."

continuously from 1827 to 1843, Andrew Johnson filled certain local offices and yet during this time he managed to accumulate a home, a tailor shop, a brick store in Greeneville, and a nice little farm containing more than a hundred acres. On the farm, which was a few miles from town, he settled his mother and step-father. Bill Johnson, his peripatetic brother, plied his chosen trade of carpenter for a short time and then set out for Texas. Before leaving, however, Bill made a massive table which he presented to his brother Andy, and to this day the curious traveler will discover this table in the Andy Johnson tailor shop and may read thereon these words, "This table was made in 1828 by William Johnson."

At the time of marriage, Andrew Johnson was doing business in a two-room building on Main Street. In the front room he conducted his tailoring establishment and "built his political fences"; the rear room was used for every imaginable purpose,—it was kitchen and dining-room, and it was also bed-chamber and parlor. In this back room, Andrew Johnson and his wife lived, and here Martha, in after days mistress of the White House, was born, and so was Charles, the first son. In about four years after marriage, Andy's prospects were much improved and he was looking about for a home of his own. This notion of a home was Andrew Johnson's big idea. "Without a home there can be no good citizen," he would say; "with a home there can be no bad one."

To secure a home and a competency, he practiced a rigid economy and bent to his tailor's job. Having been driven from his native State, as he declared, by the gaunt and haggard monster called hunger, he was resolved to provide against a return of such evil and to secure a home and a competency for himself and for those dependent upon him. Luckily, about this time a dwelling and a smithshop, down on Water Street and just a few steps from the Court House, came upon the market for sale. Johnson's attention was called to the sale by Mordecai Lincoln, who had a judgment against the property for $36.66. The sale took place on February 24, 1831, when the dwelling, known as Lot No. 77 on the city plot, and containing 70 poles, and the smith-lot, known as part of Lot

No. 68, were sold under a writ of *fieri facias* in favor of Mordecai Lincoln and other creditors against the heirs-at-law of
John T. Myrick.   At this sale Andrew Johnson became the
last and highest bidder, at the price of about one thousand
dollars.   Soon a deed was spread upon the records of Greene
County bearing this caption:

"Richard M. Woods, Sheriff
   of Greene County,   Deed
                             Registered in Book 15
         To   Page 396,
                             This February 26, 1831."
   Andrew Johnson

The property was soon paid for and the proud owners moved
their little "plunder" into their own dwelling and set up as
real housekeepers.   Pretty soon they found a building for sale,
also situated on Main Street; this they purchased and rolled
a block and a half to the smith-lot, fitting it up into a comfortable tailor shop, as it appears to-day.   Over the door of
this shop Andy nailed a sign which reads as follows:

"A. JOHNSON

TAILOR." [7]

Located under his own vine and fig tree, Andy strove harder
than ever in the work of his trade.   Every garment must be
a perfect fit, there must be no dissatisfied customer; the Andrew Johnson brand of clothes was to become a guarantee of
good workmanship.   More and more the Andy Johnson tailor
shop became the center of village politics, the gathering place
for cornfield philosophers, and the most talked about establishment in East Tennessee.   To keep himself posted on public
affairs, Andy employed a reader, paying him fifty cents a day
to read aloud while he worked at the bench.   Current newspapers, speeches of Senators and Congressmen, Government
reports, and such books as could be borrowed were thus read
aloud and devoured by the ambitious man.   Greeneville and

[7] This building, more than a century old, and the sign, which is a duplicate
of the original, are now the property of the State of Tennessee.

the tailor shop were going to know whatever was worth knowing. The "tariff of abominations," and the nullification of the same by South Carolina; the summary "hanging of Calhoun by Andrew Jackson" for threatening to destroy the life of the Nation; "Nick" Biddle and his terrible national bank; the annexation of Texas by the United States; the internal improvement scheme which hit Tennessee so hard about 1830, and the threatened bond issue for millions and millions of dollars; these and other public matters the tailor shop crowd "chewed over" in their cornfield way. Tennessee's old worn-out Constitution came in of course for abuse; that property was of more value than the life, limb and happiness of the people, and that there was a law authorizing imprisonment for debt, these were surely relics of a barbarous age and ought to be abolished.

As in England, Germany and France and in the large cities of the United States, so in the wilds of Tennessee, "the aspirations towards equal citizenship became the keynote of labor's earliest political movement," and "the wage-earner's Jacksonianism struck a note all its own." [8]

Much the most important question, however, the tailor shop tackled was, who should run the town of Greeneville, the aristocrats or the democrats, the money interests or the laborers? Undoubtedly the aristocrats had been bossing the job for a long time. Should they continue to do this, or should the democrats have a chance? To bring this matter to a head, in the spring of 1829, the mechanics and laborers brought out for the position of alderman, Andy Johnson, the town tailor. "Alexander the Great" was simply dumfounded. The idea of having a tailor for a City Father was appalling. Surely the impudence and insolence of the laboring classes were ruining the country! But despite the influence and the money of the aristocrats, Andy was elected. In fact he made such a good alderman he was elected the second time, and then reëlected, and finally was chosen Mayor of the city, filling this position for three successive terms.

[8] Selig Perlman, *Trade Unionism in the United States*, New York, 1922.

In 1833 he took part in calling a convention of the State. This convention, which met in 1834, abolished property qualifications for office, imprisonment for debt, made a fuller guarantee of freedom of speech and of the press, and in other respects reformed the old Federalist Constitution of 1796. While serving as Alderman and Mayor, Johnson grew to be the recognized leader of the laboring classes in the community. His reforms in municipal government, his fairness in dealing with every class, and his advocacy and practice of economy, created hosts of friends besides improving the town of Greeneville. His acquaintance, too, began to spread, extending throughout the County of Greene. Everywhere, from Bull's Gap to the North Carolina line, he was a welcome visitor to the homes of the mountaineers of Tennessee.

It must be said that Andrew Johnson's dream was universal democracy and that to the accomplishment of this task he was devoting his all. His local surroundings strengthened and upheld him. Not only the laborers, who gathered about the tailor shop, but political friends, in and around the Court House, had begun to recognize him as a promising Democratic leader. Into the fiber of his life, indeed, the spirit of the hills and mountains of East Tennessee and of the plains and valleys between, was passing. Climbing to the pinnacle of High Hill or some adjacent eminence, Johnson would stand alone in his favorite posture, his hands clasped behind his back, gazing in silence far away toward the sky line across the mountains of adjoining States; or in the shadow of his tailor shop he would watch the swiftly flowing stream as it ran unhindered to the sea. In sky, in mountain and in brook, everywhere, he felt that the law of nature was freedom and equality. But in human life this law seemed to him to be perverted. Men were in no sense equal. The task was to restore the balance, to give the laborer and the mechanic a chance. Nor was this a mere gesture. It was not solely an intellectual performance, it was the result of a conviction firm as life.

"Gladly I would lay down my life," he wrote, "if I could so engraft democracy into our general government that it would

1.

2.

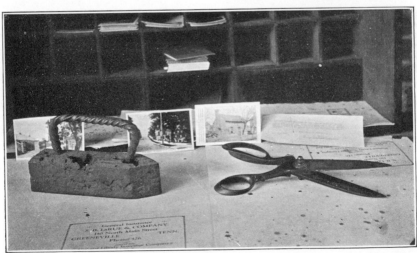

3.

1. Andrew Johnson, Runaway Apprentice.
2. Dress Coat Made by Andrew Johnson.
3. Shears and Goose, now in Tailor Shop at Greeneville, Tenn.

be permanent." Fortunately Thomas Jefferson had laid down the principles of democracy which Andrew Jackson in the White House and Andrew Johnson in his tailor shop were equally vitalizing.[9]

[9] In preparing this chapter I have consulted the Johnson MS. at Washington and at Greeneville. Johnson died in July 1875, the Johnson monument was dedicated in 1878, and in the present century Tennessee purchased the tailor shop and the National Government took over his place of burial. Both of these are now open to the public. On these occasions the facts of Johnson's early life were given to the public by the press.

CHAPTER III

SUCCESSOR TO ANDREW JACKSON

In the twenties, when Johnson moved to Greeneville, there was living in the neighboring city of Knoxville a man of such a stern sense of duty, so unaffected and ruggedly honest, he was known as "The Cato of America." And he too, like Jackson and Johnson, was a native of North Carolina. Hugh Lawson White was a very strong character. In fact, he was Andrew Jackson's right-hand man for a while, and Andrew Johnson's ideal. Aristocratic, tall, spare and dignified, with long, flowing curly locks and a benign countenance, Judge White was yet simplicity itself, and the most approachable of men. Later he was a candidate for President against Martin Van Buren.

Sometimes a law student would call at Judge White's home to be examined for license to practice law, and the judge would be away, perhaps in the cornfield plowing. Up and down the rows he would go, swinging to the wobbly plow handles and guiding "Old Dobbin" at the same time. Presently, at the end of a row he would look up, wipe the sweat from his eyes, and discover the applicant for license. "Just follow along behind me, my son," he would quietly remark, slapping his horse with the reins. On they would go, judge and student, discussing Coke and Blackstone and the Rule in Shelley's Case, and plowing the corn as they went. After an hour or so, the judge would knock off work, go back to his office, and announce the result of the examination. Of course such a thoroughgoing individual was a man after Andrew Johnson's own heart; and when the judge and Jackson "broke," Johnson wavered in his support, leaning, however, to the Cato of the plow handles, in fact, supporting him for President in 1836. But this period of disloyalty was short, and soon after entering politics Andrew Johnson became a Democrat of the Jackson kind, not a Democrat in the party sense but a universal Democrat, looking to democracy to cure all the evils of life.

26

The Johnson manuscripts in the Congressional Library, good, bad and indifferent, number more than twenty thousand. One day, when I was turning over the pages of this uncensored collection, I was struck with the frequent comparison writers made between Andrew Jackson and Andrew Johnson. Time and again I discovered letters to Johnson with such expressions as these: "You are a second Andrew Jackson." . . . "You are a man, every inch of you, standing in the shoes of 'Old Hickory.'" Occasionally I would come across a letter reminding Johnson that he was "trying to ape Andrew Jackson but cannot make the grade." Now outside of Tennessee this comparison was not instituted until Johnson had become a national figure. In Tennessee, however, the resemblance to Jackson was frequently commented on, almost as soon as Johnson entered public life.[1] Externally, of course, no two men were more unlike, Jackson being a rollicking fellow, fond of horse-racing and cock-fighting, and more fond of sports than books; Johnson, caring nothing for sports, too serious minded, and always plugging away at some problem of government.

The trait, however, that was common to both men was courage, bull-dog tenacity, the will to do or die, and the corresponding virtue of being able to take punishment without flinching. Each man also was peculiar in another respect: though he stood for the State and for States' rights to the fullest extent, he managed to place the Union above the State, and had no patience with dis-Union, whether under the guise of Nullification or Secession. Just about the time Jackson was sworn in for the first time as President, Johnson was sworn in as an Alderman of Greeneville. Some months later a great "Jefferson Day" dinner was celebrated in Washington City and Andy Johnson read the toast Andrew Jackson delivered on that famous April 13, 1830. The air was full of Nullification, and the Virginia and Kentucky Resolutions, which seemed to sanction a voluntary and peaceful separation of the States, were discussed on every street corner.

At the "Jefferson Day" dinner the toasts proposed were so revolutionary and the Republican speakers so obnoxious, the

[1] Temple, *Notable Men of Tennessee*, p. 371.

Pennsylvania delegates and other conservatives refused to attend. Calhoun, the father of Nullification, was present, of course, and the Virginia Resolutions and Madison's Report of 1798 had been responded to when the next toast was announced. "To Louisiana and the memory of him who acquired it," the toast read. This was Andrew Jackson's toast and the moment was most anxiously awaited. What would the great States' Rights Democrat do? Thus far he had not committed himself on Nullification, and neither, by look nor gesture, had he given the slightest indication of what he was going to say in response to his toast. On the back of the program having written a few words with a lead pencil, to the horror of the Nullifiers, "Old Hickory" rose and read, "Our Federal Union it must be preserved." [2]

In 1837 Andrew Jackson's second term expired and he retired from the White House to become the "Sage of the Hermitage." In his old age, however, he continued to be a dominating factor in the Democratic Party of the State and Nation. Naming Van Buren as his successor, he afterwards turned him down because of disloyalty to slavery. A little later he put his hands on the head of James K. Polk as a successor to John Tyler, and continued the Jacksonian dynasty. In the Federalist and Whig State of Tennessee, however, Jacksonian Democracy was not dominant. In 1832 the State voted against Jackson for President, and in 1840 it went against his man Van Buren, as it did against James K. Polk in 1844. The hatred of the Federalists for Jackson, and of the Whigs for Johnson, passes modern belief. We of to-day have grown accustomed to the kind of democracy these men advocated. The election of Senators and Judges by the people, the referendum and recall, public education in all its ramifications, and the principle of the income tax, are to-day commonplaces. But in the '30's and '40's when Jackson and Johnson were standing for principles of this kind they were screamed at by every Federalist paper in the land. They were called levelers, who taught and practiced principles unworthy of the Fathers, destructive of property and offensive to gentlemen. President

2 McMaster, *History of the United States,* Vol. VI, p. 32.

Jackson's New Year receptions were called, and doubtless were, coarse and vulgar. It was said that they were "orgies where the rabble gathered themselves together, drinking and swearing, smashing the White House plate and furniture, and soilings rugs and carpets with tobacco juice."

Though Jackson was not at all intimate with Andrew Johnson, now and then he would send words of approval to his youthful namesake, especially commending his backbone. In a short time after entering Tennessee politics Andrew Johnson began to conjure with Andrew Jackson's name. Thus, when he ran for office, he would arrange a ballot that stirred the fighting blood of Democrats. At the top of the ballot he would place the familiar picture of "Old Hickory," stern and fierce, with his stiff, bristly hair and his bull-dog jaw. Under the picture of Jackson, and in large bold type, would be printed these words: *"For Political and Religious Freedom."* Just below this motto would come the names of the Democratic candidates for office. In all parts of the State survivors of General Jackson's old army still lived and his political henchmen hung around almost every court house. In Greene County, for example, Richard M. Woods, who had been a Captain under General Jackson at the Battle of New Orleans, was Sheriff, and George W. Foute, a wiry, political leader, was Clerk of the Court.[3] These men and other Jacksonian leaders backed young Andy to the limit, and they encouraged the people to look to him as they had to "Old Hickory." As he rose to power and influence they hailed him as a second Andy Jackson and predicted: "Some day he will be President of the United States." Andy Johnson proudly accepted the title of a second Andy Jackson and set out to make it good.

A local historian records that on a certain Saturday, in the spring of 1835, a muster was held at Babbs' Mill a few miles from Greeneville, when the various candidates took advantage of the gathering and announced themselves.[4] That night, while the usual Saturday crowd had gathered in George Jones' store and were smoking and swapping yarns, some one came in

[3] Temple, *Notable Men of Tennessee*, p. 372.
[4] Chattanooga *Times*, January 28, 1900.

from the muster and announced "who-all" had entered the race for the legislature: Major Matt Stephenson, the then "floater," for one and Major James Britton for another.[5]   Thereupon Andy rose from his seat, and, slapping his hands together, broke out, "Boys, count me in the fight too."   The tailor shop crowd having "prevailed" on their champion to throw his hat in the ring, all that was necessary to launch a boom was a public announcement.   In those happy days, it must be remembered, there were neither conventions nor primaries.

The district which Andrew Johnson aspired to represent in the legislature was composed of two counties, Greeneville and Washington, and in the latter county the young fellow was totally unknown.[6]   The first debate took place in Washington County and, on the day appointed, the two majors and Andy were on hand, cocked and primed for the fight.   Major Stephenson, the Whig candidate and a man of wealth and large family connection, lived in that county and was on his own "dung-hill."   He led off the discussion and expounded the Whig doctrines of internal improvements, protection to home industry, a national banking system, and paternalism generally.

Johnson followed the Major and spoke so earnestly and poured out such a mass of facts and figures the crowd was amazed.   He and Milligan and John Jones had been at work on that speech for weeks.   The audacious youngster wanted to know what industries there were in East Tennessee to be protected by high taxes; he paid a tribute to "Old Hickory" for putting down South Carolina's nullification scheme and saving the Union—"the grandest government God ever made." He assured the boys that he was neither a lawyer, a major nor a colonel, but a plain man laboring with his hands, for his daily bread, that he knew what they wanted and would carry out their wishes.   He wound up by declaring the curse of the day was too much legislation and a centralized government, that the best governed country was the least governed country, and that "there are no good laws but such as repeal other laws."

5 Greeneville *Intelligence*, August 6, 1875.
6 Chattanooga *Times*, January 28, 1900.

Promising if elected to work for retrenchment and economy and for justice to the laboring man, he concluded his maiden effort.   Major Britton, seeing that the race was between Stephenson and the Greeneville tailor, withdrew, and at the polls Andy was triumphant, by a very small majority.

In the legislature Andy Johnson sounded the keynote of his life, a rigid economy, adherence to the Constitution, attachment to democracy in its simplest form and, above all, justice to the man who toiled and labored.   Individualistic, he did not intend to bind himself hand and foot to any political party or to bow down to any religious creed.   Primitive, self-confident and courageous, he proceeded to say things and to do things which would have ruined any other man.   And all the time he made his appeals to the people direct and over the heads of the politicians.   In fact, when the young fellow became convinced of a course of conduct he put no bridle on his tongue and he counted neither the cost nor the danger.   Nor did he hesitate to bed with the strangest fellows.

In 1841 the term of Senator White having expired and Felix Grundy, the other Whig Senator and Tennessee's greatest orator, having died, the legislature was called upon to elect their successors.   The Democrats had a margin in the Senate of only one vote, while the Whig margin in the House was two; the Whigs therefore had a clear majority of one on joint ballot. But the question was how to get the Democratic Senate to act, how to bring about a session of the two houses so as to take a joint ballot.   Each day the clerk of the House would convey to the Senate the request of his body for a joint session.   Mr. Reneau, a Whig Senator, would move that the Senate "do comply with the request of the House and fix the date accordingly."   The motion would be put and defeated—twelve Whigs voting "Aye" and thirteen Democrats voting "No"—the leader of the "No's" being Andy Johnson.   Finally the Democrats proposed a compromise, to let the Whigs elect one Senator and the Democrats one.   But the Whigs were not to be thus bulldozed.   During the entire session the dead-lock continued—twelve Whig Senators always voting for and thirteen Democratic Senators against a joint session.   The recalcitrant

Democrats passed into history as the "Immortal Thirteen." This strategy of Andy Johnson, leader of the "Immortal Thirteen," greatly raised him in the estimate of James K. Polk, who advocated Johnson for the United States Senate and "Old Hickory" from the Hermitage sent his blessings.[7] Now, if one understands Tennessee politics in the roaring '40's he will not be too critical of the "Immortal Thirteen." The campaign of 1840 had just ended with the defeat and humiliation of the Democrats. Log cabins and hard cider, coonskin caps, songs and dancing and general hysteria had done the work for the disgusted Democrats.

At the session of the legislature in 1835 the most important measure was a bill authorizing several millions of bonds. Out of the proceeds it was proposed to construct a system of macadamized turnpikes throughout the state. Johnson fought the bill with every argument he could think of. He doubted "the power of the legislature to impose a tax on the people without their consent first expressed at the polls" and he prophesied direful consequences should the bonds be issued. The funds would be squandered, he declared, and scandals would surely arise; sharpers and swindlers would infest the departments. Notwithstanding the "eloquence" of the young member from Greeneville, the Whigs passed the measure against Democratic opposition.

Johnson also opposed the granting of a charter to the Hiawassee Railroad and assigned as a reason the immature fears of a rustic law-giver. "A railroad!" he exclaimed. "Why, it would frighten horses, put the owners of public vehicles out of business, break up inns and taverns and be a monopoly generally." In the beginning of the session a bill to open the legislature with daily prayer had come up. Johnson, defying public opinion, boldly planted himself in opposition. If members of the legislature felt the need of religious instruction, why not go to some church and get it, he asked. For himself, he opposed the union of church and state and insisted that they should be kept as far apart as possible.

[7] *The True Whig* in May 1853 and other Whig papers assailed Johnson for his conduct as Senator.

Now this opposition to macadamized roads could not have been mere demagoguery. Johnson's home people favored them. The counties of Greene and Washington were mountain counties and much concerned about good roads. In Middle and West Tennessee, where there were water-ways over which commerce could pass, roads were not so necessary. But in East Tennessee, turnpikes were a necessity. The people, therefore, disapproved of the young Solon, and in 1837, when he offered himself for reëlection, he was badly defeated by Brookings Campbell.

But his defeat was a blessing in disguise—it gave him a chance to ripen and mature. Availing himself of spare moments, he continued to improve his mind and to acquire an education. In the legislature of 1835 he had made a number of useful friends. One of these, a member from the county of Lincoln, was a laborer like himself. George W. Jones, who served in the first legislature with Johnson, a tanner and saddler by trade, possessed a keen intellect. In large measure he guided Johnson into the Democratic party. On December 25, 1835, Johnson wrote to Jones endorsing Van Buren, the newly elected President.[8]

In 1839, with methods of thought somewhat improved, Johnson again announced himself for the legislature. His opponent was Brookings Campbell. But the canvass of 1839 was under far different circumstances from that of 1837. The tide was now setting Johnson's way. Nearly all of his predictions about the internal improvement scheme of 1835 had been fulfilled. The public funds had been mismanaged or squandered, the speculator and the swindler had been abroad in the land. The people, in no humor to follow Campbell with his high-tax program, elected Johnson by a good vote. In the legislature Johnson opposed the letting of convict labor in competition with free labor, setting forth such views as to attract general attention. The direct, personal style of the rising young laborite may be seen from a paper on the subject of convict labor prepared by him for the mechanics of Greeneville. The memorial sets forth the unfairness, in fact the deg-

[8] Letter in archives of Tennessee Historical Society.

radation, of pitting honest labor against convict labor, and winds up with a formidable list of mechanics and artisans who have rendered service to the human family. "Adam, the father of the race," Andy wrote, "was a tailor by trade, sewing fig leaves together for aprons; Tubal Cain was an artificer in brass and iron; Joseph, the husband of Mary, was a carpenter, and our Saviour probably followed the same trade; the Apostle Paul was a tent-maker; Socrates was a sculptor; Archimedes was a mechanic; King Crispin was a shoe-maker; and so were Roger Sherman, who helped to form the Constitution, and Daniel Sheffy, of Virginia; General Greene was a tinker, while General Morgan was a blacksmith." [9]

During the session of 1839 Johnson was a trifle "gun shy" in the matter of fighting internal improvements. This course had defeated him in 1837. He therefore brought forward a cautious, well-prepared scheme of internal improvements which was adopted and served a useful purpose. The money to be expended in this enterprise was to be carefully guarded and placed under the control of a wise board of trustees. In fine, Johnson's record, in the second legislature, was an improvement over his former record. In the following campaign, having become a full-fledged Democrat, he served as elector-at-large on the Martin Van Buren ticket, canvassing the State against the leading Whig orators. In 1841 he was elected to the Senate from a district composed of Greene and Hawkins Counties. With the session of 1841 and 1842 his legislative career came to an end. All during this period the feeling between Whigs and Democrats was bitter, so bitter that for two years, from 1843 to 1845, as we have seen, the State was entirely without representation in the United States Senate.

For example, in Nashville during the campaign of 1840 a leather ball almost as tall as a house was landed from a steamer and rolled through the city by a giant nearly eight feet tall while thousands of hilarious Whigs danced and shouted and sang "Tippecanoe and Tyler too" and other campaign ditties. Henry Clay, "the Mill Boy of the Slashes," addressed the

9 Frank Moore, *Life of Andrew Johnson*, p. 68.

Whig cohorts at Nashville, not in hundreds or thousands, but in acres.[10]

Not even the pulpit escaped the political rancor. On one occasion during the campaign old "Father" Aiken, a Democratic preacher, and the eccentric William G. Brownlow, a Whig parson, were conducting a joint religious meeting. Father Aiken started off the meeting with an opening prayer.

"O Lord," he prayed with great unction, "deliver us from the evils of Whiggery." "God forbid," Brownlow interjected from his knees. Turning on the "Fighting Parson," Father Aiken shouted back, "Billy, you keep still while I am praying." [11]

At the session of the legislature of 1841 Andrew Johnson began a movement for a new state to be called Frankland, to be composed of East Tennessee counties and the mountain counties of North Carolina, Virginia and Georgia. After years of intercourse with representatives in the legislature, particularly from Middle and West Tennessee, and a canvass of the State, Johnson had become convinced that there were vital issues dividing the Tennessee mountain counties from those in the plains. Before the Civil War East Tennessee in fact was more nearly akin to Kentucky and Ohio on the north than to South Carolina and Georgia on the south. These plain mountain people owned few or no slaves and did their own work. In so doing they labored under the "tyranny of a social and industrial system which held them fast." The new state of Frankland, Johnson thought, would solve this difficulty. In this new state there would be less than ten per cent. slave population; manual labor would not be in disfavor but would be dignified and honored. Moreover, in this new land, which Johnson dreamed of, worth and not family or pedigree would make the man. Johnson had scant support, however, from his fellow members for his great scheme, though he managed to get the bill through the Senate.

But the most significant measure of Andrew Johnson's leg-

[10] J. C. Guild, *Old Times in Tennessee*, p. 160; *The True Whig*, August 19, 1840.
[11] Jones, *Life of Andrew Johnson*, p. 25.

islative career was a bill offered by him affecting the white basis of representation and taxation. Under the Tennessee Constitution, similar to the United States Constitution, in estimating the population and fixing the basis of representation and of taxation negro slaves were counted as three-fifths. Thus a West Tennessee negro county with 15,000 slaves and only 1,000 freemen would be given a population of 11,000; whereas an East Tennessee white county with 5,000 freemen, that is, five times as many, but with only 1,500 slaves, would be given a population of only 6,000.

Johnson attacked this system. It was unjust to the free white man, he urged. He therefore offered an amendment to the Constitution to wipe out the three-fifths clause. As we shall see, this was no fleeting fancy of Andrew Johnson, but was a dominating influence till he passed off the stage of life. This bill met the fate of so many of his other bills and was defeated. From that day forth, however, Johnson was under suspicion by slave-holding politicians.[12]

Of the many honors that came Andrew Johnson's way none was more significant than his choice by the Democrats of Tennessee in 1840 as elector for the State at large. He was but thirty-two, had served only two terms in the legislature, and the Democratic party was full of able speakers—Cave Johnson, Aaron V. Brown, A. O. P. Nicholson and others. Yet these trained men were turned down and the Greeneville tailor was called from his workbench to lead the Democratic host.

Forthwith he issued a challenge to Spencer Jarnagan and Ephraim H. Foster, Whig electors with wide reputation as debaters, to divide time and meet him on the stump. Wily politicians that they were, they declined the proffered challenge. The Whig State of Tennessee was unwilling to furnish crowds for Johnson to address.[13] The best he could do, therefore, was to trail along behind and answer to-day what the Whig speakers had said yesterday. In this furious campaign of 1840 the Democrats were defeated, but Johnson's canvass added to his reputation. In fact, it was obvious that if the Whig party

12 *The True Whig,* June and July 1853 and 1855.
13 Temple, p. 376.

was ever to be dislodged from power plain Andy Johnson, with his personal following, was the man to do it.

And no one realized this fact more than Johnson himself. A Democrat in the sense of the Declaration of Independence, and in no party sense, he detested "whiggery," as he called the Whig party. To him whiggery meant caste. Whiggery derided and sneered at the laboring man. It was the broad-cloth party and its members owned two-thirds or three-fourths of the slaves in the South. Now and then, as in the Harrison campaign of 1840, it might masquerade as the poor man's friend, and charge that Van Buren was an aristocrat, but at heart it was exclusive and aristocratic. In this respect the Whigs of Tennessee were no whit better than the Whigs of Virginia, who professed "to know each other by the instincts of a gentleman." When old John Syme, editor of the *National Intelligencer*, was asked whether or not a Democrat could be a gentleman, he was wont to tap his snuff box significantly and reply, "Well, he is apt not to be, but if he is, he's in damn bad company." [14]

Now in order to fill the position of Democratic standard-bearer and meet the Whig orators in debate young Johnson knew he must equip himself. Accordingly, he acquired all the political literature possible. His offices he filled with speeches, essays, pamphlets, copies of the Constitution, treatises, and other reading matter on politics. Newspapers, by the score, he subscribed to and encouraged; newspaper men he welcomed. Huge scrapbooks he filled with everything—local happenings, scandal, anecdotes, clippings from North and South. One of these books he labeled, *Whiggery in Its New Dress*, printing the title in large and showy type.[15] The Greeneville *Spy*, a Democratic paper operated by Sam Milligan, could be relied on to reply to Brownlow's terrible *Whig*. The young fellow Johnson was now much in the public eye. The Democratic press were beginning to over-praise his oratory as much as the Whigs under-estimated it. To the Democrats Johnson's

---

[14] Cole, *The Whig Party in the South*, pp. 60-69; Claiborne, *Sixty-five Years in Virginia*, p. 131; Temple, *East Tennessee and the Civil War*, p. 335.
[15] Johnson MS. at Greeneville.

speeches were a "mighty Niagara" sweeping everything before them; the Whigs, however, considered them but a "spring shower."

Neither praise nor blame, however, swerved him from his course; with energies unrelaxed he went forward with his work. Nor did he neglect the people, "the source of all power." Wherever public meetings were held he was sure to be present, taking a lively interest in neighborhood affairs, mingling with the country people and interesting himself, particularly, with the younger ones. In truth, he was beginning that intimate connection with the mountain people of Tennessee which finally made him their guide—their political god. Under his molding hand they were becoming "solid, compact, petrified," even as in the days of Andrew Jackson. "He knew their names, they knew his voice." "There was an exact fitness between him and them." With a religious faith they had believed in Andrew Jackson and when "Old Hickory" died they were disconsolate, but now that Andrew Johnson had come amongst them "they hoped he would save the country." [16]

But he must pay the usual penalty of success, the dislike and envy of the select few—a situation he could not understand. Why should the rich and powerful dislike him? He would do them no harm; on the contrary, he was seeking to benefit them. He would improve labor, raise the general average of intelligence, and thereby benefit the body politic. Dr. Alexander Williams, "Alexander the Great," in particular continued to annoy the young man, losing no opportunity to slight him and to back his enemies with campaign funds. In 1836 the Doctor gave a great banquet in Greeneville. Every one was invited but Andy Johnson. The banquet was to honor Johnson's rival, Brookings Campbell. After the feast was over Andy chanced to meet on the streets of Greeneville a young Whig lawyer named Temple, and proceeded to indulge in strong talk. "Some day I will show the stuck-up aristocrats who is running the country," he said. "A cheap purse-proud set they are, not half as good as the man who earns his bread by the sweat of his·brow."

16 Temple, pp. 368-369.

1.

2.

1. Andrew Johnson's Tailor Shop at Greeneville, Tenn.
2. As It Appears Today, Encased in Brick.

Undoubtedly this slight of Alexander the Great's—as it got rumored around in the country districts—was worth thousands of votes to the young fellow. People were beginning to love him for the enemies he had made. Those who took the pains to study his record understood that he was neither a socialist nor an agrarian. His offense no doubt was deeper than socialism, it was a challenge to good society. When one has attained greatness must he kick away "the ladder of lowliness by which he has ascended"? Is it possible to be a gentleman and a cross-legged tailor at the same time?

CHAPTER IV

CONGRESSMAN

While in Nashville as a member of the legislature, Johnson kept up a brisk correspondence with his Greeneville constituents, posting them on public affairs at the Capital and asking for the local news. Among the first letters he wrote was one to his friend William Lowery, bearing date October 4, 1841. Though the handwriting is juvenile and cramped, as if written by fingers made stiff by hard labor, the letter has a tone of confidence and of buoyancy. "Governor Polk's Inaugural Address was fine," he wrote. "The Whigs are down in the mouth, and though they have a majority of one, the Democrats are going to block their game, they are planning to postpone the election of United States Senators for two years." Some months previous, Johnson had written a letter to Governor Polk. In a boyish hand, and with numerous misspelled words he wrote: "Unless I am 'rong' the terms of United States Senators expire March the 4th next," and suggested "an extra session of the legislature to handle the matter." Politics had evidently gone to the young fellow's head.[1]

In 1842, on retiring from the State Senate, Johnson began to aim at bigger game; his eye was fixed on a seat in Congress. For the past fifteen years, with his own hand, he had worked at the tailor trade. All day long he had measured customers, cut out garments and shoved the tailor's goose. Sitting on his workbench, he could be found with wax and thread, needle and thimble, in hand. Though his ears were erect and his mind alert for knowledge, he was intent on earning his daily bread. Not only not ashamed that he was a tailor but proud of it. "I always gave a snug fit," he would sagely remark, when afterwards some one joked him about his tailor days. And the business had grown and prospered. It now required five or six

[1] Johnson MS.

journeymen tailors to turn out the work. Lewis Self had been promoted to the position of manager, and a better one could not have been found.

In fact, the loyal support of Johnson's workmen and the idea of a genuine tailor, sitting in legislative halls and aspiring to a seat in Congress, spread the fame of the tailor shop far and near. The leaders, of course, had little patience with the unconventional fellow, everlastingly thrusting himself forward among his betters. Many of the Democrats among the upper classes plotted against him but were afraid to oppose him openly, fearing the man who had grown in popular favor till he was stronger than the party itself.[2] Three years he had served as Alderman of Greeneville, three years as Mayor, six years in the legislature, and one year as Elector for the State at large—thirteen years in all—and had advocated no measure and given no vote except for economy and reform and in furtherance of the rights of the laborer. On this record he proposed to enter the race for Congress.

Arriving at home, after the legislature adjourned, he called together his friends and told them that he wished to go to Congress. At Washington, he felt the field would be larger and he could serve the cause of the laborer more successfully than in the Tennessee legislature. He thought he could cut down the taxes, especially the tariff taxes on such necessities as clothing and shoes, and on sugar and coffee. Undoubtedly there should be an increase of the tax on such luxuries as silks and diamonds. In Washington, too, he would fight the battle of the homeless and the landless. He had been reading of the waste lands in the West which were uncultivated and unoccupied. These lands should be cut up into lots of 160 acres each and given to genuine settlers, thereby building up the country and furnishing a home to those without homes.

The word was therefore passed around that the First District should have a laboring man for Congress, and, from the valley of the Watauga and the Nolichucky to the Cumberland Gap, the news spread. Cheered on by the action of their brethren in Greeneville, the laborers and mechanics of the Dis-

2 Temple, p. 379.

trict passed the word along. Sheriff Woods and the Court House gang, together with Sam Milligan and William Lowery, Blackstone McDaniel and Lewis Self got behind the movement. But at this stage matters came to a halt. It was plain that the Democratic leaders were not going to allow a tailor to represent them in Congress without a stiff fight. A farmer, or even a mechanic, they could endure, but they drew the line at a tailor, nine of whom "it takes to make a man." But they little knew what was in store. If the Democratic party did not wish Andy Johnson he would run anyway, as an independent.

This brought most of the leaders to terms and in 1842 A. Johnson, tailor, was chosen the Democratic standard bearer for the First Congressional District. But the exclusive element in the Democratic party still kicked. The humiliation of having a tailor in the halls of Congress, sitting side by side with the aristocratic Winthrop, Dromgoole, and Rhett was a little too much. Uniting forces with the Whigs, the disgruntled Democrats brought out Colonel John Aiken, a Democratic lawyer and popular speaker of the neighboring town of Jonesboro. Aiken was expected to put an end to the upstart, but on election day Johnson won. The banner of the laborer and the mechanic waved triumphant, and in 1843 the Greeneville tailor took his seat in the Twenty-eighth Congress. He served five terms, until 1853.

I may here state that in the campaign of 1844 Andy Johnson's opponent was the erratic W. G. Brownlow, called the "Fighting Parson"; in 1846 his opponent was Judge O. P. Temple, a scholarly Whig; in 1848 he was Col. N. G. Taylor, likewise a Whig and a man of magnanimous nature. In 1850 the Whigs, losing hope of defeating Johnson, went into the camp of the enemy again and ran a Democrat, Landon C. Haynes, one of the most brilliant and dramatic orators in East Tennessee. Haynes likewise bit the dust. As a last resort the Whigs in the Legislature of 1851 "gerrymandered" Johnson's district. The irrepressible fellow was in Congress forever, they feared, unless they could smother his district with Whig counties. This they proceeded to do by a clever "gerrymander." Though this trick put an end to Johnson's Congressional career, it also put him in the Governor's chair, or, as the boys said, "kicked Andy Johnson up-stairs."

In 1843, when Andrew Johnson arrived in Washington, he had never seen a city of any size before except Baltimore, where he attended the National Convention of 1840. Memphis, the largest town in his State, had a population of less than eight thousand, and Greeneville was a village of less than a thousand, whereas Washington City boasted near 40,000 souls; and yet Washington was far from being a real city. Clouds of fine dust from the unpaved streets tormented the pedestrians in summer, and in winter the mud was almost impassable, while the filthy "Tiber" oozed across Pennsylvania Avenue near the Capitol. On the other hand, the public buildings were handsome and nowhere was the entertaining more elegant or elaborate than in the White House and in the residences of the great party leaders. All was therefore new and wonderful to the young and illiterate Congressman. The Library of Congress became his place of resort. In the library experts would find books for him and would run down any subject which he might be investigating.[3] His rooms were at a boarding-house on Capitol Hill and were modest and inexpensive. Here he and Abe Lincoln and other young Congressmen of small means had their homes. His table and desk were filled with books: Æsops' *Fables*, Plutarch's *Lives*, the writings of Jefferson, treatises on the Constitution and on politics; these he kept overtime, often receiving notices to renew them from the librarian.[4] While other Congressmen were off on pleasure trips to Fortress Monroe, Richmond and Baltimore, Andy Johnson was busy improving his handwriting, studying nouns and pronouns or Congressional debates. Many a day he would cross over to the Senate, and sit at the feet of Clay, Calhoun and Webster; or listen to the bombastic oratory of old Tom Benton, who was the friend and champion of their mutual friend, "Hickory" Jackson.

At this time the West was filling up with people from the Free States, and the Henry Clay compromise of 1850 was not

[3] G. W. Jones, *Address* in 1878.
[4] Johnson MS.

far away.   Kansas and Nebraska would soon be knocking at
the doors of Congress for admission to the Union.   The issue
between North and South—the issue of slavery or freedom—
was taking shape.

By the side of Andrew Johnson, during the ten years he
served in Congress, were the great actors in the tragedy then
impending.   There were Abraham Lincoln and Jefferson
Davis, W. L. Yancey, the truculent Southerner, and Robert C.
Winthrop, the courtly New Englander, Howell Cobb and
Anson Burlingame, Alex Stephens and John Sherman, Bob
Toombs, whose scarred face resembled Mirabeau's, and Owen
Lovejoy.   Johnson and Congressman Horace Greeley grew to
be friends, Greeley's simplicity, thrift, and industry appealing
to Johnson.   But in many respects the most interesting character in the House, as Johnson thought, was John Quincy
Adams, ex-President and now a Congressman from Massachusetts.   Though an aristocrat, Adams, like Andy Johnson, stood
for the plain man, the laborer and the under-dog.   During the
late '40's Mr. Adams was quite ill and did not make his appearance until the end of the session.   At length, when the old
hero appeared on the floor, Whig and Democrat rose, as one
man, to do him homage.   Andrew Johnson, having fallen heir
to one of the best seats, in appropriate words and according
to arrangement, presented his seat to John Quincy Adams.[5]

It is significant that the first speech Andrew Johnson made
favored martial law and the repayment to General Andrew
Jackson of the fine of $1,000 imposed by United States Judge
Hall.   In March 1815 General Jackson had proclaimed martial law in New Orleans; and in the war zone a citizen was arrested by military order.   The prisoner obtained a writ of
habeas corpus from Judge Hall and the Judge proceeded to
take jurisdiction.   "Old Hickory" quietly seized Judge Hall,
broke into the clerk's office, captured the writ, tore it to
pieces, and put the Judge in jail, finally sending him off eight
or ten miles, under a squad of troopers, and turning him loose
in the public road.   In a few days the war ended and Judge
Hall opened his Court again.   He then put the General in

5 J. G. Blaine, *Twenty Years of Congress*, Vol. II, p. 68.

contempt, and fined him $1,000.[6] It gave Andy Johnson great satisfaction, of course, to speak in favor of a return of this sum and interest to the old Tennessee hero; especially, since it accorded with his views that when war is waging the courts cannot function nor can the life of the nation be preserved except by the strong hand of the military. The resolution passed Congress, the fine with interest was paid to General Jackson, and the Democrats were happy.

When the subject of excluding petitions which demanded the abolition of slavery came up, Johnson took sides with the South. As the Constitution guaranteed slavery and recognized slaves as property, such petitions were calculated and intended, he alleged, to destroy property rights and defeat the Constitution. The right of a state to two Senators was not more firmly fixed by the Constitution than the guarantee of slavery itself. Confident of his ground, Johnson turned on John Quincy Adams and asked him the question, what did he imply by a recent speech before a Free Soil assemblage in Massachusetts? On that occasion he had declared that "if slavery must go by blood and war, let it come." What did he mean when he used these words? Was he not then violating the Constitution of his country? The Sage of Braintree was content not to refute the charge and recorded in his Diary that the young man Johnson was "possessed of great native ability." [7]

Though Johnson voted that such petitions be not received by Congress he was unwilling to cut off free speech. In January 1844 Giddings, in violation of Rule 21 of the House, presented a petition advocating the abolition of slavery in the District. On the following day the press carried a story that Giddings had deceived the House, that he did not disclose that the petition related to slavery. The succeeding day Giddings rose to a question of personal privilege and was going on to state that he had been misrepresented. In a moment the House was thrown into the usual confusion, southern members objecting and insisting that the affair could in no sense fall

6 First Session Twenty-eighth Congress, p. 94.
7 J. Q. Adams, Memoirs, Vol. XII, p. 240.

under the head of personal privilege. Gilmer, a leading American, doubting Giddings's word, called on the House, "man by man," to say if any one had heard Giddings announce that the petition related to slavery. Dean, a northern Congressman, affirmed that he had. The Speaker ruled that Giddings could be heard only upon a suspension of the rules. Giddings rose to explain. He declared the disorder was so great when he undertook to speak no one could hear his ears. The motion to suspend the rules failed for lack of a two-third vote, George W. Jones, A. V. Brown and Cave Johnson voting "no." Andrew Johnson alone voted to give Giddings a chance. For this vote he called down the wrath of Tennessee politicians for a dozen years.[8]

In this debate the Polk administration and the South were jeered at by Joshua Giddings, the eloquent and fiery Abolitionist. "You will fight Mexico, a poor unarmed people," said Giddings to the Democrats, "and you will fix the Texas boundary-line where you will, but England? England, you will not fight, you will not risk a war which will set free your slaves." Polk and his cabinet will "not insist on the line of 54-40 as a boundary for Oregon; they will back out. In the interest of slavery you admit the slave State of Texas, Oregon you will not admit."[9] Andrew Johnson took an active part in the debate and, because of his split with the South, attracted national attention.[10] In the platform of the Democratic party, adopted at Baltimore in 1840, the new states of Texas and Oregon were coupled together, Johnson maintained. It was there agreed that Texas should be first admitted and then Oregon.[11] The bill admitting Texas had been passed by a combination of southern and northern votes. The admission of Oregon, however, was blocked—Southerners had "jumped the coop" and refused to carry out the Democratic platform.

[8] The Nashville *Banner*, *The True Whig*, and other Whig papers, during the campaigns of 1853, 1855, 1857 and 1859, took this vote of Johnson as a standing text, proving that he was an Abolitionist and a northern sympathizer.

[9] Had the South understood when acquiring Louisiana that out of this "Purchase," called "the Great American Desert," nine or more Free States would come, the trade with Napoleon would have no doubt failed. Blaine, Vol. I, p. 54.

[10] *First Session Twenty-ninth Congress*, p. 286.

[11] Howe, *Political History of Secession*, p. 1181.

But Johnson was going to vote to admit Oregon, as he had Texas. And so he did. Almost alone among Southerners he stuck to the Baltimore platform and voted with the North to admit the free State of Oregon. Justifying his course, Johnson said: "When the admission of Texas came up, one year ago, this hall was filled with spectators. The chandelier shed forth its light on a scene of brilliancy and magnificence. I almost seemed to see the American eagle, over the President's chair; intense anxiety and breathless silence prevailed while the announcement of the final result was waited for. Texas was knocking at the door. Texas dyed in blood, bearing aloft the lone star which had waved in triumph at the battle of San Jacinto. There she stood, her presence recalling the massacre of the Alamo and the victory of San Jacinto. The Union of Texas and the United States was about to be consummated, but at this interesting period there was an *objector*. I will describe the elements of his composition and you can infer who he was; his head was the United States bank; his arms, the latitudinous construction of the Constitution; his heart and stomach, the distribution of the proceeds of the sale of the public lands; his back-bone and spine, a tariff for protection; his huge and ponderous legs, an assumption of $200,000,000 of debts of the States; his long, dirty, greasy tail, the retrospective feature of the bankrupt law.

"But despite this objector the union was consummated. Uncle Sam with the Stars and Stripes in his right hand was seen approaching in the distance, and, as he drew near the hymeneal altar, Texas, the interesting young virgin of the South, was seen leaning on his arm, the ring of 'Annexation' on her finger; and the vows are said. Uncle Sam and Texas sit down to the marriage feast. The monster objector is consigned to the grave and becomes the food for grave-worms, and Uncle Sam and Texas are conducted to the bridal chamber and there, in the arms of affection, multiply and become exceedingly fruitful." "But now," Johnson asks, "shall his back be turned on her twin sister? . . . Not that I would intimate that Uncle Sam, like King Solomon, is a polygamist, but he has lost none of his devotion to her twin sister and is still in favor of adopting the daughter of the North and admitting her into the Union of these States." [12]　Despite such platitudinous and perfervid appeals Uncle Sam turned his back on the fair damsel and Texas' twin sister was compelled to wait for another proposal.

Johnson's advocacy of the Oregon bill, the zeal with which he had been supporting homestead measures, his argument disparaging the general intelligence of the South as compared with the North, his willingness to associate with Free Soilers, such as Julian and Horace Greeley, made him the target of southern leaders.　Alert and sensitive, they felt that he was an apostate.　At an earlier date Clingman of North Carolina had undertaken the same rôle that Johnson was playing, that of independent.　Clingman had voted with the Free Soilers to admit petitions advocating the abolition of slavery.　Not only he so voted but he backed up his opinion with cogent arguments in favor of freedom of speech, freedom of the press and freedom of petition.　Hammett, the bold Congressman from Mississippi, replying, called attention to the fact that in all the South there was only one discordant note on this vital question of leaving slavery untouched and undebated.　Now, Clingman was part Indian and noted as a fighter, and fighting was the order of the day in Dixie.　Therefore when William Lownes Yancey, suave, confident, and terrible, rose to join in the attack on Clingman, and with that reserved manner and biting sarcasm which so characterized him, turned and said that he had "nothing to say with one possessed of the head and heart of the gentleman from North Carolina," every one knew what would follow.　In a short time, across the Maryland line, Clingman and Yancey fought a duel.　But Senator Clingman could not stand alone; he was duly disciplined and whipped into line.　Ceasing to be an "independent," he joined Senator Foote in the business of "arousing the South."

Andy Johnson must also be disciplined.　The man was no Southerner; at best he was but a fool and did not understand what he was about or else he was a traitor.　Jefferson Davis would destroy him by contemptuous allusions; Bayly of Vir-

[12] *Second Session Twenty-eighth Congress*, p. 288.

ginia, by fixing him with the epithet of "ally," the "ally" of John Quincy Adams and of the abolitionists. It was January 31, 1846 and the Oregon question was up for debate. Bayly had intimated that Adams was the leader in the Oregon matters and that Johnson was his ally. But, according to Johnson, Bayly "had forgotten that a prominent Southerner, Hammett, was the real leader for giving notice to England to vacate Oregon." Bayly indeed had no reason for opposing the bill except that John Quincy Adams was for it, as Johnson intimated. Bayly interrupted and brusquely asserted that the gentleman misrepresented him. "Unintentionally, I presume." "Will the gentleman specify in what particular I misrepresented him?" said Johnson. Bayly refused to answer, sitting with scowls on his face. "The gentleman's scowls and threats have no terrors for me," exclaimed Johnson. "He may go and show his slaves how choleric he is, and make his bondsmen tremble."

Johnson's reply to Clingman's attack on Polk and the Democracy also gave offense to the South. In 1845 Clingman in sheer despair because his great chief, Henry Clay, had been defeated by Polk for President, attacked the "New York Empire Club." [13] It was that club "that had carried New York for Polk," he declared. "A lot of gamblers, pickpockets, thimble-riggers, droppers, barn-burners, quibblers and repeaters." Such in fact, said Clingman, was the Democratic party generally, whereas the Whigs possessed "the intelligence and the virtue of the country." Replying, Andrew Johnson employed his old method; he relied on the facts and the figures. Selecting Clingman's State, North Carolina, a Whig state, and contrasting it with the Democratic State of Pennsylvania, he asked, "How stands this matter of intelligence? Why, in Pennsylvania only one person out of 122 is illiterate and unable to read and write, whereas in North Carolina one person out of every four is illiterate." Now this was treason to the South, and Andrew Johnson, with disagreeable census tables, disregard of southern sentiment and tradition, and with his independence and boorishness was simply a nuisance,

13 *Ibid.*, p. 170.

an out and out Abolitionist, or in the language of the '50's, a "Helperite."

In one of the running debates there was opposition on the part of some members, Johnson included, to increased appropriations to the West Point Academy, at which Jefferson Davis had graduated; and also to the employment of experts, at what was considered an extravagant price. In a reply to Johnson, Davis sneeringly asked, "Can a blacksmith or a tailor construct the bastioned field-works opposite Matamoras? . . . Can any but a trained man do this?" This slur at the laboring classes raised Johnson's ire. "I am a mechanic," angrily he replied, "and when a blow is struck on that class I will resent it." "I know we have an illegitimate, swaggering, bastard, scrub aristocracy who assume to know a great deal, but who, when the flowing veil of pretension is torn off from it, is seen to possess neither talents nor information on which one can rear a useful super-structure. . . . Sir, I vindicate the mechanical profession." Next day Johnson, who really desired to be friendly with Mr. Davis, rose and said he intended nothing unkind to the gentleman from Mississippi, but thought if he was not personal in his remarks he might at least have said that no one "unless he had a military education could command an army." "Why had the gentleman selected a tailor?"

To this olive branch, Davis replied, "I retract nothing that I said in that debate."

In the Congressional campaign of 1845 Parson Brownlow had made awful charges against Johnson. He was an infidel and an atheist. He did not believe in the Church! Why, Johnson opposed opening the Tennessee legislature with prayer. Now, after Johnson had "wooled" the "Fighting Parson" at the polls he returned to Washington to renew the attack. At the first opportunity he offered a resolution "that Congress should be opened with sincere prayer to the Giver of all Good for His blessings, and that the same should be done upon the terms as laid down in the Gospel of Jesus Christ, without money and without price, except as shall be voluntarily contributed by the members of the House individually." The previous question was moved and the resolution was tabled.

Johnson likewise continued his attack on convict labor in competition with free labor, and offered a resolution abolishing the penitentiary in the District of Columbia, "as it brings criminals and felons on a par with honest labor." This resolution was tabled on the motion of a Southerner, Jacob Thompson of Mississippi.

Despite an occasional tilt with northern Congressmen, Johnson got along better with them than with Southerners. They were usually men of simpler tastes and did not set as much store by family history. In fact, the Homestead bill which he offered in March 1846, and by hard work put through the House, was a link binding him to the Free Soilers from Boston to Ohio. As northern men cast no slurs at him or his views, but rather approved, Johnson was pleased by their attentions. He was also proud that by his own exertions, and though "smarting under the lack of an early education," he was the peer of any man in Congress and a representative of the common people of America. "Sir," he said in reply to an attack, "I do not forget that I am a mechanic. I am proud to own it. Neither do I forget that Adam was a tailor and sewed fig leaves, or that our Saviour was the son of a carpenter." [14] Evidently the homely but far-fetched notion that Adam and himself were members of the same craft pleased Andy Johnson immensely.

Johnson's defense of the veto power was prophetic, adumbrating the time when he himself would be exercising it. As he worked it out the veto was "of plebeian origin." In 479 B. C. the Roman Senate had grown so oppressive, he said, the people met on Mt. Monsacer and compelled the Senate to grant the veto power to five Tribunes of the people. In time the Tribunes were abolished and the veto power passed to the Emperor, to be used, however, not as an engine of oppression but in behalf of popular rights.[15] The veto being guaranteed by the Constitution, as Johnson declared, he would take the Constitution as it is, "and as for my country, whether right or wrong, I am for my country always."

[14] In 1866 a similar speech in Philadelphia was called blasphemous.
[15] Moore, *Life of Johnson*, p. 2.

Of the labors of Congressman Johnson as a whole it must be said that they ran true to form. He said nothing, and did nothing that "the Andy Johnson tailor shop" would condemn. When he moved to limit the price to be paid for Washington's Farewell Address to one thousand dollars and made a speech warning that unless the price was limited "by-bidders and sweeteners" would run it up, he was speaking according to his lights, and in the words of the "A. Johnson tailor shop." He was also serving the people, as he thought, when he voted against large appropriations to add wings to the Patent Office. "Great frauds have been practiced in this department," he asserted, and the money would be wasted. His opposition to the Smithsonian Institute and his resolutions to "change the same into an industrial school, for training American mechanics throughout the United States for the duties of their trade," was in line with his life work—he was doing what he set out to do, he was substituting the practical and useful for the ornamental.[16]

Because of his unwillingness to coöperate with political parties or organizations, Johnson in Congress waged but a guerilla warfare—a warfare sometimes inside the Democratic party and sometimes outside. Always, however, he stood upon the old platform, equal distribution of governmental favors, equal treatment of rich and poor, farmer, laborer, mechanic, manufacturer or what not. A strict interpretation of the Constitution and an observance of its letter had now become his guiding principle. Unlike his fellow Southerners, Johnson had come "to place the Constitution and the Union above the objects for which the Union was formed."

With these views he advocated a downward tariff to prevent monopolies. To bills which would increase the pay of clerks and other indoor laborers, he tacked riders providing that the pay of the man with the shovel and the pick should be correspondingly increased. He also offered resolutions to reduce the salary of Congressmen and to reduce the clerical force. These clerks did no real work, he asserted, "they are mere henchmen and fuglemen, going around the country blowing

---

[16] *Congressional Globe*, 1847, pp. 298 and 571.

the horn of their bosses." Nor did he stop with his attack
on clerks but assailed the Congressional perquisite system,
by which thousands were wasted. He knew a Congressman,
he said, who had "sold books and stationery, costing the Government five hundred dollars, for a hundred and fifty dollars."

His sincerity was seen in connection with an incident in-
volving the small sum of two hundred and sixteen dollars. For
services as a member of the committee to investigate a charge
against Tom Corvin of Ohio, charged with receiving fees while
serving as Congressman, Johnson was given a voucher for
seven hundred and sixty-eight dollars. He accepted only five
hundred and fifty-two dollars and returned the balance to the
government. He had earned no mileage, he said, and had in
fact served only twenty-seven days. He was handing back to
the government all of the mileage and the unearned per diem
which amounted to two hundred and sixteen dollars.[17]

Opposing the creation of a public debt, he declared that the
ideal country was a country with "a poor government but a
rich people." "Large cities are eyesores in the body politic."
"Property should not be the object of government but the life,
the liberty and the happiness of the people." "If the rabble
were lopped off at one end and the aristocrat at the other,
all would be well with the country." Though he was "not an
agrarian nor the advocate of any 'isms' or 'scisms' " he could
understand when injustice was done to the people.[18]

The administration of President Polk, though Polk was a
Democrat and from the State of Tennessee, came in for criticism. "If one could remove the lid so the people could have a
look-in and see the trickery, the jobbery, the waste and the extravagance, probably there would be a chance for the better,"
said Johnson. "Besides," as he wrote "old Mac," and this circumstance no doubt had set the Congressman against the
President, "the most outrageous appointments ever made have
been made by Polk"; "the party is without a leader and defeat
will surely come at the next election." Polk's idea of politics
was "to hang one old friend in order to make two new ones."

17 *Globe*, January 14, 1853.
18 Kenneth Rayner, *Life of Johnson*, pp. 11 and 73.

About this time President Polk was recording in his Diary that Andrew Johnson was no Democrat. "He had not appeared at the White House during the entire session." Polk, in fact, had become disgusted with the position of President and was unwilling to consider applications for office. "If I live," he wrote, "I shall tell the country about the hungry Congressmen who infest the city of Washington." Though Johnson sustained President Polk in Mexican war matters, he maintained that "the expenses of the war should be borne by the rich whose property the government protected, and not by the poor and the laborer who received little at its hands."

Johnson wrote often and freely to his son-in-law, Patterson. "Dan the God-like is considered out of the fight for President," he wrote Patterson in 1852, "and without hope of success. . . . Scott will be the nominee of the Whig party. . . . Cass at this time has the sun and is stronger than any other candidate; the difficulty will lie in getting two-thirds in convention." . . . "All agree that if Sam Houston could receive the nomination he would be elected by a greater majority than any other person; he is the only man in our ranks that can defeat General Scott, if he is a candidate for the Whig Party." Of Douglas he wrote that he was "the candidate of the cormorants," that he was "a mere hotbed production, a precocious politician, warmed into and kept in existence by a set of interested plunderers that would, in the event of success, disembowel the treasury, disgrace the country and damn the party to all eternity that brought them into power." . . . "The crowd which drinks and haugh-haughs with Douglas are fitter to occupy cells in the penitentiary than places of state." "Lank Jimmy Jones," ex-governor of Tennessee, etc., "since his arrival this winter, has been trying to play a bold game for either the first or second place on the Presidential ticket but has signally failed and fallen flat; Bell, Gentry and Watkins are dead against him here, Brownlow, Nelson and others at home." Referring to a certain person named Good, Johnson wrote that he had had "the pleasure of seeing the parson who is not worth the powder and lead it would take to kill him, he is no manner account as I am thoroughly convinced." [19]

Occasionally Andy Johnson would tire of Congressional life and of reading and studying and would take a night off. Such a night must have been November 3, 1848. On the day following he took his pen in hand and wrote eight pages to Blackstone McDaniel. This letter is dated Washington City, D. C., November 4, 1848, and begins, "Well, old Mac." It then sets out some acts of kindness the writer had done for McDaniel and proceeds to describe a visit to Baltimore the night before. "G. W. McLane and two or three others of our old companions in arms," Johnson writes, "got on a kind of bust —not a big drunk and mounted in the five o'clock train of cars were in Baltimore for supper at seven o'clock. After supper we all went up to the 'Front Street Theater' and witnessed *The Danseuses Viennoises.*' This splendid performance you will never be able to appreciate until you see it for yourself. It consists of forty-eight little girls all dressed in the richest and most gaudy manner, performing every *immagionable* evolution and arranging themselves in every circle and figure to be found in the tactics of the fashionable world, and singing with a voice so sweet—and dancing with a foot so light that *JOB* in the midst of his afflictions would have rejoiced at the scenes before him.

"The theater over and the fine Oyster supper devoured, we retired to our 'virtuous couches' and then in perfect quiet rested till six o'clock this morning. Then rose, and after we had taken a drink felt like 'giants refreshed with new wine.' At seven o'clock A.M. we again took the cars and were in Washington by nine o'clock A.M. And here I am now at eleven o'clock A.M. neither sick, drunk nor groggy, finishing my paper to my old well-tried and faithful friend and pilcher, 'Mac.' " [20]

Andrew Johnson's appearance on the floor of Congress was far from uncouth or "ludicrous," as Rhodes affirms.[21] His

[19] Johnson MS., Vol. I, p. 81.

[20] The Johnson MSS. from which this letter is taken are a store-house of uncensored material—Johnson once said to his grandson, Andrew Johnson Patterson, that no piece of writing ought ever to be destroyed.

[21] Rhodes, *History of the United States*, Vol. V, Chap. III.

attire was the last word in the dress of the day; his enemies in fact charged that he dressed in perfect form "for the purpose of adding to his strength with the masses." [22]   When in Johnson's presence one had a feeling of admiration, a feeling that he had been with a strong man and an unusual character. Even those who disliked him remarked on "the great dignity with which he bore himself and the remarkably neat appearance of his apparel." [23]

Johnson's speeches in Congress were not of high order. They were pedantic, personal and often sophomoric, and they showed a lack of training and of early education.   Besides, he was deficient in vocabulary and there was sometimes a want of the usual niceties and proprieties of debate.   These defects, however, were natural in a man of no education, who, ten years before entering Congress, could scarcely write his name.   On the other hand, the good points outweighed the bad.   No one was more diligent in preparation than Johnson; he ransacked the Congressional library and covered every point that could possibly arise.   In addition, he knew the value of repetition, of reiteration and elaboration, and he kept hammering away at his central thought till he finally brought it into shape. His honesty and the sincerity with which he addressed himself to questions under discussion likewise held his audiences.   His voice was a wonderful asset.   Rich, full and well modulated, Johnson's voice could never be forgotten.   In moments of excitement, when he was discussing a great subject, and stood before a sympathetic crowd, he rose to the height of really great oratory.

On the whole, then, it must be admitted that when the tailor Congressman, after ten years in Congress returned to Tennessee to give an account of his stewardship, he returned with satisfaction; he had pleased his friends and disappointed his enemies.   Though he was closely identified with the labor party, he was not in accord with its radical teachings.   Firmly believing in the Constitution and the laws, as to the rights of property, such leaders as Ebenezer Ford of New York he

[22] Temple, p. 461.
[23] *Magazine of American History*, Vol. XX, p. 41.

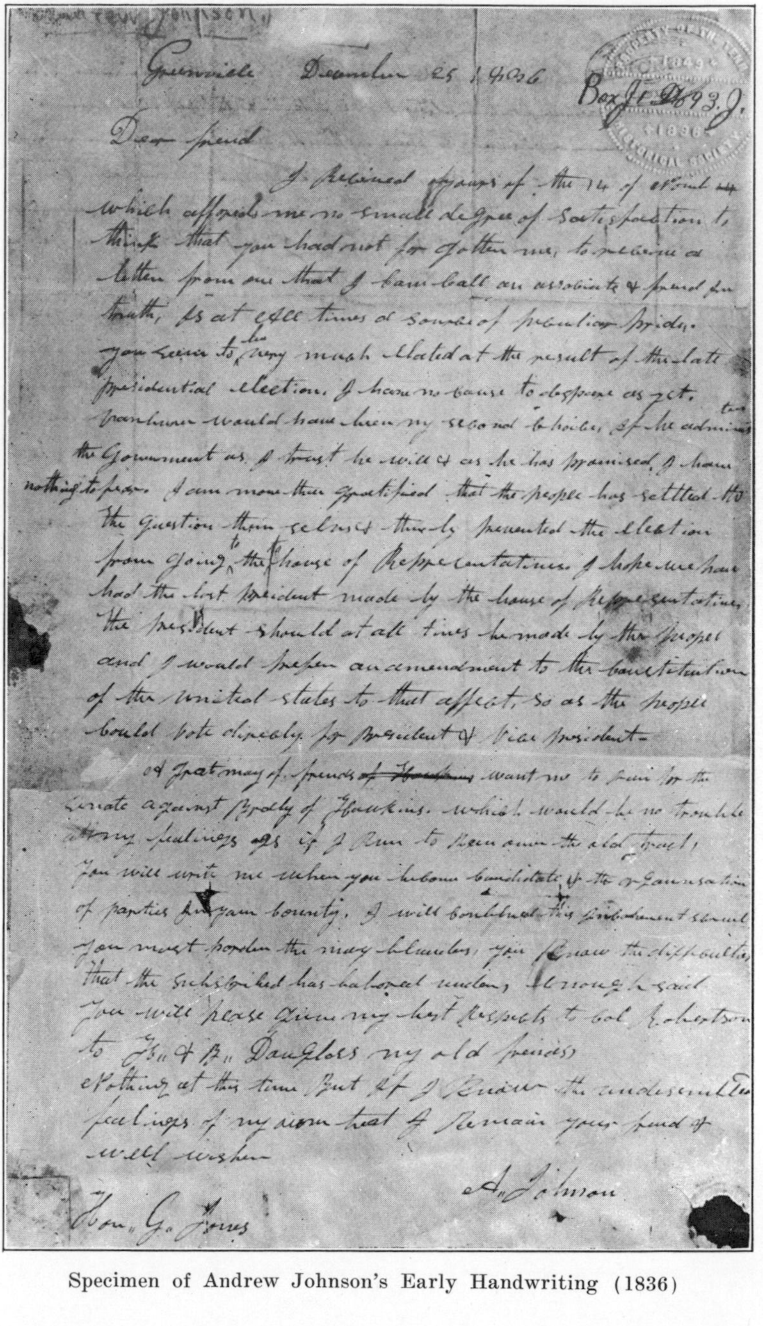

Greeneville December 25 1836

Dear friend

I Received yours of the 14 of October which affords me no small degree of Satisfaction to think that you had not forgotten me, to receive a letter from one that I can call an associate & friend in truth, is at all times a source of peculiar pride. You seem to be very much elated at the result of the late presidential election. I have no cause to despair as yet. Vanburen would have been my second choice, if he administers the Government as I trust he will & as he has promised, I have nothing to fear. I am more than gratified that the people has settled the the question them selves & thereby prevented the election from going to the House of Representatives. I hope we have had the last President made by the house of Representatives. The President should at all times be made by the people and I would prefer an amendment to the constitution of the United States to that affect, so as the people could vote directly for President & Vice President.

A great many of friends ~~of Hawkins~~ want me to run for the Senate against Brally of Hawkins. which would be no trouble to my feelings as if I Run to Run [illegible] the old track, You will write me when you become candidate & the organization of parties in your county. I will [illegible] this [illegible] soon You must pardon the many blunders. You know the difficulties that the subscriber has labored under, enough said You will please give my best respects to Col Robertson to G & B Douglass my old friends Nothing at this time But if I know the undissembled feelings of my own heart I remain your friend & well wisher

A. Johnson

Hon. G. Jones

Specimen of Andrew Johnson's Early Handwriting (1836)

would not follow. Ford's ideas that "the private ownership of the soil is barbarously unjust, that the transition of wealth from father to son is the prime cause of all our calamities, that bankers are knaves" and such like doctrines, were the exact opposite of Johnson's creed. Property Johnson would protect, but especially he would improve the condition of labor. The labor of the poor was the property of the poor. Hence he advocated equal taxation, and adequate lien law for mechanics, abolition of large standing armies, and of licensed monopolies. In short, "he placed himself in opposition to that system of capitalism which had its youth in 1830 to 1850," and was fostered, as he maintained, by the Whigs.[24]

[24] Claude Bowers, *Party Battles*, p. 50.

CHAPTER V

ON THE STUMP

Mr. Seward once declared that Andrew Johnson was the best stumper in America.[1] However this may be, Johnson lived, moved, and had his being in the home of the "spellbinder." As there were few newspapers in Tennessee before the Civil War, the stump orator was at a premium, the destinies of both political parties depending on which side could "down" the other on the stump.

Thus in 1841 when "lank Jimmy" Jones, born between the plow handles, six feet two inches tall, and weighing a scant hundred and twenty-five pounds, led the Whigs, "he made a monkey of James K. Polk"[2] and a great Whig majority was rolled up. On the other hand, in 1855 when Andy Johnson in speeches of two or three hours' length stamped his foot on the neck of Know-Nothingism, "the grand old Democratic party" was a sure winner. In fact, when Andy mounted the stump and set forth the virtues of Democracy "the crowds wept with joy"; but when he denounced the villainous and perfidious Whigs they "clutched the handles of their weapons."

During the campaign for Governor between Polk and Jones, the drollery, good temper and graveyard solemnity of "lank Jimmy" filled his party with such enthusiasm, their opponents "fled in dismay, as birds when a falcon is abroad."[3]

"And what did our man Polk say to-day?" a dismayed Polkite asked a fellow Democrat, who had ventured forth to one of the speakings.

"Oh! Polk made an ass of himself as usual," was the reply; "the idea of talking sense to a lot of d—d fools."

"And what did Jones say?"

"Jones—Jones? Why, I don't know what Jones said, nor

[1] McCutcheon, *A. Johnson at Albea*, p. 532.
[2] Temple, Chapter on "Jas. C. Jones."
[3] Temple, p. 256.

does any one else; but, if I were Polk, damned if I would allow any one to make a laughing stock of me."

Perhaps this debate was the occasion when Jones made such a monkey of Polk. At all events, in one of the joint debates Governor Polk undertook to call down the clownish Jones. Having served fourteen years in Congress and two terms as Speaker of the National House, and being then a candidate for Governor for the third time, Polk naturally felt his importance. A debate in which he took part ought to be on a much higher plane than Jones had pitched it.

"Why, fellow citizens," said the dignified Polk, "if a stranger were in this crowd to-day he would not imagine for an instant this was a campaign for the high office of Governor, but would conclude my opponent was acting the leading part in a circus."

"Agreed," said Jones in reply. "I'll be the ring-master." Then, making an imaginary ring with his long bony arms, he went on, "Yes, I accept the position of ring-master, and I will get right down in the circus ring, with my whip in my hand, and I'll trot out the little clay-bank pony; but my opponent must play his part too, he must wear the spangles, and put on the red cap and bells and take the part of the little fellow that goes round on the pony. And when I raise my whip—crack—and say, 'Go!—'" Lank Jimmy got no further. The crowd, roaring "Monkey, monkey, monkey!" imagined they saw the dignified Polk, arrayed in red cap, spangles and bells, flying around the circus ring. "Polk was so petrified, he gave up the canvass and went down in defeat." [4]

The Tennessee lawyer was as famous as the stump speaker. Once when the magnetic orator, Felix Grundy, turned himself loose in defense of a criminal, charged with murder, the scene was indescribable. The Judge on the bench "forgot his position, lolled out his tongue, and clapped his hands for joy, while a refined and enlightened gallery wept and fainted in the excess of feeling." [5] In the pulpit also the spellbinder was a second Wesley. In August, after crops were laid by, camp

[4] Temple, p. 257.
[5] *Old Times in Tennessee*, p. 84.

meetings would take place in some grove, where there was plenty of water for baptizing purposes. Pulpit orators, such as McGready, Gwinn, and Blackstone, or John and James McGee, would preach to "perishing souls" and the camp-ground would be covered with the "slain." The only safety to the "seeker," jumping up and down and jerking head, arms and legs, was to tie on to a pine sapling, scores of which had been cut off a convenient length and arranged for the purpose.[6] In the land of David Crockett, Sam Houston and Andrew Jackson, nothing was done by halves.

Amidst such surroundings Andrew Johnson was developing into a far-famed spellbinder. He did not wait until election year came on to mend his political fences, but, early in the summer before, began training the cohorts of Democracy. His organization, however, was not subject to party rules—it was personal and along the lines of "Old Hickory" Jackson. At the beginning of the campaign he would arrange a monster rally and appoint Sheriff Dick Woods master of ceremonies. Clerk Foute, Lowery, Milligan, McDaniel, John Jones and the tailor shop contingent would lend a hand. Advertised far and wide, these meetings in Greeneville attracted great interest. On the appointed day the Democracy of the mountains would arrive by the thousands in covered wagons, in carts and buggies, on horseback and on foot. A stand would be erected in the court yard and at the hour named, usually early in the morning to allow an all day meeting, Clerk Foute, in his ringing voice, would read the resolutions. These had been carefully prepared by Johnson, Milligan and John Jones. They assailed Hamilton and the Federalist party. They charged bargain and corruption between Clay and Adams, and they saw in Andrew Jackson the saviour of his country, the man who routed the British at New Orleans and knocked out the National Bank, the monster about to destroy the liberties of the people. In conclusion, they denounced Whiggery and the Whigs, dubbing them "successors to the hated Federalists who hung out blue lights to the enemy, and in 1812 tried to put an end to the war by the Hartford Secession Convention."

[6] *History of Tennessee* (1800), p. 74.

Upon these resolutions Andrew Johnson would then deliver himself. Though he stuck close to the issues, he seasoned his speech with personal anecdote and reminiscence, and he deported himself with a rough dignity and seriousness. The crowds were "spellbound," of course, and the influence of the meetings would spread to the corners of the district. Judge Temple was present on one occasion and took down Johnson's harangue. Commencing in a low soft tone, says Temple, Johnson grew louder as he warmed up. After an hour or so, his voice rang out on the air in loud, but not unmusical tones, and was heard distinctly a great distance. It seemed particularly adapted to the open air. "Without hesitation or dragging and with no effort after words," Temple continues, "Johnson went right on, the exact language coming to his lips to express the idea in his mind. As he grew warm and hurled the terrible thunder of his wrath against the old Federalists, the shouts sent up by the Democracy could be heard far and wide among the surrounding hills." As Johnson pictured the aggressions of the old Federal party and entreated the people to stand firm upon the Constitution, the "crowd would huddle closer together as if for mutual protection and plant their feet firmly upon the ground." When he warned the people that eternal vigilance is the price of liberty and that power is always stealing from the many to give to the few, "they would furtively glance around to see if any one was trying to steal from them."

In these fierce philippics Johnson never failed to use a figure drawn from the road. He would exhort the people to stand together "hand to hand, shoulder to shoulder, foot to foot, and to make a long pull, a strong pull and a pull altogether." At this allusion to the well-known custom among the farmers of that day of doubling teams, and assisting one another out of mud holes by all lending a helping hand in pushing and pulling, the old wagoners would be set "wild with delight," and the crowd would become tumultuous. Its hurrahs were like the sound of many waters, and the din and uproar became almost infernal. The enthusiasm was so great the crowds did not leave until the sun had sunk well beneath

the mountain tops. Many of those present lived twenty or
more miles away and for such a long journey, over muddy
roads, a supply of stimulants was laid in at the tavern. "When
night overtook them," Temple concludes his account, "on their
homeward way, in the bewildered condition of their intellects,
they recalled dim images of blue lights and black cockades and,
in every dark wood, they feared to see these monsters, whatever they were, confront them!"

Andrew Johnson had little trouble in campaigning with
Aiken, Brownlow, Taylor and Temple. In 1851, however,
Landon C. Haynes, his opponent for Congress, proved a
tougher proposition. Haynes was a Democratic lawyer and
had been Speaker of the Tennessee House. Subsequently, he
was a member of the Confederate Senate. A great battle was
expected when Johnson and the fiery, impassioned Haynes
"locked horns," and the crowds in attendance were not disappointed. For six hours during the hot days of June and July
the antagonists faced each other. Charges and counter-
charges, personal, social and political, flew thick and fast; but
Haynes, with his rhetoric and imagery, was outclassed. Johnson's barrage of facts, sledge-hammer blows, and adherence to
the main issue put his adversary to flight.

Other speakers, like Jones, might indulge in buffoonery or
side-splitting anecdotes, or, like Haynes, in rhetorical flour-
ishes, but Andrew Johnson wasted no time with small shot.
He was dead in earnest and he believed with his soul every doctrine he announced. Over and over he presented the strong
points till the humblest hearer grasped his meaning. One
fault with Johnson was his seriousness, his lack of fun and
humor. Though a friend to those he liked, that is to simple,
plain, unsophisticated folk, to the opposite he was a veritable
thorn in the flesh. The man who gave himself airs, the opportunist, the trifler or parlor-knight, he either shunned or
crushed. To his political opponent likewise he was too often
formal and distant, assuming a haughty air of superiority. At
the end of every canvass his blows had been so terrible, his
opponents were mortified and crushed and never demanded a
come-back. For example, when Johnson's heavy paw fell on

the neck of his fellow townsman, O. P. Temple, the young man fled from the district in which he was born. "I moved to Knoxville," the Judge naïvely admits, "to get out of politics and to avoid another race which would result in defeat."

Landon C. Haynes likewise smarted under the lashings he had received at Johnson's hands. On one occasion shortly after his defeat for Congress, Haynes was returning from Nashville, Johnson being then Governor, when he was asked how the Governor was getting on.

"Oh! fairly," he replied. "He is boarding with a butcher and skinning cattle for his board!" [7]

Even the lovable Gentry, after his defeat by Johnson, was sore. Under the influence of liquor Gentry was abusing Johnson in severe but classic phrase. Brownlow, who happened to be present, checked Mr. Gentry, insisting that instead of abusing Andy Johnson he should be praying for his soul's salvation.

"Pray for the salvation of Andrew Johnson?" Gentry mumbled. "Why, to save him would exhaust the plan of salvation and where would the rest of us be?"

Whoever indeed went up against Johnson encountered his oratorical bowie-knife. A correspondent of a New York daily, who heard Johnson speak about this time, declares that "he cut and slashed right and left, that he tore big wounds and left something behind to fester and be remembered." "His phraseology may be uncouth," said the writer, "and there may be many false Anglicisms, but his views are easily understood and he talks strong thoughts and carefully culled facts, in quick succession; . . . running his opponents through and through with a rusty jagged weapon; chopping to mincemeat or grinding to powder his luckless adversary." [8]

An incident occurred in the campaign of 1845, when the "Fighting Parson" opposed Johnson for Congress, which wounded Mr. Johnson's pride as nothing ever did. The Parson charged that Andrew Johnson was a bastard. Now this campaign of 1845 was the most exasperating of Johnson's

[7] Temple, p. 465.
[8] Nashville *Union*, May 21, 1849, citing New York *Times*.

life. That year the two old enemies, Whiggery and Democracy, were at each other's throats. Argument was thrown to the winds, and abuse and slander were the weapons of attack. If Johnson could not be defeated in open debate, he must be crushed by insinuation and by charges so foul none would vote for him. Mud-slinging, in truth, was the order of that day. Dickinson used it in his attack on Andrew Jackson, charging that Mrs. Jackson, before marriage, slept with Jackson between adulterous sheets. Called to account by "Old Hickory," Dickinson died on the field of honor.

In the campaign of 1845, therefore, it was decided that Johnson must be destroyed. The "Fighting Parson" was chosen to lead the attack and was backed, as Johnson charged, by the slave-holding oligarchy of Greeneville—Dr. Alex Williams, Foster and others. Such a campaign as Parson Brownlow and the Jonesboro *Whig* waged had never before taken place in Tennessee. Now Johnson did not resent the other accusations, but the charge that he was a bastard aroused his indignation. It seems that Johnson's enemies had started an inquiry among the Whigs of Raleigh, North Carolina, concerning this matter, and certain of the Raleigh Whigs, as bitter against the Democratic party as their brother Whigs of Greeneville, furnished rumors to give color to the charge. Andrew Johnson, they argued, could not have been the son of such humble parentage. A noble ancestor he must have had. In a word, they apotheosized Andy and made a myth of him, as is the case with all humble individuals, once they rise to fame. Honorable William H. Haywood, cashier of the bank of which Jacob Johnson had been porter, was Andy's father, so the charge was made. Any one could see Andy's likeness to the distinguished Haywood family. Why there was Dallas Haywood, afterwards Mayor of Raleigh, the nephew of William aforesaid, and as much like Andy as two peas. Undoubtedly Dallas was Johnson's first cousin. How else account for Andrew Johnson's greatness? [9]

Instead of treating this idle gossip with the contempt it de-

[9] Watterson, *Marse Henry*, Vol. I, p. 157; J. S. Wise, *Recollections of Thirteen Presidents*, p. 107.

served, Johnson, following the custom of the day, opened his batteries. His enemies and detractors were "ghouls and hyenas," he declared. "They would dig up the grave of Jacob Johnson, my father, and charge my mother with bastardy." [10] Parson Brownlow's charges fell flat, of course, and Johnson was elected to Congress by an increased majority. But so much hurt was he by the slanders, Johnson went to Raleigh and satisfied himself of their falsity.[11] In October 1845, after the campaign was over, "when the public mind was tranquil," and no election was on, he wrote an open letter to the public. The charge that he was an infidel was refuted, he argued, by the charge that he was a Catholic; no man could be a good Catholic and an infidel at the same time. Though a member of no church, he asserted that religion and "the doctrines of the Bible, as taught and practiced by Jesus Christ," he never doubted; in conclusion, he asserted that "the confidence of the people, as shown by the increased majority in the last election, has sunk deep in my bosom," and "will only cease to be cherished with my last breath."

As the next campaign was coming on, and Johnson thought of the humiliation to which he might again be subjected, he unbosomed himself to his old friend, Blackstone McDaniel, using rough words. Thoroughly conscious of the integrity of his life and of his desire to promote the interest of the whole country, North and South, he was exasperated that credence should have been given in Greeneville, where he was well-known, to the slanders of his enemy. He began his letter to McDaniel with these words: "My dear friend, if there is one left that I dare call my friend." Then he depicted a cold, gloomy Sunday in Washington, "the clouds white and angry, indicating a snow storm." "When I reflect," he goes on, "upon my past life and that of my family, and know that it has been my constant aim and desire to steer them and myself through society in as unoffending a manner as possible—this though it seems I have most signally failed—when I sum up the many taunts, the jeers, the gotten-up and intended slights to me and mine,

[10] *Open Letter of Andrew Johnson*, dated October 15, 1845, in Library of Congress.
[11] Savage, *Life*, note to Chap. I.

all without cause so far as know(n) I wish from the bottom of my heart that we were all blotted out of existence, and even the remembrance of things that were." He longs for "one obliviating draft of the waters of Lethe," and he wishes to God that Old Mac were present with him in Washington that day so he could "talk over everything"—unbosom himself as he had done on some occasions before.

"I will not enter into the details of the unpleasant state of my mind," he continues, "but I fear that the only person left to whom I can look and rely as a sincere friend is yourself; I used to think that Milligan was my friend, but how the matter really stands I have some doubts, as Milligan has taken positions in Greeneville that will ultimately carry him into the hands of those that have always been against him and against us." As to certain property on Main Street in Greeneville recently purchased and redeemed by McKinney, he declares that, "they may take and go to Hell with it for me." "I never want to own another foot of dirt in the *dam* town while I live— If I should happen to die among the dam spirits that infest Greeneville, my last request before death would be for some friend (if I had no friend, which is highly probable) I would bequeath the last dollar to some negro to pay to take my dirty, stinky carcas after death, out on some mountain peak and there leave it to be devoured by the vultures and wolves, or make a fire sufficiently large to consume the smallest particle, that it might pass off in smoke and ride upon the wind in triumph over the god-forsaken and Hell-deserving, money-loving, hypocritical, back-biting, Sunday-praying, scoundrels of the town of Greeneville. . . . Tell Patterson he must write to me. . . . Please accept assurances of my sincere friendship."   A. JOHNSON.[12]

When the campaign of 1847 came off, the Whigs were more decent to Johnson than they had been in the Brownlow campaign and his equanimity was restored. On October 9, he wrote a cheerful epistle to his friends, Milligan and McDaniel, then in Mexico serving as officers in General Winfield Scott's

[12] Johnson MS., October 15, 1845.

army.   President Polk, at the instance of Johnson, had appointed Milligan Quarter-Master General and old Mac had gone along as the General's clerk.   Writing from Greeneville to these old cronies, Andy Johnson wishes them "to accept the assurance of his high esteem, etc."   "My devout prayer is," he rambles on in a fatherly way, "that the divine arm of a protecting providence may be extended over you and that the ægis of American liberty be thrown around you throughout to preserve you from harm, from the dangers of the destructive climate, and to shield you from the assaults of a perfidious and dastardly foe."   As to the Greeneville news, he tells his old pals that "the health of the town is good," "scandal of all sorts is abundant"; and he presumes "a fair proportion of whoring is carried on, by way of variety."   "You may say to Milligan," he adds, "not to be impatient in relation to leaving his heart behind him, for rumor says that his betrothed will certainly wait until he returns from the war," etc.[13]

In the Governor's campaign with Gentry, Johnson was well prepared and made apt replies.   Indeed he was said to possess the gift of repartee and quickness, but he did not have this gift.   His mind was not light or agile; in quickness he was no match for Gentry or other quick-witted associates in Congress.   Every speech he studied and fortified with facts, and his power lay in strength, not in lightness and nimbleness. Prepared to defend any vote he had given, his replies sometimes passed for the inspiration of the moment, but were the result of unremitting toil.

In Johnson's first race for Governor, Gustavus Henry turned on him and charged that he had given a vote in the legislature which should entitle him to an immortality, "Aye, an infamous immortality."   Johnson replied that he would then be "possessed of a double immortality"; for when he was working as a tailor in the little town of Greeneville, from which he hailed, the boys used to sing a song which gave him an immortality in verse and now his opponent had given him an immortality in history.   "Perhaps my opponent," he taunted,

13 Johnson MS., p. 45.

"would like to hear the little song that the boys of Greeneville used to sing.

> " 'If you want a brand-new coat
> I'll tell you what to do:
> Go down to Andrew Johnson's shop
> And get a long tail blue.

> " 'If you want the girls to love you,
> To love you good and true,
> Go down to Andy's tailor shop
> And get a long tail blue.' "

In another debate, this time in Memphis, Major Henry sought to entrap Andy and bring him "in bad" with the Irish vote. "Why," the Major charged, "when in Congress, my honorable opponent voted against a resolution to appropriate money for famine-stricken Ireland. How could any one be so inhuman, so heartless, as to cast such a vote?"

Johnson admitted the charge; he had voted not to apply the money of the people for that worthy cause. "But that is not all of the story," he said, "for when I voted against that resolution I turned to my fellow Congressmen and proposed to give fifty dollars of my own funds if they would give a like amount, and when they declined the proposition, I ran my hand in my pocket, Major Henry, and pulled out fifty dollars of good money, which I donated to the cause. How much did you give, sir?" A few days later when Johnson discovered he was getting the better of Henry, the "Eagle Orator," he laughingly turned and said, "The Eagle Orator, indeed! Why, fellow citizens, this is the fifth appointment, five times in the pit together, but I see no blood on the Eagle's beak!" The Major replied that the "proud Eagle never feeds on carrion." This banal answer to Andy's cheap remark delighted the Whigs no little and was embalmed and passed on to posterity.[14]

Doubtless this thrust of the courtly Henry was provoked by the speeches of his opponent, Andy Johnson having badgered the Major all over the State. As we have seen, the legislature of 1851 passed a bill gerrymandering Johnson out of Congress,

[14] *Johnson MS.* at Greeneville.

—that is, Greene County, where Johnson lived, was taken from an old Democratic district and put into a solidly Whig district. Now Major Henry was known to be the father of this "gerrymander," and before taking the stump Johnson read up and posted himself on "gerrymanders." The Massachusetts Republicans in 1812, under Governor Elbridge Gerry, he read, had created a new district, which was so misshapen it looked like a salamander and the people called the trick a "gerrymander." This gave Andy a brand-new idea and the first time he met the Major on the stump he pitched into him, with gloves off.

"Fellow citizens," he said, "the Whigs have cheated me out of Congress, they have torn the county of Greene from its sister counties, and attached it to a lot of foreign counties. They have split it up till it looks like a salamander. The fact is they have "gerrymandered" me out of Congress—no, I am mistaken, they have not "gerrymandered" me out, they have Henrymandered me out!" After this shot, the "Eagle Orator" was not able to fly as high as before and in August 1852 Andy Johnson was elected the "mechanic governor" of Tennessee.

The "Know-Nothing" campaign of 1854 aroused Andrew Johnson to greater effort than ever before, and at the end of it he was securely at the head of the Democratic hosts. The doctrines of the Know-Nothing or American party were specially obnoxious to Johnson. It will be recalled that the Know-Nothings opposed foreigners, Catholics and Masons, and that this was their cardinal doctrine. Now persecution and prescription enraged Johnson and the worst form of intolerance, as he thought, was religious bigotry and hatred of foreigners. There were few Catholics or foreigners in his district. Nevertheless, while in Congress he had, time and again, expressed his indignation because of attacks on them. "Are the bloodhounds of prescription and persecution to be let loose on the Irish?" he asked, in his debate with Clingman. "Is the guillotine to be set up in a republican form of government?" Throughout the canvass with Gentry, Johnson hammered away on the same line, speaking boldly for religious tolerance and for justice to the foreigners. At Murfreesboro he said, "It is not in my nature when the poor Irishman leaves his own country and seeks America, as the home of the oppressed and the asylum of the exile, to meet him on the shore and forbid his entrance."

The debates between Gentry and Johnson covered nearly three months, the two men meeting each other sixty times and attracting attention not only in Tennessee but throughout the South.[15] The brilliant Gentry was the idol of the Whig party. Twelve years before he had served in Congress. "His voice was grand and extraordinary, and many claimed it was superior to Henry Clay's." [16] J. Q. Adams, A. H. Stephens, and other Whig leaders, who served in Congress with him, pronounced Gentry the finest orator in the body. In the presidential campaign of 1852, when Fillmore and Webster were sacrificed, at the instance of Seward and other Whigs, to General Scott, Gentry was broken-hearted. Rising in Congress, he bemoaned the fact he was "an excommunicated Whig"; he was "resolved, however, to adopt the advice of Cato to his son." He was "going to retire, content to be obscurely good, for the post of honor when vice prevails is the private station." . . . "In a sequestered valley in the State of Tennessee," he sighed, "there is a smiling farm with bubbling fountains, covered with rich pasturage and fat flocks and all that is needful for the occupation and enjoyment of a man of uncorrupted taste. There I will go and pray for 'Rome.' "

Three years later, as has been stated, this rare old Whig gentleman was prevailed upon to enter the race for Governor, against the rough-tongued tailor-politician from Greeneville. As soon as the joint debate got under way, Andrew Johnson began to refer to the gentleman who resided on the Sabine farm and was praying for Rome. His retirement to the Sabine farm and his prayer for Rome had been very short, according to Johnson, and his search for office had come hard on the heels of his denunciation of the Whig party. In reply, Gentry in-

15 *Union and American*, April 10, 1855.
16 Temple, p. 235.

sisted that Johnson had been a candidate for office oftener than he, and that, as for himself, he did not enter the race until it was manifest the people wanted him. His reason for leaving the Sabine farm and ceasing to pray for Rome he would illustrate with a true story. "Once a fearful drought afflicted Spain. The earth was parched with heat and for lack of rain streams dried up; cattle were dying and people were perishing. A pious priest, with a band of devout Catholics, traveled over the country, praying for rain. Presently they came upon a field, particularly dry and parched; the priest looked at it a moment, then raised his hands and closed his eyes, but said nothing. Opening his eyes, he surveyed the barren field again and again, closed them, raising his hands, but saying nothing. For the third time he surveyed the field and then said: 'My brethren, prayer is no good for soil so cursed and blighted as this has been; this field must have *manure*.'

"Alas! My fellow countrymen," Gentry concluded, "the State of Tennessee does not need prayers; there is a curse resting on her, parching and drying up her prosperity, and that curse must first be removed. I have come forth from my retirement and my prayers are joined with yours to remove that curse—and that curse is Andrew Johnson."

But Johnson soon evened up with Gentry. Adopting the policy of Henry A. Wise, candidate for Governor in Virginia, he fiercely attacked and destroyed the Know-Nothing party on account of its signs, its grips, its passwords, its oaths and secret conclaves, its midnight gatherings, its narrowness, littleness and proscriptiveness. He charged that the members were sworn to tell a lie when entering the order. "Show me a Know-Nothing," he exclaimed, "and I will show you a loathsome reptile, on whose neck every honest man should set his feet. . . . Why, such a gang are little better than John A. Murrell's clan of outlaws." As Johnson spoke these words the audience became "pale with rage and still as death." Many voices shouted back, "It's a lie—it's a lie." Pistols were cocked, "men ceased to breathe, their hearts stopped beating, the suspense was terrible." Johnson, unmoved, paused a minute, and, gazing around on the fearful scene he had evoked, deliberately resumed his speech.[17]

After this episode a committee of Democratic politicians waited on Johnson. He must tame down or he would be defeated; particularly he must stop defending Catholics and foreigners; in fact, certain Protestant ministers had already met to consider organizing against him. Johnson heard what his friends had to say and then, striding up and down the floor, announced his decision. "Gentlemen," he said, "I will make that same speech to-morrow if it blows the Democratic party to hell." [18]

It so happened that the next day the appointment was in a strong Whig community. Before the speaking began Johnson received notice that the Know-Nothings were not going to let him speak, that they were going to pull him off the stump. He armed himself therefore and prepared for the worst. Know-Nothingism was bearing its legitimate fruits—first the Catholics were to be suppressed, then the foreigners, and now, himself for daring to criticize. Mounting the stump, he faced the crowd: "Fellow citizens," he said, "it is proper when freemen assemble for the discussion of important public matters that everything should be done decently and in order. I have been informed that part of the business to be transacted on the present occasion is the assassination of the individual who now has the honor of addressing you. I suppose therefore that this is the first business in order—if any man has come here to-day for this purpose this is the proper time to proceed." Pausing for a moment and with his right hand on his pistol, he quietly surveyed the crowd. After a pause of a few seconds he resumed: "Gentlemen, it appears that I have been misinformed. I will now proceed to address you on the subject that has called us together."

At one of these debates Gentry charged that Andrew Johnson was not a southern man. In Congress he affiliated with Northerners and not with Southerners; his friends were the well-known abolitionists Gerrit Smith, W. H. Seward, Chase,

17 Temple, p. 386.
18 Greeneville *Sun*, February 23, 1911.

Sumner and I. P. Walker of Wisconsin.[19] Now these charges, except that Johnson was an abolitionist, were true, and would have destroyed any other southern man of the day. Johnson had advocated measures which his southern associates in Congress opposed, and for which northern Congressmen stood. To pass the Homestead bill was the ambition of his life, and yet this bill would destroy slavery; he had voted to admit Oregon as a free state; he had sneered at Bayly of Virginia, "a choleric slave-holder"; he had hurled epithets at Jefferson Davis, the southern leader, and he had advocated abolishing the three-fifths white clause in the Constitution. But all this was done while he was a Congressman, representing one mountain district only. It was easy enough to get away with such peculiar notions in East Tennessee, where the population was white and partly abolitionist.

In 1853, 1855 and 1857, however, when a candidate, he addressed an entire State, faced a slave-holding oligarchy and the assaults of the daily Whig papers, and was dependent for election on the votes of West and Middle Tennessee. And yet he made no change in his line of attack, advocating the same principles as before. An idea which he sprang on the stump, that pure democracy and theocracy were converging lines, and would some day meet and be one and the same, was pronounced by the Whig papers of Memphis and Nashville as the veriest sacrilege. Daily, for years and years, the Whig press assaulted him. He was "an apostate son of the South"; they charged he was a "mobocrat," "a Catiline, full of treason and hate against the rich"; "Robespierre was as bad, but he used chaste language." Johnson always won out, they declared, "by the votes of Catholics, Irish and thugs"—he was "low, despicable and dirty." [20]

Johnson's reply to these charges was bolder than before. "Whose hands built your Capitol?" he asked on one occasion. "Whose toil, whose labor built your railroads and your ships? Does not all life rest on labor?" . . . "I have no quarrel with

[19] Walker was included among the abolitionists though he was a southern sympathizer.

[20] *Rep. Banner*, Nashville, October 10, 1857; *The True Whig*, May and June 1853.

an aristocracy founded on merit and on honest toil, but for a rabble, upstart, mock aristocracy, I have supreme contempt;" and I call on you toiling people "to educate your sons, and especially your daughters, who will become mothers of sons to secure equal and exact justice to one and all." "There are in Congress," he declared, "two hundred and twenty-three Congressmen, and of this large number all are lawyers except twenty-three. The laboring man of America is ignored, he has no proportionate representation, though he constitutes a large majority of the voting population; the mechanic, the laborer and the farmer in Congress is only ten per cent. represented. For my own part, I say let the mechanic and the laborer make our laws, rather than the idle and vicious aristocrat." [21] The editorials of Tennessee papers, in the campaigns of 1853, 1855, 1857 and 1859, were devoted largely to Andrew Johnson and his canvass, and the news columns bristled with praise or denunciation of him.[22]

To the charge of the Whig papers, that an industrial congress of America had endorsed Johnson's course, classing him with Gerrit Smith of New York and Governor I. P. Walker of Wisconsin, "as able and tried champions of law reform and of the rights of labor and advocates of the abolition of slavery," he made no denial.[23] The jubilant Democratic papers, however, met all such charges with a bold front and with praise of their man "Andy Johnson." He was "the Mechanic Statesman"; he had "the best intellect of the day"; he was "Tennessee's greatest leader"; he had "a heart as big as a fodder stack." [24] And these encomiums they proceeded to substantiate by illustrations. Thus, an old friend who had been in California for years had just called on Congressman Johnson in Washington and wished to borrow money. Things had gone wrong with him in the far West. After Johnson heard his story, he opened his pocketbook and said, "Why, Jack, old fellow, if I had only five dollars every cent would be yours.

21 *Speech at the Agricultural Fair at Nashville* in 1857.
22 *Republican Banner*, Nashville, Tennessee, June, July and August, 1853, 1855, 1857 and 1859; Nashville *Union* of same dates.
23 *Rep. Banner*, July 14, 1855.
24 *Union and American*, April 29, 1853, and October 9, 1857.

How much do you want?" "Jack" had eight thousand dollars of good Western gold in the bank at that very moment, and was merely testing Andy.

Judge Temple declares that upon the stump Johnson never met his match. And were not Seward and Temple correct in their estimate of him? How could any one indeed hope to "down" such a man? Sprung from the people, thinking their thoughts, living their lives, voicing their needs, law abiding, and opposed to socialism in every form, he was invincible. Now stump oratory is not one of the fine arts, it will be admitted, but it must be remembered that Andrew Johnson was not contending with weaklings. In the '40's and '50's Tennessee was under the spell of men of national character. And the list is a long one: James K. Polk, John Bell, Ephraim H. Foster, Bailie Peyton, Spencer Jarnagan, Cave Johnson, Aaron V. Brown, James C. Jones, Gustavus Henry, A. O. P. Nicholson, M. P. Gentry, Emerson Etheridge, W. T. Haskell, Isham G. Harris, W. T. Senter, Landon C. Haynes, Horace Maynard, and John Netherland. And yet on the stump and at their very best—at the "perihelion of their palaver"—no man of them was the equal of "old Andy Johnson."

CHAPTER VI

GOVERNOR AND SENATOR

In April 1853 the Democratic convention of Tennessee met in Nashville to nominate state officers. Andrew Johnson, though a candidate for governor, did not attend the convention in person. The year before, when the Whigs "gerrymandered" him out of Congress, his old friend, George W. Jones, and other Democrats had urged him to run for governor and he had consented to do so. In the fall of 1852 Johnson wrote Andrew Ewing, asking him to take charge of his candidacy for governor, and adding that he "should withdraw his name if necessary to produce harmony." [1] Meanwhile Mr. Ewing's name was also mentioned for the same office, but before the convention met he wrote a letter to Johnson and also the public declining to run. [2] And so it came about that on April 14, 1853, Andrew Johnson, the Greeneville tailor, became the unanimous choice of the Democratic party for Governor, and, in August following, defeated his Whig opponent, Honorable Gustavus Henry, the aristocratic "Eagle Orator." [3]

In October 1853 the inaugural committee at Nashville were making preparation to induct Andrew Johnson into the high office of Governor. There were to be brass bands, of course, military companies, regaliaed marshals, and a procession of carriages, the Governor's equipage with the outgoing and incoming Governor leading the rest. But the gala occasion failed to materialize as arranged—the new Governor preferred to walk. If Thomas Jefferson could foot it across the square to his inaugural and Andy Jackson could ride horseback and, without fuss or feathers, take the oath, why not Andy John-

[1] George W. Jones, *Address*, 1878.

[2] *National Union*, April 15, 1853; *The True Whig*, April 29, 1853.

[3] Professor Sioussat, a student of Johnson's life and generally fair to him, states that in the 1853 Convention Johnson took advantage of a casual promise of Andrew Ewing to support the former and this caused Ewing to withdraw in Johnson's favor. *The True Whig*, June 1, 1853, sets forth the advanced platform on which Johnson ran.

76

son, as well? Walking from the hotel to the Capitol, therefore, the Governor pulled out his inaugural and proceeded to "shadow forth" his opinion as to what constitutes an ideal republic.[4]

The difference between the two political parties he found in the answer to this question, "Where should the proper lodgment of the supreme power of a nation be made?" On the one side was the Federalist or Whig party, "which maintained the old monarchical or kingly notion of Hamilton that mankind was not capable of governing himself." . . . Then "there was the Republican or Democratic party, holding with Madison, that man was honest and capable of self-government." According to the Federalists, the Governor declared, "The Constitution was but a paper wall through which they could thrust their fingers at pleasure, or a piece of gum elastic, that could be expanded or contracted at the will or whim of the legislature."

"I claim to belong to that division of the Democratic party," said the Governor, "which stands firmly by the combined and recorded judgment of the people, until changed or modified by them; . . . which is progressive, not in violation of, but in conformity with, the law and the Constitution." "There are some who lack confidence in the integrity and capacity of the people to govern themselves," he said. "To all who entertain such fears I will most respectfully say that I entertain none . . . and I will ask the question, If man is not capable, and is not to be trusted with the government of himself, is he to be trusted with the government of others? . . . Who, then, will govern? The answer must be, Man—for we have no angels in the shape of men, as yet, who are willing to take charge of our political affairs. Man is not perfect, it is true, but we all hope he is approximating perfection, and that he will, in the progress of time, reach this grand and most important end in all human affairs."

"This," the Governor declared, in an ecstasy of Democratic joy, "I term the divinity of man . . . and this divinity can be enlarged, and man can become more God-like than he is. It is

4 Temple, p. 381.

the business of the Democratic party to progress in the work of increasing this principle of divinity or Democracy and thereby elevate and make man more perfect. . . . I hold that the Democratic party proper, of the whole world, and especially of the United States, has undertaken the *political redemption* of man, and sooner or later the great work will be accomplished. In the political world it corresponds to that of Christianity in the moral. They are going along, not in divergents, nor in parallels, but in converging lines—the one purifying and elevating man religiously, the other politically. . . . At what period of time they will have finished the work of progress and elevation, it is not now for me to determine, but, when finished, these two lines will have approximated each other. At this point it is that the Church Militant will give way and cease to exist, and the Church Triumphant begin. At the same point, Democracy progressive will give way and cease to exist, and Theocracy begin."

Soaring higher, the apocalyptical Governor "confidently and exultingly" asserted that "then the voice of the people will be the voice of God." At that auspicious moment proclamation would be made "that the millennial morning has dawned, and that the time has come when 'the lion and lamb will lie down together'; when 'the voice of the turtle shall be heard in our land'; when 'the suckling child shall play upon the hole of the asp, and the weaned child put its hand upon the cockatrice's den,' and the glad tidings shall be proclaimed, throughout the land, of man's political and religious redemption, and that there is 'on earth peace, good will toward men.' "

For the young men the Governor likewise had a word. He warned them that "their wealth, and too often their preceptors," some of whom were "bigoted and supercilious and assumed superior information," inspired them "with false ideas of their own superiority, mixed with a superabundance of self-esteem, which cause them to feel that the great mass of mankind are intended by their creator to be hewers of wood and drawers of water." . . . "It will be readily perceived by all discerning young men," he proceeded, "that Democracy is a ladder, corresponding in politics to the one spiritual which

Jacob saw in his vision; one up which all, in proportion to their merit, may ascend. While it extends to the humblest of all created beings, here on earth below, it reaches to God on high; and it would seem that the class of young men to which I have alluded might find a position somewhere between the lower and upper extremes of this ladder, commensurate, at least, with their virtue and merit, if not equal to their inflated ambition, which they would occupy with honor to themselves and advantage to their country." [5]

This remarkable document was heard by Whigs and anti-Johnson Democrats with shouts of laughter and derision. They dubbed it the "Jacob's Ladder Speech," and declared that it was copied from the platform of a labor party in the North. On the other hand, the rank and file were greatly pleased and the message was broadcasted throughout the land. Though the address was censured by the conservative statesmen of this country and by the aristocratic press of England and France, democratic opinion in America, and especially in the great West, thought it "better than almost anything from Governor Johnson's pen." [6]

If, however, Johnson's inaugural was high-flown, his message to the Legislature was quite the opposite.[7] Dealing in a practical way with all these issues, the Governor made the subject of popular education his central thought. In truth, to Governor Johnson belongs the credit "of being the first Governor of Tennessee to strike an effectual blow for the common schools and for a system of public taxation throughout the State." [8] Governor Cannon in 1837 had suggested a similar remedy for the prevailing illiteracy, but the Legislature did not, at that time, act on his recommendation.[9]

Attacking Tennessee's system of public schools, the new Governor declared that it fell far short of the commands of the Constitution. The public schools were in fact doing no good but rather harm. They failed to educate the child and

[5] Johnson MS. at Greeneville; pamphlet in Carnegie Library, Nashville.
[6] *Western Democratic Review* of this period.
[7] *Message*, December 19, 1853.
[8] Jones, p. 50; Garrett and Goodpasture, *History of Tennessee*, p. 297.
[9] McGee, *History of Tennessee*, pp. 177-178; Merritt, *Tennessee and Tennesseeans*, Vol. III, p. 570.

yet prevented the people from operating private schools of
their own. To remedy this evil he urged that a tax on the
people of the whole State be levied and collected. By way of
contrast, he called attention to the new capitol building then
nearing completion. "When millions are being appropriated
to aid various works of internal improvements," he asked, "can
nothing be done for education?" . . . "With niches and ro-
tundas, for fine statues and generous paintings, and the ex-
terior, grand with carved and massive columns, and costing the
people a million and a half dollars," he urged that education
should receive like consideration. In fact, the Governor made
such a worthy plea and presented the point so clearly, and
with such danger to any politician who dared oppose, the
legislature adopted his recommendations. Thereby was begun
a modern system of common schools at the public expense.
This stand of the Governor in favor of education was no surprise to the people of Greeneville, where he had always been
interested in the subject. Soon after his arrival in Greeneville,
and for a great number of years, he served as a trustee of Rhea
Academy—a flourishing boys' and girls' school in that town.
On all occasions he coöperated in behalf of public education.

However, the "Mechanic Governor" did not stop with these
recommendations. He brought his Homestead hobby from
Washington to Nashville. Despite the attacks by the southern
press on this measure, he urged the legislature, "To instruct
our Senators in Congress and request our Representatives to
use all reasonable exertion to procure the passage of a bill
granting to every head of a family, who is a citizen of the
United States, a 'Homestead' of a hundred and sixty acres of
land, upon condition of settlement and cultivation for a number of years." Governor Johnson also recommended that steps
be taken by the legislature looking to the passage of an
amendment to the Constitution of the United States requiring
that the President and Vice-President be elected by popular
vote. Later in his career, it will be remembered, he advocated
the election of the Supreme Court judges by a like popular
vote for twelve years only. After reading the Governor's radical program, the conservatives of Tennessee were amazed. The

man was "leading a rabble against the better elements of society." He was an iconoclast of the most pronounced type, "pulling down and breaking to pieces at his haughty will." He was "a natural leveler and his theories and appeals were based on the gullibility of the masses." [10] These attacks on the Governor, however, were growing weaker and weaker. The aristocrats had learned that the more they abused him the stronger he became with the people.

During both his first and second administrations Governor Johnson reviewed the financial history of Tennessee and its existing status. Striking a balance between debits and credits, he warned against extravagance. He likewise cautioned the legislature to provide that "state banks should carry a larger percentage of gold and silver in proportion to the total bank issue." Otherwise, as he suggested, inflation would be inevitable. Governor Johnson, though much devoted to economy and reform, was not more so than to the fame of his old chief, Andy Jackson. The first speech Johnson made in Congress, it will be recalled, was urging the repayment to "Old Hickory" of the fine of a thousand dollars and interest, imposed by Judge Hall because Jackson refused to obey an order of the court and was adjudged guilty of contempt. And now an opportunity was presented to again honor Jackson. "The Hermitage," Jackson's home near Nashville, could be purchased by the State for forty-eight thousand dollars. Governor Johnson advocating the purchase, the property was bought. It is now one of the magnificent places of pilgrimage for state and nation.

In consequence of the Governor's recommendation the legislature likewise appropriated a handsome sum for the establishment of agricultural and mechanical fairs, with farm exhibits and livestock. During the Johnson administration various colleges and schools of high grade were established, and to this period must be credited the start of the public library for the State.[11] Before the administration of Governor Johnson the state library was composed almost entirely of Court

[10] J. S. Wise, *Recollections of Thirteen Presidents*, p. 107; Temple, p. 455.
[11] McGee, *History of Tennessee*, pp. 177-178.

Reports, Congressional documents and a few other books of a public nature, and of little value. In 1854 the legislature appropriated five thousand dollars for books, appointing Return J. Meigs to purchase them. Shortly afterwards Mr. Meigs was given a regular salary. From this beginning has grown the present state library of Tennessee. In the year 1857 the Tennessee Historical Society was located in Nashville and a museum of Indian relics and minerals, Confederate money, old letters, portraits and the usual accompaniments of such an institution were collected. In a word, during the Johnson administration, the affairs of Tennessee were wisely and honestly administered and progress was made. Tennessee historians, indeed, agree that "the administrations of Johnson and of Harris mark the beginning of an era of advance in learning and intellectual life, of wealth, of culture and of the development of a distinctly southern spirit and pride among the people." [12]

Having won over the heads of the leaders, the Governor did not court their favor. In fact, he went his own way regardless of party. People were beginning to say that the Democratic party of Tennessee had become the "Johnson party." Nothing better illustrates his detachment from party than an incident occurring in March 1855, when his first term as Governor ended and he had just been renominated to succeed himself.[13] The Democratic party, in convention at Nashville, failed to endorse Johnson's administration. A committee of five on resolutions was appointed and made a report, endorsing the national Democratic party but not the State. The report pointed "with pride to the achievements of the National Democratic party." It declared that "Franklin Pierce has been faithful and true, his leading measures able, enlightened and patriotic and deserve as they receive, our cordial and earnest support." Nothing, however, was said about the Johnson administration. Mr. Matthews of Bedford did introduce the following milk and water resolution:

"*Resolved*—That Andrew Johnson has been nominated for

12 McGee, p. 180.
13 *Daily Union and American*, March 28, 1855.

reëlection by the Democracy of Tennessee and that this convention registers and endorses his nomination, with pride and confidence."

The resolution was carried without a dissenting vote. When Governor Johnson accepted the nomination from the committee he threw a bit of humor into his reply. He declared that the resolutions which "endorsed and registered the will of the people, as expressed in their primary meetings in various portions of the State," were gratifying to him ". . . emanating as they do, from the true source of all political power, the people." [14] No doubt this failure to endorse Johnson's administration was intentional. His advocacy of "wild, impractical schemes" was not to the fancy of the leaders. President Polk had already written on a petition for a Homestead bill, "It is not worthy of an answer." [15]

Moreover, only a few months before, Governor Johnson had exchanged gifts and letters with Judge Pepper and had given utterance to views well-bred people could by no means approve. Mr. Pepper, now a Judge, had once been a blacksmith. Though a Whig, he was an admirer of the mechanic Governor. Doffing his judicial ermine, he went to the shop and made a shovel and sent the same to the Governor with his compliments. The Governor, not to be outdone, cut out with his own hands a broadcloth coat which he sent to the Judge with his compliments.[16] The Governor accompanied the gift with an open letter declaring that the "main highway and surest passport to honesty and useful distinction will soon be through the harvest field and the workshop." He suggested that all persons who aspired "to be leaders in political affairs shall be required to undergo such probation in order to identify them in feeling, in sentiment, in interest, in sympathy, and even in prejudice, with the great mass of people whose toil and sweat it is that produces all that sustains the government in every department both State and Federal." [17]

[14] *Daily Union and American*, April 3, 1855.
[15] "Andrew Johnson and the Early Phases of the Homestead," *Mississippi Valley Historical Review*, Vol. V, No. 3, p. 267.
[16] This coat is now in the Historical Museum of Tennessee. New York *Times*, January 2, 1927.
[17] *Letter* dated July 17, 1854, Johnson MS. at Greeneville.

Notwithstanding the dislike such undignified incidents engendered among the leaders, Johnson's administration, with the boys in the plow rows, was growing stronger and stronger. In 1856, for the first time since 1828, when Jackson carried the State, Tennessee polled a Democratic majority, casting its vote for Buchanan for President. Isham G. Harris, afterwards one of Tennessee's greatest sons, running for governor on the ticket with Buchanan, was also elected. Johnson canvassed for Harris and contributed much to his success. On the evening of July 15, 1856, Governor Johnson delivered an address before the Democratic Club of Davidson County. This speech created wide interest, was published in pamphlet, and became a campaign document.

As one reads this speech and compares it with the Governor's inaugural, in which he took such a bold stand for freedom and equality, an idea of the grip of slavery is discernible. The entire speech is devoted to the argument that the Kansas-Nebraska Act of 1854 was neither new nor startling, that the Missouri Compromise of 1820 had already been repealed by the Compromise of 1850, and that the Kansas-Nebraska Act simply reaffirmed this fact.[18]

This unfortunate speech, and Johnson's advocacy of the Jeff Davis resolutions of February 1860, that slavery followed the flag into the territories, mark the high water mark of Andrew Johnson in his progress towards the slavery position of Calhoun and Davis. However, it must be said that though, at this period of his life, Andrew Johnson was in a blind alley, neither by word nor deed did he advocate secession or stand out against the Union. Under no circumstances would he have joined with the forty-eight Southern leaders, Calhoun and Davis included, who, in 1849, in a caucus at Washington and in a manifesto to the South, threatened the life of the Nation unless southern rights were granted.[19]

Much besides politics was happening in the Governor's life at Nashville. During his first term as Governor, a brother

18 Address of Andrew Johnson on the *Political Issues of the Day*, at Nashville, July 15, 1856. In the Tennessee State Library.
19 McMaster, *History of the United States*, Vol. VIII, p. 3; Rhodes, Vol. I, p. 135.

tailor was taken sick, and, after a painful illness, died, leaving
a wife and a number of small children.   This little family the
Governor befriended, visiting them, sending them clothing and
money, and furnishing them a home in which to live.   Forthwith the tongue of scandal began to wag and "all sorts of untrue stories were circulated about him." [20]   While Governor
Johnson was living in a hotel at Nashville an incident occurred,
very much like the saving of the life of Colonel Henderson by
old Jacob Johnson at Raleigh when Andy was three years old.
One night the Governor was aroused from bed by loud cries
of fire.   Rushing from his apartment to give such aid as he
could, he saw that the hotel was ablaze.   Near by he could
hear the cries of a woman screaming for help.   Hastening to
her side, through smoke and flame, he conveyed the woman to
a place of safety, not only risking his life, but losing his trunk
and other personal effects, including $2,500 in currency, all
of which were consumed by the flames.[21]

Fortunately for his social life, several of Johnson's old
Greeneville friends had moved to Nashville and were living
there in the '50's.   Hugh Douglass was one of these.   This
young fellow moved to Greeneville, and was a new comer in the
'20's, working in the humble position of clerk in his uncle's
store.   Now Hugh was a Scotch boy, and, though of the house
of Douglass of Garalan and an aristocrat, was very poor.
In Greeneville the two youngsters had grown to be fast friends.
The first tailor-made coat Hugh ever ordered was Andy's
handiwork.   Though the young Scotchman was a Whig, he
was in no sense a politician.   A scholar and a recluse, he was
just the opposite of his young friend, Johnson.   In the larger
sense of the word he was thoroughly democratic.   Born in Ayr,
the birthplace of Burns, he, too, felt that "A man's a man for
a' that."   After a time Douglass succeeded in business and
moved from Greeneville to Nashville.   There he became a
wealthy merchant, and was called "one of the nabobs of the
town."   In the midst of riches, however, he did not forget his
old crony, Andy Johnson.   Each Christmas he would send over

[20] *Harper's Magazine*, Vol. CXX, p. 169.
[21] Johnson MS. at Greeneville.

to the Mansion a dozen red bandanna handkerchiefs, for the "sake of auld lang syne." The two men never forgot their early days, never ceased to cherish memories of their boyhood.[22]

It must not be thought that Andrew Johnson had a natural dislike for gentlemen—only those gentlemen who assumed superior airs seemed to excite his wrath. In Nashville some of the oldest families cultivated his friendship. In the '50's one of the most refined homes in the city was that presided over by the accomplished Lazinka Campbell Brown, daughter of a Congressman, a Senator, a Secretary of the Treasury under Monroe, and a Minister to Russia. As the Russian name, Lazinka, might suggest, Mrs. Brown was born in St. Petersburg and bore the name of a Russian Empress. Now Lazinka Campbell Brown and Harriott, her equally accomplished daughter, welcomed the Governor, who formed the habit of making frequent visits to their home. These good ladies and Judge W. F. Cooper once consulted together about broadening Johnson's views of life, which they agreed were extremely narrow. Accordingly the next time the Governor visited the Brown home and asked for a book to read, Mrs. Brown, carrying out the conspiracy, handed him *Sartor Resartus.* After a few days he returned the book, remarking simply, "I can't make head or tail out of it." "If it had occurred to him that there was anything in it applicable to himself, he artfully concealed the fact," the ladies declared, when they afterwards related the story.

One evening while the Governor was expounding his democratic creed, he informed the Browns that in his opinion mechanics were superior to other men. "Why, then, Governor," said the mother of the household to him, "did you make lawyers of your two sons, Charles and Robert?" "Because they had not sense enough to be mechanics," he retorted.

Perhaps in the '50's the practice of dueling in the South reached its culmination, and, under the code duello, men killed each other as courteously as they would bow to a queen. It was

---

[22] In 1869, when a daughter of Hugh Douglass married J. S. Wise, ex-President Johnson was a guest at the wedding; the aristocratic mother, though skeptical of Johnson as a wedding guest, was forced to admit that "Mr. Johnson's manners are excellent, his conversation interesting and complimentary, and his deportment dignified and decorous."—J. S. Wise, *Recollections of Thirteen Administrations*, p. 107.

one of the hallmarks of a southern gentleman "to give satisfaction" to any other gentleman who demanded it. Frequent attempts were made to draw Governor Johnson into this deadly game, and at the end of his first term as Governor it seemed that he would be forced into such a contest. The campaign of 1855 ended at the August election with the overthrow of the aristocratic Gentry and the reëlection of himself, a plain Democrat as Governor of the State. The Democrats concluded that such a splendid result ought to be celebrated. There must be a general jollification with speech-making and parades. Greeneville started off, "with its public demonstration of joy," Gen. T. B. Arnold being the presiding officer. Governor Johnson was the orator of the occasion, and everything passed off smoothly. "Three rousing cheers" were given for Greeneville's Governor. In Knoxville, the succeeding week, another celebration was held and Johnson spoke again. Parson Brownlow, though a Whig and not expected to attend a Democratic jubilee, was nevertheless on hand and wrote up the speech for the Nashville *Banner* in his best Brownlowesque fashion.

"Johnson," so Brownlow wrote the *Banner*, "called the American Party a gang of horse thieves and counterfeiters;" his speech was "a low-flung and disgraceful affair." [23] Now, according to the Democratic papers, what Johnson really said was this: "The American Party charges that both Whigs and Democrats are corrupt and claims that it is the only pure party, being made up of both the old parties. How can purity come out of corruption?" . . . "If we have one gang of horse thieves and another gang of counterfeiters, can an honest organization be formed from these two?" [24] The Whig papers in Nashville, taking Brownlow's letter as a text, also set out, at great length, Johnson's agrarian course as Congressman and Governor. They warned the people that their new Governor was "an arrant demagogue and little if any better than a freesoiler."

On August 20 it came the turn of Nashville to celebrate the Democratic victory, but the Whigs determined that the meeting should not take place. On the appointed night there was

[23] Nashville *Banner*, August 23 and 25, 1855.
[24] Nashville *Union*, August 21 to 26, 1855.

so much noise and confusion in the rear no one could be heard. Governor Johnson had mounted the stump and read the secret political oath of the Know-Nothings, in the following words: "You do solemnly swear that in all political matters for all political offices you will support the members of the Order," and was going on to say that those who took that oath were perjurers, incompetent to serve on juries or as witnesses or judges. "Such a person," he declared, "is not a free man but a slave, and his liberty is controlled by a Know-Nothing conclave." At this precise point Mr. T. T. Smiley, a Whig enthusiast, approached the speaker and begged him to moderate his language. The Governor, however, would do no such thing, but roundly denounced the high-handed attempt to bulldoze him, rubbing it in worse than ever.

Smiley challenged the Governor to fight a duel; notes passed between friends. Generals Washington Barrow and S. R. Cheatham "tendered their good offices." Mr. Smiley finally admitted that he was not present on the occasion to break up the meeting, but to hold back the infuriated Whigs; Governor Johnson met Smiley halfway, declaring that he had no particular reference to him but was referring to those who had come to prevent the speaking. The referees, feeling that the honor of each man had been preserved, wrote duplicate letters to the Governor and to Smiley, the letter to the Governor being as follows:

Nashville, Tenn., August 29, 1855.

DEAR SIR:

Having received assurances yesterday from Thos. T. Smiley and yourself to notes of the same date addressed by us to both of you, under circumstances of which you are aware, we are happy to find that there no longer exists any cause for the interruption of the personal relations existing between you previous to the evening of the 20th instant.

Very resp'y yours
WASHINGTON BARROW,
B. F. CHEATHAM

To Gov. Johnson
Pres't.[25]

25 Johnson MSS. Nos. 112 to 124. Though often challenged to fight duels, Andrew Johnson was opposed on principle to dueling and did not engage in the practice: Prof. J. G. DeR. Hamilton, Dearborn *Independent*, February 1927.

At the end of his second term as Governor, Andrew Johnson was unanimously chosen by a Democratic Legislature to a seat in the United States Senate. The Thirty-fifth Congress convened December 7, 1857. The oath was administered to the new Senator by Jesse D. Bright of Indiana. During Johnson's four years' absence as Governor of Tennessee great changes had taken place in American politics. Slavery, which Clay's compromise measures of 1850 had settled forever—as every one thought—was now the vital issue. The Kansas-Nebraska Act of 1854, repealing the Compromise of 1850, had been the occasion of border warfare in Kansas. The country was in a ferment and a new and growing political party, the Republican party, was just born. The old Whig party, South, as well as North, had nearly disbanded. In the South its members had joined the Democracy; in the North they had for the most part joined the new party. Southern Whig leaders, Alex Stephens, Clingman, and Bob Toombs, were now Democrats and, nominally at least, in the same party with Andrew Johnson. Jefferson Davis and Thomas L. Clingman, Johnson's old antagonists in the House, had been promoted to the United States Senate. Many faces confronted Senator Johnson, with whom he was shortly to have much to do: Fessenden and Hamlin of Maine; Hale and Clark, New Hampshire; Sumner and Wilson, Massachusetts; Dixon, Connecticut; Seward and Preston King, New York; Cameron, Pennsylvania; Wade, Ohio; Trumbull, Illinois; Chandler, Michigan; Doolittle, Wisconsin; and Harlan, Iowa.[26]

During the past four years Andrew Johnson had made considerable progress. He was now a better thinker and student than formerly. His handwriting was wonderfully improved, being legible, mature and well-formed. His spelling had become as good as the average. His figure, too, was rounded out. In fact, he had become a notable character, attracting attention in almost any company. Moreover, his mind was better disciplined, he was less pugnacious, and not so sensitive. If a Senator were seeking trouble he could find it, of course; but Johnson did not now go out of his way looking for trouble. And the Senate treated him with greater

26 Jas. Ford Rhodes, *History of the United States*, Vol. II, p. 283.

consideration than the House had done. They practically tendered him the chairmanship of a special committee, but he declined it. Only once in the House had he been chairman of a committee, the committee on public expenditures. Howell Cobb, the speaker in 1850, had given him this appointment, but Johnson resigned it shortly afterwards, stating that he had nothing to do. The select committee on curtailing governmental expenses, the chairmanship of which the Senate would now confer on Johnson, arose because of a recommendation of President Buchanan. Buchanan, in his message, had urged a reduction in governmental expenses, and Senator Johnson had offered a resolution to give effect to the President's message. Johnson's resolution named a certain sum beyond which the annual expenditures should not go. He declined the chairmanship of this select committee because he felt "the work should be undertaken by the judiciary committee or some other regular committee of the Senate."

Andrew Johnson's speeches in the Senate were less sophomoric and pedantic than when he was in the House. In a debate in Congress on the Oregon Boundary bill, with its well-known slogan of "54-40 or fight," Johnson had been highly dramatic. He would pit the American eagle against the British lion any day. He boasted that "when the king of birds swoops down from the Rockies the lion will be seen tucking tail and seeking the mountain coves!" On the question of admitting Texas as a state he had likewise been immature and juvenile, as we have seen, alluding to nuptial vows, Hymen's votary, and Uncle Sam's taking the lovely bride, Texas, to wife. As Senator this juvenility disappeared, and Johnson held himself better in hand. But in the Senate, as in the House, he continued to be independent and unorthodox.

Soon he found opposition in Jefferson Davis, his old antagonist. Mr. Davis, who always advocated a large and permanent standing army, offered a resolution to accomplish this purpose. The measure sharply divided the parties. Republicans feared it was a ruse of the Democrats, insisting that the Buchanan administration, controlled by the South, would use this increased army in "bleeding Kansas." Kansas would be forced into the Union, as a Slave State, under the Lecompton Constitution. When Senator Seward joined with Senator Davis and advocated the bill, Hale of New Hampshire was "pained and mortified." "Will the Senator," Hale asked, "vote seven thousand extra men to the executive of the United States who proclaims and practices such dangerous, fatal and damaging doctrines; will he lay down his fame and his reputation at the footstool of the slave power?"

Now Andrew Johnson was listening to this discussion, took part in it, and thoroughly understood that it was a fight with the North on one side and the South on the other. Nevertheless, he aligned himself with the North and against Jefferson Davis. Mr. Davis did not forget this incident.[27] In the debate on the standing army, however, Senator Johnson did not place his opposition on the same ground with Senator Hale.[28] On principle, as he declared, he turned himself against the bill. "This measure," he urged, "will entail unnecessary expense" and is "against the spirit of the people." "A standing army is an incubus, a canker, a fungus in the body politic." . . . "I want no rabble here on one hand," he declared, "and I want no aristocracy on the other." Some southern Senators, including Toombs, voted against the bill, and it was defeated. In the Senate, as in the House, Jefferson Davis and Andrew Johnson were in frequent conflict—the imperious, self-sufficient and scholarly Davis neither understanding nor caring to understand Johnson, the plebeian.

Johnson opposed the building of the Pacific Railroad, and insisted that Congress had no power, under the Constitution, to go into the business of building railroads. He suggested that politics and a desire to become President were behind many such schemes, evidently striking at Jefferson Davis. Davis and Broderick both replied to Johnson. Broderick asked how Johnson could vote for the purchase of Cuba and against the Pacific Railroad. "Why is it," he asked, "constitutional to purchase Cuba for slave purposes and unconstitutional to build a railroad to the Pacific for war purposes?"

---

27 Jefferson Davis, *Rise and Fall*, p. 703.
28 Savage, p. 99.

Mr. Davis was more personal than Broderick. He ridiculed Johnson's pretensions and insinuated that when he entered the race for President "it would be a pony race." Johnson replied with indignation. "The Presidency has become a great absorbing idea," he said, "the Aaron's rod swallowing up everything; legislation is impaired and public business ruined because Senators are president-making." . . . "Let the people attend to that." . . . "Damn the Presidency!—It is not worthy of the aspirations of a man who desires to do right." [29]

Senator Gwin of California called Johnson's attention to the fact that the National Democratic Convention of 1856 declared for the Pacific Railroad. Johnson retorted that it was true the last Democratic convention had passed a resolution recommending the completion of the Pacific Railroad, but that thereby "they hung a millstone around the neck of the party." . . . "I am no party man, bound by no party platforms, and will vote as I please," he said.

In the spring of 1858 Senator Johnson had an unfortunate colloquy with Senator Bell of Tennessee. Senator Bell was one of the few Southern Senators voting against the Kansas-Nebraska bill of 1854. In debating that measure, Bell had said that when a Senator's views were "in direct opposition to the settled sentiments of his constituency he should resign." Now it so happened that the Tennessee legislature favored the Kansas-Nebraska bill and therefore passed a resolution asking Senator Bell to resign his seat. Bell was anxious to conciliate Johnson, though he had been sneering at and belittling him for more than a quarter of a century. In discussing the Tennessee resolution which asked his resignation, Bell made certain strictures on the members of the legislature, some of them Johnson's friends. Senator Johnson espoused the cause of the Tennessee legislature and justified its action in calling for Bell's resignation. In the course of his remarks he spoke of Bell as his "competitor." Bell, replying, resented the suggestion that Johnson was his "competitor," treating the idea with scorn. Johnson, now thoroughly aroused, admonished Bell that he had had "competitors that were worthy of my steel, men

[29] Savage, p. 131.

who recognized me as such." . . . "A gentleman and a well-bred man will respect me; all others I will make do it." . . . "I stand here to-day not as the competitor of any Senator; I know my rights and I intend to learn the proprieties of the Senate, and in compliance with those proprieties, my rights, and the right of the State I have the honor in part to represent shall be maintained—to use terms very familiar with us—at all hazards and to the last extremity."

It may be thought that Johnson intended by his last remark to invite Bell to fight a duel, but such was perhaps not the case. Johnson opposed dueling on principle. In a debate with Clingman he ridiculed the field of honor and spoke of dueling as an "infamy and a disgrace." [30] While Senator Johnson took part in these running debates he was not engrossed by them. His attention was upon a larger matter—the homestead bill. The homestead bill was the goal of his ambition and when that bill passed, he declared, he would die content.

While in Congress, Mr. Johnson was injured in a railroad accident, his right arm being broken. This injury somewhat impaired his handwriting which, by constant practice, had become flowing and legible. Under treatment of surgeons in a Philadelphia hospital he was soon cured and returned to his duties.[31] At this time Johnson had high hopes of his son, Robert. He kept up a correspondence with Robert, giving him an account of his injury, and also of the politics and gossip of the day. Robert had obtained license to practice law and had been honored with the position of Secretary of the Greeneville Bar Association, of which Sam Milligan was President. He was also elected a member of the Tennessee legislature. The young man was a general favorite in Greene County, Johnson's old friends writing congratulatory letters and commending his course in matters of public concern. Mr. Johnson wrote Robert that he was going to canvass the State of Alabama for Buchanan for President; and in 1859 wrote that he had been urged to canvass Ohio for the Democratic party.

Johnson greatly admired Sam Houston, "Old Fuss and

30 *North Carolina Historical Society,* 1915-19.
31 Johnson MSS. Nos. 138 and 169.

Feathers." Houston once wrote a letter introducing Johnson to Col. A. H. Mickle. After commending Johnson to Mickle, he added, "You must make my friend cheerful while he may be with you. Thine truly, Sam Houston." Senator Johnson also kept up a correspondence with Lewis Cass; and, after the Democratic victory of 1856, Cass wrote Johnson and "gave thanks to God for the victory." Writing to his son, Robert, in 1858, Johnson expressed the opinion that Buchanan was a failure, that Douglas was a dead cock in the pit, "lost the North by advocating the Kansas-Nebraska bill and lost the South by opposing the Lecompton Constitution." Frequently during the years 1858 and 1859 Governor Harris wrote urging Senator Johnson's help in the campaign. He must come to a meeting "to harmonize and bring about the success of the Democratic party." [32] Perhaps Andrew Johnson was closer to George W. Jones of Tennessee than to any other Congressman. With Jones, once a tanner, Johnson had a common tie. They served together ten years in the House. Jones was an able and a conscientious man and was considered one of the best financiers in the House; he was known as the "watch-dog of the treasury." [33] Next to G. W. Jones, Johnson relied on the aid of A. O. P. Nicholson. Nicholson was college bred and stood high with Democratic leaders. He, almost alone among the great leaders of Tennessee, born to affluence and high station, was Andrew Johnson's constant friend. In return for this devotion, Johnson caused him to be chosen, in 1859, a United States Senator.

[32] Johnson MS., pp. 84, 136 and 175.

[33] The Tennessee Historical Society has several autograph letters from Johnson to Jones. In December, '36, he asks Jones "to pardon his blunders," as he knew the difficulties he labored under; in a letter dated February 13, 1843, Johnson advises Jones not to submit his claims to a seat in Congress to any convention, "except as a last resort."

CHAPTER VII

HOME LIFE

Martha and Charles, the first two children of the Johnson family, were born in the rear room of the small rented house on Main Street. Robert and Mary came while their parents lived down on Water Street, and Andrew, Jr., the baby, arrived during his father's governorship and after the family had moved for the third time to their permanent home. Until this last move, the home surroundings had been cramped, without yard, garden or other open space.

In September 1851, however, Congressman Johnson purchased nearly an acre of land on Main Street in the residence section of Greeneville, only a short walk from the tailor shop. On the lot at that time was an unfinished brick dwelling. The owner, being unable to complete the building, agreed to exchange it with Johnson for the Water Street property and nine hundred and fifty dollars additional. Accordingly, the trade was made and as soon as the building could be finished, probably about January 1, 1852, the family moved in. Andrew Johnson's "sweet conception," as he called one's home and appurtenances, was realized at last. He could now proclaim, "I have a home, an abiding place for my wife and for my children." [1] It was not entirely accidental that the lot purchased was the same lot on which twenty-five years before, on a September night, the run-away apprentice boy and his brother, Bill, and their mother and Turner Dougherty, her impecunious spouse, had camped. Essentially Andrew Johnson was a home-loving body, loyal not only to persons but to places.

And it was a great day, we may be sure, when Andrew Johnson and his wife, with sons and daughters, moved into their new and spacious residence, not showy or expensive, yet comfort-

[1] *National Portrait Gallery*, Vol. III. Title "Andrew Johnson."

able and homelike, with generous fireplaces, high pitched ceilings and a pleasing view from every window. There were two rooms above and two below—a pantry and serving-room were attached to the rear. Twenty "honest" steps separated the kitchen from the "Great House." This was in accordance with an old southern idea that the odor of boiled onions and cabbage should be avoided. Built on the plan of English homes, the front of the dwelling was flush with the street; the veranda was afterwards arranged on the side, overlooking the lawn some distance below. The parlor on the left, as one enters the front door, had the usual furnishings of middle-class homes of that day: the walnut chairs and sofa upholstered in mohair cloth; the inevitable walnut what-not in one corner and, in the other, an old-fashioned escritoire. The floor was covered with a flowery "store" carpet and on the neat, but cheaply papered, walls were pictures of Johnson and his wife and copies of works of the masters.

One can hear the voice of the lovable Charles, as he wanders through the new home, humming some old love song, while his mother is busying herself in the yard and garden, planting evergreens, superintending the seeding of grass, or setting out a wonderful scuppernong vine.[2] Martha, a woman of poise and superb nerve, serious-minded and devoted to duty, was the companion of her father. Charles, with his light heart and merry ways, was the idol of his mother, and a ray of sunshine to all. Though his conviviality and dissipation were a source of grief to mother and father, they did not scold or complain but met the situation philosophically.[3] Charles was now a licensed physician and druggist. Robert, a fledgling at the bar, was doing well with the help of Sam Milligan, president of the local bar association. Whiskey, however, the curse of the old South, was beginning to hold both of the boys in its clutch, drink cutting them off before they reached middle life.

From the new home Martha and Mary shortly went forth

[2] In Johnson's home and in the tailor shop are sundry mementoes of the tailor-president, such as needles, thimbles, a tailor's goose and specimens of his handiwork, including a silk vest and broadcloth coat he once made for himself and wore.—Knoxville *Sentinel*, July 30, 1922.

[3] Jones, p. 394; Johnson vs. Patterson, *Tennessee Reports*, Vol. LXXXI, p. 627.

as brides. Martha, on December 13, 1855, married David T. Patterson, eight years her senior, a circuit judge and a close friend of her father. Patterson was upright and capable, conservative and patriotic, but slow and heavy and fond of his cups. Mary married Dan Stover, a typical blue-eyed mountaineer, soon to become Colonel of the Fourth Tennessee Union Infantry. He was a man of high courage, known to fame as leader of the bridge burners. Dan, a nephew of Mordecai Lincoln, was the person of all others Andrew Johnson would have selected as a son-in-law. The Pattersons lived on a small farm a short distance from Greeneville, and Dan Stover also owned a fine plantation in the Watauga Valley, in the adjoining county of Carter. These plantation-homes, easy, hospitable, and unconventional, were a God-send to Andrew Johnson, furnishing him an outlet from cares. The Stover place especially attracted him; the winding Watauga, "the beautiful valley and the towering mountains" where the Stover place lay he never tired of.[4]

His own home at Greeneville, however, was the place where the family would gather, and most attractive it was becoming— the yard green with velvety blue-grass, the scuppernong vines spreading and covering nearly an eighth of an acre, the garden heavy with vegetables and fruits. Growing things made their appeal to Andrew Johnson. The pastoral was the corner stone on which he was building his philosophy of life. Oftentimes he would work with his own hands in the garden or he would turn the mellow soil to the golden corn, or now and then he would harness the family horse to the rockaway and run out to John Parks' or Judge Patterson's or John Jones's or up the Boone trail, sometimes going as far as the Stover place. Such were the simple recreations of the "Mechanic Governor," as the people called Andrew Johnson long after he quit the governorship. The spring in the rear, from which he first drank when he landed in Greeneville that long ago September night, he put in first-class condition. Walling it up with a new gum curb and opening the path to Water Street, he threw the rear

---

[4] *Letter from Congressman Taylor to Dr. Ensor* of Hopeton, Okla., December 8, 1925; *Journal and Tribune,* July 10, 1901; Knoxville *Sentinel,* July 10, 1901.

of the lot open to the public. It delighted him to see his humble neighbors gather on the premises, drinking from the spring and carrying pails filled with the cool water to their homes.

Near the spring he planted a willow-sprout dug from the tomb of Napoleon at St. Helena. I may anticipate and explain that this sprout soon grew into a spreading, feathery tree and that this historic willow and a number of elms, which Johnson also planted, now give welcome to thousands of tourists motoring from Bristol to Memphis to visit the old tailor shop and the home of the Tennessee tailor.

With the arrival of grandchildren, a boy and a girl in the Patterson household and a boy and two girls in the Stover home, Andrew Johnson softened and unbent, and his daughters stood less in awe of their austere parent. But, after all, the center of the family was Mrs. Andrew Johnson. When her husband was away she took his place, collecting the rents, looking after the real estate and running the household; she was also the tie that bound the family together. The influence she exerted over her husband was remarkable. When he would exhibit temper or get out of sorts she would place her hand on his shoulder and speak the word "Andrew, Andrew," and the indomitable man would instantly subside. It seemed to the partial ones, living under the same roof, that the match between the lowly tailor and the shoemaker's daughter "had been made in heaven." [5] Manifestly Mrs. Johnson's control over her husband was due to the fact that they had the same view of life. In word and deed Mrs. Johnson and Mrs. Patterson were as democratic as Johnson himself. They sustained him throughout, no matter how "plebeian" he might become. By the late '50's, with the management of these women, Johnson had accumulated an estate worth more than fifty thousand dollars, his holdings including a hotel and an office near his dwelling. This office became the hanging-out place for the old tailor-shop crowd. Though his friends, McDaniel, Milligan, Lowery, and Self, were not scholars and could not assist him in the delicate work of preparing speeches and public documents, they were safe men and just the kind Andrew

[5] W. H. Crooks, *Through Five Administrations*, pp. 85-90.

Johnson needed as storm clouds appeared in the sky. The new offices in the hotel yard, consisting of two rooms, one story high, were in the center of the town and easy to reach. In one room he arranged his books, papers, periodicals and clippings. There were thousands of these—Johnson insisting that no scrap of paper should ever be destroyed and his wife assisting him in making the collection. The other room was used as a reception room for visitors and friends.

At the time of which I am writing, about two years before the Civil War, Senator Johnson was fifty-two years of age and in robust health. He was a man of medium height, about five feet nine inches tall, with dark, luxurious hair, black, piercing, deep-set eyes, and a head large and round. His shoulders were broad, his figure strong, muscular and well proportioned, and his step elastic and graceful. Smiles and laughter were not frequent with him but when they came they were hearty and sincere. Though possessed of great dignity and gravity of manner, when he walked down the streets of Greeneville his salute to the humblest individual was as courteous as to the most distinguished.

On Saturdays or holidays when the country people came to town he would leave his office and walk slowly along, greeting the friends and patrons of younger days. Soon the crowd would gather around and he would address them as if making a speech. Every follower of his confidently expected him to be the next President of the United States; but they would anxiously enquire what would happen if Seward or Chase or Lincoln or other "abolitionist" were elected President.[6] Would South Carolina and the Far South leave the Union? If Johnson ran across a mechanic he would never pass him by without a word of greeting.

On a certain occasion he noticed a man and his wife painting a fence around the Baptist Church. The spectacle of a woman painting a fence attracted his attention and he asked what it meant. The woman replied that she was paying her subscription to the church, that she was too poor to give money, and so

[6] To the secessionist of the late '50's all Republicans were known as Abolitionists.

she was painting the fence and raising the needed five dollars. Johnson pulled out his pocketbook and handed her a five dollar bill, telling her to go home and look after her household affairs. Even to this day one will hear on the streets of Greeneville stories of Johnson's interest in the under-dog. Once he saw in Greeneville a man that had been well-to-do but was then down at the heel and working at the carpenter's trade. Taking the fellow by the hand, he told him to go ahead and learn the trade, then come back, and he would set him up in business for himself. So encouraged was the mechanic he persevered, and with Johnson's aid made a go of it. Sometimes a young fellow would be surprised to get a letter from him, perhaps offering a position as clerk or secretary or making useful suggestions. Strolling into the office of a briefless lawyer or clientless physician, he would encourage him and perhaps make a loan.[7]

In his home town, as in Washington, Andrew Johnson paid little attention to the demands of society, no doubt disapproving of the "caste" basis on which society rested. In the Senate repeated efforts were made by Jefferson Davis and other social and political leaders to win him over to the exclusive and aristocratic classes, but they could not move him.[8] His daughter, Martha, was a guest at social functions in Washington, and he himself was often invited out, but declined. In matters religious Mrs. Johnson and Mrs. Patterson affiliated with the Methodist church. Seventy-five years ago Methodism was wholly unworldly and almost as unadorned as Quakerism.

[7] I examined the final returns of Johnson's personal representatives at Greeneville and saw scores of notes returned "worthless." These notes had been made by poor people without security.

[8] In 1865 Jefferson Davis, a prisoner at Fortress Monroe, was asked by Dr. Craven his opinion of President Johnson. "He hesitated a moment, and then said that the Senators respected his ability, integrity, and greatly original force of character, but nothing could make him be, or seem to wish to feel, at home in their society. A casual word would seem to wound him to the quick when he would shrink back to the isolation of his earlier and humble life as if to gain strength from touching his mother earth. . . . His habits were marked by temperance, industry, courage, and unswerving perservance," Mr. Davis continued. . . . "One of the people by birth, he remained so by conviction, continually referring to his origin. . . . Of Mr. Johnson's character, justice was an eminent feature, though not uncoupled with kindliness and generosity. . . . He was indifferent to money and careless of praise or censure. . . . But for a decided attitude against secession, he would probably have been given the Vice-presidency."—Craven, *Prison Life of Jefferson Davis*, p. 301.

Though mother and daughter cared little for society, they did not dislike or shun it. On the contrary, they took an active part in the woman's work of the church and in community life. Doubtless down in their hearts they had as much pity for the misguided, "card-playing, theater-going, and dancing element" in their midst as these had for them—and each side was no doubt right, as such things are matters of taste. In the late '50's, however, the old factional fight between aristocrat and democrat in Greeneville had about played out. General Thomas D. Arnold, Congressman in the '30's, having become Johnson's friend, was presiding over jollification meetings in his honor. Dr. Alexander Williams, "Alexander the Great," had passed to his reward. Dicksons, Arnolds, Williamses, and Johnsons were living together in peace and friendship. Surely if Andrew Johnson could "clean up" the politicians in his home town, in the district and in the State, and could "swing around the circle" from alderman to the legislature, from the legislature to Congress, from Congress to the governorship, from Governor to Senator, and be sought after by Stephen A. Douglas as a running mate for Vice-president, he was becoming a man of some consequence.[9]

I have stated that the influence of Mrs. Johnson over her husband was unbounded, and yet into one place he would not follow her—the organized church. She might find satisfaction in such a church but he could not. Like Lincoln, if he could have found an organization based on the personality of Christ, without creed or dogma, without class distinctions or the exaltation and deification of money, he was willing to join it "with all his soul." But so far as he could make out there was no such church. Believing in a rule of right and in a revealed religion, he took Christ as a model, yet he feared that the Christians of his day were further away from the simplicity, the charity and the love of their fellows, which Christ enjoined, than many a heathen was.

[9] Judge Temple, a leading Whig, living in the '40's next door to the Johnsons, rather boasts that he never went into their house, whereas the father and mother of Judge Barton and the families of Colonel Reeves and of the Milligans were their intimate friends.—Temple. Chapter on "Andrew Johnson."

Long and earnestly he labored over the problem of linking up democracy with theocracy and of a return to the simplicity of the patriarchs. At one time he consulted spiritualists on this subject and received much useless advice. The Catholic church interested him because in it he found a saving virtue: No class distinctions in its worship. Therefore, he entered one son in a Catholic school, and sometimes attended the Catholic church himself. In fact, however, he was a Baptist, holding with Thomas Jefferson that the United States Government was organized on the same general plan as Baptist churches; that each state, like each church, was a separate entity. If there was a cure for class distinctions and snobbery, he concluded, it did not lie in the religion of his day, but in universal education. This theme he was always expounding. Early in his career, when the County Court of Greene elected him a trustee of Rhea Academy, as we have seen, he was flattered no little. He filled the position of trustee for years, with pleasure and satisfaction.

Andrew Johnson, the apostle of absolute equality, was yet a slave owner, possessing eight slaves. These people lived in a cabin, about twenty by thirty feet, located on the premises and not far from the spring. Sam and Bill, with a wife apiece and sundry pickaninnies, constituted the "crap." Johnson's relation to these domestic slaves was familiar and patriarchal. He was the head of the family, of which they were as much a part as his own children. In slave days the house servants were treated as grown up children and were greatly spoiled. With the other slaves, those who lived in the quarters, it was far different. These unfortunate people—"the field hands"— scarcely knew the name of their master and were compelled to take slavery with its narrowness and burdens. Though the domestic slaves were a part of the household, all others were considered little above a drove of horses or mules. Thus Judge Milligan advised Johnson to accept the southern argument. God had seen fit to place certain of his creatures in fixed positions—the white man in his place, the ass in his and the "nigger" in his. Why interfere with the plans of the Almighty? Why promote the "nigger" and not promote the ass? Or as a popular and liberal southern woman put the case, "Is not this unfortunate brother ass—this hirsute relative —trampled upon? Why should he not lie amidst feathers and velvet as well as the best in the land?" [10]

Now as to old Sam, Johnson's favorite slave, it was almost true that he did rest amidst velvet and feathers. In fact, according to Mrs. Patterson, it was a mistake to call Sam a slave at all. She often laughed and said that Sam did not belong to her father but her father belonged to Sam. Tall and dignified, black as a coal, Sam was one of the best known characters in Greeneville, and a thorough gentleman. He at least was an aristocrat! [11]

Johnson's other manservant, Bill, was fully as privileged as Sam. Bill's wife was the family cook and an excellent one too. When old Mas'r would rig himself out in his tall hat and long-tailed broadcloth coat, which Sam and Bill called a "jimswinger," and go abroad, Bill was sure to go too. When night came he would stir around and get a pair of blankets and make a pallet in the same room with old Mas'r. When he would get back home, tall tales Bill would tell about his trip. "Old Mas'r," he would say, "let dem po' white folks know de body servant's place was in de room wid him," wisely shaking his woolly head and ha-ha-ing with laughter. [12] When Johnson became President he rented the tailor shop to Bill. [13]

[10] DeBow, *Industrial Resources*, p. 197.

[11] After Sam was set free he bought a silk hat, a long-tailed coat, and became a church janitor, respectful and courteous. "He looked like a lord."— Jones, p. 29. Mrs. E. C. Reeves writes me that Dora, Sam's daughter, was her cook, soon after the war, and the seventy-five cents a week paid Dora was regarded as enormously high.

[12] Greeneville papers of May 1923 at the Johnson Tailor Shop celebration.

[13] In 1869 a New York *Herald* correspondent visited his shop, then battle-scarred and going to decay. He took a look at the watermill grinding corn at its door and at Spring Branch, and gave the following account of the shop itself: "The place where the famous knight of the scissors held forth was the next thing that attracted my curiosity, and so I went also to see that. 'A. Johnson, Tailor,' painted in crude letters *en imitation*, said Eureka to me, and I stopped before the magic symbol, gazing intently on the little eight by ten frame building. It is plebeian in the extreme, built very much on the style of a farmer's smoke house, of rough weather boarding, white-washed. On either end the boards are torn off in places, and the chimney is crumbling to decay. An old negro raised by President Johnson and assuming his name is the sole occupant of the building, and he is the successor in business of 'A. Johnson, Tailor.' He says, 'Massa Johnson been in the trade, de boss tailor in dese diggins.'"

In *ante bellum* days the home of every southern gentleman had its sideboard and its decanters. No guest was hospitably entertained without a glass of French brandy or a frosty mint julep, and no more was required of host or guest, on leaving a social occasion, than that he could "navigate" without assistance. Strangely enough, in the midst of such universal dissipation, Andrew Johnson was not overmuch afflicted with the drink habit. "I have never failed to publicly denounce Andrew Johnson," said Parson Brownlow, his lifetime enemy, to Judge Chase, "but I never charged him with being a drunkard; in fact nobody in Tennessee ever regarded him as addicted to the excessive use of whiskey." [14]

Squire Self had a story he loved to tell. On a certain occasion, it may have been the visit of J. M. Ashley's "smelling committee," some one came to Greeneville to interview the Squire. He wanted to know about Johnson's habits. "Wasn't he in the habit of getting drunk and making a spectacle of himself?" the visitor inquired. "Well," the Squire replied, "I'll tell you this: he never got too drunk to disremember his friends." If Johnson had been willing to join some church or let up in his advocacy of labor doctrines and plebeianism he might have saved a lot of trouble, but this he would not do and ridicule and slander continued to pile up.

A story went the rounds that when Governor he boarded at a livery stable, and "ate bacon and cabbage with his washerwoman." It seemed a pity to spoil the story but the fact is Johnson boarded at a hotel. On New Year's day, however, he did turn down an invitation to dine with Aaron V. Brown, Postmaster General under Buchanan, and took a twelve o'clock dinner with a mechanic with whom he had a previous engagement. But the story was too good to keep and in the telling was added to until it became a matter of national merriment.[15] One of the harshest statements about Andrew Johnson was made by Governor Harris, war governor of Tennessee. "If Johnson were a snake he would hide himself in the grass and

---

[14] Congressman Brownlow, in the *Taylor-Trotwood Magazine*, September 1908. No charge of drinking is in the Tennessee newspapers.
[15] Nashville *Banner*, January 20, 1910; *Harper's Magazine*, Vol. CXX, p. 171.

1.

2.

3.

1. Andrew Johnson in Masonic Regalia.
2. Mrs. Andrew Johnson.
3. Andrew Johnson's Home in Greeneville, Tenn.

bite the heels of the children of rich people," said Harris. But this cheerful opinion the Governor did not express until he had become a "secesh" and Johnson a Unionist. When the two were brother Democrats together Governor Harris was in the habit of calling on Governor Johnson to pull the party out of many a hole.[16]

Slander and abuse, however, made no impression on Andrew Johnson's home life. To his wife and family he was above reproach. And so thought the rank and file. The greater the abuse the more they looked upon Andrew Johnson as their man. "Old Andy," as they called him, "never went back on his raisin'." That was enough for them. As he was half southern and half western they were not expecting a saint. The masses loved him because, like themselves, he was a member of the human family. Of course he swore a bloody oath, but what of that? He never failed to pay an honest debt. Though he took a drink, when he felt like it, he made no concealment of the fact;[17] he despised hypocrisy and belonged to no church, but he was always with the under-dog and never ran up the white flag. On this level the plain people accepted Andy Johnson, "warts and all," and Andy bound himself to them for better or for worse.

From Bristol to Memphis every inch of Tennessee's soil was now dear to him, and whosoever assailed the fair name of Tennessee had a fight on his hands. As soon as Congress adjourned and he could get away from Washington he would run down home and mingle with the people of his beloved State. In the masonic lodges he found pleasure and comradeship. There was an earnestness and a fixedness of purpose as well as a dignity about this venerable institution he could not resist. He and Andrew Jackson entered masonry through the same lodge, the Greeneville Masonic Lodge No. 119, a fact to which he proudly and constantly alluded. As Sir Knight Andrew

---

[16] In 1861, when matters in Tennessee were going bad for the Confederacy, the citizens of Memphis demanded a king, and suggested Isham G. Harris for the job. Senator Johnson, rising from his place in the Senate, scorned the idea. "Isham G. Harris a king!" he said. "My king! I know the man— I know his elements. King Harris to be my master! Mr. President, he should not be my slave."—Savage, p. 243.

[17] His whiskey bills are filed with other manuscripts at Greeneville.

Johnson, in his sword and sash, in braid and regalia, he cut a brave figure—in masonry at least he could tolerate brass buttons. In truth, nothing of interest happened to the plain people of Tennessee but he had a hand in it, and as he climbed higher and higher he took his friends by the hand, lifting them upward. McDaniel, Barton, Reeves, Milligan, Self, Lowery, Watterson, Meigs, Witthorne, Taylor, Holtsinger and many another were assisted and sustained by this man. And their affection was returned to him fourfold; in every emergency he could rely on their aid.[18]

Andrew Johnson placed a high value on his home; he would not use it as a means of advertising or as a place for political gatherings and conferences. Business and politics must be attended to elsewhere. With the austerity of the men of his day, he looked upon a home as a spot far removed from the turmoil of life and the women of the household as guardians of his good name. In Johnson's early days he was no doubt severe and rigid, the rule of his home having been strict attention to duty and fidelity to facts. "Tell it as it is or not at all," says Mrs. Patterson, "was then the household slogan." But with age, when he grew more broad-minded and also more prosperous and had no longer to fight the wolf at the door, "his home life became as tender as a woman's." [19] Though Andrew Johnson failed, as others have failed, to inaugurate the brotherhood of man and to make democracy and theocracy coterminous, he succeeded, in a measure, in maintaining a household based on the equality of man. American homes he considered the hope of America, and certainly his home was a tower of strength; without it, and without the encouragement of his wife and daughters, Andrew Johnson could never have put up the fight he did.

Must it not be said of Eliza McCardle Johnson that she was one woman out of a million? Undazzled by wealth or position, she discarded ostentation, "added grace to merit, plainness to plenty and by the simplicity of her life illustrated

[18] In 1875, in the Tennessee legislature it was the men he had assisted who returned Johnson to the Senate. Hon. A. A. Taylor was one of them.
[19] Jones, p. 388.

the true democratic character of our government." [20]   In
younger days she was a beautiful woman.   Her soft features
and graceful form, her wavy, light brown hair and her large,
hazel eyes, her fair complexion, and above all her thoughtful
expression and pleasing address, constituted her a woman indeed, one fit to rule over the fervid nature of her husband and
to aid him in his quest of ideal Democracy.   "I should not
wonder," says the historian Schouler, "if Andrew Johnson did
not consult his wife and daughters more than he did any
fellow statesman." [21]

[20] Jones, p. 394.
[21] Jas. Schouler, *History of the United States*, Vol. VII, p. 21, covering the
reconstruction period.

CHAPTER VIII

JEFF DAVIS SPOILS THE BROTH

In December 1859 the House did not adjourn for the usual Christmas holidays. It was in no humor for merry-making. Since convening early in December it had tried in vain to organize and elect a speaker. John Sherman, leading candidate for the speakership, had disqualified himself, in the opinion of the conservatives, because of an endorsement of the *Impending Crisis.*

This remarkable publication, written by J. Rowan Helper, a poor North Carolina white, was creating almost as much trouble in Congress as John Brown's Raid.[1] In this book Helper insisted that the South was a decadent country, that slavery was gradually undermining its prosperity and destroying its soul, that it was the most backward section of the Union. Not only did he make this contention; he undertook to prove it by cold facts from the census table. His remedy was the abolition of slavery and colonization of the negro. Though his attack on southern slave-holders was untrue and unnecessary, his demonstration was unanswerable. At the bare mention of Helper's book southern Congressmen went into a frenzy, the term "Helperite" becoming the synonym for treachery to the South. Though published in 1857, the book did not come into prominence till the winter of 1859, about the time John Brown was going to the gallows in Virginia. Helper's *Impending Crisis* was Andrew Johnson's *vade mecum*—his arsenal of facts.

While the House was endeavoring to elect a speaker the greatest confusion and discord prevailed. Southern Congressmen charged that Harper's Ferry and John Brown's Raid were the direct result of Black Republicanism as contended for by Helper and by Seward and Lincoln. Seward's "irrepressible

---

[1] *First Session Thirty-sixth Congress*, p. 574.

conflict" and Lincoln's "house divided against itself" utterances were regarded as unspeakably false and treasonable. During the spring session, bowieknives and pistols flashed in Congressional halls and challenges to fight duels were not infrequent. Potter of Wisconsin accepted the challenge of Prior of Virginia and chose bowieknives. Prior refused the challenge, being unwilling to engage in "so barbarous a method of warfare." On one occasion Owen Lovejoy, an Illinois Congressman, brother of Elijah Lovejoy, murdered by an anti-abolition mob, crossing over from his seat, stood facing the Democratic side of the Chamber: "The principle of slavery," said the exasperated man, "is the doctrine of devils as well." There is no place in the universe "outside of the five points of hell and the Democratic party where the practice would not be a disgrace." Prior of Virginia angrily exclaimed: "The gentleman shall not approach this side of the House"—shaking his fist—"it is bad enough to be compelled to sit here and hear a member use treasonable and insulting language; but he *shall not*, sir, come upon this side of the House shaking his fist in our faces." Potter of Wisconsin rushed forth to the help of Lovejoy, followed by a score of Republican Congressmen. Barksdale of Mississippi, with bowieknife in hand, led a dozen angry Southerners to the rescue. The confusion was great. It seemed as if a terrible encounter was about to take place on the floor of the House.

After order was restored, Lovejoy broke forth again. "You might," he exclaimed, "put each crime perpetrated among men into a moral crucible and dissolve and combine them all and the resultant amalgam is slave-holding. . . . It is the violence of robbery." *Prior:* "You shake your fist at us, go to your side." *Barksdale:* "Order that black-hearted scoundrel and negro-stealing thief to take his seat or—" Again discord and confusion broke out. A motion to adjourn was made. Congressmen gathered in hostile array as before. Lovejoy resuming, abated not a jot of his denunciation. "You speak of us who labor as greasy mechanics," he scowled, "filthy operatives, and you jeer at us as worse than slaves. . . . Slavery must die. *'Carthago delenda est.'* " *Barksdale:* "The meanest slave in the South is your superior." *Singleton:* "May I ask a question?" *Barksdale:* "I hope the gentleman will hold no parley with the perjured negro thief."

After the usual holiday recess the Senate convened with two important measures confronting it. The first was the Homestead bill, whose fate I shall discuss in the next chapter, the other was the slavery question in all its ramifications. This being election year, platforms were to be written, candidates chosen and a President elected. If the election of 1856 had been held in September or October of that year instead of November it had been believed that Frémont, the Republican, would have defeated Buchanan. As the canvass proceeded, however, the conservative element became alarmed. Fear of a dissolution of the Union, in the event of Frémont's election, drove thousands to vote for Buchanan. Throughout the South open threats had been made that the Union would be dissolved if a Black Republican were elected. Now, in this opinion Andrew Johnson did not concur; in fact, he regarded such threats as idle and vain. He did not think that the Union was in danger in 1856, nor did he think it in danger in 1860. Moreover, he was decidedly of opinion that the great principles of government, such as the Homestead bill, should be considered on their merits and not under threats of dissolving the Union. Though he voted for the compromise measures of 1850 he did so with reluctance. He was never a compromise man. Addressing the Senate in 1858, he said, "In 1820 we had a compromise; the republic was agitated; dissolution threatened before it was made, and when it was effected it became a permanent subject of contention—until it was repealed . . . In 1850 several measures were passed as compromise measures; they produced a great agitation; a dissolution of the Union was threatened; in 1851 some great pacificators came forward on another compromise and that compromise has been a continual and increasing source of agitation."

"Compromise!" he exclaimed. "I almost wish the term was stricken out of the English language." "Let us agree to abide by the Constitution of the country and have no more compromises." . . . "We have been compromised and conservatized until there is hardly any Constitution left." . . . " 'The Union! the Union!' is the constant cry. Sir, I am for the Union; but in every little speech I have to make I do not deem it necessary to sing peans and hosannas to the Union. I think the Union will stand uninterrupted. It will go on as it has gone on without my singing peans to it; and this thing of saving the Union I will remark here has been done so often that it has gotten to be entirely a business transaction." [2]

John C. Calhoun, father of the nullification doctrine, Johnson regarded as a mere logician, "more of a politician than a statesman," "often wrong in his premises," "the founder of a sect, not of a great national party." "If Calhoun were now living," said Johnson, "he and all the men in the United States could not put a government into successful operation under the system he laid down.[3] The Union," Johnson exclaimed, "it cannot, it cannot be dissolved."

Though Andrew Johnson deplored the waste of time in the discussion of Davis' resolutions, such debates in Congress were not unusual. Foote's resolution on the public lands gave rise to the Webster-Hayne debate; Calhoun's resolution of January 23, 1833, condemning the high tariff measure and justifying the action of South Carolina in nullifying the same, provoked the Calhoun-Webster debate.

These resolutions of Calhoun declared that the American government is a compact to which the sovereign states are parties and each state has a right, in case of a violation of the compact, to choose its own mode of redress.[4] Hereunder, Calhoun advocated, as the mode of redress, not Secession but Nullification. That is, the aggrieved state would nullify the obnoxious law but, at the same time, remain in the Union. This was not Jefferson Davis' idea at all. His school differed from Calhoun as to the relation of the states to the general government. According to Davis, each state was sovereign and above the government. In 1787, upon entering into the agreement to form a Union, each state contracted with each other state,

[2] *Congressional Globe, First Session Thirty-fifth Congress,* 1858.
[3] Savage, *Life of Johnson,* p. 147.
[4] *Niles Register,* Vol. XLIII, p. 170.

but not with the general government. In a word, a compact was then formed between Sovereign States. The general government was a mere agent, a mere stake-holder or trustee and no more. It made no contract nor was it under any obligation to the states; it was but a wisp of hay, binding the bundles together. In case of a breach of this contract, therefore, according to Mr. Davis, the following results would appear: If the United States government should break the contract the aggrieved state would seek redress *inside the Union*, that is, by nullification. On the other hand, if a Sovereign State should breach the contract, *ipso facto* the contract would be abrogated, and the injured state might withdraw from the Union. It would then become a foreign power.

Accordingly, the Davis school, speaking through Rhett and Keitt of South Carolina, insisted that in 1860 the United States had not broken the contract; that certain of the northern States had broken it; and in so doing, they had absolved the other states from their obligations.[5] Indeed, these men insisted that under the Fugitive Slave law of 1850 the general government was not to blame for failure to return fugitive slaves. This duty of returning fugitive slaves devolved, under the Constitution, on each state. When the State of Vermont or New Hampshire or Massachusetts or Rhode Island or Connecticut or New York or Michigan or Ohio refused to return escaped slaves that state thereby annulled the compact. When John Quincy Adams asserted that "Massachusetts men are not to be made slave catchers of" he was speaking as a citizen of Massachusetts and not as a citizen of the United States.

Now Andrew Johnson did not agree with Calhoun nor did he agree with Jefferson Davis. Though a state's-rights man, he held that each state had parted with such attributes of sovereignty as related to the continuity and perpetuity of the national government, but no more. Johnson looked to the people as the source of all power. Agreeing with Webster, he maintained that the opening words of the Constitution declared by whom the instrument was formed. "We the people of the United States," Johnson read to mean that the people

[5] *Great Political Debates*, Vol. XXI, p. 103.

were sovereign and not the states. Though he was in the habit
of writing to Sam Milligan and making fun of the "Divine
Daniel," at heart he agreed with Webster that there was an
indestructible Union of indestructible states. In 1788, when
Patrick Henry read the proposed Constitution and discovered
that these words, "we the people," were written therein, he set
up a great howl. "It squints at despotism!" the old patriot
exclaimed. "Why change the wording of the articles of Confederation? Why substitute the words, 'We the people of the
United States,' for the names of the states themselves?"

It is generally conceded that Mr. Davis' resolutions were
offered to destroy Douglas; but may they not have been
offered for a double purpose? The Democratic party in the
South was being crowded with Whigs. These Whigs were
driven from their party by the attitude of Seward and other
northern Whig abolitionists. In fact, an acceptance of the
Wilmot Proviso, excluding slavery from the territories, had
almost become a prerequisite to admission into the Whig party
at the North.[6] This heterogeneous mass needed to be welded
together and made coherent. Andrew Johnson was an insurgent; Clingman had been. These men and all other kickers
must be rounded up. Johnson in particular was troublesome
and must be made to show his hand. The Davis resolutions
would force the issue. In a debate with Congressman Stanley
Andrew Johnson had used treasonable language. Stanley had
moved to organize the House by dividing out the offices, which
motion Andrew Johnson had opposed. It was "but a bargain
and sale," Johnson insisted, and it "would cut out the Free
Soil party." Stanley, who was not averse to the field of honor,
retorted that a man like Andrew Johnson "would not blush
at anything." [7]

If the Davis' resolutions would destroy Douglas, force the
hand of Andrew Johnson and other weak-kneed Southerners,
and write a new platform, the South could present an unob-
structed front against the North, and Jefferson Davis would

6 T. L. Clingman, *Life and Letters*, p. 341.
7 *Thirty-first Congress, Congressional Globe*, Part I, p. 34.

not suffer in the shake-up.[8]   In the '50's, at a Quitman banquet in Georgia, he had been toasted as "the game cock of the Confederacy."   As Secretary of War he had dominated the Pierce administration, making it possible for Douglas to push through the Kansas-Nebraska bill.   In January 1859 he had advised the Mississippi Legislature, in the event of the election of an abolitionist to the Presidency, to seek safety outside of the Union.[9]   Dignified and austere, Jefferson Davis, in appearance and in intellect, was more northern than southern.   Seven years of study, after leaving the army, had weakened his constitution.   One eye was gone.   Swathed and bandaged, he often came to his duties in the Senate chamber, a sick man.   Tall and spare, pale and emaciated, he caused many to remark a resemblance to Senator Fessenden of Maine.   His language was chaste and restrained.   Unforgiving and Cassius-like, he had few friends—almost none among his equals.   He was not of gentle birth, his father having been a wandering Kentucky tenant.   Not till past fifty years did he leave the church of his father, the Baptist church, to join Saint James' church, Richmond.   Around him as the center and the chief apostle of slavery gathered the fiery and truculent Wigfall and Iverson, the smooth and wily Benjamin and Slidell, the cultured and aristocratic Mason and Hammond, proud of the slightest nod of approval.

Jefferson Davis firmly believed that there were two allegiances, one to the State and the other to the United States. He likewise held, as a corollary, that there were two kinds of treasons, one against the State and the other against the United States.   In the conflict between State and Nation, he stood with the State.[10]   But he was now playing a desperate game.   He was matching slavery against the Union and laying down terms to the North which, if rejected, might bring on a conflict.   From the old and safe position of his party that Congress had no right to legislate slavery *out* of the territories, he had advanced to the new position that Congress must

8 Rhodes, Vol. II, p. 27; Quitman was a Northerner turned southern "fire eater."

9 *Ibid.*, p. 348.

10 Craven, *Prison Life*, p. 114.

legislate slavery *into* them.   This the North called a "national slave code."

Would the North yield to this demand?   Constitutions and Dred Scott decisions to the contrary, would the North become a partner in the slavery business? That the North should bow to the Constitution and return run-away slaves, property of high value, to their masters, thereby obeying the Supreme Court, Andrew Johnson stoutly maintained.   But if the North refused to do these things, would the South make good its threat of secession?   This was the dilemma Johnson now faced. To this extremity was he brought by the zealots in his own party, and he must shortly decide what course he would pursue, for an event soon took place indicating that the fiery Southerner from the Cotton States was going to throw the sword into the scales.

Nearly four years had passed since Buchanan's election and conservative men were again asking if the Union could be saved in 1860 as in 1856.   Would appeals to the thoughtful business element prevent a split in the Democratic party and the defeat of "black Republicanism"?   Abraham Lincoln, in his Cooper Union speech in February 1860, had announced the Free Soil or Republican doctrine: Though slavery could not be interfered with in the states, it was morally wrong and should not be extended.   Douglas in September 1859, unhappily for himself, restated his "squatter sovereignty" idea: [11] The Constitution neither establishes nor prohibits slavery in the territories but leaves it to the people thereof to decide. On this platform the Democrats had elected Buchanan in 1856 and on it Douglas expected to succeed Buchanan in 1860. But a disturbing influence had arisen since 1856—the Dred Scott case had been decided.

In this case the Supreme Court, in an effort to put the slavery question at rest forever, had held two things. *First*, that a negro was not a citizen of the United States and could not be—that the Constitution was not made for negroes. *Secondly*, that slavery was guaranteed by the Constitution and was beyond the control of Congress.   The result naturally

[11] *Harper's*, September 1859.

followed that all existing legislation prohibiting slavery in the territories was unconstitutional, null and void. The Missouri Compromise of 1820, prohibiting slavery north of 36° 30', was void. So was the Clay Compromise of 1850. The fathers were in error. Monroe and his cabinet,—John Quincy Adams, Crawford, Calhoun, Thompson of New York, McLean of Ohio, and Wirt, advising that said compromise was constitutional, were likewise wrong. So were Henry Clay, Daniel Webster and others who enacted the Compromise of 1850. In fact, every one was wrong on the subject except Jefferson Davis, W. L. Yancey and their followers. John C. Calhoun, when he in 1848 originated the doctrine and thereby overruled his opinion to Monroe that the Missouri Compromise was unconstitutional, was correct.[12]

What then was Jefferson Davis, leader of the Democratic party, to do? Was he to move the party from the caucus platform of 1856—plant it on the Dred Scott decision—or was he to lie down and surrender the advantage vouchsafed by the court's decision? Davis naturally chose the former course— that is, he took advantage of the Dred Scott opinion. On February 29, 1860, he offered his famous resolutions in the Senate. The chief one declared "that neither Congress nor a territorial legislature has the power to annul the constitutional right of citizens to take slaves into the common territory, but it is the duty of the Federal Government to afford to slaves as to other species of property the needful protection."[13]   In view of the fact that the Democratic convention was to meet at Charleston, in April following, and that Stephen A. Douglas was almost sure of nomination on the platform of 1856—in direct conflict with Davis' resolutions—a fight of immense proportions was anticipated. Every one knew that the resolutions if adopted would defeat Douglas' chances for the Presidency, and would split the Democratic party. Some charged that the Davis resolutions were offered for that purpose and for

12 Rhodes, Vol. I, p. 468.
13 *Con. Globe, First Session Thirty-sixth Congress*, p. 658.

the further purpose of creating a secession of the Southern States and the disruption of the Union.[14]

Before these resolutions were offered Mr. Davis conferred with President Buchanan, who concurred in their adoption.[15] Senator Slidell of Louisiana was called into the conference; he too approved. This conference, and the subsequent caucus of certain Senators and Congressmen from the far South, Clingman, a Democratic Senator with union proclivities, called "the conspiracy of Buchanan, Douglas and Slidell," a conspiracy "surpassing in insanity and wickedness," he declared, "all other events in the history of humanity." [16] But the significance of the conspiracy was not understood by those on the outside; only the insiders knew its real significance. The North was fooled and so was Andrew Johnson. Regarding the movement as a mere abstraction, a political ruse to defeat Douglas, Johnson had no idea that the Union was in danger.[17] President Buchanan, no doubt, also regarded it as a mere trick to kill off Douglas; he certainly could not have understood that the first step in breaking up the Union had been taken. Edmund Ruffin, however, knew what was up. "You must disrupt the Democratic party," he said, "before you disrupt the Union." [18]

On May 8, 1860, while Andrew Johnson was urging the Senate to allow his Homestead bill to come forward and insisting that mere abstractions like the Davis resolutions should not displace it, and that an expression of opinion on the territories was an idle performance, his Democratic colleagues, headed by Jefferson Davis, were in fierce controversy with Senator Douglas.[19] "We know," said Senator Douglas, "for what object this matter is brought up now. It is all under-

14 Wilson, *Rise and Fall*, p. 230; A. Johnson's July 27, 1861, speech; President Taylor, Davis' father-in-law, made a like charge in the '50's; Rhodes, Vol. I, p. 135.

15 A. H. Stephens, *War Between The States*, Vol. II, p. 271.

16 Clingman, *Life and Letters*, p. 48.

17 J. S. Schouler, *History of the United States*, Vol. VI, p. 84; Johnson attended no disunion caucus.

18 Johnson MS., Josiah Turner's "Petition for Pardon." Ruffin claims "to have pulled the first lanyard at Sumter."

19 *Thirty-sixth Congress*, Part III, p. 1971.

stood; the country understands it; the Senate understands it."
Davis: "I do not, I wish you would state it." *Douglas:* "If the
Senator doesn't understand it I am not aware I am under any
obligations to furnish him with information on that point."
Davis: "I desire it." (Mr. Mason here made a signal to Mr.
Davis.) *Douglas:* "I will see what the Senator from Virginia
has to say." *Senator Mason:* "I was talking to the Senator
from Mississippi." *Douglas:* "Talking too loud, in violation
of the courtesies of the body." *Mason:* "You are welcome to
hear it." *Presiding Officer:* "The Senator from Virginia will
address the chair." *Senator Mason:* "He interrupts me, sir,
that is all." *Douglas:* "His manner does not carry any terrors
for me."

Andrew Johnson had little sympathy with these Davis resolutions. Insofar as they would injure Douglas' chances at
Charleston he was in favor of them. As an abstract proposition, and wholly harmless, he had no objection to them, but
as the subject of serious debate they were a mere waste of
time, and so he referred to them. "Why," he asked, "should
the business of the country be delayed while the Senate indulges in the expression of an opinion on the territories." In
fact, Johnson thought, as many others, that the matter in dispute involved "the protection of a nameless 'nigger' in a nameless place." As all western lands, suitable for slaves and slavery, had already passed out of a territorial condition and become States, every one understood that the matter was of no
practical importance. When a ballot was taken on the Davis
resolutions, however, Andrew Johnson voted with the South.
Indeed, all Democrats so voted except Pugh and Douglas. As
Andrew Johnson's Homestead bill was at this time in an acute
stage, no doubt his vote was cast to hold as many Southerners
as possible in line.

If Andrew Johnson, a southern man living among the
negroes, had been free to discuss slavery, and to do with it as he
pleased, he would no doubt have been, like Mr. Lincoln, unable to say what to do. "If you liberate the negro," he once
asked, "what will be the next step?" . . . "What will we do
with two million negroes in our midst?" . . . "Blood, rape and

rapine will be our portion. You can't get rid of the negro except by holding him in slavery."

Dear as was the Homestead to Johnson, strong as was his opposition to the Wilmot Proviso and other measures invading the constitutional rights of the South, love of the Union was dearer and stronger than these. "The preservation of this Union ought to be the object that is paramount to all other considerations," Johnson had urged, when discussing the Wilmot Proviso. Debating the John Brown raid, he further declared: "Our rights must be safeguarded and preserved, not outside, but always inside the Union." While these words were falling from the mouth of Andrew Johnson, news from home came that he was going too far in these matters. "Some of our papers are not strong for you," wrote W. M. Lowery in the spring of 1860.

When the Democratic convention met at Charleston April 23, 1860, Andrew Johnson was in Washington busying himself with his homestead measure. His son, Robert, had written from Greeneville that he felt sure his father would be nominated, in fact had a presentiment to that effect. Johnson, however, did not think so. He did not expect to me nominated for President.[20] Notwithstanding this doubt, he had made arrangements to have his claims presented to the convention. Robert was to attend. General Sam Milligan, a delegate-at-large, was supplied with funds to meet expenses. Andrew Ewing and W. C. Witthorne were chosen to place Johnson in nomination. The State Democratic convention at Nashville, had already endorsed Johnson for the Presidency. Therefore, he would start off with twelve votes at all events.

On January 27, 1860, soon after the Nashville convention adjourned, Lowery wrote and gave an account of the meeting: "Good feeling and harmony prevailed throughout; it was the largest convention ever held in the State." The resolutions written by Lowery and "endorsing the Governor were unanimously adopted." . . . "The delegation, however, was not satisfactory," Lowery wrote, and he was "not altogether

20 Johnson MS., p. 250.

pleased with the delegation." [21] On the day of the Charleston convention William Lowery wrote again that he was surprised at the course of the Memphis *Avalanche*. "It has done much to give tone to things in Alabama, Arkansas, Mississippi and Texas; it has acted badly and ought to have stood up manfully for Tennessee's nomination."

After the Tennessee delegation arrived at Charleston it was evident that some of its members were at heart opposed to Andrew Johnson. Sam Milligan wrote Governor Johnson that Isham G. Harris at heart was not for him; Robert wrote that Watterson, Andrew Ewing and Jones of Overton "fought manfully, being much better friends than some whose pretensions were greater." In truth, it was soon manifest that the convention had not met to elect but to defeat. From start to finish it was riding for a fall.[22] Douglas, who four years before, because of his Kansas-Nebraska measure, was the prime southern favorite, was now in disrepute. The strength of Buchanan's administration was being hurled against him. The Davis resolutions, pending in the Senate, were rendering him hateful to the people of the South.[23] Andrew Johnson's antipathy for Douglas was purely personal. As to national politics they were not in great disagreement. Johnson disliked him because he considered him an opportunist, skillful in catching on his feet. As he wrote Patterson, interested plunderers were "throwing their arms about his neck along the street"—"reading pieces to him in the Oyster Cellar of a complimentary character, which are to be sent off to some subsidized press for publication"; if Patterson were present where "he could see some of the persons engaged and the appliances brought to bear for the purpose of securing Douglas' election," he would involuntarily denounce the whole concern.

Was man ever worse treated than Douglas by the slave party of the South? He had fought its battles on a hundred stumps and on the issue of slavery he had just met and defeated Lincoln for the Senate. But in the eyes of southern leaders Doug-

---

21 Johnson MS. at Greeneville.
22 *Life of Thurlow Weed*, p. 618.
23 *Caucuses of 1860*, p. 76; Clingman, p. 484.

las had committed two grievous sins: He had opposed the Lecompton Slave Constitution for Kansas and he had declared that Squatter Sovereignty would survive despite the Dred Scott decision. What though slavery be guaranteed by the Constitution, so that Congress cannot shut it out of the territories, he had said, nevertheless an adverse sentiment in such territories will destroy slavery. When President Buchanan informed Douglas he was going to sustain the contentions of the slave power the latter replied that he would then denounce such policy in the Senate. Buchanan bluntly reminded Douglas that "no one has ever survived who opposed an administration of his own choice," and cited the case of Reeves and Tallmadge. Douglas, putting an end to the interview, emphatically remarked: "Mr. President, I wish you to remember Andrew Jackson is dead." [24]

Never was there such a madcap crowd as gathered in picturesque Charleston that April day, 1860. And never a more academic issue. "A fight to protect a nameless 'nigger' in a nameless country"—a "quarrel over goats' wool." Many of the Western delegates had never seen the "Sunny South" before. Plain, hardy men, living on the corn lands of Iowa and Illinois, some of them raising hogs and cattle for a livelihood, they were interested and bewildered by the spectacle of Charleston. Though a city of only about forty thousand people, it was the most aristocratic center in America. The Battery set in its gem-like harbor, old Saint Michael's church, Magnolia Gardens, with tropical plants and palmettoes, elegantly gowned women and gay equipages, these were in sharp contrast to the work-a-day surroundings of the great western prairies. Despite its elegance and reputation for hospitality, however, Charleston made no effort to entertain the delegates, the haughty bearing of Charleston towards the Tammany Braves and the uncouth western delegate being obvious throughout.[25] Yet politically the aristocratic Southerner and the democratic Westerner were further apart than socially.

24 Rhodes, Vol. II, p. 282.
25 *Ibid.*, p. 441.

On the morality of slavery they were indeed as far apart as the poles.

The platform, therefore, was the bone of contention. Would it be the platform of 1856, or would it be the Jefferson Davis resolutions? Before the convention met a caucus of anti-Douglas delegates was held, when it was decided to support these resolutions. Though Davis was not at the convention, Senator John Slidell of Louisiana was on hand to guide and direct. Smooth, cunning, adroit and wealthy, Senator Slidell was the man for the job. Having secured the committee on platform, the Yancey-Davis forces wrote the majority report, and Avery of North Carolina submitted it to the convention. This report covered practically the same ground as the Davis resolutions. The minority report substantially covered the national platform of 1856, that is to say it affirmed Douglas' Squatter Sovereignty idea, as embraced in the Kansas-Nebraska bill of 1854. The debates on the proposed platforms were earnest and exciting. Yancey of Alabama was the southern champion; Senator Pugh of Ohio, the northern. In the early '50's Yancey had been in Congress; he had likewise attended other national Democratic conventions and he was the product of a northern college. Heretofore his radical views had made him a dangerous, even an unwelcome leader. Now he was more than welcome. The "Yancey" doctrine, for which Yancey and R. B. Rhett of South Carolina had vainly contended for a score of years, was now the Jefferson Davis doctrine. Could Yancey secure its approval in the convention hall?

When the great southern orator rose to address the convention, every seat was taken and the aisles were crowded. A plain, mild-mannered man, unruffled, never out of humor, rose to address the convention. In a smooth, southern voice which filled every corner of the hall he advocated the majority platform. The spectacle was dramatic beyond description. The fate of a great party—the fate of the Nation, perhaps—hung on his words. He spoke for nearly two hours, not concluding till the gas jets were lighted. Setting forth the southern view of slavery, he declared that it was of God, embedded

in the Constitution, upheld by the highest court.   On it the
South had builded the greatest civilization known to man.
Would this benign institution survive or would northern fanatics tear it to pieces?   Addressing northern Democrats, he
exclaimed: "You have made a fatal mistake in admitting slavery to be wrong; you have greatly erred; it is divine and it is
right.   No more pandering to abolitionists.   Go back and
preach that doctrine and win the North."   Yancey had swept
the convention; the applause was deafening.   Replying, Senator Pugh reached the climax of his speech when he declared,
"You mistake us, sir, we will not do it."   Pugh's speech was
strong and logical.   Admitting the constitutional right of
slavery, agreeing that the fugitive slave law should be obeyed,
advocating the continuance of slavery in the states, nevertheless he would not, for himself or for his people, admit the
morality of slavery or that slavery should be extended.   The
re-opening of the African slave trade he regarded with abhor-
rence.   Richardson of Illinois and Payne of Ohio likewise
championed the cause of Douglas.[26]

On a proposition, sponsored by Yancey, to re-open the slave
trade, Virginia and the Border States were in violent opposition.   A delegate from Georgia, named Gaulden, got the floor.
An honest, straightforward slave-holder and dealer, without
concealments, he declared that he was for the African slave
trade and that he understood the attitude of Virginia.   "Virginia is after the dollar." . . . "She wants to breed and sell
niggers at two thousand dollars a head when I can go to Africa
and buy a better article for fifty dollars a head." . . . "Go
with me home, gentlemen, and I will show you some darkies I
purchased in Virginia, some in Georgia, some in Alabama and
some in Louisiana, and then I will show you the native African,
noblest Roman of them all.   In Virginia he costs me twelve
hundred dollars and in his native wilds, only fifty dollars—and
I make a Christian of him besides."   Roars of laughter greeted
the Georgia delegate, in fact he had "let the cat out of the
bag."   Shortly afterwards he was repudiated by the State of
Georgia.

[26] *Political Textbook,* 1860.

When the platform was voted on the minority won and the Far South seceded from the convention. That night the city of Charleston was all excitement; "she never enjoyed herself so much as over the idea of Secession." A meeting was held at the Court House and there were loud calls for Yancey. Mounting the platform, Yancey again addressed the people. Calling the convention, which he had just left, a "Rump convention," he uttered a characteristic thought, in characteristic words: "Perhaps even now," he softly insinuated, "the pen of the historian is nibbed to write the story of a new Revolution." Three cheers for the Independent Southern Republic were called for and given with a will.[27]

When balloting began Andrew Johnson received twelve votes, the entire vote of Tennessee, for President, and at one time a Minnesota delegate rose and declared that he wished to cast one of Minnesota's votes for Andrew Johnson. On the sixth day Johnson's friends communicated with him by wire. On April 29, W. C. Witthorne telegraphed as follows: "Have you declared for Douglas in the event of adoption of minority report? Six or more states will withdraw. What ought Tennessee to do?" To this telegram Johnson wired: "I would hold on and acquiesce in result. Nicholson, Wright and Avery concurring."

On the second of May W. H. Carroll sent the following wire to Johnson: "We have withdrawn you. Douglas has majority. Ought we support him?" On the next day and in response Johnson wired: "The delegation present, with all facts before them, are better prepared to determine what course to pursue than I am." On the thirty-sixth ballot Johnson's name was withdrawn from the convention.

During the month of May sundry letters were received by Andrew Johnson, giving him an account of the Charleston convention; in fact, Washington and Charleston were in constant communication at that time. Sam Milligan wrote: "I fear the election is lost, all due to the extreme South." He likewise suggested a convention in Tennessee in June "to speak out on Union or dis-Union." A. G. Graham of Jonesboro

27 *Caucuses of 1860*, p. 64.

wrote and said, "you can be nominated for Vice-president though I hear that you will not accept it." On May 8, Robert Johnson wrote from Greeneville: "The Charleston convention was a general row and injured the Democratic party more than anything that has happened to it for years. . . . I was sorry to see the southern States permit such a man as W. L. Yancey of Alabama lead them by the nose wheresoever he saw proper. I would have had more independence than that, and if I had wanted a leader I would have selected a different man—but he, in the opinion of some is a very great man—in my judgment he is no man at all." Robert likewise informed his father that "some of the Tennessee delegates were stricken with the fire-eating movement and were ready to go off with the others but better counsel prevailed"; he also sent some distressing news from home. Charles had gotten on a spree at Charleston and given him considerable trouble. But they were "at home again now and would have to make the best of it as it could not be remedied. Mother and myself," he added, "would have started to Washington this week if he had kept straight but as it is we cannot say when we will get off but I hope in a short time."

While letters and newspapers were advising Johnson of the insane course of the Democratic party at Charleston, he was sticking to his post, endeavoring to hold the discordant forces together in order to pass his Homestead bill. To his disgust the Senate had resolved itself into a mere debating society. The Charleston convention and the "Yancey Platform" were almost the sole subject of discussion. Lyman Trumbull, a Democratic Senator from Illinois, declared that he was opposed to the Senate's directing party conventions.[28] Wigfall and Judah P. Benjamin continued to pour out their wrath on Douglas. Senator Doolittle, quoting Benjamin that since the Charleston convention Douglas was dead, wished to remark that if Douglas was dead, "then it is the biggest funeral procession I ever attended."

It was becoming plainer and plainer that April 30, 1860, at Charleston, was the beginning of a new epoch in the United

---

[28] *First Session Thirty-sixth Congress*, Part III, p. 2234.

States.   Northern Democrats having left the slave-holding Democracy, slavery was doomed to destruction.[29]   By slavery the Democratic party was being split in two as nearly all the churches had been.   In the Senate Mr. Davis continued his fight on Douglas.   In an exciting debate with Douglas he declared: "I have a declining respect for platforms; I would sooner have an honest man on any sort of rickety platform you could construct than to have a man I did not trust on the best platform which could be made."   "If the platform is not a matter of much consequence," Douglas retorted, "why press that question to the disruption of the party?   Why did you not tell us in the beginning of this debate that the whole fight was against the man and not upon the platform?"   Teasingly and sneeringly Davis rejoined: "I am only a small man.   I speak for myself only."   Amid such trifling scenes Andrew Johnson was fretting his life away, anxious that the Senate should devote itself to matters of state.   "Is it not possible," he complained, "that these idle abstractions shall give place to my Homestead bill?"   But, as we shall see, his Homestead bill was not destined to become the law at this session, not in fact till 1862, after all southern Congressmen had retired from Congress.   Thus Congress dragged itself along till late in June, when it adjourned.

Douglas, at the Charleston convention, had not been able to secure the requisite two-thirds.   The convention, after a ten days' session, adjourned to meet in Baltimore on June 18, when Douglas and Herschel Johnson were nominated.   The Whig party nominated for President and Vice-president, Bell of Tennessee and Edward Everett of Massachusetts.   The insurgent Democrats nominated Breckinridge and Lane and the Republicans nominated Lincoln and Hamlin.   Though Sam Milligan, Robert Johnson, Witthorne and other friends of Andrew Johnson attended the adjourned Baltimore convention, Johnson's name was not presented.   On June 18, Johnson wrote to General Milligan and requested that such course be taken.   After thanking Milligan and his associates

[29] Von Holst, *Constitutional History of the United States*, p. 138; *Thirty-sixth Congress, Second Session*, p. 265.

for their support, he expressed apprehension for the welfare and perpetuity of the government, declaring that he would not suffer his name to add to the difficulties and embarrassments of the situation. "I feel that it is incumbent upon you, and upon me," he wrote, "to do everything that can honorably and consistently be done by us to secure unity and harmony of action, to the end that correct principles may be maintained, the preservation of the only national organization remaining continued, and above all, that the Union with the blessings, guarantees, and protection of its Constitution, be perpetuated forever."

Well might Andrew Johnson feel that the Union was in danger and that the Charleston convention was the beginning of the end. Opinions then differed widely as to what the further development of the struggle would probably be. "But there was no difference of opinion . . . that in the whole history of the Union, from the adoption of the Constitution, scarcely an event could be found that could be compared in importance with this event of the Charleston convention." [30]   But the convention at Charleston was as disastrous to Johnson's Homestead as to the Democratic party. As that convention was bottomed on slavery and as the Homestead was bottomed on freedom, the two were in deadly conflict. "In fact, the Homestead was more destructive of slavery than the Wilmot Proviso." Yet Johnson advocated both the Homestead and slavery—a position alike delicate and ambiguous.[31]

[30] Von Holst, p. 138.
[31] *North American Review*, Vol. CXLI, p. 182; Blaine, Vol. II, p. 4.

CHAPTER IX

FATHER OF THE HOMESTEAD

One of the most interesting problems of the early American statesman was what should be done with vacant government lands. In 1803 France had ceded Louisiana to the United States; in 1819 the Floridas had been purchased and thereafter, by the Mexican War, the Oregon Boundary, and the Gadsden Purchase, much other territory was added.

In 1821 Missouri had become a state, and, lying on the outskirts of civilization, was particularly desirous of attracting settlers. Thos. H. Benton, long a Senator from Missouri, was an early advocate of homestead legislation.[1] Benton proposed the "Graduation Plan"; a sale but on a graduated scale. The best unoccupied lands would be sold at a fair price, the waste or left-over land at a smaller price, and lands occupied by squatters, who claimed title but in fact had none, at a nominal figure. Benton went so far as to advocate a donation of lands to settlers, after a certain number of years' residence.[2] The minimum price of lands before 1820 was $2.00 an acre, with liberal terms of credit; but in 1820 the credit system was abolished and a price of $1.25 cash was fixed.

Graduation homestead bills were frequently offered in Congress in the early part of the last century. The famous Webster-Hayne debate of 1830 was upon resolutions of Foote of Connecticut relating to and criticizing public land legislation. These resolutions inquired as to the advantage the West was getting in the sale of such lands. At that time the issue was not between North and South,[3] Southerners not then dreaming that the "Great American Desert," as the recent Louisiana Purchase was called, was a territory larger than the

[1] *Mississippi Valley Historical Review*, Vol. V, p. 282.
[2] Benton, *Thirty Years' View*, Vol. I, pp. 102-103.
[3] William McDonald, *Jacksonian Democracy*, p. 109.

thirteen original States and that valuable land subject to homestead rights lay within that Purchase. The relation of the South to the North was intimate and cordial in those days. As time passed, however, and nine territories grew up demanding admittance into the Union, it became apparent that the influx of free men would make the West free and give the North the whip-hand over the South. When this discovery was made southern politicians stood aghast, and debates in Congress became sectional. When Senator Hale of New Hampshire, at a later date, wanted to know of Senator Wigfall of Texas, "What wrong has the North done you?" the fiery Texan came back with an answer. "Inhabitants of the new territories," he replied, "gathered from every quarter of the world, from the five points of New York and the purlieus of London, under homestead bills have squatted and undertaken to say what is and what is not property, in open violation of the Constitution." In the '40's, as Wigfall stated, foreigners had begun to crowd American shores, famine in Ireland, and dissensions in Europe driving three hundred thousand refugees to America in 1850.

But before the sectional issue arose Southerners as well as Northerners advocated homestead bills. Henry Clay, with his internal improvement views, proposed a sale and distribution of the proceeds among the States. Calhoun, always an advocate of increasing the power of the states, would surrender to the states such lands as were within the organized boundaries. President Polk favored a sale, and out of the proceeds the payment of the costs of the Mexican War. Efforts were also made to combine the two leading ideas—the raising of revenue and at the same time the assistance of *bona-fide* settlers. Considerable quantities of land were disposed of under homestead bills subject to preëmption laws—that is, the right of occupants to hold the lands on complying with the law. But primarily "public lands were regarded as the basis of a very large revenue." [4] In 1841 the passage of Clay's Distribution Act was "an indication of a policy hostile to a reduction of the price of lands, as there would then be much

[4] *American Historical Review*, Vol. VI, p. 19.

less to be distributed." [5]   In 1844 the question whether lands
should be sold or donated was not active, indeed was not an
issue between the Whigs and Democrats.

Such was the condition of land legislation when Andrew
Johnson entered Congress in 1843.   On March 27, 1846 he
offered his famous homestead measure, at which he kept driving ahead till it became an absorbing issue.   This issue was
greatly complicated, however.   First of all, there were the
land-speculators and big land owners, North and South.
These opposed any free-land bill.[6]   Trans-continental railroads began to "grab" the public lands; Free Soilers to demand them for genuine settlers; slave-holders to condemn
homestead legislation as a policy hostile to the South, and
"Know-Nothings" to dread an influx of Catholic immigrants.
The tariff also entered into the fight.   If the lands were sold
and the proceeds placed in the national treasury there would
be no need for tariff taxes.

Subject to these handicaps, Andrew Johnson set to work to
pass an out and out homestead bill, a measure in the interest
of "the landless."   Andrew Johnson's Homestead bill was
simple and uncomplicated. Its distinguishing feature was benefit to settlers and not revenue.   The Government's western
lands should be divided up and provide homesteads to *bona-fide*
settlers—without money or price. One hundred and sixty acres
should be thus granted to every head of a family, being a citizen of the United States, upon condition of settlement and
cultivation for a number of years.   This homestead idea Johnson came by very naturally.   He knew what it was to be
without a home and to feel the gnawings of hunger!   Besides
the Homestead was a Tennessee idea.   Throughout Tennessee
there were tracts of land, for which no grant from North Carolina had been issued.   These vacant lands were subject to entry
and thousands of enterers were occupying them with no other
title than naked possession.   Johnson's bill would quiet their
titles and make them real owners.

[5] *American Historical Review*, Vol. VI, p. 26.
[6] Carl Sandburg, *Abraham Lincoln*, Vol. I, p. 455.

Congressman Andrew Johnson had rough sledding to reconcile and hold together the advocates of his measure. Jefferson Davis, the Mississippi slavery apostle, and Thad Stevens, the New England abolitionist, sleeping in the same bed, surely made a dangerous pair. In fact, one day when Stevens, the "Vermont cobbler," then representing a Pennsylvania District, addressed the House on Johnson's Homestead, he all but "threw the fat in the fire." "Slave countries never can have a yeomanry," said Stevens. "There is no sound connecting link between the aristocrat and the slave." . . . "True there is a class of human beings between them but they are the most worthless and miserable of mankind." . . . "The poor white is the scorn of the slave himself. For slavery always degrades labor. The white population who work with their hands are ranked with the slaves, . . . they are excluded from the society of the rich; and feel that they are degraded and despised." Forestalling Helper's *The Impending Crisis*, Stevens described what the South would be but for slavery. He praised the soil, the climate and the harbors of Virginia, spoke of her early achievements and of her present decay. "In Virginia there are no new towns, no improved highways, no public schools." . . . "Ask us the cause, sir, and I will abide the answer," the great orator declared. "Education is necessary to civilization and there can be no education on big plantations. The children of rich men cannot associate with poor whites, that would be an offense, hence there must be private tutors." . . . "The sons of Virginia instead of seeking for the best breed of horses and cattle to feed on her hills and valleys must devote their time to slavery and growing lusty sires and the most fruitful wenches to supply the slave barracoons of the South." . . . "And this is not my picture," Stevens solemnly warned, "but the description of a Congressman from Virginia, a statesman who pathetically laments that the profits of this gentle traffic 'will be greatly lessened by the circumscription of slavery.' "

On July 25, 1850, Johnson addressed the House on his bill, and gave expression to his humanitarian ideas. "Every man is entitled to a home," he asserted. When "the government fails to supply a home it makes war on the interests of those it is bound to protect." [7]   Standing with General Jackson on the land question, he urged that America should learn a lesson from poverty-stricken Ireland. The argument that revenue would be lost by a gift he met with the assertion that there would be more revenue in taxes from western lands, when occupied and cultivated, than from a sale at $1.25 an acre. "There were 1,442,216,116 acres of public lands on September 30, 1848," he declared, "which at $1.25 an acre would be $1,802,707,000;" but "when these lands are put in cultivation they will be worth many billions more." He rested his case, however, not on revenue but on the right of the thing. "Like the air or like the heat, the public domain," he said, "is the property of all, intended to be used and enjoyed by all." It was this feature of Johnson's Homestead—free land for free laborers—that distinguished it from all previous measures.

Holding his unruly forces together, Congressman Johnson succeeded in passing his measure through the House, though only Jones and Clements, of the Tennessee delegation, voted for it. In the Senate it was defeated. At almost every subsequent session the House would act favorably on the bill and the Senate, unfavorably. In 1854, while Johnson was Governor of Tennessee, the House again passed the bill. The Senate again set it aside for a substitute, providing that after a *bona-fide* occupancy for five years the tenant could purchase at twenty-five cents an acre. But nothing further was done towards the passage of the bill. Thus homestead legislation halted and stood still in Congress, during the four years Johnson was Governor of Tennessee. Meanwhile his efforts as labor leader and as a champion of the Homestead had given him recognition throughout the Union.[8] At a convention of a labor party held at Albany in June 1851, he received three votes for President of the United States.[9] In the preceding month, at the invitation of George Henry Evans, exponent of

[7] *First Session Thirty-first Congress*, Part II, p. 1449.
[8] *Mississippi Valley Historical Review*, Vol. V, p. 3.
[9] New York *Tribune*, June 2, 1851.

land reform in America, and editor of the *Working Man's Advocate,* and of Greeley, of the *Tribune,* he had gone to New York to address a land reform association.

When accepting this invitation Johnson wrote to Chairman Evans and expressed the wish that the meeting should be gotten up as "a homestead gathering without connection with any of the 'isms' of the day." The meeting was to be held in a public park, but a rain-storm drove the reformers indoors. A fair-sized crowd was in attendance, and the New York papers carried good accounts of the speeches. The *Tribune* in an editorial commended Andrew Johnson and his work. Shortly after this, Johnson, with pride and satisfaction, wrote to Sam Milligan that he was in New York sometime since, "and had quite a pleasant time of it in the Empire City and was treated there with marked kindness and attention." [10] But if Johnson received marked kindness in the North, in the South he was suspected of abolitionism and of treachery to his native land. In the South Johnson's scheme was called "wild agrarianism," "socialistic." "It was an infamous and a nefarious scheme." "Who would own a farm in North Carolina when he can get better in the West for nothing?" it was asked. Johnson himself was called "the greatest of national humbugs" and the "pioneer insurgent." [11]

Nothing better shows the confusion into which Andrew Johnson had been thrown by circumstances beyond his control than his attempt to ride two horses at the same time. As between the two, however, there is no doubt of his choice. His advocacy of slavery was perfunctory, his advocacy of the homestead, spontaneous and whole-souled. In the '50's the South had passed under the dominion of the slave power, Middle and West Tennessee being as much controlled by it as other sections of the South. Old abolition ideas no longer prevailed. A good negro fellow, "sound in wind and limb," who in the '30's or earlier—before the cotton gin or the spinning jenny—would have brought three or four hundred dollars, was now fetching

10 Johnson MS.
11 *Raleigh Register,* June 2, 1852; McMaster, *History of the United States,* Vol. VIII, p. 109; Richmond *Whig,* May 15, 1852; Wilmington *Journal* (N. C.), same date.

twelve or fifteen hundred. Free negroes had been disfranchised, slave laws were harsher and more rigid. To teach the
slave to read or write was a misdemeanor and, in the Far
South, to advocate freeing the negro was a felony punishable
with death. These laws were necessary to preserve slavery.
Educated slaves were an impossibility. Therefore, through
necessity, Andrew Johnson was an advocate of slavery.
Doubtless he would have taken this position anyway, despite
public opinion. He stood by the Constitution and "that sacred
document," as he called it, recognized slavery. "But for the
protection of slavery in the Constitution," the Supreme Court
had said in substance, "southern slave states would not have
come into the Union, and there could have been no United
States."

For these reasons Johnson was with the South on the slavery
issue. If his attitude towards slavery was compulsory, on the
other hand the Homestead appealed to his fighting blood. For
it he stood heart and soul. Looking upon the white race as
superior to the black, so far as he was concerned, he had settled
that matter. It was the duty of the North to obey the compromise measures of 1850 and return fugitive slaves.

In not obeying this law Ohio, Michigan, Massachusetts and
other states were law-breakers and violators of the Constitution. If the abolitionists succeeded in emancipating the slaves
and turning them loose on the South, "the non-slaveholder
would join with the slave-owner and extirpate them," he had
said; and "if one should be more ready to join than another
it would be myself." [12] This usual southern view, I may add,
explains the attitude of poor whites during the Civil War;
they fought, as they thought, for racial integrity. If slavery
were abolished either the poor white or the free negro must be
exterminated, and they stood by their race.

In a debate with Senator Trumbull Andrew Johnson once
quoted that Senator to the effect that "politically the races
are equal." He then asked, "If Arizona were populated by
negroes would the Senator admit it as a state?" Trumbull
assented that he would not and declared that "there is a dis-

[12] *Thirty-sixth Con. Globe*, Part II, p. 1367.

tinction between white and black, made by omnipotence itself."
"Ah," Johnson retorted, "the difference then begins with the
deity, and the whole ground being conceded, all this claptrap
falls to the ground." When Sam Milligan read this speech he
wrote Johnson "not to try to justify slavery by the Bible but
by the laws of nature." . . . "Slavery advances civilization
because it improves the ignorant, vicious negro, who can be
thus and thus only used." [13] That Andrew Johnson knew
slavery to be a curse appears from his Texas "gateway" speech
in the '40's. "Texas in the end," he declared when advocating
the admission of Texas, "may prove to be the gateway out of
which the sable sons of Africa are to pass from bondage to
freedom." [14] Though Johnson toyed with slavery, the homestead idea moved his soul; "free land for free labor," he tackled
in dead earnest. In touch with Free Soilers and well posted
on the land question, he was ready to show his colors, on this
great issue, in the South as well as in the North.[15]

A Free Soil Democracy had existed for some time and in
1848 had nominated Hale of New Hampshire for President
and Chas. F. Adams for Vice-president. This party seceded
from the Democrats but did not join the Whigs. In 1852
they nominated Hale for President and Julian for Vice-president, on a platform advocating Johnson's plan, "land to landless settlers, free of cost." In 1856 this party and the Whigs
merged and out of this merger came the Republican party.

On returning to the Senate in 1857 Johnson offered his
Homestead bill again, determined to make any sacrifice in its
behalf. Addressing the Senate he endeavored to show that the
measure was not sectional because many great Southerners,
Andrew Jackson for example, had favored it. Economically
too the bill was sound, he urged. More and more, however,
the incongruity of a slave-holder's advocating the Homestead
bill appeared. Thus in February 1859 Wade, the noted abolitionist, moved to postpone prior orders and vote on Johnson's
Homestead—the prior order was a proposition to purchase

13 Johnson MSS., January, 1860 and February 9, 1860.
14 Savage, p. 32.
15 Johnson MS.

Cuba for slave purposes. Every one knew that the Cuba bill, to which Johnson was committed, could not pass, yet it was used as a buffer to defeat the Homestead bill. Seward joined with Wade and urged that the Homestead bill take precedence over the Cuba bill. "The Homestead bill," said he, "is a question of homes for the homeless, of land for the landless; while Cuba is the question of slaves for the slave-holders."

The leonine Toombs, incensed by Seward's thrust, paid his respects to demagogues. "If you don't want to give thirty millions for Cuba," he declared, "say so, but don't sidetrack Cuba with your plea of 'land for the landless.' Don't divert us from a great public policy by pretext or by the shivering in the wind of men in certain localities." "We are 'shivering in the wind' are we, sir," said Wade, "over your Cuban question? You may have occasion to shiver on that question before you are through with it. The question will be, shall we give 'niggers to the niggerless' or 'land to the landless.' You can no more run your party without niggers than you can run a steam engine without fuel; that is all there is of democracy. . . . Are you going to buy Cuba for land for the landless? What is there? You will find there three-fourths of a million of niggers, but you will not find any land—not one foot, not an inch." [16] What must have been the feelings of Andrew Johnson while listening to this debate between his friend and "ally," bluff Ben Wade, and fiery Bob Toombs, the favorite son of Georgia? Anyhow, Cuba won out. The Senate determined to debate slavery and postpone the homestead. Five times the vote was taken on the question, "Shall the Senate consider the Cuban question or the homestead question?" Five times Cuba won. Once there was a tie, twenty-eight to twenty-eight, broken by Vice-president Breckinridge in favor of Cuba. In 1860 Johnson made a comprehensive speech in favor of his bill, pleading, conciliating, and quoting facts and figures. "Take a million families," he suggested; "in the East they can hardly procure the necessaries of life. Place them each on a quarter section and how long before their condition will be improved so as to make them able to contribute something to the support

[16] *Congressional Globe*, Vol. XXXVIII, p. 1354.

of the government?" After depicting the future grandeur and permanency of America's free institutions, he exclaimed, "Who dares say this is not our destiny if we will only permit it to be fulfilled? . . . This great work of interesting men in becoming connected with the soil" must go on; they must "be interested in remaining in mechanic shops; prevented from accumulating in the streets of your cities," and thereby this will dispense "with the necessity of all your pauper systems." Replying to Senator Hammond, who had called the poor white man the "mudsill of society" and commended him for his honesty, docility and fidelity, Johnson said that such remarks were "invidious." . . . "Laboring with the hands does not make one a slave," he replied; if so, "Paul was a slave and Archimedes." [17]

Nevertheless, Andrew Johnson must have felt that his Homestead bill was doomed to defeat. Its advocates, differing as the poles, would have brought this to pass. "Bluff" Ben Wade, who sponsored the bill, was perhaps the most disliked man in the South; Seward was almost as obnoxious, and Julian the Free-Soiler was in the same case. As the debate proceeded friction between North and South increased. Senator Johnson of Arkansas declared that Andrew Johnson's Homestead was "so strongly tinctured with abolition no southern man could vote for it." Doolittle of Wisconsin advocated the measure, but by his frankness gave much offense to Johnson. "Slavery is the curse of America," said Doolittle, and "the Homestead bill by giving free land to free men will remedy the evil." By this time Senator Andrew Johnson's patience was well-nigh exhausted. He could not understand why the bill was not debated on its merits. "Why lug slavery into the matter?" he asked. He verily believed that if the Ten Commandments were up for consideration "somebody would find a negro in them somewhere"; the chances were "that a Northern man would argue that they had a tendency to diminish the area of slavery; to prevent the increase of the slave population and in the end perhaps to abolish slavery." On the other hand, "if some Senator from

[17] Savage, pp. 66-67; Cf. Hammond, *Plantation Manual*, in the Library of Congress.

the South would introduce the Lord's Prayer," . . . "somebody would see a negro in it somewhere; it would be argued upon the Ten Commandments or the Lord's Prayer that the result would be a tendency to promote or advance slavery, on the one hand, or, on the other, to diminish or abolish it." Wigfall vigorously replied to Johnson's attack on southern statesmen. Wigfall, indeed, possessed a vocabulary of unusual words and a torrent of uncontrollable eloquence. Jeering and scoffing at the money-loving North, the fierce, scarred-faced southern orator called the roll of southern soldiers sitting about him in the Senate Chamber. "Colonel Jefferson Davis, General Joe Lane, and Colonel Hemphill,—these I discover," he said. But who, "on the other side of the Chamber? Who among you is a soldier or a fighter? . . . I stand here and, on my conscience, say I do not believe a black Republican can ever be inaugurated President of these United States. . . . An irrepressible conflict indeed!" he exclaimed. "The North would be a barren waste without the South." Despite such turbulent scenes Johnson did not despair. He kept his eye on the raging contest and on his Homestead.

His bill had already passed the House by a vote of 115 to 90, but in the Senate it was evident the House bill could not pass. Therefore Johnson proposed a substitute which gave to actual settlers the right of preëmption at twenty-five cents an acre.[18] Senators attacked the bill by argument and by motions to lay on the table and to adjourn. But finally, on May 10, the bill came to a vote. Forty-four Senators voted for the bill and eight against it.[19] All of the negative votes except one were from the South. Johnson, with the aid of Brown of Mississippi, had run the politicians to cover, making it plain that the poor man was about to get a raw deal.

On May 21 the House took up the Senate bill and by a vote of one hundred and three to fifty-five adopted a substitute. As amended, the bill, storm-tossed and scarred, entered the harbor. It passed Congress on June 19, 1860. Andrew Johnson could "now die content," as he had often written his

---

[18] J. B. Sanborn, *American Historical Review*, Vol. VI, p. 34.
[19] *Thirty-sixth Congress*, Part III, p. 2043.

son-in-law, Patterson. The Homestead had passed Congress. The labors of many years had been rewarded by victory, and he had "been the means of giving homes to thousands of worthy families." In the language of Senator Brown, spoken when the measure passed, Johnson was "the Daddy of the baby," "the Father of the Homestead."

But even while Johnson was rejoicing Southerners were besieging President Buchanan to veto the bill. This he did and the veto was sustained. "The slave-holding interests were so strong, Buchanan felt justified in overriding Congress." [20] It was charged that Buchanan's main object in his veto was to destroy Douglas' chances to be elected President. The veto was a labored affair. It was based largely on the ground that the measure was not constitutional and that the public lands when disposed of should be sold.

Johnson was not only indignant, he was enraged. A President and a Democrat, whom he had in a measure elected and who had formerly stood for the Homestead, had gone back on him. This conduct was inexplicable, except that he had "sold out" to the slavocracy. His "veto message," Johnson declared in debating it, "is monstrous and absurd." When the veto was voted on in the Senate, Senator Davis reversed himself, voting to sustain the President. Senator Toombs, in high feather, objected to Johnson's moving a reconsideration, though Johnson had voted "aye" to enable him to make the motion. "As Senator Johnson is the defeated party," Toombs sneered, "he has nothing to reconsider." I will now anticipate events and add that in June 1862 after southern Senators and Congressmen had gone out with their states, Johnson's bill was passed almost without a fight. "Free land and free labor" was the slogan in 1860 and on it Lincoln and the Republicans had won.[21]

In the sense that Andrew Johnson popularized and "put across" the idea of land for the landless, he is the acknowledged Father of the Homestead. Not that he was the first to offer a

---

[20] Stephens, *Political History of Public Lands;* Sanborn, *Congressional Grant of Lands;* Cowan, *Economic Beginnings of the West,* p. 360.

[21] Cowan, *Economic Beginnings,* p. 365.

bill donating land,—Felix Grundy McConnell anticipated him by more than two months, having introduced a bill in Congress similar to Johnson's on January 9, 1846. But neither Mc-Connell's bill, nor others of like kind, except Johnson's, became the law. To Andrew Johnson therefore is due the credit of a workable homestead law, "copied from no other nation, distinctly American and with the merit of originality." [22] Johnson's Homestead is "the concentrated wisdom of legislation after eighteen years." . . . "It protects the government, fills the new territory with homes." . . . "It builds up communities" and by "yielding ownership of soil to occupants lessens the chance of social and civil disorder." Between 1867 and 1874 "one hundred and sixty-eight thousand families, native and foreign, had settled in the Far West and twenty-seven million of Quarter Sections had been occupied." Johnson's Homestead "admits of no favoritism, has promoted an amount of emigration the like of which the history of the world affords no other example," and it has "produced to the United States a revenue which has averaged about a half million sterling per annum." . . . "It appears to combine all the chief requisites of the greatest efficiency." [23]

During the discussion of Johnson's Homestead and after its passage Congressmen and Senators gave him the credit for its enactment. The Senator from Iowa returned his thanks to "a mechanic struggling with poverty, working with the hands which God gave him . . . the most able and faithful member of Congress." Senator Johnson appeared to another enthusiastic Senator as Lycurgus, when "returning through the fields just reaped; . . . and he is entitled to and receives the homage of my poor esteem," he added. Senator Brown declared that Johnson's "reward in the future must be the lowly inscription of his name with those who loved the people." But in June 1860, when Congress adjourned, the future was dark to Andrew Johnson; he could not divine the events I have just described. So far as he could see he was but a defeated man. The labors of a life had come to naught and at the hands of his

[22] Donnalson, *Public Land Commission*, p. 350.
[23] *Mississippi Valley History*, Vol. V, Part III, p. 254.

party associates. The veto was an act of his own President, and the failure to override the veto was due to the change of Jefferson Davis with whom, thirty days before, Johnson had joined hands in the famous February resolutions. At the last moment Mr. Davis had changed his vote on the Homestead— unwilling to fellowship with Free Soilers. Truly Andrew Johnson was sailing in rough weather, but he was also growing tougher and stronger to meet a more angry sea.

CHAPTER X

IMPASSE

With the disruption of the Democratic party at Charleston, and the defeat of the Homestead bill, on which he had staked his all, Andrew Johnson was a man at sea without chart or compass. Out of tune with southern sentiment, without the backing of a political party, and having no ability to organize, he was now playing a lone hand. So far, the best he had been able to do was to raise his voice against special privileges and for the absolute equality of persons of the white race. The negro he did not consider entitled to the blessings of freedom. This attitude on slavery, though an error, was an error of the times. In 1858, when he voted for the Lecompton Constitution to fasten slavery on the free State of Kansas, he made a mistake, but he was following the highest court in the land. Slaves were not persons, they were but things, and "they had no rights which the white man was bound to respect." Thus the Dred Scott opinion was interpreted by the people.

Though Johnson was willing to protect slavery as property, he was unwilling to imperil the Nation's life on the issue, and he was equally unwilling to fall down before slavery, worship it and call it an institution of God. He considered it an evil, but to get rid of it by setting the negroes free and leaving them a source of constant irritation was as great an evil as slavery itself. The argument of southern men, like Alex Stephens, that there was no such thing as slavery and that the question was "one relating to the proper status of white and black" sounded strange and specious to Andrew Johnson.

Almost any day he could go down to slave pens and auction sales in Washington and see negroes sold as if they were cattle or sheep. And yet he knew from his own experience that southern masters were kind and indulgent and that house servants in particular had "many advantages over the white race of like rank in Europe." This fact Sir Charles Lyell had confirmed after seeing the plantation system at work.[1] Often Johnson had fooled himself with the thought that slave labor in the South and free labor in the North fitted into each other, a fallacy he soon rid himself of. Yet there was a world of difference between him and southern men on the subject of slavery. To him slavery was an incident, a thing impossible to get rid of; whereas, to most southern leaders slavery was vital, the foundation of southern greatness, and well worth fighting for.

In the month of June 1860, as Andrew Johnson journeyed home from Washington, passing through Staunton, Roanoke, and Bristol, he traveled along the upper Shenandoah. A land of plenty spread before his eyes. In the meadows sheep and cattle were grazing, comfortable farm-houses dotted every hillside, and plantation melodies could be heard as the slaves followed the plow or swung the cradle in the wheat fields. All was peace and plenty in that favored land. The low tariff of 1857, though hurtful to the manufacturing North, had benefited the agricultural South.

As Johnson reflected on his career, strange thoughts must have come to mind. He could no doubt have been on the ticket with Douglas at that very moment; why had he not acquiesced and run for Vice-president? [2] Why was he not willing to drift with the tide, why worry because the President had vetoed his Homestead bill, why fight the battles of labor and contend that the working man's wages should be increased and put on a level with clerks and sheltered employees? Why continue to set himself up against the evils of the day—hypocrisy and extravagance; caste and cheap aristocracy? "If I cannot live in peace," he must have said to himself, "why not go to the Northwest where notions like mine will be respected?" [3] No doubt he considered himself one born out of time. Poverty, ill-treatment, and hard luck had been the portion of his early

[1] Rhodes, Vol. I, p. 334.
[2] Johnson MSS., May 19 and 28, 1860.
[3] Blaine, Vol. II, p. 4.

life. Did the impressions of that period still pursue him? He was called a demagogue and a sans-culotte—a traitor to the South urged on by obstinacy and unholy ambition. Since entering public life the Whigs had taken him as a target, and justly so, they maintained, because he among southern leaders stood alone.

In truth, the man Andrew Johnson found himself in the plight of the Roman judge who saw both sides of a disputed question and whom both sides put to instant death. Though Johnson had often voted and acted with the North, he knew that the North was as blameworthy as the South. He cherished the hope that Vermont and other Free States would repeal their laws making it a crime to return fugitive slaves, and agree to put a guarantee in the Constitution to protect slavery. He reflected that many Northern States had been high-handed in the matter of refusing to return fugitive slaves. Though Congress had passed statutes requiring that they should do this, under heavy penalty, they had flatly refused. In fact, so far as Massachusetts was concerned, Missouri, which came in as a Slave State in 1821, had never been in the Union at all.[4] As Johnson read and pondered these anti-fugitive slave laws his perplexity must have increased. What should be thought of a state which made it a crime to do that which the United States made it a crime not to do? Thus the Vermont law provided that, "Every person who may have been held as a slave, who shall come or who may be brought into this State, with the consent of his or her alleged master or mistress, or who shall come or be brought, or who shall be in this State, shall be free."

Not only so, but it was further provided that "Every person who shall hold or attempt to hold, in this State, in slavery, as a slave, any free person in any form or for any time, howsoever short, under the pretense that such person is or has been a slave, shall, on conviction thereof, be imprisoned in the State Prison for a term not less than five years, nor more than twenty, and be fined not less than one hundred dollars, nor more than

4 *Massachusetts Statutes* of this date so declaring.

ten thousand dollars." Thus were State and Nation "at grips."

Johnson knew the argument of Chase and Wade and Julian. These abolitionist friends of his were always preaching of the beauty of freedom, depicting the horrors of slavery and urging its abolition. But to him the Constitution was the supreme law and that instrument was dead against their position. If the Constitution was flouted, the American Government must go to pieces. That proposition seemed too plain for argument. The abolition appeal indeed got nowhere with him; if he had his way he "would punish southern fire-eater and northern abolitionist" to the limit. "I would chain Massachusetts and South Carolina together," he once said in Congress, "and I would transport them to some island in the Arctic Ocean, the colder the better, till they cool off and come to their senses."

Arriving at home, Andrew Johnson found the State of Tennessee in a turmoil. His old running-mate, Governor Harris, and his friend, W. C. Witthorne, were bitten by the serpent of Secession and were declaring that the election of an abolitionist as President should dissolve the Union. Even A. O. P. Nicholson and George W. Jones, Union men, were bending to the popular wrath. Though he was beginning to lose confidence in the Democratic party, and though the Charleston convention had opened his eyes to strange sights, he had not yet arrived at the conclusion that Wigfall, Iverson, Slidell, and Jefferson Davis were plotting to break up the Union. Before the summer was ended, however, he had almost made up his mind to that effect.

"The blood of secession at the Charleston convention is not on my head," he declared. "The Democratic party has made a fearful mistake; it ought to have stuck it out at Charleston and not gone to pieces." [5] At a political meeting in Norfolk, and again at Raleigh, during this turbulent period, some one asked Stephen A. Douglas if he favored disunion in the event of Lincoln's election. "Never, never," Douglas answered. "No circumstances can justify such a course." In Tennessee, Yancey of Alabama was abroad stumping it for Breckinridge

[5] Nashville *Banner*, October 2, 1860.

and Lane.   Consumed with wrath and overwhelmed by a conviction that the South was being humiliated and trampled upon by the North and that Lincoln's election meant the destruction of slavery and a rending to pieces of the Constitution, Yancey was nevertheless as mild as a dove.   At Knoxville he was interrupted in his speech by a written question passed up to the speaker's stand.   It was the usual question agitating the South at that moment, "What do you advise, Mr. Yancey, if Lincoln is elected?"

"Come forward, sir," said the great orator.   The man obeyed, as every one else seemed to do when Yancey ordered. "Who prompted you to this, sir?" said Yancey.   The names were given—Judge Temple, Parson Brownlow, and three other Union Whigs.   "Let Judge Temple and the Reverend Mr. Brownlow come forward," said the imperious Yancey.   Dutifully the "culprits" came up to the stand, in the midst of secession applause.   "Judge Temple," said Yancey, "have you the honor of John Bell's acquaintance?" "I have, sir," Temple meekly answered.   "Is he a worthy man, one to be trusted and followed, sir?" "He is."   Drawing a paper from his pocket, Yancey read a letter from Bell practically urging secession in the event of Lincoln's election.   Temple was dumfounded, but the Fighting Parson was not.   Straightening himself up and staring Yancey in the eye, he exclaimed, "If a Secessionist from Alabama or anywheres else undertakes to march through the State of Tennessee it will be over my dead body."   For the first and only time, William G. Brownlow and Andrew Johnson were getting together on the same platform.[6]

As the canvass proceeded, there were urgent calls for Senator Johnson to take the stump.   Why was that voice which swayed the masses hushed and silent, why was the man who had converted the Whig State of Tennessee into a Democratic commonwealth sulking in his tent?   At last the great Tribune came forth to his task, entering the contest for Breckinridge and Lane.   But his heart was heavy within him; a new issue had arisen.   He might urge the people to vote against Whiggery and John Bell, the candidate of the Whigs, because this

6 Temple, *East Tennessee and the Civil War*, p. 316.

was the old fight of the classes and the masses, yet no one was interested. The burning question was, what shall be done if Lincoln is elected? And in West and Middle Tennessee, only the fire-eater could answer this question to the satisfaction of an infuriated people.

Though Johnson claimed that Breckinridge and Lane were better Union men than Bell and Everett, and deserved to be elected, the people did not so understand it. On every stump he exhibited "Campaign Document Number Sixteen." This paper asserted that Breckinridge and Lane were devoted to the Union, that they would not destroy it but "would lengthen it and strengthen it." But Johnson could get up little enthusiasm, his speeches lacked punch; he was not red-hot on the main issue. Being nothing of a fire-eater, using no epithets or braggadocio, he could not keep step with the secession orators of the day. Others might call names and vilify the North, but not he. The term "Black Republican," applied to Lincoln, he cut out. The popular statement that if war came the North would not fight, and if they did one southern man could whip half a dozen Yankees, and that the South was strong and growing stronger, while the North was weak and growing weaker, he did not believe a word of. In the House, he had frequently shown from the census that the Free States were surpassing the Slave States. Having made a study of *The Impending Crisis* and compared Helper's figures with the census table, he knew that Helper was right and that the blight of slavery was upon his native land.

During the canvass Johnson spoke in the city of Memphis, which he loved so well. The people of that growing city were the owners of slaves by the thousands, and were therefore red-hot Secessionists. When Johnson arrived they sounded him out on the great issue, "What do you advise, Senator Johnson, if Lincoln is elected?" "As for myself," he replied, "I shall stay inside the Union and there fight for southern rights. I advise all others to do the same," he added, quickly passing to other issues.[7] In a speech at Meridian, Mississippi, he went a step further and declared that both Breckinridge and Doug-

_____
[7] Nashville *Banner*, October 20, 1860.

las were bolters and that any Democrat was at liberty to vote
for whom he chose. The people were disappointed. *The Mer-
cury* and *The Banner*, Whig papers, quoting Johnson's
speeches, interpreted him as opposing the Breckinridge
platform.[8]

Once or twice the Senator spoke from the same platform
with Nicholson, but these meetings were not a success. Finding
that the political situation was unbearable, he returned home
to think matters over. Concluding that Tennessee was destined to cast her vote for Bell, the Whig candidate, unless the
Democrats could get together, he dispatched his son, Robert,
to confer with the managers of Douglas and of Breckinridge
and to arrange for a fusion between the two. This could not
be worked out, however, and was abandoned. Urging this
fusion, Johnson declared that both Douglas and Breckinridge
were good men, differing only on their interpretation of the
Dred Scott case. He declared that Breckinridge construed the
decision to mean the Constitution carried slavery into the territories, whereas Douglas insisted that the matter of slavery was
for the people of such territories to decide.

Sad at heart, when the canvass was over, Johnson returned
home. He had accomplished nothing, added no new laurels.
November 6, 1860, arrived. It was election day and Lincoln
was elected. Boston, the capital of Massachusetts, and
Charleston, the chief city of South Carolina, rejoiced and were
exceedingly glad—Boston because the slave power would be
curtailed, Charleston because the accursed Union would be
dissolved. Immediately South Carolina took steps to withdraw from the Union. December 17 was fixed on as the date
when a convention should meet to arrange the details. The
Far South would probably follow South Carolina.

In a few days the Senate would be in session and Johnson
would be called upon to take sides. From the Far South
exultant cries of dis-Union rolled up, but the Border States
held back. A thousand conflicting emotions swelled in Andrew
Johnson's breast, but one dominated all others: In a slave em-

8 Nashville *Banner*, October 17, 1860; *Tennessee Historical Magazine*, October 1926.

pire what chance for the "mud-sill"? [9] Was he going to surrender the principles for which he had always struggled? Was he willing to live in a slavocracy where popular education would be impossible, where there was no equality of man, and where the laborer's rights would not be respected? In a border state, as Tennessee would be in the new Confederacy, when fugitive slaves escaped to free territory, would there not be border warfare as in Kansas? In Johnson's mind all was discord and confusion; others seemed sure, others had no doubt of the course to pursue. They understood it all, Johnson did not. Indeed, had not his life always been confusion? Had he not advocated measures, assembled facts, adduced arguments fitting in with freedom and not with slavery? His Homestead bill, would it not kill slavery? Would not a repeal of the Three-fifths White clause be an admission that slavery was wrong in principle? Was he not a southern man with northern principles? Yancey had no doubt about what he wished, nor did Giddings. Yancey would dissolve the Union and make a slave empire, reopening the African slave trade and multiplying the happiness and wealth of the new nation; Giddings would dissolve it, making a free northern republic without the taint of slavery. But Johnson had no such assurances; he felt no such satisfaction.

In those fast-fleeing November days, doubtless the mountains about Greeneville, clothed in their fall garments, never looked fairer. His own home was never more inviting and his surroundings never more propitious. Just out of town, his son-in-law, Patterson, had a good farm and he and Martha were rearing a little family; Dan Stover's place over in Carter County was a perpetual comfort. In Greeneville his sway was supreme. As he walked down the main street of the town and on by the Court House, a turn to the right took him to Water Street where his little tailor shop was still doing business. A few steps up Spring Branch from the shop was the famous town spring. How beautiful and wonderful, bolder than the boldest! From its bowels a million gallons of mountain water, pure and cold, gushed forth every twenty-four hours. Over

[9] Johnson MS.; Statement of Senator A. G. Brown at Greeneville in 1861.

pebbly bottoms it rushed, washing the foundation of the tailor shop and turning a mill wheel a few paces below.[10]   Only a few yards to the north was High Hill.   Towering a hundred feet or more in the air, this was a restful place in the long summer days.   His mother had died in 1856 and his stepfather about the same time.   He buried them in the village churchyard hard by.   Now and then his stroll would be to the other end of the town; over in that section there was a knoll, with a fine view of the mountains.   Like a great dome this knoll shot up into the air.   Though little given to sentiment, he pointed out this spot to a friend, saying that there he wished to rest and to take his final sleep.   Searching out the owner, he acquired this property, and took a deed to the same.[11]

On Monday, November 5, 1860, the day before the election, Andrew Johnson and Col. J. J. Turner spoke at Gallatin, and the Colonel invited the Senator to tea.   That evening the conversation was almost wholly about the election to take place on the morrow and on the probable result if Mr. Lincoln were chosen President.   In the conversation, Johnson gave it as his opinion that Lincoln would be elected, "that the South would seize upon his election as a pretext to secede and that he did not believe a state had the right to secede."   At this point he paused in his remarks and rose from his seat.   "When the crisis comes," said he solemnly, "I will be found standing by the Union."   He intended to go to Washington and "come out distinctly in opposition to a dissolution of the Union."   Concluding, he prophesied: "The attempt to secede will fail, as the South has no resources, can not manufacture arms and will probably be cut off from the whole world. . . . Slavery will find no friends anywhere." [12]

Colonel Turner was greatly alarmed at what Senator Johnson had said and at once wired Governor Harris to meet him in Nashville on the following day.   The Governor, startled at Johnson's attitude, wired to Senator Nicholson to come to Nashville at once.   Nicholson came.   He and Harris did their

10 It is to-day Greeneville's sole source of water supply.
11 Johnson MS. at Greeneville.
12 *Ibid.*

utmost to dissuade Johnson from declaring himself in favor of the Union. Johnson was immovable. "Nothing could be done with him." [13]

The Senate convened on Monday, December 3, Vice-president Breckinridge, defeated candidate for President, presiding. Hannibal Hamlin, just elected Vice-president, was a Senator from the State of Maine, "attracting much attention and endeavoring to escape notice"; General Joe Lane, defeated Democratic candidate for Vice-president, was a Senator from Oregon. Southerners from the Far South were jubilant. The agony was over, the battle for southern rights as well as won. Away with the accursed Union! Senators from South Carolina were conspicuous by their absence. Northern Senators and southern Senators scarcely bowed to each other as they passed. The election of Lincoln was bearing fruit. A group of Senators would gather here and another group would gather there, Abolitionists flocking with Abolitionists, Free Soilers hobnobbing with Free Soilers, Fire-Eaters swaggering around with Fire-Eaters, Compromisers whispering to Compromisers. Andrew Johnson sat alone. In the entire body there was no one to whom he could go. Would the unlettered Tennessee tailor defy the combined wisdom of the South, would he set up his opinion against the world and tread the wine-press alone?

[13] *Johnson MS.* at Greeneville.

PART II: ALONE
1860-1865

CHAPTER I

TESTING TIME

As soon as the South Carolina legislature called a Secession convention, the North became thoroughly alarmed and sobered. So often had idle threats to secede been made, both in the North and in the South, the cry of "Wolf! Wolf!" had lost its terrors. But now at last the "wolf" was at the door and what was to be done? The obvious thing was to comply with the constitutional demands of the South, as Andrew Johnson and other Unionists insisted.

On December 17 Congress, by an almost unanimous vote, requested the abolition states to repudiate their Personal Liberty Laws. The offending states set about complying with this request and all of them, except possibly Massachusetts, would have repealed these unconstitutional statutes. But the concession came too late. Southern Senators like Davis and Iverson let it be known that the proposition would be rejected. "The progress of this revolution would not be stopped," they declared, "if every Personal Liberty Law were repealed to-morrow." [1]   Thurlow Weed, Republican Congressman from New York, and a partner of Senator Seward, proposed to go further. Weed offered resolutions, extending the Missouri compromise line to the Pacific and providing that compensation be paid to owners of run-away slaves by counties refusing to deliver up such fugitives to their masters. Crittenden, the patriarchal Senator from Kentucky, offered a famous resolution to amend the Constitution. The Crittenden Amendment, as it is known, would have prohibited slavery in existing states north of 36° 30′, and south of that line would have protected slavery irrevocably and without the possibility of repeal. The territory north or south of that line, not yet states, should be

[1] *Cong. Globe*, December 5, p. 11.

formed into states with liberty to admit or exclude slavery as they elected.[2]

Before coming to Washington Lincoln had said to Weed that he would not accept the Crittenden Amendment. Slavery being morally wrong, he declared it ought to be restricted; no doubt it would in time be abolished by slave owners, and the slaves colonized. Lincoln was unwilling to bind future generations to slavery. This he made known to Weed, who went to Springfield in the winter of 1860 to get the new President's assent to the compromise. In this conclusion Lincoln was voicing the decree of his party as registered in the November election. His views on the subject he also set forth in a correspondence with Alexander Stephens and John A. Gilmer. "You think slavery right and ought to be extended," he wrote Gilmer, "while we think it wrong and ought to be restricted." [3]

In the present emergency much depended on President Buchanan. Under the Constitution he was Commander-in-Chief of the army and clothed with the duty of suppressing insurrections, a serious responsibility indeed. What would he do? On December fourth his message was read to Congress. In its discussion of slavery, the one absorbing issue, it was a fine example of running with the hare and holding with the hounds. As Wade read the message, the President laid down three general propositions: (1) South Carolina had just cause to secede. (2) She had no right to secede. (3) The United States had no right to prevent her from seceding. As time passed, clouds gathered in the southern sky and dis-Union appeared nearer and nearer. Men began to cry out: "Oh, for an hour of Old Hickory Jackson!" At the same time that Crittenden proposed his resolution the Senate adopted another resolution appointing a Committee of Thirteen to consider the grievances between the slaveholding and the non-slaveholding states and to suggest some remedy. A strong and representative committee was appointed by Vice-president Breckinridge —three from Border States, two from the Far South, five Republicans and three northern Democrats. This committee

2 S. ℂ. Cox, *Three Decades of Federal Legislation*, p. 66.
3 Λ. H. Stephens, *War Between the States*, Vol. II, p. 267.

began work late in December and, upon the motion of Jefferson Davis, it was decided that no report should be adopted without the approval of a majority of the Republicans.[4] This motion may not have tied the hands of the committee, but at all events the committee accomplished nothing. Being unable to agree, they were discharged before the first of the year.[5] As Hale of New Hampshire declared, "When the committee was appointed it was determined that the controversy should not be settled in Congress."

While Congress and the Committee of Thirteen were discussing the state of the nation, the Ship of State seemed to be headed for the rocks. At least three of Buchanan's official family were committed to the right of a state to secede—Floyd, Secretary of War; Cobb, Secretary of the Treasury, and Thompson, Secretary of the Interior. The commercial North was now anxious to heal the breach.[6] Many northern people, who had voted for Lincoln in November with enthusiasm, were now in despair. The prospect of a dismemberment of the nation was not a pleasing one. Buchanan's course gave satisfaction neither to the North nor to the South. Soon his cabinet disagreed and went to pieces. On December 8 Cobb, an able Georgian, resigned because the President would not surrender the Charleston forts to South Carolina. A week later Lewis Cass, Secretary of State and in 1852 the Democratic candidate for President, likewise resigned, but for quite a different reason. He opposed Buchanan's surrender to Jefferson Davis and the South.[7] He and Attorney-General Black and Joseph Holt advised fortifying and holding the South Carolina forts and a thorough-going Jacksonian policy. General Scott wrote to the President, calling his attention to the situation that confronted Jackson in the '30's when South Carolina was engaged in the same business of becoming a "sovereign" state. With due apologies the General would inform the President that "on that occasion Jackson had sent the

4 Cox, *Three Decades*, p. 69.
5 Rhodes, Vol. III, p. 170.
6 *Ibid.*, p. 171.
7 *Annual Encyclopedia for* 1861, p. 700.

sloop of war *Natchez* with two Revenue cutters to Moultrie to prevent the seizure of that fort by the Nullifiers." [8]

But the aged and distracted President, alternately praying and crying, hesitated. Meanwhile the people grew suspicious and critical. It was currently rumored that the President had lost his mind and was unable to transact business. The country at large was as much divided as the cabinet. Some were for peaceful secession. Others would bring the South back into the Union if every demand had to be acceded to. Still others, like Seward, were for a do-nothing policy, relying on the healing influence of time. The "Georgia" idea was to take the South out of the Union for a season, so as to get better terms, and presently to bring her back home again. Nearly every northern paper concurred with Horace Greeley and the *Tribune:* "Let the erring sisters go in peace." Chase likewise favored this course. Ex-President Pierce wrote "Jeff." Davis that if an attempt were made to coerce the South, blood would flow in northern cities. It was well-known that few if any Republicans in Congress were in favor of coercing a state.[9] The stalwart Abolitionists to a man favored a dissolution of the Union in order to get rid of slavery.

To them Lincoln was simply despicable. His universal heart, his ability to see both sides of the slavery question, were specially objectionable. Shortly after Lincoln's nomination, Garrison, editor of the *Liberator,* wrote an article on him and headed it, "The Slave Hound of Illinois." "We gibbet a northern hound to-day side by side with the infamous Mason of Virginia," the implacable Abolitionist wrote. Wendell Phillips was quite as severe. "Who is this huckster in politics?" he asked, referring to Lincoln, "Who is this County Court advocate?" In a word the Abolitionists placed human freedom above the Union and above the Constitution. To them the Constitution was "a covenant with death and agreement with hell." [10]

Time passed. It became certain that South Carolina would

[8] Rhodes, Vol. II, p. 189.
[9] Howe, *History of Secession,* p. 560.
[10] Howe, p. 441; Rhodes, Vol. I, p. 74.

leave the Union and that other southern states of the Far South had caught the secession contagion. Yet no effort was made to suppress them. The old flag had no advocate. The Far South was eager to depart. To avoid war, public interests in the North and East were willing to let her go. New York was arranging to become a free city like Venice. A panic was upon the country. Banks were failing, money was hard to borrow at twelve per cent. United States vessels were scattered. Secretary Floyd and Secretary Thompson were actively cooperating with South Carolina. Mr. Barnwell, of that "sovereign" state, was pressing Buchanan so hard to evacuate Sumter "he didn't have time to say his prayers." [11] Northern papers were filled with sentiments against coercion. "Not a Democrat in the North would raise his hand against his Southern brothers," they were asserting. "The Crittenden amendment is the least the South should ask." [12] In Albany a public meeting was held. It resolved that the North were "the revolutionists and not the South"; that the idea of coercion, "as all men know, the founders of the government . . . would have rejected with scorn." Governor Seymour of New York asked if northern coercion was less revolutionary than successful secession and "whether revolution can be prevented by overthrowing the principles of the government."

The Senate was cross and in bad humor. A simple resolution to print the usual number of copies of the President's message brought on a long and heated debate. Threats, taunts and jeers were indulged in.[13] Iverson, the terrible, declared that five states would be out of the Union before March 4. "Texas' secession is now clogged by Governor Houston," he roared, "and if he does not yield some Texan Brutus will rise to rid his country of the hoary-headed incubus." [14] Senator Davis suggested that threats were inappropriate "as between ambassadors of sovereign states"; that he expected to be out of the Senate in ten days. Wigfall proposed that all Southerners

[11] *War Records*, Vol. I, pp. 90-100.
[12] Bangor *Union*, February 4, 1861; Detroit *Free Press*, February 4, 1861; Carr, *Life of Douglas*, p. 118; *Annual Encyclopedia*, 1861, p. 700.
[13] *Thirty-sixth Congress*, Part I, p. 12.
[14] Savage, *Life of Johnson*, p. 206.

withdraw at once and form a New Treaty. Senator Lane wanted to get Lincoln's election before the Supreme Court, claiming that "undoubtedly it is unconstitutional and void." Amidst derisive laughter by northern Senators, Lane shouted, "The gentlemen may laugh but it is not contemplated that a sectional President on a sectional platform should be elected." Hale of New Hampshire grew belligerent. "If the will of the people," he said, "as expressed at an election held under the Constitution will not be submitted to and war is the alternative, let it come." At this threat the Senate, which had not yet found itself, stood aghast. The idea of coercing a state! Brown of Georgia declared that the South asked no more than to be allowed to "depart in peace and let God defend the right." Iverson enthusiastically quoted Hammond of South Carolina, who had not returned to his seat at this session, "The State of South Carolina has gone out high and dry." "But," Iverson comforted, "there will be no war. Like Senator Seward, the North has too much common sense for that." Iverson, closing a defiant attack on northern aggression, exclaimed with Toombs, "Seize the forts and to your tents, O Israel." "Bluff" Ben Wade declined to say whether he would enforce the Fugitive Slave law or not, but intimated that "the South might take her slaves and go her way and the Free North would go hers." "The Free States would offer to the world a homestead law," he declared, "and they would invite the laboring white man from every quarter of the globe." . . . "The Slave States might go on with their system alongside, and the world would judge which system was most consonant with human happiness." [15] Senator Andrew Johnson rose, sad at heart, and asked that his new homestead bill be referred to the committee on public lands. The motion was agreed to.

Powell, making a strong plea for the old Union in a spirit of compromise, declared that "the Union has cost blood and money"; Senator Douglas, joining in this plea, declared that he was for the Union and did not wish to hear the word party again. Senator Jeff Davis corrected the Senators: "The Union cost no blood, no time, no treasure," he asserted, "the

[15] Savage, p. 209.

Revolution cost blood, time and treasure but the Union cost nothing." Referring to the proposed coercion and degradation of the South, Davis wished to know "who would keep a flower which has lost its beauty and its fragrance and in their stead had formed a seed-vessel containing the deadliest poison?" Sumner read a letter of "Old Hickory" Jackson's. "Now it's the tariff," the letter ran. "The next excuse to destroy the Union will be slavery." Wade asked, "Why is the South kicking? She controls the nation, including Congress and the courts. As for the President, why you own him as much as you do the servant on your plantation." The second day after the genial Hale made his warlike speech, he got "cold feet" and rose to explain. He had been misquoted. He did not intend to say a state could be coerced. "I agree with the speech of Senator Davis," he insisted. Thus for weeks did the Senate sidestep the great issue, "What ought the government to do? In the present emergency is she going to assert her integrity or is she going to surrender to South Carolina? Is she going to continue to function or lie down?"

Nor is this attitude to be wondered at. Before 1860 there was no American Nation—there was but a confederacy. During the first years of the Republic few doubted the right of a state to leave the Union for just cause, of which the state itself was the judge. The Hartford Convention of 1814 was an inchoate expression of this right. "From the beginning of the ratification of the Constitution to the end there never was a moment when the people of the whole United States acted in their collective capacity or in any other manner than as people of sovereign states." [16] The great idea that the people and not the states ratified the Constitution was Marshall's distinct contribution to American constitutional law.[17] Certainly it did not lie in the mouth of Senators Wade and Chase to harshly criticize South Carolina. Rather than engage in the inhuman business of catching and returning runaway slaves, as the United States statutes directed, they would have favored the

16 Professor McDonald, *Jacksonian Democracy*, p. 109.
17 *McCulloch vs. Maryland*, Wheat IV, p. 316, decided in 1819.

withdrawal of Ohio from the Union.[18]   These men were actuated by a high purpose, and this purpose was of greater value, as they thought, than obedience to the Constitution.   The truth is, the Irresistible and the Immovable at last stood facing each other.   Freedom and slavery were at each other's throats. No written constitution, no compromise however tightly drawn, not even Henry Clay himself, could reconcile freedom and slavery.   The stars in their courses were against slavery.   The South failed to see this fact and South Carolina, the "Harry Percy" of the Union, went rushing to her doom.

On December 17, 1860, another convention met in Charleston, but a far different one from that of eight months before.[19] Now there was no debate, no uncertainty, everything was clearcut, everything settled.   Governors, Senators, Chancellors, Judges, and other wise men, Senator Hammond included, were unanimous.   The position of R. Barnwell Rhett of Charleston, taken years before and continuously advocated by him, was correct.   The "accursed" Union must be dissolved.   To celebrate the event the city of Charleston was taking a day off. Business was suspended; the city was gay with bunting; joy was unconfined.   The blue cockade was on every gentleman's lapel; guns roared; Saint Michael's bells pealed forth, reverberating across the Battery and far out into the harbor. South Carolina had left the Union, the first step had been taken to construct a Southern Confederacy "whose corner-stone was to be slavery and whose mudsill was to be the poor white." [20]

Washington City was likewise aflutter,—a Secession town, she was backing South Carolina, the "Game-Cock."   Events were happening so fast no one could keep track of them. To-day it was certain that the Charleston forts would be evacuated and turned over to the "sovereign" State of South Carolina; to-morrow it was equally certain that Major Anderson,

[18] Cox, *Three Decades*, p. 63; Chase's Speech before Peace Conference, February, 1861.   In 1855 Wade advocated the right of a state to secede.   He then declared "that a state is not only the judge of an unconstitutional statute, but of the remedy in such cases."—*Second Session Thirty-third Congress*, p. 214, *Appendix*.

[19] Rhodes, Vol. II, p. 440.

[20] Cox, *Three Decades*, p. 115; Alex Stephens' *Corner-stone Speech* at Augusta in 1861.

The "Secession Movement"

Published by Currier & Ives

in command at Fort Moultrie, would be succored, that provisions and reënforcements would be sent him.

In the Capital of the Nation things were going on for the cause of Secession about as well as in Charleston. Before the Crittenden Amendment was offered in the Senate, favorable action on it had been forestalled and foreclosed. On December 14, four days before the Crittenden Amendment, extending the Missouri Compromise line, was offered and a week before the first vote on the measure was taken, twenty-nine southern Senators and Congressmen, Jefferson Davis among them, had met, consulted and devised a plan which would smother the infant amendment in its crib. Reuben Davis, a Mississippi Congressman, declared that this manifesto was issued to kill off the peace resolutions which had been adopted by the House Peace Committee of Thirty-three. These resolutions had set forth a desire "that all troubles might be composed, the Constitution obeyed, rights guaranteed and the Union restored." [21] If adopted by Congress they would have prevented war. Whatever the purpose of the southern manifesto, its language was plain: "The argument is exhausted," it declared. "All hope of peaceful relations extinguished. . . . Nothing is left but speedy and absolute separation from a Union of hostile states, and the organization of a southern confederacy." [22]

News from the Charleston convention was eagerly awaited. It was the habit of wealthy southern gentlemen to reside in Washington during the sessions of Congress, with their wives and daughters. These devoted women often filled the galleries of Senate and House. As they followed the debates the hot southern blood surged through their veins. Who could make the welkin ring like Toombs or Wigfall? "Coerce the South?" these gallant gentlemen would scornfully ask. You may try it but "we will welcome you to the harvest of death" and "future generations will point to a small hillock upon our border showing the reception we have given you." . . . "Even as the sons of Hamilcar were sworn on the altar to die for country," so the sons of the South, "for home and fireside."

[21] Rhodes, Vol. III, p. 177.
[22] Savage, p. 210.

Of this scene Andrew Johnson was a part. Full well he knew what it meant if he stood in the way. Thirteen years he had spent in Congress and he had not failed to observe the temper of his southern associates. Abuse, proscription, violence, a duel, more than likely death, these might be his portion. Nevertheless he had made up his mind. He was going to stand for the Union. Come what might, this would be his course. Like the man in the boat he would no longer look one way and row another. Every consideration impelled him to this course. The Union gone, and Tennessee in the Southern Confederacy, what would happen? He would be a citizen of a slaveholding oligarchy. What then would become of the mudsill? South Carolina was the leader in this movement. In South Carolina he himself could not hold office. Before one could sit in the legislature of that State and make laws he must be the owner of a hundred acres of land and of ten negroes. Johnson owned only eight. Would laws made by such land-owners and slave-owners bear equally upon high and low? Had not the problem of the southern slave-holding oligarchy always been, how can the few, and the relatively always becoming fewer, rule the greater number, and the always relatively growing greater? Great principles were at stake, the dignity of labor, the homestead law, free land for free men. Dissolve the Union and his life work would be blotted out. Preserve the Union and abolish slavery and the white man as well as the slave would be set free and his beloved Tennessee would bound forward. No doubt she would equal Ohio, Pennsylvania or Illinois.

While these thoughts were disturbing Johnson's mind, the Senate chamber was in a constant hubbub. When Wigfall would cry out that the "blood bought Union cannot be held together with hemp" the galleries would resound with cheers. When he was ridiculing the Peace Committee of Thirteen, declaring that "the states and not that committee must settle the differences" and that " whipt syllabub is not the remedy for the patient," and that "if you of the North wish long to live in our company you must abolish your so-called liberty laws, abolish all your abolition societies and abolish all newspapers advocating abolition," Free Soil Senators roared with mock laugh-

ter. As the laughter continued the excited Texan exclaimed,
"Let the Border State Senators take notice of the mockery with
which southern rights are denied. . . . Not only do you spurn
our constitutional rights, you laugh at us for demanding them.
Sirs, we will no longer submit; . . . we will quietly withdraw
from the constitutional compact and establish a government
for ourselves and, if you then persist in your attempt, we will
leave it to the *Ultima ratio regum* and the Southern States will
settle that question,

> Where the battle's wreck is thickest
> And death's brief pang is quickest,

and when you laugh at these impotent threats, as you regard
them, I tell you Cotton is King . . . and there is no crowned
head of Europe that does not bow the knee in fealty and
acknowledge allegiance to that monarch. . . ." (Long and
continued applause in the gallery.)   "South Carolina has laid
her hands on the pillars and she will shake it till it totters
first and then topples."   During this speech of Wigfall's the
galleries almost took possession of the Senate, as the Vice-
president half-heartedly rapped for order.   Amidst such turbulent scenes December 18 arrived.   On that day South
Carolina was "laying hands on the pillars of the Union"; a
reign of terror existed in southern cities, northern men fleeing
for their lives.   On that day also Andrew Johnson got the
floor and addressed the Senate.

"Mr. President," he began, as the galleries, brilliant with
the élite and chivalry of the South, looked down with hate and
scorn upon him, "I am opposed to Secession." [23]   "No state
has the right to secede from this Union without the consent of
the other states which ratified the compact. . . . If the doctrine of Secession is to be carried out upon the mere whim of a
state this government is at an end," he thundered.   "It is no
stronger than a rope of sand, its own weight will crumble it
to pieces and it cannot exist.   If a state may secede why, as
Madison asks, may not other states combine and eject a state
from the Union? . . . South Carolina if she succeeds might

[23] S. S. Cox, *Three Decades*, p. 70.

and will negotiate with a foreign power. . . . Both sides in
this contest are wrong, sir. The North is wrong in enacting
so-called liberty bills, in the teeth of the Constitution and
United States Statutes. Vermont has such a law." Here Collamer of Vermont entered a mild denial, but Johnson read the
Statutes of 1850 and of 1858 which made it a felony in Vermont to return a run-away slave to its master. Collamer subsided.

"The South is equally wrong," Johnson continued. "Florida, Louisiana and Texas, bought and paid for by the United
States, are now endeavoring to back out of the contract." [24]
. . . "Will not Louisiana and Mississippi close the mouth of
the great river and what then will become of the Northwest?
. . . Florida and Louisiana were territories before they were
states and if they withdraw from the Union, what condition will
they assume on such withdrawal? Will they be states or mere
territories?" Senators Slidell, Yulee, Wigfall and others here
interrupted and indeed interfered so often with Johnson's
speech, badgering and hectoring him, it was two days before
he could conclude. Finally Wigfall in disgust turned to
Yulee and said, "Let him alone!"

"What then is the issue?" Johnson went on with scorn and
emphasis, but still claiming to be a part of the South. "It is
this and only this, we are mad because Mr. Lincoln has been
elected President and we have not got our man. If we had
got our man we should not be for breaking up the Union, but
as Mr. Lincoln was elected we are for breaking up the Union!
I say, no, let us show ourselves men and men of courage. . . .
What sort of a slave-holding nation is proposed to be formed
anyway? If it is based upon the aristocratic laws of South
Carolina it would be a mere slave-holding aristocracy. . . .
The voice of South Carolina, like that of Sempronius, is still
for war but when the battle comes Tennessee, the quiet Lucius,
will be found doing the fighting. . . . Am I to be so great a
coward as to retreat from duty? No, sirs! Here I will stand
and meet the encroachments upon the institutions of my country at the threshold. Shall I desert the citadel and let the

24 *Second Session Thirty-sixth Congress*, Part I, pp. 116-143.

enemy come in and take possession? No! Instead of laying hold of the columns of this fabric and pulling it down, though I may not be much of a prop, I will stand with my shoulders supporting the edifice as long as human effort can do it. Though I fought against Lincoln I love my country; I love the Constitution. Let us therefore rally around the altar of our Constitution and swear that it and the Union shall be saved as 'Old Hickory' Jackson did in 1832. Senators, my blood, my existence, I would give to save this Union."

How did the man make so bold a speech? How dared he stand in that presence and deliver such an utterance? At all events, no sooner were the words spoken than they swept the country. North and South were alike astounded. The best politician in America, his enemies declared, had deserted the South and joined the Union. Surely the North must stand a chance to win if Andy Johnson, the wily old politician, had picked her out as a winner. Why, sixty days before he was stumping Tennessee for Breckinridge and Lane, now he was a "Lincolnite." Senator Green called the speech infamous. Senator Brown called it damnable. The New York *Herald* said that it was "the talk of every circle in Washington and was uniformly condemned by southern men." Senator Clingman declared that until that speech the North was paralyzed and afraid. As Johnson left the Senate chamber his southern associates refused to recognize him.[25] Scowls and hisses greeted him on every side.[26] As he walked down the avenue towards his rooms in the Kirkwood House, insults and indignities were offered to him.

Soon the expected attack on him began in the Senate. Jefferson Davis opening up on "the southern traitor," and seeking to destroy him at home, called Johnson the "ally of Ben Wade," the hated Ohio abolitionist. "Men of that class," Senator Davis intimated, "are but miserable recreants nailed to the cross." Ridiculing the idea which Johnson had suggested that the city of Washington might be besieged by the army of the seceding states, Davis said he was "glad the school

[25] New York *Herald*, December 20, 1860.
[26] Savage, p. 226.

girls of Washington can still turn out and walk the streets in safety without the danger from Johnson's imaginary army." Senator Lane followed, charging that Andrew Johnson had never accomplished anything in life, that he "knows nothing except the Homestead bill," . . . that he had "always acted with the North and against the South." The idea of coercing a sovereign state was monstrous. Wigfall charged that Johnson did not represent true southern sentiment. In the last campaign he was false to the South; his speech at Memphis was treasonable. "In that campaign," Wigfall exclaimed, "did Johnson declare that if Lincoln were elected President the South should secede? He did not; on that subject his lips were sealed. But, sir, I did then and I do now so declare." Benjamin, more diplomatic, endeavored to coax Johnson back into the ranks. "The Senator," so Benjamin urged, "has been unfortunate in the impression his speech has created upon the country. Surely, he did not mean to imply that a sovereign state could be coerced?" To these attacks Andrew Johnson interposed no interruptions, but sat quietly in his seat.

Meanwhile the influence of that December 18 speech was covering the land from New York City to San Francisco. Senator Clingman of North Carolina afterwards charged that Johnson's speech brought on the Civil War and was the most effective speech ever made on any subject. Alexander Stephens considered that it hardened and solidified the North. Senator Simon Cameron called Andrew Johnson the "lion-hearted" Johnson.[27] Johnson was now Seward's "noble friend." Letters from everywhere came pouring in to congratulate and to encourage "the only Union Senator from the South." Mechanics and laborers especially blessed his name. A Baltimore laborer wrote that "the poor working man will no doubt be called on to fight the battles of the rich." An opponent from Memphis declared that "it was labor that achieved our independence and the laborers are ready to maintain it." The New York Working Man's Association voted a resolution of thanks. An illiterate old mountaineer wrote that he wanted some "publick dociments" . . . "to set the people

27 Johnson MS. No. 1057.

rite in this section, so I want to be poasted as how things is going on at Washington." A hundred men from Jacksborough wrote as follows: [28]

Jacksborough, Tenn., May 2nd 1861.

Hon Andrew Johnson:
SIR,

As old friends, and enemies, in a political point of view, we now address you as political friends assuring you that we are with you in heart and feeling in your efforts to save the government from overthrow, and transmit to posterity the blessings of liberty. And it is our desire you should make this in your appointment. Come to Jacksboro and address the people on the great question of Union and Liberty, or Disunion and Despotism.

We ask you to come, with all the power and force of the English language, with Super added emphasis to the word COME!

Yours Truly &c

P.S. We could have got any amount of signatures but time will not permit.

The Minnesota legislature sent resolutions of endorsement and commendation, signed by the Speaker of the House and the President of the Senate. Copies of the speech were eagerly demanded. The *Gazette* at Chattanooga had received orders for a thousand copies; H. M. Watterson desired a hundred and fifty copies; a New York Senator wished a half dozen speeches; Montgomery Blair called for five hundred speeches in Maryland; the Cincinnati *Times* eulogized the speech; Benjamin Rush from Philadelphia urged that the speech be scattered. Scores compared Andrew Johnson with "Old Hickory" Jackson. A Nashville man who had been Johnson's political opponent ordered five hundred copies at his own expense, likening Johnson to "fiery, faulty Andy Jackson." Many declared he would mount higher and higher, that in 1864 he would supplant Douglas and be President of the United States.[29] Southern sympathizers were quite as abusive as the Unionists were friendly. He was called "a Tom Thumb trying to wield the sword of General Scott." It was charged

---

[28] Johnson MS., Vol. II, p. 2358.

[29] These letters may be found in Volumes I, II and III of the Johnson MSS., the numbers ranging from 579 and thence onward. They fill nearly three volumes.

that but for his speech the North would have accepted the Crittenden Amendment and that it would have been adopted by Congress. He was burned in effigy in Memphis, in Lynchburg, in Nashville; and, as Wigfall boastfully declared, "I know not how many other places." [30]

Letters from home were specially encouraging. Sam Milligan advised that he was burnt in Memphis and Nashville and they tried to burn him in Knoxville but the Union men prevented it. "All the Whigs are for you." Writing again, Milligan said that "the Whig papers copied the speech but the Democratic papers called it infamous and refused to publish it." . . . "In certain quarters they are giving you thunder," Milligan wrote. "All you or any one else were ever hurt by being burned in effigy amounts to nothing. When you and I are gone and I fear our government too and the Constitution under which we live torn in pieces, the doctrines of that speech will remain unchanged and its wholesome teachings will be seen in stronger light than the burning fires of the author's effigy." Robert Johnson was delighted at his father's course, and congratulated him for not changing his mind on the Union. Blackstone McDaniel, full of enthusiasm, suggested that "that dam fool 'Crow' Ramsay ought by all means be turned out of office." From far away Texas, brother Bill Johnson wrote, "as a brother to a brother," and "cussed out Texas," declaring, "I am against Secession but am going to vote for it and let the slaveowners fight it out."

Early in January Senator Seward delivered a prepared address.[31] The substance of this speech was that nothing rash should be done, "that we should sit on the bank till the rising tide of Secession flows by." Of this address it has been declared that it was as patriotic and as important a speech as has ever been delivered in the walls of the capitol.[32] That it was patriotic no one can deny, but in comparison with Andrew Johnson's speech of a month earlier, can it be called important? The "Georgia" idea, which Seward approved, that the south-

30 Johnson MS. No. 685.
31 *Congressional Globe*, p. 341; Bancroft, *Seward*, Vol. II, p. 216.
32 Howe, *History of Secession*, p. 496.

ern states would play a child's game—withdraw from the
Union, organize a Confederacy, elect a President, Congress and
courts and get fully under way, and then return again into
the Union—seems fanciful. The North would certainly not
yield more than the Crittenden Amendment and this the South
had already rejected.[33] If the Union was worth preserving,
the occasion needed a *man* in the halls of Congress, as it needed
one in the White House. In Congress that man was Andrew
Johnson, the most indomitable, the most thorough-going and
the most determined individual of his age. In the White
House the man was Abraham Lincoln. The Democratic revolution, begun by Andrew Jackson, it must be admitted, was
bearing fruit. The destiny of the state was passing into the
keeping of the rank and file—the "Rail-splitter" and the
"Tailor."

On January 21, 1861, Jefferson Davis withdrew from the
Senate, delivering a farewell message which brought tears to
many eyes. Shortly afterwards Benjamin likewise departed
for his home in New Orleans. On February 5 Andrew Johnson
charged in the Senate that Davis, Lane, Benjamin and Wigfall had attacked him by preconcert. "The scene was pretty
well gotten up and was acted out admirably," he asserted.
"The plot was executed to the very letter." He then proceeded
to show that since the election of Lincoln, Benjamin had
lauded the Union, praising it to the skies. In fact, Benjamin,
in a public speech in November 1860 had referred to those who
would attack it as "silly savages who let fly their arrows at the
sun in the vain hope of piercing it! and still the sun rolls on
unheeding in its eternal pathway, shedding light and animation upon all the world." To Davis and Lane, who had charged
that he was disloyal to the South and an ally of Ben Wade,
Johnson retorted that he was an ally of any man who stood
for the Constitution and the Union. He likewise showed that
Davis and Lane had been inconsistent in this matter. In May
1860 they had voted that no legislation was needed to protect
slavery in the territories. Yet they were now going to secede

---

[33] Rhodes concludes otherwise, but Secession in the Far South, I think, was
inevitable after Lincoln's election.

because Congress would not do what they said was necessary
to be done.[34]   Johnson concluded his speech on February 5.
The next day but one, Wigfall rose to reply.   Never before
were more vituperative or bitter words spoken in the Senate.

Davis, Lane and Benjamin had hurled tufts of grass; Wigfall let fly stones, rocks, and boulders.   If Johnson could not be
stopped by argument he must be destroyed by abuse.   Denouncing Johnson as a "Black Republican," "a renegade
Southerner," "a Helperite," in fact "more treasonable than
Helper," Wigfall took up Johnson's argument that Alabama,
as a people and not as a state in 1819 adopted the Constitution
and was bought and paid for by the United States government.   "Shame, where is thy blush!" he exclaimed.   "Why, my
cheeks would burn with shame if I would attempt to palm off
a fraud of this kind on the people I represent."   Quoting
Æsop's Fable, that the bugler blowing the horn for peace was
the first to be put to death, he asserted that Johnson could not
raise the issue, "that slaveholding is not sound except at the
risk of his neck, in the South.   Why, sirs," he went on, "his
speech was offensive to every southern state-rights man, to
every southern Democrat, and caused his effigy to be shot,
burned, to be hung in his state I do not know how many times."

Flouting the suggestion that Andrew Johnson was to be
another Andrew Jackson, he spurned the very thought.   "How
it maddens me to see a popinjay speak of guns and drums
and wounds.   After six weeks he attacks the noble Davis, no
longer here to reply;" . . . like the jackal "he preys on the
carcass his royal master has left."   If he had dared "to vilify
the Senator from Mississippi to his face the reply would have
been, 'Lord Angus, thou hast lied,' to prince or peasant or
plebeian."   At this point the Senate could sit quiet and submit no longer.   It broke up in disorder and confusion.   Finally
order was somewhat restored when the intrepid Texan resumed.
"A mousing owl, striking at the proud eagle!" he shouted.
"The vilest of Republicans, the reddest of Reds, a sans-culotte,
for four years past he has been trying to please the North with
his Homestead and other bills.   When war comes he'll not be in

[34] Savage, p. 224.

the breach, he'll not take up arms.   In truth when Tennessee
adopts the ordinance of secession he will have sworn to support any constitution the last time during his natural life."

Senator Wigfall resumed his seat.   The expected had happened, a tornado had swept the Senate.   No man had yet escaped who attacked the institution of slavery.   Johnson was to
go the way of all others who had assailed it.   Broderick fell
at the hands of Terry, Sumner at the hands of Brooks.   A challenge to fight a duel would perhaps follow.   Clingman had
challenged Yancey, Branch had challenged Grow, Prior had
challenged Potter, Barksdale had challenged Burlingame, in
each case the controversy arising out of slavery.   As Wigfall
had denounced Johnson, so Barksdale had denounced Lovejoy.
Foote had presented his derringer at Benton's breast.   On
more than one occasion scores of southern Congressmen had
surrounded Northerners, while weapons gleamed, and men
held their breath.   Such scenes authorized Hammond to write
to Lieber, "Every Congressman is armed with a pistol or a
bowie knife, some with both."

The New York *Herald* of February 8 declared that a duel
would take place between Wigfall and Johnson.   But Johnson sent no challenge to Wigfall.   His courage did not have to
be bolstered by a duel, it had been tested before.   Besides, he
had work on his hands.   In a moment the United States seemed
to have turned to him as its savior.   His mail grew to immense
proportions.   Letters, telegrams, resolutions of endorsement,
invitations to speak, were pouring in upon him.   "Thousands
in New England mention your name with benediction," a
broker wrote Senator Johnson.[35]   The citizens of Cincinnati
invited him and Crittenden to address them.[36]   People began
to crowd his rooms at the hotel and to seek him out.   Charles
Francis Adams called and "was impressed with his dignity,"
his "quiet composure" and "the neat clothes" he wore.   "Who
is this fellow Johnson anyway?" some one inquired.   "Is he the
famous Cave Johnson, Congressman from Tennessee?"   "Not
a bit of it," was the reply.   "There isn't any 'cave' in Andy
Johnson."

[35] Johnson MS., February 26.
[36] Johnson MS. No. 1417.   See Appendix "A" for the copy of Governor
Hicks' letter to Senator Johnson.

CHAPTER II

LION-HEART

During the last days of February Lincoln arrived in Washington and took rooms at the Willard Hotel, half a mile or more from the Capitol. Though divinely appointed to save the Union, Mr. Lincoln, at that time, had not found himself. Either he did not know the seriousness of affairs or he was putting up a bold front. On his way to Washington he had made several inconsequential and unsatisfactory speeches. "There is no crisis but an artificial one," he had said at Columbus. "There is nothing going wrong." [1] But when he arrived in Baltimore he had a rude shock. As he passed through that city his life was in danger. Everything was going wrong; America did not know her own mind. Each day brought distressing news. South Carolina had been joined in secession by Mississippi and other states, and the Crittenden Amendment was practically dead. It had been killed by the manifesto of December 14, and by a combination of Secessionists and Abolitionists—Benjamin and five other secession Southerners combining with Wade, Sumner, Thad Stevens and other unyielding Abolitionists.

Toombs, wiring the Georgia Legislature, shouted, "War! War! War!" The much touted Peace Conference, which Virginia had suggested, ended in nothing. The discussions served but to show how wide apart Southerners and Northerners were on the extension of slavery. President Buchanan was beside himself. "Either a fool or an idiot," the New York *Herald* of December 24 had declared; "drawing Secession to a head like a milk and bread poultice." In January Postmaster-General Blair had threatened to leave the cabinet unless Fort Sumter was garrisoned; [2] and the President had dispatched the *Star*

[1] Rhodes, Vol. III, p. 304.
[2] Gideon Welles, *Diary*, Vol. II, p. 13.

of the West, a side-wheel merchant steamship with provisions for that fort. The gallant Anderson, without orders from the President, had previously removed his small force from Fort Moultrie to Sumter, a much stronger position, determined to strike a blow for the Nation's life. This change of base had incensed the South Carolina government. It likewise raised an issue of veracity as to who had dared order the seizure of property belonging to a sovereign state. Before the boat left port, Jacob Thompson, Secretary of the Interior, and Wigfall, a United States Senator, had not thought it disloyal to the government they served to notify the Charleston people that provisions were on their way and to look out for the incoming steamer. Consequently, when the *Star of the West* arrived off Charleston harbor everything was in readiness for a fight. But the "tub," being unarmed, withdrew and limped back to New York, after a few shots had passed over her bow. No one was killed in this engagement, as Major Anderson from Sumter did not fire in return. Had an engagement then taken place no doubt the Civil War would have begun in January instead of April. Both sides were sparring for position, each anxious to force the other to strike the first blow. The abortive attempt to reënforce Sumter did not greatly arouse the North.

January 2 Buchanan plucked up courage to remove Floyd, Secretary of War, actively coöperating with the Confederacy. Joseph Holt, a staunch Unionist from Kentucky, was appointed in his stead. It was then that Wigfall wired to South Carolina, "It means war; cut off supplies from Anderson and take Sumter as soon as possible." On February 8 a provisional Confederate government was formed at Montgomery, Alabama, composed of South Carolina, Mississippi, Florida, Alabama, Georgia and Louisiana. Jefferson Davis was elected President and Alex Stephens Vice-president. Walker, Confederate Secretary of War, was boasting that Washington would be occupied by Confederate troops before May 1, a boast repudiated by Davis, as he was expecting peaceful secession. Nearly all southern Congressmen had resigned and departed for their homes. Confidence in the new government was above par; in the old government it was a vanishing quantity. "Let South Carolina go over a Bridge of Gold," the delighted abolitionists were saying.[3] Alone in his opinion, the optimistic Seward, soon to be Secretary of State, was more optimistic than ever. "In sixty days all will be well," he cheerily declared. And yet every one knew this was not the case, and that Seward's wish was father to the thought. In truth, the Far South was gone from the Union and gone forever. Prior to the firing on the old flag at Sumter, most of the northern states were unwilling to stand for war on their southern brothers.[4]

The situation in the Border States before April 15 was more hopeful for the Union. Yet southern fire-eaters knew they held the cards. At any moment they could drive the Border States into line. "Sprinkle a little blood in their faces," a turbulent Southerner had suggested. "Blood is all that is necessary." He knew that when fighting began, no matter when or by whom started, the South would rush together as one man. The outlook in Tennessee was still favorable to the Union. Though the legislature, coöperating with Governor Harris, had ordered an election to vote "for" or "against" convention, on February 8 the convention was defeated by a vote of 54,156 for and 67,369 against. Early in the session Robert Johnson, a member of the Tennessee legislature, wrote his father that a resolution had been offered requesting his resignation as Senator but that it had been dropped.[5] In January Senator Johnson wrote to his son, Robert, that probably the Crittenden Amendment would pass Congress and the young patriot was correspondingly happy.[6] "All is well and you need not come home," Robert replied; but added that his brother, Charles, had been on a spree again.[6a] Many were urging Senator Johnson to come to Tennessee, stating that

[3] Moore, p. 262.

[4] U. S. Grant, *Memoirs*, p. 227.

[5] Johnson MS. No. 749; the resolution was adopted in May, 2nd Extra Session, p. 157.

[6] Johnson MS. No. 761.

[6a] Charles Johnson, now a practicing physician, was a lovable character, a musician of talent, and, though like many young men addicted to drink, the idol of his mother's heart.—J. S. Jones, *Address*.

intimidations had been used in the February election.[7]   Neill
S. Brown, former Governor, wrote, congratulating Johnson on the February elections.[8]   Belligerent old Blackstone
McDaniel wrote "there is a dam' Secession postmaster by the
name of Gordon holding on, turn him out."   But even in Tennessee the secessionists were so active the conservatives were
intimidated.   It was manifest that in a short time a new election would be called to vote for another convention.   Many
peace-loving Whigs were joining the secession Democrats and
catching the fever.   Some were like Colonel Gentry, Johnson's
old opponent for Governor.   Colonel Gentry, explaining his
course in quitting the Union and joining the Confederacy, declared that he never had the least idea of doing so.   "I was
always a Union man," he declared, "but one day a wheezy old
side-wheel steamer, labeled Secession, came puffing along and
hove up at the wharf.   As every one else was jumping aboard I
jumped too; and all hands went to hell together."

As a last effort for peace the gallant Crittenden determined
to let the people of the United States vote on his proposed
amendment.   That is, he would call a national plebiscite.   As
southern fire-eaters and northern fanatics had joined hands
and smothered his measure in the committee, he would carry
the same over their heads directly to the floor of Congress.
He hoped thereby to have an election ordered.   But the extremes, North as well as South, again blocked his pathway.
In the Senate Clark of New Hampshire offered an insidious
resolution to the effect that the Constitution itself furnished
sufficient guarantees for the protection of slavery.   This resolution was adopted by one vote and Crittenden's patriotic
labors came to naught.   Six southern Senators sat by and
refused to vote on the Clark substitute.   One of these was
Senator Benjamin.   Andrew Johnson, whose seat was near
Benjamin's, spoke out and said, "Senator Benjamin, why
don't you vote?"   Benjamin tartly replied that it was none
of Johnson's business.   "Vote, sir!   Vote," said Johnson,
"and show yourself an honest man."

[7] Johnson MS. No. 986.
[8] *Ibid.*, No. 1073.

While affairs were in this chaotic condition, and the Union apparently tottering to its fall, Andrew Johnson was busy preparing himself to strike a blow for his country.[9] It was March 2 and, though Congress would adjourn on the fourth, Johnson was determined to rouse the patriotism of America. Whether in New England or the great West, in the eastern cities or on the plains, in the Border States or elsewhere, he had a message for the plain man, and as usual he would go over the heads of the leaders and appeal directly to the people. The Union was in danger. The issue was not well defined. The leaders were blinding the people's eyes. The old shibboleth, "a state cannot be coerced," was being twisted so as to befog and anger the masses and disrupt the Union. Northern abolitionist and southern fire-eater were in accord. The pacifist, the Copperhead and the "dough-face" were playing into the hands of ambitious Southerners. If steps were not taken to arrest the progress of secession, in sixty days, there would be no Union. The Confederacy would be so firmly established nothing could overthrow it.

To galleries filled with spectators, Senator and General Lane of Oregon, a gallant officer in the Mexican War and a Virginian by birth, had just concluded a spirited attack on Andrew Johnson. Seizing upon Johnson's illustration that if President Washington, with force and arms, had put down the Pennsylvania whiskey rebellion, why should not President Buchanan put down the South Carolina rebellion, General Lane exclaimed, "My God, Mr. President, what can I say to a man who likens the secession of a state to a whiskey rebellion? One whose mind cannot discover the difference between a local affair such as the whiskey rebellion and the secession of a great state is triumphantly ignorant and exultingly stupid. . . . Why, such a man never had a correct idea in his head. . . . Why, sirs, his December speech has so encouraged the North and the Black Republicans it has prevented peace and peaceful Secession; that infamous speech has been scattered broadcast all over the country, and its author, Andrew John-

---

[9] Geo. W. Julian, *Recollections*, p. 189; *Johnson MS.* No. 1301, Johnson was in daily conference with Secretary Stanton.

son, is now the noble friend of Seward, the New York abolitionist, forsooth. . . . A tyro understands a state cannot be coerced. . . . Would you forcibly hold the South in the Union, put her in the same relation to the Union that Ireland occupies to England, Greece to Turkey, Italy to Austria, Poland to Russia, the Netherlands to Spain? . . . Sir, like Esau, Andrew Johnson has sold his birthright." [10]

As soon as Lane concluded, Johnson dashed into the fight, charging that there was a conspiracy against him, a conspiracy joined in by sundry Senators, by Davis, Benjamin, Wigfall, and by Lane, by dis-Unionists from everywhere.[11] "Sir, it must be apparent, not only to the Senate, but to the whole country," he declared, "that, either by accident or by design, there has been an arrangement that any one who appeared in this Senate to vindicate the Union of these states should be attacked. Why is it that no one in the Senate or out of it, who is in favor of the Union of these states, has made an attack upon me? Why has it been left to those who have taken both open and secret ground in violation of the Constitution, for the disruption of the Government? Why has there been a concerted attack upon me from the beginning of this discussion to the present moment, not even confined to the ordinary courtesies of debate and of senatorial decorum? It is a question which lifts itself above personalities. I care not from what direction the Senator comes who indulges in personalities towards me; in that, I feel that I am above him, and that he is my inferior."

As Johnson vigorously uttered this last sentence the galleries, filled at last with Unionists, broke into loud applause. The presiding officer rapped with his mallet and ordered the galleries cleared. After some debate Johnson began where he had left off. "Mr. President," he boldly went on, "I was alluding to the use of personalities. They are not arguments; they are the resort of men whose minds are low and coarse. I have presented facts and authorities and upon them I have

[10] I abridge these speeches for the sake of brevity, but retain the language as far as possible.
[11] Savage, p. 409; *Thirty-sixth Congress, Second Session,* Part II, p. 1351.

argued; from them I have drawn conclusions; and why have they not been met? Why abandon the great issues before the country and go into personalities? In this discussion I shall act upon the principle laid down in Cowper's Conversation where he says:

> " 'A moral, sensible and well-bred man
> Will not affront me; and no other can.'

"But there are men who talk about cowardice, cowards and all that kind of thing; and in this connection I will say once for all, that these two eyes never looked upon any being in the shape of mortal man that this heart of mine feared."

As Johnson uttered the words "these two eyes," a spectator in the gallery thus describes the scene: "Johnson here rose to full height, pointing with two right fingers at Lane, and smote his breast with a blow that reverberated through the Senate chamber." . . . "Sir," he then went on, "have we reached a point of time in which we dare not speak of treason? Our forefathers talked about it; they spoke of it in the Constitution of the country; they have defined what treason is. Is it an offense, is it a crime, is it an insult to recite the Constitution that was made by Washington and his compatriots? What does the Constitution define treason to be? Treason shall consist only in levying war against the United States, and adhering to and giving aid and comfort to their enemies. Who is it that has been engaged in conspiracies? Who is it that has been engaged in making war upon the United States? Who is it that has fired upon our flag? Who is it that has given instructions to take your arsenals, to take your forts, to take your dock-yards, to seize your custom-houses, and rob your treasuries? Show me who has been engaged in these conspiracies; show me who has been sitting in these nightly and secret conclaves plotting the overthrow of the Government; show me who has fired upon our flag, has given instructions to take our forts and our custom-houses, our arsenals and our dock-yards, and I will show you a traitor!"

When Johnson plumped out the word "traitor," bedlam broke loose. Senator Clingman in an angry voice rebuked the gallery. "Why, the Senate chamber is becoming but a theater," he sneered. Douglas replied that the Senator seemed to want applause for dis-Union but not for Union.[12] Bigler of Pennsylvania declared that, on his soul, if he had been in the gallery he should have joined in the applause. Senator Bayard was for law and order and for the people, but against popular clamor. Senator Rice said a word for the galleries. They had come to hear and they ought to be permitted to stay. The Chair on motion ordered the galleries cleared. Senator Bayard insisted that the order be carried out. Douglas appealed from the Chair's ruling to the Senate. Bayard called for the ayes and noes. A motion to recess was made. Then a motion to adjourn.[13] During this senatorial tangle Johnson stood his ground while Lane nervously walked to and fro in the aisles, his hands clasped behind, exclaiming, "Let the galleries hear, they can't move me if all were armed. I am for the right; any other Union except with each state having full right is an insult. I have nothing to fear." Bright, a Senator from Indiana, joined in with those who would cut Johnson off. At length the motion of Douglas to suspend the order to clear the galleries prevailed and Johnson resumed his speech—hammer and tongs, the galleries now standing on tiptoe.

Lane's reference to Johnson's "triumphant ignorance and exulting stupidity" the latter turned with fine effect. "Whatever may be the character of my mind," said he, "I have never obtrusively made it the subject of consideration. I may, nevertheless, have exhibited now and then the exulting stupidity and triumphant ignorance of which the Senator has spoken. Great and magnanimous minds pity ignorance. The Senator from Oregon, rich in intellectual culture, with a mind comprehensive enough to retain the wisdom of ages, and an eloquence to charm a listening Senate, deplores mine; but he should also be considerate enough to regard my humility. Un-

---

[12] *Second Session Thirty-sixth Congress*, Part II, p. 1351.

[13] Twelve columns of the *Globe* are filled with the discussions of the motion to clear the gallery, indulged in by Senators Doolittle, Douglas, Clingman, Bright, Crittenden, Bayard, Bragg, Bigler, Mason, Baker, Collamer, Rice, Grimes, Clark, Trumbull, Hale, Thompson, Kennedy, Fessenden, and Johnson of Arkansas.

pretending in my ignorance, I am content to gaze at his lofty flights and glorious daring without aspiring to accompany him to regions for which my wings have not been plumed nor my eyes fitted. Gorgeously bright are those fair fields in which he revels. To me, alas! his heaven appears but as murky regions, dull, opaque, leaden. My pretension has been simply to do my duty to my State and to my country.

"The Senator has not discovered that I ever introduced or projected any great measure except the Homestead. I infer that he is now opposed to the homestead policy. It has been an object long near my heart to see every head of a family domiciliated. Less gifted than the Senator from Oregon, I did not perceive that when, in the Senate, in the House of Representatives, and before the people, I advocated a measure that I thought had a tendency to alleviate and ameliorate the condition of the great mass of mankind, I was incurring the censure that is due to a crime. Lamentably devoid of his wisdom, if I had succeeded in accomplishing the great object I contemplated, the measure of my ambition would have been full. I have labored for it long; I labor still. In 1846 in the House it had few friends, in 1852 it received two-thirds vote of the House; it came to the Senate and during the last session forty-four Senators were for it and only eight against. The Senator from Oregon himself, though he doubted and wavered, recorded his vote for it; but he is opposed to it now. I think it was one of the best acts of his life; and if it had succeeded, I think it would have been better for the country. He intimates that I have been acting with Senators who are not so intensely southern as he pretends to be. Sir, look at his course this morning, who is trying to defeat peace measures, to eject the olive branch, why does he not stand with his noble colleague when this measure of peace is presented to the country? He refers to my State of Tennessee, he seems exceedingly solicitous about Tennessee; I am inclined to think that on twelve o'clock Monday next, or a few minutes before, when the hand of the dial is moving round to mark that important point of time when his term of office shall expire, instead of thinking about the

action of my State, he may soliloquize in the language of
Cardinal Wolsey, and exclaim:

> " 'Nay, then, farewell!
> I have touch'd the highest point of all my greatness;
> And, from that full meridian of my glory
> I haste now to my setting; I shall fall
> Like a bright exhalation in the evening,
> And no man see me more.'

"Yes, Mr. President, I have alluded to treason and traitors,
and shall not shrink from the responsibility of having done so,
come what will; and while I, her humble representative, was
speaking, Tennessee sent an echo back, in tones of thunder,
which has carried terror and dismay through the whole camp
of conspirators. I have been held up, and indirectly censured,
because I have advocated those measures that are sometimes
called demagogical. I would to God that we had a few more
men here who were for the people in fact, and who would legislate in conformity with their will and wishes. Certain men,
having signally failed in being President and Vice-president
of the United States as the people have decided against them,
have reached the precise point of time at which the Government ought to be dissevered and broken up. It looks a little
that way. And how has Secession been brought about except
by usurpation? A reign of terror has been inaugurated, the
freemen of the country have not been heard, the voice of the
people has been suppressed. I suppose it is demagogism to
talk of the people but I say they too have been overslaughed,
borne down, and tyranny and usurpation have triumphed.
It was so with Louisiana; so with Mississippi; with Alabama;
with Georgia.

"In some of those states, even the flag of our country has
been changed. One state has a palmetto, another has a pelican,
and another has the rattlesnake run up instead of the Stars and
Stripes. On a former occasion, I spoke of the origin of secession; and I traced its early history to the garden of Eden,
when the serpent's wile and the serpent's wickedness beguiled
and betrayed our first mother. After that occurred, and they
knew light and knowledge, when their Lord and Master ap-

peared, they seceded, and hid themselves from his presence. The serpent's wile and the serpent's wickedness first started secession; and now secession brings about a return of the serpent. Yes, sir; the wily serpent, the rattlesnake, has been substituted as the emblem on the flag of one of the seceding states; and that old flag, the Stars and the Stripes, under which our fathers fought, and bled, and conquered, and achieved our rights and our liberties, is pulled down and trailed in the dust. Will the American people tolerate it? They will be indulgent; time, I think, is wanted; but they will not submit to it.

"A word more in conclusion. Give the Border States that security which they desire, and the time will come when the other states will come back; when they will be brought back— how? Not by the coercion of the Border States, but by the coercion of the people; and those leaders who have taken them out will fall beneath the indignation and the accumulating force of that public opinion which will ultimately crush them. The gentlemen who have taken those states out are not the men to bring them back.

"I have already suggested that the idea may have entered into some minds: If we cannot get to be President and Vice-president of the whole United States, we may divide the Government, set up a new establishment, have new offices, and monopolize them ourselves when we take our states out. Here we see a President made, a Vice-president made, cabinet officers appointed, and yet the great mass of the people not consulted, nor their assent obtained in any manner whatever. The people of the country ought to be aroused to this condition of things; they ought to buckle on their armor; and, as Tennessee has done, God bless her! by the exercise of the elective franchise, by going to the ballot-box under a new set of leaders, repudiate and put down those men who have carried these states out and usurped a government over their heads. I trust in God that the old flag of the Union will never be struck. I hope it may long wave, and that we may long hear the national air sung:

" 'The star-spangled banner, long may it wave,
    O'er the land of the free and the home of the brave.'

"Long may we hear Hail Columbia, that good old national air; long may we hear, and never repudiate, the old tune of Yankee Doodle! Long may wave that gallant old flag which went through the Revolution, and which was borne by Tennessee and Kentucky at the battle of New Orleans. And in the language of another, while it was thus proudly and gallantly unfurled as the emblem of the Union, the Goddess of Liberty hovered around, when 'the rockets' red glare' went forth through the heavens, indicating that the battle was raging, and the voice of the old chief could be heard rising above the din of the storm, urging his gallant men on to the stern encounter, and watched the issue as the conflict grew fierce, and the result was doubtful; but when, at length, victory perched upon your standard, it was then, from the plains of New Orleans, that the Goddess made her loftiest flight, and proclaimed victory in strains of exultation. Will Tennessee ever desert the grave of him who bore it in triumph, or desert the flag that he waved with success? No, never! she was in the Union before some of these states were spoken into existence; and she intends to remain in, and insist upon—as she has the confident belief that she shall get—all her constitutional rights and protection in the Union, and under the Constitution of the country." Here the galleries broke forth again, and the presiding officer ordered them cleared. Johnson then said: "I have done." As the grim old warrior spoke these last words, "I have done," the applause was renewed and was louder and more general than before. Hisses were succeeded by applause. Cheers were given and reiterated. "Such a scene was never witnessed in the Senate chamber before." Johnson had called a spade a spade. To his untutored mind Davis was a traitor and a conspirator and the crowd had agreed with him. Grinnell of Iowa, a spectator in the gallery, jumped to a bench, waved his hat and shouted, "Three cheers for the Union and for Andy Johnson of Tennessee!" The galleries joined in the demonstration. The presiding officer pounded his desk and ordered the arrest of the offenders. Charles Aldrich, also a spectator in the galleries, jumped to his feet, and yelled back, "Arrest and be damned! We are ready to go now."

To fully appreciate such a scene this must be remembered: southern fire-eaters, such as Wigfall and Iverson, had been mocking and bullying the Senate and deriding the Union until conditions were intolerable. "Gentlemen of the Republican party," Wigfall had sneered a few hours before, "the old Union is dead. . . . The only question that concerns any one to-day is as to its burial. Shall we have a decent Christian funeral or an Irish wake; it is for you to decide." Johnson had undertaken to answer these taunts and his speech came like sunshine after a tempest. Of this occasion Senator Harlan of Iowa affirmed: "I never saw anything to approach it, nor do I believe it has ever been equaled in this country." [14]

In fact, it seemed as if every Union man, North or South, was anxious to extend the glad hand to Andrew Johnson. He was compelled to employ a special clerk to look after his mail. Benjamin Rush urged that Johnson's speech and the speech of Senator Baker of Oregon should be printed together, circulated, and preserved. [15] Newspapers throughout the North were asking for sketches and photographs. Johnson was elected a member of various societies and clubs in Kentucky, Philadelphia and elsewhere. Open letters were addressed to him in the New York papers. Boston invited him to address the citizens. Littell's *Living Age* copied complimentary verses from the New York *Advertiser;* E. Little of New York wrote: "Your voice in the Senate sounds like a trumpet of defiance to treason and it is paralyzed before us! Let us hear it again, brave and faithful Senator! Marshal the patriot host and lead us to the rescue of our insulted nationality." Enthusiastic patriots from New York and Philadelphia declared that they were in ecstasy while they read his last speech. [16] The New York *Times* of March 4 referred to Johnson as "the greatest man of the age." Others who had formerly been friends wrote and warned him that he could not ride on the trains, that resistance to the Confederacy would not be tolerated. In Tennessee his old friend, John L. Hopkins, who had been ap-

[14] *Magazine of American History*, Vol. XXV, p. 47: Johnson's speech made him Vice-president and President of the United States.
[15] Johnson MS. No. 2085.
[16] Johnson MSS. Nos. 2265-2310, 2325-2326.

pointed United States Attorney by Lincoln, refused to serve under a Black Republican. On the other hand, Blackstone McDaniel, on the recommendation of Sam Milligan, accepted the position of United States Marshal. Both Milligan and McDaniel recommended that none but Union men be appointed to office. Johnson had now become Mr. Lincoln's agent in naming the officers for Tennessee, and the sole authority on southern affairs.

CHAPTER III

FIGHT FOR TENNESSEE

With a divided North on his hands Lincoln's task was delicate and difficult. He knew not which way to turn. Being both wise and cautious, however, he concluded that the first thing was to get the lay of the land, and not to formulate a policy till he knew all the facts. One thing at least was clear, he must play for time, and by no means was he to offend the Border States. Then, too, he must hold in line northern Union Democrats, such as Douglas and Pugh, and southern Whigs, such as Bell, Gilmer and Stephens. Andrew Johnson's bold, defiant utterances, though cheering and stimulating, were premature and rather warlike. Lincoln would wait for a united North and he would put the South in the wrong by making her the aggressor. As to succoring the Charleston forts, Seward might toll that matter along, encouraging the South Carolina Commissioners to think the forts would be evacuated. At the right time he could fortify or evacuate as the state of the country demanded.[1]

Secretary Stanton who, in Buchanan's cabinet, had been a tower of strength for the Union, was now in opposition. He had been left out of the Lincoln cabinet and was pouting. Double-faced, tyrannical and with an inordinate desire for office, this strange man set about undermining Lincoln's administration. Almost daily he was writing to Buchanan, his old chief, belittling Lincoln and lauding Buchanan and the Buchanan administration.[2] His pet term for Lincoln was "a gorilla." "Why should Paul du Chaillu have to go to Africa for an ape?" he asked. "He has a better specimen in Washington."[3]

[1] Rhodes, Vol. III, p. 345; Douglas states that Lincoln promised to evacuate, but Rhodes discounts this statement. Douglas recommended evacuation.

[2] Blaine, Vol. II, p. 563.

[3] Welles, Vol. I, XXXI; D. M. DeWitt, *Impeachment*, p. 260. Subsequently Stanton became the "Great War Secretary" under Lincoln—perhaps the most efficient officer in Lincoln's cabinet.

State of Mississippi, Feb. 3. 1861

Dear Sir

I have a mulatto slave remarkable for his impudence. This you know is often the case with africans having anglo saxon blood Witness the Case of Hannibal Hamlin. As a means of humiliating my slave it has been recommended to me, to send him to Washington City, with a Cowhide, and instruct him to give your back & shoulders some marks of his attention, with the instrument aforesaid. It is thought that his Coming in Contact with you, will do effectually disgrace him, that the effect on him will be so humiliating, that he will make a good obedient slave.

Thinking the Suggestion a good One, I have concluded to try the experiment. If he shall happen to wound you badly in the encounter, employ Senator Sumner to send daily bulletins of your Condition to your friends about

Grand Junction.

A Threatening Letter Sent to Andrew Johnson in 1861

To the restoration of the Union, therefore, Mr. Lincoln addressed himself. His inaugural was a marvelous exhibition of love and charity. In it he poured out his feelings to America. He besought her sons to be at peace and to stand for a united country. But even this liberal state paper failed to give general satisfaction. The New York *Herald* declared that it was "crafty and cunning" and suggested that Lincoln "had better to have told a funny story and let it go at that." [4] To the Radicals it was much too conservative—to the Conservatives it was too radical. In the South it was interpreted to mean war. If the South Carolina forts were to be occupied and held by the United States the Confederacy would be at an end. To this the secession government naturally objected. What right had a foreign country to own a fort in the sovereign state of South Carolina?

As soon as the Senate adjourned Johnson hastened home to Tennessee and he was badly needed. His December, his February, and his March speeches, characterizing the leaders in secession as traitors, had been broadcasted over the land. They were the topic of general conversation. His journey home lay through Virginia. In Lynchburg and at other places along the route, as the cars stopped and it became known that Johnson, the traitor, was aboard, crowds of toughs rushed into the train, insulting and ridiculing him. Once an attempt was made to assault him but, being well armed, he protected himself. Full well he understood what was coming to him in the South. Before leaving Washington he had received warnings and threats of which the following is a sample:

State of Mississippi, Feb. 3, 1861.
DEAR SIR:
I have a mulatto slave remarkable for his impudence. This you know is often the case with Africans having Anglo Saxon blood. Witness the case of Hannibal Hamlin. As a means of humiliating my slave it has been recommended to me, to send him to Washington City, with a *Cowhide*, and instruct him to give your back & shoulders some *marks of his attention*, with the instrument aforesaid. It is thought that Coming in Contact with *you*, will so effectually *disgrace* him, that the effect on him will be so humiliating, that he will make a good obedient slave.

4 New York *Herald*, March 5, 1861.

Thinking the suggestion a Good One, I have concluded to try the experiment. If he shall happen to wound you badly in the encounter, employ Senator Sumner to send daily bulletins of your condition to your friends about [5]

Grand Junction.

Face of envelope reads: Hon. Andrew Johnson
U. S. Senate
Washington, D. C.
Endorsed: Signed Grand Junction
Threatened assault
From Mississippi
Attended to.

After receiving this letter it must have been refreshing for Senator Johnson to open his mail and get a word of encouragement from a Tennessee "mudsill." In halting words and in wretched penmanship many letters such as the following came:

Cleveland Tennessee
Feb. the 17th 1861.

Hon. Andrew Johnston Dear Sir
exciting election Has past of which you have Seen and I will assure you your Speach that you Dilivered In Congress was a Standerd your name was Mentioned in the Short canvass a Million of times and the More it was Mention the Brighter it Shind—a few More Such Speach wont Leave a Disunion Man in Tennessee except a few Small pollitions as Such as John Croizen and Bill Swan of Knoxville Tennessee. We have grate confidence in the Deligates that is in conference at Washington at presant Sir the corse that you Have taken in the presant Congress is Rich your name Grows Higher and Higher with the Masses a letter from you would be a Rich presant to an old freind of your on the State of the fairs of our belove country if you Have any thing that is favoring a compromis Let me know
Your Obedt Servant
A. A. Clingan [6]

Arriving in Tennessee Johnson traveled about, speaking in behalf of the Union. The crowds were often belligerent. "At one point an attempt was made to belittle and degrade him by

[5] Johnson MS., Vol. VI, p. 869.
[6] *Ibid.*, Vol. V, p. 1068.

pulling his large and conspicuous nose." The assailant failing in his effort and "noticing that Senator Johnson was assuming a threatening attitude, made a rapid stride for the car door. Others crowded around Johnson, jeering and insulting him, when a shot from his pistol plowed its way through the door-sill as the train hastened away on its journey." [7]

In West and Middle Tennessee a new political alignment had taken place. The Democrats were against Johnson and for Secession, while the Whigs were for him and for the Union. He must therefore join forces with his old political enemies—John Bell, Horace Maynard, Gentry, Nelson and even the "Fighting Parson," old line Whigs. At his home in Greeneville he was delighted to find unity in his own household—wife, children, sons-in-law, all were standing behind him. On momentous occasions it was his custom to consult his wife and daughter, Martha; and now they agreed with him in his determined course. They were for the Union. Truth to say, Mrs. Eliza Johnson was as much of a Democrat as Johnson himself. She it was who constantly urged him on in his fight for the laboring man.[8] Though nervous now lest her husband should be slain, because of his stand for the Union, she nevertheless urged him to fight on and never to quit. The February election, Union or dis-Union being the issue, had been an exciting affair, but the Whig leaders had fought a good fight and had won. Generally throughout the State, as we have seen, the Democrats were Secessionists, but Johnson's old friends, in Greeneville, to a man, and regardless of politics, were for the Union. McDaniel, Milligan, Park, Self and the old tailor-shop crowd were adamant. Governor Harris, W. C. Witthorne, Gustavus Henry and other Democratic orators had been powerless to detach Tennessee from her ancient moorings. She was determined to abide in the ship.

Presently distressing news came. Sumter had been fired on. The first blow had been struck. War had begun. Charges were made that Seward and Lincoln had not kept faith with the South Carolina Commissioners. They had promised

---

[7] *Journal and Tribune*, May 23, 1923.
[8] *Famous Loves of Famous Americans, Globe-Democrat*, April 28, 1914.

not to reënforce Fort Sumter, nevertheless they had sent troops and provisions. In this matter perhaps Seward broke his word. Therefore, on ethical grounds, the forts ought not to have been fortified. On the other hand, should the Union have been dissolved to enable Seward "to keep faith with Sumter"? Anyway, Lincoln did not think so. In the South the charge was everywhere made that Lincoln and Seward had changed front, and the reason for this change of front was two-fold. First, the speeches of Andrew Johnson in the Senate—discordant and belligerent, encouraging the North, dividing the South and detaching the Border States. And second, an assembly of seven Governors from seven northern states who, by their "mischievous machinations caused Mr. Lincoln to change his purpose as to the evacuation of Fort Sumter and caused him to fail to 'keep faith as to Fort Sumter.' This was the conspiracy which inaugurated the war. It was a conspiracy well typified by the Seven-headed Beast in the Apocalypse!" [9] Whatever caused the Lincoln administration to change it finally did so. It concluded with Andrew Johnson that the men who seized United States forts and seized arsenals were traitors and should be dealt with accordingly. Nothing except war was left, if the life of the nation was to be preserved.

The most terrible moment in the history of the United States was the firing on the flag at Sumter and Lincoln's call for troops. In the South the "call" was interpreted to mean coercion and invasion; in the North, the Sumter episode was an insult to Old Glory. The South was now fighting against invaders, for home and for fireside. The North was fighting to protect the flag. Z. B. Vance, the North Carolina Union patriot, on April 15 was addressing a multitude. He was beseeching them to abide in the ship. Both hands were extended to Heaven in prayer. A messenger boy was seen running toward the crowd with a piece of yellow paper in his hand. It was a telegram announcing that Lincoln had called for 75,000 troops. "When these two arms fell by my side," afterwards Vance sadly declared, "they fell by the side of a Secessionist." Thousands of other southern leaders believed as Andrew John-

[9] Stephens, *War Between States*, Vol. II, p. 84.

son did, and would perhaps have done as he did, remained in the Union, but a certain loyalty to caste forbade. It had been taught, and was believed in the South, that the North was bullying the southern states. What right had the North to teach morals to the South? Slavery was a southern, not a northern, institution. When Southerners got ready they would free the negroes, without advice or orders from the North. Was the South a coward? Was she going to free her negroes under compulsion? Would any one be so base as to desert her?

Now Andrew Johnson had no such thoughts as these, no such scruples. The social pull, the tug of *noblesse oblige*—stronger to the aristocrat than death itself—did not move Johnson. The much overworked idea of the sacredness of slavery, the aura which was supposed to encircle the head of a slave civilization—was to him a sham and a fraud. Out of slavery had developed an aristocratic leadership. Such civilization spurned the mechanic and regarded the poor white man as but a mudsill, a fit foundation for the aristocrat to build upon. "Vigor," "docility," "fidelity," these were all that were required of poor whites. Away with the aristocrat, therefore, and down with his proud scornful ways! Away with slavery, the breeder of aristocrats! Up with the Stars and Stripes, symbol of free labor for free men!

To Lincoln's call for troops Governor Harris made a spirited reply: "Tennessee will not furnish a man for purposes of coercion, but 50,000, if necessary, for the defense of our rights and those of our southern brothers." Thus the proud Tennessean made reply. No truer, no braver man than Governor Harris. In making this reply he was but standing by his State. He was doing his best to protect her honor he imagined and to preserve her from internecine warfare. Forthwith the Governor called the legislature in special session and ordered another election for June 8. He also seized the reins of government, assumed the dictatorship and made an alliance with the Confederacy. Dealing with this great question, Johnson and Harris, each in his own way, was serving the State as best he could, and doing his duty as he saw it. If

Tennessee must fight let her fight strangers and not kindred, was Harris' thought; and this was likewise the thought of Robert E. Lee. Men like Lee and Harris would not draw the sword against their native States. Not so with Johnson. In some inscrutable way wisdom had been given to this plain man. He saw what others failed to see. He did what others failed to do. He had the vision of a united country, a great country stretching from sea to sea—not a few scattered, distracted and broken states. Therefore, plunging into the fight and taking the stump, during the months of April and May, he waged relentless warfare on Secessionists and on Secession. "Hell-born and hell-bound," he called them. Far to the west he could not go. There he would have been shot as an outlaw. But in the mountain counties and in portions of Middle Tennessee he spoke night and day. Johnson was now "simply god-like," says Judge Temple. He spoke as one inspired. The conspiracy of Davis, Slidell and Yancey, Johnson denounced. Governor Harris he denounced also as a traitor and a despot—"taking Tennessee out of the Union before the people could be heard." "What is the oppression of the North upon the South," he asked, "the aggression on southern rights, as compared with this act of tyranny and oppression by Governor Harris? . . . The people of Tennessee are to be handed over to the Confederacy like sheep in the shambles, bound hand and foot, to be disposed of as Jefferson Davis and his cohorts may think proper. . . . Money has been appropriated," he charged, "to enable him to carry out his diabolical and nefarious scheme, depriving the people of their rights, disposing of them as stock in the market. . . . Talk about slaves and slavery, but when a slave changes his master he has the privilege of choosing his next master; in this instance the people of a free state have not been allowed the power or privilege of choosing the master they desire to serve."

At many of the speakings T. A. R. Nelson of Knoxville joined in the canvass. Judge Nelson was slightly lame. He was a Union Whig and a man of moving fiery eloquence, and greatly beloved. He made a fit companion for Johnson—as Whig and Democrat were thus drawn together. Horace May-

nard, likewise, was on the stump, and Parson Brownlow. But
the number of Unionists, among the leaders, had fearfully
dwindled since the fall of Sumter. Everywhere excitement ran
high and the blood of men was at fever heat. Secession speakers under Gustavus Henry flooded the mountains. There was
speaking on every stump. East Tennessee was a great stake—
at every cost it must be held for the Confederacy. Virginia
had already seceded. East Tennessee and Southwest Virginia
were the "hog and hominy section" of the South—the granary.
The main line of railroad, from West to East, passed through
East Tennessee, through Greeneville, Jonesboro, Johnson
City, and Bristol. Cut this road and a wedge would be driven
into the heart of the Confederacy. Daily, soldiers were passing
through East Tennessee, over the Virginia and Tennessee
railroad, on the way to Richmond. Trains loaded with provisions and supplies were likewise transported. If Andrew
Johnson's efforts to hold East Tennessee succeeded it would
result in cutting this artery and crippling the southern cause.
His treachery was therefore double-dyed. He was an outlaw
and should be treated as such. Constantly his life was in
danger. But for the warnings of friends he would no doubt
have met his death.

At Rogersville an immense crowd from Hawkins and the
surrounding counties had gathered. Here the Union sentiment was overwhelming and the Court House was full of armed
men. Johnson was addressing the crowd and excitement was
running high. Suddenly Captain Fulkerson of the "Hawkins
Boys" marched to the door of the court room, at the head of
his company. Shoving his way through the packed crowd, the
Captain ordered the speech to stop. The air was charged "as
with an electric thrill," says an auditor. Johnson raised his
right hand for silence, and pointing his finger at the Captain,
said: "Captain Fulkerson, I have been a Democrat all my life
and accustomed to the rule of the majority; if a majority of
this crowd want me to stop speaking I will stop, but if a majority want me to continue I will speak on, regardless of you
and your company." Without giving the Captain time to
reply Johnson asked those of the crowd who favored the speak-

ing to follow him to the right side of the Court House and those opposed to go to the left. A large majority pressed to the right, the Captain saw the complexion of the crowd and, turning and walking out of the court room, led his company away from the scene.[10]

A pathetic incident occurred on June 7, the day before the election, illustrating how danger draws together bitter enemies. On that day the "Fighting Parson" saved the life of Andrew Johnson. On June 7 Johnson spoke at Kingston, a small place off the railroad. That afternoon he had engaged passage on a public hack for Louden. From Louden he was to take the cars next morning for Knoxville and Greeneville. There was only one train a day over the Virginia and Tennessee railroad. A son of Parson Brownlow happened to mention to his father that on the incoming train two thousand Confederate soldiers were expected. Brownlow, Sr., knowing that Johnson was to be on this train and that his life was not worth a pin's-value if he was, dispatched his son, posthaste. He must stop Johnson before he boarded the train and bring him through the country. Young Brownlow, afterwards an editor, writing of this trip, told how Johnson thanked him for his trouble. The stern old fighter swore a bloody oath: He would be damned if he would be driven "from traveling on the railroad by the damn traitors of the Cotton States." Finally Nelson and Trigg prevailed on Johnson not to take the train, not needlessly to risk his life. East Tennessee would need his services in Washington. The result was Johnson yielded and he and young Brownlow jogged along, over forty miles of muddy roads, till they reached Knoxville. It developed that two desperadoes, serving the Confederate government and living in Knoxville, one a Spaniard, named Columbus Carlos, and the other named William Parker, had gone to Louden to incite the soldiers to take Johnson's life.[11]

At the June election Tennessee was taken out of the Union. East Tennessee, however, went strong against Secession and for the Old Flag. But chaos and confusion at once set in. All

10 *Johnson MS.* at Greeneville.
11 *Ibid.*

government was gone. There was neither a United States nor a Confederacy to uphold the law. Every man's hand was raised against his neighbor. Johnson became a marked man. His mail was rifled—his name forged to letters. A wealthy banker in Boston, named Amos Lawrence, had "sent Andrew Johnson a thousand dollars of Yankee money and this he had used in the election." Such was the charge made to discredit Johnson and to break him down. The letters to Mr. Lawrence, soliciting money and purporting to be signed by Johnson, were soon shown to be forgeries. In a moment the State of Tennessee had left the United States and become a Confederate state. The efforts of many loyalists aided by Johnson, to form an independent state of East Tennessee failed. But the famous Knoxville-Greeneville Convention was organized to effect this purpose and survived for a year or more. Soon the Confederate Government began the work of conscription. The loyal Unionists resisted the conscription officers. Many fled to the mountains, some went over into Kentucky and Ohio. Cumberland Gap was filled with refugees. From the tall peaks, round about, sadly and sorrowfully, these brave men looked towards Tennessee and their little homes in the valley. Many of them were abolitionists and owned no slaves. All were opposed to the war. Yet they were compelled to fight. They were hunted down like wild beasts. The iron entered into their souls—35,000 of them joined the Union army. Of this number 13,000 were old Andy Johnson Democrats—his personal followers. These 13,000 to a man followed him into the Union army.

Parson Brownlow was cast into prison. His paper, the Knoxville *Whig*, was destroyed. On Sunday, December 22, 1861, in his prison-cell the Parson wrote in his Diary: "Brought in old man Wampler, a Dutchman 70 years of age, from Greene County, charged with being an Andrew Johnson man and talking Union talk." Nelson, just elected to the United States Congress, was captured on his way North and sent to Richmond. There he was lionized by the Confederates, and finally turned loose on a promise to fight the Confederacy no more. Searching parties were scouring the mountains, looking for Dr. Charles Johnson, who was recruiting for the Union. Robert Johnson, having raised a regiment and been elected Colonel of the first Tennessee Cavalry, was an object of Confederate search. Dan Stover, now a Colonel and in the mountain-fastnesses of Tennessee, was leading the mountain boys—tearing up railroad tracks, burning railroad bridges, doing the Confederacy all the damage he could. "The Chiefs of the Bridge-Burners" he and Colonel Carter were called. Judge Patterson was in jail. "Shall I hang the traitor?" his captor was wiring to headquarters. Jails were filled with Unionists. Sundry bridge-burners were hung. Many Unionists were shipped to the Far South; houses were burned, crops abandoned. Able-bodied Unionists who did not escape were captured and sent to the Confederate army. Only old men, women and children remained at home. Despair reigned. As in Italy, when Guelph and Ghibelline cut each other's throats, so in the fair regions of East Tennessee. Finally the Confederate army moved into the country and took possession.

Soon after the election Andrew Johnson received the following letter:

Memphis, June 19th 1861.

Andrew Johnson Esqr
    Late U. S. Senator &c
        Greenville, Tenn.
Sir:
    The patriotic sense of all this portion of Tennessee being fully developed, and that of the whole State becoming rapidly right, it has become dangerous to the persons of Traitors to remain longer within her borders. I therefore take the liberty of warning you, in the language of your friend Lincoln at Washington, "to disperse in twenty days"; and I suggest further, that your personal safety might require you to leave much sooner.

    Our own self respect as *gentlemen and freeman,* as well as a proper regard for the purity of our Commonwealth and the respectability of our State Sovereignty imperatively require that you should leave Tennessee at once and forever. You can probably find a Congenial home and associations among your Northern Allies.

                Yours   JNO. R. McCLANAHAN
                                        of the Memphis Appeal [12]

12 *Johnson MS.,* Vol. II, p. 2394.

With this letter in hand, coming from the highest source, what was Johnson to do? Was he to submit or was he to fight to the death, leaving home and wife and children? Not a moment did he hesitate.

Bidding adieu to wife and little ones, Johnson left home and became a "fugitive from tyranny." Escorted by three brave men, Colonel Carter, Captain McLelland, and Reverend J. P. Holtsinger, he started off by the country road, unable to travel by rail. He was headed for Cumberland Gap. On the way he was several times fired upon from ambush, but escaped. He seemed to have a charmed life. At the home of his old friend, John Park, the cavalcade stopped for a moment. Johnson spoke words of encouragement; he assured his old friend that "retribution would certainly come." He placed his hands on the head of young James Park and blessed the lad. He besought him to do as his father had done, "to stand up for his country and never to desert the Old Flag." [13] The little band moved on. Presently they reached Cumberland Gap. Here Johnson was likewise fired upon. From the summit of the Cumberland mountains his eyes wandered towards Greeneville and his old home—alas, he was not to see them again in eight terrible years. In a few months likewise the sorrowing women and the children were to be turned out of home and into the streets. In Tennessee war was war.

Johnson's destination was Washington City. He was hastening to headquarters to put the facts before President Lincoln and to arrange for an army to be sent into East Tennessee. With a Union army at Knoxville, the Knoxville-Greeneville convention would function. There would then be no trouble in organizing the new state, as West Virginia was organized from Virginia.[14]

On his way North the people crowded around him. His fight for the Union, the dangers and trials he had undergone, and his expulsion from home had made him an object of curiosity, wonder and admiration.[14a] In a speech at Lexington, on

[13] The facts above set out I gathered from James Park, the lad on whose head Johnson placed his hands that terrible June day.

[14] O. P. Temple, *East Tennessee and the Civil War*, p. 160.

[14a] Frank Moore, Chapter II; Savage, p. 241.

June 18, he denounced the doctrine of Secession. "Secession is a heresy," he declared, "a fundamental error, a political absurdity, an odious, an abominable doctrine. . . . Making war upon everything that tends to promote and ameliorate the condition of mankind. It is disintegrate, universal dissolvement." On the nineteenth a general reception at Cincinnati was tendered him. "Have we a government in the United States?" he asked, "or only a pretext of a government? If it is a government its authority should be asserted so as to let the civilized world know that it is a government. Let us dispel the delusion under which we have been laboring since our government was founded in 1789—that ours is an ephemeral government, that we imagined we had a government but when the test came it frittered away between our fingers and quickly faded in the distance." . . . "Rewards are out for my capture, I am told. Officers with warrants are hunting me down, but I am no run-a-way, no fugitive—except a fugitive from tyranny, and I thank God the country in which I live is with me. . . . On June 8 the county of Greene gave two thousand seven majority against the odious, diabolical, nefarious, hell-born and hell-bound doctrine called Secession."

The New York *Herald* of June 22 announced that Andrew Johnson, "that staunch and fearless United States Senator," had run the gauntlet and was safe in Cincinnati, Ohio.[15] When he arrived in Washington reporters called and interviewed him. News from Tennessee was eagerly sought. "What is happening to the 'Fighting Parson,' is he still in jail?" every one was asking. "Would Horace Maynard be elected to Congress in August, or be put in jail or be forced to run away, as Johnson had been?" Calling on the President, Johnson unbosomed himself to Lincoln. He told of the trials, the deprivations, and sufferings of the people of East Tennessee, described the value of that section to the Union cause, set forth the valor and heroism of his people, and pointed out their services as fighters if they only had arms and munitions. Mr. Lincoln was greatly impressed with Johnson's recital of conditions. In fact, it became Lincoln's "cherished plan" to throw an army from Ken-

15 *Johnson MSS.* Nos. 2399 and 2776.

tucky into East Tennessee and thereby cut the Confederacy in twain.[16] Military operations in Washington, so far as Tennessee was concerned, were turned over to Johnson. He busied himself at the Postoffice Department and at the War Department. Postmaster General Blair declared that it was Johnson's "prerogative to lead in Tennessee matters." Cameron, Secretary of War, assured him that his applications for arms and munitions for Tennessee had been duly filed.[17] The army to defend the Cumberland Gap, indeed, was now spoken of as the Andrew Johnson army.[18] Secretary Chase wrote Senator Johnson that "our great and good friend Lincoln expressed the strongest wish to gratify you and to approve the order for arms," and that he wrote "approved A. Lincoln" on the order.

Funds poured in from the North to relieve the distress in East Tennessee.[19] From Pittsburgh, from New York, from Boston and from other places assistance was furnished. A warrant on the treasury for the sum of $100,000.00 was drawn at Johnson's instance. Envelopes of patriotic design contained letters of praise, of cheer, and of substantial aid. On these envelopes flags, bunting and other patriotic symbols appeared. There were also snatches of verse; buglers on horseback; pictures of George Washington and of the Capitol. At this time Andrew Johnson remitted $1,800.00 to Amos Lawrence, as it was not then needed.[20] He was elected a guest of the Loyal Society of Indiana, invited to come and live with various people, "to share their homes and hearthstones." [21] Return J. Meigs, an old friend from Nashville, living on Long Island, and a fugitive from Tennessee, offered "to divide his shelter and his bed" with Johnson; patriotic citizens from Philadelphia, Chicago, Brooklyn, Cambridge, wrote inviting him "to spend the entire summer" with them.[22]

In the midst of scenes like these there also came heart-rend-

---

[16] J. W. Fertig, *Secession*, etc., p. 30.
[17] *Johnson MSS.* Nos. 2776 and 2538.
[18] *Ibid.*, Nos. 2473, 2538, 2776.
[19] *Johnson MS.* No. 2468.
[20] *Ibid.*, No. 2666.
[21] *Johnson MSS.* Nos. 2666 and 2740.
[22] *Ibid.*, Nos. 2528b, 2860 and 2862.

ing letters from the East Tennessee fugitives. They were without food, shelter or clothes; the United States army had not come as promised. Oppressed, living in mountain caves like wild beasts, they asked was not succor ever coming? [23] Some of the East Tennessee soldiers were growing suspicious. From his family, imprisoned in Greeneville, no word had come to Johnson; he knew not whether wife, daughters and grandchildren were living or dead. Judge Patterson, of course, was fast in jail; but as to Colonel Dan Stover, Colonel Robert Johnson and Dr. Charles Johnson, somewhere on the confines of Tennessee and Kentucky, God only knew what had become of them.

Thus passed the trying days of war. Johnson was straining every nerve to cripple the Confederacy, to strengthen the Union and to relieve the loyal people of the South. He was not only a Senator but a commissary, a fiscal agent, a relief society, a comforter of his people. And bitter as was the cup, he never lost faith. This most unnecessary war was the crime of southern leaders, not of the people, he insisted. By these leaders secession had been planned for years. He saw it all, now. The people had been deceived. "Conscious traitors" were criminals and should be dealt with as such. As for the plain people they were not at fault. "His faith in the people never wavered." [24]

Early in October Johnson left Washington City on a speaking tour. First he visited Camp Dick Robinson in Kentucky where the First and Second Tennessee Union Infantry regiments were encamped. These regiments were made up largely of East Tennessee Unionists—refugees from home, Johnson's friends and supporters. From Camp Dick Robinson he crossed over into Ohio, everywhere urging the people to rally around the Old Flag. At Columbus, Ohio, to an immense crowd, he described the emotions that swelled in his bosom while he was visiting Camp Dick Robinson and mingling with

[23] *Johnson MS.* No. 3058.
[24] Judge Temple claims, and no doubt correctly, that the first meeting of the Knoxville-Greeneville Convention in December 1860, and the support of the plain people, encouraged Andrew Johnson to make his December 18, 1860, speech.

the Tennessee refugees and witnessing their distress and sufferings.

"The other day," he said, "when I stood in the presence of two thousand Tennesseans, exiled like myself from the homes of comfort and the families of their love, I found that my manhood and sternness of mind were all nothing, and that I was only a child. There they were, my friends and fellow-citizens of my beloved State, gathered upon the friendly soil of Kentucky, from the tender stripling of sixteen to the gray-haired father of sixty, all mourning the evil that has befallen our land and our homes, but all seeking for arms wherewith to go back and drive the invader from our fields and hearth-stones. I essayed to speak to them words of counsel and encouragement, but speech was denied me. I stood before them as one dumb. If it be true that out of the fullness of the heart the mouth speaketh, it is also true that the heart may be too full for the utterance of speech. And such were ours—two thousand of us exiled Tennesseans, and all silent as a city of the dead! But there was no torpor there. There were the bounding heart and throbbing brain; there were the burning cheek and the blazing eye; all more eloquent than ever were the utterings of human speech. Each of that throng of exiles, who had wandered among the mountains and hid in their caverns, who had slept in the forest and squeezed themselves, one by one, through the pickets of the invader, each one was now offering comfort and pledging fidelity to the other. Youth and age were banded together in a holy alliance that will never yield till our country and our flag, our government and our institutions are bathed in the sunlight of peace, and consecrated by the baptism of patriotic blood.

"There were their homes, and there, too, is mine—right over there. And yet we were homeless, exiled! And why? Was it for crime? Had we violated any law? Had we offended the majesty of our Constitution or done wrong to any human being? Nay, none of these. Our fault, and our only fault, was loving our country too well to permit its betrayal. And for this the remorseless agents of that 'sum of villanies,' Secession, drove us from our families and firesides, and made us exiled wanderers. But the time shall soon come when we wanderers will go home! Depend upon it, my friends, this monstrous iniquity cannot long exist. Some bolt of Heaven's righteous vengeance, 'red with uncommon wrath, will blast the traitors in their high estate.' But whatever they may do— though they may ravage our State and make desolate our homes, though they convert the caves of our mountains into sepulchers and turn our valleys and plains into graveyards, there is still one thing they cannot do—they never can, while God reigns, make East Tennessee a land of slaves." [25]

[25] Moore, *Rebellion*, Vol. III, p. 13: "Johnson's able and patriotic speeches in the fall of 1861 created immense enthusiasm."

CHAPTER IV

SENATORIAL WHIP

Heretofore Senator Johnson had been in the minority, a free lance and a man without a political party. But with the breaking out of war he stepped to the front, and disputed the leadership of the Senate with Collamer, Sumner, Fessenden and Hale. In matters pertaining to the war in Tennessee and the West his wish became a command.

On April 15 Lincoln had called for 75,000 troops to suppress insurrectionary combinations; on the 19th and 27th issued proclamations setting on foot a blockade of southern ports; on the 27th authorized the Commanding General to suspend the writ of *habeas corpus* between Washington and Philadelphia; on May 1 called for 42,034 volunteers. Under these proclamations action had been taken, arrests made on suspicion and without legal authority. In Border States, particularly, the people were in an uproar. On April 22 the Sixth Massachusetts Regiment, passing through Baltimore to Washington, were attacked by a mob and several lives were lost. Baltimore, a city with southern sympathy, was in a frenzy, Washington in danger of capture. It was agreed by the Washington and Baltimore authorities that no more troops should pass through the latter city but should go around it. Hundreds of secessionists in Maryland were cast into prison, without judge or jury. The writ of *habeas corpus* was a dead letter. Civil officers, being powerless to over-ride the military, returned such writs "unexecuted for lack of power to enforce." Mr. Lincoln, now "a military dictator," as his enemies charged, declared he was not going to give up the government "till he had played his last card." Finally he could play a lone hand no longer and called a special session to meet July 4.

In the Senate Andrew Johnson took an active part, pleading

for the loyalists of the South. "The loyal citizens of the rebellious states," he said, debating a resolution of his to send arms to the Tennessee mountaineers, "feel that the United States should protect them against invasion and should guarantee a Republican form of government."[1] Without verbiage, circumlocution or controversy, the Senator spoke seldom but his soul was aglow for his country. He was as anxious to put down the Rebellion as Lincoln himself. And this the Senate understood and appreciated. Senator Wilson called up Johnson's bill No. 38 to appropriate a blank sum, the amount not named, to transport arms and ammunition to southern loyalists and asked Johnson what amount he suggested. "Two million dollars to begin with," Johnson replied. This was "entirely satisfactory" to Wilson and his committee and the resolution was adopted unanimously.

When a joint resolution was offered to endorse President Lincoln's acts, during the recess of Congress, an acrimonious debate broke out. Indeed the President's course in suspending the writ of *habeas corpus* was never endorsed by Congress, and other acts could only be endorsed by tacking amendments of endorsement to various bills to increase the pay of private soldiers. Though Congress was sympathetic with the President, voting men and money as he called for them, it was averse to approving acts in violation of the Constitution. At this period but for the fortitude of President Lincoln, sustained by loyal men like Andrew Johnson, the Union would undoubtedly have gone to pieces.

On July 22 Senator Johnson offered a resolution the importance of which cannot be over-stated. It is the foundation of Johnson's subsequent conduct. No understanding of the object of the war, as it appeared to Lincoln or to Johnson, is possible without a knowledge of this resolution. Indeed it runs the dividing line between Stevens and Sumner, fighting for Abolition, and Lincoln and Johnson, fighting for the life of the Union. "The present deplorable Civil war," Johnson's resolution reads, "has been forced upon the country by the dis-Unionists of the Southern States, now in revolt against the

[1] *First Session Thirty-seventh Congress*, Part I, p. 216.

Constitutional government and in arms around the Capital; in this National emergency Congress, banishing all feeling of mere passion or resentment, will recollect only its duty to the whole country; this war is not prosecuted upon our part in any spirit of oppression, nor for any purpose of conquest or subjugation, nor for the purpose of over-throwing or interfering with the rights or established institutions of those states, but to defend and maintain the supremacy of the Constitution and all laws made in the pursuance thereof, and to preserve the Union, with all the dignity, equality and rights of the several states unimpaired, and as soon as these objects are accomplished the war ought to cease." Other resolutions on the subject were offered and discussed; one totally different from Johnson's, by Breckinridge, late candidate for President, now Senator from Kentucky. Breckinridge's resolution provided that all United States troops should be withdrawn from the South.

In his message to the special session Lincoln had used language so plebeian that Johnson himself might have written it. "The plain man in the South," President Lincoln asserted, "had he known the facts, would have opposed the war;" and in "no state except South Carolina would the people, except by coercion, have left the Union." Of this message Copperheads and Conservatives were alike critical and censorious. The New York *Times* on July 5 declared that there "was never a message less important." At an earlier date President Lincoln had used words quite as suggestive of Andrew Johnson's doctrine of government. "This is essentially the people's contest," he had declared. . . . "On the side of the Union it is a struggle for maintaining in the world that form and substance of government, whose leading object is to elevate the condition of men; . . . to lift artificial weights from all shoulders; . . . to clear the paths of laudable pursuit for all; . . . to afford all an unfettered start and a fair chance in the race of life. . . . Yielding to partial and temporary departures from necessity, this is the leading object of the Government for whose existence we contend." How cheerfully Andy Johnson could enlist under "Abe" Lincoln's banner.

While resolutions and proclamations were discussed in Congress the Civil War was getting under way. In June and July General George B. McClellan had won a few minor victories in Virginia and the North was much elated. There was a demand that the government run the Confederates under Beauregard from the gates of Washington and put an end to the war. McDowell, in command of the Union forces around the Capital, was loath to engage in a fight. The Confederate General Joseph E. Johnston might break away from the Valley of Virginia, he feared, and join forces with Beauregard and prove too strong. General Scott, Commander-in-Chief of the Union forces, though not urging a fight, promised that he would "arrange to hold Johnston off"; if Johnston moved toward Beauregard he would "have General Patterson at his heels." Thus in response to a precipitate demand for a fight the first great battle of the war took place—the battle of Bull Run. Johnston, eluding Patterson, joined Beauregard and the Union forces were utterly routed. Pell-mell they rushed back into Washington. With blanched cheeks Senators and Congressmen, out on a holiday to witness the triumph of Union arms, scampered back to their homes, wiser men.[2]

It was now clear that southern troops under trained officers like R. E. Lee, Johnston, and the redoubtable Stonewall Jackson were going to fight to the last ditch. That the country was in for a four years' war. Washington City was in a panic. The New York *Times* of July 26 and 27 declared the Capital was in imminent danger. Debates in Congress reflected the general terror. Border State Congressmen were for compromise and peaceful secession, a course nearly all northern Democrats favored. Senator Polk of Missouri and Senator Powell of Kentucky bitterly denounced the dictatorship of Lincoln. They charged him with precipitating a "cruel, useless and bloody war"; he was "a dictator violating the Constitution." Only Congress, they maintained, could declare war.

On July 16 J. C. Breckinridge, speaking on the resolution to endorse Lincoln's war measures, asked "how was it possible

2 Cox, *Three Decades*, p. 156.

for the legislative department to make the unconstitutional acts of the Executive constitutional and valid?" [3] Breckinridge quoted Webster and Stephen A. Douglas, "A President has no power to suspend the writ of *habeas corpus*." . . . "The Supreme Court," Breckinridge exclaimed, "has just held, through its Chief Justice, that this could not be done. . . . There stands the opinion, unanswerable; and it will add to the Chief Justice's renown. . . . In the name of the people I represent I protest," he went on. "Jails are filled with victims unable to get out because we have no civil law; our country is a mere despotism. . . . These resolutions do not state the facts; . . . the South is not the aggressor, the North is the aggressor; this war is waged by the North. . . . So far from resolutions being passed ratifying and approving the President's acts, I think the Chief Executive of the country, and I have a right, in my place to say it, Sir, should be rebuked by the vote of both houses of Congress." Thus were the Democrats, even the gallant Breckinridge and others, obstructing Lincoln's efforts to preserve the Union.

One day while such utterances were ringing through the halls and corridors of Congress, encouraging the new Confederate government, Senator Baker of Oregon, Colonel of a Union regiment, "in blue fatigue cap and riding whip in hand, came from his camp and took his seat in the Senate chamber." Unbuckling his sword, he laid it on the desk and sat in meditation, while the speech of Breckinridge continued. "Why coerce the South," Breckinridge was saying. "Why endeavor to whip her back into the Union? Will you whip her back into love and fellowship at the point of the bayonet?" Breckinridge closed and Baker rose to reply. "Suppose," said Colonel Baker, "a Senator, with the Roman purple flowing over his shoulders had risen in his place and declared that Hannibal's cause was just and Rome's wrong?" "He would have been hurled from the Tarpeian Rock!" Fessenden, the coolest Senator of them all, broke in. Colonel Baker—resuming— asked, "How could courts and juries fight a war? War is a

[3] *Thirty-seventh Congress, First Session,* p. 138.

one man's job; it is the duty of the President and not of Congress to put down this insurrection." [4]

John Sherman, Senator from Ohio, declared, "It is better that all we have should perish, and you and I and all, than this noble country of ours." Senator Doolittle was "unable to see why the President's call for troops was unconstitutional. "Answer me this, sirs," he said, "with thirty thousand men under arms in Virginia, less than thirty miles away, cannot I as an individual, not as an executive, call a hundred thousand men if necessary to go out and suppress this rebellion or even take the lives of the rebels?" In the Senate Chamber the only member from a seceding state was Andrew Johnson of Tennessee. All others were gone. But a different man he was from heretofore. A fugitive from home and from State, an implacable foe to secession and to the Confederacy, the gaze of the nation was upon Andrew Johnson. He had fought, he had suffered, as no other American, to save the life of the republic. Peculiarities of speech, repetition, personal controversies, these were overlooked, in fact had disappeared. His utterances were now short, direct and to the point. Neither force nor threats had swerved him, nor had the lust of power or place seduced him. Home, wife, children had been surrendered in behalf of the Union. Everything, he had abandoned for country.

Johnson's resolution, declaring the objects of the war, was treated by the Senate with unusual deference; Senators "would follow him wheresoever he led." They proposed to adopt the resolution just as it came from his hands.[5] Senator Clark of New Hampshire might not like the wording of the resolution, "but if it suits the honorable Tennessean," he declared, "and his people I am for it." Senator Howe declared that "when Senator Johnson gives expression to his sentiments he gives expression to my own." Doolittle and the West Virginia Senators objected to the word "subjugation" in the resolution. But Johnson insisted that it remain and the objection was withdrawn. Certain Senators objected to the words, "in arms

[4] *American Oratory*, Vol. IV, "Insurrection and Sedition Bill," S. B. 33; Blaine, Vol. I, p. 345.

[5] Blaine, Vol. II, p. 339.

around the capital," but these words were also retained, Johnson exclaiming, "Why, sirs, we heard the guns last Sunday roaring around the capital. . . . In fact, we are pretty near having some in the capitol who are against the government— almost in this chamber."

Senators opposing Johnson conceded his courage and genuine worth and spoke in terms of high praise. Senator Harris of New York, in reply to Johnson, said of him, "He is a man to whom my heart goes out in warmer and more gushing sympathy than to any other man on this floor." Senators who loved the Union most admired Senator Johnson most, discovering in him "a spirit noble, lofty, patriotic and self-sacrificing." The distinguished Senator Saulisbury declared that he esteemed Johnson much and always had.[6] And the new and untried position of leadership Senator Johnson filled most acceptably. A sense of responsibility now steadied and sobered him and the desire to save his country, his home and his family made him wise and strong.

On July 27 Andrew Johnson got the floor on his resolution declaring and defining the objects of the war: The war is to be waged not for oppression nor for conquest, not to overthrow or establish institutions, but to maintain the Constitution and preserve the Union with the rights of the states unimpaired. When these things are done the war ought to cease. In offering this resolution two thoughts, as we have seen, dominated Andrew Johnson. First, to destroy the Southern Confederacy. Death he would gladly suffer rather than see Tennessee, and his home, in a slave-holding, oligarchical empire, such as he feared would be established. His resolution would solidify the Border States. And second, to restore the United States government under the Constitution of the fathers. Slavery was secondary. In truth, if the Union was restored, on Lincoln's platform, slavery would be outlawed anyway. Either way, therefore, slavery would soon be gotten rid of. Probably "the sable sons of Africa would pass into freedom by the gateway of colonization," as Johnson had said in his speech on the annexation of Texas.

6 *Second Session Thirty-seventh Congress*, Part I, p. 645.

On the resolutions of endorsement of Lincoln, Johnson stood shoulder to shoulder with the ultra-Unionists. "Not until your forts were surrendered," said he, addressing the Senate, and "not until the President of the so-called Southern Confederacy was authorized to call out the entire militia, naval, and military forces, one hundred thousand strong, did President Lincoln call for seventy-five thousand men to defend this capitol." . . . "Are we for the Government, or are we against it? That is the question. . . . With your forts taken, your men fired upon, your ships attacked at sea, and one hundred thousand men called into the field by the so-called Southern Confederacy, Senators talk about the enormous call of President Lincoln for seventy-five thousand men and the increase he has made of the army and navy! Mr. President, it all goes to show, in my opinion, that the sympathies of Senators are with the one Government and against the other. Admitting that there was a little stretch of power; admitting that the margin was pretty wide when the power was exercised, the query now comes: Are you willing to sustain the Government? . . . Senators complain of the violation of the United States Constitution. Have you heard any intimation of complaint from those Senators about this Southern Confederacy—this band of traitors to their country? Have you heard any complaint about violations of constitutional law on the other side? Oh, no! . . . But we must stand still; our Government must not move while they are moving, with a hundred thousand men. While they are reducing our forts, and robbing us of our property, we must stand still; the Constitution and the laws must not be violated! . . . When our enemies are stationed in sight of the capitol, there is no alarm, no scare, no fright. Some of us would not feel so very comfortable if the rebels were to get this city. I do not think I could sleep right sound if they were in possession of it. I do not believe there would be much quarter for me! Let us look at the question plainly and fairly. Suppose the rebels advance on the city to-night; subjugate it; depose the existing authorities; expel the present Government; what kind of government have you then?

"How eloquent my friend Breckinridge was upon Constitutions! He told us the Constitution was the measure of power, and that we should feel constitutional restraints; and yet when your Government is perhaps within a few hours of being overthrown, and the law and Constitution trampled under foot, there are no words of rebuke for those who are endeavoring to accomplish such results." . . . "No, sirs," said Johnson, "it is not Lincoln but Davis who is overthrowing our Government and making of it a despotism. And what is Davis' objective, what is he driving at? He proposes to erect a slave oligarchy. . . . Russell of the London *Times*, traveling through the Southern States, correctly sizes up the would-be Secession leaders. . . . They despise a republic. What they want is a monarchy like England, not a republic like the United States. . . . Toombs has declared for a monarchy and so have scores of southern newspapers." Johnson continued, "If we had had ten thousand stand of arms and ammunition in East Tennessee, when the contest commenced, we should have asked no further assistance. We have not got them. Our population is homogeneous, industrious, frugal, brave, independent; but how powerless, and oppressed by usurpers. You may be too late in coming to our relief; they may trample us under foot; they may convert our plains into graveyards, and the caves of our mountains into sepulchers; but they will never take us out of this Union, or make us a land of slaves—no, never! We intend to stand as firm as adamant, and as unyielding as the mountains that surround us. Yes, we will be as fixed and as immovable as are they upon their bases. We will stand as long as we can; and if we are overpowered and liberty shall be driven from the land, we intend before she departs to take the flag of our country, with a stalwart arm, a patriotic heart, and an honest tread, and place it upon the summit of the loftiest and most majestic mountain. We intend to plant it there, to indicate to the inquirer in after times, the spot where the Goddess of Liberty lingered and wept for the last time before she took her flight from a people once prosperous, free and happy. . . .

"We ask the Government to come to our aid. We have confidence in the integrity and capacity of the people to govern themselves. We have lived entertaining these opinions; we intend to die entertaining them. . . . The battle has commenced. The President has placed it upon the true ground. It is an issue on the one hand for the people's Government, and its overthrow on the other. . . . We have commenced the battle of freedom. It is freedom's cause. We are resisting usurpation and oppression. We will triumph; we must triumph. Right is with us. A great and fundamental principle of right, that lies at the foundation of all things, is with us. We may meet with impediments, and with disasters, and here and there a defeat; but ultimately freedom's cause must triumph, for—

> " 'Freedom's battle once begun,
> Bequeathed from bleeding sire to son,
> Though baffled oft, is ever won.'

"Yes, we must triumph. Though sometimes I cannot see my way clear in matters of this kind, as in matters of religion, when my facts give out, when my reason fails me, I draw largely upon my faith. My faith is strong, based on the eternal principles of right, that a thing so monstrously wrong as this rebellion cannot triumph. Can we submit to it? Is the Senate, are the American people, prepared to give up the graves of Washington and Jackson, to be encircled by a combination of traitors and rebels? . . . I say, let the battle go on—until the Stars and Stripes shall again be unfurled upon every cross-road, and from every house-top. Let the Union be reinstated; let the law be enforced; let the Constitution be supreme. . . .

"If the Congress of the United States were to give up the tombs of Washington and Jackson, some Peter-the-Hermit would arise and appeal to the people. He would point to the tombs of Washington and Jackson in the possession of those who are worse than the infidel and the Turk, who hold the Holy Sepulcher, and urge their recapture. I believe the American people would redeem the graves of Washington and Jackson and Jefferson, lying within the limits of the Southern Confederacy. . . . Do not talk about Republicans now; do not talk about Democrats now; do not talk about Whigs or Americans now; talk about your country and the Constitution and the Union. Save that; preserve the integrity of the Government; once more place it erect among the nations of the earth."

The influence of this speech of Johnson's, as that of his former Union speeches, was great. Often during its delivery the galleries applauded so loud and long the Vice-president ordered them cleared. When Johnson said, "God being willing and whether traitors be few or many I intend to fight them to the end," Jefferson Davis' idea that there might be a peaceful Secession or a compromise vanished into thin air. The North was awakened to duty at last. Johnson's resolutions passed the Senate by a vote of 35 to 5.

The special session adjourned in August. During the vacation Johnson was busy making speeches for the Union, and also with the affairs of East Tennessee. That great State was entering upon a scene of desolation not equaled anywhere. The regular session of Congress met in December. On the nineteenth instant a joint select "Committee on the Conduct of the War" was appointed. It consisted of Senators Wade, Chandler and Andrew Johnson, and of Congressmen Covode, Odell, Gooch and Julian. This committee occupied much of Johnson's time until the following February. He then went to Tennessee as Military Governor.

Before quitting the Senate Johnson was as eager in the cause of the Union as a youth of eighteen. No one can contemplate the days of 1861 and not feel that Johnson knew the lay of the land better than any of his associates. The expulsion of Senator Bright is a point in hand, but for Johnson Bright might have escaped punishment. When Johnson, however, told the Senate that Bright—who it will be recalled was Johnson's friend, presenting him in 1857 to the Senate—was at heart a rebel, it was all up with the Senator from Indiana. "On December 19 last," said Johnson, "when I raised my feeble voice for the Union, where was Senator Bright? . . . With a bevy of Confederates he stood, with frowns and scowls and expressions of indignation and contempt for me; as cold as an iceberg—he gave me no look of recognition." By a vote of

32 to 14 Bright was expelled from the Senate. His offense was the authorship of the following remarkable epistle:

Washington, March 1st 1861.

My dear Sir:

Allow me to introduce to your acquaintance my friend Thos. B. Lincoln of Texas. He visits your Capitol mainly to dispose of what he regards a great improvement in firearms. I recommend him to your favorable consideration as a gentleman of first respectability and reliable in every respect.

Very truly Yours,
JESSE D. BRIGHT.

To his Excellency Jefferson Davis
President of the Confederate States
(December 16—1861)

Every scrap of news favorable to the Union, in those early days of war, Johnson gathered and sent to the clerk's desk to be read.[7] He wished every one to be doing something—if they could not fight let them cheer and huzza. At his urgent request $10,000 were voted to celebrate Washington's Birthday and to awaken the people to a patriotic sense of duty. When news of Federal naval victories in January and February reached Washington, he was beside himself with joy, offering a resolution of thanks "to the brave officers and sailors who carried the flag."

Grimes and Fessenden objected; the news was not authentic, they urged; and it would be better to let Congress attend to its own business. Fessenden, in fact, thought such resolutions inept, "unless our minds are so upset by the news we cannot do business." Johnson admitted that was precisely his case. "I am free to say I am pretty much that way," he said, and the resolution was passed.[8] The capture of New Bern, Elizabeth City and other Confederate ports had stirred his patriotic blood; he could hear Farragut, the gallant Tennessean, in Mobile Bay thundering, "Steam ahead!—Damn the torpedoes!" and he could catch visions of a reunited country.

[7] *Thirty-seventh Congress, Second Session*, Part I, p. 738.
[8] *Ibid.*, p. 846.

CHAPTER V

MILITARY GOVERNOR

At the August elections the Confederates conceded the election of two Union Congressmen from East Tennessee, T. A. R. Nelson and Horace Maynard. Shortly after his election Nelson was captured on his way to Washington. Maynard, however, was duly seated as a Representative from the State of Tennessee. This action of Congress was in line with the resolutions of July. Tennessee had not been out of the Union and could not get out. Maynard, a native of Massachusetts, had represented a Tennessee district in Congress for some years. His judgment was sound, he had been a Henry Clay Whig and he was devoted to the Union. Tall, and of swarthy complexion, with long black hair, he seemed of Indian extraction. Hastening to Washington, Maynard sought out Andrew Johnson, his old political opponent. The two straightway went to the President, as Johnson had already done. They wished arms for East Tennessee and they requested that a Union army be sent to protect the loyal citizens of that section.

Mr. Lincoln was impressed with the importance of complying with their request and of saving East Tennessee to the Union. Going to the War Department, he left a memorandum as follows: "On or about the fifth of October (the exact date to be determined hereafter) I wish a movement made to seize and hold a point on the railroad connecting Virginia and Tennessee, near the mountain pass called 'Cumberland Gap.'" This suggestion of Lincoln was forwarded to General Buell in Kentucky, but he temporized. Promising to obey orders, he finally notified the President it was impossible to do so. To seize and hold a position within the enemy's line would violate the first rule of warfare. The President, however, was not satisfied with General Buell's decision. He agreed with Johnson and Maynard that East Tennessee could be held if the

217

loyal mountaineers were supplied with arms and backed up by an army. On December 7 Johnson and Maynard wired General Buell as follows: "We have just had interviews with the President and General McClellan, and find they concur fully with us in respect to the East Tennessee expedition. Our people are oppressed and pursued as beasts of the forest. The Government must come to their relief. We are looking to you with anxious solicitude to move in that direction." To this telegram General Buell gave an encouraging reply, but did nothing. Johnson and Maynard wrote bitter letters to Buell complaining of his delay. On December 20 the War Department asked General Buell if he needed more regiments. To this he replied that he was not willing to say that he did. General McClellan and Mr. Lincoln continued to press the matter of relieving East Tennessee upon Buell's consideration. On December 29 General McClellan telegraphed Buell, "Johnson, Maynard, etc., are again becoming frantic, and have President Lincoln's sympathy excited—better get the East Tennessee arms and clothing in position for distribution as soon as possible." General Buell replied that he would need more troops in Kentucky. On January 4 the President took a hand, sending the following telegram to Buell: "Have arms gone forward for East Tennessee? Please tell me the progress or condition of the movement in that direction. Answer." To this telegram General Buell wrote that as long as the Confederate line from Columbus to Bowling Green held it was dangerous to seize Knoxville. Thereupon President Lincoln sent the following wire: "Your dispatch of yesterday has been received and it disappoints and distresses me—my dispatch, to which yours is an answer, was sent with the knowledge of Senator Johnson and Representative Maynard, of East Tennessee, and they will be upon me to know the answer which I cannot safely show them. They would despair; possibly resign to go and save their families somehow, or die with them. Yours very truly, A. Lincoln."

This wire of President Lincoln's was followed by another dispatch to Buell from General McClellan, urging immediate action. To McClellan's telegram General Buell sent rather a dubious answer. The result of the matter was that on February 1 General Buell wrote that the scheme could not be carried out as it would take at least 30,000 men for East Tennessee and thousands of wagons.

General George H. Thomas, however, concurring with Lincoln, undertook to capture Knoxville. The plan as developed was for General S. P. Carter, Colonel Dan Stover and the Tennessee Bridge-Burners, on the night of November 8, to burn the railroad bridges. At the same time General Thomas was to march south from Kentucky and join the loyal Tennesseans. On the night mentioned Carter and Stover did their work well, burning several bridges; but General Sherman and General Buell refused to permit the army to advance within the enemy's territory, as long as the Confederate line remained intact.[1]

The situation in East Tennessee was daily growing more desperate. To add to the discomfiture of the mountaineers their Western brethren had become exasperated; they could not understand why East Tennessee was holding back from the Confederacy and was so obstinate. As early as May 30, while the Greeneville-Knoxville Convention was meeting in Knoxville and taking steps to organize a new state, a Confederate army was standing almost at the convention door with bayonets fixed. This famous convention, of which Robert and Charles Johnson were members from Greene county, would have carried out its plan, no doubt, of forming a new state but for the interference of the Confederate troops. After its second meeting in Greeneville the convention adjourned to meet again at the call of any one of its officers, but war prevented. No meeting was again held for three years. The stoutest Union men had joined the Confederacy. John Bell, George W. Jones, Governor Neill S. Brown, all had left the Union. The gallant General Zollicoffer, staunchest of Union men hitherto, wrote with a sad heart: "We must not, we cannot stand neutral and see our southern brothers butchered." In these words General Zollicoffer voiced the sentiment of the militant and heroic South. East Tennessee was Zollicoffer's

1 O. P. Temple, *East Tennessee and the Civil War*, p. 378.

home and thither he was sent to win the mountaineers to Secession, but he made little progress.

After Congress adjourned Washington City became Andrew Johnson's headquarters. But he was constantly on the go—speaking in Ohio, Indiana and Kentucky. Notices of writs of execution, issued by the Confederate courts and served on his property, were received by him. The following is a copy of the finding of the court in the case of

Confederate States of America
vs.   } Judgment.
The Estate of Andrew Johnson, an alien enemy.

After reciting the facts the court adjudged Andrew Johnson to be an alien enemy. It likewise decreed that "all the property rights and credits belonging to him, either at law or in equity, are hereby sequestrated under the acts of Congress . . . and the receiver is directed to proceed to dispose of the same as provided by law."

A New York attorney, Lorenzo Sherwood, wrote a letter making suggestions to Senator Johnson: "Why do you not offer resolutions in Congress boldly affirming that this war will free the poor white man? There is a great deal of mawkish sensibility over the negro. . . . It is the poor white man, in shirt sleeves, who must be protected from the Southern oligarchy." Accompanying the letter was a set of resolutions carrying out Mr. Sherwood's suggestions.[2]

In the fall of 1861, and the winter of 1862, the situation in East Tennessee had become hopeless. No Union army had been sent and the Confederacy had raised thousands of troops, many of whom were now in East Tennessee. By September 1st 22,000 troops had been raised in Tennessee, 18,000 had come over from Mississippi, and 14,000 had been requested from Richmond. Five millions of dollars had been expended in equipping the troops. General Pillow was in command. The Confederate army, coöperating with conscription officers during the fall, created such terror Union men fled from their homes, seeking the mountain heights. Every gap and pass seemed to be guarded by the vigilant Confederates, yet

[2] *Johnson MSS.* Nos. 2974 and 2911.

thousands eluded the guards and joined the Union army. Hundreds of Unionists were in jail, their offense being that they were for the Union.

On January 18, 1862, however, General G. H. Thomas, one of the safest, and judged by results, the most successful of Union Generals, with a superior force shattered the Confederate line at Mill Springs, defeating and slaying General Zollicoffer. At that time General Grant, serving under General Halleck, was in command of an army at Cairo on the Mississippi, a few miles north of the Confederate line of defense. General Joseph E. Johnston, the pride of the South, had fortified Forts Henry and Donelson to prevent Union gunboats from running up the Tennessee and Cumberland rivers and coöperating with the land forces.

In the first days of February, however, Grant—the sledgehammer of the North—moved with gunboats and transports filled with troops, up the Tennessee river and on the way to Fort Henry. On February 6 Fort Henry surrendered. Most of the Confederate troops, however, escaped to Fort Donelson, ten or twelve miles away on the Cumberland river. On February 16 Federal gunboats and transports, having steamed up the Ohio and Cumberland rivers, in conjunction with land forces under Grant, invested Fort Donelson. General Floyd, President Buchanan's Secretary of War, fled for his life. He feared he would be shot as a traitor to the Union. General Buckner assumed responsibility and surrendered the fort. The Confederate defenses were destroyed, the Confederate army was cut in twain, Colonel Forrest refused to surrender however and escaped with his cavalry. Nashville, the capital, only a few score miles away, was open to the Union forces. The Confederate legislature adjourned from Nashville to Memphis. General Grant advanced up the Cumberland river and General Buell soon occupied Nashville. The Confederate government in Tennessee had come to an end. Some six months it had lived and then it expired, hammered to death by Union troops, many of whom were East Tennessee boys. But the whole of East Tennessee was still held by the Confederacy. In fact, only such portions of Western and Middle Tennessee were under

Union control as Federal gunboats on the rivers and massed troops could protect. The body of the people of Tennessee were still hostile to the old Government. The Confederacy was determined that Buell's troops in Nashville should be driven out at all hazards. The Confederate flag must fly over Tennessee's capital again.[2a]

Before the fall of Donelson General Floyd had demanded of Grant the terms he would require for the surrender of the fort. "Unconditional surrender," Grant replied. When these words, "unconditional surrender," were flashed to the North, with the news that 15,000 Confederates had been captured, the Confederate line broken, and Tennessee was no longer under foreign flag, no two men were happier, we may be sure, than President Lincoln and Andrew Johnson.[3] The Border-State policy was vindicated; the way to whip the South had been discovered: Flank her, attack her in the rear. The failure to pursue this course in the East had resulted in defeat. The war in Virginia, under McClellan and others, had gone badly for the Union. No frontal attack could overcome the invincible Army of Northern Virginia.

Forthwith President Lincoln set about winning Tennessee back into the Union. This he would do not only with military rule but also by civil government, as far as possible. Sending for Andrew Johnson, President Lincoln urged him to go to Tennessee to act as Military Governor and Brigadier-General, and to restore the State to the Union. Not a moment did the heroic man hesitate. The ease and comfort of Washington life he was willing to sacrifice to serve his country. The terrors of an armed camp, the threats and hatred of an implacable foe, all these he would face in an effort to save the Union. "This act of self-sacrifice gave him unexampled popu-

---

[2a] Rhodes, Vol. III, p. 600.

[3] In reply to criticisms of General Albert Sidney Johnston, for evacuating Bowling Green and failing to destroy Grant at Shiloh, his son William Preston Johnston declared that "The army of General Albert Sidney Johnston had been weakened by the necessity of keeping thousands of troops in East Tennessee to overawe the Union population of this section so as to guard the only line of railroad communication between Tennessee and Virginia"; and that "East Tennessee, like a wedge, penetrated the heart of the Confederacy, flanked and weakened General Johnston's line of defense, requiring constant vigilance and repression."—*Century*, February 1885; *Johnson MS.*

larity at the North." [4] Accepting the position tendered him
by the President and resigning his seat in the Senate, the
new Military Governor, early in March 1862, in company
with Horace Maynard and Emerson Etheridge, set out for
Nashville, Tennessee. The Senate had confirmed his appointment under a commission with ample powers to crush
rebellion and restore Tennessee to the Union. In fact, it
might be said that Andy Johnson had become the executive,
legislative and judicial functionary of the State of Tennessee.
Among other duties he levied taxes, took control of railroads,
built a seventy-five mile railroad from Nashville to the Tennessee river, thereby connecting the capital with the gunboats, issued military proclamations, put violent Secessionists
in jail, without court or jury, ordered elections, declared the
civil law enforced, here and there, and appointed sundry officers. [5] Besides this he had free hand to draw on the United
States' Treasury for funds as they were needed. Mr. Lincoln,
implicitly trusting his Brigadier-General, asked no questions
except that he hold Tennessee in the Union. Missouri was a
safe and loyal state, and so were Kentucky and Maryland and
West Virginia. Tennessee, however, the most unruly, the
most warlike of the Border States, needed attention. Could
Andrew Johnson ride the fiery steed?

Now, long before the fall of Forts Henry and Donelson it
was felt in Tennessee that the indomitable Johnson, with a
Union army, was going to swoop down and capture Nashville.
In September 1861 General Beauregard wrote Jefferson Davis
that "Andrew Johnson has secured 10,000 muskets for East
Tennesseans." The papers in Tennessee were filled with
threats and accounts of what would happen to Johnson on his
arrival. [6] Assistant Secretary of War Scott wrote Stanton that
Johnson would certainly be killed if he went to Tennessee as

[4] Blaine, *Twenty Years*, Vol. II, p. 7.

[5] This road was built with the approval of Stanton, who was now Lincoln's
War Secretary; in the charges against Johnson, during the impeachment
investigation, the building of this road was included. In June 1864 Johnson wrote Lincoln introducing Michael Burns, president of this railroad.
August 3, 1864, Lincoln wrote on the back: "Hon. Sec. of War, please see and
hear bearer, Mr. Burns."—Letter in Mrs. W. W. Dismukes' possession.

[6] Moore, *Rebellion Record*, Vol. I, p. 43; *Johnson MSS.* Nos. 51 and 1023;
C. R. Hall, *Military Governor of Tennessee*, p. 39.

Military Governor.[7] The Tennessee papers were "delighted at
the indignities offered to Governor Johnson" the year before
and they were glad that "some elderly men at Bedford county,
Virginia, prevented a mob from hanging him and left it to
Tennessee to deal with him." . . . "Tennessee would do the
proper thing by Andrew Johnson." [8] On September 30, 1861,
the Memphis *Avalanche* contained a peculiar item: "Yesterday
a procession of several hundred stout negro men," it boasted,
"marched through the streets of Memphis, in military order,
under the command of Confederate officers. A merrier set
never was seen, shouting for Jeff Davis and singing war songs.
They were going to dig trenches to inter carcasses of Abolitionists and other Paul Prys, no doubt."

Arriving in Nashville, about March 12, the new Military
Governor took possession of the deserted State House, over
which, some years ago, he had presided as civil Governor. Mr.
Lincoln's first experiment in State Reconstruction had begun.
Tennessee had been a wayward sister, Lincoln concluded, but
she had not got out of the Union. From June 8, 1861, to
February 1862 certain misguided individuals had "thrown the
State out of proper relations to the Union," but this was the
action of individuals and not of the government.[9] The State
of Tennessee, being an entity, had no power to get out of the
Union. The night of his arrival Andrew Johnson addressed
the people of Nashville in a conciliatory speech. On the eighteenth of the month he issued an "Address to the People of Tennessee," thousands of copies of which were printed and circulated. In words wise and temperate he invited the sons of the
state to come back into the Union, promising amnesty and
pardon to all except "conscious leaders in treason," and adduc-
ing weighty reasons why they should do so.[10] Quite a number
of prominent men accepted the invitation. Governor Johnson
was delighted to shake the hand of ex-Governor Campbell, ex-
Governor Neill S. Brown, W. H. Polk, brother of President
Polk, and Bailie Peyton. Governor Brown had several sons in

[7] Stanton MS., March 4, 1862; Memphis *Avalanche*, April 25, 1861.
[8] *Johnson MS.* at Greeneville.
[9] J. W. Burgess, *Reconstruction*, p. 8.
[10] See Appendix "A" for this address.

the Confederate army and the local papers announced that his youngest son "was going to disinherit his father for going into the Lincoln government." But most of the leaders refused to return to their allegiance, and, as for the Confederate government, "it was but beginning to fight." The press and the clergy were specially rebellious and so were all civil officers of the Confederacy. It was important that the city government of Nashville should be loyal to the Union. The Governor therefore required the council to come forward and take the oath of allegiance.[11] This they refused to do and the Governor dismissed them, putting loyal men in their place. Six ministers likewise refused to take the oath. The Governor ordered the last mother's son of them to jail. A Judge with secession proclivities was elected; Johnson gave him his certificate and then put him in jail, also. Other Confederates, refusing to take the oath of allegiance, were expatriated, to be treated as spies if they returned. The Nashville *Times*, a belligerent Confederate paper, was suspended under the Governor's restrictions.[12]

There was much destitution among the wives and children of Confederate soldiers. To support these dependent ones Governor Johnson levied large assessments on wealthy Secessionists. The sums thus collected, running into the thousands, he distributed among the poor and needy and destitute. The lowest office and the highest he filled with Union men. As far as he could, he discharged the disloyal. With a heavy hand he came down upon "conscious traitors," but to the humble man and to the ignorant he was tender and merciful. Incidents of a humorous character as well as the pathetic demanded his attention. One day a woman of immense size, wife of one of the wealthiest and most prominent Secessionists in Tennessee, came in to ask a pass that she might visit her husband in a northern prison. Turning to his secretary, the Governor said, "Make out a pass for this woman to leave Nashville over the Granny White Pike."

"And return," added the giantess.

[11] J. W. Fertig, p. 38.
[12] New York *Times*, March 26, 1862.

"We don't want you to return," said the Governor.

The lady was furious, exclaiming, "Andrew Johnson—do—you—know—what—I—ought—to—do? I ought to take you across my knee and give you the biggest spanking you ever had in your life."

"Madam," the Governor replied, "it would take the whole Union army to spank you."

After she had received her pass to go and *return*, Johnson said to his Secretary: "If her husband had any sense of gratitude, he'd send me a letter of thanks for sending him to a northern prison."

On another occasion a famous beauty of the region, a rich widow, named Mrs. Carter, of Franklin, called to see the Governor. Mrs. Carter was constantly asking for a pass between Franklin and Nashville. Now if there was one thing more irresistible with the Governor than another it was a pretty woman. One day she came in and said she wished a permit to carry home six barrels of salt—salt being a very scarce article in the South. The request was granted.

"Give Mrs. Carter the permit for six barrels of salt," said the Governor, to his Secretary, "they won't be of much service to the Confederacy. Besides, Mrs. Carter is a lovely woman."

About a month afterward the lady came back for twelve more barrels of salt, explaining that she owned nearly a hundred slaves and was salting down pork and beef. The Governor was again consulted. "Mrs. Carter is a lovely woman," said he, "but she can have a permit for only six barrels. . . . You might tell her gently that she won't have to feed her slaves much longer." When the Governor's message was delivered, Mrs. Carter, in her coyest manner, wished to know if two permits might not be made out, each for six barrels. Mrs. Carter being a lovely woman, Governor Johnson ordered that the two permits be made out.

In April 1862 General E. Kirby Smith issued an order that Mrs. Andrew Johnson, Mrs. Horace Maynard, Mrs. W. G. Brownlow and Mrs. Colonel Carter, and their families, leave their homes. Nothing better shows the horror of the brothers' war than this order of so gallant and humane an officer.

"Madam"—the order served on the Johnson family reads—
"by Major E. Kirby Smith I am directed to respectfully require that you and your family pass beyond the lines of the
Confederate army, through Nashville if you please, in thirty-
six hours. Passports will be granted you at this office." Meanwhile Governor Harris from his camp in Memphis was firing
the southern heart. In a stirring call to his people, he exclaimed, "Tennesseans, follow me! Shall the black banner
of subjugation wave in triumph over your altars and your
homes? By the memory of your glorious dead, by the sacred
names of your wives and children, by our own faith and manhood, No." [13]

But Johnson, the Union Governor, met words with words,
blows with blows. When guerrilla bands, under Forrest and
Morgan, swarmed through the State, "arresting Unionists and
maltreating and plundering them," he issued a proclamation of
retaliation—"In every instance in which a Union man is arrested and maltreated by marauding bands," the Governor
proclaimed, "five or more rebels, from the most prominent in
the immediate neighborhood, shall be arrested, imprisoned and
otherwise dealt with as the nature of the case may require. . . .
This order will be executed in letter and spirit and all citizens
are hereby warned, under heavy penalties, from entertaining,
receiving or encouraging such persons so banded together, or
in anywise connected therewith."

When Morgan's men entered the town of Pulaski and dam-
aged and seized property of Unionists, Johnson levied a fine
on the place to compensate for such damages. "It is well
known," Johnson announced, "that such bands only go and
remain in places where they have sympathizers." [14] When he
put the "assumed ministers of Christ" in jail because they
"were corrupting the female mind" with treason; poisoning
and "changing them into fanatics," he ordered that "no visitors be admitted to comfort and lionize them, and that no
special favors be granted them." [15]

Sometimes the Governor tried to work a bluff on the Con-

[13] Johnson MS.
[14] Ibid., No. 4525.
[15] Ibid., No. 5281.

federates, and frighten them back into the Union by threats of confiscating their lands.[16] "Who has not heard of the great estates of Mack Cockrill, situated near this city," he exclaimed, one October night in 1864, to thousands—laborers, mechanics, wandering slaves, and not a few slave-owners—"estates, whose acres are numbered by the thousand, whose slaves were once counted by the score? And of Mack Cockrill, their possessor, the great slave-owner and, of course, the leading rebel, who lives in the very wantonness of wealth, wrung from the sweat and toil and stolen wages of others, and who gave fabulous sums to aid Jeff Davis in overturning this Government? . . .

"Who has not heard of the princely estates of General W. D. Harding," he proceeded, amidst shouts of approval, "who, by means of his property alone, outweighed in influence any other man in Tennessee, no matter what were that other's worth, or wisdom, or ability. Harding, too, early espoused the cause of treason and made it his boast that he had contributed, and directly induced others to contribute, millions of dollars in aid of that unholy cause. . . . It is wrong that Mack Cockrill and W. D. Harding, by means of forced and unpaid labor, should have monopolized so large a share of the lands and wealth of Tennessee; and I say if their immense plantations were divided up and parceled out amongst a number of free, industrious, and honest farmers, it would give more good citizens to the Commonwealth, increase the wages of our mechanics, enrich the markets of our city, enliven all the arteries of trade, improve society, and conduce to the greatness and glory of the State.

"The representatives of this corrupt, and if you will permit me almost to swear a little, this damnable aristocracy, taunt us with our desire to see justice done, and charge us with favoring negro equality. Of all living men they should be the last to mouth that phrase; and, even when uttered in their hearing, it should cause their cheeks to tinge and burn with shame. Negro equality, indeed! Why, pass any day along the sidewalks of High Street where these aristocrats more particularly dwell,—these aristocrats, whose sons are now in the bands of

16 Moore, *Life*, p. XXXVIII.

guerillas and cut-throats who prowl and rob and murder around our city,—pass by their dwellings, I say, and you will see as many mulatto as negro children, the former bearing an unmistakable resemblance to their aristocratic owners." . . . "Thank God," he exclaimed, "the war has ended all this . . . a war that has freed more whites than blacks. . . . Suppose the negro is set free and we have less cotton, we will raise more wool, hemp, flax and silk. . . . It is all an idea that the world can't get along without cotton. And, as is suggested by my friend behind me, whether we attain perfection in the raising of cotton or not, I think we ought to stimulate the cultivation of hemp (great and renewed laughter) ; for we ought to have more of it and a far better material, a stronger fiber, with which to make a stronger rope. For, not to be malicious or malignant, I am free to say that I believe many who were driven into this Rebellion, are repentant; but I say of the leaders, the instigators, the conscious, intelligent traitors, they ought to be hung." (Cheers and applause.)

On the stump and in the field Andrew Johnson went forward in his fight to crush the rebellion and restore the Union. Not many miles from Nashville the Confederate army was still quartered, Morgan and Forrest, the most dreaded of Confederate raiders, were dashing here and there. Often they rode within a few miles of the gates of Nashville. Fighting between the Union forces, in and around Nashville, and the Confederates was of frequent occurrence. The citizens of Nashville expected, at any moment, Johnson would be captured and executed. While he was penned in Nashville, what a scene was enacted throughout Tennessee! The battles of Donelson and of Shiloh were fought and Albert Sidney Johnston killed. Chickamauga, perhaps the bloodiest twenty-four hours of the war, was also fought. Widow Hunt's mill-pond, at the foot of Snodgrass Hill, ran red with the blood of American heroes. Battles around Chattanooga, the "Battle above the Clouds," and "Murfreesboro" and "Nashville"—all marked the valor of the American soldier. Tennessee had become the cockpit of America. On her devoted soil seven hundred engagements are said to have taken place, of which one hundred might be designated as battles.   Over at Greeneville, Andy Johnson's home, a secession paper, called the *Tri-Weekly Banner*, was preaching a strange doctrine.   On July 11, 1862, it made the following announcement:

"From Cumberland Gap we learn, from a gentleman who arrived here a day or so ago, from this important position, that the Yankee army had all skedaddled from there and gone to parts unknown." *The Daily Register* from the neighboring town of Knoxville, on July 29, 1862, announced that Andy Johnson and his General Dumont "both slept upon the cars in anticipation of Stearnes' arrival at Nashville in order to take an early start for safer quarters, near 'Abraham's bosom.'" This paper likewise stated that one or two of the officers "have already laid claim to Andy's scalp, when the army reaches Nashville."

The women of Nashville, as with all women in times of war, were braver than the men.   They would not yield an inch.   By them the fighting spirit was kept at white heat.   But for the women, whom a Union General called the "pouters," there would have been little trouble; "the men would have grounded arms and come back into the Union." [17]

Soon after Johnson's arrival in Nashville "Fighting Parson" Brownlow came down from the North, whither he had fled the fall before.   While in the North he had written and published a book called *Parson Brownlow's Book*, giving a graphic account of the fight to save the Union in Tennessee. He and Governor Johnson had not spoken to each other in twenty-five years; they had been as bitter and uncompromising as Whig and Democrat ever got to be.   Arriving at Nashville, the Parson hastened to the capitol.   He wished to see his ancient enemy.   They were fellow sufferers now.   Hunted, persecuted, fleeing for their lives, a price set on their heads, their families turned out in the streets, they now had a common tie. Meeting in the Governor's office, they spoke not a word, but fell into each other's arms and wept like disconsolate women.[18]

In October 1862 the Governor's family also arrived at Nash-

[17] Reid, *After the War,* p. 46.
[18] Temple.   Chapter on "W. G. Brownlow."

ville. Suffering, exposure and anxiety had told on the noble mother of the family. She was now in the first stages of consumption and so, likewise, was little eight-year-old Andy, called Frank. Colonel Dan Stover in a few months was to die of the same disease. But now the family were together in Nashville again. Their son, Charles, and their other son, Robert, would run in and out from their duties in the camp and visit father and mother in the Capitol. The thread of family life was taken up again. The boys were now a comfort to their parents. Colonel Robert Johnson, in fact, was a much loved officer of the First Tennessee Cavalry. He was perhaps the first man to lead a Tennessee Regiment over the Kentucky line and into his home state.[19] As the First Tennessee Cavalry crossed over from Kentucky into their native state the boys broke into tremendous cheering. "Colonel Robert Johnson mounted a stump and made a short, characteristic and eloquent speech. The boys sang a medley, the chorus being:

> " 'Somebody is after Van—y
> Somebody is there I know
> It surely is old Sigel
> For I hear his cannon roar.' " [20]

The eyes of the nation were now on Tennessee, on Nashville, and on Andrew Johnson. The New York *Herald* sent a special correspondent. Arriving at Nashville in April 1862, he immured himself within the walls and for six months kept a diary of what took place. The importance of holding East Tennessee had become more and more apparent. To the Confederates the capture of this strategic position meant that troops and provisions from the South, going to the battlefields of Virginia, must pass a circuitous route through Augusta, Georgia, and the Carolinas, instead of moving directly through Knoxville and Bristol.

Following his old tactics, Governor Johnson determined to take the question of the Union to the people of Tennessee— to stump the State for the Union. But, as he went from place to place, guerilla bands lay in wait for him. At one point

[19] *Union*, January 29, 1863.
[20] *Johnson MS.*, Greeneville.

seven Unionists were killed by the guerillas. At another, four were slain. The railroad track was torn up and the train on which Johnson was traveling narrowly escaped destruction. Minnesota and Michigan regiments escorted him to the trains, acting as a bodyguard. When the Sixty-ninth Ohio regiment, under Colonel Campbell, arrived in Nashville, Governor Johnson delivered a patriotic address. Leading Tennesseans participated in the reception. W. B. Stokes, Bailie Peyton and others sat upon the platform. At Murfreesboro, Columbia, Shelbyville and Nashville "the great old commoner" rose to heights of popular oratory. "While he was depicting the sufferings and agony of the loyal people of his State," as the *Herald* reporter wrote, "strong men shook with emotion and cried as distressed children." "What confidence should Tennesseans have in Jeff Davis?" Johnson exclaimed. "In secret session, the people of Tennessee were lashed to the car of his hybrid despotic government. . . . Tennesseans are now in the dungeons of Alabama, bound in irons and fed on rotten meat and diseased bones. . . . No sound comes to cheer them; no sound to relieve them of their sad and weary confinement, save the clanking of the chains that confine them. . . . What sin, what crime, what felony, have they committed? None! None! In the name of God, none, except they love the flag of their country (great applause). . . . What do the Secessionists propose to do? They are ready for a return to a monarchy and the establishment of an aristocracy that should control the masses. . . . Are you willing," he asked, "to quail before treason and traitors and surrender the best Government the world ever saw?" (Cries of "Never, never.") "If the Union goes down," he continued, "we go down with it. There is no other fate for us. Our salvation is the Union and nothing but the Union. The only inquiry must be, Are you for the Union and willing to swear that the last drop of your blood should be poured out in its defense?" (Applause long continued.) . . . "The Confederates went to my home while my wife was sick, my child, eight years old, consumed with consumption. They turned her and the child into the streets, converted my house, built with my hands, into a hospital and barracks.

My servants they confiscated. It was with much suffering my wife and little boy were able to reach the house of a relative, many miles distant. Call you this Southern rights? If so, God preserve me from another such infliction." The audience was silent as a tomb, as the Governor related this portion of his personal experience, and the sensation was profound.

On his visit to the camps he addressed the soldiers and declared, "Never shall we surrender the cause we are fighting for. . . . If it were my destiny," he exclaimed, "to die in the cause of liberty I would die upon the tomb of the Union, the American flag as my winding sheet." [21] . . . "This is the people's Government, they received it as a legacy from Heaven, and they must defend and preserve it, if it is to be preserved at all. I am for this Government above all earthly possessions and if it perish I do not want to survive it. I am for it though slavery should be struck from existence—I say, in the face of Heaven, Give me my Government and let the negro go!" [22]

In January 1863 a great sorrow came to the Johnson family, when their son Charles was thrown from a horse and killed. Despite his dissipated ways Dr. Charles Johnson was the favorite son. His mother never fully recovered from the shock of his death; the affection between her and her son Charles was almost supreme. Some time previous to this sad event, General Grant, the hero of Donelson, called on General Johnson and was given a right royal reception. Johnson impressed Grant as "a short stocky man with smooth face, swarthy complexion and an air of obstinate determination." [23]

Carl Schurz also called and a contrast it was when the two men met—Johnson, a Cromwell, fearless, inflexible, a man of destiny; Schurz, "a citizen of nowhere and of everywhere," "playing the piano and singing, 'I love thee, oh, I love thee!'" Or, as he described himself, "sitting on the fence with clean boots watching for a nice place to jump." [24] Though Johnson

[21] This speech was received with vociferous applause and at its conclusion the soldiery and citizens joined in singing "Hallelujah," with a grand chorus and thrilling effect.—Glenn's *Diary*.

[22] I am indebted to Savage's *Life of Johnson* for much of this chapter.

[23] Schouler, Vol. VI, p. 448.

[24] *Taylor-Trotwood Magazine*, September 1908; *Reminiscences of Carl Schurz*, Vol. III, p. 329.

was quite sober, at the time of the call, he was "so dignified and so well groomed," Schurz, *as he afterward recorded*, "concluded he had been on a spree," and "had gotten himself up for the occasion." At this time the reporter of the New York *Herald* was writing that Johnson was "a model of abstemiousness," "was working twelve or fourteen hours a day," was literally "sleeping on a bed of revolvers and bayonets," and "had raised twenty-five regiments of Union troops." . . . "He is drinking about as much stimulant as a clergyman at a sacrament." [25] In fact, Andrew Johnson was never more in earnest than when Nashville was besieged. He made up his mind that he would not be taken alive, that before he would suffer Nashville to be surrendered he would burn every house in the town. So courageous and efficient was he his critics complained of his influence with the President. They declared that Johnson's "sturdy patriotism and brutal energy gave him influence with President Lincoln." [26]

As to whether, from a military point of view, East Tennessee, after the death of Zollicoffer, could have been held by the Union army, experts differ. At all events, Andrew Johnson's unalterable conviction was that East Tennessee could be held. His energetic letters to Washington so impressed the War Department that Lincoln, Stanton, and the North generally were eager for the movement on Knoxville. Undoubtedly the loyal mountaineers of twenty-five East Tennessee counties would have opened their cribs and smoke houses to a Union army. There seems no reason why "the richest grain field in the South except the valley of Virginia should not have furnished wheat and corn, hay, beef and bacon, as well as horses and mules for a Union army, as it did for the Confederate army." . . . "From June 1861 to September 1863 more than ten thousand Confederates, located in Tennessee, were supplied from this region and there were large shipments of provision and forage to armies in other sections." [27] As time passed, and the Confederates fortified the mountains and Buell

---

[25] Savage, p. 278.
[26] Rhodes, Vol. IV, p. 183.
[27] *East Tennessee and the Civil War*, p. 454.

remained inactive, Johnson's indignation exceeded bounds. Buell was a traitor, he declared, and Mr. Lincoln must remove him. On March 29, 1862, Johnson wrote from Nashville to Stanton, Secretary of War:

"SIR,—This place as I conceive has been left almost defenseless by General Buell. There are a few regiments left in detached positions without a single piece of artillery. There are one or two regiments at Camp Chase, Ohio, and one at Lexington, Kentucky, that might be forwarded to this point. In addition to these forces here, there should be one brigade complete. In this opinion Brigadier-General Dumont, left in command, fully concurs."

A. JOHNSON, *Military Governor*.

At length Governor Morton of Indiana likewise charged that Buell was a traitor and many other prominent men, including Tod, Governor of Ohio, and Yeates, Governor of Illinois. The soldiers under Buell joined in the charge. General Buell was therefore removed by the President.[28] But so difficult was the task of taking Knoxville and so slow were the Union armies in reaching Tennessee it was not till the fall of 1864 Rosecrans entered that city. The scenes of joy as General Rosecrans entered Knoxville exceed belief. By the tens of thousands people gathered from mountain and cove— fathers, mothers, brothers, sisters, torn from each other for three long weary years, were now re-united. "Glory to God, Glory to God," was on every lip. Rosecrans was not a conqueror, but a deliverer. "The officer in charge reported that he had often heard of tears of joy but never before had witnessed such a sight." . . . "Colonel Littrell, Mayor of the city, brought forth the Old Flag. As it was unfurled the crowds yelled with a perfect fury of delight." [29]

On three occasions it was determined by the military authorities of Nashville that the city would eventually have to be evacuated. Tennessee could not be held by the Union forces at the expense of larger movements. In 1862 when General Bragg invaded Kentucky every Union troop was required to halt that invasion and Nashville was left open to attack. At

[28] Buell was generally endorsed by the army officers.—Force, *Sherman*, p. 193; Rhodes, Vol. IV, p. 174.
[29] *East Tennessee and the Civil War*, p. 479.

another time it was likewise exposed, Morgan, like a whirl-wind, swept through Kentucky and Missouri, and Union troops left Tennessee in pursuit. From September 15 to November 14, 1862, Nashville was in a state of complete siege—cut off from the outside world. It was then Andrew Johnson grew to a hero's stature. The capitol building at Nashville, then called Fort Johnson, was fortified, and in the cupola the Governor and his staff often slept without removing their clothing. "By his wise and energetic measures," said the correspondent, "Johnson inspired every one with confidence and courage." On November 5, 1862, a concerted attack on the city was made, Morgan and Forrest in command. It was reported that 50,000 Confederate troops under Breckinridge were near at hand. As the Confederates approached the city Johnson and his staff ascended the cupola of the capitol and watched the battle line, surging and wavering to and fro. Presently the Union troops gave way and fell back towards the city. All was despair. Nashville must capitulate and surrender. But not so. From his place, in the dome of the capitol, the lion-hearted Johnson thundered out, "I am no military man but any one who talks of surrender I will shoot." What appeared to be a repulse proved a ruse of General Negley, the Union commander. The Union troops rallied, the Confederates were repulsed, and, "for a third time the city was saved by the inflexible firmness of Governor Johnson." [30]

The diary of Glenn, the imprisoned correspondent of the *Herald* is moving and exciting:

"*October 21, 1862.*—Days, weeks, nay, months, roll round, and there seems to be no change for the better in this important city. Cut off from communications with the outer world, our supplies have become exhausted. We are deprived of almost all articles of luxury and even comfort, and are subject to the ill-disguised sneers and taunts of Union haters. Rebel hosts are reported to be menacing us. Governor Johnson's wise and energetic measures, coupled with the activity of General Negley, inspire courage and confidence among Union men. We

[30] I have made free use of the diary of Mr. Glenn, reporter of the New York *Herald*. From the cupola fine views of the battlefields may be had.

The Capitol, Nashville, Tenn., Under Siege: Fort Andrew Johnson

hear that Breckinridge is around us with fifty thousand men; that Anderson, mortified at his defeat at Lavergne, declares that he can and will capture the city; and Forrest, incensed from the same cause, roughly swears that he will have Nashville at all hazards, if he falls himself at the first fire. But those who are in the confidence of Governor Johnson know that the enemy, if they should capture the city, will achieve an empty triumph, amid blackened and crumbling ruins. The coolness and calmness of the Governor amid these trying scenes are beyond all praise. He does all he can to preserve order; but, notwithstanding this, midnight assassinations are frequent. There were six murders one night recently. The other day a party, belonging to an Illinois regiment, broke down the door of a room in which were a Secessionist and his mistress. The Secessionist shot and killed two of the Illinoisians. The exasperation of their comrades cannot be portrayed. A rope was procured, and the nearest lamp post would have witnessed the unfortunate man's end but for the interference of Colonel Stanley and a strong detachment of soldiers. Amid the wildest excitement he was taken before Governor Johnson's Provost Marshal, Colonel Gillem, at the capitol, and secured against the results of mob violence. Although the act was calculated to lessen Governor Johnson's popularity with the troops, he unhesitatingly endorsed the conduct of Colonel Gillem, declaring that there was a legal and proper way to punish the offender, and so long as he had the power he would see it enforced. These facts are mentioned to show Governor Johnson's sense of justice and his determination to exercise it under the most trying circumstances.

"*November* 4.—The enemy have made several attempts to drive in our pickets, without material loss on either side. A rebel siege train has arrived at the Lunatic Asylum, about three miles from the city, where the enemy have thrown up intrenchments. A rebel attempt to capture the city by a *coup de main* in the rear has been thwarted by the timely action of General Negley.

"Great activity prevails at the capitol. Governor Johnson, with his private secretary, Mr. Browning; one of his aides, Mr. Lindsley; Provost Marshal Gillem; Captain Abbott, First

Tennessee Battery; Assistant Provost Marshal B. C. Truman; Volunteer Aid Mr. Glenn, together with the officers of the Governor's bodyguard, the First Tennessee infantry, under command of Colonel Gillem, are on duty night and day at the Governor's room, ready for any service that the Governor may require. . . . All hands are engaged in cleaning firearms, sharpening cutlasses, etc. Four Rodman guns have been placed in position to defend the capitol, which is also protected by lines of earthworks and breastworks of cotton bales. The capitol will be defended to the last extremity. The cool and determined demeanor of Governor Johnson is the admiration of all.

"*November* 5.—The enemy made two attacks on Nashville to-day. One attack was made by Morgan, on the Edgefield side of the river, with a view probably of destroying the new railroad bridge. Morgan was repulsed with considerable loss. About the same time the enemy under Forrest approached the city by four routes, viz.: the Franklin, Murfreesboro, Lebanon and Nolansville pikes. They were in great strength, and seemed bent on capturing the city. General Negley and Governor Johnson determined they should not. Fort Negley prepared to welcome them, with the Tenth Illinois as a garrison. Forts Browning and Lindsley and the two enfilading works, known as Forts Truman and Glenn, were garrisoned by the gallant Nineteenth Illinois and detachments of other regiments. Fort Andrew Johnson (the capitol) was garrisoned by the First Tennessee, Colonel Gillem, with a reserve of artillery under command of Captain Abbott, of the First Tennessee battery. Governor Johnson and staff, including the writer, took position in the cupola of the capitol, and had a splendid view of the conflict going on about two miles distant." Presently, as I have said above, the Confederates were repulsed, the siege raised and Nashville ceased to be the center of rebel attack.

Andrew Johnson's office as Military Governor was anomalous. How could a Military Governor, wholly dependent on the army, function side by side with a General in charge of such army? In fact he could not, without constant friction. But Military Governor Johnson was unwilling to take a sub-

ordinate place—he was to be the real Governor or nothing.[30a]
One by one those opposing him were turned out by the Washington authorities, General Buell, Captain Greene, Postmaster Lellyet, General Rosecrans, Colonel Truedail, the latter charged by Johnson with speculating in cotton against the Government.

When Major Stearns came down to organize negro troops the Governor, thinking enlistment of troops was to be taken from his hands, wrote Secretary Stanton that the matter ought to be left "to the General commanding and to the Military Governor Johnson." [31]   Stanton promptly acceded to Johnson's demands. "Upon your judgment in matters relating to the State of which you are Governor," Stanton wrote, "the department relies, in respect to whatever relates to the people, whether white or black, bond or free." [32]   Another complainant, Captain Dickson, was severely rebuked by the War Department: "The Military authorities," Secretary Stanton telegraphed the captain, "had no right to interfere with the questions which belonged to General Johnson, in whose discretion and judgment the department has full confidence." Ere long Mr. Lincoln put Johnson in charge of amnesty in Tennessee. Governor Johnson appointed ex-Governor Campbell, Commissioner of Pardons, and many releases were arranged for.[33]

It would serve no useful purpose to set forth in greater detail the struggles through which the Governor went before Tennessee had reconstructed herself, or to describe the many duties he performed. Suffice it to say, Governor Johnson handled millions of dollars and accounted for the last penny, coming out of his office poorer than he went in. In Tennessee civil war was at its worst. Davis confiscated the property of Unionists and Lincoln, through Governor Johnson, confiscated the property of Secessionists. Cities, towns, and counties would be over-run and devastated by a Confederate army to-day and by a Union army to-morrow. Each side vied with the other in acts of terror and outrage. The Unionist re-

30a Hall, *Military Governor*, pp. 68-70.
31 *Johnson MSS.* Nos. 74, 75.
32 *Johnson MS.* No. 7481.
33 Hall, p. 194.

garded the Confederate as a rebel, destroying "the best government under Heaven"; the Confederate regarded the Unionist as a traitor to the South, and both were equally honest. But for gifts of food, clothing, and money from the North, East Tennessee would have gone naked and perished. In that distracted land there was no business but war. Try as he might, the Governor could not restore order and civil government in such conditions. He could not organize a civil government sooner than he did. Temple and others, criticizing him in this matter, have been "hardly just to Johnson. . . . No one who knew the conditions could justly have charged the Governor with unnecessary delay." [34]

By August 1863 the Union party in Tennessee had split asunder. Radicals and Conservatives were lined up against each other. Emerson Etheridge, a Union man differing with Governor Johnson as to the test oath and the manner of organizing the State, set on foot a general election. Ex-Governor Campbell was declared elected civil Governor. Etheridge thereupon went to Washington to get the President to recognize Campbell. His mission failed, of course. I. G. Harris, Confederate Governor, was understood to be the power behind this movement. The dread of both Lincoln and Johnson was that the people of Tennessee, at an election, would vote against the war, thereby recognizing the Confederacy and peaceful secession. Governor Johnson was doing all in his power to bring the plain man from the Confederacy back again into the Union; and "was disposed to smooth the path for the return of the rank and file of the disaffected." [35] He believed that the masses at heart were Unionists; and yet "he dared not make a speech in any place ten miles distant from a Federal encampment."

After November 1863, when the Confederate army under Bragg was routed at Lookout Mountain and Missionary Ridge and driven into Georgia, President Lincoln thought surely the time had come to restore civil government. He therefore telegraphed Governor Johnson to that effect. But he added some precautionary words: "The whole struggle for

[34] Hall, p. 210.
[35] *Ibid.*, p. 102.

East Tennessee," he wired, "will have been fruitless to both
State and Nation if it so ends that Governor Johnson is put
down and Governor Harris is put up." It required much
caution to do what the President requested. Despite a vigorous campaign by the Governor the masses of the people
adhered to the Confederacy. In truth, only a decided Union
victory and the departure of the Confederate armies could
restore Tennessee. The middle and western sections were as
devoted to the southern cause as the eastern section was to the
Union. As a matter of fact, civil government was not restored
until more than a year after the defeat of Bragg's army. The
reason for this was partly because of internal dissensions
among the Unionists. Some of these insisted that the polls be
thrown wide open, without an iron-clad oath; others opposed
the method of calling the convention and insisted that only a
legislature could do this. Johnson's fight in this matter was
almost as severe as his fight with real enemies. In these con-
tests the Governor was no doubt harsh, stern and thorough-
going. But no other course seemed possible.[36] Both he and
the President were in constant dread of an adverse vote by the
people. Certainly the Military Governor could not afford
to have himself voted an interloper.

On November 12, 1864, the East Tennessee Union Executive
Committee, which had been formed by the Knoxville-Greeneville
convention of 1861, called a convention, to meet in Nashville
on December 19, 1864, and name a ticket for a convention.
Almost immediately, however, ill-fated East Tennessee was
again over-run by the Confederates. Breckinridge surprised
and defeated General Gillem, a man unacquainted with the art
of war. Knoxville passed into Confederate hands.[37] The
misery and want of East Tennessee were now sickening to the
heart. But preparations for the convention went forward. It
was to be "a meeting of Tennessee loyalists," the call disclosed,
"to restore the State to its once honored status in the American Union." When December 19 came, however, General
Hood was thundering at the gates of Nashville and the convention was postponed until January 8, 1865. By that date

36 *Ibid.*, p. 214.
37 *Johnson MS.* No. 1357.

Hood had been driven out of West Tennessee by General Thomas, and Breckinridge out of East Tennessee by Rosecrans. The only enemy the Unionists of Tennessee now had in their midst was themselves.

The convention met on the day appointed and wrangled over the details. Some attacked the call of the convention. The Radicals replied that the people of the State had the right, in a crisis, to meet of their own motion. At length four amendments were prepared and submitted to the meeting. In substance they provided (1) that slavery should be abolished; (2) that no right of property in man should exist; (3) that certain officers should be appointed by the Governor, with the consent of the Senate, and (4) that all citizens, who had borne arms for the United States should be allowed to vote; color should not disfranchise any person, who was a competent witness in the courts.

The first and second amendments were adopted but the last two provoked long and bitter discussion. It was feared that the convention would not be called. But the Radicals had Governor Johnson in reserve. He was "their final thunderbolt." When the decisive moment to launch this thunderbolt came the Governor, who had taken no active part in the proceedings, was invited to address the convention.[38] His speech was magnificent. "It would not be an overstatement to say that never did a political speech bring more decisive results. Opposition immediately dissolved and disappeared and the radical plan was put through, with slight modification and with little further deliberation." [39]

Thus, during three years did Andrew Johnson ride the whirlwind. "When the loyalists of Tennessee were perplexed, and also demoralized, he stood firmly and saw clearly, and by these merits won the confidence of Lincoln and Stanton, and was thus able to hold the leadership, overcome all opposition, and command the course of events." [40]

[38] Hall, p. 167.
[39] *Ibid.*, p. 169.
[40] *Ibid.*, p. 222. Slavery in Tennessee was not abolished by Lincoln's Proclamation, because Johnson requested it be not, besides the cession of Tennessee to the Union (December 12, 1789), deprived Congress of the right to emancipate slaves.

CHAPTER VI

LINCOLN AND JOHNSON

"No man has a right to judge Andrew Johnson in any respect," said Lincoln on one occasion, "who has not suffered as much and done as much as he for the Nation's sake." [1] Now in June 1864, when Lincoln spoke these words, no one knew better than he whereof he spoke. Two years before he had taken Johnson from a bomb-proof seat in the Senate and transferred him to the enemy's country. During that time the two men had been in almost daily communication and a common understanding had arisen between them.

Totally unlike in mental equipment and in physical proportions, Lincoln and Johnson were nevertheless bound together during the Civil War with hoops of steel. They first became acquainted in 1847, when Lincoln was a Whig Congressman from Illinois, and Johnson a Democratic Congressman from Tennessee. As they were men of small means they set up no establishments in Washington, nor did their wives accompany them during the session of Congress. Small rooms at a boarding house and "a mess together on Capitol Hill" were the best they could afford. [2] Now a Whig Congressman who voted forty-two times for the Wilmot Proviso, as Lincoln did, and a Democratic Congressman who voted forty-two times against that measure, as Johnson did, were not likely to be very intimate. In fact, they seem to have had little acquaintance at that time, certainly no intimacy.

But in March 1861, when they next came together, they had a common purpose, the task of saving the Union. [3] Scarcely had President Lincoln arrived in Washington when Senator Johnson's bugle note sounded down Pennsylvania Avenue and

[1] *Life and Services of Andrew Johnson* (anonymous), p. 209.
[2] Tarbell, *Lincoln*, Vol. II, p. 2.
[3] Julian, *Recollections*, p. 221.

throughout the land. "Show me the man who fires on our flag and I will show you a traitor," Andy Johnson was thundering on that March day. Before the nation's consciousness was aroused and when it seemed that President Lincoln was without friends, there was one southern man at least unafraid, one to whom Lincoln could tie. And from the day of that speech Andrew Johnson dwelt in the heart of Abraham Lincoln.[4] At a flag-raising at the capitol in June following, Lincoln insisted that Johnson should be present and make one of his patriotic speeches.[5] During the dark days of July, after Bull Run was fought and lost and Washington was trembling for its life, Johnson was chosen by Congress to serve as a member of the important committee of seven on the conduct of the war. This committee often met with Lincoln and his cabinet, and urged a more vigorous campaign.[6]

Strong men in the North, moved by Johnson's fight for the Union, were urging President Lincoln to send him as Ambassador to England. In February 1862 Fort Donelson was captured by Grant, and the way opened for civil government in Tennessee. In that happy hour no other name, except that of Andrew Johnson, came to Lincoln to serve as Military Governor. Well did Lincoln know that if the Civil War was won the plain people must win it. Who better typified this class than Andy Johnson, the Tennessee tailor, mouthpiece of the mechanic and the artisan? Often in 1863 and 1864 Governor Johnson would run up from Nashville to Washington and confer with Lincoln, discussing Tennessee affairs and the conduct of the war.[7]

In September 1862, after the battle of Antietam had forced General Lee out of Maryland, and Lincoln had issued his Emancipation Proclamation, Johnson was consulted and his advice followed.[8] Johnson advised Lincoln, perhaps unwisely as the sequel showed, that it was best not to include all negroes

---

[4] Blaine, *Twenty Years*, Vol. II, p. 4; Dunning characterizes Blaine's book as "useful but untrustworthy."—W. A. Dunning, *Essays*, p. 145.

[5] *Johnson MS.*

[6] Julian, *op. cit.*, p. 203.

[7] *Ibid.*, p. 204; Nicolay and Hay, *Lincoln*, Vol. V. p. 60.

[8] Moore, *Life of Johnson*, Chap. XXVIII; Blaine, *Twenty Years*, Vol. II, p. 7.

in the Emancipation Proclamation, but only those engaged in actual warfare. He suggested that the Emancipation Proclamation was a war measure and, in issuing it, the President was acting as Commander-in-Chief of the army. Therefore, it could only operate in war territory. He also advised that to free the slaves in Border States would give offense to the loyalist slave-owners. As to Tennessee, she ought to have the honor of freeing her own negroes without coercion by the general Government. Under Lincoln's Emancipation Proclamation about one-twentieth of the slaves, that is to say about 200,000, were manumitted. Other slaves, those not in the actual war zone, were not affected thereby.[9]

On the one absorbing proposition, that the war should be fought to a finish and peaceful Secession should never be thought of, Lincoln and Johnson were in accord, as they were on the conduct of the war itself. Each agreed, as we have seen, that the Border States were necessary to the existence of the Union, and should be held at every cost. Each likewise agreed that the freeing of the negro was a matter secondary to the salvation of the Union. And when three hundred and odd thousand Border State soldiers joined Grant, Sherman and Thomas, the wisdom of Lincoln's course was verified. Had not the Border States remained in the Union, would Sherman have been able to march to the sea? Upon this record of Andrew Johnson, were not Lincoln and his great War Secretary Stanton correct when they asked, "What man in America has done more for the Nation's life than Andrew Johnson?" But for the battles fought on the soil of Tennessee,—Mill Springs, Shiloh, Donelson, Chattanooga, Lookout Mountain, Franklin, Nashville,—would the morale of the Confederacy have been destroyed? It was Sherman's March and Sheridan's route of General Early, in the Valley, that overthrew the Confederacy. In January 1865, when Vance, War Governor of North Carolina, read that Sherman's March met no resistance in Georgia, he urged that fighting cease. As no bridge was burned, no road blocked, no provisions destroyed and there was passive

---

[9] A. H. Stephens, *War Between the States*, Vol. II, Appendix; Jones, *Life of Johnson*, p. 88.

submission by the people "the will to fight is gone," said Vance. Every gun fired thereafter was murder; and this plight of the Confederacy was a condition which border warfare had created. In fact, the war was won in the West and not in Virginia.

Lincoln's letters to Johnson, while Military Governor, were hearty and cordial. Johnson was his "good friend." Lincoln spoke of him as "wise and patriotic." On September 11, 1863, Lincoln wrote the Governor, "I see you have decided in favor of emancipation in Tennessee, for which God bless you. Get emancipation in your new State Constitution and there will be no such word as fail." [10] Another letter written September 19, 1863, was full of endorsement of Johnson's plans. During the summer of 1861 Johnson had constantly furnished Lincoln with information as to Tennessee affairs, and Lincoln, replying to Johnson's request for arms, had said he hoped "such arrangements would be satisfactory to him." [11]

As time passed it became certain that the State of Tennessee would return to the Union. It was then the people came to the parting of the ways. Those who had never left the Union, such men as Brownlow and Maynard, became "radicals." Nothing short of an iron-clad oath would suit these fiery Unionists. They would exclude from the polls all rebels, in fact exclude every one except Union soldiers in West and Middle Tennessee. While Governor Johnson favored a vigorous test oath, he would not shut out such rebels as had become repentant and were willing "to come back home." When this question was put up to President Lincoln he approved Johnson's plan. "I have seen Andrew Johnson's plan," he wrote, "and I approve of the same. You had better stick to it." In the midst of worries and perplexities Mr. Lincoln had no trouble with Governor Johnson. At all times Lincoln and Stanton "listened to Johnson and Johnson had his way with them." [12]

Though Andrew Johnson held the toughest and the most disagreeable job of the war he acquitted himself so well Stan-

[10] Nicolay and Hay, *op. cit.*, Vol. VII, p. 441.
[11] C. R. Hall, *Andrew Johnson, Military Governor*, p. 70; Nicolay and Hay, Vol. VII, p. 441.
[12] Hall, *op. cit.*, p. 68; *Johnson MS*. No. 4944.

ton, "the Iron Secretary," was full of praise of him. "This department called you from the comparatively safe and easy duties of civil life," Stanton wrote Johnson in 1865, "to place you in front of the enemy." "In a position of personal toil and danger, perhaps more hazardous than was encountered by any other citizen or military officer of the United States, you have maintained yourself. Through unparalleled trials you have gallantly periled all that is dear to man on earth. . . . Your services have been patriotic and able, you have been worthy of the confidence of the Government, and the thanks of the department are extended to you." [13]

In 1861 and 1862 the war situation seemed dark indeed for the Union. Stonewall Jackson and Early were chasing Pope, Burnside, and Banks here and there, and McClellan was unequal to Lee. In that hour Lincoln said to Speaker Colfax, "Andrew Johnson has never embarrassed me in the slightest degree." [14] Undoubtedly it was the stubborn Johnson who held Tennessee in line, and it was Missouri, Tennessee, Kentucky, Maryland and West Virginia that broke the backbone of the Secession movement, and gave courage to the flagging cause in Virginia.[15] By holding the Border States Lincoln was expecting to build a wall around the Confederacy and then to choke it to death. If Lincoln's plan of holding these states in the Union succeeded, one could start in Maryland, on the Atlantic seaboard, and travel on Union territory through Maryland, West Virginia, Tennessee, Arkansas, and Louisiana, to the mouth of the Mississippi. After the battles of Lookout Mountain and Missionary Ridge, Lincoln issued the following proclamation:

"Executive Mansion, Washington, D. C.,
"Dec. 7, 1863

"Reliable information being received that the insurgent force is retreating from Eastern Tennessee, under circumstances rendering it probable that the Union forces cannot hereafter be dislodged from that important position; and esteeming this to be of

[13] *War of the Rebellion*, Ser. III, Vol. IV, Serial No. 125, p. 1221.
[14] Johnson MS. No. 4944.
[15] Temple, *East Tennessee and the Civil War*, p. 203.

high national consequence, I recommend that all loyal people do, on receipt of this information, assemble at their places of worship, and render special homage and gratitude to Almighty God for this great advancement of the national cause.

"A. LINCOLN" [16]

Little wonder a disappointed abolition preacher, returning from an interview with Lincoln, declared that the President "would like to have God Almighty on his side but must have Kentucky."

During the siege of Nashville an incident occurred that gave Mr. Lincoln a hearty laugh. It seems, according to Lincoln who dressed up and told the story, that a fighting Methodist parson, named Granville Moody, had been marooned in Nashville during the siege. One day, when everything seemed lost, the Parson sought comfort in the Governor's office. As he entered the Governor was walking to and fro, greatly excited. "Moody," the Governor exclaimed, turning on the Parson, "we are sold out! Buell is a traitor! He is going to evacuate the city, and in forty-eight hours we'll be in the hands of the rebels." As the Governor spoke, he continued to pace up and down, like a caged lion. Presently he halted and turned to the Parson again, "Moody, can you pray?" he queried. "As a minister of the gospel, sir, that is my business," said the Parson. "Well, Moody, I wish you would pray," said the Governor and the two went down on their knees. The prayer became warmer and warmer. Johnson in Methodist style responded "Amen! Amen!" and crawling on his hands and knees to the Parson's side, put his arms around him. After a while the prayer ended with another hearty "Amen!" The two penitents rose, and Johnson, taking a long breath, said, "Well, Moody, I feel better!" Then turning, as if he had forgotten something, he added, "Oh, Moody, don't think I have become a religious man because I asked you to pray. I'm sorry to say I'm not religious and never pretended to be and no one knows that better than you, Moody. But there is one thing about it—I do believe in God Almighty and in truth, and I'll be *damned* if

16 Savage, *op. cit.*, p. 282.

Map of Greeneville, Tenn.

Star marks spot where General Morgan fell.

Nashville shall be surrendered!" *And Nashville was not surrendered.*[17]

On September 4, 1864, a messenger rushed into the White House, from the War Department, with news for President Lincoln: General John H. Morgan, the noted Confederate raider, was dead—killed by Andrew Johnson's bodyguard and under circumstances dramatic and tragic. A few weeks before Governor Johnson had procured from President Lincoln an order promoting Colonel A. C. Gillem of the Governor's Guards to Brigadier-General. The Governor's plan was to organize a separate unit for the purpose of capturing Morgan. General Gillem was to be in command. Accordingly, during the first days of September 1864 Gillem and his troop of cavalry set out from Nashville for the Tennessee mountains. On September 3 they reached Bull's Gap, fifteen or twenty miles from Greeneville, and went into camp. That night an East Tennessee Union lad, some twelve or fourteen years old, slipped into headquarters and called for the General. The name of this young boy was James Leady. Riding a mule with a sack of corn on its back and pretending that he was going to the mill, the lad had nearly passed the Confederate out-posts when he was captured. He rendered first one excuse and then another and at length was turned loose to make his way to Union headquarters. Breathless he told his story. Morgan, the raider, and his men were certainly in Greeneville, and no doubt about it—Morgan was right over at Dr. Alex Williams' and the town was full of rebels. As General Gillem listened to this story he shook his head. His Lieutenant-Colonel, W. G. Brownlow, however, knowing the loyalty of the mountain folk, offered to back the boy with his life. A night attack was agreed upon.

The night of September 4 was dark and stormy. About midnight a storm swept over the mountains. The lightnings played and the thunders rolled. At five o'clock in the morning Gillem's men, after a fifteen-mile march, burst into the town, breaking through the Confederate pickets stationed on High

---

[17] Jones, *op. cit.*, p. 83; "Siege of Nashville" in *Campaigns of Kentucky and Tennessee,* p. 275.

Hill. Rushing up Water Street and on by the A. Johnson tailor shop, they poured into Depot and Church streets, crossing Main Street and thence on to Irish Street. Main Street, Railroad Street, Irish Street and Church Street were filled with Union troopers and the Williams' house was surrounded. As the gray dawn was breaking the hoofs of horses rattled on the pavements. Carbines cracked, men ran hither and yon, confusion reigned. Morgan was awakened by the screams of the women of the Williams household.

"The enemy are upon you!" they shouted. "The house is surrounded by the enemy." Throwing his military coat about him, the gallant son of Kentucky slipped out the back door, a pistol in each hand—dodged from tree to tree, looking for a way of escape. Reaching the large scuppernong arbor, some two hundred feet from Depot Street, he crouched close to the ground. The bushes and leaves rattled and shook; probably he exposed himself to view. In an instant, "Crack, crack!" went a rifle in the hands of Andrew J. Campbell, an Irish Sergeant of Company G, Thirteenth Tennessee Cavalry. The noble trooper fell dead. The sturdy Irish Sergeant, astride his horse on Depot Street, obeying orders, had shot to kill. "Morgan must be captured dead or alive," was the command. For his courage and daring Campbell was promoted by General Andrew Johnson to a Lieutenancy. By a strange coincidence the spot where the fierce Morgan fell was only two blocks north of the confiscated and deserted home of Andrew Johnson. A few days later Lincoln issued a proclamation of thanksgiving and prayer, because it had "pleased Almighty God to recently vouchsafe great triumphs to the national arms in the capture of Mobile Bay, Weldon Railroad, and Atlanta, and the killing of the marauder, John Morgan, and the defeat and rout of Wheeler and his raiders." [18]

As Lincoln contemplated Andrew Johnson during these years of war and persecution he was no doubt amazed and awestruck. How could a human being endure what he endured? Of the public men of Tennessee if not of the South he stood

[18] This account I get from living witnesses and from various written sources. I think it is accurate.

alone. Defying the Secessionists, he had gone into their midst and dared them to do their worst. T. A. R. Nelson and Temple were over-run and silenced; Sam Milligan remained quietly at home; so did McDaniel, Lewis Self, and Johnson's other Greeneville friends; Horace Maynard was not a son of Tennessee but of Massachusetts. Alone at the President's request the Greeneville tailor had dared all, suffered all, sacrificed all, for country. A seat in the Senate, he resigned; the chances of capture and certain death, if captured, he underwent. His estate, including eight slaves, was confiscated and sold; from his wife and children he was separated; disease and death invaded his household. The taunts and jeers of the people of Tennessee and of the South were heaped upon him, and of these facts Abraham Lincoln was aware. Johnson's nervous strain must have been almost unbearable, yet he went his indomitable way. Nor did he repine or play the martyr or sulk in his tent. His faith in the people never wavered. Though he despised conscious traitors and leaders in rebellion, the rank and file he pitied, encouraged and succored. No doubt if he could have laid hands on Jeff Davis or John Slidell or Iverson they would have fared badly.

And yet Andrew Johnson bore his troubles no more heroically than his wife and daughters bore theirs, unprotected in their Greeneville home and surrounded by spies and enemies. These women were as loyal to the Union as though they carried a musket. In 1862 when Union troops, under General Orlando B. Wilcox, had chased the Confederates out of Greeneville, Mrs. Johnson placed her home at the General's disposal. In the early morning the colored maid passed through his room and opened a trap door. She went to the cellar below, when the General received a greeting "in various tongues of pigs, fowls and puppies." Whether his breakfast that morning "was pig, puppy or duck" the General never knew. The bed he slept on also attracted the General's attention. Raised high in the air by wheat and corn stored beneath the mattress, it presented a two-story appearance.[19]

In January 1864 Johnson spoke to the people of Nashville,

[19] This incident furnished by Colonel Reeves.

urging them to return to their allegiance and follow "Old Abe." "Abraham Lincoln is an honest man," he said, "and is going to put down this infernal rebellion. He is for a free government and I stand by him. . . . As for the negro I am for setting him free but at the same time I assert that this is a white man's government. . . . If whites and blacks can't get along together arrangements must be made to colonize the blacks. . . . They tell you cotton is king, but I say 'No,' bread and meat are king! If we look over in Rebeldom now we will find that a little bread and meat would be more acceptable than cotton. . . . In 1843, when I was candidate for Governor, it was said, 'That fellow Johnson is a demagogue, is an Abolitionist.' . . . Because I advocated a white basis for representation—apportioning members of Congress according to the number of qualified voters, instead of embracing negroes, they called me an Abolitionist. . . . What do we find to-day? Right goes forward; truth triumphs; justice is supreme; and slavery goes down. The time has come when the tyrant's rod shall be broken and the captives set free. Why this feeling on the part of the leaders in the rebellion against Abraham Lincoln?" he asked. "It is because Lincoln is a Democrat in principle; he is for the people and for free government and he rose from the masses."

Soon after Johnson's appointment as Governor conditions seemed favorable for Military Governors in North Carolina, Arkansas and Louisiana. Federal gunboats having captured Roanoke Island, Elizabeth City and New Bern in North Carolina, and New Orleans and other places in Louisiana and Arkansas, in the spring and early summer of 1862, Governors for these states were appointed. But as the prospects of victory seemed sure Congress began to ask, what shall be done with the Seceding States? Shall they come back without more ado or shall they be reconstructed? Sumner, Stevens and other Radicals were bringing forward the "state suicide" doctrine and the theory that the rebel states had lapsed into a territorial condition. That is, they insisted that the Crittenden-Johnson resolutions should be repudiated. Andrew Johnson considered this course treachery. The idea of changing the principle on which the war was begun, and had been fought, was to him unthinkable.

Johnson, therefore, wrote Montgomery Blair, Postmaster-General, "I hope the President will not be led to make territories out of the rebellious states." [20] In this Lincoln concurred with Johnson and refused to follow Sumner and Stevens. Lincoln's famous ten per cent. government proclamation is dated December 8, 1863: "If one-tenth of the qualified voters, as shown by the Presidential election of 1860, take an oath of fealty to the Constitution and obedience of acts of Congress and of the proclamations of the President as to slaves and shall reëstablish state governments such shall be recognized as the true government of the state." [21] This was Lincoln's well-known "Louisiana plan," substantially. When the Radicals in Congress attacked this conciliatory policy it gave Johnson much concern. Though the Union was safe, Johnson was beginning to inquire as to the future of the Constitution. As the Union was the child of the Constitution and each necessary to the national life, if the radicals destroyed the Constitution the government would end in centralization. Though the Wade-Davis bill, attacking Lincoln's "Louisiana Plan," passed both Senate and House, it was defeated by a "pocket veto."

The administration of Governor Johnson, by the year 1864, was attracting universal attention. In the North he was lauded; in the South, bitterly denounced. Lincoln and Stanton, as we have seen, endorsed his vigorous policy. Lincoln, who managed men by diplomacy, and Johnson, who drove them by force, were now agreed that force was necessary. [22] Lincoln's only fear was that Governor Johnson had been high-handed and tyrannical, as the Confederates were charging. If he had not been a tyrant, Lincoln proposed to honor him as he had never honored another, he was going to name Johnson as his next running-mate. Sundry visitors came to Nashville while Johnson was Governor, but no one so vital to Andrew Johnson's future as General Daniel E. Sickles. In the spring

[20] McPherson, *Political History*, p. 199.
[21] Nicolay and Hay, Vol. IX, p. 111; Rhodes, Vol. IV, p. 484.
[22] Hayes, *Life of Lamar*, p. 139.

of 1864 Sickles was sent to Tennessee by Lincoln to investigate
the Governor's record.   The President's object, however, was
not disclosed to the General.   After reflection Lincoln had
concluded that Andrew Johnson was, of all others, the man to
run on the ticket with him for Vice-president.   The Union
was going to pieces and Johnson would strengthen the ticket
and bring in a new element of voters.

Lincoln first thought of General B. F. Butler as a running
mate, but soon changed to Johnson.   Several reasons induced
him to turn to Governor Johnson.   A candidate on the ticket
from a seceding state would impress England and Europe that
the South itself was split and divided and that the national life
was in no danger.   Besides, Johnson was a life-long Democrat
from a Border State.   He had been a staunch Union man
from the start and was a well recognized labor leader.   In fine,
Johnson "had the goods" and unless he had been a military
tyrant would make an ideal candidate.   The ticket of Lincoln
and Johnson would not be sectional and would represent the
body of the people.   Hannibal Hamlin of Maine had made a
satisfactory Vice-president, but he had been a Democrat only a
short time and was from the North.   Other names were considered, Dickinson of New York and Joseph Holt of Kentucky.   After an investigation of Governor Johnson in Nashville Sickles reported to the President that his record was good
and that he had been no more stringent than the circumstances
required.

Thereupon Mr. Lincoln quietly set to work to have Johnson
placed on the ticket with him; he informed a few friends that
he wished Governor Johnson for Vice-president, and not Hannibal Hamlin.   The National Union Convention met in Baltimore on June 6, and Congressman Pettis, one of the delegates, called by the White House on his way to the Baltimore
convention.   "Whom do you desire put on the ticket with you
as Vice-president?" Pettis asked President Lincoln.   "Governor Johnson of Tennessee," Lincoln replied, leaning forward and answering in a low but distinct tone of voice.   I
will run ahead of the story and state that it was not till September 1889 that Vice-president Hamlin learned that Lincoln

had made choice of Andrew Johnson in 1864 in preference to himself. Judge Pettis in 1889 received a letter from Hamlin in which the latter said, "Undoubtedly Lincoln was alarmed about his reëlection and had changed his position; . . . I was really sorry to be disabused." [23]

At the Baltimore convention Lincoln was nominated without open opposition, though many of the leaders were dissatisfied. Radicals opposed the policy of Mr. Lincoln because of his ten per cent. government proclamation and really favored the nomination of an out and out Abolitionist. At that time John C. Frémont was in the field, as the nominee of the Abolitionists, for President, and if he had been a less erratic man would have given Lincoln trouble. The political situation was also complicated because the war in Virginia was going badly for the Union; General Grant was making little progress toward the capture of Richmond, and Jubal Early with his cavalry force was soon to dash entirely around the Capitol, at Washington. Lincoln was almost sure that he would be defeated in November and the Union would go to pieces. These fears he expressed in a private memorandum written some time in August 1864. "This morning," Lincoln wrote, "as for some days past it seems exceedingly probable that this Administration will not be reëlected. Then it will be my duty to coöperate with the President-elect so as to save the Union, between the election and the inauguration, as he will have secured his election on such grounds that he cannot possibly save it afterwards." Signed, Lincoln.

Despite secret opposition and the disgust of Radicals Mr. Lincoln's conciliatory policy prevailed at the National Union Convention in Baltimore: The Border States were to be further conciliated, the South invited back into the Union, and sectionalism and party spirit done away. To this end everything must bend. The convention was called to meet in Baltimore, a southern city; a mild platform was adopted; Rev. Dr. Breckinridge, a Border State War Democrat, presided. The party name was changed. In his opening address the presiding offi-

---

[23] *Globe Democrat*, November 15, 1891. For an account of Lincoln's conferences with McClure, Cameron and others, see McClure, *Lincoln*, p. 471.

cer let it be known that if the convention was to be a Republican convention, or a party affair, he wished it understood he would not preside. The sole object in view must be the restoration of the Union, he insisted. Along the same line Mr. Tremain, a Democrat from New York who presented Dickinson's name for Vice-president, also spoke. Mr. Tremain declared that it had been well said by the temporary and by the permanent chairman that "we meet here not as Republicans; . . . if we meet as Republicans I have no place in this convention. I have been a lifelong Democrat."

During previous campaigns the organization had been called the Republican party, henceforth it was to be known as the National Union party.[24] Under such circumstances Lincoln was nominated for President and Johnson for Vice-president. The fight in the convention arose when the Border States delegates sought admittance. The motion to admit was granted and the delegates were seated. C. M. Allen, a delegate from Indiana, presented the name of Andrew Johnson for Vice-president. Horace Maynard seconded the nomination. "When Andrew Johnson sees your resolutions," said Maynard, "he will adhere to those sentiments and to the doctrines therein set forth as long as his reason remains unimpaired and as long as breath is given him by his God." [25] "Fighting Parson" Brownlow, another delegate from Tennessee, then, and at no other time supporting Johnson, was a tower of strength. The nomination of Johnson was brought about by the State of New York. As the choice of Vice-president lay between Johnson and Dickinson, the latter a citizen of New York, and the selection of Dickinson meant the defeat of Seward for Secretary of State, the New York delegation gave Johnson a majority of its votes.

On the first ballot Johnson received two hundred votes, Hamlin one hundred and fifty, Dickinson one hundred and eight, scattering sixty-one. Before the result was announced all delegates but twenty-six went to Johnson and the result was

24 Professor Dunning, *American Historical Review*, Vol. II, p. 575.
25 Jones, *Life of Johnson*, p. 120.

Ticket for President, 1864

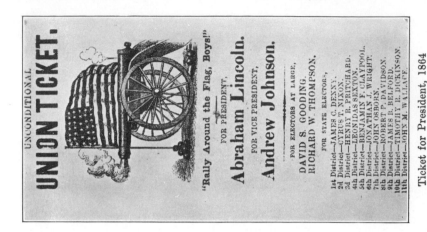

Tennessee Ticket for Governor in 1855

unanimous.[26] When Thad Stevens heard of the nomination of Johnson, he sneeringly asked, "Can't the Republican party find some one for Vice-president without going into a damned little rebel Territory to pick him out?" The New York *World* and other Copperhead papers declared that the ticket was composed of "Gawks, rail-splitters and tailors." Blaine, however, took a different view of the matter. "The choice of Andrew Johnson for Vice-president," said Blaine, "tended to nationalize the Republican party and thus give it great popularity throughout the nation." Andy Johnson's comment on his nomination was characteristic. "What will the aristocrats do with a rail-splitter for President and a tailor for Vice-president?" he wanted to know.

In his letter to the committee of notification Johnson accepted the nomination, planting himself firmly on the resolutions of the convention. Those resolutions expressed a determination "not to compromise with the rebels or to offer them any terms of peace except such as may be based upon an 'unconditional surrender.' " "It is the highest duty of every American citizen," the Resolutions declared, "to maintain, against all their enemies, the integrity of the Union and the paramount authority of the Constitution and the laws of the United States; and that, laying aside all differences of political opinions, we pledge ourselves, as Union men, animated by a common sentiment and aiming at a common object, to do everything in our power to aid the Government in quelling, by force of arms, the Rebellion now raging against its authority, and to bring to the punishment due to their crimes the rebels and traitors arrayed against it."

In 1864, as we have seen, the Union men of Tennessee split to pieces, some of them coming out for McClellan for President against Lincoln and on a platform which declared that the war was a failure. These men named an electoral ticket with the following electors: ex-Governor William B. Campbell, T. A. R. Nelson, J. T. P. Carter, John Williams, A. Blizzard, Henry Cooper, Bailie Peyton, John Lellyet, Emerson Etheridge and

[26] Rhodes, Vol. IV, p. 470; Rhodes asserts that "a severe scrutiny of Johnson's personal character would have prevented his nomination."

John B. Perryman. Governor Johnson was disappointed at the conduct of men who had recently been coöperating with him. Their course, however, was inevitable as they were not yet ready to make the final plunge against the South. Governor Johnson, scenting treason, prepared an oath which must be taken before one could participate in the election. He was determined that Lincoln and Johnson should not be defeated in Tennessee by disloyal votes; and one must conclude, after reading Johnson's oath, that he accomplished his purpose.

The elector was required to swear he would support the Constitution and defend it against the assaults of its enemies; that he was "an active friend of the Government and ardently desired the suppression of the rebellion;" that he "sincerely rejoiced in the triumph of the armies and navies of the United States, and in the defeat and overthrow of the armies, navies, and of all armed combinations of the so-called Confederate States;" that he would "cordially oppose all armistices or negotiations for peace with rebels in arms until the Constitution of the United States and all laws and proclamations made in pursuance thereof should be established over all the people of every State and Territory embraced within the National Union," and that he would "heartily aid and assist the loyal people in whatever measures might be adopted for the attainment of those ends;" and further, that he took the oath "freely and voluntarily and without mental reservation—so help me, God."

Naturally the electors for McClellan objected to this oath. The Governor, however, was obdurate. The McClellan crowd hastened to Washington to put the matter up to the President. After reading the oath and their protest to President Lincoln, the committee insisted he call down his high-handed Military Governor. When the committee had finished Lincoln took a hand. "May I inquire," said he, "how long it took you and the New York politicians to concoct that paper?" The committee stammered that "the paper was concocted in Nashville." "Well," said Lincoln, "I expect to let the friends of George B. McClellan manage their side in their own way and I will manage my side in my way." In a few days the President, at the request of the committee, wrote an open letter. He had nothing to do with Tennessee matters, he said. He lauded Governor Johnson as "a loyal citizen of Tennessee," and assured the committee that if they would be peaceable and loyal Governor Johnson would not molest them but would protect them against violence as far as in his power. The McClellan boom thereupon burst. The electors withdrew their names, and in November Lincoln and Johnson carried the State by an estimated majority of twenty-five thousand.[27]

In the fall of 1864, whenever political meetings were held scenes of wild disorder occurred. With pistols, clubs, and stones, Radicals broke up Conservative meetings and Conservatives dispersed Radical meetings. Governor Johnson was now the object of more bitter attack on the part of the rebels than ever before, but his friends came to his rescue. On the night of October 24 a torchlight procession in his honor was staged. Thousands of people lined the streets of Nashville—mostly laborers, mechanics, and slaves. As Andy Johnson rose at the south entrance of the beautiful Capitol to address that mottled assemblage, the poverty-stricken condition of the poor southern whites, under years of slavery, rushed in upon him—lords and overlords, masters and slaves, but no place for the poor white. In that highly organized society the poor white had been but a mud-sill, a something upon which a civilization for the few might be built. Johnson's early life rose before him and he recalled the slurs, insults, threats and sufferings of later days. "What crime have I committed to merit such treatment?" he asked, addressing the crowd. "Has not my life been devoted to uplifting my fellow man, and to improving the general average? As the least of you, my countrymen, have I not conducted myself? Does my fight to save the Union deserve rebuke? Perhaps as Military Governor I may have 'appeared to be brandishing a club to frighten the people into submission,' but is that not necessary? How else can rebellion be crushed?"

As Johnson's wrath kindled, indignation vexed him like a

---

[27] Returns from the November election were meager but Lincoln and Johnson carried Memphis by a majority of about twelve hundred and the Tenth Tennessee Regiment by a majority of eight hundred. On this basis the majority in the State would be as above given.

thing that was raw, and he proceeded to depict the evils of slavery and to point out the increase of mulatto children in Tennessee, "bearing a resemblance to their masters." Presently he came to the impulse of his life, the elevation of the masses. "Would to God," he exclaimed, recurring to Old Testament imagery in which he so much delighted, "that some Moses might arise to lead you from the land of bondage to the promised land of freedom." "You will be our Moses!" shouted the excited crowd. "Well, then," the Governor answered back, "humble and unworthy as I am, if no better shall be found, I will indeed be your Moses, and lead you through the Red Sea of war and bondage to a fairer state of liberty and peace." Extravagant words to be sure. To be read, however, in the light of letters Johnson had been writing to his consumptive wife and family at Greeneville. "My mind is tortured and my body exhausted," he wrote his wife. "Sometimes I feel like giving all up in despair, but this will not do. We must hold out to the end; this rebellion is wrong and must be put down, let cost what it may in the life and treasure. I intend to appropriate the remainder of my life to the redemption of my adopted home, East Tennessee, and you and Mary must not be weary; it is our fate and we should be willing to bear it cheerfully." [28]

Critics, seated in easy chairs, have spoken harshly of this speech of Johnson, on that weird October night, and undoubtedly his words were bitter. Were they not, however, in keeping with every act of his life? Did he not aspire to be the Moses of the mechanic and of humble folk everywhere? The idea of dividing out the lands of rebels, which the Governor often threatened, was but war hysteria, the aftermath of every great conflict. Nothing more than a gesture. Nor was he primarily fighting for the enslaved blacks; slavery was not uppermost in his mind. Like Lincoln he favored emancipation in order to save the Union and to free the white man and no further.[29] "Damn the negroes," he once said when charged with race equality. "I am fighting those traitorous aristocrats,

---

28 Hall, *Military Governor*, p. 155.
29 Johnson's speech to a Virginia delegation in April 1865; Julian, *Political Recollections*, p. 243.

Pendleton   Little Mac   Old Abe   Grant   Andy Johnson   Vallandigham

Copperheadism vs. The Union

their masters." [30]   During the campaign of 1864 Johnson went
into Ohio and canvassed the State with John Sherman, "making patriotic speeches to great audiences. . . . His arraign-
ment of the slave autocracy of the South was very effective." [31]
Whether in Tennessee or elsewhere the people flocked around
the much-talked-of man and heard him depict the dangers
of electing McClellan President.   Such a calamity, he declared,
would end the war, permanently establish slavery, and degrade
honest labor.

At the North the ticket of Lincoln and Johnson was a drawing card.   In primitive cartoons "Ole Abe" would be exhibited
splitting rails to mend the national fences.   "Andy" would be
seen sewing up the torn garment of the Constitution.   One
cartoon was very effective.   It was called "The Rail-Splitter
and Tailor, repairing the Union."   On a table there was a
large covered globe with the cover, a map of the Union, rent
and torn.   Andy was sitting on top of the globe, busy with his
needle and shears, while Abe was prizing the rent together.
"Take it quietly, Uncle Abe," Andy was saying.   "I will draw
it closer than ever and the good old Union will be mended." [32]
At the polls the combination of the rail-splitter and the tailor
proved irresistible, capturing 213 electoral votes out of a total
of 234.   Every state except Delaware, Kentucky and New
Jersey went for the National Union ticket.[33]

At the February election, Tennessee ratified the action of
her Constitutional Convention.   Thereby she liberated her
slaves, placing herself in position to come back into the Union,
as Johnson had suggested to Lincoln would be the case.   This
result gave Governor Johnson much pleasure and he would
share it with his chief at Washington.   "Thank God the
tyrant's rod has been broken," he wired President Lincoln,
as soon as the result was known.[34]

[30] Palmer, *Recollections*, p. 127.

[31] John Sherman, *Recollections*, Vol. I, p. 348.

[32] *Great Debates*, Vol. VI, p. 199, N. Y. Society collection.

[33] General Sherman and General Sheridan really carried the election, at that
very time having routed the Confederates in Georgia and in the Valley of
Virginia, practically ending the war.

[34] *O. R. Series III*, Vol. IV, p. 1050.   The vote for ratification was 25,293,
and against ratification, 48.   On April 3, the legislature met and elected Johnson's son-in-law, Patterson, and G. S. Fowler to the United States Senate.
—*Annual Encyclopædia for* 1865, p. 778; Fertig, *Secession in Tennessee*, p. 54.

But no human being could endure Johnson's labors without a collapse. Four years of fighting had produced a tortured mind and a disordered body. The iron man could fight no longer. Shortly after the campaign, in which he had taken so active a part, he fell ill of fever. Unable to attend the inauguration of President Lincoln, he wrote to W. Hickey, Chief Clerk to the Secretary of the Senate, to know if it were possible for him to take the oath in Tennessee, and whether a Vice-president had theretofore failed to attend an inauguration. In reply the Clerk sent a list of the Vice-presidents who had been sworn in after the inauguration of the President:

> John Adams, March 4, 1793; sworn in December 2, 1793.
> George Clinton, March 4, 1809; sworn in May 22, 1809.
> Elbridge Gerry, March 4, 1813; sworn in May 24, 1813.
> David Tompkins, March 4, 1821; sworn in December 28, 1821.
> Martin Van Buren, March 4, 1833; sworn in December 16, 1833.
> William R. King, March 4, 1853; died before December.[35]

Mr. Lincoln, doubtless learning that Johnson did not intend to be present at the inaugural exercises, wrote him and also wired, requesting that he come to Washington on the fourth of March if possible. With this request the Vice-president elect complied, setting out from Nashville five or six days before the inauguration and arriving at the Capitol about March the first.[36] Before leaving Nashville, the Governor issued a friendly letter to the people of Tennessee, filled with sound advice. (See Appendix "B" for this letter.)

[35] Johnson MS.
[36] *Taylor-Trotwood Magazine*, September 1908; Lincoln's letter is set out in Nicolay and Hay's *Life*.

CHAPTER VII

VICE-PRESIDENT

On a certain occasion it was said of Martin Luther that he was not a nice man; the obvious reply was, "No, and he did not have a nice job." So might it be said of the job of Andrew Johnson, when he set himself against southern tradition, defied southern chivalry, ridiculed caste, lauded the mechanic, and placed himself on the side of manual labor. According to accepted standards, he was not then in accord with "good form," nor engaged in a nice business. The hand of little employment hath the daintier sense. But an emergency had called for an absolute man, and in the fires of civil war the timid had had no place. As General Sherman remarked, "You cannot make an omelette without breaking eggs." Whether or not some other Southerner could have played the part of Andrew Johnson is beside the question; the fact remains that no other prominent southern official did. Out of a population of about eight or ten million he has the distinction of standing alone. And he has the greater distinction, as I have pointed out, of being Abraham Lincoln's choice for running mate in the greatest crisis of our history.

Arriving in Washington about March 1, Andrew Johnson registered at the Kirkwood House, a hotel four or five stories high, situated in the heart of the city at the corner of the Avenue and Tenth Street. The Hotel Raleigh now covers the same lot.[1] His rooms consisted of a reception room and sleeping apartments and were on the second floor, in the most public part of the house.[2] Washington, expecting daily to hear of the collapse of the Confederacy, was supremely happy; she had on her gala clothes. Sherman had taken Atlanta, marched

[1] Bryan, *History of the National City*, p. 445.
[2] Attorney Doster's address in the "Assassination Trial," June 23, 1865.

through to the sea and was thundering on his northward course to smash Joseph E. Johnston. Petersburg was under siege.

Amidst these auspicious surroundings, March 4th, inauguration day arrived,—typically cold and raw. The exercises took place on the south front of the capitol and Chief Justice Chase administered the oath to President Lincoln, now the acknowledged leader and hope of the nation. His address delighted the admiring and enthusiastic thousands who hailed him as Father Abraham. Even in the flesh a halo had gathered about the brow of him who had piloted the ship safely into harbor. In the Senate chamber an hour earlier the simple exercises of swearing in the Vice-president took place. The oath was administered by the Chief Justice. Vice-president Andrew Johnson rose to address the Senate and the distinguished array of visitors, cabinet officers, judges, congressmen, diplomats, representatives of foreign governments, scholars and savants. It was observed that the Vice-president had no manuscript in his hand. Evidently he was going to speak *ex tempore*, to take the matter to the people, as down in Tennessee.

In substance the Vice-president declared that he wished it well understood that he was but an humble man and a plebeian and that but for the plain people that occasion would never have been. He himself had risen from the humblest walks, and his life illustrated the strength and the glory of our Government. "Here even the humblest has a chance with the mightiest," he affirmed. "In fact, you, Mr. Secretary Stanton, and you, Mr. Secretary Welles, and you, Mr. Chief Justice Chase, owe what you are or will ever be, to the people." He did not claim to be wise or learned, he went on. In fact he knew little about parliamentary law and as Vice-president would have to depend on the indulgence of the Senate. More, in this wretched stump-oratory vein, he spoke, to the disgust of the cultured and critical audience. Impatience and disappointment were on every face. It was plain that Johnson was disguised in stimulants. That which would have been but a poor speech at a crossroads gathering was entirely out of place on a dignified occasion.

As this is perhaps one of the most unfortunate "drunks" a mortal ever indulged in, furnishing the theme of endless oratory, verse and self-righteous sermonizing, I trust I may be allowed to say a word for the unhappy offender. That the speech was in execrable taste none can deny. It was no occasion for "climbing Jacob's ladder" and discoursing on the millennial dawn when "Democracy and Theocracy would meet." Yet when Johnson declared that the people were above presidents, cabinets and judges he was running true to form. *In vino veritas.* Moreover, as we have seen, he had just arrived from Tennessee, a weary and a sick man. He came to the Capitol that morning in the carriage with the retiring Vice-president, Hannibal Hamlin, and before leaving the hotel had taken no stimulants. On the way to the capitol he told Mr. Hamlin that he was ill and his physician had prescribed whiskey. Hamlin found a flask of brandy and the result was Johnson made a spectacle of himself.[3]

In a few days Vice-president Johnson, in company with his friend Preston King, went out to Silver Spring, Maryland, the home of Frank Blair. Here he remained till the special session adjourned on the eleventh of March. Colonel McClure intimates that the Vice-president was forbidden to preside over the Senate, but the record does not confirm the suggestion. A caucus, however, was held and some of the Senators discussed the question of asking him to resign. Shortly afterwards a resolution was offered in the Senate prohibiting whiskey in the restaurants.[4] Vice-president Johnson was so concerned about the incident that, from a bed of fever, he had his secretary write to the Senate reporter asking for a verbatim copy of his remarks. He does not seem, however, to have given out any public statement or to have rendered any excuses or apologies, or even to have alluded to the occurrence. Johnson was neither an apologist nor a conciliator.[5]

Shortly after the swearing in of Vice-president Johnson,

---

[3] *Century*, Vol. LXXXV, p. 199, article by General Henderson; *Littell's*, Vol. LXXXIV, p. 13.

[4] *Rise and Fall of the Slave Power*, Vol. II, p. 478; *Life and Services of Andrew Johnson*, p. 129; Ward Hill Lamon, *Recollections of Lincoln*, p. 1; "Vice-President Johnson" in *Southern Historical Review*, Vol. IX, 1905.

[5] Johnson MS. No. 24,489.

Secretary McCulloch called on President Lincoln and referred to Johnson's unfortunate speech, intimating that Johnson was disguised in stimulants. "Oh, well," said Lincoln, "don't you bother about Andy Johnson's drinking. He made a bad slip the other day, but I have known Andy a great many years, and he ain't no drunkard." [6] "For six weeks after Johnson became President," Secretary McCulloch writes, "he occupied a room adjoining mine and communicating with it in the Treasury Department. The President was there every morning before nine o'clock and he rarely left it before five. There was no liquor in his room. It was open to everybody. For nearly four years I had daily intercourse with him, frequently at night, and I never saw him when under the influence of liquor. I have no hesitation in saying that whatever may have been his faults, intemperance was not among them." [7]

Returning to Washington from Silver Spring improved in health, the Vice-president took part in the closing scenes of the war. He had been on the firing line in Tennessee for four years and he had been a refugee and an outlaw for five years; war hysteria therefore gripped him. The hemp rope which he had twisted down in Tennessee, tight and strong for hanging conscious traitors, he had brought along with him to Washington. He made no concealment of the fact that treason should be made odious. Everywhere he advocated a vigorous policy and the hanging of Jeff Davis and the leading rebels in short order. It must be noted, however, that these broad threats were made in March and early in April 1865. Johnson, at that time, was Vice-president and clothed with no authority in the premises.[8]

Soon the ill-starred Confederacy fell; on Sunday, April 2, 1865, Jefferson Davis and his cabinet fled from Richmond and the Confederacy was no more. On the ninth Andrew Johnson,

---

6 McCulloch, p. 373; *Taylor-Trotwood Magazine*, September 1908.

7 I have dealt with the subject of Johnson's intemperance at some length in Part III, Chap. II, "Swinging Round the Circle"; see also a collection of the authorities on this subject by Schouler in his *History of the United States*, Vol. VII, pp. 1-10.

8 The Radicals afterwards used these utterances as though Johnson were then President.—Schouler, Vol. VII, Chap. I.

The Tailor and Rail-splitter Mending the Union

at the request of Mr. Lincoln, joined the presidential party for a visit to Richmond, the capital of the Confederacy.

With the firing of guns and with patriotic speeches by William Lloyd Garrison and Henry Ward Beecher, on April 14, the fourth anniversary of the fall of Sumter, the Stars and Stripes were again raised over that historic fort. That afternoon Andrew Johnson spent in the Vice-president's rooms at the capitol. In the evening he and ex-Governor Farwell of Wisconsin, also a guest at the Kirkwood House, conversed for a short time. Presently the ex-Governor went to Ford's Theater, about two blocks away, to see Laura Keene in "Our American Cousin." It was understood that Mr. Lincoln would attend this play. The Vice-president retired early. A desperate character, named Atzeroth, assigned to murder Johnson, it may be stated, had taken room No. 126, in the Kirkwood House. In about two hours, and after the Vice-president was in bed asleep, a vigorous knocking was heard at his door. It was Governor Farwell. Greatly excited, having run with all speed from the theater, he called out and said he had an urgent message and must see Johnson at once. The Vice-president opened the door, and the ex-Governor rushed in. "Some one has shot and murdered the President," he exclaimed. The two men almost beside themselves, clung to each other for support.[9] Five hundred people soon gathered in the hotel. A number of friends were admitted to the Vice-president's rooms. Johnson despatched Farwell to ascertain the President's condition. In a short while he returned. Mr. Lincoln was in a dying condition. Secretary Seward had been assaulted. There was a plot to murder the Vice-president and all the heads of the departments. The excitement was indescribable. Against the remonstrance of friends the Vice-president insisted on going to President Lincoln's bedside. Accompanied by Major O'Bierne, Andrew Johnson left his apartments and made his way through vast crowds to the deathbed. Here he found that the President was beyond hope. The little dwelling in front of Ford's Theater, whither he had been hastily carried, was crowded with relatives and with cabinet officers. The weeping

[9] Testimony of Governor Farwell in the Surratt trial.

and terror-stricken populace filled the streets. After gazing upon the pale face of his chieftain, whom he loved and served so well, Johnson returned to his hotel.[10]

Early next morning, Saturday April 15, Secretaries McCulloch and Speed came to the Kirkwood and officially notified Andrew Johnson of the death of Lincoln and of his ascension to the Presidency. The written notification was signed by McCulloch, Secretary of the Treasury; Stanton, Secretary of War; Weeks, Secretary of the Navy; Dennison, Postmaster General; Usher, Secretary of the Interior, and Speed, Attorney-General. Secretary Seward, having been injured in a fall and wounded by one of the assassins, was too unwell to sign his name. At Johnson's request, the oath of office was administered at the hotel. About eleven o'clock on Saturday, in the parlors of the Kirkwood, Chief Justice Chase, in the presence of McCulloch, Speed, Foote, Hale, Francis P. Blair, Sr., and son, Montgomery Blair and others, administered the oath.[11] Andrew Johnson impressively kissed the book at the twenty-first verse of the eleventh chapter of Ezekiel. The ceremony ended. The Greeneville tailor was President of the United States. Chief Justice Chase extended his hand. "You are President," he solemnly declared. "May God support, guide and bless you in your administration." The President spoke a few simple words. He was almost overwhelmed by the sad event

[10] *American Historical Review*, Vol. XXIX, p. 515: "Andrew Johnson was present a short while at Lincoln's bedside"; *Chronicle*, August 26, 1865: "D. Massey, a witness, talked with Andrew Johnson a half hour after he returned from the deathbed"; *National Intelligencer*, edition two-thirty o'clock A.M., April 15: "The Vice-president has been to see Lincoln, but all company except the family, the cabinet and a few friends have been excluded." Senator Sumner wrote to John Bright, "About two P.M., the Vice-president called at the dying President's bedside"; Pierce, *Sumner*, Vol. IV, p. 241. The drawing of Lincoln's deathbed scene has Andrew Johnson in the group of attendant mourners; Washington *Star*, April 16: "Andrew Johnson was at the President's bedside"; J. S. Jones, *Life of Johnson*, to the same effect; ditto, Savage, *Life*. On the contrary, in Barton, *Life of Lincoln*, Vol. II, p. 343, it is stated that Johnson was not present, and that the artist was mistaken. In Stewart, *Reminiscences*, p. 194, it is said that Andrew Johnson had been drunk a month, was "in with the conspirators," "did not know of the President's death until seven or eight o'clock next day," when Stewart, Stanton, Chief Justice Chase and Foote woke him! That Stewart went to Johnson's rooms at the Kirkwood House, roused him from a drunken sleep, took him to the White House and Stanton sent for a tailor, a barber and a doctor! It may be here stated that Johnson did not occupy the White House until May 25.

[11] Rhodes, Vol. V, p. 150.

which had so recently occurred, he said. As to an indication of his policy, he went on to declare, that would develop as the administration progressed. He could offer no assurances for the future but his past life, one of toils and labors. He hoped "that the present perils will bring about greater freedom for the masses. . . . Toil and a hearty advocacy of the principles of the free government have been my lot. . . . The duties have been mine," he declared, "the consequences are God's." Craving "the encouragement and support of all who were present" and feeling that "all patriots and lovers of right, all who are in favor of a free government for a free people" would hold up his hands, "he favorably impressed all who were present." On this solemn occasion he was "calm and self-possessed" and his manner indicated that he was "grief stricken." [12] The daily papers were greatly gratified "at the manner in which the new President was conducting himself." [13]

A cabinet meeting was held in the office of the Secretary of the Treasury the same day. The President stated that he wished to carry out the policy of his predecessor. [14] He therefore earnestly requested each member of the cabinet to continue in office. So anxious was he to pursue Mr. Lincoln's policy, he at once tendered the office of Secretary of the Interior to James Harlan. Secretary Usher had signified his desire to resign and Mr. Lincoln had spoken of Harlan for the position. At this first meeting of the cabinet, as ever afterwards, Johnson was "patient, courteous and considerate," deporting himself admirably, or, as Sumner said, "His manners were excellent, even sympathetic." As the White House was still occupied by Mrs. Lincoln and her family, the President was assigned rooms in the Treasury building, next to Secretary McCulloch, where he remained until May 25. At that time he and his family moved into the White House.

On May 26 the last Confederate army, under General E. Kirby Smith, surrendered and the Civil War ended. Three days before a grand military review of the armies under Grant

12 McCulloch, p. 376.
13 Evening *Star*, April 15, 1865.
14 Dunning, *Reconstruction*, p. 74.

and Sherman took place in Washington—a scene perhaps transcending in grandeur anything before witnessed in the country. President Johnson and other officials reviewed the parade. The great armies were disbanded and melted away into the body politic. At once delegations from everywhere began to pour into Washington, bent on interviewing the President and offering suggestions. Henry Ward Beecher called. Radicals like Wade, Sumner and Chase undertook to formulate a policy for the reorganization of the Southern States and of emancipation and negro suffrage. War Democrats were thick around the White House; Reverdy Johnson of Maryland, General F. P. Blair and his son Montgomery Blair, Preston King of New York, were sure of the President's ear. Liberal Republicans, Dixon, Doolittle and others, offered suggestions. From the conquered and prostrate South came scores of delegations composed of old line Whigs and Union men generally, pleading for mercy and a restored Union and a speedy admission into the affairs of government. In truth, all sorts and conditions, except original Secessionists and northern Copperheads, frequented the White House. To these divergent and conflicting interests the President gave due attention.

Without exception, however, he declined to commit himself to any line of policy; his policy "would unfold page by page." "In regard to my future course," he declared to an Illinois delegation, "I will now make no pledges, no promises." He would impress one fact, however, on all: "I was sprung from the people and every pulsation of the popular heart finds an immediate answer in my own." As to treason and traitors, he never failed to declare that the former was a crime and that "conscious traitors"—the "head devils"—should be punished. The murderer of President Lincoln should suffer the severest penalty, "that is the response that swells in every bosom."

Having no aptitude for diversions or sports, the President devoted himself to his daily tasks. This, indeed, was also his pleasure. He did not attend the theaters, he was not fond of society, and with difficulty was prevailed upon by his associates to go on week-end excursions down the Potomac. His daily routine was a full one. Rising at six, he would read the newspapers till breakfast at seven-thirty. After breakfast he would begin the labors of the day. Bundles of letters were to be read and replies dictated, applications for appointments considered. Promotion and discharges from the army and navy, political advice, petitions for executive clemency and innumerable other subjects engaged his attention. Before these matters were half completed visitors commenced to flock into the anterooms and thrust their cards upon him. "Pardon seekers swarmed on every hand; former owners of confiscated property paced up and down before his rooms, and females with indescribable effrontery insisted upon immediate audiences." The more important business disposed of, "visitors were admitted one by one, and the President submitted himself to the artesian process." At three o'clock or thereabout the doors of his apartment were opened and the whole crowd admitted. "At such times Colonel Robert Johnson or Colonel Brown would stand near the President and take memoranda as dictated by him." The whole scene resembled a dense throng "at the post-office window. . . . The President's manner at such times was always pleasant and gave confidence to the most timid. His decisions were quick and every individual who laid his case before him learned in half a dozen courteous words the final decision. . . . When all had been listened to and the halls were once more empty the President turned again to the papers on his table." At four o'clock dinner was served. After dining, he returned to his office where he remained until eleven o'clock. In addition to all these duties, "distinguished visitors constantly presented themselves. Representatives of foreign courts, Governors, Senators, Generals, and hundreds of lesser magnitude must be received, each having some important subject requiring care and deliberation, while over all towers the great and ever-present problem of reconstruction."[15]

Thus it will be seen the President was resolved to take the people into his confidence. To this end he changed the rules so that each day, from ten to three except on Tuesdays and Fridays, the public might call and transact business. The

[15] Washington *Star*, November 14, 1865, "A President's Busy Day."

natural result was that by October, "hundreds of pardon-seekers were crowding the anteroom and by March 1866 the crowds had simply inundated the entire establishment, the press of those imposing on the President's patience being unprece-dented." [16]

The Southern States engaged much of the President's time. During the first month of his administration he issued a procla-mation removing trade restrictions in the seceding states; on May 29 an amnesty proclamation was issued. "To all persons engaged in rebellion amnesty and pardon, with restitution of rights of property, except slaves" was granted, provided they took the oath prescribed. This oath provided that the affiant would support the Constitution and all laws with refer-ence to emancipation. Certain classes of Confederates, how-ever, were excepted from the proclamation: Civil or diplomatic officers of the Confederacy who left judicial stations under the United States; officers above the rank of Colonel; United States Congressmen who left their seats in Congress; those who re-signed the United States army or navy; those who treated pris-oners unlawfully; those absent from the United States aiding rebellion; military and naval officers who were educated at West Point; Governors of seceding states; citizens who left the United States and went into the Confederacy to aid re-bellion; those destroying commerce on the high seas or making raids in the Confederacy; prisoners of war or under bonds as such; those voluntarily participating in rebellion and the esti-mated value of whose property was over $20,000.00; those who had not kept their former amnesty oath.

At the end of this proclamation was appended a paragraph providing that special application might be made to the Presi-dent by persons belonging to the excepted classes and that clemency would be liberally extended. The provision that rebels worth above $20,000.00 should be excluded created much com-ment in the South. This was President Johnson's own idea, it not having been included in Lincoln's amnesty Proclamation of 1863. "President Johnson is wreaking his vengeance on rich slave-holding aristocrats," it was charged. But there was

[16] Esther Singleton, *Story of the White House*, Vol. II, p. 101.

a reason for this exception, the President concluded. But for this provision there would be no punishment for "conscious rebels"—for the leaders in rebellion. This the President explained to a Virginia delegation which called and urged its repeal. To one of this delegation the President justified excepting from the amnesty provisions persons worth above $20,000.00. He asked the delegate if he did not know "that men aided the rebellion according to the extent of their pecuniary means." The delegate replied, "No, I do not know it." Thereupon the President rejoined, "Why, yes, you do. You know perfectly well it was the wealthy men of the South who dragooned the people into Secession." Though the executive mansion was always crowded with pardon seekers, the President carefully investigated each case and administered his high prerogative with care." [17]

As month after month passed and the President discovered, from intercourse with the visiting delegation, that the Southerners were on their knees and repentant and that the Union element was in the ascendant and the Secessionists in the discard, he grew more lenient. Some are disposed to credit Mr. Seward with softening the heart of President Johnson. No doubt the influence of Secretary Seward was potent. But, after all, Johnson was a southern man and "loved the southern people." After becoming President and after a full investigation, he had become convinced that the southern people had undergone a complete change of mind. As Judge Frost of South Carolina in June 1865 expressed it, "Certain delusions have been dispelled by the Revolution; among them that slavery is an element of political strength and moral power"— another delusion, viz., "that cotton is king" had likewise vanished in mist. "We are to come back with these notions dispelled and with a new system of labor," said Frost. Thus Johnson came to realize that in the South the principles for which he had contended had conquered, that the war had liberated poor southern whites as well as blacks. A more controlling thought undoubtedly came to the President: Not only had

[17] Rhodes, not a friendly critic agrees, Vol. V, p. 535, that Johnson "wisely exercised the pardoning power."

the South changed her mental attitude but she was now prostrate and in actual want.

Her railroads were torn up or worn out, her public buildings and colleges in ruins, her banks broken and closed, her commerce destroyed, farms grown up in weeds and briers, ditches stopped, plantations abandoned. Much more than this, her morale was gone. Millions of slaves were roaming over the land idle and vicious, "trying out their new freedom." The South's vast social, economic and industrial system was disrupted. In a word, such was the desolation in the South, there would have been much loss of life but for Government aid. Four million slaves, valued at two billion dollars, had been liberated. Bonds and other securities to fully as large an amount had been rendered worthless.[18] Instances of individual suffering were heart-rending. "White families of widows and children were often found wandering through the woods without food or shelter." In one instance a large landowner, one distinguished for generations, was now penniless, "his slaves all gone and he the scion of the family stands on the corner of the old homestead and peddles molasses by the quart and tea by the pound to former slaves to gain a little bread." [19]

Two hundred and fifty thousand men had been killed, wounded and maimed and there was general demoralization from the letting down of social standards. With facts such as these, President Johnson was eager, at the earliest moment, to restore the land of his birth to its place in the nation.

Those who had wrought desolation he still maintained should be punished. Meanwhile Jefferson Davis was held as a prisoner at Fort Monroe and General Miles, his jailer, was unusually harsh and cruel. Miles had put the rebel chieftain in irons. He kept Mr. Davis in a dark casement, a light burning in his room, and a sentinel watching every movement. Of this treatment, however, President Johnson had no knowledge until the last of May. Such matters were under the super-

---

[18] Fleming, *Reconstruction*, p. 64; Pike, *Prostrate South*, p. 117; *The Sequel of Appomattox*, p. 3; DuBois, *Reconstruction, American Historical Review*, Vol. XV, p. 784.
[19] Pike, *op. cit.*

vision of the War Department.[20]   On May 28 it came to the
President's attention, for the first time, that Mr. Davis was in
irons.   At once the President communicated with General
Miles, asking if Davis was in irons and if so, why?   The General answered that the doors of the cell were made of wood and
that irons were necessary.   The President at once ordered the
irons removed.   He also dispatched Secretary McCulloch to
Davis to investigate and report his condition.   Though President Johnson regarded Davis as "the head devil of Secession
and the one above all others that ought to be hung," nevertheless he insisted that he ought not to be brutally treated while
in prison.[21]   To Mrs. Jefferson Davis the President was as
courteous and considerate as the nature of the case allowed.
On June 17, 1865, she wired him for permission to go North.
The request was granted.   On September 4, having heard that
Mr. Davis was afflicted with carbuncles, she was allowed to
visit him.   On September 13 she wrote to President Johnson
expressing thanks.   "You have refused no reasonable request,"
she declared.   Mr. Davis, himself, however, was implacable.
To the last he refused to apply for a pardon.[22]   "I have done
nothing wrong, why should I seek pardon?" he asked.   Indeed,
in the 1880's, speaking of his course in the Civil War, he said
that "considering all the blood that was shed and all the
treasure spent," he would do the same thing over again.

In 1865, if Johnson could have done so, he would have hung
the President of the Confederacy.[23]   When Attorney-General
Speed advised that Jefferson Davis could not be tried by military court-martial [24] the President consulted General B. F.
Butler, at that time a favorite of the North.   Butler devised
an original scheme.   Davis should be tried by court-martial for
treason and sentenced to be hung.   The President should then

20 Oberholtzer, Vol. I, p. 37.   Oberholtzer lays a part of the blame of Davis'
treatment on the President.—Craven, *Prison Life*, p. 25; Oglesby, *Shackling of
Davis*, p. 13.
21 McCulloch, p. 410; O. R., Part VII, p. 904, etc.
22 In 1869 President Johnson suggested that Davis make application.   He
would not, dying as he had lived, an unrepentant "rebel."—Professor W. E.
Dodd, *Life of Davis*, p. 369.   In contrast General Lee applied for pardon, at
once.
23 *Century Magazine*, January 1913.
24 McCulloch, p. 408.

recognize the writ of *habeas corpus*, and permit Davis to take the case to the Supreme Court. If the Court held that the military commission had jurisdiction, Davis would be executed, otherwise he would be discharged.[25]

President Johnson went so far in his effort to punish conscious traitors he asked Grant if Lee could not be punished. Grant replied that Lee was a paroled prisoner and therefore could not be tried. The President did not further press the matter. At first General Lee was included with Davis in the same bill of indictment, but to the credit of the United States government a *nol. pros.* was entered as to General Lee and he was never molested. President Johnson lauded General Lee's conduct after the war. He would hold Lee up as an example to rebellious and disloyal Southerners, deserting the South and fleeing to other lands. "Why didn't you do like General Lee?" he said to a belligerent southern woman. "General Lee is not fleeing from the South." [26] No one more appreciated the magnanimity of Lee after Appomattox than President Johnson. Lee's patriotic course at Appomattox was indeed winning all hearts. On April 9, for the last time, mounted on old "Traveler," Lee rode down the thin gray line. Thousands of brave Union troops stood at attention, doing honor to their gallant foe. To his ragged veterans Lee turned and said farewell: "Men, I have done the best I could for you," he said, "but we have been defeated. You have made good soldiers and now you will make good citizens—when you reach home remember the war is over and the United States is our country." A few months later, when President of Washington and Lee University, Lee was writing to the southern people, endorsing Andrew Johnson and his administration. "Every one approves of Andrew Johnson's policy," Lee wrote to a friend.[27]

[25] *Ben. Butler's Book*, April 1865.
[26] *Harper's Magazine*, Vol. CXX, p. 179.
[27] Jones, *Life of Lee*, p. 216; Rhodes, Vol. VI, p. 72.

CHAPTER VIII

THE EXECUTION OF MRS. SURRATT

While President Johnson was busy with executive duties, the War Department had been busy running down and trying the assassins of Mr. Lincoln. After murdering Lincoln at Ford's Theater on April 14, John Wilkes Booth jumped upon the stage and mock-heroically exclaimed, *"Sic semper tyrannis."* In the excitement, though his leg was caught in the drapery and broken, he made his escape, crossing the Long Bridge and reaching Dr. Mudd's twelve miles away in Maryland. Next day the War Department got on the trail and arrested eight persons, David E. Herold, Edward Spengler, Lewis Payne, Michael O'Loughlin, Samuel Arnold, George A. Atzerodt, and Dr. Samuel A. Mudd. John H. Surratt, though suspected, escaped to Europe.

On April 27 Booth and Herold were surrounded in a barn on the Virginia side and Booth was shot to death by Burton Corbett. Corbett was First Sergeant of his company, an eccentric gloomy personage, who afterwards killed himself, first shooting up a state legislature. When called to account for killing Booth, he replied, "Colonel, Providence directed me!" Booth's body was wrapped in a blanket and taken to Washington. When it reached there "Dr. John Frederick May examined it. He recognized Booth's features and also a scar on his neck, the result of an operation the doctor had performed." [1] The body was secretly buried under the old penitentiary. In Booth's pockets were found various articles—a pipe, a spur, a compass, and a diary. Four years later President Johnson gave Edwin Booth, brother of John Wilkes, leave to remove Booth's body. One midnight in February 1869 Edwin Booth and the family dentist went to the grave and exhumed the body and thoroughly identified it. There were gold fillings in the teeth which the dentist knew to be his work. The long raven-

[1] *Lincoln Obsequies*, in Library of Congress, p. 97.

black, curly locks were unmistakable. Edwin Booth buried
the bones of his mad brother in the Booth burial ground in
Baltimore.[2] As late as 1925 it was claimed that Wilkes Booth
was not captured or killed. Some other body had been passed
off for his; and Booth escaped and lived to be seventy years old.
In fact a "body of Booth," carefully embalmed, was exhibited
to the public![3]

John Wilkes Booth, son of an English tragedian, was a violent, emotional, half-crazy Southerner, living in Baltimore.
He originated the assassination plot, giving to each conspirator his part.[4] Booth's part was to kill Lincoln. To acquaint
his associates with the place where the murder was to occur, he
accompanied them, a few days in advance, to Ford's and looked
it over. He himself had often acted there. To Payne he gave

[2] Washington *Star*, January 5, 1907; Benn. Pittman, *The Assassination of
President Lincoln*, p. 197; Oldroyd, *Assassination of Lincoln*, p. 209.

[3] Two accounts of Booth's escape and later life have been written: 1. Bates,
Finis L. Escape and suicide of John Wilkes Booth, assassin of President
Lincoln. Memphis, Pilcher Printing Co., 1907, 309 p. The author claims that
John Wilkes Booth was not killed at the Garrett house in Virginia in 1865,
but that he was living under the name of John St. Helen at Glenrose Mills,
Texas, 1872-1877, and committed suicide at Enid, Oklahoma, in 1903 as David
E. George. 2. Oklahoma the Mecca for men of mystery; John Wilkes Booth,
escape and wanderings until final ending of the trail by suicide at Enid,
Oklahoma, January 12, 1903. [Oklahoma City, 1922] 144 p. (Travelers series,
number seven.)

An official statement in the matter is that to be found in v. 46. pt. 3 of the
series bearing the title: "The war of the rebellion: a compilation of the
official records," Washington, Government printing office, 1894. The following is copied from p. 989 of that volume:

Headquarters Middle Military Division,
Washington, D. C., April 27, 1865.

Bvt. Maj. Gen. W. H. Emory, Cumberland, Md.:
  The following is sent for your information:

War Department,
Washington, April 27, 1865—9:35 A.M.

Major-General Dix,
      New York.
  J. Wilkes Booth and Herold were chased from the swamp in Saint Mary's
County, Md.: pursued yesterday morning to Garrett's farm, near Port Royal,
on the Rappahannock, by Colonel Baker's force. The barn in which they took
refuge was fired. Booth, in making his escape, was shot through the head
and killed, lingering about three hours, and Herold captured. Booth's body
and Herold are now here.

EDWIN M. STANTON,
Secretary of War.

  By command of Major-General Hancock:

DUNCAN S. WALKER,
Assistant Adjutant-General.

  (Same to Brevet Major-General Torbert, Winchester, Va., and Brigadier-
General Stevenson, Harper's Ferry, W. Va.)

[4] DeWitt, *Assassination*, p. 40.

the task of murdering Seward; Atzerodt was to kill Andrew Johnson; O'Loughlin was to kill Grant; Herold was to show Payne the Seward residence and then assist Atzerodt. The guilt of Payne, Atzerodt and Herold was beyond dispute, as each knew of the plot to kill and participated in it; but Mrs. Surratt's guilt was more than doubtful. Payne murderously assaulted Seward; Herold and Atzerodt that night rode wildly around the city on horseback. Herold afterwards accompanied and assisted Booth in his flight. Earlier in the night Atzerodt had engaged room No. 126 at the Kirkwood House, deposited his weapons in the room, and looked over the sturdy man whom he was assigned to murder. But he went no further.

One fact must be kept in mind. There had once been a plot to abduct Lincoln, and carry him off to Richmond but not to murder him. This, as Booth thought, would end the war. This plot failed because the conspirators could find no favorable opportunity. Several times they had followed Lincoln's carriage but the President happened not to be an occupant. The reason Booth reorganized his band to kill Lincoln was this: On April 11 President Lincoln declared in his last speech that he favored the more intelligent negroes and negro soldiers voting. Booth was present and said to a companion, "That is the last speech Lincoln will ever make." At once he set about to murder Lincoln. Now with this change of plan Arnold and O'Loughlin were not acquainted; on the fourteenth Arnold was at work at Fortress Monroe, and knew nothing of the plot to kill. He had, however, been connected with the plot to abduct. The evidence against O'Loughlin was slight. Though he knew of the plot to abduct, he did not know he was expected to kill Grant, and his only connection with the murder was that he happened to be in Washington on Thursday and Friday of the fatal week.

Spengler, however, and Dr. Mudd were implicated as accessories after the fact. Spengler tried to hinder the pursuit of Booth and to prevent his identification. Dr. Mudd set Booth's leg the night of the fourteenth when he and Herold fled from Washington. The Doctor was a Union man. He and Booth were slightly acquainted, and yet he claimed not to have recognized Booth that night or the next morning. For his services in setting the broken leg the Doctor was paid twenty-five dollars. When he cut the boot from Booth's broken leg, inside the boot he saw written, "John Wilkes ———." Next morning, April 15, the wounded actor called for a razor and shaved off his mustache; he also put on false whiskers. These facts, Dr. Mudd asserted, he learned from his wife. At first it was thought John H. Surratt assaulted Seward, but afterwards Seward's bellboy identified Payne as the assailant.

We now come to Mrs. Surratt's connection with this affair. Unfortunately for her, since October 1864 she had run a boarding house in Washington, at 602 H Street N. W., near the Capitol. She also owned a tavern at Surrattsville, Maryland, about twelve miles distant from Washington. Boarding with her in Washington were several of the conspirators, including one Weichman, who afterwards became the chief, if not the only, witness against her. Booth did not board with Mrs. Surratt, but at the National Hotel. The evidence of Mrs. Surratt's guilt hardly amounted to a scintilla. Though she ran the boarding house, where one or more of the conspirators and the man Weichman boarded, and though her son John was implicated in the plot to abduct Lincoln, yet the evidence of her guilt extended little further. This evidence may be summarized as follows: Two days after the murder and while the police were searching her home, a shocking looking fellow, dirty and disguised, came in with a pickax on his shoulder. He had come to do some work for Mrs. Surratt, he said. The police arrested him as a suspect and took him to the station where Mrs. Surratt had already been taken. She was confronted with the stranger and was asked if she knew him. She said she did not. This man proved to be Lewis Payne, the assailant of Seward. In the March previous he had been to Mrs. Surratt's house at least once, and was passing off as the son of a Baptist preacher. This denial of acquaintance by Mrs. Surratt was suspicious but not necessarily criminal.

In addition to this circumstance there were two others. Weichman, Mrs. Surratt's favorite boarder, testified that on the Tuesday before the fatal Friday he and Mrs. Surratt had driven out to Surrattsville, where she had a private talk with Lloyd, her tenant, which he did not hear. Lloyd, all but frightened to death, stated that Mrs. Surratt said, on that occasion, "Get the shooting irons ready, parties will call for them." Afterwards, when he and Weichman were threatened with hanging if he did not tell more, he changed the statement and swore she said, "Get the shooting irons ready, parties will be wanting them soon." Weichman also testified that on Friday, April 14, about noon, while he and Mrs. Surratt were in a buggy and about to start for Surrattsville, Booth came along and put a package in the buggy, and they carried the package to Surrattsville. This package when afterwards opened was found to contain Booth's field glasses.

Secretary of War Stanton and Joseph Holt, Judge Advocate General, had skillfully and expeditiously done the work of detecting and capturing these conspirators. But their attempt to implicate Jefferson Davis and others was a farce. At Stanton's request President Johnson had offered $100,000 for the capture of Davis and smaller sums for C. C. Clay, J. P. Benjamin and others.[5] Stanton and Holt had worked themselves up to believing Davis and Judah P. Benjamin in Richmond had hired the conspirators to commit the crime. Stanton, nervous and timid, was wild with excitement; he was guarded by special police. Judge Holt, his assistant, was merciless and cruel. A man of harsh, forbidding countenance, Holt had prosecuted and disgraced Fitz-John Porter. No one who bore the name of "rebel" had any rights, he thought. In 1864 he refused the request of an 18-year-old "rebel" girl to attend a marriage in her family.[6] Judge Holt expected "to hang the murderers before Lincoln was buried." [7]

Holt and Stanton assured President Johnson that they had evidence to convict Davis, Benjamin, Clay and others, and in consequence of this statement the President offered the rewards. This extraordinary conclusion of the War Department was based on the statement of one Sanford Conover "who was going to produce at least three witnesses of unimpeached

[5] Welles, *Diary*, Vol. II, p. 300.
[6] *O. R. Series II*, Part VIII, p. 839.
[7] Welles, Vol. II, May 9, 1865; Schouler, Vol. VII, p. 26.

character who submitted to Davis a proposition to kill the President." [8] Conover, it is needless to say, was a suborner of perjury.[9]

In order to include Davis and the others, whether present or not, in the murder of Lincoln, Judge Holt charged a conspiracy. Now when a criminal conspiracy is proven every conspirator, though absent when the crime is committed, is bound by the acts of his co-conspirators. In May, Jefferson Davis was captured in Georgia and was informed of President Johnson's reward. "Why, Johnson knows better than that," said the fleeing Confederate chieftain, "he knows I much prefer Lincoln as President, to him." [9a] Booth having been killed and John Surratt having fled to Europe, only eight persons remained to be tried. They were rough characters, except Mrs. Surratt and Dr. Mudd. She was a refined woman and a devout Catholic, and he was a man of character. All were huddled together in the old prison, at the foot of Seventh Street, on the banks of the Potomac, and were tried by a Military Commission, without judge or jury.

This court-martial was perhaps the most important and far-reaching military trial in American annals. Mr. Lincoln, the victim, was the foremost personage in the world; his murderer was John Wilkes Booth, brother of Edwin Booth, the impersonator of Hamlet; the court was composed of ten officers, none with the rank of less degree than General, except two who were Colonels. One member of the court was Lew Wallace, author of *Ben Hur;* General Winfield Scott Hancock, afterwards Democratic candidate for President, was sheriff or marshal. The commission was organized May 8 and was in session nearly sixty days; the trial provoked unending discussion and out of it came hundreds of books, pamphlets and newspaper articles. It likewise entered into politics, greatly irritating President Johnson and injuring the usefulness of

[8] Jones, *Life of Andrew Johnson*, p. 150.
[9] DeWitt, *Assassination*, p. 173.
[9a] Union soldiers who captured Davis certify that he was not disguised, but bore himself like a gallant soldier. J. Wm. Jones, *Memorial of Jefferson Davis*, p. 401.

Judge Joseph Holt, John A. Bingham, special prosecutor for the Government, and Edwin M. Stanton, Secretary of War.

Each day the eight prisoners would be brought into court in shackles. Only two days had been allowed them to get ready and employ attorneys. When Reverdy Johnson, a Union Senator from Maryland, came in to represent Mrs. Surratt, he was ordered out of the case. Under the rule he was advised no one could appear as attorney who had not taken the iron clad oath. Johnson was afterwards readmitted but refused to appear. Evidence of the most remote kind was heard. In fact, Mrs. Surratt and her associates were made responsible for the acts of southern rebels during the war,—for the "horrors of Southern prisons" and the like.

During the torrid days of June the court room was packed with public officials, generals of the army, society leaders, curiosity seekers, brides and grooms.[10] Mrs. Surratt's daughter Anna was also present. As near as she could approach her mother, this devoted woman dragged herself, almost dying of grief and sorrow. John L. Bingham and Major H. L. Burnett appeared for the United States, and seven attorneys for the defendants. The trial was a farce. Recorder Holt, whose duty it was to see that justice was done and no innocent person convicted, taxed his ingenuity to suppress evidence that would hurt the Government's case or help the defendants.

He had in his possession the diary of John Wilkes Booth, taken off the dead body of Booth and written just after the murder. This diary would have shown that Mrs. Surratt had no knowledge of the plot to assassinate Lincoln, that Booth's change of plan after April 11 had not been known to her. This was not brought to light, nor offered to the Court.[11] Commenting on this diary, General B. F. Butler, on a noted occasion attacking Bingham, declared, "It might not have been legal evidence, yet it was moral evidence carrying conviction to the moral sense, and if Mrs. Surratt did not know of the change of purpose, and there is no evidence that she knew in

---

10 Oldroyd, *op. cit.*, p. 316.

11 DeWitt finds as the motive for the suppression of Booth's diary that both Stanton and Holt wished to convict John Surratt, and that this could not have been done if Booth's diary were put in evidence. DeWitt, *Impeachment*, p. 215.

any way of the assassination, she ought not in my judgment to have been convicted." Judge Bingham addressed the Commission in his impassioned manner, for five or six days, concluding his speech on July 3.

The Military Commission then retired to consider their verdict. They found all eight guilty. Mrs. Surratt, Payne, Atzerodt and Herold were guilty in the first degree and should be hung; three of the others should be imprisoned for life, and one for six years. This sentence had to be approved by the President before it could be carried out. On July 5 the diligent Holt gained admittance, by a side door, to the White House—the President though sick must sign the death warrant. President Johnson, anxious as Holt or Stanton to punish Mr. Lincoln's murderers, came from his sick bed, and signed the warrant, under circumstances I will presently explain.

The friends of Mrs. Surratt on July 5 and 6 moved heaven and earth to secure her release. Many hastened to the White House to implore the President to exercise mercy, but were refused admittance. Preston King and Senator Lane guarded the White House entrance. The President, since June 26, had been confined with bilious fever. Anna Surratt threw herself fainting on the steps of the White House. Other friends applied to Judge Wylie to issue a writ of *habeas corpus*, to inquire into the legality of a court-martial in times of peace. The writ was issued and directed to General Hancock to execute. The General, with the great writ in hand, called on Attorney-General Speed for advice. The legal department advised that the writ had been suspended by Lincoln "and specially in this case by Johnson." Therefore the General, after explaining matters to the Judge, returned the writ unexecuted.[12]

All hope for Mrs. Surratt was now gone. The President would not hear her appeal for mercy and the courts were suppressed. Judge Wylie complained that he was treated with contempt, but did not further defy the Government. July 7,

[12] In 1880 when Hancock was the Democratic candidate for President this circumstance injured him in some sections.

1865, was a hot, blistering day; on that day Mrs. Mary Surratt was to die on the gallows.   Bound and shackled, the four doomed persons approached the place of death—two in front and two behind.   At one o'clock General Hartranft, Provost-Marshal, cut the rope and the four bodies fell with a thud. Thousands from trees and rooftops gazed at the gruesome spectacle.   Their bodies were buried on the spot.   The four lesser culprits were sent to the Dry Tortugas, off the coast of Florida.[13]   The pardoning of these parties in 1869 by President Johnson "created not a ripple." [14]

The public and the press in July 1865 "approved the finding of the court-martial and the execution of the four murderers." [15]   "So far as heard in the public marts," said the reporters, "people approve the trial, and the sentence gives general satisfaction;" "of the guilt of the criminals and the justice of the sentences there was ample evidence." [16]   The agony of Anna Surratt, fainting on the steps of the White House, moved not the hearts of an outraged people.   Yet her friends felt that Mrs. Surratt had been murdered.   The Surratt home was draped in mourning that July day, and church bells tolled her death.   But it was a day of tragedy and Lincoln's murder must be avenged.   "Thousands of relic hunters visited the Surratt home and chipped chips from the portico until the police were called to disperse them." [17]   But the sequel to this trial is its most interesting feature.

Two years after the execution of Mrs. Surratt, her son John was captured in Italy, as a member of the Pope's Guards, and brought back to Washington.   He was indicted and tried before a civil court and a jury for conspiracy to murder Lincoln. At this trial startling disclosures occurred in connection with the court-martial of Mrs. Surratt.   For the first time it came

---

13 In March 1869 Andrew Johnson pardoned Dr. Mudd, who had risked his life in a yellow fever epidemic on the island, and also Spengler and Arnold; O'Loughlin had died in the yellow fever scourge.

14 Oldroyd, *Assassination*, etc., p. 161; DeWitt, *Assassination*, in the last chapter.

15 Washington papers, July 8, 1865.

16 *National Republican*, July 26; *National Intelligencer*, July 7.

17 *Evening Star*, July 8; the superstitious noted that Senator Lane and ex-Senator King, who acted as janitors at the White House and kept Anna Surratt from the President, soon killed themselves.

out that John Wilkes Booth had left a diary and that this diary would have acquitted Mrs. Surratt, and that the diary had been suppressed. A second fact came to light. There had been a recommendation for mercy, signed by five of the military commission. This recommendation had likewise been suppressed. As the evidence against Mrs. Surratt was meager and related to matters prior to April 11, 1865, when Booth changed his plans, it was manifest that she had been improperly convicted—"murdered!" Holt and his associates had suppressed evidence, it was charged, they had offered the pipe, the field glasses and the spur, taken from Booth's body, but the diary they had not offered. In Holt's safe it had lain for two years, known to no one except Holt, Bingham and Burnett. John Surratt was set free by the court.[18]

The suppression of the recommendation for mercy came to light in this way. Richard T. Merrick, John Surratt's attorney, in his address to the jury, referred to the change in Booth's plans. "Mrs. Surratt had no earthly connection with the plot to kill formed after the 11th of April," he asserted. Bingham, counsel for the Government, replied that "the whole matter of Mrs. Surratt's guilt or innocence had been passed on and reviewed by President Johnson." "Here I hold in my hand the original record," he exclaimed, "a record presented to the President and laid before his cabinet. . . . Every single member voted to confirm the sentence and the President with his own hand wrote his confirmation of it and with his own hand signed the warrant."

Now this was the first knowledge the President, the cabinet or the public had of such a paper. Though during the early days of July 1865 there had been wild rumors of such a recommendation, these rumors soon died out and were discredited. President Johnson was as much astonished as the public by Bingham's statement. At once he sent to the War Department for the original records in the court-martial of Mrs. Surratt.[19] In the records he found the recommendation for mercy. Here, then, was a bad situation—a woman hung, hung because evi-

[18] Laughlin, *The Death of Lincoln*, p. 396.
[19] W. G. Moore, *Diary*, August 5, 1867.

dence had been suppressed and a recommendation for mercy withheld.

What then was the truth of this matter? Only July 5, 1865, when Judge Holt called President Johnson from his bed and requested him to sign the sentence of death against Mrs. Surratt, did he suppress the recommendation for mercy? Again was the recommendation for mercy submitted to the President at a cabinet meeting, as stated by Bingham, and approved by them? The President always declared he never saw or heard of the recommendation for mercy until it was called to his attention by the newspapers on August 4, 1867. Holt asserted that the President had seen it. The facts of this wretched affair seem to sustain the President. To begin with, there was no cabinet meeting on the last Friday in June 1865. In fact, after the finding of the court-martial and before the hanging of Mrs. Surratt there was no cabinet meeting at all, as the records show. During that time it is conceded the President was sick with fever and that he got out of a sick bed on the fifth and signed the death warrant. Therefore, the statement that the cabinet approved the execution was erroneous.[20]

A most pregnant fact is this: The recommendation for mercy was never printed nor referred to in the newspapers. The *Star* of July 10, 1865, had a long account of the trial, New York and other papers, likewise, were full of it, but no reference was made to a recommendation for mercy. If it had been in the file, surely reporters would not have missed so important a point. But perhaps the public could not gain access to the War Department to inspect the file? That suggestion is met by another circumstance. In August 1865 Benn Pittman, reporter to the military commission, asked leave of Judge Holt to print the trial. The Judge granted leave but imposed two conditions: First, Pittman "must publish every word, omitting nothing"; second, in order to see that nothing was changed or omitted, "Major Burnett of the commission must inspect the proof." This was carefully done; Major Burnett inspected the proof of Pittman's book, *The Trial of the Assassins*, and

<hr/>

[20] Welles, *Diary*, Vol. II, p. 324; Oberholtzer, *History of the United States*, Vol. I, p. 17.

certified to its "faithfulness and accuracy." Yet nowhere in the publication does the recommendation for mercy appear. Other publications of the trial, some profusely illustrated, were issued, but in none was there a recommendation for mercy.

In the spring of 1926 I inspected the original of this military court-martial, on file in the War Department at Washington. It presents a curious aspect. Each day's evidence, consisting of about twenty-five foolscap pages, is written in longhand and bound together; the fastenings are blue ribbons, inserted through three slits at the top of each page. This is true of all the proceedings except after the evidence and the argument of counsel—that is to say from June 30 to July 5. These last six days' proceedings, nineteen pages, relate to matters after the argument. They include the names of the culprits, the connection of each with the assassination, the finding of the court-martial, the sentence imposed upon each prisoner and the recommendation for mercy. Now these nineteen pages are not at this time bound together, though it is apparent that at one time they were. Furthermore, at the top of the nineteen pages are not only three perforations for ribbons similar to the other pages, but also three holes or eyelets for brads. Evidently this part of the file was at one time bound together with ribbons and then was taken apart and afterward bound with brads. At present each sheet is separate and unbound. The outside page or covering indicates rough treatment; it appears to have been ground by some one's heel into a gritty floor.

A controlling circumstance may now be stated. In the file is a private report of Adjutant-General Holt to the President. Its language is significant. Judge Holt uses these words, "Having been personally engaged in the conduct of the foregoing case as Judge Advocate of the commission, I deem it unnecessary to enter in this report into an elaborate discussion of the immense mass of evidence submitted to a consideration of the Court. . . . There were fifty-three days of the evidence and three hundred or four hundred witnesses. . . . The rights of the prisoners were watched and zealously guarded by seven able counselors. . . . The opinion is entertained that the proceedings were regular and that the findings of the commission were fully justified by the evidence.   It is thought that the highest considerations of public justice as well as the future security of the lives of the officers of the Government demand that the sentences based on these findings should be carried into execution."   Holt likewise reports that he was present at all times during the trial and speaks of his own knowledge.   Holt's report is bound with one brad and covers everything necessary for the information of the President, except the recommendation for mercy.   In Holt's report this recommendation is not alluded to, and it is so written and placed on the back of a page, that when signing the death warrant the President could not see it.

On the whole, it seems clear that the President had no knowledge of the recommendation for mercy until two years after Mrs. Surratt's death and at the trial of John Surratt on August 4, 1867.   It is significant that on that date the President discharged Stanton from office.   Relying on the report and recommendation of his official advisers, and on the findings of ten officers, constituting the military tribunal, the President signed the death warrant.   It does not follow that he would have pardoned Mrs. Surratt had he seen the recommendation for mercy—he wished Lincoln's assassins hung—but he was entitled to have seen it.   It seems plain that at the interview between President Johnson and Judge Holt on July 5, 1865, the original file was not inspected by the President.   He relied upon the personal and intimate report of his official adviser and this did not call the recommendation to his attention.   In fact, Holt urged the President to sign the death warrant, giving his personal assurance that Mrs. Surratt was guilty and should be hung.   As soon as Judge Holt obtained the President's signature he carried the original file to his office and locked it up.   This file remained in his safe till the John Surratt trial, when, as we have seen, it was brought out by Judge Bingham.

My own theory is this.   In August 1865, when Pittman asked leave to publish the trial, Holt furnished him with the entire record but retained the recommendation for mercy.   In fact, no copy of the recommendation was made, as was the case with the other papers, and the original, attached to the court-martial proceeding, was perhaps not subject to inspection by the public. In justification of the conduct of Judge Holt in not calling the attention of the President to the recommendation for mercy, it may be said that he imagined he was serving the country and avoiding a scene. It was then generally thought that Mrs. Surratt was guilty, and in this opinion Holt, Bingham and Stanton concurred. One member of the commission declining to recommend mercy was General Lew Wallace, perhaps the ablest of the tribunal. Besides, it must be said that disinterested lawyers had arrived at the conclusion that Mrs. Surratt kept "the nest in which treason was hatched." [21] On the other hand, Payne on his way to the scaffold told General Hartranft that Mrs. Surratt had no earthly connection with the assassination plot, a fact which was shortly after the death of Mrs. Surratt communicated to President Johnson.

In August 1867, when John Surratt was tried, the public began to remember many circumstances connected with the trial of Mrs. Surratt—that the prisoners were bound and shackled and brought into court surrounded by men under arms, that their cells were padded, and that sacks had been tied around their heads leaving a small opening through which food was passed into their mouths; that Mrs. Surratt's lawyer, Reverdy Johnson, appearing for her without pay, had been badgered by the court and insulted, and that the whole proceedings—certainly as to Mrs. Surratt—were disreputable, being but the mockery of a trial.

Andrew Johnson urged the execution of Lincoln's murderers, a fact he often stated. If he is censurable in connection with the death of Mrs. Surratt, it would seem to be because he relied upon his official advisers. Attorney-General Speed furnished an opinion in writing that a military commission was the proper tribunal to try the case and that it ought not to yield its jurisdiction to a civil court, that Washington City was in a state of war, and was an armed camp, that Lincoln at the

21 Oberholtzer, Vol. I, p. 2.

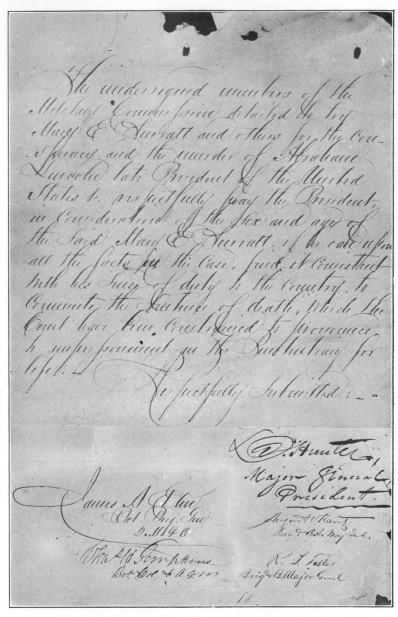

The Recommendation for Clemency in the Surratt Trial

time of his death was the Commander-in-Chief of the army, and
that to slay the Commander of the army "was to violate the
common law of war." On this opinion the President relied.
Should he have done otherwise? As to the guilt or innocence of
Mrs. Surratt, he put that up to the duly constituted authorities. They having declared her guilty, in this opinion he concurred. His war minister and his Adjutant-General, together
with the private prosecutor, were lawyers of national reputation. Johnson was not a lawyer. Would he have been justified
in over-ruling experts in the law and setting himself above
Attorney-General Speed, Judge Holt, Judge Bingham and
Secretary Stanton? [22]

In after years, when attacked for "murdering" Mrs. Surratt, Johnson boldly asserted that he relied on his Attorney-
General and on the Military Department. Secretary McCulloch, however, states that the incident was grievous to Johnson and that "he deeply regretted it." [23] In connection with
this court-martial, it is doubtful if the Supreme Court would
have declared it illegal, had the writ of *habeas corpus* come
before it. At that time the war was still raging. Washington
was an armed camp and there the Commander-in-Chief had
his headquarters. The opinion in *Ex Parte Milligan*, subsequently delivered, went no further than to hold that courts-
martial were illegal in states where war was not raging, as in
Missouri.[24]

[22] *Vindication*, in Washington *Chronicle* of July 26, 1872, and *Refutation*,
published in 1873, in pamphlet form, give Holt's side; President Johnson's
reply in the *Chronicle* of November 12, 1872, is a document of conviction;
North American Review, July 1888.
[23] McCulloch, *Memoirs*, etc., p. 226.
[24] Warren, *The Supreme Court*, Vol. III. *Ex Parte Milligan.*

CHAPTER IX

HERO OF AN HOUR

One August day in 1865 two carriages drove up to the White House. Tom Pendel, the old doorkeeper, opened wide the doors, the servants bustled around in obsequious welcome, and the President hastened from his busy desk—the entire Johnson family, eleven in number, had arrived. Exiles, fugitives, three years driven from their Tennessee home, but now together again and under one roof. Five robust children, happy and open-eyed, swarmed through their magnificent new home, twelve-year-old Andy, cured of infantile consumption, leading the rest. Mrs. Johnson, weary with travel and worn with disease, was assisted from the carriage and soon retired, having chosen a small quiet bedroom on the southwest, overlooking the grassy lawn and the wonderful elms, with the Mall and the Potomac in the background.

What a contrast the renovated White House was to that of President and Mrs. Lincoln's days. Then there was anxiety, war and destruction; now had come smiling peace. Then, only three sat at table, Mr. Lincoln, Mrs. Lincoln and little Tad; now there were a round dozen. Colonel Robert Johnson, about thirty years of age, was to assist the President in routine work; Andrew, Jr., was entered at a Catholic school in Georgetown; D. T. Patterson, a son-in-law, was a Senator from Tennessee. His wife, Mrs. Martha Patterson, and her sister, Mrs. Mary Stover, were to relieve their mother, as mistress of the White House. A private tutor had been engaged for the children old enough to enter school. These were Mary Belle, a beautiful young girl, and Andrew Johnson Patterson; and then the Stovers, Sara, Lillie S. and Andrew Johnson—rollicking, wholesome, fun-loving urchins, devoted to "Grandpa" and "Grandma" and always out for fun and sport.[1] Indeed these

[1] *Recollections of Col. W. H. Crook; Saturday Evening Post,* June 18, 1910.

little ones soon drew their over-worked grandparent out of himself.[2] As a result of the care of his wife and daughters, and to the exercise he received in his drives and tramps with the children, the President grew fit and strong, and by the coming of winter was in excellent health. To Rock Creek Park, to Pierce's Mill, and now and then to Silver Spring, the home of Frank P. Blair in Maryland, Grandpa and the children frequently drove. Weather and duties permitting, the President's carriage, running over with children, could be seen wending its way into the country for a picnic frolic. The little ones, pulling off shoes and stockings, as the officer of the White House writes, would "wade in the soft waters of Rock Creek, skate flat stones over its surface, fish for frogs, minnows and water bugs," while the President "would wander through the woods, enjoying their happiness. . . . When twilight closed in and the merry party, with a carriage filled with wild flowers, moss and lichens, would return to the White House, the little ones would hasten to Grandma's room with their wonderful adventures. No one in all the world was quite like Grandma, with her sweet gentle ways, her simplicity, patience, common sense, and never failing sympathy. Though frail in body, the little woman, as she quietly knitted or crocheted in her corner, was the center of the household. To the guiding hand and mind of this motherly old lady was due a remarkable fact. Three families lived together under one roof without friction or disputes for nearly four years. This may sound extraordinary—it is extraordinary—but it is true. For example if one of the boys or girls would suddenly shout, 'Come along and have a roll!' all the rest of them would jump up with an answering shout and off they would romp to the slopes south of the White House, where they would throw themselves down on the green turf and roll over and over, laughing and whooping like a lot of wild Indians." [3]

Mrs. Eliza Johnson's influence over her husband was boundless. So devoted were they, "they seemed as two souls and

[2] *Century*, Vol. LXXXV, p. 440; Colonel W. H. Crook (Disbursing Officer of the White House), *Through Five Administrations*, pp. 88-90.
[3] *Through Five Administrations*, p. 90.

minds merged as one." "The nearest approach to ideal married life I've ever seen or known," said the officer of the White House, "was in the case of Andrew Johnson and his wife, and yet they were as unlike temperamentally as was possible for two human beings to be." "She looked after everything for him—his room, diet and dress." In fact, she was "an angel of a wife." [4] In the matter of dress President Johnson "was particular to the point of fastidiousness—wearing a frock coat, a stiff collar, well-fitting boots and carefully cut trousers." The newspaper reporters, of course, sought to interview the President's wife, but got little satisfaction. "We are plain people from Tennessee," she quietly observed, "temporarily in a high place, and you must not expect too much of us in a social way." This simple speech found its way into the hearts of men everywhere and, we may be sure, did not detract from the popularity of her husband. In such an atmosphere there was no place for pretense and "airs." Simple living, industry and economy, as in the old Tennessee home, was the life of the White House. Mrs. Patterson, real head of the establishment because of her mother's illness, gave close attention to household duties. She purchased two jersey cows, installed them on the premises, and supplied the family with milk and butter. Not conceited because of the high place they filled, they were just normal folk, regardful of the poor and the humble, and, as singular as it may sound, they were ever longing to be back again in Tennessee, at the Dan Stover place or in the old home in Greeneville, overlooking the mountains.

"Crook," Mrs. Johnson would say to the disbursing officer, "it's all very well for them who like it, but I don't like this public life at all. I often wish the time would come when we could return to where I feel we best belong." Sometimes the dear soul, laying aside needlework and book—for she was a great reader and of the best literature—would wander down to the kitchen, "as though she wished to have a hand in making the doughnuts and pies!" "Her kindness to those in distress was unusual; inquiries, delicacies, flowers, she constantly sent to the sick and needy." White House domestics, when taken

[4] *Bookman*, Vol. XXXIV, p. 399.

sick, were to be treated "just as members of the household."
When Slade, the old and infirm colored butler, grew ill he was
given every attention and at his humble burial the President
of the United States was a sincere mourner.[5]

One afternoon, as the President's carriage was returning
from a drive through Rock Creek Park, a summer thunder-
storm broke; rain fell in sheets and thunders rolled. By the
roadside a woman, poor and ragged and dripping wet, with a
babe in her arms, was making her way towards town. The
President, discovering her plight, stopped the carriage, and
the poor creatures were stored away in a seat, fronting his
own. At Boundary Street, between Fourteenth and Fifteenth,
mother and babe were delivered at their humble home. Reaching the White House, the President issued orders for a hot
whiskey toddy to be served to the rain-soaked coachman.[6]

With customs and manners so unconventional, so simple and
democratic, one might imagine the dignity and traditions of
the White House would suffer. The contrary is true. With
one voice the people of America acclaimed the Roman mother
and her daughters. Always they dressed well, appeared well
and maintained the best traditions of their exalted station.
Their gowns were of "simple but rich material" and were constructed "by the best dressmakers in Washington." "The
honor and dignity of the nation lost nothing in the hands of
these plain people from Tennessee."[7] They were every inch
women, "kindly and gracious," fully understanding "what was
required of the President of the United States and equal to
any emergency." "One of the finest characters that ever
graced the White House was Eliza Johnson, wife of Andrew
Johnson."[8] A Senator who knew the family intimately declared: "All parties agree that the White House was never
more gracefully kept and presided over than by Mrs. Patterson"—a perfect lady, a model of a Republican mistress of the
White House.[9] Of such a helpmeet and such daughters An-

[5] A. H. Stephens, *Recollections*, p. 536.
[6] Johnson MS.
[7] *Independent*, Vol. LVI, p. 727.
[8] *Cosmopolitan*, Vol. XXX, p. 410.
[9] Senator Doolittle in an Address in 1869.

drew Johnson "was proud and justly so." "More sensible or unpretending women never occupied the White House." [10]

The President would informally call on members of his cabinet and on the Blairs and other friends. He also attended a reception given by General Grant. Now that the war was over, society had undergone a complete transformation. At the President's receptions "aristocracy and democracy were alike represented and titled dames and republican wives and mothers were scarcely distinguishable in the crowded rooms of the presidential mansion. The ladies displayed a large variety of toilets from the plain parlor to the extreme evening or party dress. There were velvets, satins, pearl, lavender, crimson, garnet and black silks in profusion, as well as tulles and tarletons. These adorned with diamonds and other ornaments, with their neatly arranged coiffures, presented an attracting and fascinating scene." [11]

On these occasions the President, dressed in plain black with straw-colored gloves, usually stood near the entrance in the Blue Room. Mrs. Patterson and Mrs. Stover, on the right and rear of the President, assisted in receiving the guests. Mrs. Patterson, attired in black velvet, low neck and short sleeves, with illusion bodice and her hair ornamented with flowers and back curls; Mrs. Stover wearing a rich black silk trimmed with lace, with hair tastefully arranged and back curls. The Cabinet usually remained in the Blue Room. Noted promenaders were conspicuous. Sometimes one would observe Governor Sharkey and lady, the latter dressed in rich pearl-colored silk, long trail with velvet border and trimmings, "with steel edging, with an elaborate coiffure;" or Mr. and Mrs. General Banks, the latter "attired in rich salmon silk with pink flowers, low neck and trail and coral necklace." Frederick Bruce and Lady Thurlow attended a reception, and Señor Romero, the Mexican Minister, was seen "escorting the lady of President Juarez, who was attired in lavender silk richly trimmed, with long trail and diamonds; Hon. L. D. Campbell also had a Mexican lady on his arm. She was dressed in a blue silk, long trail,

10 McCulloch, *Men and Measures*, p. 406.
11 Singleton, *Story of the White House*, p. 107.

and fluted trimmings round the bottom, with diamond pin.
Mr. Labantree, of the State Department, also escorted a Mexican lady, who attracted considerable attention. The brunette
countenances and well-formed features of these Montezuma
ladies furnished a contrast with the American ladies, and made
them the center of attraction." [12] "The President never appeared to be in better spirits than when mingling with the
people," the reporters noted; and "the ladies of his household
received the guests in the same frank and unostentatious manner that has heretofore gained for them the respect of all
visitors."

When Queen Emma of Hawaii, widow of King Kamehameha
IV, visited Washington on her way home from a trip around the
world, the President gave her a reception. "She arrived with
her suite at half past eight o'clock, and was received by Mr.
Stanbery, the Attorney-General, who escorted her to the Red
Room, where the President, Mrs. Johnson, Mrs. Patterson,
Mrs. Stanbery, Secretary and Mrs. Gideon Welles and other
ladies and gentlemen were assembled. The dusky queen was
dressed in a rich black silk with low neck, a broad mauve ribbon
across her breast, a jet necklace and a diamond brooch. A
jet tiara and white lace veil were worn upon her head. Contrary to custom, the doors of the White House were thrown
open to as many as could be accommodated in the reception
room, so that all who pleased might witness the ceremony." [13]

In December 1865 Congress appropriated thirty thousand
dollars for the renovation and refurnishing of the White
House. In a few months the newly decorated rooms were on
view for the first time. As the weather was most inclement, the
new carpets were prudently covered, for the house warming
which then took place. On this occasion Mrs. Patterson and
Mrs. Stover were dressed "with unexceptionable taste and elegance and very nearly alike. Each wore a black corded silk
dress with tight-fitting basques, splendidly embroidered with
a border of leaves of a new and exquisite pattern. The em-
broidery extended around the skirt a little distance below the

12 *Ibid.*, p. 108.
13 *Ibid.*, p. 109.

waist, and descended in a double border down the front of the skirt, widening into a graceful curve on either side, and continued in a deep border near the bottom of the skirt. Mrs. Patterson's dress was embroidered with narrow white braid forming a vine of leaves bordered with white on the black ground of the dress. Mrs. Stover's dress was embroidered in violet silk, the leaves of the vine being worked solid. Each of the ladies wore narrow collars fastened with a brooch. Mrs. Patterson had a spray of mignonette in her hair, and Mrs. Stover's hair was ornamented with a white japonica." [14]

The renovation of the Mansion and the decoration of the rooms had been under the supervision of Mrs. Patterson, and the work of improvement was thorough and on a most extensive scale. "The ceilings have been newly frescoed," the newspapers announced, "the heavy cornices newly painted and gilded; the walls which were formerly covered with paper of red velvet and gold, are now laid off in panel work, surrounded by a rich border of black and gold, giving to the room a most brilliant effect; the furniture has been revarnished and freshly covered with flowered silk, of a color corresponding with the name of the room; the mirrors have been regilded, and some that were of a rather ancient pattern have been replaced with others of a new and elegant design." As elegant as the new mansion was, the President insisted that the masses should be admitted without restraint; and so dense became the crowd it was uncontrollable. Both policemen and soldiers were kept on duty at the door of the Red Room "to prevent the visitors from rushing through." Nevertheless, his family were swept away "and carried on with the living tide to the Blue Room, where the throng was as dense as elsewhere."

Soon after the Civil War an orgy of speculation and extravagance set in. Gambling in stocks, bonds and other securities, wildcat and fraudulent schemes, were the order of the day. Favorable legislation was necessary for the success of these schemes and lawmakers and other officials were presented with rich gifts. Now this practice was specially distasteful to President Johnson. What though gifts were accepted

[14] Singleton, *Story of the White House*, p. 110.

by Admirals and Generals? Each man must judge of such matters for himself. Therefore, when certain wealthy persons in New York presented President Johnson with a coach and four, of the value of six thousand dollars, he returned the gift. True to form, as in the '40's when he sent back to the Government an overpayment of three hundred and twenty-six dollars for services as a committeeman in the investigation of Thomas Corwin, he would have nothing he had not earned.

If in little things Andrew Johnson was the hero of an hour, much more so was he in his great office as President. During all his days he had stood for economy in government. In 1858, when fighting the Jefferson Davis bill to increase the army, he denounced "extravagance, profligacy, corruption, and improper appropriation of the people's money." In the progress of events it had come to pass that he was now in position to carry out his teachings, and to tighten the purse strings. To this task he set himself. Public expenditures were cut at the rate of a million a day. The army and the navy were reduced as fast as the disturbed times permitted. The civil list was purged of idlers and supernumeraries.[15]

In April 1865, when Johnson became President, it must be said he was far from popular. Indeed, he was suspected and disliked. To the triumphant North it seemed a cruel paradox that their great and good President Lincoln had been murdered by a southern man and succeeded by a southern man from a slaveholding state. But this feeling of resentment and distrust did not long continue. In a short time suspicion and dislike passed away. Nearly every class began to find something admirable in "Old Andy Johnson," the Tennessee tailor. First, the North was propitiated. The progress with which northern prisons were filled with southern rebels and the speedy trial and execution of President Lincoln's assassins did much to appease northern sentiment and to mollify the Radicals. In fact, it was at first feared that the President would be too severe in punishing rebels. Ben Wade advised the President not to execute more than "a round dozen of the rebels." Even before Mr. Lincoln was buried a caucus of the Radicals had

[15] Rhodes, Vol. V, p. 533.

been called and a free exchange of opinions made. Ben Wade was delighted. On leaving the caucus, he turned to the President and exclaimed, "Johnson, by the gods we have faith in you; there will be no further trouble with rebels now."[16]

Even the South, where a few years before Andy Johnson's name was a synonym for hate, and where he was burned in effigy by a negro slave, was soon joining in the chorus of praise. His efforts to rehabilitate that section, his amnesty proclamation, his proclamation looking to the readmission of North Carolina and other states into the Union, the generous sentiments expressed to visiting southern delegations—"I love the southern people, I know them to be brave and honorable, I know that they have accepted the situation and will come back into the Union in good faith"—were winning for him golden opinions among southern people. War democrats, of course, were delighted, and hailed the President as one of their own faith. He was ruling the nation wisely and well. Such leaders as Thurlow Weed, Frank P. Blair, Senator Dixon, Senator Doolittle, Reverdy Johnson, and S. S. Cox were loud in praise of the President's course. Old line Union Whigs, Seward, Raymond, General Thomas Ewing, Sherman and Fessenden joined in the chorus.[17]

People praised the President's "dignity, his patriotism and his high purpose." They recalled "the golden opinions he had won as Military Governor of Tennessee.[18] Southern legislatures, where a few months before Andrew Johnson had been denounced as "the drunken Tennessee tailor" and "the vulgar renegade," now vied with each other in praise of him. His administration was "wise and patriotic"; it was "marked by liberality and magnanimity." "By the sense of justice he was attaching the South to the Union by cords stronger than triple steel." "He was endeavoring to stem the tide of fanaticism."[19] Secretary Seward's proclamation of December 18, that three-fourths of the States had ratified the Thirteenth Amendment

---

[16] Most of Johnson's threats were made while he was Vice-president.—Schouler, Vol. VII, Chap. I.

[17] Flanders, *Observations*, etc., p. 6.

[18] McCall, *Stevens*, p. 250; *American Historical Review*, Vol. XI, p. 575.

[19] New York *Tribune*, December 8, 1865, *ibid.*, December 1.

and that slavery had been forever stamped out, was hailed with joy unspeakable. "Glory to God" was on every tongue. The President came in for his share of the praise. Because of his activity, and that of his provisional southern Governors the result, it was conceded, had come about. South Carolina was the first southern State to ratify the amendment. This was on November 13, 1865. Then followed North Carolina on December 1, Alabama on December 2, and Georgia on December 6. The requisite three-fourths being thus secured, slavery was abolished; abolished, too, by the aid of southern slaveholding states. Not only was slavery abolished, but at President Johnson's request, if not command—for it was no less than a command—all debts in aid of rebellion were canceled and Secession ordinances repealed.

In May the President had appointed provisional Governors for the seceding states. By them conventions had been called. Legislatures were elected, Congressmen and Senators chosen, and civil government restored. The South was pulling herself together. On December 6, when Congress met, nearly every southern state was represented. Southern Senators and Congressmen were standing at the doors and knocking for admission. Though the overzeal and impetuosity of many Southern leaders, especially in South Carolina and Mississippi, had greatly embarrassed the President's work of rehabilitation, it had, nevertheless, proceeded, as he declared, "with more willingness and greater promptitude than under the circumstances could reasonably have been expected." His embarrassment had been of this kind. The Mississippi Legislature had insisted that Davis should be pardoned by the President; Perry, the Military Governor of South Carolina, had expressed sorrow and pain at having to bring his state back into the Union. Surely these were unwise utterances from rebels seeking favors! For the most part, however, the President's embarrassment came not from the obstinacy or opposition of southern rebels and northern copperheads—but from overpraise—from too much approval. "What business had rebels and copperheads praising a Union President?" northern Radicals were asking. When such papers as "The Copperhead" *World* changed front and began to praise Andrew Johnson, and when southern legislatures endorsed him, and southern rebels claimed him as their own, it was high time for lovers of the Union to beware.

Praise and applause, however, continued to fill the President's ears. "Take him all and all," said a Virginia delegate returning to Richmond in May, from an interview with the President, "I do not believe any proud monarch of Europe, whose race of kings by divine right has flourished a thousand years of time, has a clearer conception of his duties and knows better how to temper mercy with justice than Andrew Johnson of Tennessee." [20]   Of this portion of the President's life—the summer and autumn of 1865—a not too favorable historian asserts that "the President labored with industry, tact and patience to heal the great sectional wound and cure the body of the state." [21]   In truth, his words and acts merit this encomium for "he reasoned with and counseled his provisional Governors by turn . . . as he praised and congratulated them when they did well." [22]   "God grant that the southern people will see their true interest and the welfare of the whole country, and act accordingly," he wired to Governor Holden of North Carolina, urging the adoption of the Thirteenth Amendment. "I do hope the southern people will see the position they now occupy, and avail themselves of the favorable opportunity of once more resuming all their former relations to the Government," he telegraphed Governor Sharkey, in November. "If I know my own heart and every passion which enters it," he telegraphed Governor Perry, "my earnest desire is to restore the blessings of the Union and to tie up and heal every bleeding wound which has been caused by this fratricidal war." [23]

The President's course provoked not only the admiration of America but of Europe. Here was a man "generous and judicious" and with godlike attributes, one who knew "how to be forgiving to enemies." [24]   Not only had he issued a general amnesty proclamation, but had specially pardoned thousands

[20] Savage, p. 407.
[21] Oberholtzer, Vol. I, p. 143.
[22] *Ibid.*, Vol. I, p. 143.
[23] *Senate Executive Document, Thirty-ninth Congress, First Session*, No. 26, pp. 221, 234, 254.
[24] Schouler, Vol. VI, p. 32.

excepted from its provisions—pardoned the men who had
abused and insulted him, set a price upon his head, called him
a renegade, and sought to destroy him.   Count A. de Gasparin, in an open letter, "bowed before the wisdom of such a
policy. . . . It is simple like everything that is great, it is
resolute like everything that is good." [25]   Beecher from his exacting pulpit exclaimed, "Thus far the Lord hath led us—I
have faith in Andrew Johnson."

In the midst of so much praise President Johnson delivered
his first message to Congress.   This remarkable state paper astonished every one.   How was it possible for an illiterate man
to conceive such generous thoughts and to express himself so
smoothly and so aptly?   This message indeed "put a climax to
the President's popularity."   "Nothing better has been produced since Washington was chief and Hamilton his financier,"
exclaimed Charles Francis Adams, generous as the Adamses
ever are.   "It was smooth, eloquent and dignified," all agreed.[26]
Metropolitan Dailies—the *Times* and the *Tribune* likewise
praised the message.   "It is full of wisdom," they wrote.

In language plain, but not offensive, the President restated
his views of what constitutes a state and of the relation of a
state to the Union.   "The sovereignty of a state is the language of the Confederacy," he asserted, "and not the language
of the Constitution. . . . Though the people ordained and
established the Constitution the states had to give their assent. . . . The best security for the permanent existence of the
states is the supreme authority of the Constitution. . . . So
long as the Constitution endures the states will endure, the
destruction of one is the destruction of the other; the preservation of one is the preservation of the other."   Dealing with
the newly liberated slaves, the President enjoined "patience
and no hasty assumption that the two races can not live side by
side with mutual benefit and good will." . . . "Let nothing be
wanted," he urged, "to make a fair experiment."   If dissatis-

[25] *Loyal Publications, Serial Number 87, No. 3;* Pierce, *Sumner,* Vol. IV,
p. 250.
[26] *Historical Review,* Vol. XI, p. 575; Cf. *Historical Review,* Vol. XI, p. 951
for a criticism of the "frivolous manner" in which Professor Dunning disposes of Johnson's "plagiarism."

fied, let the negro migrate but let migration and emigration be purely voluntary. "I know that sincere philanthropy is earnest," he admitted, "for the immediate realization of its remotest ends, but time is always an element, in reform. . . . Our Government springs from, and it was made for the people, not the people for the government." Monopolies, perpetuities and class legislation are "contrary to the genius of a free people and ought not to be allowed." For the reason that the system of slavery created "a monopoly of labor," this was the inherent defect of that system. "When labor was the property of the capitalists the white man was excluded from employment or had but the second best chance of finding it; and the foreign emigrant turned away from a region where his position would be so precarious." With great satisfaction the President advised Congress that military rule in the South had ended, that steps had been taken to return the states to their constitutional relations to the Union by participation in the high office of amending the Constitution. "The adoption of the amendment reunites us beyond all power of disruption. It heals the wound that is still imperfectly closed; it removes forever the element which has so long perplexed and divided the country; it makes of us once more a united people, renewed and strengthened, bound more than ever to mutual affection and support."

"The amendment to the Constitution being adopted," he reminded Congress that "it would remain for the states, whose powers have been so long in abeyance, to resume their places in the two branches of the national legislature, and thereby complete the work of restoration. Here it is for you fellow citizens of the Senate and for you, fellow citizens of the House of Representatives, to judge each of you for yourselves of the elections, returns, and qualifications of your own numbers."

On December 6 when this message was read President Johnson had rounded out less than eight months of his term. By that date or shortly thereafter, nearly every southern state had called conventions, as I have said, elected Senators, Congressmen, Governors, and other civil officers, and were functioning, with little aid from the general government. Though the writ of *habeas corpus* was still suspended and troops were kept at some parts of the South, to assist in preserving order, yet the body of the people, lately at war with the North, had signified an earnest desire to come back home. Belying the old prophecy that the South could not be brought back into the Union against its will—could not be pinned to the Union with bayonets—the southern people had shown unmistakably that, instead of hating, they loved and respected the Union, and longed to get back into the fold. A few unrepentant rebels had fled to South America, to Mexico and to Europe, but scarcely one in a thousand remained. Afflicted with an attack of nostalgia, they were applying to "Andy Johnson," their ancient enemy, for pardon, and returning to the land of their birth, to the old flag, and to the Union.

While these mighty changes were taking place—shackles broken from the limbs of four million slaves, southern states rehabilitated and knocking at the doors of Congress—what of Andrew Johnson, the captain of the craft? How did he conduct himself? Had the office of President gone to his head? Were his thoughts of self or of country? From the office of Military Governor of Tennessee he had come out poorer than he went in. But now greater opportunities presented themselves, would he reveal his true character at last? Would he prove himself to have been a demagogue, "feather his nest," and build up a political party to boost himself, or would he tread the winepress alone? The answer is not difficult. To a delegation of South Carolinians in October he said, "If I could be instrumental in restoring the Government to its former relations, and see the people once more united, I should feel that I had more than filled the measure of my ambition. If I could feel that I had contributed to this in any degree my heart would be more than gratified, and my ambition full." [27]

Regardless of self he stood, like Lincoln, four-square to every wind, the Union and the Constitution his only guide. No Union, no Constitution; no Constitution, no Union. "I want the people of the world to know," said he to a Virginia delegation, "that I stand where I did of old battling for the

[27] New York *Tribune*, October 14, 1865.

Constitution and the Union of these United States. . . .
While I dread the disintegration of the states I am equally
opposed to centralization or consolidation of power here, under
whatever guise or name," and "if the issue is forced, I shall
fight it to the end." [28]

[28] If Johnson had favored the Fourteenth and Fifteenth Amendments in
1866 civil war would have resulted. It required two years of negro misrule
to convince the North that the negro was unfitted for governmental action.—
Moore and Foster, *Tennessee*, p. 517.

Johnson Is Crowned King, as Wade Predicted

CHAPTER X

THAD STEVENS POCKETS CONGRESS

Radicals in the Thirty-ninth Congress were greatly alarmed. Would it be possible to head off the aggressive President? If not, they feared direful results. The Republican party would be defeated by a combination of southern Rebels and northern Copperheads, and the negro would remain a slave. Perhaps the national debt would be repudiated and bonds issued to compensate the slave-holders. The bare thought of these things had put Thad Stevens and Charles Sumner in a towering passion. "Rebellion has vaulted into the saddle," said Sumner. "If something isn't done," Wade wrote Sumner in the early fall, "the people will crown Johnson king before Congress meets. So much success," he complained, "will reconcile the people to anything."

In April Wade and Sumner, after interviews with Johnson, had been sure he would coöperate and be as unrelenting as could be wished. But Thad Stevens was doubtful—Johnson did not so impress him. Early in the summer he wrote the President from Philadelphia, "I have not found a single person who approves of your policy! Wait for Congress." During the summer "a campaign of misrepresentation was begun to discredit Presidential reconstruction, to keep alive war hatred and to build up a radical organization." [1] In February 1865 the doctrine was spread in the West that the Southern States were conquered territories. They should be held as such "as a public example," "for the dignity and safety of the Government," "as an act of justice to the freemen and the loyal Southern whites, and to protect the national debt from repudiation." [2] At Dartmouth College the Phi Beta Kappa address, dealing with reconstruction problems, called loudly

[1] Fleming, *Sequel of Appomattox*, p. 83.
[2] John Y. Smith, *Address*, pamphlet.

307

for action in favor of negro suffrage. "No waiting, but *now*, waiting means no action."[3] "Shall the horrors of Salisbury and Andersonville prisons, the murdering of innocent prisoners," it was asked, "be forgotten and forgiven to unrepentant or lip-serving, lying rebels, whose oath is as naught under compulsion"? Stevens in Pennsylvania was teaching a similar doctrine.

Senator Morton, then a friend of the President, "repelled the insinuation that Andrew Johnson was disloyal or had left the Republican party." "The President was going to submit his acts to Congress," said Morton.[4] Chase, however, wrote that Andrew Johnson's face "was set as flint against the good cause." Charles Kirkland, in an open letter to Peter Cooper, made a list of the rebels to be hung: Jefferson Davis and his cabinet; also Judge Campbell and two members of Buchanan's cabinet. A baker's dozen in all. The Chicago *Tribune* threatened to convert the South into "a frog pond" unless it treated the colored man better.[4a] In this state of confused public opinion Thaddeus Stevens undertook to maneuver the Republican party into a compact phalanx. In the radical House he felt safe, but the Senate was more conservative and troublesome. In that body there were four groups. Radicals, led by Sumner of Massachusetts, Wade of Ohio, and Howe of Wisconsin; Conservative Republicans of whom Fessenden of Maine, Grimes of Iowa, and Trumbull of Illinois were types; administration Republicans, consisting of such leaders as Doolittle of Wisconsin, Cowan of Pennsylvania, and Dixon of Connecticut; and Democrats led by Johnson of Maryland, Guthrie of Kentucky, and Hendricks of Indiana.

On Friday December 1, 1865, Stevens and about thirty radical associates held a caucus in Washington to lay plans to thwart the President and revive the Republican party. The caucus appointed a committee, with Stevens as chairman, to prepare resolutions to bind each House not to admit southern

---

[3] A. Crosby, *Phi Beta Kappa Address*, pamphlet.
[4] *Globe, Second Session Fortieth Congress*, p. 726.
[4a] A joint resolution of the Tennessee Legislature proposed that nine "Rebels" be put to death: Davis, Mason, Hunter, Toombs, Cobb, Benjamin, Slidell, Lee and Breckinridge.—Moore and Foster, *Tennessee*, p. 531.

representatives till the other House had come to the same conclusion.[5]   On the next evening, Saturday, December 2, the
regular Republican caucus was held and a committee, with
Stevens again as chairman, was appointed to consider what
should be done with the southern Representatives.   Stevens,
quietly and without alluding to the previous caucus, proposed
his caucus resolution and it was adopted unanimously.   Such
stupidity as the astute Raymond, serving on Stevens' committee, was guilty of in not fighting this bottling-up of the
conservative Republicans was hardly ever witnessed.[6]

On Monday, December 4, when Congress met, the floors, the
ante-rooms and galleries were filled with spectators to witness
the return of the "erring Southern Sisters" to the Union.
But they were disappointed.   When the roll was called Edwin
McPherson, the clerk, omitted the names of the newly elected
Congressmen from the South.   Horace Maynard, the Tennessee loyalist, Congressman elect from his Union District,
holding in his hand a certificate of election from Governor
Brownlow, addressed the clerk and asked that his name be
called.   The clerk turned a deaf ear, though Maynard had represented his district in Congress during the early years of the
war and had been a delegate to the 1864 Baltimore Convention
which nominated Lincoln and Johnson.   "Does the clerk decline to hear me?" Maynard shouted.   The clerk adhered to his
ruling.

Brooks of New York, the minority leader, insisted that
southern members should be admitted; that as the South had
complied with the prerequisites to admission as promulgated
by the President, Congress could not exclude them.   "If Tennessee is not in the Union," said Brooks, "and has not been in
the Union, and is not a loyal State, and the people of Tennessee are aliens and foreigners to the Union, by what right
does the President of the United States usurp a place in the
White House?"   This embarrassing question did not seem to
trouble Congress in the least; in fact, it refused to hear Maynard in his own behalf.   At this stage the "blue-eyed, light,

[5] Kendrick, *Committee of Fifteen*, p. 139.
[6] *Sequel of Appomattox*, p. 126.

sunny-haired clerk" turned to Stevens for further orders. "I wish to know when the matter of admitting southern members will be taken up," he inquired. "I have no objection to answering the gentleman," said the audacious Stevens. "I will press the matter at the proper time." [7]

This cut-and-dried program having been carried out, and the roll-call exhibiting 176 members present—a quorum without the presence of the Southerners—the speaker, "Smiling" Schuyler Colfax, foreshadowed what the Radicals were going to do to Andrew Johnson's reconstructed southern states. "The duty of Congress," said the Speaker, "is as plain as the sun's pathway in the Heavens; the door having been shut in the rebel faces, it is still to be kept bolted. . . . Establish a republican form of government and put the rebel states anew on such a basis of enduring justice as to guarantee every safeguard and protection to the loyal people." These words provoked loud applause.[8] That which Lincoln had done in Tennessee, Louisiana, and Arkansas, and Johnson in the other southern states to restore civil government was to be wiped out and everything done "anew."

Meanwhile "Old Thad Stevens," his wig awry, was sitting complacently in his place. Presently the House was organized and he offered his caucus resolution. Dawson of Pennsylvania moved to defer action till the President's message was received. This was promptly voted down.[9] Niblack of Indiana moved that pending the question of "admitting persons claiming seats in Congress, such persons be entitled to the privilege of the floor." This was likewise voted down. The Stevens resolution was carried by vote of 129 to 35. Thereby a Joint Select Committee of Fifteen was provided, who were to inquire into "the condition of the so-called Confederate States and to report by bill if any were entitled to be represented in Congress; . . . and until that time no member to be received into either house." A similar resolution was offered in the Senate by Charles Sumner of Massachusetts. The Senate, however, refused to adopt

7 Oberholtzer, Vol. I, p. 151 and citations.
8 Blaine, Vol. II, p. 112.
9 *Ibid.*

the last provision, admitting members only upon a joint vote. William Pitt Fessenden, a wise and just Senator from Maine, killed this unusual provision. He advocated the Anthony motion to strike it out. This motion was passed by the Senate and accepted by the House.

Thus early did Congress put itself on record that the reconstruction of southern states was the business of Congress and not of the President. Thereby a contest was precipitated "that transcended any in the history of the country." [10] Congress became a one-man-power Congress and every resolution relating to southern affairs had to be referred to this committee, there to be buried "as in a tomb." The Committee of Fifteen became a "Central Directory," as Senator Cowan declared, "carrying in its girdle the keys to the Union, without which the erring Sisters could not enter." Four years of war had been waged to bring the seceding states back into the Union, "a four years' war was to be waged to keep them out. . . . By this political dexterity of the Radicals no opportunity was afforded the Conservatives to get together and support the President," though "Congress at that time was in a frame of mind to do so." [11]

The Joint Select Committee consisted of six Senators and nine Congressmen. Its head, however, was Thad Stevens. The members of the committee were Senators Fessenden, Howard, Harris, Grimes, Johnson and Williams; and Representatives Stevens, Washburne, Morrill, Grider, Bingham, Conkling, Boutwell, Blow and Rogers. In the cause of the negro, Stevens, with the aid of Sumner, was an ideal leader. Their aim was to abolish all racial prejudices and distinctions.[12] "In a moment's time the civilization of two centuries" in the South was to be uprooted.[13] Looking upon the Constitution as a covenant with hell, nothing to Stevens or Sumner was wrong or "unconstitutional which advanced the cause of freedom." In behalf of the negro, Sumner was a pernicious philanthropist, a

---

[10] McCall, *Stevens*, p. 250.
[11] *Sequel of Appomattox*, p. 121.
[12] Haynes, *Sumner*, p. 317.
[13] Blaine, Vol. II, p. 80.

mere theorist. Personally he cared nothing for the colored man.

Not so Thad Stevens. "He had no objection to the closest contact with negroes." [14] To destroy Copperheadism, to re-build the Republican party, to establish freedom for all men, and to punish the slaveholding aristocrats, confiscating their estates and giving to each freeman "forty acres and a mule,"— this was Stevens' program. Fierce, "vindictive and unscrupulous," "bitter in speech and possessing in a supreme degree the faculty of making ridiculous those who opposed him," Stevens "had a countenance of iron," and the tongue of Voltaire.[15] Hitherto "a party leader, hereafter he became the dictator of the nation."

Thus by the partisan leadership of Thaddeus Stevens were the labors of Johnson and his cabinet wiped out. Though the seceding states had complied with the President's demand, adopted the Thirteenth Amendment, repealed Secession ordinances and abolished war debts, they were not to come in the Union until Congress gave consent. They were to be deemed *States* sufficient to adopt the Thirteenth Amendment, but no further. History was repeating itself. In 1863 Lincoln had done in Louisiana precisely what Johnson was now doing. He had established a form of civil government, formed the nucleus of self-governing states, and relied upon the magnanimity and manhood of the Southerners to deal fairly and honestly by the dependent and newly manumitted slave. For this, in 1864, the Radicals in Congress assailed Lincoln and endeavored to tear down his work.

"A President has no authority to admit rebel states into the Union," said Congress in 1864 as in 1865. "This is the work of Congress alone." The Wade-Davis bill of February 1864 attacking Lincoln passed both Houses, as I have stated, but was defeated by President Lincoln's pocket-veto. Lincoln though

---

[14] Fleming, *Sequel to Appomattox*, p. 125; J. G. deR. Hamilton, *Reconstruction*, p. 81. On his death bed Mr. Stevens was attended by colored people, and was then baptized by one of them; his honorary pallbearers were colored and a majority of his active pallbearers; his "housekeeper" was a negress.—Stewart, *Reminiscences*, p. 205. By his Will, he was buried in a cemetery with the colored people.—Last chapter of Woodburn's *Stevens*.

[15] Fleming, *op. cit.*

"not wedded to any particular form of reconstruction," was not willing to surrender to Congress. The work of the loyal men of Louisiana should not be wiped out. In November 1864 at the polls Henry Winter Davis, author of these attacks on Lincoln, was defeated and Lincoln triumphed. It is interesting to speculate upon what might have happened if the radical Wade-Davis bill, though, as a matter of fact, it was not at all radical, had become the law. It did not enfranchise the negro. Nevertheless, had it become law, might not the negro have fared better at the hands of southern whites, than at the hands of the National Government? Though the Wade-Davis bill provided that the negro should be set free, yet the right to vote was limited to "the loyal *white* male citizen of the United States." If the returning Confederate soldier and not the negro had been put in control of the South, would not a more satisfactory system of reconstruction have resulted? [16]

Now President Johnson, with the approval of his cabinet, Secretary Stanton included, had followed Lincoln's "Louisiana Plan." The action of Congress, therefore, in repudiating his course and overturning civil governments in the South was a blow to him. Though he expected a fight with the Radicals, he did not expect a fight with moderates—these he counted on to support his policy. But a fight from every quarter had come and the Radicals had drawn the first blood. Particularly was the President wounded because it seemed to him Congress had ceased to be patriotic and become partisan, that it was more concerned in saving the Republican party than in saving the country. For, as the New York *Times* put it, "The very success of Johnson's policy proved to be one element of later weakness;—the Republicans were against him because the Democrats were for him."

I have stated that partisan politics defeated the program of reconstruction, but this is only partly true. Party politics alone could not have defeated a plan so far reaching and generous. In 1865 elemental forces were at work in our country. At that time the guns were just silenced. Hatred stirred the

[16] McDonald, *Documentary Source Book,* p. 482; Rice, *Sumner,* Vol. II, p. 441.

hearts of men; and Até was come "hot from hell." The passions of half a century had found vent in four years of war. Billions of property had been destroyed. Hundreds of thousands of men had been killed or wounded. The land was full of widows and orphans. These evils the North regarded as the work of southern rebels; men who had precipitated a useless and a bloody war, with slavery as its basis.[17] Even the gentlewomen of the North were asking vengeance on the rebel South. "Tell President Johnson," wrote Mrs. Doolittle to her son the Senator, "to be sure to have Jeff Davis tried and executed."[18] "God bless you, sir," wrote one correspondent to Johnson when he approved the hanging of Mrs. Surratt.

That the rebels who wrought this desolation and destruction were now knocking for admission to Congress, the North regarded as traitorous and wicked. To admit into Congress four Confederate generals, five Confederate colonels, six of the Confederate cabinet, and fifty-eight Confederate Congressmen, none of whom was able to take the oath of allegiance, seemed to the North unthinkable. And yet a situation of that kind confronted Congress. The case of Alex H. Stephens, late Vice-president of the Confederacy, was especially aggravating. Four months before he had been a prisoner at Fort Warren. Pardoned by the President, he waited not a moment to repent but returned to Georgia, was elected to the United States Senate, and was now asking admission—asking to govern the country he had been trying to destroy. To grant this request, said the North, would be stretching forgiveness to the breaking point.

This condition of affairs in the South, however, except in the Border States, was not only natural but unavoidable. War in the South during four years had become a test of manhood and of loyalty to home. The braver the fighter the truer the man. "The hope of the nation lies in the Confederate soldier," said Colonel W. H. Truman, in his report to the President in 1866. "From the returning soldier the people of the South are learning the lesson of charity and brotherhood, as the

[17] Rhodes, Vol. IV, p. 79.
[18] Oberholtzer, Vol. I, p. 19.

people of the north do from returning northern soldiers." [19] In the spring of 1865 Vice-president Johnson had shared this feeling of vengeance against "the head devils of the rebels." But when war hysteria wore off and he saw the true condition of the South and of the southern people, he ceased to regard them as conscious rebels or, except Davis and a few others, as criminals deserving punishment.

As one looks back on the summer of 1865, it must be said that there was much confused thinking and writing. Conservative papers which praised the President's course read something into his messages which was not there. They declared that his first message was non-committal and hence open to changes and to the "coöperation of Congress." The opposite was true. The message was final, and Johnson so intended. "The South must be Americanized," said the candid *North American Review*, attacking the message.[20] "The North is not to be cheated out of its victory." It is not "to be deluded by specious promises or by oaths taken to be broken." Though Andrew Johnson is "not a tool like Buchanan or a tyrant like Jackson," said Lowell, yet "the North is in no temper to submit to 'black Codes' or to the burning of negro schools"; the President "ought to have recommended negro suffrage in his message."

A genuine note of defiance came from abolitionists such as Wendell Phillips. When Johnson, in his message, failed to advocate full social and political freedom for the negro, Phillips delivered a blistering lecture. "The South Victorious," he tauntingly called it. When invited to Washington, he refused to go. He "would rather not breathe the same atmosphere with them," he declared.[21] "Slavery is being reëstablished by Congress and there is a specter walking over the country in its shroud. . . . If the President succeeds he shall write his name higher than Burr or Arnold."

Radicals were strengthened by the report of General Carl Schurz. This report was published and widely circulated. In

[19] Fleming, *Sequel of Appomattox*, Chap. I; Truman, *Report*.
[20] Vol. CII, p. 258.
[21] Oberholtzer, Vol. I, p. 159.

the summer of 1865 Schurz had been sent South by the President to ascertain conditions. The accomplished German had indicated to the President that he approved Presidential Reconstruction. After visiting portions of the South and consorting, it was claimed, mostly with Federal Bureau Agents and others hostile to the President's course, he made his report. There is "no loyalty among leaders or masses," he reported, "except such as consists in submission to necessity." By means of new legislation "the South is establishing a form of slavery like the old chattel slavery" and this "can only be prevented by a national law and by national control." The negro, according to Schurz's report, "cannot protect himself without suffrage and this the South will not of itself grant." To induce the South to grant suffrage "it must be made a condition precedent to admission." In 1872, it may be here stated, the versatile Schurz presided over the Greeley Convention, organized to defeat President Grant and disrupt the Republican party. "This is moving day," he then said. But he had then become "a southern man with southern ideas." In 1872 he was opposing the Republican party for doing that which in 1865 he had urged it to do—make the negroes the equal of the whites.[22]

General Grant, in his report, drew conclusions opposite to Schurz's and reported to the President accordingly. The General had also been requested by the President, while on duty in the South, to examine into affairs. Though his visit was not of such length as that of Schurz; he was satisfied "that the mass of the men of the South accept the situation in good faith —the right of a state to secede they regard as settled forever." In Grant's opinion "the officers of the Federal Bureau are a useless and dangerous set and should be dismissed and military officers substituted." The report of Major Truman, who traveled extensively over the South, was the fullest and most comprehensive of the three reports. Truman drew a wise distinction between patriotism and loyalty. He found and declared that the South was "thoroughly loyal." "To the disbanded regiments of the old rebel armies," he said, "I look with

22 *Reminiscences of Carl Schurz*, Vol. III, pp. 321-341.

great confidence as the best and altogether the most hopeful element of the South, the real basis of reconstruction and the material of worthy citizenship."

Radical leaders made a great ado over Carl Schurz's report and paid little attention to Grant's. Grant's report was meager, they said. Of Johnson's message accompanying Grant's report Sumner declared it was "like the white-washing message of Franklin Pierce with regard to the enormities of Kansas." This statement *Harper's* deprecated, declaring that the President was "patriotic and should be sustained." [23] With Schurz's report in hand, and a promiscuous mass of letters filled with negro outrages on his desk, Sumner admonished the Senate: "An angry God could not sleep while such things find countenance." He besought the President, if he was "not ready to be the Moses of an oppressed people not to become its Pharaoh."

The situation in the South in the winter of 1865 and 1866 was this. Mississippi, where negroes were in a majority and "were wandering around lazy, vicious and waiting for their forty acres and a mule," had enacted Black Codes. None of the other states had enacted such laws. But, as a none too friendly critic of Johnson's policy puts it, "this Mississippi legislation does not appear as far from what was natural and even necessary, as Mr. Stevens and his followers made it out." [24] As to disorders in the South in 1865 and 1866, "they were no more than were usual in the South and in new countries, except in Memphis and Mississippi." [25] It is also to be said that in 1865, when the Mississippi Black Code was enacted, the status of the negro was undefined; though he was not a slave he was not a citizen. The Black Codes "extended rather than restricted the negroes' rights." [26] "The Southern vagrant acts were quite similar to those in Maine, Rhode Island and Connecticut." [27] It is also pointed out by modern historians that

[23] *Harper's Weekly*, March 10, 1866.
[24] Burgess, *Reconstruction*, p. 53.
[25] Fleming, *Sequel to Appomattox*, p. 83.
[26] Woodrow Wilson, *History of the United States*, Vol. V, p. 20.
[27] As to the necessity for such laws, consult Herbert, *Reconstruction*, pp. 8-31; Fleming, *op. cit.*, p. 1; Rhodes, Vol. V, p. 556; Garner, *Reconstruction*, p. 116.

these codes were not enacted "from hate of the North but to protect Southern whites." Professor Hamilton also points out, that no reference, in the Congressional debates of 1865, to Black Codes was made.[28]

While Congress and the North were agitating themselves about the freedman—"God's image in ivory" as he was then called—Thad Stevens and his Directory sat complacent, playing for time. They knew that the impoverished South, overrun by armies, staggering under the race problem and outlawed by Congress, must soon break out into disorder and that this would play into the hands of the Radicals.

Conservative members of the committee like Fessenden were anxious to bring about reconstruction without going to the extent of negro enfranchisement and social equality, but they were over-ridden by the Radicals. From the first Sumner, the theorist, openly avowed his purpose to effect absolute equality of black and white. Later, when his bill guaranteeing such equality was defeated, "he hastened from the Senate to his home where his disappointment found vent in tears." [29] Stevens was more practical than Sumner. He fought each inch of ground for the negro, taking what he could get. As soon as one rampart was scaled Stevens moved to the next. First, freedom for the negro; next, protection through the Bureau; then, Civil Rights, to be followed by Military Rule, the Fourteenth Amendment and the Fifteenth—and, if he could have had his way, confiscation. Forward and ever forward the heroic old man pressed, till halted by an aroused public conscience.

In a speech on December 18, 1865, Stevens laid his cards on the table.[30] "The Republican party and it alone can save the Union," he declared. " 'Do you aver the party purpose?' some horror-stricken demagogue asks me. 'I do.' " Thus spoke the candid man. To save the country the Republican party must control Congress, and southern members must be excluded. If southern Representatives were admitted the Republican party

28 Herbert, p. 13: Pennsylvania, Ohio, Connecticut and other northern States in 1865 voted against negro suffrage.
29 Haynes, *Sumner*, p. 317.
30 Fleming, *Sequel*, p. 125.

might be defeated. In the Senate there were 39 Republicans and 11 Democrats, in the House 141 Republicans and 43 Democrats. To the Democrats must be added certain weak-kneed Republicans who were supporting President Johnson; such men as Dixon, Cowan, Doolittle and, at that time, Morton. If southern Representatives were admitted 22 Senators and 58 Congressmen would be added to the Democratic column. Thus Congress might pass under Democratic and Copperhead control.[31] That the negro should not count if he did not vote Stevens regarded as a truism. He averred that "the idea of a white man's government is as atrocious as the Dred Scott decision—a decision that has damned the late Chief Justice to everlasting fame and I fear everlasting fire."

While Congress was debating the loyalty of the South, while the press was full of it and it was the talk of every northern home, President Johnson had information unknown to the public. Into his ear were pouring the sorrows and the agony of Southerners from Texas to Maryland. To the White House they daily came. They admitted that the war had been a mistake, that the President had been right and, as General Lee afterwards testified before the Reconstruction Committee, but for the politicians no war would have taken place, that if the people could have settled the matter war would have been avoided. These visiting delegations told of scenes of desolation in the South. During the war every available dollar —trust funds included—had gone into Confederate securities and had been lost. "Everything to eat and everything to wear had been consumed. When the war ended, suddenly, there was nothing left but poverty and nakedness. Famine had followed and suffering beyond computation—the story of which could never be told." [32] In truth, the President was satisfied that the Secession element of the South was discredited beyond resurrection.

Judge Reade, the loyalist President of the 1865 North Carolina Convention, had sounded the keynote: "My friends," said he, in his opening address, "we are going home, we are going

---

[31] *Thirty-ninth Congress, First Session*, p. 74.
[32] Pike, *Prostrate State*, p. 117.

home." And so President Johnson concluded. Had the affairs of Tennessee, North Carolina, Kentucky, Maryland, West Virginia, Louisiana, Arkansas been left to the South, the North would never have regretted its generosity. Had those Border States been permitted to manage their own affairs without force or violence they would have "come back home." The names of fire-eating Secessionists, who once boasted of "having pulled the lanyard that fired the first gun at Sumter," would have been anathema. Andrew Johnson foresaw all this and, foreseeing, was willing to risk the affairs of the Nation in the hands of the loyal men of the South, though they had been in Confederate armies. Charles Sumner's assertion that such men were "not so far changed as to be fit associates," the President did not approve of.

And yet this must be said. Andrew Johnson himself had changed his views as to the punishment of rebels. He was, therefore, in no condition to blame those who—without his inside information—would not follow him. President Johnson, in December 1865, was not bloodthirsty as was Vice-president Johnson in April previous. At all events, there was an honest difference of opinion between patriotic men of the North and of the South on the subject of Reconstruction. Nevertheless the President, having worked faithfully and unselfishly, having won the epithet of "Angel of Light," undoubtedly expected an endorsement by Congress. The critical New York *Nation* had said of his policy and of his first message, "We do not know where to look in any part of the globe for a statesman to seize the points of so great a question and state them with so much clearness and breadth as this Tennessee tailor." "If the President were to commit to-morrow every mistake or sin which his enemies have feared," the *Nation* continued, "his plan of reconstruction would still remain the brightest example of humanity, self-restraint and sagacity ever witnessed—something to which history offers no approach." With such words of praise sounding in the President's ear the attitude of Congress grated harshly upon him.

On December 21 Senator Voorhees offered a resolution endorsing Johnson's policy and declaring "his message was able and patriotic," that he was entitled to thanks for his wise and patriotic efforts to restore civil government and "we pledge ourselves to aid and uphold him in his policy to give harmony, peace and unity to the country." Bingham offered a substitute, but Thad Stevens objected to any recognition of Andrew Johnson. Stevens asked that both the motion and the substitute go to his committee. On January 9 the motion of Voorhees was voted down and the House passed the Bingham substitute. It damned the President with faint praise. The House was satisfied, the resolution read, "that in the future as in the past the President will coöperate with Congress." From this time, January 9, 1866, "the relation of the dominant party in the North to President Johnson was changed; and any coöperation between him and Congress became extremely difficult." [33]

About this time an ominous situation arose in the cabinet: Stanton was looking one way and rowing another. That is, in the cabinet, he was supposed to be an out and out Johnson man; but with Sumner, he was an out and out Radical.[34] Sumner, Stanton's sponsor, was a frequent visitor to Secretary Welles. He accused Welles of misrepresenting New England sentiment. On the other hand Welles concludes that "Sumner was vain and egotistical." Though he boasted, said Welles, of having read everything "on what constitutes a Republican government, from Plato to the last French pamphlet," he was thoroughly "unpractical." [35] Sumner did not fail to pay his respects to Andrew Johnson, calling him "the utterly unprincipled and wicked author of incalculable woe to the country." [36]

[33] Blaine, Vol. II, p. 137.
[34] Welles, *Diary*, Vol. II, p. 394.
[35] *Ibid.*, Vol. II, p. 393.
[36] Haynes, *Sumner*, p. 213.

PART III: UNBOWED
1865 and After

CHAPTER I

PRESIDENTIAL RECONSTRUCTION

In a speech in lighter vein, in which Seward often indulged, he declared that Congress was quarreling with President Johnson though it had had its way. This reminded him of an irate individual who had won his lawsuit but continued out of sorts. "Damn it," the man said, "I won my case but I didn't win it my way." Mr. Seward's wish, in this matter, was undoubtedly father to his thought.

The differences between the President and Congress were basic. It must be admitted that Johnson opposed any fundamental change in the Constitution. Therefore, the Freedmen's Bureau bill and the Civil Rights bill he vetoed on principle. He saw clearly that the first of these bills was only the advance guard "of a long procession of others that were even more obnoxious to him. . . . He knew it was impossible to avoid the issue eventually and he determined to meet it firmly at the outset." [1] The President's mistake was in thinking the Freedmen's Bureau bill a measure for which the Radicals alone were responsible. "As a matter of fact there were very few Republicans who did not desire such modification of the President's policy as would give protection and assistance to the newly emancipated negroes." [2]

Congress would never have consented that the Southern States return to the Union by simply abolishing slavery, repealing secession ordinances, and repudiating confederate debts. Indeed, as we have already seen, Congress assailed Lincoln's Louisiana Plan of reconstruction. Certainly the committee, dominated by Thad Stevens, would have demanded more than the Louisiana plan and would have insisted that such demands be put in the Constitution. Even the conserva-

[1] *Congressional Globe*, February 21, 1866.
[2] Kendrick, *Committee of Fifteen*, p. 235.

tives on the committee, Fessenden, Bingham and Roscoe Conkling, insisted on radical changes in the Constitution. They would place the rights of the citizen in the keeping of the Federal Government. The radical members would go further. They would follow Stevens, not only reconstructing but punishing the South. An analysis of the committee shows it was composed of George S. Boutwell of Massachusetts, a cold and calculating fanatic, a professional politician dependent on office for a livelihood; Williams of Oregon, whom the acrimonious Welles designates as "a third-rate lawyer weak and corrupt"; Grimes of Iowa who, at that time, was quite radical; and Howard of Michigan, classed as a protégé of Zachary Chandler, one of the most vulgar and reckless of Radicals, in the vanguard of the extreme negrophiles. The other Republicans on the committee, some of them also radical, were of little importance in shaping reconstruction legislation. They were Morrill of Vermont, Washburne of Illinois, Blow of Missouri, and Harris of New York. The Democratic members were Johnson of Maryland, Grider of Kentucky, and Rogers of New York.[3] Johnson was the ablest of the Democratic Senators and was not a strict party man.

In addition to the negro question there was this vital issue between President and Congress: Should the southern states be restored under the old Constitution or should they be reconstructed? Should the old Union remain intact, that is, should each State be a judge of citizenship and of its local affairs? Or, should citizenship become national and the general government regulate the internal affairs of the states? In a word should America become a *Nation?* In this contest there could be no doubt as to where Andrew Johnson would stand. As in the past, he would be for the old Constitution and the old Union. The Constitution had been his pole star. By it he had guided his political course. It was too late to expect him to break away from the simple, uncomplicated Democratic doctrines of Jackson and take up the complex, paternalistic and federalistic principles of Adams. He had always opposed indirect taxation. Tariffs and other revenue taxes were his

[3] Kendrick, *Committee of Fifteen*, p. 190.

abomination. He maintained now as he had when in Congress that there were too many laws and that the general government should not supplant state governments. No more amendments to the Constitution were necessary, he thought, except one to change the basis of representation because of the liberation of the slaves under the Thirteenth Amendment.

In this course Johnson was not changing front. Mr. Seward was not "softening him," as it was charged. Neither were "southern aristocrats and rebels flattering him to reverse himself." In 1864, when Military Governor, he had urged Lincoln not to follow Stevens and Sumner but to treat the rebel states as states. His July 1861 resolutions defined the purposes of the war to be simple restoration, a principle which his message to Congress in December 1865 reaffirmed. In the White House, and in official life his associates were not rebels, not Southerners and not Copperheads. His friends and associates were Unionists and war men—many of them the attached friends of Lincoln. In February 1861, when Lincoln passed through Baltimore, and faced a threatening mob, he chose one man to stand by and guard his life. Armed to the teeth, the courageous Ward Hill Lamon, Lincoln's partner and "particular friend," was the man so chosen by Lincoln. Lamon soon became Johnson's particular friend also. Seward, Welles and McCulloch had been Lincoln's friends and advisers, they were also Johnson's. Browning was Lincoln's manager in Illinois, and he was put in Johnson's cabinet. So with the Blairs, Grant, Sherman, Cowan, Dixon, Ewing, Doolittle and others; they had been Lincoln's advisers, and they became Johnson's. President Johnson's fault was not that he had changed but that he had not changed and would not change. For this he was attacked, and so were all others who followed Lincoln. For refusing to follow the Radical program, at a later date, Henderson, Trumbull, Fessenden, Grimes, Ross, Fowler, Doolittle, Chase and others became, like Johnson, traitors, unworthy and discredited; [4] Ward Lamon was almost hounded to his death.

It must also be remembered that the struggle between the

[4] Schouler, Vol. VII, Chap. I.

President and Congress touched the latter at a vital point. President Johnson was endeavoring to supplant or to dwarf Congress. This Lincoln had done during the war, and this Congress was determined should not continue. Now that the war had ended, Congress meant to reassert itself, to put the President in his place and take the southern situation in hand. Moreover, the President's course in re-admitting the rebel states would be ruinous to the Republican party. This was a vital point. In December 1865 when the Thirteenth Amendment was adopted, setting free the slaves, a curious result followed. Twenty-nine additional Representatives were thereby added to the South.[5] The three-fifths rule no longer operated. If no other amendments were adopted, all the negroes would be counted in apportioning representation, and the amendment would work an injury of the party which passed it. The struggle was fiercer because of one other fact I have mentioned: The ancient social structure of America lay in hopeless ruins; conditions after the war were totally different from those before the war. The days of individualism were gone. The rise of Nationalism was manifest in Europe and in America. Andrew Johnson did not appreciate this fact. He set himself against a force which has controlled the world from that day to our own, against the Nationalization of his country.

In the process of reconstruction curious changes of position occurred. Whatever the Constitution declared on the subject of Secession or whatever either side contended, the North had fought to prove and by success had proved, that no state could withdraw from the Union: "Wherefore the seceding states continued to be states after Lee's surrender just as they had been before invalid votes had undertaken to effect an unlawful Secession. . . . The Radical view that the southern area was no longer an aggregation of sovereign states but conquered territory to be re-organized and dealt with as the victors might choose, was illogical and contrary to the theory on which the war was fought."[6] And yet the working out of the former

[5] Kendrick, *Committee of Fifteen*, p. 198.
[6] Welles, *Diary*, Preface by Morse, p. xlvi.

theory, that is the perdurance of a state, was utterly impracticable.   Something must be done by the rebel states, besides laying down arms, before they could come back into the Union.

The question was, What should be done by the rebellious states and who should pass on the matter, the President or Congress.   Now the initial steps taken by Mr. Lincoln "in the readjustment after the termination of hostilities were guided by the widespread northern belief that the old Union had been maintained," but the "final steps in reconstruction revealed with unmistakable clearness the truth of the southern view that a new Union had been created." [7]   In fact, "a condition never contemplated by the framers of the Constitution had to be disposed of in pretended accordance with an instrument which had not a word to say concerning such problems." [8]   Nevertheless, it seems safe to conclude, *arguendo*, that the work of bringing the states into their proper relations with the Union was for the President and not for Congress.[9]

No one knew better than Andrew Johnson that the war had been inaugurated by President Lincoln, that is, that President Lincoln, and not Congress, in April 1861, adjudged that the states were in rebellion and declared war.   If the President had this right, Johnson inquired, why not the corresponding right to say when the states were no longer rebellious but fit to return to their proper places in the Union? The President is Commander-in-chief of the army and navy, he must take care that the laws be faithfully executed; he takes an oath to support, protect, and defend the Constitution, and the Constitution guarantees to each state a Republican form of government.   Therefore, did it not follow, as Lincoln held, that reconstruction was his job, that it was his right to restore the states to their places in the Union, and to see that a Republican form of government was maintained? [10]

At all events, President Johnson concluded that this was his duty.   He put the case this way.   No state has ever been out

---

[7] Dunning, *Reconstruction*, p. 5.
[8] John T. Morse, *supra*.
[9] Lincoln's *Proclamation* of December 8, 1863.
[10] Kendrick, *op. cit.*, p. 17.

of the Union nor can it get out. Each state "went into rebellion with slavery and by the operation of rebellion lost that feature, but it was a state when it went into rebellion and when it came out, with the peculiar institution it was still a state . . . its life breath had only been suspended." [11]   Therefore, in tackling the problem of reconstruction, "President Johnson was under no necessity of devising a solution, the plan already applied by Lincoln being ready to hand. He took up the work at the precise point where his predecessor had left off." [12] Easy it would have been to float with the tide, to join with the Radicals, to agree with Congress, to control administration patronage and to succeed himself as President. To do this, however—to compromise, to become a Federalist—would not have been Andrew Johnson.[13] President Johnson was pleased that his plan concurred with Lincoln's. The two had worked together harmoniously since February 1862, when Johnson became Lincoln's War Governor and agent in Tennessee. Johnson, therefore, determined to follow Lincoln.

Without doubt the plan of reconstruction adopted by Lincoln and followed by Johnson was the martyr President's last will and testament. Whoever opposed it incurred his displeasure.[14] In 1863 General Butler called an election in Norfolk, over the head of Provisional Governor Peirpoint. President Lincoln rebuked him, as he did military authorities in Tennessee for interfering with Governor Johnson, and in Arkansas for interfering with Governor Steele. These states, having shown a loyal disposition, had, as Mr. Lincoln concluded, regained their right to statehood. Congress itself had considered the southern states merely rebellious and not out of the Union and had endorsed Lincoln's plan of reconstruction. This is shown by many facts. At the special session in July 1861 Andrew Johnson, from the rebel State of Tennessee, had been admitted as a Senator and so had Maynard and Clements, as Congressmen. In 1862 Hahn and Flanders had

[11] April 1865 speech to the Indiana delegation.
[12] Dunning, *Reconstruction*, in the *American Nation*, p. 35; Rhodes, Vol. V, p. 527; Burgess, *Reconstruction*, p. 36.
[13] Speech to committee of Philadelphia Convention, August 1866.
[14] Nicolay and Hay, *Lincoln*, Vol. IX, p. 437.

been admitted from Louisiana.[15]   In 1864 Andrew Johnson of the rebel State of Tennessee, had been nominated for Vice-president of the United States; and on July 8, 1864, Lincoln had issued a proclamation in which he maintained that Louisiana was a state of the Union.   He would not yield to Wade and Davis, he would not consent to abolish what loyal Louisiana had done.   Louisiana should forthwith come back into the Union.

Undoubtedly, therefore, the war had been begun and prosecuted on the idea that there was and could be no disruption of the Union by invalid ordinances of secession.   In July 1861 the basic principle on which the war was to be fought was declared by Congress.   As Andrew Johnson's resolution sets forth: It was to be, not conquest, not oppression, but the suppression of rebellion and the restoration of the Union.   Even prior to then, in his December 18, 1860, speech to the Senate, Andrew Johnson had given notice to the world that in his judgment the Union existed only by virtue of the Constitution and that without the Constitution there could be no Union.[16]

Again, early in February 1865, a bill declaring that no Representatives should be admitted from the rebel states till Congress so declared had been defeated by a vote of 80 to 65. In the same month, Senator Trumbull, from Lincoln's State, moved that Louisiana be admitted as the President recommended.   This bill would have passed but for Charles Sumner. He defeated it by a filibuster.   Forming a combination, as Trumbull charged, with Wade and two or three other radical Senators to defeat a great public measure, Sumner and the Radicals had their way.   This bill was called up again on February 27 and was postponed by a filibuster "until to-morrow."   But to-morrow never came.[17]

On Sunday, April 9, General Lee surrendered and the people rejoiced.   But Lincoln did not rejoice, the reconstruction of the southern states bore too heavily on his heart.   "He was

15 Burgess, p. 14.
16 Fleming, *op. cit.*, Vol. I, p. 116.
17 Nicolay and Hay, Vol. IX, p. 462.

glad Congress was not in session," . . . "he wished Southern matters closed without much discussion," . . . "the breach between the North and South must be speedily healed." [18] From the White House steps on Tuesday, April 11, he read to cheering thousands his last public speech, thoroughly prepared, and a generous, gracious document. First he argued that Louisiana and the repentant southern states should be at once admitted to seats in Congress, on complying with his proclamation. Proceeding, he said: "Now if we reject and spurn the southern whites we do our utmost to disorganize and disperse them. We in effect say to the white man, 'You are worthless or worse; we will never help you nor be helped by you.' To the blacks we say, 'This cup of liberty which these your old masters hold to your lips we will dash from you and leave you to the chance of gathering the spilled and scattered contents in some vague and undefined when, where, and how.' If this course, discouraging and paralyzing to both white and black, has any tendency to bring Louisiana into proper practical relations with the Union, I have so far been unable to perceive it. . . . We must energize and feed, nourish and cherish the twelve thousand loyal men in Louisiana. . . . Granting that the negro desires the franchise, will he not rather attain it by holding what he has than running backward over his old masters?"

On April 14 Lincoln's cabinet met for the last time. Stanton, always diligent and efficient, had a draft of the proclamation admitting North Carolina, Virginia, and other states to representation in Congress. It was objected by the conservative members of the cabinet that Virginia and North Carolina should not be coupled together in one bill. This would impair their territorial boundaries. While the matter was being discussed, Mr. Lincoln took occasion to outline his policy toward the South. "No one need expect me," he said, "to take part in hanging these men. Drive them out of the country, open the gates, let down the bars, scare them off,"—throwing up his hands as if to scare sheep. He deprecated the disposition to hector and dictate to the people of the South who were trying

[18] Nicolay and Hay, Vol. X, p. 283.

to right themselves. He urged that Congress should admit the southern states. No harm would follow, he insisted, because "Congress has the right to accept or reject such members as present themselves." That night Lincoln, the friend of mankind, was murdered and the South lost its best friend. Forthwith the wrath of the North was poured out as never before.

In less than sixty days Wendell Phillips was declaring that it was "better, far better, for Grant to have surrendered to Lee than President Johnson to North Carolina." [19] The humane proclamations of Lincoln and Johnson to admit the southern states and to leave it to the honor and virtue of the southern white man to work out the negro problem, Phillips and his associates scouted. Radicals, abolitionists, negrophiles, and philanthropists were gathering their forces to fight Andrew Johnson and his policy as in 1863 and 1864 they had fought Abraham Lincoln.

Meanwhile, the country was kept in a ferment. The Reconstruction Committee was taking evidence, mostly partisan, tending to show disorder and disloyalty on the part of the impoverished and helpless South. The press was insisting that the revolution should not go backward, that the South should not escape punishment—forgetting the misery, the poverty, and the desolation of the southern people. In Congress the Shellabargers and the Stevenses were waving the bloody shirt, coining war hysteria into partisan advantage. According to men who "had remained a safe distance from the battlefields," southern soldiers had "carved the bones of your unburied dead into ornaments and drank from goblets made out of their skulls." [20] In the Senate, Conservatives, like Doolittle of Wisconsin, were vainly urging a conciliatory course, the approval of Lincoln and Johnson's plan, and the putting of thirty-six actual, not sham, stars in the National Flag. "Is the flag as it floats," Doolittle indignantly asked, "a truth or a flaunting, hypocritical lie?"

Wade, Sumner, and the Radicals were insisting that it rested with Congress to decide what government is the established one

[19] *Life of Trumbull*, p. 235.
[20] Shellabarger in January 1866 debate.

in a state, and were threatening to remove the President by impeachment if he stood in the way. In fact, Congressman Yeates was for harsher means—"The President should be taken out of the way," he put it, "though I will not say how." [21]

In the background of this confusion and dissension—if not its real cause—was the newly liberated slave. What should be done with him? Lincoln had insisted on colonization. In April and in July 1862, Congress had put $600,000 in his hands to be disposed of "as his judgment might direct in settling the negroes recently emancipated in the District of Columbia beyond the limits of the United States." [22] Andrew Johnson concurred with Lincoln in this view but was, nevertheless, in favor of first trying out the experiment of gradual enfranchisement by the states. He favored giving the ballot "to colored soldiers, to the more intelligent negroes, and to those owning $300 of property." [23] If this experiment failed, after an honest effort, then Johnson favored voluntary colonization.[24] In this conviction—that enfranchisement *en masse* of the ignorant negro would be a great wrong and would lead to bloodshed and riot—men like Henry Ward Beecher and Governor Andrew of Massachusetts concurred. Though they wished fair treatment for the blacks, they also wished fair treatment for their white brethren of the South.

Relying on the President's promise that she would be taken back into the Union, the South had adopted the Thirteenth Amendment and otherwise complied with the President's demands. Notwithstanding this the Radicals were determined to block the pathway and if necessary to overthrow the policy of the President and resort to force and a military government. In this policy Stevens was a leader, though in December 1865, when opposing the admission of the Southern States, he had said, "They will not and ought not to live up to the Thirteenth Amendment." "The President has forced the amendment upon them," he said. "No one who has any regard

[21] *Thirty-ninth Congress, Second Session*, pp. 315-317.
[22] Oberholtzer, *History of the United States*, Vol. I, p. 75.
[23] *Senate Executive Documents, Thirty-ninth Congress, First Session*, No. 26, p. 229; Fleming, *Documentary History of Reconstruction*, p. 177.
[24] Oberholtzer, Vol. I, p. 75.

for the freedom of elections can look upon these governments forced upon them in duress with any favor." In fact, Stevens agreed that southern whites "should disregard laws and constitutions put upon them at the point of the bayonet." "It would be," said he, "both natural and just if the South will scorn and disregard their present constitutions forced upon them in the midst of martial law." [25]

Mr. Beecher, at this time in sympathy with Johnson, was often in Washington, saw southern men in the White House, and knew how deeply repentant they were. In the last conversation Beecher had with Lincoln and Governor Andrew, President Lincoln said that he was inclined "to the policy of immediate reconstruction." The great preacher, visualizing the situation, with prophetic insight expressed himself in noble words. "We that live at a distance," said he in an open letter, "may think that the social reconstruction involved in the emancipation of four million slaves is as simple and easy as it is to discourse about it, but such a change is itself one of the most tremendous tests to which industry and society can be subjected, and to its favorable issue is required every advantage possible. . . . No army, no government and no earthly power can compel the South to treat four million men justly if the inhabitants, whether rightly or wrongly, regard these men as the cause or even the occasion of their unhappiness and disfranchisement. But no army or government or power will be required when the Southern States are honorably restored, and are prospering in the renewed Union. Then the negro will be felt to be a necessity to southern industry, and interest will join with conscience and kindness in securing for him favorable treatment from his fellow citizens." [26] For uttering these sentiments, Plymouth Church called on Beecher to explain and recant. This he would not do. But he restated his position in milder language, and joined in the popular abuse of Johnson's "obstinacy."

The word "if" plays a great part in history. If Mr. Lincoln had not been assassinated, what would have happened?

[25] Stevens' speech, December 18, 1865.
[26] *Two Letters of H. W. Beecher.* pamphlet.

Could he have commanded enough votes in December 1865 to readmit the Southern States? Was a compromise possible, or was a show-down between Radicals and Conservatives inevitable? That Lincoln would have imposed no harsher terms on the South than his Louisiana plan is certain. That the Radicals would not have yielded is equally certain. In other words, it is fair to conclude "that Lincoln would have aligned himself with Johnson and Secretary Welles, and that a fight on his policy would have resulted." [27] "The truth is that the Radicals of Johnson's day were really thinking of votes and were only talking of negroes." Radical caucuses of the time were shocking affairs, full, reckless, and venomous. It required a brave Congressman to disobey their mandates. When old Thad Stevens took the floor and sneered at Andy Johnson and Andy Johnsonism every Congressman "fled the sheep-fold—or the goat-fold." "Do not, I pray you," said he, "admit those who have slaughtered half a million of our countrymen, until their clothes are dried and until they are reclad. I do not wish to sit side by side with men whose garments smell of the blood of my kindred. Only six years ago when the mighty Toombs, with his shaggy locks, headed a gang with shouts of defiance on this floor, he rendered this hall a hell of legislation." "Ah, sir, just before they went out to join the armies of Cataline, just before they left this hall, with weapons drawn, and Barksdale's bowie-knife gleaming before our eyes, it was one yelling body and all because a speech was made for freedom. Would you have these men back again so soon to reënact this scene? Wait until I am gone, I pray you. I want not to go through it again. It will be but a short time for my colleague to wait. I hope he will not put us to that test."

In truth, to the blood-thirsty Stevens universal amnesty and "universal Andy Johnsonism" were the same thing and each equally diabolical and sinister. He delighted to ask if loyal blacks had not "quite as good a right to choose rulers and make laws as rebel whites." "Centuries ago," he exclaimed in reference to Johnson's first veto, "had such an utterance been made to Parliament by a British King, it would have cost him his

[27] Welles, *Diary*, Vol. I, Preface, p. lxiv.

head." Sumner declared that the President's plan of admitting the southern states was the greatest and most criminal error ever committed by any government and insinuated that "the negroes of Georgia are better qualified to establish and maintain a Republican government than the whites." [28] In a word the Radicals—and they were dominant—were fixed in their determination to undo all that President Lincoln and President Johnson had done and to enfranchise the negro, literate and illiterate, *en bloc*.[29] And it must be admitted that freeing the slaves and thereby increasing the strength of the South by more than thirty votes and yet denying to the negro the ballot was a great hardship on the Republican party and a natural element of discord. This condition, however, Johnson realized and proposed to remedy. He would change the basis of elections from population to qualified voters.[30]

But the President's troubles were not all frontal; many came from the rear and flank. The Copperheads continued to embarrass him. Though he would not join them or endorse them, he could not prevent their endorsing him. Time and again the irrepressible Vallandigham had to be admonished that he was not wanted.[31] Again, when Raymond, the liberal New York Congressman, rose to speak, he was terribly handicapped. A Copperhead Congressman, one who had done what he could to disrupt the Union, got the floor first, making a cheap exhibition of himself, and discrediting the cause he advocated. On the principle that one is known by the company he keeps, Raymond's defense of the President was at a disadvantage and fell on a hostile nation. Shellabarger's fierce and lurid picture of southern atrocities and outrages swept all before it. The Conservatives made no impression upon the country.

The very honesty and manhood of the South were attributed by the Radicals to sinister motives and to disloyalty to the Union. In the fires of war it had been forgotten at the North that there was a justification for Secession; that Secession had

28 Welles, Vol. II, p. 393.
29 *Ibid.*, p. 415.
30 Schouler, Vol. VII, p. 26.
31 Oberholtzer, Vol. I, p. 46.

been a debatable question; that slavery was a condition brought about by North and South alike; that but for Boston and New Bedford sailing vessels the infamous slave trade could not have been carried on; and that, in the far South—as in the North in earlier days—practically all men considered the right of Secession a constitutional one and themselves, in exercising it, not traitors, but patriots. Though the North had forgotten these things, the South had not, nor had Andrew Johnson. Having always been a state-rights Democrat, Johnson, with his one-track mind, had held uniformly to the doctrine that a state is as necessary to the Union as the Union to a state, and that each state should manage its own affairs without outside interference. The Southerners, however, in their demands on the President, went much too far. Though thoroughly loyal they conceded nothing, admitted no guilt. In May 1865 they were grievously wrong in asking the President to restore the rebel states without more ado than the laying down of arms. If they were entitled to come back in May 1865, why not in May 1863, during the battle of Chancellorsville?

At a conference of the President with three Unionists from North Carolina in May 1865, this fact was brought baldly to light.[32] When the President exhibited his plan to restore North Carolina, B. F. Moore, the chairman of the committee, objected and urged that it was unconstitutional. The Legislature should first meet and call a convention, he insisted, as provided by the Constitution. The President took the ground that the legislature of North Carolina had no legal status. "Besides," said the President, no doubt recalling his experience as Military Governor of Tennessee, "suppose I recognize the legislature and it refuses to conform to the terms deemed necessary?" To this the North Carolina Unionist replied, "Such a thing in the loyal State of North Carolina is unthinkable. Why, sir," he said, "there is no one of that body who might not be led back into the Union with a silken thread."

---

[32] Hamilton, *Reconstruction in North Carolina*, p. 106; Senator Pool in a pamphlet asserts that the South accepted every thing favorable and rejected every thing unfavorable.

On the next day, when the President appointed Holden provisional governor, Moore and his associates left the room, declining to take any part in the proceedings. And, logically, of course, Moore was right.

Here, indeed, was the weak point in Lincoln's and Johnson's plan. If the southern states were now states, having become loyal to the Union, what right had Congress or the President to impose terms and conditions—even the Thirteenth Amendment—on a sovereign state? If the President had the right to require the states to abolish slavery as a condition of readmittance to the Union, why had not Congress the right to impose other conditions? The reply of Lincoln and Johnson that that was their business and not Congress's is not convincing. Surely neither the President nor Congress has the right to impose terms on a *State* not imposed by the Constitution. Raymond undertook to justify the President's action in an ingenious argument. Undoubtedly, as he contended, the President, as Commander-in-chief, had the right, under his war powers, to destroy rebel arsenals and all other implements of warfare and agencies for maintaining Secession. "Now," said Raymond, "slavery was more an implement of war than the deadliest gun. Slavery, indeed, was the cause of the present war and if allowed to continue, will cause other wars. Hence, slavery must go with Secession and guns." At all events, Johnson, having worked out the matter as his predecessor had done, put down his foot, defying the world, the flesh, and the devil.

No doubt Johnson had visions of succeeding himself as President, but this was not his operating motive.[33] Here and there the matter was being discussed and in the spring of 1866 a definite organization, the National Union party, was started in Washington, looking to Johnson's nomination in 1868, but he paid little or no attention to the project. If he won, it must be on his record, not on any party caucus or fiat of the leaders.[34] Being a man without a party, he knew that his chances of success were slim. The National Union party

[33] Schouler, Vol. VII, p. 10.
[34] Johnson MS.

could not spring into being and win in a moment, and the Republican party was the dominant factor in politics. Yet he refused to ally himself with that dominant party. To do so would be "to give the lie to his whole life and to the policy on which he understood the war was fought." Time and again Republican leaders assured him that if he would partake of their radicalism and coöperate with Congress, all would be well. In fact, John Sherman and others, who valued Johnson's unselfish and patriotic services for the Union, were convinced that he would finally do this—that he would cease to obstruct legislation. But this he would not do, he would not yield. "I was born a state-rights Democrat and I shall die one," he declared. Yet he would not join the Democratic party. Though he could not coöperate with the Republicans to humiliate, disgrace, pauperize, and Africanize the South, yet he could not join with the Democracy of the South and thereby keep alive the fires of sectionalism.[35]

So it came about that Andy Johnson in the White House was the same Andy Johnson as in the Tennessee tailor shop. In Tennessee the leaders had been against him. In Washington like conditions existed and he must tread the wine press alone. There was, however, one bright spot in the political sky. Nearly all the great Union generals and fighters were backing him. General Grant endorsed his action and so did General Sherman. Indeed, Sherman was convinced of the loyalty and manhood of the South. After a conversation with Lincoln in April 1865, he had entered into a "convention" with General Joseph E. Johnston, the Confederate leader, at Durham, N. C. In this convention it was agreed that the old Union should be restored and the southern states readmitted without any reconstruction whatsoever. Schofield, Meade, Hancock, Ewing, and Thomas—these great Generals likewise endorsed the President's southern policy. So also, substantially, did Andrew, the war Governor of Massachusetts. "Before I support Grant," said General Ewing in 1868, "I wish to know

---

[35] Cameron and Chandler, in a conversation with Congressman Brownlow, declared that President Johnson would have succeeded himself if he had not opposed Congress. Letter dated November 27, 1897, and copied in the Nashville *Banner*, January 20, 1910.

if he approves the reconstruction measures. If he does, I cannot support him." [36] In 1865 Schofield from Raleigh advised Grant of the "total unfitness of the negro as a class to exercise the ballot." [37]

While the Reconstruction Committee was slowly incubating —their policy being one of delay "and to preserve and perpetuate the Republican party"—the Thirty-ninth Congress was not idle.[38] Its task, indeed, was next in importance to the First Congress which organized the government under the Constitution. Yet it was engaged in an impossible undertaking. Legislation which was clearly outside the Constitution and could not be justified except under war powers, was the concern of Congress. Despite the line of decisions, culminating in the Dred Scott case, Congress was engaged in legislating upon matters expressly forbidden to them by the Constitution.[39] It was this feature of Congressional action that alarmed President Johnson. He had almost as soon the Union itself was blotted out as a state. That a state should manage its own affairs had been the rock on which he stood. On this principle he had fought the Whig party, and on it he had destroyed the Know-Nothing party in Tennessee. While he conceded to Congress the right to legislate for territories, he did not concede this right as to a sovereign state. In his opinion, the war being over, all war powers were at an end, and the Constitution *suo vigore* was the law of the land.

And yet, even this patriotic thought was not without a flaw. At that moment in the South United States troops were stationed and the writ of *habeas corpus* was suspended—a condition incompatible with civil government.[40]

Entertaining these old-fashioned views of the Constitution, the President could do no less than veto the very first reconstruction measure, the Freedmen's Bureau bill. This bill passed Congress in February 1866. It was unconstitutional

[36] Pollard, *Lost Cause Regained*, p. 166; *Memoirs of General Sherman*, p. 375.

[37] Oberholtzer, Vol. I, p. 141.

[38] Kendrick, *Joint Committee*, p. 141; Barnes, *The Thirty-ninth Congress*, p. 442.

[39] McDonald, *Documentary Source Book*, p. 415.

[40] W. A. Dunning, *Essays*, p. 89.

beyond cavil, as it really superseded civil authority throughout the South. In fact, it was formulated on the Stevens idea that the South was conquered territory, and it was a blow to Presidential reconstruction. The President's veto reached Congress February 19. Though the bill had passed the House by the large vote of 137 to 33 and the Senate by 37 to 10, it was defeated, after the veto. Two-thirds of the Senate refused to over-ride the President. Thus did Johnson triumph over Congress and block their progress. It was thought the Radicals were now at the end of their row. But the case was far otherwise. Congress had just begun to fight.

On the next day Congress responded to the veto by passing a cast-iron resolution that the rebel states should have no representation in either House until both Houses so declared. Thad Stevens, advocating the measure, said "its passage would put an end to a disturbing question agitating the country and that rebel Congressmen would be admitted when Congress said so, not before." Many inducements had been held out to the President not to veto the Freedmen's Bureau bill. Senators and Representatives from Tennessee would be admitted, he was promised, if he would withhold his disapproval. Three of his cabinet indeed joined in the request not to veto—Stanton, Harlan, and Speed. But the unyielding man could be neither bribed nor intimidated. "He would not do wrong," he declared to the cabinet, "to secure right." [41]

Forthwith the country became a political debating society. Sumner, on his weekly visit to Welles, to detach him from the President, exhibited articles of impeachment against Johnson. Gideon Welles, the brave and puritanical Secretary, wanted to know if Sumner "really thought Massachusetts could govern Georgia better than Georgia could govern herself?" Sumner thought she could. In fact, "this is Massachusetts' mission." [42] The New York *World*, endorsing the President, dubbed the Congress, sitting without the eleven Southern States, a "rump Congress." The Committee of Fifteen was likened to the

[41] Welles, Vol. II, p. 434.
[42] *Ibid.*, p. 430.

French Directory. It was called "a red cabal" and its "mission was to grind the southern white man in the dust." [43]

Washington's Birthday was fixed upon by the President's friends, and the conservatives throughout the Nation, as a suitable time to make a grand demonstration in his behalf. A monster meeting was held in Cooper Union, New York City. David Dudley Field presented resolutions endorsing the President's policy. Seward, Dennison, and Raymond spoke. The New York Aldermen passed resolutions endorsing the President's "conservative, liberal, enlightened, and Christian policy." One hundred guns were fired on February 21 and one hundred on February 22. The President's mail was packed with letters of approval. Johnson was, they declared, "greater than 'Old Hickory.'" "He was on the highest pinnacle of the mount of fame"; "his feet were planted on the Constitution of his country"; "he was a modern edition of Andrew Jackson bound in calf." Preachers prayed for him, women named their babies for him, he was "suffering all things as Christ did." [44] Unfortunately for the President's cause, too much of this praise came from rebel states and from Copperheads of the North. Indeed, it was said by the Radicals in reply to the Democratic fireworks that "more powder was burned in honor of the veto by the Copperheads than they had consumed during the four years of war."

In Washington City thousands gathered at the White House to cheer and encourage the President. There were music and shouting and a great demonstration. Andrew Johnson was the second Andrew Jackson—"a man not to be bullied or intimidated." Calls went up for a speech. Senator Doolittle had urged Johnson to make no speech, but Welles had insisted that he should publicly state his position. [45] Appearing on the White House terrace and looking into the faces of the cheering people, the deterministic man forgot he was the ruler of millions of people. He was in Tennessee again. He was fighting the battles of the Union, standing for the Constitution and the

43 *Ibid.*, pp. 424, 425, 432.
44 Johnson MS.
45 Welles, *Diary*, Vol. II, p. 421.

old flag—the glorious old flag, 36 stars intact, not one plucked from its place. Having dared all, suffered all for a reunited country and now standing in Lincoln's shoes pleading for peace and harmony, why should he be dictated to by men who had sacrificed nothing in the great cause—by the Covodes, the Boutwells, the Wades, the Sumners, the Stevenses, the Shellabargers, the Ashleys, and the Colfaxes? It was the old fight against him, he felt, the fight of the leaders, not of the people. If the people only knew the facts, he would triumph, and please God they should know the facts—know exactly what he was doing for them.

Girding up his loins and addressing the excited crowd, he asked: "What usurpation has Andrew Johnson been guilty of, what is his offense? His only usurpation has been standing between the people and the encroachments of power." . . . "The wicked rebel has been put down by the strong arm of the Government," he declared, "the rebel armies defeated in the field, but now another rebellion has started, a rebellion to overthrow the Constitution and revolutionize the Government. . . . In 1861 I said in the Senate that the states had no right to secede and that question has been settled and determined. Thus settled and thus determined, I cannot turn around and give the lie direct to all that I profess to have done during the past four years. . . . Though I am opposed to the Davises, the Toombs, the Slidells and the long list of such, yet when I perceive on the other end of the line men still opposed to the Union, I am equally against them, and I am free to say I am still with the people."

"Name three of the men you allude to," came from the crowd.

"The gentleman calls for three names and I will give them to him. I say Thad Stevens of Pennsylvania, I say Charles Sumner of Massachusetts, and I say Wendell Phillips of Massachusetts."

Great applause greeted this thrust. Indeed, throughout the speech there was wild cheering, laughter, and applause. Especially when some one asked how about Forney—once the

President's friend, now his worst detractor. "Forney?" the President replied. "I do not waste my fire on dead ducks."

Urged on by the enthusiasm of the crowd, feeling that the people were with him and that he could rout the leaders, the President grew more personal. He declared that the American people by instinct knew who were their friends and that Andrew Johnson, in all positions from alderman to President, had been their friend. "I have occupied many positions in the Government," he said, "going through both branches of the legislature—" "And was once a tailor," some one interrupted. "Some gentleman here behind me says that I was once a tailor. Now that don't affect me in the least. When I was a tailor I always made a close fit, was punctual to my customers, and did good work." (A voice) "No patchwork!" (The President) "No, I did not want any patchwork. But we pass by this digression." Concluding this unusual, not to say revolutionary and yet wholly characteristic and natural appeal to the country, the President declared that he could wish the thirty million American people "could sit in an amphitheater and witness the great struggle now going on to preserve the Constitution of our fathers, in which struggle I am but your instrument." [46]

In due time, James Russell Lowell, speaking for the North, asked, "Shall we descend to a mass meeting?" "The North would remind the South," said Lowell, "that occasion is swift, that something happened these last four years, that the United States is determined, by God's grace, to Americanize you. By yourselves or us, your prejudices must be conquered." [47]

To the South and to northern Copperheads the Washington Birthday speech gave great satisfaction. "In the estimation of thoughtful people, however," as Secretary McCulloch records, "it hurt the President." [48] Nevertheless the New York *Herald* called the speech "bold, manly, outspoken"; the *Times* "strong, direct, manly." Thurlow Weed, declared it "a glori-

[46] *Annual Encyclopædia*, 1866, p. 752.
[47] *North American Review*, Vol. CXLI, p. 534.
[48] McCulloch, *Men and Measures*, p. 393.

ous speech." "Traitors will now seek hiding places and the Government is safe." Seward, strong for Johnson as a stumper, "heartily approved the speech." Even the less enthusiastic Welles considered it "earnest, honest, and strong."

From this time, as was to be expected, a fiercer war between Congress and the President was waged. This, however, was a warfare not of Johnson's seeking. Had not Congress struck the first blow, had it not gone back on the Republican platform of 1864 on which he was nominated for Vice-president? Had it not tied the hands of the President, and created a Central Directory from whose girdle hung the keys of the Nation? At all events, Johnson considered Congress the aggressor, and if he must die, he would die defending the Constitution, and with boots on. Even while the Judiciary Committee of the House was investigating him, with the view to impeaching and removing him from office, he was vetoing every bill he regarded unconstitutional. The Civil Rights bill soon passed Congress. He vetoed it as he did the second Freedmen's Bureau bill, and the bills admitting Colorado and Nebraska. And this he did though Ashley was running down every rumor he could get wind of—Johnson's alleged drunkenness and licentiousness, even his private letters and papers undergoing scrutiny.[49] Stevens was irritating and insulting the President as only Stevens could. Referring to Johnson's Washington's Birthday speech, Stevens surprised the House. He praised Andrew Johnson. "His patriotism and honesty no man will question," he declared. Called to account by a brother Radical, the "Old Commoner" quizzically retorted, "Why, it's all a hoax, our President didn't make it; it's a contrivance of the Copperhead party which has been persecuting our President!"

[49] The evidence taken by this committee is on file in the Document Room at Washington; none of it, however, was embraced in the charges against the President in the Impeachment Trial.

CHAPTER II

SWINGING ROUND THE CIRCLE

Andrew Johnson had a notion that everything goes in a circle—that unit and universe are round. Delighting in elaboration and reiteration, he would tackle problems from every angle, and, if given time, would swing around the circle to a mathematical, but oftentimes, an unworkable conclusion.[1] Now in 1866 he proposed to handle the issues between himself and Congress in the old way. Concealing nothing, he would take the people into his confidence, swing round the circle, and fight a good fight, as he declared "for one country, one flag and a union of equal states." He would like, of course, to have a second term, but, as Schouler concludes, "he made no effort to ingratiate himself with one set or another." . . . "Under a tremendous pressure of political apostasy, he refused to Tylerize the party," but "filled the cabinet and national offices with Republicans, worthy men of high character." . . . "Copperheadism made no head with Andrew Johnson."[2]

In the beginning it seemed that the President's course would be sustained at the polls. Even so radical a Senator as O. P. Morton became now endorsed him, advising that he employ every power and instrumentality to sustain his position. "I cannot be mistaken in the opinion," he wrote, "that the great body of the people North will endorse your doctrines and this the members of Congress will find before they are ninety days older."[3] Ex-Justice R. B. Curtis, perhaps the most highly respected judge of the day, advised Senator Doolittle that he endorsed the President, and "after much reflection must declare that the Southern States are in the Union." Stanton

[1] Temple, p. 459.
[2] *Bookman*, Vol. XXXIV, p. 500.
[3] Johnson MS. No. 8146.

declared that Johnson's measures "received the cordial support of every member of the Cabinet." [4]

A new Congress was to be elected in November and it was all important for the Presidential plan that the Radicals should be turned out and Conservatives chosen. Early in the Spring there were held in various cities mass meetings in which the people expressed themselves on the veto of the Freedmen's Bureau bill and on the February speech. The resolutions partook of the character of the representatives in the respective states. In Massachusetts and Pennsylvania, represented by Sumner and Stevens, the President's course was usually condemned. In Illinois and New York, the homes of Trumbull and Seward, respectively, it was endorsed. On March 13, while the country was still agitated over the veto and the Washington Birthday speech, Congress passed the first Civil Rights bill. The President vetoed this bill on March 27. This act made citizenship a United States and not a state affair, and guaranteed certain civil rights to the negroes. The President's veto was overridden by a two-third vote of the Senate on April 6 and by the House on April 9. The President placed his veto on constitutional ground. In fact, Congress had touched the President in a vital spot, as I have stated, affection for States' Rights. An advocate of the doctrine that each state was the judge of citizenship and that the general government could not encroach on the states in such matters, the President was consistent in his veto. The Civil Rights bill was so manifestly repugnant to the fundamental law "Constitutional lawyers stared and gasped." [5] To make the act particularly obnoxious, its language was copied from the Fugitive Slave Law of 1850. It was intended to give vitality to the Thirteenth Amendment.[6]

The President's veto of this bill gave much offense to Senators like Stewart, who had voted to sustain the veto of the Freedmen's Bureau, with the understanding that the President

[4] Fleming, *Documentary History of Reconstruction*, Vol. I, p. 86.

[5] Dunning, *Essays*, p. 65. An act similar to this was afterwards declared unconstitutional by the Supreme Court.—*Civil Rights Cases*, Reports, United States, 109, p. 37.

[6] Gorham, *Stanton*, Vol. II, p. 294.

was not to veto the Civil Rights bill.[7] Lyman Trumbull was so sure the President would not veto the Civil Rights bill, he publicly announced the fact. But these Senators must have misunderstood the President. At no time, according to the record, did he commit himself to such a course, whereas time and again he declared "for the old Union as it was." [8] The veto was an able and a dispassionate document. The President planted himself on the Constitution. Nevertheless, the North was greatly concerned over this veto, having fully expected the President to approve the measure. Governor J. D. Cox and Henry Ward Beecher had urged the President to sign the bill. All the Cabinet, except Welles, had joined in a similar request.[9]

The action of Congress in overruling the veto of the President upon a constitutional question was epochal and revolutionary. It was the first instance of the kind on record. What right had the Legislative Department, more than the Executive Department, to play the part of a court—to declare an act Constitutional or otherwise? Why should a President enforce an act which he considered manifestly violative of the highest law of the land? Anyway, the President acquiesced in the action of Congress and threw no obstacles in the way of enforcing the Civil Rights Act.[10] The Radicals were now in high glee. Having a two-third majority, they could legislate over the President's head—Stevens and Sumner "had crossed the Rubicon and taken the entire army with them."

On April 30 Stevens reported the Fourteenth Amendment to the House. It was the result of the labors of his Committee of Fifteen.[11] This committee had been sitting in Washington since January, inquiring into the affairs of the rebel states.[12] On June 14 a joint resolution passed the Senate and the House proposing the Fourteenth Amendment to the states for adop-

7 Stewart, *Reminiscences*, p. 199.

8 August 1866. Reply to a Committee of the Philadelphia Convention.—Kendrick, *Journal*, p. 259.

9 Schouler, Vol. VII, p. 56; Rhodes, Vol. V, p. 583.

10 Rhodes, Vol. VI, p. 60. This situation moved President Johnson to recommend an Amendment to the Constitution. In Constitutional questions the disputed matter should be certified to the Supreme Court and forthwith passed on by it.—*Address*, March 4, 1869, "To the people of the United States."

11 McCall, *Life of Stevens*, p. 271.

12 For an analysis of the Fourteenth Amendment, *vide post*, p. 518.

tion. The resolution, however, gave no assurance that its adoption would admit the Southern States. Though Stevens offered a bill to admit them upon the passage of the Amendment, it is believed that he was merely playing politics. Certainly he did not approve of the bill. At this time the radicals in Congress were indulging in flouts and jeers at the Constitution.[13] The President opposed the Fourteenth Amendment and made no concealment of the fact. Telegraphing Governor Parsons of Alabama, he said that to pass the Amendment would do "no possible good." That there should be "no faltering on the part of those who are honest in the determination to sustain the several coördinate departments of the Government in accordance with its original design." [14] Nevertheless, the President directed the Secretary of State to certify the Amendment to the states for their action. Though he loved the Constitution much, he loved the Union more.[15]

After six months' deliberation the Joint Committee of Fifteen had no program. Though Congress had rejected Johnson's plan of admitting the rebel states, it had no substitute to offer for it. In the circumstances the commercial North was growing restless. Eleven southern states were treated as mere conquered territory and there was no prospect of a change. Though mails were carried, courts functioned, postoffices were open, and taxes collected, representation in Congress was denied the South. Conservative Northerners were asking what Congress proposed to do. Was the South to be held in perpetual bondage, its territory divided up among the negroes, and the whites expelled as Stevens and the Radicals insisted? [16] If not, why did not Congress speak out, formulate a platform, let the South know what to expect? The South had adopted Presidential reconstruction, what else was in store? Evidently, things were working well with Thad Stevens and there was no hurry.

[13] Dunning, *Essays on Reconstruction* in *American Nation*, p. 60; MacPherson, *History of Reconstruction*, Vol. I, p. 152; Dunning, *Essays*, p. 84.

[14] Fleming, *Documentary History of Reconstruction*, Vol. I, p. 237.

[15] The removal of Stanton was the only instance in which President Johnson disregarded a Statute of Congress, no matter how unconstitutional. He did, however, exercise the pardon power, which Congress forbade.

[16] Fleming, *op. cit.*, p. 151.

Nevertheless, as the summer campaign was coming on, Congress was afraid to adjourn without some show of reconciliation between the sections. Therefore they turned to the question of admitting Tennessee, the most loyal of the seceding states. In January 1866, Governor Brownlow had wired Congressional leaders to admit Tennessee and save a break with Johnson. In April 1866 an arrangement had been made, in the Senate and House, whereby the passage of the Civil Rights bill would insure the admission of Tennessee into the Union.[17] To aid in carrying out this arrangement, Governor Brownlow, who had become a pronounced southern Radical, on July 19, by high-handed methods, had forced the Tennessee legislature to adopt the Fourteenth Amendment. When he wired the news to Congress he also sent his "respects to the dead dog in the White House," meaning President Johnson. Evidently the war-time friendship of Johnson, the states-rights Democrat, and the Fighting Parson, an old-line Whig, had been of short duration.

As might be expected, the southern people, "many of whom were idle and starving," were growing desperate.[18] In the halls of Congress they were criticized by the radicals for wearing rebel uniforms, when often they had nothing else to wear. They were besides denounced as unrepentant rebels—perjurers taking the test oath to break it, and unfit to associate with loyal people. In southern cities the late slaves had gathered in numbers and were often idle, boastful and dangerous. In such case, conflicts between whites and blacks were unavoidable. In the country districts, where there was no congestion, conditions were much better. During the last of April, a riot occurred in Memphis. There the negro soldiers were rowdy and disorderly and unfortunately the police were fighting Irishmen. On April 30 four Irish policemen had jostled negro soldiers on the sidewalks. Next day, another collision with the negroes occurred. The police were joined by a white mob. An attack was made upon the negro population and forty-six negroes were killed outright. This riot created a revul-

17 Kendrick, *Journal*, p. 259.
18 Fleming, *Documentary History*, Vol. I, p. 17; Oberholtzer, Vol. I, p. 378.

sion in the North. A Committee of the House investigated the matter and there were two reports. The majority reported that the whites were not only disloyal but "bear undying hate to the black race." The minority reported that the negro soldiers began the riot and that the policy of Congress in disenfranchising the better element of the South was the cause of ill feeling.

In this condition of affairs the President's position was growing more precarious every day. If he adhered to the principles of a life-time and opposed the rising tide of nationalism he was sure of a fall. Only by yielding his convictions and joining the Radicals could he hope to succeed himself as President. Extremists like General Frank Blair, the brave Unionist, were urging that he ignore the "rump Congress" and recognize Senators and Congressmen from the southern states. It was urged that the southern Representatives, added to the northern Democrats and to conservative Republicans, would constitute a majority in Congress, and that the combination could run the country, on a constitutional basis. Others urged the President to pursue the opposite course and to yield to Congress, even to the extent of approving bills which were admittedly unconstitutional. Northern Copperheads continued to be a thorn in the President's flesh. In the South also a new party called the Radicals had organized to advocate negro suffrage and "to secure its fruits." [19] These southern Radicals were specially dangerous as they had the ear of Stevens, Sumner and their followers. In the South they were known to be mostly scalawags, carpet-baggers, buffaloes and deserters from the Confederate army. In the North, however, where they were unknown, and therefore idealized as the only true southern loyalists, they commanded respect.[20]

The President's advisers were also at variance. His Cabinet was divided. Welles insisted that the President stand firm, Seward advised a milder course. Nearly all of the Democrats contended that Seward was an obstruction and should leave the

[19] Fleming, *Documentary History*, Vol. I, p. 164.
[20] In the mountain sections of Tennessee, Kentucky, North Carolina and Virginia, there were many excellent citizens who became Radicals.

Cabinet. To these conflicting counsels, the President gave a too patient ear, but after much deliberation arrived at the only conclusion possible to a man of his antecedents. He would carry the question directly to the people. He would "swing round the circle," as he had so often done in Tennessee.

The failure of the President to endorse the Fourteenth Amendment and his veto of the Civil Rights bill are generally considered his greatest mistakes, and are pointed to as evidence of obstinacy and bullheadedness.

In taking the issue to the people two major movements were to be set on foot. A Union mass convention was to be held in Philadelphia on August 14. This was to be followed by a public campaign conducted by the President himself. The former movement has passed into history as the "Arm and Arm Convention," the latter, as the "Swing round the Circle." The idea behind the Philadelphia convention was the organization of a great Union party to be made up of old Whigs, the disrupted Democratic party, and conservative Republicans. Its name was to be the National Union party. This was its name at Baltimore in June 1864 when Lincoln and Johnson were nominated, and the name was to be retained. The movement originated in Washington in the Spring of 1866 with A. W. Randall, Assistant Postmaster-General, as its leader. In a short while another club was organized in Washington called the National Union Johnson Club. This club had Democratic antecedents and was headed by Montgomery Blair, Charles Mason of Ohio, T. B. Florence of Pennsylvania, Charles Knapp, and Ward H. Lamon of Washington. The two clubs consolidated under the name of the National Union Club, with A. W. Randall as president, and with sundry vice-presidents, members of the executive committee and other officers.

Forthwith extensive preparations began. Meetings were held and two delegates from each Congressional district and four at large from each state were chosen to attend the Philadelphia Convention. As the fourteenth approached, the movement assumed gigantic proportions. A special wigwam, two stories high, was erected on Girard Avenue with a seating capacity of ten thousand. The interior was decorated with the

United States flag and thirty-six commonwealths rose above the Speaker's chair. The day before the convention met, delegates began to arrive and by Tuesday noon, the fourteenth, an enthusiastic and patriotic crowd had assembled. The temporary chairman was General John A. Dix, who, as Secretary of War in April 1861, had made the Nation tingle by his order to shoot the first man who pulled down the flag at Sumter. Senator J. R. Doolittle was chosen permanent president. The keynote of the convention was the Constitution and the old Flag, thirty-six stars, not one erased—the Union as it was. How could this be done except by turning the Radicals out and electing a brand-new Congress? Reverend J. P. Holtsinger, Chaplain of the First Tennessee Union Regiment, who had fought to rescue Andrew Johnson from the rebels in June 1861, offered a prayer for his old friend and comrade-in-arms. "Give him the head, the heart and the hands to accomplish the mighty work assigned to him to perform," he prayed. From East Tennessee no delegates reported. President Johnson's course toward the rebels was much too considerate for those fierce mountaineers. But two old Union Tennessee friends, Governor W. B. Campbell and Governor Neill S. Brown, came as delegates at large.

"A few minutes before twelve o'clock, as a band of music stationed in the gallery gave the National air, Governor Randall announced from the platform that the delegates from Massachusetts and from South Carolina were entering the hall arm in arm." This announcement produced great excitement; "cheer after cheer went up. Members stood upon the benches, hats were thrown into the air, ladies waved their handkerchiefs, the band commenced the air 'Rally Round the Flag,' and followed it with the 'Star Spangled Banner' and 'Dixie.' Major General Custer jumped upon a bench and called for cheers." General Dix, the Chairman, came forward and declared that the Confederate States, having accepted the condition imposed upon them by the President, were entitled to exercise their legitimate function as members of the Union, that the enaction of new conditions "was unjust and the violation of the faith of the Government, subversive to the purpose of our political system, and dangerous to the public prosperity and peace." . . . "Is this the government our fathers fought to establish?" he exclaimed. "Is this the government we have been fighting to preserve?" What an inspiring and yet what an impossible scheme! How noble the thought! In twelve months men who had been cutting each other's throats had become the best of friends. Yet how absurd to expect that Copperheads, like Fernando Wood and C. L. Vallandigham, could organize a National Union party and take charge of a Nation that had been saved, despite their efforts to disrupt it.

Indeed the incongruousness of the thing was such that delegates Wood and Vallandigham withdrew, under pressure. But there remained another class of delegates almost as obnoxious to the North—the rebel element from the South. Men like Alexander Stephens, Vice-president of the Confederacy; J. B. Gordon and Richard Taylor, gallant Confederate generals; Colonel McIntyre and Major Pendleton. Should rebels and Copperheads lay down laws for Union men? In fact, the call for the convention, which was largely a Democratic call, was itself an offense to the triumphant North, and many wise men, like William Cornell Jewett, so wrote and advised the committee in charge. Horace Greeley fairly blistered the pages of the *Tribune* with maledictions. It was a "bread and butter" convention and it was "composed of ninety per cent. Rebels and Copperheads"! Notwithstanding these handicaps, the convention was a success. Senator Reverdy Johnson, the President's personal manager, was well pleased. Randall wrote the President that "if the convention got through without a split" they would "have easy sailing thereafter." In response to a wire from secretaries Browning and Randall, the President replied, "The finger of Providence is unerring and will guide you safely through. The people must be trusted and the country will be restored." While the Convention was sitting Colorado was reported to have elected a Conservative to Congress over a Radical and there was great applause.[21] The declaration of principles was wise and strong and the address to the

[21] *The National Union Convention, its History and Proceedings* (Barclay and Company, publishers), Philadelphia, 1866.

people in excellent style and taste.   Both were the work of
Henry J. Raymond, Chairman of the Resolutions Committee.
Samuel J. Tilden rose and proposed three cheers for Raymond
and they were given with a will.

"History affords no instance," so the resolution read, "where
a people so powerful in numbers, in resources, and in public
spirit, after a war so long in its duration and so adverse in
its issue, have accepted defeat and its consequences with so
much of good faith as have marked the conduct of the people
lately in insurrection against the United States."   And yet "no
people has ever existed whose loyalty and faith the treatment
accorded them by Congress would not alienate and impair.
The ten millions of Americans who live in the South would be
unworthy citizens of a free country, degenerate sons of a heroic
ancestor if they could accept with submission the humiliations
sought to be imposed upon them.   Resentment of injustice is
always and everywhere essential to freedom; and the spirit
which prompts the states and the people lately in the Insurrection, but insurgent now no longer, to protest against the
imposition of unjust and degrading conditions, makes them
all the more worthy to share in the government of a free commonwealth, and gives still firmer assurance of the future power
and freedom of the Republic."

The convention adjourned, well pleased with its work, having appointed a committee of two delegates from each state, of
which Reverdy Johnson was chairman, to present an official
copy of the proceedings to the President.   On the eighteenth
the committee went over to Washington.   They assured the
President that there was unanimity and unbroken harmony,
that every heart was full of joy, every eye beaming with patriotic animation, that the men of Massachusetts and of South
Carolina came in the convention hand in hand, filling thousands
of eyes with tears of joy which they neither "could nor desired
to repress; for the time had arrived when all sectional differences had ceased and there was unbounded pride in a common
Union." . . . "In you, Mr. President," the committee declared, "the convention recognize a chief magistrate devoted to
the Constitution and laws and the interests of the whole coun-

try. The course of Congress in holding ten states as subjected provinces is at war with the very genius of our Government and prejudicial to the peace and safety of the country."

The President, accepting the proceedings, spoke with vigor and feeling. He had taken his stand upon the broad principles of liberty and the Constitution, he declared, and "there is not power enough on earth to drive me from it. . . . Having placed myself upon that broad platform I have never been awed, dismayed or intimidated by either threats or encroachment, but have stood there in conjunction with patriotic spirits, sounding the tocsin of alarm when I deemed the citadel of liberty in danger. . . . My race is nearly run, I have passed through every position from village alderman to President . . . if I wanted authority or if I wished to perpetuate my own power, how easy it would have been to hold and wield that which was placed in my hands by the measure called the Freedmen's Bureau bill! With an army which it placed at my discretion, I could have remained in the Capitol and with fifty or sixty millions of appropriations at my disposal, with the machinery to be worked by my own hands, and with my satraps and dependents in every town and village, and then with the Civil Rights bill following as an auxiliary, I could have proclaimed myself dictator. . . . But, gentlemen, my pride and my ambition have been to occupy that position which retains all power in the hands of the people. . . . I acknowledge no superior except my God, the author of my existence, and the people of the United States." As the President proceeded, the committee followed him with rapt attention, particularly when he said how visibly he was affected when he received a despatch informing him that the convention, distinguished for intellect and wisdom, was at times so overcome that "every eye was suffused with tears on beholding the scene." . . . "I could not finish reading the despatch," the President admitted, "for my feelings overcame me."

But there were seams in the President's armor, seams which the rapier of the Radicals soon pierced. In the course of his speech he had said that Congress was "a body called or which assumes to be the Congress of the United States, but in fact a

Congress of only a part of the states, a body hanging on the verge of government." Why, the man who could give expression to such sentiments was a traitor and ought to be ejected from office without a trial! Accounts of the "arm and arm convention" filled every paper. By the Conservatives Johnson was pictured as a patriot. By the Radicals he was depicted as "King Andy"—in purple and velvet with the trappings of royalty. "Tears, idle tears," Greeley wrote. "No doubt, tears of grief at the murder of loyal men in Memphis and throughout the South!" Thomas Nast, the cartoonist, had a fine subject for ridicule. *Harper's* bubbled over with fun. Its readers could not get enough of the "arm in arm convention." It was pictured from every angle, but always in tears. Governor Orr of South Carolina, large and benevolent with chin whiskers, *a la* Horace Greeley, and General Couch of Massachusetts, kindly, humane, dreamy-eyed, both locked in fond embrace, were cartooned leading a procession of tearful delegates. A lion and a lamb, likewise arm in arm, then came along. In the corner a pussy cat was weeping, as though her heart would break; while the dicky bird, on the mantel, shook with grief. The great writer, James Russell Lowell, descended from his lofty tripod, appealing to man's lower nature, even making fun of the Chairman's name—"Doolittle!" . . . "He was a Doolittle indeed!" and much more of like kind.[22]

Unfortunately for the President, on July 30, while meetings were being held in New Orleans to select delegates to the Philadelphia convention, a terrible riot occurred in the former city. Nearly forty people, almost all negroes or Unionists, were killed. The blame of the affair was sought to be laid by the Radicals at the President's door.[23] The New Orleans Riot is but the history of the age-old conflict between whites and blacks. In 1864 a constitutional convention, called by the Military Governor, had been held in New Orleans, and, after finishing its work, adjourned to be reconvened, "if the work of the convention is not ratified by the people," at the call of the presiding officer. But the work of the convention was ratified

---

[22] *North American Review*, Vol. CII, p. 520.
[23] New York *Tribune*, July 31, 1866.

at the polls.[24]   Nevertheless, two years later the presiding officer was asked to reconvene the convention, the object being to
give the negroes the ballot, thereby placing New Orleans under
negro rule.   This the President refused to do.   He held that
the convention was *functus* and had no right to meet again.

A few members of the 1864 convention then met and attempted to elect a new presiding officer.   This officer, though
it was claimed he was not a delegate to the convention, issued
a call for the convention to meet on Monday, July 30, to ascertain how many vacancies had occurred since 1864 and to transact other business.   Up to this stage the affair was considered
harmless and more or less of a joke, but when the Governor
took a hand and issued a call for an election to be held on
September 3 to fill vacancies in the convention, matters grew
serious.[25]   Was New Orleans to become Africanized?   Was
Louisiana to pass into corrupt and alien hands, as Arkansas
had done?

In this situation Judge Abell, a member of the convention
and also a state Judge, charged the grand jury at New Orleans
to present the members of the convention, about to assemble,
that such assembly was unlawful and that the overt act of lawlessness was the mere gathering together of the delegates without authority and for unlawful purposes.   He called attention
of the grand jury to the law as declared in *Russell on Crimes*,
"The mere assembly of persons to do an unlawful thing is a
disturbance of the peace." [26]   The military authorities then
arrested the Judge.   In this controversy, the Lieutenant-Governor and the Mayor stood in with the whites, and both sides
seemed anxious to be sustained by the National Government.
In New Orleans at this time, as General Sheridan reported to
General Grant on August 1, the negroes were led on by whites,
"who were political agitators and revolutionary men," and
"the action of the convention was likely to produce breaches
of the peace." [27]

Three days before the convention met, Dr. Dostie, a radical

[24] New York *Times*, August 1, 1866.
[25] *Ibid.*, July 31-August 10, 1866.
[26] New Orleans *Times*, July 28-August 10, 1866.
[27] Johnson MS. No. 11,939.

leader, addressing the negroes, advised them to come to the convention armed to fight the "hell-born" rebels. . . . "We have four hundred thousand to three hundred thousand," he exclaimed, "and we cannot only whip but exterminate the other party." . . . "We want brave men and not cowards Monday. . . . There will be no such puerile affair as at Memphis and . . . if we are interfered with the streets of New Orleans will run with blood." The crowd of excited negroes shouted back that they would be there.[28] President Johnson did what he could, by letter and wire, to prevent the convention from assembling. The civil authorities were evidently anxious to avoid bloodshed, as were the military. After Judge Abell was arrested, on July 25, the Mayor wrote to General Baird, in command during the temporary absence of General Sheridan, that he, as mayor, felt it his duty to arrest the delegates and "suppress the unlawful assembly provided they met without the sanction of the military authorities." General Baird replied that he could not see what business the Mayor had to interfere, that "the Governor ought to take the initiative and the United States Government ought to decide."

Each side got in touch with Washington, General Baird wiring Secretary Stanton and the Lieutenant-Governor, and the Mayor wiring the President. The Mayor's wire to the President, dated 2 p.m., July 28, 1866, advised that "the President was bitterly denounced"; that the whole matter would be moved before the grand jury, but it was "impossible to execute civil process without certainty of a riot. Contemplated to have members of the convention under process from the Civil Court. Is military to interfere to prevent process of court?" To this wire, the President replied at once, "The military would be expected to sustain and not to obstruct or interfere with the proceedings of the court."

To General Baird's telegram, Secretary Stanton made no reply. Baird's telegram notified Stanton that a convention had been called with the sanction of Governor Wells for Monday. "The Lieutenant-Governor and city authorities think it unlawful and propose to break it up by arresting the dele-

[28] Fleming, *History of Reconstruction*, Vol. I, p. 231.

Reconstruction and How It Works

gates." So Baird's wire read. And it went on: "I have given no orders on the subject, but have warned the parties I should not countenance or permit such action without instructions to that effect from the President. Please instruct me by telegraph." The President's wire to the Mayor was exhibited to General Baird on the forenoon of July 28. Stanton made no reply to Baird's telegram, claiming that he did "not understand from the wire that force or resistance would be used to break up the convention;" [29] nor did he communicate its contents to the President.

General Baird declared that he would arrest any officer who interfered with the delegates. In consequence of this, as the Mayor claimed, he turned the matter of policing New Orleans on the thirtieth over to General Baird, who promised to have troops at that time. On the day of the convention the delegates assembled at twelve noon without disturbance. At this time there were neither police nor soldiers around Mechanics' Hall where the convention met. No quorum being present, an adjournment was taken for an hour and a half. Meanwhile a large crowd of negroes armed with pistols and clubs marched to the convention hall. On the way down they either knocked or shoved a white boy from the sidewalk. The offending negro was arrested, but before he could be taken in hand by the officer the negroes fired one or two shots. This was the first shooting of the day. Immediately a call was sent in for the police force, which had been armed in advance. A battle ensued between the police, assisted by a large number of whites, and the negro rioters. The negroes fled to the convention hall. A white flag was run out of the window; the police went forward to make the arrest, and were fired upon from the convention hall. Infuriated whites broke into the building and killed and butchered without mercy. Only one policeman was killed. General Sheridan reported that the Mayor was "a bad, disloyal man" and that "three-fourths of the mob of

[29] *Tribune Tracts* No. 1; *History of New Orleans*, Vol. I, p. 267; *Report of the Committee of the House, Second Session Thirty-ninth Congress*, Document No. 1304, p. 27 and also p. 252.

whites were ex-Confederates," who "instead of quieting the riot aided it."

Before the convention assembled General Baird stated that if a riot occurred it would be "a serious hurt to reconstruction." President Johnson and Secretary Welles, commenting on the affair, insisted that the riot was deliberately arranged by the Radicals for political effect. The Radicals, on the other hand, laid the blame on Johnson's telegram. President Johnson did not know of General Baird's wire to Secretary Stanton until the middle of August, and he bore resentment to Stanton for failing to call it to his attention. Time and again the President declared that if he had known the contents of the Stanton [30] telegram he would have put the city under military rule on July 30. One of the strangest incidents connected with the affair is that Baird claims he thought the convention was to meet at 6 o'clock at night. He admits that he made no inquiry as to the time.[31] The negro rioters were indicted by the Grand Jury, which made a report exonerating the whites. The police were not arrested. The influence of this terrible affair upon the minds of the nation was overwhelming. In all its horrors it was photographed in the magazines. By the Radicals it was held up to the North as the direct result of Andy Johnsonism. The *Tribune* called it a "rebel riot." It was not a riot, it subsequently said, but "a cold-blooded murder." No doubt the convention of 1864 was a defunct body, but the violence with which the police set upon the badly advised negroes was wholly without excuse.

The New Orleans massacre furnished a rallying point for the two Republican conventions which were shortly after held, one in Philadelphia by the "True Southern Loyalists" and the Soldiers' and Sailors' convention in Pittsburgh. This last convention was the most enthusiastic and best attended of all the conventions of the year. It declared: "We will dare maintain our country and when we follow Congress we follow the same flag and principle we did during the war." The Southern Loyalists convention proclaimed Andrew Johnson a traitor to his

---

[30] W. G. Moore, *Diary*, p. 98.
[31] Rhodes, Vol. VI, p. 613.

country, the speech made by Fighting Parson Brownlow on this occasion being as violent as anything ever uttered by Thaddeus Stevens.   The Parson gave notice that unless the new rebels were put down nothing was left to the National Government but to send out an army with compass and rule, and cut up the South into small lots and sell these off to pay the expenses of the war.

Early in July three of the cabinet, unwilling to oppose the radical policy of Congress—Dennison, Harlan, and Speed— resigned and were replaced by Randall of Wisconsin, Browning of Kentucky, and Stanbery of Ohio.   In the reorganization of the cabinet, "the President had no recourse to the Democracy; none of the new members had ever affiliated with that party, Johnson exhibiting an immovable fidelity to the conditions under which he attained to his high office." [32]   The subordinate offices under the new secretaries were, however, filled by persons friendly to the President, who contributed what they could to the building up of a party favorable to him.   Stanton did not resign but remained to plague the administration.[33]   Advised by the Radicals to "stick," he stuck.   Welles, Preston King, the Blairs, and others urged the President to remove him, but Seward opposed and prevailed.[34]   In pursuing this course, and retaining the Republicans, the President was undoubtedly correct.   Being a southern man and under suspicion at the North, had he yielded to Welles, he could not have weathered the storm of northern indignation as long as he did.[35]

In the midst of such excitement and discussion the event known as the "Swing Round the Circle" took place.   Promptly at seven-thirty A.M. on August 28, in compliance with an invitation of the Douglas Memorial Association, President Johnson and his party pulled out from the Washington station in coaches attached to the regular train for Chicago.   Accompanying the President were his daughter, Mrs. Patterson, together with General Grant, Admiral Farragut, Secretaries Seward, Randall, Welles and Mrs. Welles.   Some fifty others,

---

32 Dunning, *Reconstruction*, p. 73.
33 Welles, *Diary*, May 14, 1866, and Rhodes, Vol. V, p. 611.
34 *Ibid.*, Vol. III, p. 492.
35 *Magazine of American History*, Vol. XX, p. 40.

more or less prominent, many accompanied by their respective wives, were also of the party. The pageant, as Secretary Welles calls it, was approved of by Seward, Stanton, McCulloch and Stanbery, but he, Welles, was "greatly disinclined to go along." [36]

It was, however, the event of all others President Johnson welcomed; he wished the chance to meet the people face to face. Forgetting that war hysteria had not subsided in the North as it had in his own bosom and that revolutions never go backward, he was going forth with the United States flag in one hand and the Constitution in the other, pleading for the old Union just as it was. Incidentally, he was breaking up the Republican party and organizing a new party in which neither Jeff Davis, Thad Stevens, Charles L. Vallandigham, nor other Rebel or Radical or Copperhead, would be tolerated. Since taking up Lincoln's task he had striven to follow the middle course with malice towards none and charity for all, the expounding of this policy being one object of his present trip. Scarcely, however, had the trip begun before it was plain the Radicals were determined to ridicule it and belittle it, as they shortly did at Philadelphia, and finally to break it up.

In Baltimore the people turned out, one hundred thousand strong. Cannon boomed and the air was rent with cheers. The President rode in a carriage through the main street and on to Fort McHenry. General Grant and Admiral Farragut, when presented by Seward, who uniformly acted as master of ceremonies, were wildly cheered. A number of mechanics and laborers, breaking through the crowd, clasped the President by the hand amidst great applause.[36a] The Metropolitan press carried columns describing the great tour with its orations, banquets and pageants. In Philadelphia the crowds were immense, but there, as in Baltimore, Republican leaders were conspicuously absent. On August 29, in New York, half a million people greeted the party. There were speeches by the President, General Grant, Farragut and Seward, a great ban-

[36] Welles, *Diary*, Vol. III, p. 588.
[36a] New York *Herald*, August 29, 1866.

quet at Delmonico's and a serenade to the President, together with a reception along the Hudson.

The gist of the President's remarks wherever he spoke was, "Let there be a common feeling—our country first, our country last, our country all the time—disregarding party for the public good." This sentiment usually met with vigorous applause. Commenting editorially on the President's course, the *Herald* called Andrew Johnson "the fearless patriot, steadfast to his trust and in the fiery days of war like

> " 'Abdiel, faithful found
> Among the faithless faithful only he.' "

But the Radicals were bent on his destruction. The Republican party, which had won the war and broken the shackles from the ankles of four million slaves, must not be destroyed by a combination of Copperheads and Rebels led on by a turncoat President. Forgetting that Johnson's policy at that moment was the same as in 1865 when he was the national hero, Horace Greeley called him a traitor and pooh-poohed the idea he was following in Lincoln's footsteps. Other Radical and Jacobin journals used violent, dangerous and threatening language, pointing to Charles I as a warning. The New York assembly voted down a resolution welcoming the President to the state. A Senator, who had been a Wall Street speculator during the war, intimated that Johnson would be murdered if he attempted to cross upper New York.[37] Thad Stevens pulled himself out of a sick room to make a single speech. Dubbing Johnson's swing around the circle a traveling circus, with Seward and Johnson as the two clowns, he sneeringly paraphrased the President's speeches. "He has been everything," he tells us, "alderman, constable, legislator—God help that legislature—and in Congress and now is President; but he has never been a hangman and so he wants to be that, and hang Thad Stevens." [38]

Conservative Republicans of the James Russell Lowell type lost their poise, declaring that Seward's "awkward attempts at familiarity," "his tumbling efforts to be droll," and Johnson's "Jack-pudding tricks," as they swung around the circle, were

[37] *Ibid.*, August 31, 1866.
[38] McCall, *Stevens*, p. 281.

disgusting. Johnson's plan of reconciliation, which the cartoonists labeled "My Policy," they called treasonable. There should be no policy. "The boyish and conceited Southerners," they asserted, "would treat Johnson's leniency as cowardice." . . . "The South called for war," said Lowell, "and we have given it to her. We will fix the terms of peace ourselves and we will teach the South that Christ is disguised in a dusky race." [39]

On the way to Chicago the President spoke in sundry cities, sometimes from the rear end of the platform. "I leave in your hands the Constitution and the Union," he would uniformly say, "and the glorious flag of your country, not with twenty-five but with thirty-six stars." On September 6 at Chicago he delivered the address before the Douglas Memorial Association, crying out: If Andrew Jackson or Stephen A. Douglas knew what was going on in our country to-day "they would shake off the habiliments of the tomb and declare 'the Constitution and the Union, they must be preserved.'" Everywhere he made it plain that the Radicals in Congress must be defeated and Conservatives elected, indulging in personal experiences to point his remarks.

By the time the party set out on the return trip to Washington the President's opponents were well organized. In opposition to the new National Union party stood forth a mighty phalanx: Party men like Fessenden, Blaine and Garfield, who saw death to the Republican party in the new Johnson movement; philanthropists like Beecher, Gerard and Greeley, who felt that the colored man needed further protection than the Thirteenth Amendment; radicals like Wade, Stevens, Chandler, Shellabarger, who hated the South on principle; negrophiles such as Chase, Sumner and Julian. Besides these there were millions of Union soldiers, some crippled and wounded, together with their families, who were unwilling to trust their future in the hands of the Democratic party. General Dix, who presided at the Philadelphia convention, charged that faith was not kept with that convention, that the new party had been captured by the Democrats. But what

[39] *North American Review*, Vol. CII, p. 520.

could Johnson do? As the tour proceeded it was becoming more and more evident that he could not shake off the copperheads and the rebels, and that these constituted nearly all that was left of the promising National Union party. As Hogan, the Irish Congressman from St. Louis, with his strong lungs, would introduce the President to the crowd, General Grant took grave offense. "I can stand a rebel," said the General to Welles, "but a Copperhead like Hogan I cannot forgive." [40]

On the return trip the crowds were sometimes boisterous and unruly. The Radical press had ridiculed the President's idea of immediate and peaceful restoration until the boys in the streets laughed and jeered without knowing what it was all about.[41] At Philadelphia the President, reverting to his stock illustration and addressing the mechanics, declared that Adam was the first tailor and sewed fig leaves together. "No," he said, "this is not entirely satisfactory, for we read in the twenty-first verse of the third chapter of Genesis that God Almighty was the first tailor and that 'unto Adam also and his wife did the Lord God make coats of skin.' Therefore God Himself was the first member of the craft!" [41a] Clearly this was blasphemy, the Radicals declared, and "the use of such language showed that Johnson was desperate."

The President so often referred to what he had done and suffered for the Union, Forney of the Philadelphia *Press* headlined accounts of the tour with only one word, "I," "My," or "Me." He charged that Johnson's speeches were a continued rigmarole of "My policy." The Memphis and New Orleans riots were again brought forward by the press. *Harper's* had blood-curdling cartoons, sometimes covering two pages. One of these was labeled, "Andrew Johnson's Record—How it works." Skeletons of starving Union soldiers, starved at Andersonville, were depicted.[41b] Negro men and women were seen tied to a stake while the bull whip was being poured on

[40] Welles, *Diary*, Vol. II, p. 591.
[41] Blaine, Vol. II, p. 239.
[41a] It will be noted that this is the same speech that Johnson delivered in Nashville in 1857; Hubbard, *Tale of Two Tailors*.
[41b] The per cent. of deaths in northern prisons and in southern was practically the same.

their naked backs. In hospital wards negroes, wounded or killed at Memphis and New Orleans, were shown.

As Johnson read these attacks upon himself and heard his motives impugned by "slackers" he hurled back the charges. The radical press he called mercenary and subsidized. "The foul rebellion at the South," he declared, "headed by the traitor, Jeff Davis, had been put down and this new rebellion headed by Stevens and Sumner must also be put down. . . . I fought the southern traitors and whipped them," he said, "and, God being willing and with your help, I intend to fight out the battle with northern traitors." Presently hecklers began to interrupt the speaking. "What about the New Orleans riot?" they asked. "Don't get mad, Andy," they jeered. "Three cheers for Congress," they cried. Sometimes they cried, "Traitor! Traitor!" One of the hecklers shouted, "Why don't you hang Jeff Davis?" "I am not the Chief Justice," Johnson retorted, "I am not the prosecuting attorney, nor am I the jury."

At Norwalk, Ohio, the President was saying that it was time to stop the sacrifice of blood and treasure when a rowdy broke in and asked, "Why don't you stop it at New Orleans?" Johnson called for the fellow and denounced him in a most un-Presidential way. At Cleveland, when some one yelled out that his speech did not become the dignity of a President, Johnson answered, "When I am insulted I do not care about dignity." To a person in the crowd who constantly interrupted the speaking Johnson hurled back that one who would stop free speech had "ceased to be a man and had shrunk into the dimensions of a reptile." At St. Louis he replied to an interruption relating to the New Orleans riot, saying that the blood of that riot was not on himself but on Congress, that the Radicals in Congress held a caucus just before the riot and knew that the unlawful Louisiana convention was called to meet, and approved of its object, and that the object was to disfranchise the whites and enfranchise the blacks.

At Cleveland it was charged that ruffians had been hired to heckle the President.[42] At Pittsburgh, where the great

[42] Oberholtzer, *History*, Vol. I, p. 409.

Soldiers' and Sailors' convention was soon to meet, the speaking could not take place. Along the route it was plain that Grant and Farragut were more popular than the President, and for the first time Grant began to think of the Presidency for himself. On September 10, while the President was at dinner at Indianapolis, a riot broke out in the lobby of his hotel and several persons were killed or wounded. The Indianapolis *Herald* of that date declared that it was a radical plot and "the whole thing preconcerted."

As the Presidential party came further South the complexion of the crowds changed and there was great enthusiasm. At Louisville, Kentucky, "the reception was magnificent," as it was all through Kentucky, Maryland and in parts of Pennsylvania. While the tour was in progress, southern radicals were not idle. Parson Brownlow, who had become a leader of the radical wing, headed a counter tour, its object being, he declared, "to wipe out the moccasin tracks of Andrew Johnson and William H. Seward." [43]

The New York *Herald* spoke of the journey and the speechmaking tour of Brownlow and Jack Hamilton of Texas as "the journey of the negrophiles and the miscegines." And truly the course which they then advocated was a bloody one. The Fighting Parson declared that when the next northern army went South, he "wanted to have a finger in the pie." "Let them go armed with small arms and with heavy artillery," said the Parson, "in order to do the killing; and with spirits of turpentine and pine knots to do the burning." [44]

After passing through York and Baltimore, amidst great enthusiasm, on Saturday, September 15, the Presidential party arrived in Washington. Great preparations had been arranged by the city council and patriotic organizations to make the President's homecoming a hearty welcome. Guns were fired at the navy yard. Poets shrieked popular lines,

> "Thrice welcome back
> To thy national home
> Our brave magnanimous President."

[43] *Herald*, September 12, 1866.
[44] New York *Times*, September 13, 1866; Oberholtzer, Vol. I, p. 405.

Mayor Wallach, delivering the address of welcome, declared that the whole population of Washington had turned out for the occasion. "We have come out to greet you, Mr. President," he said, "to welcome you home and to cheer you in your efforts to restore eleven states to their places in the Union." [45] After the President had made a short and appropriate reply the enthusiastic crowds marched up Pennsylvania Avenue to the White House. They passed under banners on which were inscribed, "The Constitution and Andrew Johnson now and forever," and like patriotic sentiments. At the Mansion the crowd called out the President again. He spoke briefly and well, thanking them for their presence and bidding them good-night.

Taking the tour as a whole, Secretary Welles thought it was a success. "In some cases party malignity showed itself, but it was rare and the guilty few in number." . . . "It was evident," said Welles, "that in most of the cases—not exceeding a half dozen in all—the hostile party manifestations were pre-arranged and precipitated by sneaking leaders." . . . "The President spoke freely," said Welles. "He wished to address the people face to face, a plan with which he had been familiar in Tennessee and the Southwest. . . . When he stated the true issues to the people they were obviously with him." [46] Not only Welles but the President himself, "had sanguine belief that he had aroused his countrymen." Unfortunately, the President was mistaken. Though the people were aroused, it was not in his behalf. It would have been far better for the President's cause had he remained at home. Despite enthusiastic peace and union meetings in New York on September 17 and elsewhere during the fall, in the November election "Andyjohnsonism" was turned down. In 1861 and in 1862, Johnson's rough tongue, in the cause of the Union, had delighted the North and he was then called "glorious old Andy Johnson." In 1866 the same sturdy patriot had become a blackguard!

45 New York *Herald*, September 16; *National Intelligencer*, September 17; *Evening Union*, September 15.
46 Welles, Vol. II, p. 590.

As the southern states voted against the Fourteenth Amendment, it was defeated, for lack of the requisite three-fourths. Thus the Radicals won a temporary victory. But was it not at a sacrifice? Having rejected Lincoln's advice, having "spurned and rejected the southern whites" and said to them, "You are worthless, or worse," the Radicals molded a solid South, resurrected the defunct and despised Democratic party, and created those unhappy conditions in the South which have not yet fully disappeared.[47]

Rhodes, the historian, characterizes this trip as an "indecent orgy," and positively asserts that Johnson was intoxicated at Cleveland. In this Rhodes was mistaken, as we now know. All trustworthy accounts are that these charges of drunkenness are "wholly unfounded," that there was no eye-witness and "no responsible charge of drinking." In fact, Schouler "challenges the proof of such a cruel statement." While Johnson's harangues and colloquies "were vehement and inappropriate," they were "clear and to the point," and far from "incoherent or maudlin." [48] I might add that in the Impeachment trial newspaper reporters testified that there was no drinking on this trip. Indeed, the presence of the wives and daughters of those participating repels the suggestion of a "drunken orgy."

[47] Blaine, *Twenty Years*, Vol. II, p. 242: The 1866 election was vital; "had it gone Democratic there would have been no more amendments or reconstruction laws."

[48] Major Truman, *Century Magazine*, January 1913, p. 438; McCulloch, *Men and Measures*, p. 393; DeWitt, *Impeachment and Trial*, p. 420; Schouler, Vol. VII, p. 74; Oberholtzer, Vol. I, p. 404.

CHAPTER III

VETO FOLLOWS VETO

The November elections in 1866 went overwhelmingly Republican, and the Radicals had things their own way. Old Thad Stevens, rising in Congress, drolly remarked, "I was a Conservative at the last session of this Congress, but I mean to be a Radical hereafter." The President's course had been so thoroughly condemned at the polls that conservative papers were urging him "to forego his plans." He could now "tuck ship and sail with the wind," they declared; "why sharpen acrimony by further resistance?"[1] The radical press was jubilant, boasting that "King Andy" was dead, that the sot, the beast, the renegade, the dirty dog and the copperhead, as they called the President, together with "my policy" and "I," "Me," and "My" had been buried forever.[2] He had "reeled" into the Presidency and been repudiated.

Threats made during the campaign, "We'll hang the d——d traitor," were again heard and the Governors of several states held an imprudent and violent meeting.[3] The President being a traitor to his party, his office should be sequestered, he should be turned out and tried afterwards. On the other side unwise friends were still urging the President to meet force with force. Congress was a Rump and it was his duty, they insisted, not to recognize the unlawful assembly or to approve any bill until the southern states were admitted. He was admonished "to keep his powder dry" and "to issue a call for five hundred thousand troops to defend the country."[4] Advice of this kind came from the North, however, the South having had war enough for the present.

In this state of confusion the President kept his head and

[1] New York *Herald* and *World*, November 8, 1866; *Times*, November 9.
[2] Oberholtzer, Vol. I, p. 416.
[3] *Ibid.*, p. 417.
[4] Johnson MS.

wisely held his tongue though he issued orders to Secretary Stanton "to take such steps as were adequate for the protection and security of the Government." [5]   Neither radicals nor conservatives understood President Johnson.   Though he was stubborn and pugnacious he was loyal, through and through, and his country was more to him than personal success.   He had been ill treated by Congress but he would not follow those advising that he use the army to reorganize that body. Neither would he follow the radicals and run the steam-roller over the Constitution and the southern states.   If he must be a martyr, so be it, he was willing to go down with the Constitution.

Besides, Johnson foolishly concluded that the people had been deceived and would reverse themselves when they knew the facts.   Even war hysteria he imagined could be overcome by the facts.   He was sure that time and patience would disillusion the North as to the negro and show that Lincoln was right.   He realized that not an inch could the South be driven, but anywhere it could be led, by kindness and generosity. Among Democratic leaders the President relied mostly upon Senator Reverdy Johnson of Maryland, who was daily pleading for conciliation without force or coercion.   "Let us take our southern brethren to our bosoms and trust them," he was saying, when opposing the Civil Rights bill.   "And as I believe in my existence you will never have occasion to regret it.   If we do this we will look back with delight on our course for we will be prosperous and have a national fame of which the world furnishes no example." [6]

In a word, President Johnson's policy was very unlike that proposed by the radical leaders.   "The Radicals would base the new governments upon the loyalty of the past, plus the aid of enfranchised slaves; he would establish the new régime by

[5] Letter to Stanton dated November 1, 1866.   Oberholtzer concludes from this letter that the President "took counsel of his fears as he was wont to do," a charge Johnson's enemies did not make.   Governor Morton, one of the impeaching Senators, together with John Sherman, Blaine and other stalwart Republicans who knew Johnson personally, declare that he was "distinguished for courage and bravery."—*Memorial Addresses* in the Senate on Andrew Johnson, p. 14.

[6] Barnes, *The Thirty-ninth Congress*, p. 386.

the loyalty of the future." Like Governor Andrew, he thought
that restoration must be effected by the willing efforts of the
South. Johnson would aid and guide but not force the people.
If the latter did not wish restoration, under Lincoln's terms
and his, they might remain under military rule. There should
be no forced negro suffrage, no sweeping disfranchisement of
whites, no "carpetbaggism." [7]

When Congress met in December 1866 the President sent in
a message whose conservatism and dignity surprised the radicals. They had been looking for an outburst of temper. First
he recounted the steps he had taken with a view to the gradual
restoration of the states. Having done these things, "he had
done all that was within the scope of his constitutional authority." One thing, however, "yet remained to be done before
the work of restoration could be completed," and that was
"the admission to Congress of loyal Senators and Representatives from the South." "More than one-fourth of the whole
number of states," he declared, "remained without representation and the seats of fifty members in the House and twenty
members in the Senate are yet vacant. . . . Their admission
would have accomplished much toward the renewal and
strengthening of our relations as one people; it would have
accorded with the great principles in the Declaration of Independence that no people ought to bear the burden of taxation
and yet be denied the right of representation. . . . Each state
shall have at least one representative . . . and no state without its consent shall be deprived of its equal suffrage in the
Senate." These provisions, the President reminded the Senate,
were "intended to secure to every state the right of representation. So important was it that not even by an amendment of
the Constitution can any state, without its consent, be denied
an equal voice in the Senate."

The President next quotes his resolutions of July 1861,
which declared the principles upon which the war was waged:
"Not in any spirit of oppression nor for conquest or subjugation nor to overthrow or interfere with the rights or institutions of the states but to defend the Constitution and preserve

[7] Fleming, *The Sequel of Appomattox*, p. 68.

the Union with the rights of the states unimpaired." All of these things having been accomplished, in the language of the resolution, "the war ought to cease." The message then calls attention to acts of Congress which, from time to time during the war, recognized the existence of Tennessee and other loyal southern states, and also to the action of the executive department of the Government recognizing such states. "The recognition of the states by the judicial department of the Government," the message continues, "has also been clear and conclusive in all proceedings affecting them as states. . . . Upon this question so vitally affecting the restoration of the Union and permanency of our present form of government," the President declares, "my convictions heretofore expressed, have undergone no change, but, on the contrary, their correctness has been confirmed by reflection and time. If the admission of loyal members to seats in the respective Houses of Congress was wise and expedient a year ago, it is no less wise and expedient now. If this anomalous condition is right now—if in the exact condition of these states at the present time it is lawful to exclude them from representation—I do not see that the question will be changed by the efflux of time. Ten years hence, if these states remain as they are, the right of representation will be no stronger, the right of exclusion will be no weaker." [8]

This was Andrew Johnson's view of the Constitution and of his duty as a Constitutional President, and from this position he would not budge. According to his way of thinking no state had committed suicide nor was the Constitution permanently dead. During the Civil War the rebellious states temporarily lost their standing in the Union. When the war ended such states regained their statehood and the Constitution became the supreme law. "On the question of punishing rebels," as has been well said, "the Radicals may have had cause of complaint that Andrew Johnson, in action, had turned out so differently from Andrew Johnson, in speech, but not on the question of reconstruction. Upon that question his course had been perfectly consistent and straightforward throughout." [9]

[8] Richardson, *Messages and Papers*, Vol. VI, p. 448.
[9] "Vice-president Johnson," *Southern Historical Association*, Vol. IX, 1905; Schouler, Vol. VII, p. 28.

As to the matter of pardons, he was liberally extending pardons in individual cases. Freely and wisely he was exercising this great power.[10]

Republican organs, commenting on the message, characterized it as "a dreary, lifeless document and on a par with one of Franklin Pierce's." . . . "The President has been reduced to a cipher," they boasted, "and Congress will deal with him so as to make him realize his defeat and future insignificance."[11] Accordingly, the Radicals or Jacobins in Congress set about to make Johnson a figurehead, a thing it must be admitted they were fully capable of undertaking. Stevens, mocking at Johnson's attempt at restoration as he had mocked Lincoln's effort to organize Virginia and give constitutional life to the ten per cent. governments; Sumner "unpractical, theoretical, not troubled by constitutional scruples"; Henry Wilson, "the Natick cobbler," who considered the Republican party divine, "created by no man or set of men but brought into being by Almighty God himself"; Morton, who had changed front, and Wade, "bluff, coarse and ungenerous"; Boutwell, "fanatical and mediocre"; Ben Butler, "a charlatan and a demagogue," and Shellabarger, who had convinced himself that "the Confederates had framed iniquity and universal murder into law, poisoned northern wells, put mines under the prisons of Union soldiers, ordered the torch and yellow fever to be carried into northern cities, to kill women and children, and plan one universal bonfire of the North from Lake Ontario to the Mississippi."[12] An unfortunate aggregation to be sure! Writing to his wife, the rising young Congressman Garfield, made this comment, "The Radicals must do some absurdly extravagant thing to prove themselves Radicals, but I am trying to be a Radical and not a fool."[13]

Undoubtedly the recent election was an endorsement of the plan of the radicals. The southern states were either conquered provinces or had committed suicide. In either event there was no law and no constitution for them, except such as

10 Rhodes, *History*, Vol. VI, pp. 60 and 535.
11 Oberholtzer, Vol. I, p. 422.
12 Fleming, *Sequel*, p. 124.
13 Smith, *Garfield*, p. 397.

the conquerors might vouchsafe. With this mandate from the people Congress needed no further urging. In order to bring to a test vote his plan of treating the late Confederate States as conquered provinces Stevens opened an attack upon the Johnson governments in the South. On December 13, 1866, he offered a bill to abolish the government in North Carolina and to reconstruct that State. On February 6, 1867, he reported from the joint committee a general reconstruction bill. This great measure is so important I have reserved it for a separate chapter. During the years 1866, 1867 and 1868 the Thirty-ninth Congress, treating the southern states as conquered provinces and unprotected by the Constitution, placed various statutes on the book.[14] These statutes were logical and necessary, the Radicals concluded, to carry out the mandate of the people and to give full effect to the Thirteenth Amendment liberating the slaves. As they were mere statutes, however, and not yet a part of the Constitution it was understood that they were temporary, being police regulations and awaiting their embodiment in the fundamental law. The Fourteenth Amendment, just submitted to the states but not adopted by them, had it been enacted, would have accomplished this end in part.

These acts were manifestly unconstitutional, if there were a Constitution in those horrid days. Courts and lawyers therefore "could only stare and gasp"; [15] and historians exclaim, "Oh, monstrous!" [16] To each and every one of them the President entered his protest. With delicate irony he would say to Congress, "The Constitution makes it the President's duty to recommend to Congress such measures as he shall judge necessary and expedient and he knows of no measure more imperatively demanded than the admission of loyal members from the

[14] The dates of these Acts are as follows: First Civil Rights Act, April 9, 1866; First Reconstruction Act, January 31, 1867; Tenure of Office Act, March 2, 1867; Conduct of the Army Act, March 2, 1867; Second Reconstruction Act, March 23, 1867; Third Reconstruction Act, July 19, 1867; Fourth Reconstruction Act, March 11, 1868; The Act Admitting North Carolina, etc., July 25, 1868; Joint Resolution Excluding Electoral Vote of Louisiana and other states, July 20, 1868.—MacDonald, *Documentary Source Book*, pp. 501-535.

[15] Dunning, *Essays*, p. 65.
[16] Burgess, *Reconstruction*, p. 127.

now unrepresented states." He would also raise the question whether there was a Congress at all or only the part of a Congress, eleven states being unrepresented.

"The President of the United States represents all the people," he would blandly suggest, and "a Senator or Congressman represents only one state or one district." While he would not interfere with the discretion of Congress with regard to the qualification of members, nevertheless when admittedly loyal persons were asking admission, why reject them?" . . . "Disquiet and complaint would arise in the nation if any indefinite or permanent exclusion was enforced and a sentiment against the Government might arise." In the President's opinion the rebel states had been restored to the Union, "and if they have not," said he, "let us get together and secure that desirable end." [16a]

In his veto of the Civil Rights bill the President declared that its details were fraught with evil. Suddenly to uproot a civilization was dangerous and time only could adjust the relations between the blacks and their late masters. He also called attention to this effort of Congress to abrogate the local laws of the states. "In many states there are laws forbidding marriages between the races," he reminded Congress. Did Congress propose to change this law? Quoting Chancellor Kent, that marriages between whites and blacks are forbidden by law in most of the states, and, "whether forbidden or not, are revolting and regarded as an offense against public decorum," [17] the President asked, "Does Congress propose to go into a state and overturn its domestic and local policy?" "Is not Congress endeavoring to change the Constitution by a short cut?" he enquired. By a mere statute it was undertaking to annul the precise meaning of the phrase, "citizen of the United States" as defined in the Dred Scott case. Congress would make citizenship a national and not a state matter and it would place citizenship beyond state influence.[18] "There are

[16a] In December 1927, when the Senate undertook to pass on the qualifications, other than constitutional, of Senators Smith and Vare, it raised the very question confronting Congress in 1865.

[17] Richardson, *Messages*, Vol. VI, p. 407.

[18] Dunning, *Essays*, p. 96.

no citizens of the United States," he reminded Congress, "only citizens of states—as the Supreme Court has held." Why unsettle this matter of citizenship?

Johnson's vetoes of the Civil Rights bill and of other measures relating to the negro were not because of animosity toward the race, but because of a reverence for the Constitution. "He was earnest in his desire that the negro should be properly treated," and "he enforced all statutes relating to the negro, though he had previously vetoed such statutes." [19] Even as to so-called southern Black Codes, Johnson well knew that these codes, far from embodying any spirit of defiance for the North or any purpose to evade conditions, which the victor had imposed, were in the main "a conscientious and straightforward attempt to bring some sort of order out of the social and economic chaos which a full acceptance of the results of the war involved." [20]

In vetoing this mass of unconstitutional legislation, how far into the future did President Johnson peer? Congress was engaged in overturning a proud and self-contained civilization, one which had produced Washington, Marshall, Jefferson, Henry, Madison, Andrew Jackson, and Robert E. Lee. When Johnson warned Congress of the danger of this task and of the folly of thrusting the ballot into the hands of four million ignorant blacks, at a time when negro suffrage was not generally allowed in the North, "engendering a hatred between the races, deep-rooted and ineradicable, preventing them from living together in a state of mutual friendliness," did he foresee conditions as they are to-day? "The sudden gift of the ballot to men wholly unprepared to use it," said Dunning of Columbia University in 1901, "was a most dangerous policy. . . . It is equally apparent that insofar as partisan motive was dominant in the transaction, partisanship has paid the penalty. . . . In the South the negro enjoys practically no political rights, the influence of the negro in political affairs is 'nil' and the Republican party but the shadow of a name." [21]

[19] Rhodes, Vol. VI, p. 27; Schofield, *Forty-six Years*, p. 420.
[20] Dunning, *Reconstruction*, p. 58.
[21] "The United States is doing with the Filipinos what the South is doing with the negro. Why may not South Carolina and Mississippi apply the

The connection of Stanton, the great War Secretary, with the Tenure of Office Act exhibits the temper of that wretched period. Stanton first advised with the radicals as to the passage of this measure; after its adoption he wrote the message vetoing it. After the veto was overruled he stuck to his job, though ordered to vacate, becoming bolder and more open in opposition to the President.[22] This veto is "the masterpiece of political logic." [23] It may be added it put Congress in a hole from which it never extricated itself—and destroyed Secretary Stanton, as will presently appear.

If there had been no negro problem reconstruction would have been less difficult. When the Thirteenth Amendment set the negro free he became, as we have seen, a full unit in estimating the population and not three-fifths of a unit as in slave days. Hence southern representation in Congress, by virtue of this amendment, would be increased more than thirty per cent. Yet the negro could not vote. Manifestly this was unjust to the North and this Johnson was willing to rectify, as appears when he requested Congress to meet him and "arrange terms of amicable settlement." The President wished to estimate representation according to population, excluding any class not allowed to vote. This position he made plain on numerous occasions.

In vetoing these acts of Congress Johnson maintained that he was not obstructing legislation but advancing it, and keeping faith with the new South. As he reasoned, in such matters he was also acting especially for the people. In Roman days, as he once showed in a speech to Congress, the Tribunes of the people exercised the veto power for the public good and not for the king or the ruling classes. In the thirties, when Congress censured Andrew Jackson for vetoing the Bank bill, "Old Hickory" entered his protest to such censure. As the law-making power, under the Constitution, consisted of both Congress and the President, no bill could become a law with-

shot-gun policy as well as the United States?"—*Atlantic Monthly*, Vol. LXVIII, p. 434. "The North has had a change of mind and heart," says Burgess, p. 298.

[22] DeWitt, *Impeachment*, pp. 202 and 270; Welles, Vol. III, p. 54; Dunning, *Reconstruction*, p. 91; *American Historical Review*, December 4, 1885.

[23] Burgess, *Reconstruction*, p. 127.

out the President's signature, except by a two-thirds over-riding vote. As President Johnson was a part of Congress in this matter of enacting laws, he could not understand how he was censurable for exercising his constitutional veto power.[24] The popular idea that Johnson is the "veto" President is not correct, at least so far as the number of bills vetoed is concerned. At the end of Cleveland's administration there had been four hundred and thirty-three vetoes. Of these Johnson had vetoed twenty-one bills, Grant forty-three, Cleveland three hundred and one. The remaining vetoes are divided out among the other presidents; Jefferson vetoed no bill but left such matters to Congress. Two of Andrew Johnson's vetoes prevented a New York mining corporation getting illegal control of certain Montana lands.[25]

Johnson's state papers, including vetoes, were uniformly in good temper, conservative, historical and well considered. In the preparation of them he made use of every person on whom he could lay his hands. Bancroft wrote the first message to Congress; Jerre Black, the hero of *Ex Parte Milligan*, wrote the reconstruction veto; Seward, the precise scholar, supervised much that the President wrote; Stanton, the practical lawyer, wrote the bill to admit North Carolina and other states into the Union in 1865; the Attorney-General, Welles, Secretary of the Navy, and other members of the cabinet he frequently used. Neither a lawyer nor a statistician, Johnson relied on the legal profession to furnish the law and on the experts to make reports on their various departments. In pursuing this course, and in fighting the enemies of the Constitution with his might, the President was following precedent. Hamilton's hand is plainly seen in Washington's farewell address; Livingston wrote Jackson's Nullification Proclamation; and, in later days, Olney is discovered in Cleveland's Venezuela message, and Hay in McKinley's state papers. Webster's connection with President Taylor's inaugural is well known. As Mrs. Seaton, at whose house Webster was staying, tells the story, Mr. Webster came in one day after having read and corrected Taylor's vo-

24 *Harvard Historical Monograph*, "Veto Power of the President," p. 33.
25 *Veto Power, supra*, p. 133.

luminous inaugural manuscript, abounding in allusions to Roman history. "You look worried, Mr. Webster," she said. "Has anything happened?" "If you knew what I have done," Webster replied, "you would think so. I've just killed seventeen Roman pro-consuls." [26]

That Johnson openly requested his cabinet to write certain of his state papers would seem to rebut the idea, so widely circulated, that he was endeavoring to conceal the fact that he did not compose them. Certainly, when he filed away among his valuable papers his first message to Congress, largely in the handwriting of Bancroft, he was not endeavoring to deceive the public as to its authorship.[27] As a matter of fact, Bancroft's part in this message was to whip it into shape. He took Johnson's speeches on the Constitution and Union and threw them into a connected and attractive whole. This will appear from a study of the message itself. The last fourteen paragraphs, relating to the work of the departments, are purely technical.

The introduction is the work of Bancroft alone. Johnson did not write smoothly and flowingly as in that first paragraph. The next paragraph, covering a full page, and also paragraph twelve follow Johnson's speech of December 18 and 19, 1860. The illustrations throughout and references to Jefferson were constantly in Johnson's mouth during the war. The third paragraph is thoroughly Johnsonian. Reference to "the suffering revolutionary patriots," to "arbitrary power," to the "absorption of state governments by the general government" and to the fear that "the states might break away from their orbits," suggest one of Johnson's old Tennessee mountain speeches in the "Roaring '40's," when "Federal blue lights were burning low." Paragraphs four and five contain extracts from Jackson's Nullification Proclamation which Johnson often quoted.

The sixth paragraph and part of the seventh are formal. The last part of the seventh is taken from an interview with

---

[26] *Nation*, Vol. LXXXII, p. 91; *American Historical Review*, Vol. II, p. 951; *Bookman*, Vol. XXXIV, p. 500.

[27] This paper may now be seen among the Johnson manuscripts at Washington.

the Indiana delegation in April 1865. Paragraphs eight to eleven merely state the President's views on reconstruction, and are not significant. Paragraph thirteen suggests the famous Stearns interview in October 1865 which Johnson signed with his own hand. Paragraphs fourteen to sixteen explain the acts of his administration and are not significant; the sixteenth paragraph also calls to mind Johnson's address in April 1865 to Loyal Southerners. Thus it will be seen that the entire message is the product of Andrew Johnson, though its literary flavor is due to the historian, Bancroft.[28]

In the fall and winter of 1866 and 1867, when the southern states and some of the northern states refused to ratify the Fourteenth Amendment,[29] Conservatives like Fessenden, Sherman, and Garfield considered that Congress had done its duty by the South. The South had been given a chance on liberal terms and had refused it.[30] Radicals began to run a race to see which could prove himself the most radical, oftentimes becoming vindictive and going to useless lengths. On January 8, 1867, Sumner "nagged" the District of Columbia bill through Congress over the President's veto. This act gave the ballot to the negroes in the district,[31] though there was no demand for such legislation and the proposal had been voted down a few weeks earlier by a vote of 6525 to 35 in Washington, and 812 to 1 in Georgetown.[32] So unprepared were the negroes in Washington for the ballot that fraud, corruption, and violence followed in the wake of this statute. In 1874 Congress repealed the act, and placed the Capitol under a board of three commissioners.

The Tenure of Office Act, of March 1867, undertaking to tie the President's hands and to make his subordinate officers independent of him, was vicious legislation. Not only was it unconstitutional and so declared by the courts, but "it was not at all necessary." . . . "It grew out of a family quarrel in the

---

[28] I have followed the *American Historical Review*, Vol. XI, p. 952, in this analysis.

[29] Kentucky, Maryland and Delaware rejected this amendment and in January 1868 New York and New Jersey withdrew their approval.

[30] Blaine, Vol. II, p. 475.

[31] Dunning, *Reconstruction*, p. 94.

[32] Fleming, *Sequel to Appomattox*, p. 134; Burgess, *Reconstruction*, p. 109.

heat and excitement of the day and was intended to worry and insult the President." [33]   At this time Congress was angered at the Supreme Court "because of decisions adverse to their radical theory," [34] and was determined to make a cipher of that court as well as of the President.[35]   Though little legislation was enacted hostile to the Supreme Court it was made to understand that Congress would tolerate no interference.[36]   Well might the court fear a Congress which deprived it of jurisdiction in a criminal case, in order to save reconstruction legislation from being overturned.   This Congress did after the matter had reached a hearing.[37]   Congress likewise reduced the court from nine to seven to prevent Conservatives from being added to it by the President.

Perhaps the veto of the Civil Rights bill created more bitterness than any other veto.   Stewart of Nevada, who had been the President's supporter, in the Freedmen's Bureau matter, turned against him, pursuing him ever after, writing newspaper articles and his own *Reminiscences* full of bitterness as well as of misstatements.[38]   Sherman, Trumbull and Fessenden, who had also been friendly to the President, became antagonistic.   Radicals of the Ben Wade type were furious. When a vote was to be taken on this veto a conservative Senator rose and requested a postponement of the matter for one day to allow a sick member an opportunity to be present. Thereupon Wade indulged in a tirade beyond precedent. Gloating over the sickness of the absent Senator, Wade exclaimed, "I feel justified in taking advantage of what the Almighty has put in my hand and I will tell the President if God Almighty has stricken one member so he cannot be here to uphold the dictation of a despot, I thank Him for his inter-

[33] Blaine, *Twenty Years*, Vol. II, p. 274; *Civil Rights Cases*, United States Reports, Vol. 109, p. 3; *Myers vs. United States*, decided in October 1926.

[34] Dunning, *Essays*, p. 121; Dunning, *Reconstruction*, p. 90.

[35] *Ex Parte Milligan*, 4 Wall. 2; *Cummings vs. Missouri*, 4 Wall. 277 and *Ex Parte Garland*, 4 Wall. 333; Dunning, *Reconstruction*, p. 89.

[36] Dunning, *Reconstruction*, pp. 256-258.

[37] *McCardle Case;* Dunning, *Essays*, p. 137; *Burgess*, p. 197.

[38] The quotation, in my Introduction, that Johnson, at the time of President Lincoln's death, was intoxicated and that Stewart and his friends took him to the White House may illustrate other statements by Senator Stewart. At that time, as I have stated, Mrs. Lincoln was occupying the White House and remained more than a month.

position." The Senate was shocked. The golden-hearted Mc-Dougall, Senator from California, and the most brilliant man in the body though sometimes intemperate, steadied himself to reply:

"The Senator from Ohio," said McDougall, "is in the habit of appealing to his God in vindication of his judgment and conduct. It is a common thing for him to do so. But in view of his demonstration it may well be asked who and what is his God—Ormudz or Abriman, the god of lightness and beauty or the god of death? . . . Well or ill, God has made him ill, sir, and the god of evil and of death is his god. I never expected to hear such objections raised by an honorable member—to hear such things in this hall—and I rise simply to say that such sentiments were to be condemned and must receive my condemnation and if it amounts to a rebuke, I trust it may be a rebuke." Immediately the Senate adjourned till the next day.

In February 1867 an effort was made by the Conservatives of North Carolina to formulate a plan to take the place of the defeated Fourteenth Amendment.[39] There is no direct evidence that the plan had Johnson's approval. Anyway, the Legislature refused to accept it doubtless asking, what is the good? In 1865, though it had adopted one plan, it had been turned down by Congress. Why try another? The proposed amendment is nevertheless interesting. It provided that (1) no state could of its own will leave the Union or be ejected from it; (2) the public debt of the United States should be observed and paid; (3) citizenship should be as provided in the defeated Fourteenth Amendment; (4) numbers should be the basis of representation and if any class were not allowed to vote it should be excluded. A part of the plan was that a state amendment should likewise be adopted that "any male citizen who had been one year in the state, six months in the county and could read the Declaration of Independence and the Constitution and write his name or who may be the owner of two hundred and fifty dollars of taxable property shall be

[39] My father, Patrick Henry Winston, President of Governor Worth's Council of State, was with the Committee which prepared this measure.—Hamilton, *Reconstruction*, p. 187.

entitled to vote." [40]   Rhodes is correct in his condemnation of
Johnson if he approved this measure; [41] but the Raleigh *Sentinel*, a Johnson paper, on February 7, 1867, announced that
the President "was standing by his own plan."   The North
Carolina plan embraces Johnson's position, however, except as
to citizenship.   It puts reconstruction up to the states, guarding and protecting the intelligent negro in his ballot.

To enforce and maintain the supremacy of negro governments in the South, Johnson well knew, and so advised Congress, that it would require an expenditure of two hundred
million dollars a year, besides the evil consequences that would
result from the effort to Africanize one-third the country.[42]
At all events, Johnson stood by the Constitution.   And after
the southern states in 1865 had accepted presidential reconstruction, in good faith, and the Civil War had ended, was he
not right in his course?   Would not Lincoln have kept faith
with a repentant South, as he did with Louisiana in 1865?
Despite Memphis and New Orleans riots and the unsettled condition of the Southern States—growing out of the war, and
out of the shock of freeing the slaves—these states were nevertheless loyal.   There were not sufficient reasons, as we of to-day
see, for excluding the southern Representatives from Congress.
When Congress met in December 1865 not only was the South
loyal but the original Secessionists were in disrepute.   This
is a cardinal point, one that I must urge again. Wigfall, Iverson, Toombs, Slidell, Rhett, Yancey, Yulee, Mason, even
Jefferson Davis—less belligerent in 1860 than earlier—none
of these were in evidence.   It is true that Alex Stephens, the
unhappy Vice-president of the late Confederacy and Mr. Lincoln's old Whig and Union-loving friend, was in Washington
knocking at the door of Congress.   So was that other Whig
lover of the Union, W. A. Graham, late of the Confederate
Senate.   General Gordon, a Unionist, through and through,

[40] *Annual Encyclopædia*, 1865, p. 132.
[41] Rhodes, Vol. VI, p. 11.   This proposition was submitted by North Carolina in February 1867 to avoid the Reconstruction Act, then pending and certain to pass.
[42] Blaine ridicules Johnson's position, but must it not be said that the unsettled negro question has cost the nation more than the President estimated?—Blaine, Vol. II, p. 300.

and a handful of other lesser Confederate lights had also been elected to Congress. But these men, too, were loyal to the Union. They had espoused the Confederate cause by force of circumstances, when every attribute of manhood drove them to that course. After it was decided in that Brothers' War that the southern man must fight with his state or against it these lovers of the Union with a sad heart had joined the Confederacy. President Johnson knew that Horace Maynard, W. A. Graham and Alex Stephens were as true to the Union in 1865 as they had been before the Civil War. Though Secretary Seward, of kind and optimistic nature, encouraged President Johnson in his conciliatory course toward the South, he needed no such outside aid. Johnson was a kind and a forgiving man, as Secretary McCulloch declares. "When the fight was over he bore no malice." [43]

Before the southern states accepted presidential reconstruction, in the fall of 1865, it was doubtful as to what course the President should take in dealing with these states. Theoretically either the extreme Radical like Stephens was correct or the extreme Copperhead like Vallandigham. That is, either the South was conquered territory, to be dealt with as such, or else it was as much a part of the Union as before the Civil War. Johnson followed Lincoln and the Constitution, and put natural and necessary terms of restoration upon the South. These terms appear to have been acceded to in good faith. Under these circumstances should not Congress have followed the advice of the martyred President, should they not have hesitated a long time before dashing from southern lips the cup which had been extended to them? [44] In 1862, to save the Union, Lincoln had torn the Constitution to shreds and put

---

[43] Stanton was perhaps Johnson's most implacable foe and yet the President in December 1868 attended Stanton's funeral and made a short talk. It is reported as follows: "He was my friend, a friend who did not always understand me. He was one of the most able men I ever knew and one of the most honest men I ever knew. If he had faults they were of the head and not of the heart. And now all we remember is his zeal, his earnest zeal for the good, his upright intellect, his matchless ability of brain. Let love mingle with memory and peace be accorded his ashes."—Hubbard, *The Tale of Two Tailors*, p. 12; at the end of his bitter campaign in 1853, Johnson and his opponent shook hands and went their ways.—*True Whig*, August 4, 1853.

[44] C. F. Adams, *Address on Lee at Lexington, Va.;* Rhodes, Vol. IV, p. 240.

men in jail without the semblance of law; in December 1865, after the war was over, would he have trampled on the Constitution to save the Republican party?

There were many noble men in Congress—Fessenden, Henderson, Sherman, Grimes, Trumbull—who would not follow Lincoln's last public advice. They contended that Lincoln would have changed his mind had he lived, that "he would have rejected without hesitation any system of which the fruits were a little more than a nullification of his decree of emancipation." [45] Is it not more charitable to conclude that Mr. Lincoln would not have reversed himself in this matter; that he would have been well pleased at the loyalty of the South in the fall of 1865, that he would have kept faith with the National Union party, a party composed of Whigs, Free Soilers, and War Democrats? This party had solidified the nation in July 1861, saved the Union at the polls in 1862, brought several hundred thousand Border soldiers into the Union army, and reëlected Lincoln President in 1864.[46]

The plea that Congress was justified in going back on its resolution of July 22, 1861, was met by President Johnson in his message to Congress in 1867. He reminded Congress that the resolution was "a solemn, official pledge of the national honor" and he could "not imagine on what grounds the repudiation of it is to be justified." . . . "If it be said," the President went on, with fine irony, "that we are not bound to keep faith with the rebels let it be remembered that this pledge was not made to rebels only. Thousands of true men in the South

---

[45] McCarthy, *Lincoln's Plan of Reconstruction*, p. 487; McCarthy intimates that the July 1861 resolutions, defining the objects of the war, were passed, not in good faith, but as a means of winning the war; that when the South continued to fight circumstances were so changed there was no longer a reason for sticking to the original bargain.

[46] On the day after the November 1862 election the New York *Times* declared that "a feeling of gloomy anticipation surrounds the administration." At that time Illinois, Mr. Lincoln's state, toyed with Copperheadism, electing eleven Democratic Congressmen and only three Republicans. New York went against the war and, "in the great cordon of Free States beginning with New York and New Jersey on the Atlantic and extending to Missouri the Copperhead majority in Congress was twenty-three." This majority, however, was overcome by Union victories in the Border States and thus, and thus only, Mr. Lincoln was enabled to carry on.—Julian, *Recollections*, p. 215; McCall, *Stevens*, p. 221; Rhodes, Vol. IV, p. 163.

were drawn to our standard by it and hundreds of thousands in the North gave their lives in the belief it could be carried out." Regardless of warnings, however, Congress went its precipitate way, passing laws, which, as Rhodes remarks, must have made Conservatives exclaim,

> "Oh, most wicked speed!
> It is not nor it can not come to good."

CHAPTER IV

THE GREAT RECONSTRUCTION

Two years had gone by since Lee surrendered, and the Southern States were still out of the Union and the fight between the President and Congress growing fiercer. After the 1866 election Johnson realized that his "swing around the circle" had not worked and that the people as well as the politicians seemed to be against him. But he was determined to fight on and, with his back to the wall, meet the enemies of the Constitution. In this conflict he had the support of his entire cabinet except Stanton. Gideon Welles, "the old bushy-bearded Connecticut deacon," as Governor Andrew laughingly called him, was more aggressive than Johnson himself; Seward was equally loyal, though Welles declared he was "always dancing around the Radicals"; and so were Attorney-General Stanbery, McCulloch, Randall and Browning. The cabinet, in fact, were becoming genuinely attached to the fearless, lonesome and determined President. His abstemious and heroic life, the loyalty of his wife and daughters, their wholesome, unpretentious lives, and the general atmosphere of the White House appealed not only to the cabinet but to thoughtful people in the country at large. It was a fine thing to see Spartan virtue and simplicity in high place.

After his unfortunate speeches in 1866 the President conducted his controversy in courteous and parliamentary language. Yet he gave offense to the practical, conservative Republicans who wished the deadlock ended. These men were wounded because the President constantly referred to the legislative body as only a part of Congress. They knew that Congress, as then constituted, had legislated for many years. Fessenden, Grimes, Henderson, Sherman, Bingham and other Senators and Congressmen, who knew and appreciated what Johnson had done for the Union, were personally fond of him,

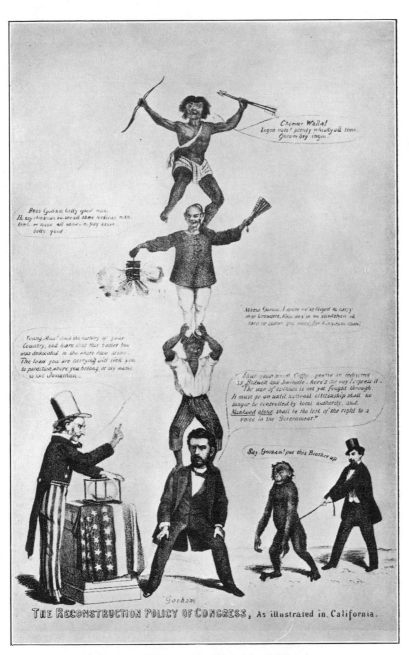

Reconstruction, as Illustrated in California

but were beginning to regard him as a theorist and an obstinate theorist beside. Though they disliked Stevens' and Sumner's radicalism, little by little they were forced to follow it. No other course was open. In December 1866 Congress grew alarmed at the President's action in vetoing bills and passed a resolution that the Fortieth Congress should meet March 4, 1867, instead of in December 1867 as usual. This was done in order to keep watch over him. On March 4 Congress met and by the thirtieth had completed its work and was ready to adjourn. The Radicals were unwilling to this. They dared not leave the Government a single day in the hands of this "bad man," as Sumner called the President. Therefore an adjournment was taken until July 3 and on the thirtieth of that month, all business being finished, Congress was again ready to adjourn *sine die*. Sumner, Howard and others objected and an adjournment was taken to November 25. These adjournments caused the people to fear that there was a secret danger, known only to Congress, and tended to add to the general sense of uneasiness.

In his veto of the Army bill the President had spoken his mind to Congress, condemning their effort to legislate him out of office and to make a cipher of the Executive. "While I hold the chief executive authority of the United States," he declared, "while the obligation rests upon me to see that all laws are faithfully executed, I can never willingly surrender that trust or the powers given for its execution. I can never give my assent to be made responsible for the faithful execution of laws, and at the same time surrender that trust and the powers which accompany it to any other executive officer, high or low, or to any number of executive officers." This statement of the President Congress construed as a threat to overthrow the government by force.

In March 1867 an event of the greatest consequence had occurred: A general plan of reconstruction was formulated and adopted by Congress. Previous to that time there had been much delay, either for partisan reasons or because no agreement could be reached. In May of the previous year, as we have seen, the Reconstruction Committee, having finished its labors and reported its work to Congress, ceased to function for the remainder of the year. Their labors consisted of the Fourteenth Amendment and this the southern states had refused to adopt. Therefore the work of the committee was blocked. That Johnson did what he could to defeat this amendment is true, but that his influence caused its defeat by the South is more than doubtful. After the summer of 1865 the southern states were acting for themselves and were constantly running counter to the President's wishes. In the fall of that year North Carolina, Johnson's native State and more devoted to him than any of the other states except Tennessee, repudiated Holden, Johnson's candidate for Governor, and elected Worth. In Alabama and Mississippi the President's candidates had likewise been defeated.[1]

In truth the only time the southern people were really frightened was immediately after the collapse of the Confederacy. "After the 1866 elections they regarded the Fourteenth Amendment as inevitable, and negro suffrage as a possibility, but it does not appear that they ever seriously considered that they would again be placed under military rule, their state governments overthrown, and new governments established in which apostates to their cause, northern adventurers and negroes would have the controlling influence." [2] If Congress, in 1866, had coupled with the Fourteenth Amendment a provision that upon its adoption the Southern States would be admitted into the Union, it is probable the amendment would have been adopted, despite the disfranchising clause.

But at no time did the Radicals consider the Fourteenth Amendment the complete plan of reconstruction. "It was but the first step and others were to follow." [3] If this amendment was not a final settlement of reconstruction, it may be asked what then was it? An answer to this question was given by the New York *Herald* of June 12, 1866. "This Congressional proposition," said the *Herald*, "is an ingeniously contrived

---

[1] Oberholtzer, *History*, Vol. I, p. 125.
[2] Kendrick, *Committee of Fifteen*, p. 351: "Those writers who attempt to shift upon the South a part of the blame for the evils of reconstruction are hardly justified."
[3] *Ibid., Committee*, p. 314.

party platform for the coming fall elections." In New England it was understood that the amendment was not final, and the *Independent*, the Radical organ, of November 18, 1866, scouted the idea.[4] In fact, the Stevens bill accompanying the amendment, and declaring the same to be a finality, was laughed at by the author himself, kicked around in the House, delayed, postponed and finally tabled by a vote of 101 to 35. Morton and possibly Blow in the Senate were the only members willing to keep the faith. "Thus sank into eternal sleep the luckless Reconstruction bill." [5]

During the preceding two years radicalism had greatly advanced. "At the end of the war the northern people would have supported a settlement in accordance with Lincoln's policy; eight months later a majority, but a smaller one, would have supported Johnson's work had it been possible to secure a popular decision on it." [6] How then did the Radicals gain the victory over the Conservatives? James Ford Rhodes asserts that three men are responsible for the Congressional policy of reconstruction: Andrew Johnson, by his obstinacy and bad conduct; Thad Stevens, by his vindictiveness and parliamentary tyranny; and Charles Sumner, by his pertinacious, misguided humanitarianism. Yet radicalism, as we know, did not begin in the Johnson administration. Lincoln had felt its covert opposition throughout the war. That Johnson is responsible for a failure to compromise with Congress may be true, though it is not probable, as I have endeavored to show. Was not the conflict between President and Congress fundamental, was it not a fight between Andrew Johnson, a strict constructionist, and the spirit of modern nationalism? Was not reconstruction a struggle between the individualism

---

[4] Dunning, *Reconstruction*, p. 85; Schouler, Vol. VII, p. 83; Kendrick, p. 314; Oberholtzer, Vol. I, p. 427.

[5] Kendrick *supra;* Blaine asserts that the Fourteenth Amendment if adopted would have put an end to reconstruction legislation.—Blaine, Vol. II, pp. 243-245. In discussing the amendment, however, Congressman Blaine appears to have been of a different opinion. He then called attention to objections to the amendment and said that the obligation of "the Federal Government to protect the loyalists of the South was supreme" and that "the gift of free suffrage must be guaranteed."—*Globe, Thirty-ninth Congress*, p. 53.

[6] Fleming, *Sequel*, p. 119.

of ante-bellum days and the governmental and industrial concentration, unification and coöperation of our own times?

Whatever the cause of the growth of radicalism, the fact of such growth was manifest, and Stevens could hardly hold back his radical followers. Grinnel was asking, "Are we to allow rebels to come here and take their seats, rebels unwashed, unrepentant, unpunished, unpardoned and unhung?" (Laughter.) Boutwell was telling Congress, "You might as well expect to build a fire in the depth of the ocean as to reconstruct loyal governments in the South until you have broken down disloyal despotisms." "There are eight million and more of people," he exclaimed, "writhing under cruelties nameless in their character." [7] Stevens was calling attention to the loyalists of the South, "driven from home by the rebels." . . . "These loyal men you see flitting about you in your cities, melancholy, depressed, haggard, like the ghosts of unburied dead on this side of the river Styx. If we neglect to protect these people we shall be responsible to the civilized world for the greatest neglect of duty that ever a great nation was guilty of before, to humanity." While Mr. Stevens was speaking these perfervid words, President Johnson well knew that "the relations between the races in the South were better than conditions indicated." [8] For, as General Bob Taylor, of Confederate fame, put it, it seemed, according to the Radicals, "that about 1866 every man, woman and child in the South began to kill niggers." [9]

At all events the time had come when the most radical of radicals conceded that something must be done with the South, that a complete plan of reconstruction should be formulated. The people were demanding this and further delay was dangerous. Now the fight between the President and Congress had come to a draw. Though Congress, without southern votes, could pass a statute, it could not enact an amendment. The southern states not only could but would block any change

[7] *Globe*, p. 1122.
[8] Fleming, p. 47.
[9] *Cf.* Fleming, pp. 100-117. As to the Black Laws or Codes often complained of by the Radicals, "they were never enforced but were suspended from the beginning by the army and the Freedmen's Bureau."—*Ibid.*, p. 97.

in the Constitution which made the late slaves the rulers of the whites. 'Though Stevens was sure the southern "provinces" need not be consulted in the enactment of an amendment and wished to declare the Fourteenth Amendment valid though less than three-fourths of the states had adopted it, wiser ones knew better. They knew that the Supreme Court had just held in the Milligan case that the Constitution was still the law and that under the Constitution three-fourths of all the states must ratify an amendment before its adoption.

The great question before Congress therefore was how to put through an amendment protecting the rights of the freedmen despite the southern states. Secretary Welles thought this would finally be done as Stevens suggested, that is, by disregarding southern states.[10] "If the southern states should be put to the ban by Congress and declared territories," Welles wrote, "the Radicals would not then have completely accomplished their purpose, for Mordecai the Jew will still be in their way. Andrew Johnson must be disposed of and impeachment must be effected." Welles concluded that "as the states were excluded from Congress in disregard and defiance of the Constitution, the same Radicals could, with as much authority, exclude them from passing on the Constitutional changes." But in this Welles was mistaken. Congress was unwilling to take any chances, they were afraid of the Supreme Court. Therefore they adopted a simpler and less dangerous way of meeting the situation. Congress proposed to coerce the South, and to enforce consent to its legislation. That is, they would disfranchise the whites, enfranchise the negroes and put the amendment up to this new and strange electorate—a composition of late slaves, scalawags, carpetbaggers, and a few decent natives.

On February 6, 1867, Thad Stevens, for the Committee of Fifteen, presented to the House a military reconstruction bill, out of which the great reconstruction measure grew. An uncomplicated bill, it was nevertheless, "thorough." As Garfield said of it, "It was written with an iron pen, made of a bayonet." "This measure is so simple," said Stevens when offering it,

10 Welles, Vol. III, p. 636.

"one night's rest after its reading is enough to digest it." The Stevens bill proposed to wipe out the work of two Presidents, to wipe out all that had been done in the South towards rehabilitation in the last two years, to change the ten southern states into five military districts—these to be ruled by five Generals of the army. So far as this bill provided, it was without limit as to time, military rule was to be indefinite. Fortunately for the peace of the country, Blaine offered his historical amendment. The "Blaine Amendment" provided substantially that any southern state could come out from under military rule and into the Union upon adoption of the Fourteenth Amendment and changing its state constitution so as to admit white and black alike to the polls.[11]

But Stevens and his followers voted down the Blaine Amendment and whipped the original bill through the House. In the Senate Williams of Oregon proposed the Blaine Amendment and then withdrew it. Thereupon Reverdy Johnson offered it again. After a long and fierce debate, in which the whole ground of Presidential reconstruction as opposed to Congressional reconstruction was gone over, the matter was referred to Senator Sherman to prepare a substitute. The "Sherman Substitute" passed the Senate, with amendments. After conferences and further amendments the House adopted the Stevens-Blaine-Sherman bill. Thus for the first time definite terms upon which the rebel states could come back into the Union were outlined. The bill reached the President March 2 and though he might have killed it by a pocket veto, he sent it back to Congress with his objections. This veto, written by Jerre S. Black, was "stronger than all arguments that had been made against the amendment in both Houses." [12] The bill was immediately passed over the veto and on March 2, 1867, the Great Reconstruction measure became the law of the land. It is idle to waste words as to the unconstitutionality of an act which was "passed purely for political purposes"; [13] which was enacted when matters in the South "did not justify it"; [14]

---

[11] Blaine, Vol. II, p. 256.
[12] *Ibid.*, p. 261; *American Historical Review*, April 1906, p. 585.
[13] Dunning, *Essays*, p. 139.
[14] *Ibid.*, *Reconstruction*, p. 95.

and which advocates of the "conquered territory" theory admit was "distinct usurpation." [15]

In due time the Southern States accepted the terms of the Act and returned to the Union. On July 28, 1868, the requisite three-fourths having concurred, the Fourteenth Amendment became a part of the Constitution. Of this amendment it must be admitted that, for good or evil, it transformed the United States from a Confederation into a Nation; that it has been the source of more litigation than any other amendment; that it overrules all that was said about citizenship in the Dred Scott case, abolishes the much disputed three-fifths clause in the Constitution, makes citizenship a matter of national and not of state concern, places the citizen of each and every state, his life, his limb and his property under national protection and gives to all persons the equal protection of the laws of the United States. But it does more, as concerns Andrew Johnson and his views of the Constitution. It is the utter destruction of the old dogma of States' Rights. It is a return to the Federalistic and Whig doctrine of protection to American industries. Before this amendment there was legally no such thing as a citizen of the United States. One was then a citizen of a state but not of the United States. Nothing in the old Constitution defined or implied national citizenship, as distinct from state citizenship; but from the adoption of the Fourteenth Amendment a great change took place.[16]

I might add that the amendment as construed by the Supreme Court has given the world a decided surprise. Construing the amendment strictly, the Court holds that it furnishes little protection to the negro, that it operates on a *state* only. It prohibits a state, not a person or corporation, from denying equal rights to the black man. On the other hand, the Court holds that the amendment must be liberally construed to place corporations under its protecting ægis, free from unjust and unequal state laws.[17] Hence under the provisions of this amendment, and the protection of United States courts, Big

---

[15] Burgess, *Reconstruction*, p. 197.
[16] *Civil Rights Cases;* 16 Wall., p. 73; United States Reports, Vol. 109, p. 3.
[17] *Santa Clara vs. Railroad,* United States Reports, Vol. 118, p. 394; Kendrick, p. 27.

Business has flourished. The individual in business has disappeared. As a natural consequence Andrew Johnson's little tailor shop, down in Greeneville, closed its door, the overshot mill wheel, hard by his residence, ceased to turn, the cobbler no longer made shoes for the neighborhood. Blackstone McDaniel, the village plasterer, Johnson's only pal, went out of business or took orders from the local union.

The Fourteenth Amendment was carefully drawn and is worthy of the great subject it disposes of. A part of the world movement for nationalization and expansion, begun in the '60's, the instrument breathes a broad and liberal spirit. If we omit the fifth section, which merely authorizes Congress to enforce the amendment by appropriate legislation, there are four short sections. The first section declares that all persons who are citizens of a state are likewise citizens of the United States, and that no state shall make any law which shall abridge the rights of such citizen or deprive any person of liberty or property without due process of law or deny the equal protection of the laws. Section two declares that representation shall be apportioned among the states according to numbers, but if the right to vote is denied, the basis of representation shall be reduced accordingly. Section three deprives of holding any office all persons who previously had taken oath in certain capacities to support the Constitution and thereafter engaged in rebellion. By a two-thirds vote of each House this disability might be removed. The fourth section declares that the validity of the debt of the United States shall not be questioned, but that none of the Confederate debt or any claim for the emancipation of the slave shall ever be allowed. On the same day, March 2, 1867, that the Reconstruction Act was passed, the Tenure of Office Act and the Command of the Army Act were likewise passed over the President's veto.

The great Reconstruction Act was twice amended to meet defects. These amendments were likewise vetoed by the President. To prevent a judicial decision upon the original act or the amendments Congress provided that no court should have jurisdiction over the same. For about one year after the act was passed the South was under military rule and during this time "a Radical party was organized composed of negroes, scalawags and carpetbaggers." [18] Under the supervision of the army a new electorate was enrolled, elections were held, and conventions, composed of the above-named individuals, met and framed for the Southern States new constitutions in harmony with the acts. The white man was practically turned out of house and home.

The great Reconstruction Act was passed under strange surroundings. Senator Sumner spoke no word in its behalf— Sumner, who for a dozen years had insisted that whites and blacks sit together in the theaters and other public places of amusement, in the common schools and public institutions of learning, in railroad coaches, in the churches, that they occupy beds in the same benevolent institutions and be buried in the same cemeteries.[19] The act was too mild for Sumner. On the other hand, Reverdy Johnson, the Conservative, was a staunch supporter of the act. He contended that the South should act quickly and accept the bill, or worse was in store for her. The incorrigible Welles saw in Senator Johnson's course apostasy to the administration. He called Johnson "an old political prostitute" currying favor with the Radicals "to get his son-in-law confirmed by the Senate, as United States District Attorney."

The course of Senator Johnson, however, was not so bad as Welles pictured it. Johnson knew that the military bill would pass anyway and set himself to work to limit the operation of the same through the Blaine amendment. As the discussion proceeded he dealt effective but courteous blows. In the conduct of Senator Williams of Oregon, a champion of the "downtrodden" negro, Senator Johnson discovered an inconsistency. "The honorable Senator from Oregon," said he, "is the champion of the negro in this hall and yet if I mistake not in the State of Oregon from which the Senator comes no negro is allowed to enter, or to vote or to contract or to sue. Is not the Senator's State sinning against the light of the times, tramp-

18 Fleming, *Documentary History*, p. 397.
19 Storey, *Sumner*, p. 403.

ling upon the inalienable rights of man, denying manhood suffrage?"

During the debates on this measure so much diversity of opinion arose in the Republican party, Stevens grew discouraged. "If I don't change my mind," he said, "I will tomorrow move to lay the bill on the table." But after the passage of the act the "Old Commoner" was himself again, the greatest parliamentary leader before whom Congress ever bent the knee. When the bill was enrolled he lifted himself, on his club foot, pursed together his terrible lips and exclaimed, "Mr. Speaker, I rise to inquire if it is in order for me now to say that we endorse the language of good old Laertes, that Heaven rules as yet and there are gods above." During the entire discussion he had been the guiding spirit. With wit, ridicule, sarcasm, and invective, he had lashed the House into partial obedience. Referring to the charges that the bill was harsh and unconstitutional and to the provision that the rebels should not vote till 1870, he declared that this provision was not too harsh. "My only objection to it," he said, "is it's too limited in time. I might not submit to the severity of the Military Governor of Tennessee, I mean the late lamented Andrew Johnson of blessed memory, but I would have in it the security of section three. Give me section three or give me nothing."

While Stevens was bullying his party associates in the House, the voice of McDougall in the Senate was heard in a wise appeal to the future. "There is no such thing as coercing an unwilling people," he declared. "The South has been punished and has come to us as the prodigal son; we make no feasts for them but have met them with curses and we pronounce excommunication. Will that policy be a success? . . . You cannot conquer the human will. Brave men when vanquished can surrender and yield and become obedient but they cannot be degraded. . . . Would you put twelve millions of Anglo-Saxons—men of your own color—under their late slaves? . . . Half a century hence when hundreds of thousands of Chinese have landed in the State of California will Congress place these Asiatics above the whites?"

Other minority leaders were as effective as McDougall.

Senator Saulsbury would not "touch, taste or handle the unclean thing." It "sounded the death knell of civil liberty." Because he disapproved of other men Saulsbury declared that he would not come in to usurp the seat of Almighty God and cast "the thunderbolts of damnation upon their land." "Great God, has it come to this," Senator Doolittle passionately exclaimed, "a dictatorship and a despotism for the South?" As Doolittle saw the situation, the measure "was born of unforgiving hate and lust for despotic power"; the disfranchisement of the whites and negro domination will produce "such a horrible state of things as no language could describe and which it has never entered into the heart of man to conceive." Senators like Wilson of Massachusetts, on the other hand, discussed the problem of overturning the southern civilization as academically as if it were a game of checkers. Thus when Doolittle asked Wilson this question, "Suppose the Southern States refuse to accept this bill or to adopt the amendment what then will happen?" Wilson retorted, "Make them! . . . Settle the controversy, do not keep it open. Cut out the cancer." [20] Thad Stevens spoke the last words in reply to the Democrats, and "his tongue dripped venom." He was not satisfied with the way the Senate had treated his bill. Instead of allowing the power of appointment of officers who should command in the South to remain with General Grant where the House had placed it, the Senate had preferred to entrust this duty to the President of the United States. "How will the President execute this law?" Stevens asked. "As he has executed every law for the last two years, by the murder of Union men and by despising Congress and by flinging into our teeth all that we seek to have done. . . . I will make no pledges as to the future to these outlawed communities of robbers, traitors and murderers," Stevens continued, "but I am not done with the hope that at least some of those who have murdered the brothers, fathers and children of the North will be imprisoned and hanged and their property confiscated." [21]

It will be noted that the act did not pass until it was pro-

[20] Oberholtzer, Vol. I, p. 432.
[21] *Ibid.*, p. 433.

vided that the leading whites should not vote in the conventions to be called or in the legislatures following such conventions, and not until equal rights were guaranteed to the negroes. The negroes, *en masse*, educated and uneducated, should vote. Is it to be wondered at that the Fourteenth Amendment, adopted under such circumstances, and the Fifteenth, adopted under like circumstances, have ever been inoperative and nugatory— a dead letter? In 1865 Thaddeus Stevens had predicted that such would be the case. In December 1865 he had said that the southern people ought not to submit to the Thirteenth Amendment forced upon them, that he would lose respect for them if they did. Now, Andrew Johnson could not foresee the consequences which would follow from the reconstruction legislation. Yet his state papers indicate that he understood the matters in controversy better than those Senators and Congressmen who were far removed from the scene of the problem and were undertaking to adjust the delicate relations between the races offhand.

Though party expediency might demand that the old Constitution be shattered, though philanthropy and humanity joined in the cry, and though the spirit of nationalism would not be hushed, President Johnson knew that the scheme, put through by force, would not work. Therefore he stood out against it. Years before in Congress he had pictured the dangers of setting free four millions of negroes and injecting them into a white civilization. And now as President he reminded Congress that "some people considered this legislation so important, a violation of the Constitution is justified as a means of bringing it about; but that that morality was always false which excused a wrong because it proposes to accomplish a desirable end." . . . "We are not permitted to do evil that good may come," he said; "but in this case the end itself is evil as well as the means." As he saw it, the subjection of the states to negro domination was "worse than military despotism," and the people "would endure any amount of military oppression rather than degrade themselves by subjection to the negro race. . . . While the blacks in the South should be well and humanely governed and have the protection of just laws it is now proposed that they shall not merely govern themselves but rule the white race, make laws, elect officers and shape the destiny of the country to a greater or less extent. . . . Would such a trust and power be safe in such hands?"

The President likewise reminded Congress that the United States had prospered under the old Constitution, "which is well adapted to the genius, habits and wants of the people—combining the strength of a great empire with the imperishable blessings of local self-government;" and that to enforce the Constitution and the laws "there must be an intelligent and honest electorate." "Are the four millions of black persons who yesterday were held in slavery that had existed for generations sufficiently intelligent to cast a ballot?" . . . "Intelligent foreigners coming to our country," the President reminded Congress, "are required to remain five years and to prove good moral characters before they can be admitted to citizenship. . . . To give the ballot indiscriminately to a new class wholly unprepared by previous habits and opportunities to perform the trust which it demands is to degrade it and finally to destroy its power, for it may be safely assumed that no political truth is better established than that such indiscriminate and all-embracing extension of popular suffrage must end at last in its destruction." [22]

The South was stunned by a return to military government. Two states took steps to have the acts tested by the Supreme Court. In April 1867 Mississippi asked leave of the Court to file a Bill in Equity to enjoin President Johnson from executing the acts. About the same time Georgia brought suit against Stanton, Grant and Pope to enjoin them as individuals from enforcing the same.[23] As the court had decided in the McCardle case that it would take jurisdiction and enquire into the legality of a trial by court martial, it was hoped it would also pass on the Reconstruction Acts. Cautiously, and no

[22] Richardson, *Messages of the Presidents,* Vol. VI, p. 566; General Lee, General Hampton, Alexander Stephens and his brother Linton Stephens together with many other Southerners, particularly those in the Border States, agreed with President Johnson that the intelligent negro of character or who had accumulated even the small sum of two hundred and fifty dollars should be given the ballot.

[23] *Mississippi vs. Johnson,* 4 Wall. 475; *Georgia vs. Stanton,* 6 Wall. 51.

doubt wisely, the court declined to interfere. In the Mississippi case it was suggested by the court that if it should restrain President Johnson and he should refuse to enforce the acts a conflict between the executive and the legislature might arise, and the President might be impeached. In that case, "would the court restrain by injunction the Senate of the United States from sitting as a court of impeachment?"

Though military officials in the South were supreme, superseding the civil authorities, reconstruction did not work as badly as had been feared. Legislatures elected during that period were admittedly ignorant and corrupt, entailing no end of trouble, but the Generals, appointed by the President, were honest and usually fair minded. The President first appointed Generals Schofield, Sickles, Pope, Ord and Sheridan, but afterwards changes were made. Some of the Generals were radical; others, moderate and tactful. The most extreme were Sheridan, Pope and Sickles; the most conservative Hancock, Schofield and Meade, Hancock's benign administration of Virginia affairs winning for him the Democratic nomination for President a few years later.

CHAPTER V

IMPEACHMENT OF THE PRESIDENT

The three departments of government are supposed to be equal, but they are far otherwise. Thus during times of war the President as Commander-in-Chief of the army is supreme. In April 1861 President Lincoln seized the reins of government and saved the Union. Though it was the duty of Congress to declare war, he usurped this power, calling for seventy-five thousand troops to wage four years of warfare. Again, in times of peace the courts are supreme; in 1857 the Supreme Court overrode all precedent, declaring legislation relating to slavery in the territories illegal, and setting itself up as supreme. And yet after all is said the legislative department is the final arbiter. It controls the purse, has the power to impeach presidents and judges and to deprive courts of jurisdiction. Except when war is actually raging and an army is in the field, the popular assembly, standing closest to the people, is the ultimate source of power.

Possessing this great power, Congress was bent on using it. Nothing should stand in "its way of reconstructing the South with a negro on top and a white man on the bottom." [1] If necessary the courts and the President should be reduced to ciphers, and the checks and balances of the Constitution destroyed. In 1866 when the Supreme Court decided the Milligan, Cummings and Garland cases, holding that military tribunals were illegal and could not function in times of peace, and that no *ex post facto* or similar laws could be passed, because the Constitution forbade, Radicals were beside themselves. The calm judicial statement of Justice David Davis that military tribunals had had their day seemed to the mind of Sumner, "an alliance offensive and defensive between the Supreme Court and the President." Wendell Phillips was for abolishing

[1] DeWitt, *Impeachment*, p. 135.

the court.   Thaddeus Stevens regarded the Milligan opinion
"as more dangerous than Dred Scott, placing the knife of the
rebel at the throat of every man who now or ever had declared
himself a loyal Union man."   And, so far as the Radical party
is concerned, this fear was well grounded.   If the Supreme
Court had been allowed to pass on reconstruction legislation
it would have given it a complete knockout.   A majority of
the court at that time, including Chief Justice Chase, were of
the conviction that reconstruction acts were unconstitutional.[2]

It therefore became necessary to silence the Supreme Court.
A bill was offered in the House requiring a unanimous opinion
of the court on all matters relating to reconstruction, and a bill
passed the House requiring a two-thirds vote in such cases.[3]
But a more satisfactory manner of disposing of the court was
soon arranged.   Congress by statute deprived the court of
jurisdiction in reconstruction matters.   In a case from Mississippi, the McCardle case, there was no way for the court to
sidestep the doctrine of the Milligan case.   Either it must
stultify itself by overruling Milligan or it must face the issue,
take jurisdiction of reconstruction, and probably overturn it.
In the fall of 1867 McCardle, a Mississippi editor, was arrested
by military order for opposition to reconstruction.   McCardle
sued out a writ of *habeas corpus* in the United States Circuit
Court, charging that military reconstruction was unconstitutional, that he was unlawfully detained, and asking his discharge.   The military commander refused to obey this writ and
held the prisoner.   An appeal was taken to the United States
Supreme Court and, after an argument of four days by some
of the ablest lawyers in America, the court decided that it had
jurisdiction and must pass upon the issue.   But before the
day of hearing Congress repealed the law allowing appeals in
such cases and the Supreme Court bowed in silence.—As Judge
Curtis said of this McCardle affair, Congress by the ac-
quiesence of the people "overcame the President and subdued

---

[2] Fleming, *The Sequel*, p. 159; in 1875, 1882 and 1883 "the Supreme Court
came to the aid of the Democrats with decrees which drew the teeth from
the Enforcement Acts, and in 1894 Congress repealed what was left of this
legislation, restoring Home Rule to the South.—Fleming, *op. cit.*, p. 303.

[3] *Second Session Fortieth Congress*, p. 489.

the Supreme Court."[4] Now if Congress would thus hector and degrade the highest court, what would it not do to Andrew Johnson, whom they regarded as an "incubus"?

Though the first resolutions of impeachment were not offered until January 1867, at all times, since the President and Congress came to the parting of the ways, the Radicals had been urging impeachment and removal from office. All during the year 1866, Boutwell, of the judiciary committee, and Ashley had been keeping their eye on the "great malefactor." The Republican victory of 1866 having inspired Congress to go any length against the President, it passed numerous resolutions and bills to vex and harass him. Perhaps the most astounding legislation on record was the act relating to the President's military functions, requiring that the Commander-in-Chief should consult the Senate before giving certain orders to his subordinates. As Professor Dunning characterizes this act, it is "without parallel in our history for its encroachments on the constitutional powers of the executive or for inherent preposterousness." "But," says Dunning, "its source is even more astonishing than its content; for it was secretly dictated to Boutwell by the President's official adviser, Edwin M. Stanton, Secretary of War."[5] On the first day of the session in 1866 Congress likewise undertook to deprive the President of his constitutional right to grant amnesty; but he proceeded to extend pardons as before, disregarding the resolution. As we have seen, the President would veto offending measures and each veto would give fresh offense. Finally, on January 7, 1867, when he sent in a veto to the bill extending the ballot to the negroes of the District, the explosion came. This measure was a pet of Sumner's. The negrophiles regarded it as a forerunner of negro suffrage throughout the Union, a step "without which the nation could not long endure." In his veto the President called the attention of Congress to the folly of enfranchising illiterate negroes,

[4] Prentis, *Life of Curtis*, p. 421. The act of February 5, 1867, was passed to enable the black man to appeal from local courts to the United States Supreme Court. It was repealed in March 1868 to prevent the white man from exercising the same right of appeal.—Curtis, "Executive Power," cited in Rhodes, Vol. IV, p. 170.

[5] Dunning, *Reconstruction*, p. 91; Boutwell, *Reminiscences*, Vol. II, p. 108.

good and bad without distinction, and intimated that there was danger that Congress would soon assume all power to itself "and create a despotic government."

This veto enraged the House no little. Lone and Kelso, Radicals from Missouri, attempted to offer resolutions of impeachment, but failed. Thereupon Ashley of Ohio, soon to be known as the self-appointed "scavenger of the smelling committee," rose to a question of personal privilege. "I have a painful but solemn duty to perform," he declared. "I impeach Andrew Johnson in that he has usurped power and violated the law, that he has corruptly used the appointing power and the pardoning power, has corruptly interfered in elections, that he has corruptly used the veto power and has corruptly disposed of the property of the United States." [6] Ashley's resolutions were adopted and a sub-committee of the Judiciary appointed to take evidence. As soon as this episode was closed, the House without debate overrode the President's veto, and on January 8, 1867, suffrage was extended to the negroes of Washington city.

Armed with authority to investigate the President, Boutwell and Ashley were satisfied they would have the bad man out of office and probably on the gallows before the new year. They were already on the track of most astounding disclosures. They had discovered facts and circumstances which satisfied them that Andrew Johnson was one of the murderers of Abraham Lincoln. This conclusion they arrived at while the committee was investigating the complicity of Jefferson Davis and Benjamin in the assassination. To the inflamed mind of Boutwell, and also of Ashley, there was no doubt of the guilt of Davis and Benjamin, and probably of Johnson as well. Judge Holt had produced before the committee one Sanford Conover. This person brought with him seven depositions setting forth that the deponents were in Richmond in the spring of 1865, at an interview between Davis and Benjamin, when the plot was formed to murder Lincoln.[7] Now one of these precious witnesses of Conover was a fellow named Campbell. But on com-

6 *Second Session Thirty-ninth Congress*, pp. 319-321.
7 DeWitt, *Impeachment*, p. 138; Welles, Vol. II, p. 299.

ing before the committee Campbell broke down and confessed
that the depositions were fabricated by Conover, that he himself was going under an assumed name, and so was Conover,
whose real name was Dunham.   When confronted with Campbell, Dunham took to his heels but was soon caught, tried, and
given ten years in the penitentiary for perjury.   Campbell had
been paid six hundred and twenty-five dollars and Snivel, another of the scoundrels, four hundred and seventy-five dollars
by Holt's Department of Justice.

Now this perjury and villainy in no way dashed Boutwell's
ardor, or Ashley's, nor did it divert them from their pursuit
of Andrew Johnson.   "Why does not Johnson cause the arrest
of John Surratt?" they asked themselves.   "Surratt has been
located in Europe, why shall he not be brought back to America
and hung as his mother was before him?"   The obvious answer
was because Andrew Johnson was afraid of Surratt, afraid that
Surratt would "give him away."   Who but Andrew Johnson
had a motive to kill President Lincoln?   Did not Lincoln's
death make Johnson President?   Was not Johnson a bad man,
just the man for such a deed, and had he not been drunk when
sworn in as Vice-president?   Undoubtedly, according to Boutwell and Ashley, he was at the bottom of the assassination plot.
Ignoring the advice of Stanton and Holt, that John Surratt
should not be brought back to America for trial as no jury
would convict him on the evidence, and that the fifty thousand
dollar reward for his arrest be withdrawn, Boutwell proceeded
gravely to inform the House "that the executive had not used
due diligence" in arresting Surratt.[8]   Boutwell indeed died in
the belief that Johnson was implicated in the assassination of
Mr. Lincoln.

Under the impeachment resolutions the judiciary committee
busied themselves to sustain Ashley's absurd charges.[9]   Shortly
it was given out by Boutwell and Ashley that the President was
suspected of assassinating Lincoln.   Thereupon Dunham, who

[8] Boutwell, *North American Review*, Vol. CXLI, p. 573.
[9] Blaine declares that every one present felt that Ashley's charges "were
gross exaggerations and distortions of fact and could not be sustained by legal
evidence or indeed by reputable testimony of any kind."—Blaine, Vol. II,
p. 342.

was not yet in the penitentiary but in jail awaiting his departure thence, became a star witness. Ashley and others visited him in his jail quarters. Dunham and his wife let it be known that they could supply the missing testimony to convict Johnson. A man named Adamson had a letter, Dunham assured the judiciary committee. This letter he had seen. It was written during the war by Military Governor Johnson to Jeff Davis. In this letter Johnson offered to surrender Tennessee to the Confederacy and assured the sendee, he "was going to join them." A colored servant of Parson Brownlow's son had stolen the letter from Johnson's desk before it was sent. Chief Detective Baker, a moving party in this malodorous investigation, had also seen this letter. While Baker was out looking for the man, Adamson, the committee went cheerily ahead taking evidence against the President. It raked over the New Orleans riots, investigated the President's bank account and private papers, inquired into his opposition to the Fourteenth Amendment, his restoration of captured lands to southern rebels. And his construction of the Nashville, Chattanooga and Northwestern Railroad in 1863 and 1864. Of course Adamson was never found. The whole affair was the froth and scum that float to the surface after all great human cataclysms. Though the committee was wholly without evidence to sustain Ashley's charges, a majority asked, and obtained leave of Congress, that the committee be continued until the Fortieth Congress, Ashley intimating that the President was a party to Lincoln's assassination.

While the House was busy nosing around for proof of its charges, radical Senators, under the leadership of Ben Wade, were equally busy packing the Senate to convict, when the House voted to impeach. Daily it was becoming more plain to radicals such as Sumner, Wade and Chandler that conservative Senators were deserting them. Therefore the greater the necessity that the Senate be purged and made "loyal." A two-thirds majority must be maintained at all hazards. Accordingly, the seat of Stockton, a Democratic Senator from New Jersey, was contested by the Republicans, and Stockton was unseated under disreputable circumstances. A pair, which

Morrill, a Republican Senator of Maine, had arranged with a Democratic Senator, was ignored and broken and by this disgraceful trick Stockton was unseated and a Republican put in his place.   Likewise, in July 1866, Nebraska, with a population of less than one-fourth of an authorized Congressional district, was admitted as a state over the President's veto. Thereby two more Republican Senators were added to the list. The scheme to admit Colorado, with a less population than Nebraska and to add two more Republican Senators, was defeated by a close call.

At midnight on the last days of Congress Wade, who would succeed to the Presidency if Johnson were removed, called up the bill to admit Colorado and insisted upon an immediate vote. Senator Fessenden protested on account of the pressing nature of the bill under discussion.   And, besides, it was called to the Senate's attention that Senator Riddle was ill with rheumatism and Senator Grimes was likewise ill and absent.   Therefore Senator Hendricks proposed that a vote be taken "at half past twelve to-morrow."   Wade bluntly informed the Senators that he expected to get a vote that night.   "I want to be frank and plain about it," he said.   "I am better prepared to-night than I will be to-morrow to decide this question."   Senator Doolittle replying to Wade, called attention to the absence of the two Senators who were ill and to the lateness of the hour, almost midnight.   "Right in the midst of the business of the Senate upon an important measure," he declared, "to have pressed upon us by surprise a motion to postpone and to take up the Colorado bill is beyond anything I could ever have anticipated." . . . "Sir," said he, "the world stands looking on. The people of the United States know what is transpiring in this body; and there are peculiar reasons which connect themselves with the Senator from Ohio, which will draw some attention to him, and to the course he is pursuing on this occasion. We all know, time and again, that Senator, in pressing this matter of Colorado, has said over and over that his purpose was to reënforce a majority in this body, already more than two-thirds.   And for what, sir?" [10]   Doolittle was proceeding

[10] *First Session Fortieth Congress*, p. 497.

to furnish a bill of particulars, the chief item of which was that Wade was scheming to be President, when the latter backed down and said that "as many of his friends did not agree with him he withdrew his motion." In truth, a caucus had been held on this measure; Fessenden, Harris and Morgan had kicked out of radical traces and Wade knew that he could not override the veto. The next day the President's veto was sustained by a vote of 29 to 19, Edmunds, Fessenden, Foster, Grimes, Harris and Morgan, all strict Republicans, voting "No." "The two-thirds majority was broken. The Colorado bill was lost. The high-water mark of impeachment had been reached," [11] and America continued to be a representative and not a parliamentary government.

Now in these political upheavals the Republicans themselves were far from united. They allowed no one to oppose their program; on such an offending member they turned as they did upon the Democrats. The proud Conkling was almost run out of the party for defending Milligan. Fessenden and Grimes, for liberal votes, were lashed in a merciless manner. Though Senator Fessenden was perhaps the ablest Senator on the Republican side he was defeated for President *pro tem.* by Wade, who frankly admitted that "he did not know any parliamentary law," and he was roundly abused by Zach Chandler. "The conservative Senator from Maine!" Chandler would sneer a dozen times when referring to Fessenden. The "conservative Senator from Maine," according to Chandler and others was "standing in" with the administration to keep friends and relatives in office.[12] Charles Sumner continued the attack in a Boston interview.[12a] Senator Fessenden, Sumner insisted, was "afflicted with chronic dyspepsia. He runs to personalities as a duck to water, he comes into the debate as the Missouri enters the Mississippi and discolors it with temper, filled and surcharged with sediment. . . . He is of much finer fiber than Andrew Johnson but resembles the President in prejudice and combativeness."

11 DeWitt, *Impeachment*, p. 179.
12 Fessenden, *Life of Fessenden*, Vol. II, p. 136.
12a Boston *Advertiser*, August 30.

Perhaps the queerest instance of the intolerance of the Radical with the Conservative was seen when Ben Butler ran afoul of Bingham. The House was debating a bill for the relief of destitute persons in the South, whether loyal or disloyal. Bingham, supporting the bill, wandered over to the Democratic side of the chamber. Butler, who opposed the bill, remarked that the gentleman from Ohio had "got over on the other side not only in body but in spirit." Judge Bingham, who it will be remembered was the Judge Advocate who prosecuted Mrs. Surratt and the other alleged assassins of President Lincoln, had grown tired of such flings. He therefore retorted that "it does not become a gentleman who recorded his vote fifty times for Jeff Davis, the arch traitor in this rebellion, as his candidate for President of the United States, to undertake to damage this cause by an imputation on either my integrity or honor." "I repel with scorn and contempt any utterance of that sort from any man," said Bingham, "whether he be the hero of Fort Fisher not taken or of Fort Fisher taken."

This fling at General Butler, who, as was well known, had voted fifty times at the Charleston convention in April 1860 for Davis for President, and had not taken Fort Fisher, aroused the incorrigible man's wrath. In reply he admitted he had voted fifty-seven times for Jeff Davis for President, "hoping thereby to prevent disunion," but he asserted that the difference between himself and the honorable gentleman from Ohio was this: "While Jeff Davis was in the Union, a Senator of the United States and claiming to be a friend of the Union, I supported him." . . . "I left him as soon as he left the Union," Butler explained; "but the gentleman from Ohio now supports him when he is a traitor." . . . "I did all I could and the best I could," he went on, "and I feel exceedingly chagrined because I could do no more; but if during the war the gentleman from Ohio did as much as I did in that direction I should be glad to recognize that much done. But the only victim of that gentleman's prowess that I know of was an innocent woman hung upon the scaffold, one Mrs. Surratt. And I can sustain the memory of Fort Fisher if he and his present associates can sustain him in shedding the blood of a woman tried by a military commission and convicted without sufficient evidence, in my judgment."

Butler's onslaught stunned Bingham and he corrected his remarks for the record. Butler then renewed the attack, intimating that Bingham and his associates had withheld Booth's diary from the court and had mutilated it by tearing out leaves to shield Johnson, the instigator of Lincoln's murder. "Who spoliated the book?" Butler bellowed. "Who suppressed the evidence? Who caused an innocent woman to be hanged, when he had in his pocket the diary showing the purpose of the main conspirator in the case?" Along this line Butler cavorted, as only Ben Butler could. When he had finished his remarkable tirade Bingham rose to make reply. "Such a charge as the gentleman makes," said Bingham, "is only fit to come from a man who lives in a bottle and is fed with a spoon"—evidently referring to General Grant's contemptuous remark about General Butler's soldiering and to Ben Butler's well-known reputation in New Orleans.[13]

The impeachment committee had been making slow progress. The election of the radical Wade President *pro tem.* over Fessenden and the absurd stories of Dunham and Baker had almost put an end to the investigation. "Bad as President Johnson is," the Republicans were saying, "Wade as President would be worse." But in November 1867, after the election, interest in the investigation was revived in the following manner: The Republicans having lost heavily at the polls—New York and New Jersey going Democratic, and Maine, Republican, by only eleven hundred—the President's friends gathered about him, congratulating and calling for a speech. From a written manuscript Johnson boldly, but unwisely, referred to the "military despotism controlling the country" and to "the arbitrary power of Congress." Concluding, he said he was still hopeful "that in the end the rod of despotism will be broken and the heel of power lifted from the necks of the people and the principles of a violated Constitution preserved."[14] "Treason!" the impeachment committee exclaimed.

13 DeWitt, *op. cit.*, pp. 215-216.
14 *Impeachment Investigation*, p. 1175.

"That utterance alone is sufficient to warrant impeachment."
A meeting of the committee was hastily called and the irrepressible Baker again appeared as a witness. "One Matchett,"
he said, "had seen a witness, a Mrs. Harris, who knew all
about the treasonable Andrew Johnson letter to Jeff Davis
but who would not come as a witness for less than twenty-five
thousand dollars, paid in advance." This was too much, even
for Ashley, and the witness Baker was dismissed for good.

At this stage of the investigation Ashley himself took the
stand and became a witness in his own behalf. "The evidence
against Andrew Johnson though not legal," he testified, "sat-
isfies me that he was implicated in Lincoln's murder." Ashley,
however, stated this in explanation, "I always believed that
President Harrison, President Taylor and President Buchanan were poisoned and were poisoned for the express purpose of putting the Vice-president in the presidential office."
It seems incredible that upon such balderdash a majority of
the committee should have reported to the House a recommendation that Andrew Johnson be impeached, but so they did.
The minority report, prepared by Republican Senator Wilson
was adopted. On December 7, 1867, Ashley's resolution to
impeach failed by a vote of 157 yeas and 108 nays. Forty-
one Democrats and sixty-seven Republicans voted in the negative, including such prominent representatives as Banks, Bingham, Blaine, Garfield, Dawes, Washburn and Wilson.

Little wonder Ashley has been denounced by historian and
biographer. As an expert at double-crossing he was without a peer. While Dunham was in jail in Washington and
had not gone to the Albany penitentiary, "Ashley and Co."
urged the President to pardon him "because of valuable assistance in Mrs. Surratt's case." The President declined to do so
and Dunham was sent to Albany. The worm then turned and
stung. Dunham attacked Ashley, Holt, Butler, and Matchett.
He declared that they had been using him as a tool to destroy
the President. Ashley had manufactured evidence and had
said it would be easy to prove four facts against Johnson: That
Booth paid Vice-president Johnson several visits at the Kirkwood House, that Johnson corresponded with Booth, that on

April 14, 1865, Atzerodt put weapons in his room as a blind to divert attention from Johnson, and, lastly, that Booth had stated in New York that Johnson was acting with him. "If you will procure this evidence," Ashley said to Dunham, "you shall be pardoned." Such was Dunham's story. He also went on to say that he wrote down what Ashley dictated and procured two witnesses to commit it to memory.

At all events, these two witnesses came to Washington and were examined by Ben Butler and Ashley. Matters then came to a halt because Dunham refused to go on unless his pardon was first forthcoming! In 1869 President Johnson pardoned Dunham both on account of ill health and because it was plain that he had been made a dupe of by Ashley and Co.[15] It may be said that Ashley was called the scavenger of the smelling committee because he investigated idle and remote rumors such as this: Did prostitutes have access to Johnson's back stairs and thereby sell pardons to rebels? Did a woman named Perry request the President to make an arrangement with her to handle the New York Custom House, and did the President agree to do this? Johnson filed these Perry letters and wrote on them "Blackmail." [16]

During this year, 1867, no less than five other attempts at impeachment failed, not for lack of a desire to impeach, but for lack of a scrap of evidence. If the House Committee could only lay hands on some specific offense, short shift it would make of "the renegade." And this specific act Johnson himself soon furnished. In the teeth of a resolution of the Senate, passed January 13, 1868, that the President had no power to remove Stanton from his office as Secretary of War and to appoint a successor, Andrew Johnson issued an order to Stanton to vacate and another order to General Lorenzo Thomas to take possession. The explosion which followed took place on February 22, 1868.

It is necessary to recite the circumstances leading up to this event. For a long time Secretary Stanton had been a thorn in the President's flesh. Since the summer of 1866 Welles and

---

15 DeWitt, *Impeachment*, p. 280.
16 Johnson MS; Oberholtzer, Vol. II, p. 65.

others had urged his removal, but the President held on to the popular War Secretary, despite such warnings. After the Tenure of Office Act, March 2, 1867, which made Stanton secure, as he thought, the Secretary of War had become more open and defiant of the President and "assumed the task of inspiring in Congress the belief that his chief, the President, was a desperate character, bent on overriding the majority by military force." [17] At a cabinet meeting in the summer of 1866, for example, when the question of the government's supplying bunting for the Philadelphia Union National Convention was up for discussion, a significant conversation occurred. "Let the navy furnish the bunting," said Stanton, sneering at Welles's attachment to Johnson. "The navy never refuses to show its colors," Welles retorted. As time passed Stanton drew nearer to Sumner and "collogued with the Radicals," in fact acted with such duplicity as "to strongly suggest the vagaries of an opium-eater." [18] It must be said, however, that, though Stanton was acting as a spy on the Johnson administration, Congress, as a whole, sought to justify him in so doing. He had a right to do so and indeed he was moved so to do by high and patriotic motives, the Radicals affirmed.

The strained relations between the President, supported by his cabinet, and the Secretary of War continued till Monday, August 5, 1867, when the President suspended Stanton from office, and appointed General Grant in his place. On that day, as we have seen, John Surratt was on trial for assassinating Lincoln, and his attorney was charging that the Government dared not put Booth's diary in evidence as it would acquit Surratt. In reply Judge Bingham, for the Government, holding in his hands the record in the Mary Surratt trial of two years before, had called attention to it. "Why, this entire record was presented to the President, at that time, including the recommendation for mercy;" Bingham said, "and the judgment approved by the chief executive." Next day's papers carried an account of the trial, laying special stress on the recommendation for mercy. Before then, as I have stated,

[17] Dunning, *Reconstruction*, p. 92.
[18] *Ibid.*, p. 91.

the President had never heard of the recommendation and was dumbfounded. Did the war secretary know of the recommendation and conceal it from him? Holt certainly knew of it, as he often admitted. Must Stanton not have known of it also? Anyway, on that very day, Stanton was suspended and General Grant appointed *ad interim*, in his place. General Grant served as Secretary of War, with great satisfaction to the administration, for about four months. At the time of this incident the President likewise suspended General Sheridan as military commander at New Orleans for discourteous remarks concerning an opinion of Attorney-General Stanbery upon the Reconstruction Act. This action of the President gave great offense to the North and was displeasing to General Grant.[19]

On December 12, 1867, the President sent a message to the Senate, informing them that he had removed Stanton and appointed Grant, giving his reasons. Stanton at the same time, submitted his reply to the Senate. On January 13, 1868, the House, in a great state of excitement, resolved that the President had no right to remove Stanton or to appoint a successor and sent formal notice of its action to the President, to General Grant, to Stanton, and to General Thomas. On the next day, Secretary Grant, fearing that he might be fined ten thousand dollars and imprisoned five years, as prescribed in the Tenure of Office Act, resigned. Going into the War department office, he locked the door, then turned the key over to his first assistant, and Stanton came back in as Secretary of War. Now this was more than the resolute President could endure. He was going to fight. The Constitution authorized him to select his official family and Congress should not deprive him of the right.

Specially was his wrath kindled against General Grant, of whom he was both fond and proud. Poor men they had been, and plain men; Grant a tanner, Johnson a tailor, and both Democrats. But Grant had gone back on him in this matter, he concluded. When he was appointed secretary *ad interim* he had promised Johnson if Congress interfered to hand the

19 DeWitt, *Impeachment*, p. 315.

office back and not to deliver it over to Stanton. This would enable the President to test, through the courts, Stanton's right to hold the office. Sending for General Grant, the President interrogated him before the assembled cabinet. Why had he not complied with his agreement? A controversy arose between the two friends. In this controversy all the cabinet sustained the President.[20] General Grant's pride was wounded and forthwith he joined his old enemy, Stanton, and the Radicals, Thad Stevens declaring "we will now admit you into the church." The loss of General Grant's influence was an immeasurable injury to the President's administration.

In this crisis the President had the coöperation of his entire official family. Welles considered the Senate "a debauched, debased, demoralized body without independence, sense of right or moral courage. . . . A Radical body subject to the dictation of Sumner who is imperious and Chandler who is unprincipled." The cabinet had just advised the President "that he could not be removed from office except on impeachment," as the Constitution provides; that, "pending impeachment, he could not be suspended"; that "if he should be suspended he ought to maintain his authority" and that "such suspension and arrest would be a crime, no less a violation of the law by Congress than if effected by private parties." [21]

After the retirement of General Grant as Secretary of War on January 14, the President offered the place to General Sherman. Sherman declined. As a last resort on February 21, Stanton was again removed and Lorenzo Thomas, titular Adjutant-General, was appointed Secretary of War, under the act of 1789. Now, the Senate being in session, the President could not remove Stanton if the Tenure of Office Act was applicable and constitutional. He and his advisers, however, concluded that the old act of 1789 covered the case and not

20 Moore, *Diary*, p. 118; Oberholtzer, Vol. I, p. 489.

21 Jones, *Life*, p. 245; Rhodes stigmatizes this conduct of Johnson, in not surrendering to Congress, as "vindictive resentment." "Johnson was surrounded by office-seeking sycophants," says Rhodes, "and was driven to do what he did by obscure busy-bodies, beggars for place."—*Cf.* The opinion of the Supreme Court in the fall of 1926, in *Myers vs. United States*, sustaining Johnson's course, cutting up the Tenure of Office Act by the roots, and declaring that no President could run the government with such a law hanging over him.

the Tenure of Office Act, and that he could remove and fill the office at the same time.[22] It is probable that General J. D. Cox of Ohio if appointed, as Sherman and Ewing recommended, might have been acceptable to the Senate, but Cox was under Grant's influence, Welles insisted. Therefore, he was not appointed.[23] Ewing and Sherman, much concerned, now undertook to get the President out of trouble, urging him to let Stanton alone and "not adopt rash measures." Chief Justice Chase also warned "of the coming avalanche." [24] But Andrew Johnson was not to be humiliated or disgraced. Congress might chop him to mincemeat but he would not play the coward. "Damn it," he would say, to those suggesting that he might be impeached, "I am tired of such talk, let them go on and impeach if they want to." . . . "If the people do not entertain sufficient respect for their Chief Magistrate to uphold him in his course," he said to his secretary, "he ought to resign." [25] To the New York *World* he said that he had "the constitutional right to remove Stanton and that if a contest arose it would be settled in the courts."

It was February 21 when Stanton was summarily dismissed and his successor Thomas appointed. Now Thomas, the new appointee, a fair-weather warrior, was a gentleman of the old school—convivial in his habits and somewhat garrulous. Under his administration events moved along rapidly and merrily. Going over to Stanton's office, he demanded possession, exhibiting his authority. At first Stanton seemed disposed to yield but asked time to consider the matter. The General, swelling with the importance of the high honors thrust upon him, went his way. Stanton put himself into communication with the Senate and House, furnishing to them copies of the President's order of removal. The response was instant and vigorous. Many Congressmen rushed to the War department to back up the War Secretary. Sumner forwarded a letter with the single word "Stick."

The night following these important events General Thomas,

[22] DeWitt, *Impeachment*, p. 340.
[23] Welles, *Diary*, Vol. III, p. 231.
[24] Warden, *Chase*, p. 618.
[25] Moore, *op. cit.*, p. 120.

in fantastic garb, attended a masque ball in Washington, enjoying the luxury of his new position and the sensation he was creating. To those crowding around him and asking what he proposed to do if Stanton resisted, he replied, "Break down the doors!" In fact, as it afterwards appeared, "the eyes of Delaware," his native State, "were upon him!" But in the early morn the General's sleep, after a night of carousal, was disturbed by the arrival of the sheriff, armed with an order of arrest, sworn out by Stanton. In due time the General gave bond to appear before Judge Cartter. First, however, he asked the Judge if the order of arrest forbade him "having it out" with Secretary Stanton. Advised by Judge Cartter that it did not, the General conferred with the President who was glad "Stanton had taken the matter to court." "That's just where I wish it," he said. "The Tenure of Office Act will now be tested. When you are taken in custody we will sue out *habeas corpus* and the courts will settle the matter."

Forthwith the gay old warrior crossed the street again to try his luck with Secretary Stanton. But Stanton would not budge an inch. Thomas demanded of Secretary Stanton to surrender the office. Stanton replied that he himself was Secretary of War and ordered Thomas out of the office. Thomas refused to go. Stanton wanted to know, "Do you mean to use force?" Thomas replied that he did not care to use force but his mind was made up what he should do. After a while the controversy grew tiresome and the Congressmen who had witnessed the scene returned to the House. What followed their departure it was left to Thomas to relate, and this he did as a witness in the Impeachment trial. Stanton handed him a note, dated the day before, forbidding him from acting as Secretary of War *ad interim;* and then the conversation continued as follows:

"I said, 'The next time you have me arrested, please do not do it before I get something to eat.' I said I had had nothing to eat or drink that day. He put his hand around my neck, as he sometimes does, and ran his hand through my hair, and turned to General Schriver and said, 'Schriver, you have got a bottle here; bring it out.'

"Schriver unlocked his case and brought out a small vial, containing I suppose about a spoonful of whiskey, and stated at the same time that he occasionally took a little for dyspepsia. Mr. Stanton took that and poured it into a tumbler and divided it equally and we drank it together.

"A fair division, because he held up the glasses to the light and saw that they each had about the same, and we each drank. Presently a messenger came in with a bottle of whiskey, a full bottle; the cork was drawn, and he and I took a drink together. 'Now,' said he, 'this at least is neutral ground.' " [26]

Soon after this warlike episode, the President sent to the Senate the name of General Ewing, W. T. Sherman's father-in-law, to be Secretary of War. The appointment was not acted upon, sterner matters demanding the attention of Congress. On the twenty-first, when the President appointed Thomas, he likewise sent to the Senate his veto of the resolutions of Congress disapproving of Stanton's removal. In this document he gave warning to the Senate and to the House to do its worst. "Whatever be the consequences personal to myself," he declared, "I could not allow them to prevail against a public duty so clear to my own mind and so imperative. If what was possible had been certain, if I had been fully advised when I removed Mr. Stanton, that, in thus defending the trust committed to my hands, my own removal was sure to follow, I could not have hesitated, actuated by public considerations of the highest character." [27]

It was February 22 when this message was received, and it threw Congress into an uproar. Covode immediately offered impeachment resolutions, and in two hours the Great Reconstruction Committee, now at last a unit on removing Johnson, appeared in the House and through its spokesman Thaddeus Stevens recommended that "Andrew Johnson, President of the United States, be impeached of high crimes and misdemeanors in office." All Washington was now on tiptoe. The country at large was greatly excited. Andy Johnson meant fight; at that very moment, he was consulting with General

26 DeWitt, p. 356.
27 *Ibid.*, p. 375.

Emory, and preparing to resist the action of Congress. The debate on Covode's resolutions to impeach occupied a day and a half. Stevens arraigned the President as the "first great political malefactor"; a man "who was possessed by the same motive that made the angels fall." . . . "Who dare to hope that the Senate will dare to betray its trust?" he asked. . . . "Will disgrace itself in the face of the nation? Point me to one who dare do it and I will show you one who will dare the infamy of posterity." One Radical Congressman was in favor of "the official death of Andrew Johnson without debate." Another was wagering that Ben Wade would be President within ten days. Sumner in the Senate was exclaiming, in his lordly fashion, that this was "one of the last great battles with slavery." "Why higgle over words and phrases?" Sumner insisted. "It is wrong to try this impeachment on any articles."

Democrats and conservative Republicans, on the other hand, were much concerned. It seemed to the Democrats that "they stood in the midst of a red tribunal," that Congress had "silenced the courts," "murdered ten Southern States" and now "proposed to put the President out of office." Hubbard of Connecticut spoke words of great earnestness. "I take it upon myself to say," the Connecticut Congressman declared, defending Andrew Johnson's manhood, "that the first instinct of a man of honor similarly situated would impel him to eject by force and arms, with hot and honest indignation, any contemptible individual who should presume, with brazen and shameless impudence, to seek to intrude into his family of confidential advisers. Nay, sir," Hubbard continued, "if the old hero of New Orleans were to-day seated in the President's chair, he would find a sharp and speedy remedy for such a nuisance, in the toe of his boot, and not by the tardy process of law."

On the following Monday, February 24, at five o'clock in the afternoon, a ballot was taken on Covode's resolution. It was carried by a vote of 126 to 47. Every Republican voted aye and every Democrat no. A committee of two, consisting of Stevens and Bingham, was appointed to communicate the action of the House to the Senate. Next day Thaddeus Stevens and Bingham appeared at the bar of the Senate. Stevens, "looking the ideal Roman, with singular impressiveness, as if he were discharging a sad duty," approached and said, "In the name of the House of Representatives and of all the people of the United States we do impeach Andrew Johnson, President of the United States of high crimes and misdemeanors in office; and we further inform the Senate that the House of Representatives will, in due time, exhibit particular articles of impeachment against him and make good the same." Wade the President *pro tempore* replied, "The Senate will take order in the premises." [28]

While these momentous matters were happening in Congress, the ubiquitous Thomas was also playing his part in the drama. Accompanied by his lawyers, on the day fixed for the trial, he appeared in Judge Cartter's court to answer the charge of Secretary Stanton for a violation of the Tenure of Office Act. Stanton was not present in person, but by attorneys. Thomas, coming forward, surrendered himself to the court. "Hold," said the astonished attorneys for Stanton, seeing a *habeas corpus* staring them in the face, "we have not asked for imprisonment." "Very well," Thomas's attorneys replied, "we then ask the prisoner's discharge." The court so ordered. Thomas was then released and Andrew Johnson's effort to test the law was again foiled by the Radicals. Stanton, understanding that possession was nine points of the law and that so long as he was in the office no court would put him out, stuck to his job. Whereas, if Thomas had been put in custody he could have had his imprisonment inquired of, under the writ of *habeas corpus*. This great writ no judge would dare deny. Thus ingloriously ended the famous lawsuit of *Edwin M. Stanton vs. Lorenzo Thomas.*

Thomas out of the way and the danger of a writ of *habeas corpus* removed, Congress could go forward without molestation. Seven managers were next elected, Bingham, Boutwell, Butler, Logan, Stevens, Williams, and Wilson. General Grant's contempt for Ben Butler had kept the hero of Fort

[28] Rhodes, Vol. VI, p. 111.

Fisher off the committee to formulate charges, but Butler had succeeded in being appointed a manager. Next in order came the formulating of charges and this was a specially troublesome task, requiring several days. The issue must be narrowed for sensible lawyers knew that if the President were charged with petty offenses, provable by rumor, it would take as long to try him, "as it did to try Warren Hastings." It was therefore agreed to limit the charges to eleven. Ten of them were formulated on the first day and adopted. Ben Butler's pet specification was rejected. But on the morning of March 4, after a night's reflection, the ten charges sounded so scant and meager, the House reversed itself and adopted Butler's charge, based upon the President's political harangues. Jenkes, who had a habit of referring to the President as "the person exercising the duties of the executive office," wished to broaden the charges so as to inquire into the motives of the President. "Beastly Ben Butler," discussing the question of what constituted an impeachable offense, expressed himself as usual, in the language of the fish market. "I had thought," said he, "this old dogma that the President was impeachable only for indictable crimes dead and buried—I knew it stunk." (Laughter.) This was Butler's idea of the way to proceed in deposing the Chief Executive of forty millions of people.

Though there were eleven articles, there was really but one offense—the removal of Stanton and the appointment of Thomas. The first article charged the removal in so many words; the second article charged the writing of a letter to Thomas to take possession; the third article charged the actual appointment of Thomas. Articles four, five, six, seven, and eight are known as the "conspiracy articles" as they charge a conspiracy to do what the three first articles already charged. The ninth article charged illegal advice to General Emory. The tenth article, included at the earnest solicitation of Butler, charged that Andrew Johnson, in a loud voice, delivered sundry speeches on February 22, 1866, and during his "swing round the circle." Article eleven was fathered by Thad Stevens and is known as the "omnibus article." It charged a design to prevent the reinstatement of Stanton after the Senate had concurred in his suspension, as shown by the Grant-Johnson correspondence.[29]

Now these charges were based on a violation of the Tenure of Office Act of March 1867, an act which deprived the President of power over appointments and would even keep an enemy in his official family. At the time the bill passed the House in 1867 it provided specifically that the President should not remove any one of his cabinet without the Senate's consent. The Senate, however, struck out this provision. After a conference a compromise was arranged, as appears in the proviso to the first section. Discussing this proviso, Voorhees suggested that the provision was not clear and that some cabinet officer might hold over, "though ordered out by the President." Sherman replied that such a thing was impossible, that he did not see "how any gentleman could do it." Williams declared, "that he had no doubt any cabinet minister, with a particle of self-respect, would decline to remain in the cabinet after the President signified his presence no longer needed." [30] Hendricks, hinting at Stanton, stated "that the very person who ought to be turned out was the very person who would stay in." And so it eventuated, Stanton claiming that he was not within the exception.

This famous Tenure of Office Act declares in substance that the President shall not remove any officer except his cabinet, and, as to them, they shall "hold their offices respectively for and during the term of the President, by whom they may have been appointed and for one month thereafter, subject to removal by and with the advice and consent of the Senate." The act further provides that if any officer, during the recess, shall be guilty of misconduct the President may suspend him and appoint his successor until the case can be acted on by the Senate and in such case the President, in twenty days after the Senate meets, shall report the suspension and his reasons to the Senate; that if the Senate fail to concur in the removal the removed officer shall resume his duties; and, finally, that

29 DeWitt, *Impeachment*, p. 386.
30 *Globe, Second Session Thirty-ninth Congress*, p. 1039.

any person who violated the Act or attempted to do so should pay a fine not exceeding ten thousand dollars and be imprisoned for not more than five years.   It will be noted that in February 1867, when Stanton was finally removed, the Senate was sitting.

By 12 o'clock midnight on Wednesday, March 4, everything had been arranged—resolutions of impeachment adopted, managers elected, charges formulated.   On the morrow, March 5, 1868, at high noon, the President of the United States would face his accusers before the Senate sitting as a High Court of Impeachment with Salmon P. Chase, Judge presiding.

CHAPTER VI

THE TRIAL

On Thursday March 5, at one o'clock, the Chief Justice
entered the Senate Chamber, every Senator rising to his feet.
Mr. Justice Nelson accompanied his chief and Pomeroy, Wilson, and Buckalew acted as a senatorial escort. On taking the
chair the Chief Justice said, "Senators, in obedience to your
notice I am present for the purpose of forming a Court of
Impeachment and am now ready to take the oath." A deep
and abiding interest followed this statement. Did the Chief
Justice propose to change the Senate into a court, to overrule
the radical contention that the Senate was a mere political
tribunal with none of the attributes of a court? Undoubtedly
he did, for after taking the oath he turned and said, "Senators,
the oath will be administered to the Senators as they will be
called by the secretary in succession." Yielding obedience to
a force greater than politics or partisanship, the Senators came
forward, one after another, and the Senate was transformed
into a high court of impeachment.

A brilliant spectacle was presented: the Chief Justice, imposing in appearance, of great natural dignity and easily conscious of the awe and veneration his presence inspired; the
prisoner at the bar, the chief executive of forty millions of
people; the jury, fifty-four Senators representing twenty-seven
sovereign states; and the accusers, one hundred and ninety
members of the House. In the audience were diplomats, ministers of foreign courts, splendidly gowned women, and people
of all ranks, filling every inch of space. As the roll was called
and the name of Senator B. F. Wade—President of the Senate
and next in succession to the presidency—was reached, objection was made. If Senator Wade were allowed to take his seat
as a member of the court, it was urged, he would be trying his
own case. The Constitution was quoted to the effect that when

the President is impeached the Vice-president shall not preside. In deference to the spirit of this provision it was thought Wade should not sit as a member of the court. Several of the conservative Senators, however, insisted that he should, and objection was withdrawn. On the sixth he was sworn in and took part in the case. That he was within his legal rights no one can deny.

The composition of the Senate sitting as a court having been arranged, the Sergeant-at-Arms made proclamation, "Hear ye! hear ye! all persons are commanded to keep silence on pain of imprisonment while the Senate of the United States is sitting for the trial of the articles of impeachment against Andrew Johnson, President of the United States." Senator Howard moved that the secretary notify the managers that the Senate was now ready to proceed. The Chief Justice interposed, feeling it to be his duty, he said, to submit a question as to the rules of procedure. "In the judgment of the Chief Justice," said Chase, speaking with the impersonality and detachment of a disinterested judge, "the Senate is no longer the Senate, but is a distinct body, under a different oath, and the presiding officer is not the president *pro tem.* but the Chief Justice; though the Senate has heretofore adopted rules of procedure, such rules are not the rules of this body. The Chief Justice may be in error," he said, "and if so, he wishes to be corrected; and therefore, if he may be permitted to do so, he will take the sense of the Senate on this question—whether the rules adopted by the Senate on March the second should be considered the rules of this body." . . . "Senators," the Chief Justice went on, putting the question, "you who consider such rules the rules of this body will say 'aye,' contrary, 'no.' The ayes have it by the sound." Thus a second time the majesty of the law prevailed over the turbulent passions of politicians and it was apparent that Ben Wade's place was filled by a self-respecting Judge. Notice was given to the managers that the Senate was ready to proceed and a summons was ordered to be issued for Andrew Johnson to show cause on March 13 why he should not be removed from office and otherwise dealt with.

Thousands had been drawn to Washington to witness the

great Impeachment trial. "The city was a seething caul-
dron." "The most memorable attempt of an English-speaking
people to dethrone their ruler" was a drawing card. Though
Andrew Johnson's head could not be chopped off, as with
Charles I and Louis XVI, he could be disgraced, removed, and
in a jury trial fined ten thousand dollars and imprisoned for
five years. But the matter had a deeper significance, it involved the very existence of the executive office. Radicals,
especially, were in evidence, rejoicing that the House "had had
the nerve to go forward and that the madness of Johnson had
compelled Congress to face the great duty of removing him." [1]

And yet while feeling was running high against the President and General Schenck was calling him "an irresolute
mule and a devil bent on the ruin of his country," a discordant note was sounded in a most unexpected quarter. On
the night of March 4 Chief Justice Chase gave a reception and,
about the midnight hour, the master of ceremonies, waving
other guests aside, announced, "The President of the United
States!" In came Andrew Johnson and he was cordially
greeted by his old abolition friend Chase. Next day the city
of Washington was set by the ears. Undoubtedly the Chief
Justice was no fit person to preside at a trial "to enforce party
discipline." [2]

On the thirteenth the trial began. Wade again vacated the
chair and the Chief Justice looked down upon fifty-four Senators seated as near the presiding officer as convenient. On
the left were the managers, on the right the lawyers for the
President. The Sergeant-at-Arms made proclamation, "Hear
ye! hear ye! Andrew Johnson, Andrew Johnson," but Andrew Johnson came not. Obeying his attorneys, he was remaining discreetly away, attending to his duties in the White
House. While this call for Andrew Johnson was echoing
through the chamber, "Ben" Butler popped in the door and
halted in mid-air, seemingly at a loss to conceive why so
offensive a name should be hurled at him in so offensive a
manner." The crowd tittered and enjoyed the joke on "old

[1] Julian, *Recollections*, p. 316.
[2] Washington papers of March 5.

Ben," as every one called him. Presently Stanbery rose and read a paper, signed by himself and B. R. Curtis, Jeremiah S. Black, William M. Evarts, and Thomas A. R. Nelson, attorneys for the President. They asked forty days to file an answer. Butler, rolling his cock-eye at the gallery, exclaimed, "Forty days, as long as it took God Almighty to destroy the world by a flood!" No one could fail to mark the contrast between Henry Stanbery and "Beast" Butler—Butler, "insolent, intolerant, audacious"; Stanbery, "courteous, gentle and dignified"; so refined and cultured indeed, Welles was alarmed "lest he would prove no match for Butler." [3]

Butler's effrontery and audacity were much relished by the crowd and strangely enough by the great old man Stevens, who had now adopted Butler as his successor and spokesman. Thin, pale and haggard, his face scarred with the crooked autograph of pain, Stevens would die content could he but kick Andrew Johnson out of the White House. [4] Each morning he had to be carried upstairs and to his seat by two negro men, to whom he would grimly remark, "Boys, I wonder who will carry me when you are dead and gone?" [5] Though his eye flashed and his bull-dog mouth snapped as of old, his mighty spirit was flickering and was soon to take its flight. From a tumbler by his side he must sip strong brandy to whip himself along. Butler and his associates regarded themselves as "vice-gerents of the people." Besides, as DeWitt puts it, "They knew their Macaulay and were resolved to be the Burkes and Sheridans in this trial of another Warren Hastings." Manager Logan was known as "a wild horse." He had an unruly temper and a mad hatred of the Democratic party, which he had just quit; Boutwell was the typical stump orator; James F. Wilson had always opposed impeachment and "was now the sinner come to repentance"; [6] he was saner than the others. Manager Williams was both ornate and bitter. Of Judge Bingham much was expected, but he soon took a back seat, Butler admitting no peer.

[3] Welles, *Diary*, Vol. III, p. 308.
[4] Cullum, *Fifty Years*, p. 1256.
[5] Julian, *Recollections*, p. 313.
[6] DeWitt, Chapter VI.

The President's request to be allowed forty days to answer was turned down. The managers insisted that no time be allowed as the eighth rule required an immediate trial. Judge Curtis called attention to a rule of all courts to allow a reasonable time to answer, and suggested it was not well to put an important matter through with railroad speed. "Railroad speed!" Butler grunted. "Sir, why not? Railroads have affected all other business, why not trials? In every other business of life we recognize that change, why not in this?" The Senate decided ten days sufficient. The case then went over until March 23, to allow the President time to file his answer.

During this interval the President and his attorneys were busy with the defense. Though the fated man was beset by enemies he did not waver; he went about his business as usual, reserved and calm. He was going to put up a fight for the Constitution and for his own good name—a fierce fight but a fair one. Soon he was advised that the Radicals were endeavoring to exert influence over the Senate to work a conviction and he was urged to meet the situation by fighting the devil with fire. "I had rather be convicted than resort to fraud, bribery or corruption of any kind," he replied.[7] A great comfort to him in these trying days was his daughter, Mrs. Patterson. No matter how late the conferences or how protracted the sittings of the court, she remained by his side, ministering to him without rest or sleep. The worn and invalid wife could render no aid, but his daughter Martha never failed him; when the lawyers and cabinet had gone he would tell her of his troubles and she would assist in bearing his heavy load. Often till morning she would busy herself making a pot of coffee or arranging some delicacy, awaiting the end of a protracted conference.[8]

Henry Stanbery, who had resigned as Attorney-General to defend the President, was likewise a joy. Living no great distance from Johnson's Tennessee home, and being a true friend of the President, this whole-hearted Ohio gentleman would

[7] Moore, *Diary*, p. 129.
[8] Johnson MS.; Schouler, Vol. VII, p. 21.

enter the White House and by his excellent spirits encourage his Chief. "Everything will come out right," he would say; "I feel it in my bones. . . . I confess at first I felt a misgiving about this act of impeachment," he would declare, "but now, Mr. President, I see in it nothing but good. It gives you the great opportunity to vindicate yourself,—not only before the American people but before the entire world . . . an opportunity such as you could never otherwise have had to show whether you are a traitor or not." On another occasion he said, "If I can only keep well for this trial, Mr. President, I will be willing to be sick the balance of my life. I know, Sir, that you will come out of it brighter than you have ever shone." [9]

The President had hoped that his old friend Jerre Black, whom he selected as his main attorney, would be a stay and support. An unfortunate circumstance, however, removed Judge Black from the case and came near producing serious results. Black, it will be remembered, had been a staunch Democrat and had assisted the President in his messages to Congress. In truth, there was no stronger constitutional lawyer in his day than Jerre Black, the hero of *Ex Parte Milligan*. Now, shortly after Black was retained, his law firm imprudently urged the President to assist them in recovering a small Guano island, called Alta Vela, in the Caribbean Sea. Black's firm wished United States war vessels to be sent to capture the island, otherwise their client would lose his debt. Accompanying the request to the President was a letter urging favorable action. This letter was signed by Ben Butler, Stevens, Bingham and James G. Blaine. It must be kept in mind that this letter was dated March 9, several days after the impeachment trial had got under way. The President refused Judge Black's request. He was not to be made a tool of by him or any one else. The Judge withdrew from the case, even severing further social relations with the President.

Very little evidence was offered, about twenty-five witnesses for the managers and sixteen for the defendant. These were wholly unimportant. The case was based upon the record and

9 Moore, *Notes*, p. 124.

not upon living witnesses. By March 31 the written evidence was in. This consisted of the President's oath to support the Constitution; the act of March 2, 1867; the order removing Stanton and appointing Thomas and other evidence of that kind. On April 4 the witnesses for the managers had been examined and their case closed. One fact at least the managers had developed, that in his "swing round the circle" the President was coolly sober. "There was no drinking on that trip," the newspaper reporters testified. The first decided setback the prosecution received was when Butler offered to show that General Thomas had gone with his commission in hand to Stanton's office with intent to take forcible possession.[10] Stanbery objected. The Chief Justice held against him. "The evidence will be heard unless the Senate think otherwise," he ruled. Senator Drake, an extreme Radical, took exception to the presiding officer's "undertaking to decide a point of that kind. It is for the Senate," he insisted. The Chief Justice ruled against this position. Drake appealed to the Senate and demanded a vote. Fessenden insisted that Drake was out of order. Senator Johnson "called the Honorable Member to order." "The question is not debatable in the Senate," said Senator Johnson. "I am not debating it," retorted Drake, "I am stating my point of order." The Chief Justice rapped sharply upon his desk. "The Senator will come to order," he commanded. "If the President please," said Manager Butler, "is not this question debatable?" "It is debatable," said the Chief Justice, "by the managers and by the counsel for the defendant, not by the Senators." After further discussion Senator Drake again declared he objected to the presiding officer's ruling.

"The Senator is not in order," the Chief Justice tartly ruled. "I wish that question put to the Senate, sir," the recalcitrant Senator persisted. "The Senator will come to order," the Chief Justice sternly said. Senator Drake subsided and from this time forth no Senator undertook to debate the case. At this juncture the Senate retired for conference and by a vote of 30 to 20 adopted a rule in accordance with the Chief Jus-

[10] Supplement to *Globe, Second Session Fortieth Congress*, p. 59.

tice's suggestion, that is, the presiding officer would first pass upon disputed points and the Senate, on appeal, would review him. Despite the ruling of the Chief Justice that he was sitting as a judge and presiding over a court the managers and the radical Senators continued to address him as "Mr. President." Oddly it sounded to hear Senator Reverdy Johnson or Mr. Evarts say, "Your Honor," or "Mr. Chief Justice," and to hear Senator Conness and Senator Sumner address the Judge as "Mr. President."

The managers undertook to make a great deal out of General Thomas's threats to batter down Secretary Stanton's door. When it appeared, however, that "the eyes of Delaware" were upon General Thomas, and that the old gentleman was more concerned about the masquerade ball and the sensation he was creating than all else, evidence of this kind proved a boomerang. In fact when it came out in evidence that the gallant General and the Secretary of War "met on neutral ground" and took "a drink from the same flask," and that it "was an equal divide," it was apparent that the managers could not rely upon the charge of force or conspiracy. The charge that the President had directed General Emory to disobey the law, in opposition to a resolution of Congress, fell to the ground when Emory testified to his conversation with the President. "Have you been receiving orders from any one other than myself?" the President had asked Emory. "To this," said Emory, "I replied, 'The command of the army has been taken from you, Mr. President, and given to General Grant.'" "But," said the President, "is that not unconstitutional?" "Nevertheless," Emory replied, "I must obey Congress. The lawyers all advised that I must." Such was the terrible Emory episode!

On Friday April 10 the defense began its case. Mr. Stanbery called witnesses to show that the President had acted in good faith, under the advice of his cabinet, and with no thought of violence. Return J. Meigs, Clerk of the District Supreme Court, was called for this purpose. He produced the papers in the case of Stanton against Thomas, also the *habeas corpus* proceedings taken out by Thomas. Butler ob-

jected to this evidence. The Chief Justice ruled in favor of
the President—"no Senator being heard to object." [11] "Does
your Honor understand that the affidavit in the case is admitted?" Manager Butler gasped. The Chief Justice did. It
seemed that this ruling would go unchallenged, but not so. "I
heard one Senator ask for the question to be put," Butler insinuated. The truculent Senator from California, Conness,
admitted that he wished the question put. The Senate by a
vote of 34 to 17—Roscoe Conkling one of the seventeen, however—overruled the Radicals. Butler then sneered, "Mr.
President, I wish it simply understood, that I may clear my
skirts of this matter, that this all goes in under our objection
and under the ruling of the presiding officer." To this insolent
insinuation the Chief Justice quietly replied, "It goes in under
the direction of the Senate of the United States." [12]

On the same day another ruling of the Chief Justice was
sustained, and under this ruling the testimony of General
Sherman was admitted. On January 27, after Grant had
turned the office back to Stanton, it will be recalled, Johnson
tendered the place to Sherman. Sherman after a talk with the
President declined it. "Why do you not test the matter in the
courts?" Sherman had then inquired. "That's precisely what
I'm trying to do," the President replied. The force of this evidence is apparent. It showed the President's lawful motives.
Now at the conferences of the lawyers they had tried in vain
to devise some plan to induce the Senate to hear evidence of
this kind. All during the morning of April 18 General
Sherman had been interrogated about his conversation with the
President. But all questions and answers relating to this matter had been excluded.

During the afternoon, however, and while the General was
still in the hall, Reverdy Johnson asked to recall him, for a
question. "When the President tendered to you the office of
Secretary of War," Senator Johnson asked, "did he, at the very
time of making such tender, state to you what his purpose in

11 *Globe*, p. 168.
12 DeWitt, *op. cit.*. p. 441.

so doing was? If he did, state what he said his purpose was." [13]
These searching questions—relating to the *res gestae*, as the
lawyers would say—threw the managers into a passion. Ben
Butler grew indignant and insulting. "In this matter," he
snapped, "Senator Johnson is acting as the attorney of the
President." The Senate by a vote of 26 to 24 directed Sherman to answer the questions. As framed, it will be observed,
they related to the *res gestae*; that is, the transaction itself was
speaking. General Sherman proceeded to testify: "On the
twenty-seventh and thirty-first of January the President had
said, 'General Sherman, I wish you to serve as Secretary of
War, to protect the army and the navy; I cannot work in harmony with Stanton and I beg you as the General of the army
to accept this office for the good of the country.'" This evidence disposed of all the charges except numbers one, two and
three. When General Sherman left the stand Bingham rose
and apologized for Butler's remark. "Senator Johnson was
strictly within his rights in asking his questions," said Bingham, "and the managers have no grievance against him."
Secretary Welles was next called but was not permitted to
testify, nor were the other members of the Cabinet. These
witnesses would have sworn that the Tenure of Office Act, when
first passed in March 1867, was discussed by the President and
cabinet. Stanton was then present. The cabinet were unanimous that the Secretary of War was not included in the
protection of the act. Of all members of the cabinet Stanton
was the most outspoken in this opinion.

During the trial the suspicious Welles witnessed a scene in
the streets of Washington which made him so indignant he
hastened home to record it. "When I was coming up H
Street this evening, between four and five," Welles records, "I
came upon Conkling and Benjamin F. Butler, who were in
close conversation on the corner of 15th Street. It was an
ominous and discreditable conjunction,—the principal manager, an unscrupulous, corrupt, and villainous character, holding concourse with one of the Senatorial triers, a conceited

[13] *Globe*, p. 170.

coxcomb of some talents and individual party aspirations. They both were, as Jack Downing says, stumped, and showed in their countenances what they were talking about and their wish that I had been on some other street,—or somewhere else."

A little while before Welles had made another entry in his diary: "The Constitution-breakers are trying the Constitution-defender," he wrote; "the law-breakers are passing condemnation on the law-supporter; the conspirators are sitting in judgment on the man who would not enter into their conspiracy, who was, and is, faithful to his oath, his country, the Union, and the Constitution. What a spectacle! And if successful, what a blow to free government! What a commentary on popular intelligence and public virtue!"

Towards the last of the trial Stanbery was taken sick and Evarts asked that no more testimony be taken during the day. This simple request aroused Butler's anger and he delivered what Evarts called a harangue, "such as was never heard before in a court of justice." [14] "While these delays are taking place," Butler said, "and the Senate being courteous to lawyers, the true Union men of the South are being murdered. On our hands and on our skirts is their blood. Gentlemen of the Senate," he roared, "this is the closing up of a war wherein 300,000 men laid down their lives to save the country." . . . "My mail is filled with threats of assassination," he whined. " 'Butler, prepare to meet thy God; Hell is your portion, the Avenger is abroad on your track;' these are the threats I daily receive, but I am a free man and it is known that the threatened dog lives the longest." [15] As Butler indulged in these daily tirades conservative men were dreading more and more the placing of Ben Wade in the President's office with Ben Butler as his chief adviser.[16]

As soon as the evidence was closed it was clear that the case was one wholly of law. The conspiracy articles, numbers four, five, six, seven and eight disappeared under the evidence of General Sherman, Thomas, and others that the President's purpose was to have the courts test the matter. Besides, if

14 DeWitt, p. 442.
15 *Globe* Supplement, *Second Session Fortieth Congress*, p. 208.
16 Rhodes, *History*, Vol. VI, p. 152.

there had been a conspiracy General Grant was one of the conspirators. He had served as Secretary of War for nearly four months. There was no evidence under article nine. It appeared that the President in his dealings with General Emory was trying to keep and not to break the peace. Article ten, that the President had made a number of speeches, using rough language, and speaking "in a loud voice," as Ben Butler charged, provoked a smile. "It is certainly a novelty in this country," Evarts blandly remarked, "to try anybody for making a speech." The last article, known as the omnibus article, was too general to base an argument upon. In a word, the case finally came down to this, "Was the President guilty of a high crime and misdemeanor in removing Stanton and appointing Thomas?"

One phase of the case, however, was giving the defense some trouble. In the summer of 1867 when the President first removed Stanton he seemed to be placing himself within the provisions of the Tenure of Office Act. The Senate was not then in session. When it met in December the President reported his action to the Senate, as the act provides—apparently operating under the act. If the President had removed Stanton before March 1867, the date of the obnoxious act, or if he had removed him outright under the Act of 1789 and regardless of the Act of 1867, it is probable he would not have been impeached.[17] But this mistake of the President in first proceeding under the Act of 1867 was not regarded as fatal. In February 1868 he finally removed Stanton under the Act of 1789 and was on safe ground, no matter what he had done in August 1867. The old Act of 1789 had not been repealed. For more than half a century Presidents had removed officials at their pleasure. Johnson's conduct in first proceeding under the Tenure of Office Act, though a mistake, was not a crime. By one's conduct one can not estop himself so as to transform innocent conduct into a violation of the law.

As the trial progressed the President grew restless, his calvinistic blood was stirred. To be charged with treason to a Union which he had fought to save was bad enough. To be

---

[17] McCulloch, *Men and Measures*, p. 392

charged with complicity in Lincoln's murder was more than he could stand. In 1862, at Mr. Lincoln's request, he had quit the quiet life of a Senator in Washington to go into the hot furnace of Civil War. There he had stood like adamant while his prosecutors were safe in bomb-proof places. Now these parlor-knights were hounding him. "He hoped to God he might be convicted," he said to Colonel Moore. "He would like to see what a just God would do to his persecutors." . . . "Bring me in a list of the murderers of Charles I," he ordered; "I'd like to see how many of them came to an untimely end." Several times he was on the eve of going to the Senate to manage his own case. At night he sought to soothe himself with Addison's "Cato," and works on immortality.

Crook, the President's secretary, makes the astounding statement that during this trying time the President would frequently hand a letter to him and say, "Crook, here's a letter for General Butler, take it and wait for an answer." Crook would go to Ben Butler's house, at I Street near Fifteenth, ring the bell and "a curious cross-eyed chap like his master would answer." Crook would deliver Butler's answer to the President who would read it and tear it up. Now considering the time and the circumstances it seems plain that the President's secretary has mixed his dates. These occurrences took place in April 1865 and not in April 1869. At the former date the President and General Butler were frequently passing notes, but not at the latter date.[18]

Each evening Warden, the President's domestic, would come in from the Senate, no matter how late, and report what had taken place. "Well, Warden," the President would cheerfully say, "what are the signs of the zodiac to-day?" Warden would give an account of the day's doings. One evening Warden told of Boutwell's speech. Boutwell had just assaulted the President for dismissing Judge Black from his case. He had charged that Johnson had treated Black tyrannically and therefore the President had lost his chief attorney. "Andrew Johnson has but one rule of life," said Boutwell: "To use every man of power. If the conservative flee or the brave re-

[18] *Private and Official Correspondence of General Butler,* Vol. V, p. 602.

sist, they are utterly ruined; he spares no one. Already this purpose of his life is illustrated in the treatment of a gentleman who was counsel for the respondent, but who has never appeared in his behalf." These charges of Boutwell flew on the wings of the wind. Yet the President sat silent.[18a]

After the exclusion of the testimony of Secretary Welles, no other evidence of consequence was offered. The case was then turned over to the lawyers. The taking of testimony had consumed but half a dozen full days. Butler assumed the responsible task of making the opening speech. Curtis replied to Butler. Butler had declared he was going to try the case, as he would a "horse case." He did not belie himself. As Evarts remarked, at the end of Butler's three-hour speech, "The air was filled with epithets and the dome shook with invectives." The General, however, made a strong plea from manuscript, which he read, and was specially severe on the President for language used in his speeches while "swinging round the circle." In Pickwickian phrase "old Ben" declared that the President was simply blasphemous. His reply to the crowd in Cleveland, that "if he was a Judas, Thad Stevens, Wendell Phillips or Charles Sumner must have been the Christ, was shocking!" "But," said the pious Butler, "I will not pursue this shocking exhibition any further."

A high crime or misdemeanor Butler defined as "one which is highly prejudicial to the public or is the abuse of discretionary powers for improper motives." [19] The strength of the General's position lay in this: The President stood self-convicted. He had committed the crime above defined. He had been disloyal to the Government, had defied Congress, opposed the Fourteenth Amendment, vetoed wise and necessary laws, and was a public enemy. "If the President commit a crime, no matter how trifling," said Manager Butler, "he may be removed from office. Shall he escape when he has committed offenses a thousandfold greater than technical crimes?" . . . "Senators, you are bound by no law," he said, "by no law statute or common. . . . Johnson was elected to his high office,

18a Burgess, p. 178.
19 DeWitt, *Impeachment*, p. 409.

not by the people but by murder most foul." Not only was he probably a party to the crime of Lincoln's murder but in a speech in Cleveland had referred to his accession to the Presidency "as fortunate." "The liberties, the welfare, of all men hang trembling on the decision of this hour," Butler dramatically concluded.

Judge Curtis rose to reply. Dignity and character marked his effort. "I am present," he quietly began, "to speak to the Senate of the United States, sitting in its judiciary capacity as a Court of Impeachment, presided over by the Chief Justice of the United States, for the trial of the President of the United States. This statement sufficiently characterizes what I have to say. Here party spirit, political schemes, foregone conclusions, outrages, biases, can have no fit operation. The Constitution requires that here should be a 'trial,' and as in that trial the oath which each one of you has taken is to administer 'impartial justice according to the Constitution and the laws,' the only appeal which I can make in behalf of the President is an appeal to the conscience and the reason of each judge who sits before me."

Curtis then proceeded to demonstrate that no high crime or misdemeanor had been proven, unless the removal of Stanton constituted such offense. The only real charge against his client was such removal and the appointment of Thomas. Under the old Act of 1789 it had never been contended, until recently, he declared, that the power of removal was lodged in no one. On the contrary, it had been the custom for the President to exercise this power without consulting the Senate; this and no more the President had done. Besides, Stanton was not protected by the Act of 1867, he was appointed by President Lincoln. By the very terms of that act his office expired a month after Lincoln's death. From that date he was an occupant of the office by sufferance. It would be as unreasonable, he declared, to call Johnson's possession of the Presidency President Lincoln's possession, or Johnson's administration Lincoln's administration, as to call Johnson's term Lincoln's term. President Johnson's right to remove was undoubted. But if the President was in error, Curtis continued, "he was not criminally in error; no one could test the Tenure of Office Act but the President. He, in good faith, was anxious to do this in the courts, but was thwarted. When Thomas was arrested, on Stanton's oath, and taken before Judge Cartter, the President expressed satisfaction. The case was where he wished it to be, in the courts. Stanton dropped the case against Thomas. Therefore, the President could not test the matter, except by removing him. This he had attempted to do under the law." To meet this position, Butler, "the learned manager had declared that you are no court and bound by no law." . . . "Will you please state," Butler rose and interrupted, "where I said the Senate was bound by no law." "You stated that the Senate was a law unto itself," Curtis replied. Evidently, Judge Curtis had almost persuaded Butler he had no case. At the end of Curtis's address no one doubted that the President would be acquitted unless the Senate took the law into their own hands, as Butler had urged they should do.

William M. Evarts added to his already great fame. Conscious of the righteousness of his case, this master of courts realized that to lose so good a cause would reflect on his reputation. Evarts was the wit of the occasion. His unfailing humor made the ponderous machinery of impeachment appear ridiculous. His reply to Boutwell's lurid speech produced such peals of laughter it came near breaking up the court. To this day Boutwell's effort is called the "Hole in the sky" speech. Boutwell had no fear of a conviction of Johnson. What disturbed him, however, was what to do with Johnson after conviction. Finally he worked it out. The guilty man must be banished to outer darkness. "In the southern heavens, near the southern cross," said the impassioned orator, "there is a vacant space which the uneducated call the 'hole in the sky.' There the eye of man with the aid of the most powerful telescope has been unable to discover nebulæ, or asteroid, or comet or planet, or star or sun. To this dreary region of space I consign Andrew Johnson, the enemy of mankind."

Now throughout the trial Boutwell had been sneering at the lawyers, men "whose intellects were sharpened but not enlarged by the practice of the law." With what satisfaction therefore Evarts replied to Boutwell's extravagant hole in the sky metaphor. "If I might be permitted to do so," said Evarts, "I would inquire if there might not be some difficulty in executing the sentence proposed by the learned manager. The sergeant-at-arms is not, I believe, an expert astronomer and perhaps does not know the way to the 'hole in the sky,' so eloquently described by my honorable friend. I see no way out of the dilemma unless the honorable manager will consent to serve as a special deputy to execute the sentence of the court and to convey the President to his doom. And as the honorable and astronomical manager, with the President securely lashed to his strong and ample shoulders, shall take his flight from the dome of the capitol, the two houses of Congress and all the people assembled will shout, *'Sic itur ad astra!'* As he passes through the constellations, what thinks Bootes as he drives his dogs up the zenith in their race of sidereal fire?" No doubt Boutwell wished to his dying day his contemptuous sneer at men "whose intellects were sharpened but not enlarged by the practice of the law," had been left unsaid.

Evarts's tribute to Johnson's patriotism was fine. "Though his mind is not enlarged by the culture of the school," said Evarts, "thrice daily with Eastern devotion he bows to the Constitution." Dealing with the charge against the President, as set forth in article ten, that he had used violent language in his Washington Birthday speech and in his "swing round the circle," Evarts explained that they were made in 1866, and that they related to a Congress which had passed out of existence. These speeches were a subject in the report of the judiciary committee to the House, from which the House voted that they would not impeach. This matter, therefore, had been adjudicated. Further, said the incorrigible orator, "Though these speeches of my client may be crimes against rhetoric, against oratory, against taste and perhaps against logic, the Constitution of the United States, neither in itself nor by any subsequent amendments, has provided for the government of the people of this country in these regards."

The addresses of Nelson, Groesbeck and Stanbery were not

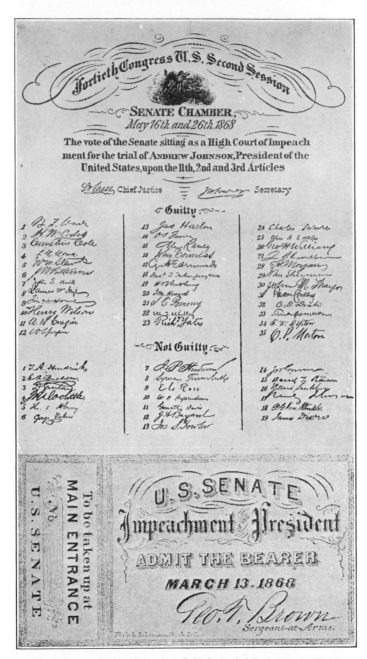

The Vote on Impeachment and Ticket of Admission to Trial.

as effective, from a legal point, as Curtis's and Evarts's. Their
words of praise and sympathy were wasted. No Senator was
willing to acquit the President unless compelled to do so by
his oath. Nevertheless, these speakers measured up to the
occasion. They addressed the Senate in impassioned and dramatic efforts. Henry Stanbery was just from a sick bed.
"He was a man of surpassing beauty of person and emphasis
of presence." In a "weird meaning and abstracted manner he
conjured up, in the Senate chamber, a scene memorable in the
annals of American oratory." "Unseen and friendly hands
seem to support me," he declared, "voices inaudible to others
I seem to hear. They are whispering words of consolation, of
hope, of confidence; they seem to say, 'Feeble champion of the
Right! Hold not back! A single pebble from the brook is
enough in the sling.'

"Listen for a moment," he softly continued, "to one who
perhaps understands Andrew Johnson better than most of
you; for his opportunities have been greater. When nearly
two years ago he called me from the pursuits of a professional
life to take a seat in his cabinet I answered his call under a
sense of public duty. I came here almost a stranger to him
and to every member of his cabinet except Mr. Stanton. From
the moment that I was honored with a seat in the cabinet of
Mr. Johnson not a step was taken that did not come under my
observation; not a word was said that escaped my attention.
I regarded him closely in the cabinet, and in still more private
and confidential conversation. I saw him often tempted with
bad advice. I knew that evil counselors were more than once
around him. I observed him with the most intense anxiety.
But never in word or deed, in thought, in action, did I discover in that man anything but loyalty to the Constitution and
the laws. He stood firm as a rock against all temptations to
abuse his own powers or to exercise those which were not conferred upon him. Steadfast and self-reliant in the midst of
all difficulty, when dangers threatened, when temptations were
strong, he looked only to the Constitution of his country and
to the people.

"Yes, Senators, I have seen that man tried as few have been

tried. I have seen his confidence abused; I have seen him handle day after day provocations such as few men have ever been called upon to meet. No man could have met them with more sublime patience. Sooner or later, however, I knew the explosion must come and when it did come my only wonder was that it had been so long delayed. Yes, Senators, with all his faults the President has been more sinned against than sinning. Fear not, then, to acquit him. The Constitution of the country is as safe from violence in his hands as it was in the hands of Washington. But if you condemn him, if you strip him of the robes of his office, if you degrade him to the utmost stretch of your power, mark the prophecy! The strong arms of the people will be about him. They will find a way to raise him from any depths to which you may confine him, and we shall live to see him redeemed and to hear the majestic voice of the people, 'Well done, faithful servant, you shall have your reward!' " Here Stanbery, the sick man, paused and gathered strength for a parting word.

"But if, Senators," he concluded, "as I cannot believe, but has been boldly said with somewhat official sanction, your votes have been canvassed and the doom of the President is sealed, then let not the judgment be pronounced in this Senate chamber; not here, where our Camillus, in the hour of our greatest peril, single-handed, met and baffled the enemies of the Republic; not here where he stood faithful among the faithless; not here where he fought the good fight for the Union and the Constitution; not in this chamber whose walls echo with that clarion voice that in the days of our greatest danger carried hope and comfort to many a despondent heart, strong as an army with banners! No, not here! Seek out, rather, the darkest and gloomiest chamber in the subterranean recesses of this Capitol, where the cheerful light of day never enters! There erect the altar and immolate the victim!"

When it came Judge Nelson's turn to address the court it was apparent that one friend was pleading the cause of another. No man knew Johnson's life better than Nelson. No one knew better what Johnson had suffered and sacrificed for the Union. No one felt more outraged at the treatment the

President was receiving at the hands of Congress than this Tennessee Unionist. In truth, Judge Nelson's zeal almost consumed him. The charge that the President had been dishonorable in discharging Black aroused Nelson to the use of harsh and unparliamentary language. Plainly he recited the facts. Stevens, Butler and Bingham had joined with Black in requesting the President to do what the President considered wrong. For this reason and for no other Judge Black had withdrawn from the case. Nelson concluded, and next day Butler, in great dudgeon, rose to a point of personal privilege. He accused Nelson of "deliberate falsehood." "He is the veriest tyro in the law," said Butler, "and from the most benighted portion of the southern country. He dare 'insinuate calumny' against me!" . . . "I deny that I signed the request to the President after I was made manager. The letter must have been signed in February before." Thereupon Nelson produced the letter and handed it to the Senate. It was signed by B. F. Butler and others. It bore date March 9, five days after the trial began.[20] Unfortunately Nelson also lost his temper in the encounter, "hurling back Butler's imputations with scorn" and practically offering to fight him. Though Charles Sumner moved to expel Nelson from the case, "old Ben," always a good sport, would not hear to it. "The matter must be dropped," he said. Accordingly, it was.

Groesbeck, for the defense, followed the belligerent Nelson. He spoke but a few simple words, words of great power, however. Many regarded it as the ablest argument on either side.[21] Manager Williams read a ponderous, solemn oration. He described the awful scene if Andrew Johnson were acquitted. He pictured "his ascent to the capitol, like the conqueror in a Roman triumph, dragging not captive kings but a captive Senate at his chariot wheel." Williams, likewise, impugned the President's patriotism. Stevens, too weak to read or stand, handed his manuscript to Butler. "Johnson is the offspring of assassination," said Stevens. "Any Senator who votes to acquit will be tortured on the gibbet of everlasting obloquy."

[20] Supplement to *Globe*, p. 341.
[21] Oberholtzer, Vol. II, p. 112.

On May 4 the great Bingham was to address the Senate, and close the case. The building would scarcely hold the crowd. Of Bingham Thad Stevens had declared he could excel any living man "in his appeals to the gathered wisdom of the ages." And well did Judge Bingham perform a difficult task. He moved the spectators to outbursts of applause never before witnessed on such an occasion.

"Go on! Go on!" the Radicals would shout whenever the speaker showed signs of quitting. "The written order for the removal of the Secretary of War and the written letter of authority' for the appointment of Thomas to the office," Bingham declared, "are simply written confessions of guilt. And in the light of that which I have already read from the record, no man can gainsay it. . . . I ask you, Senators, to consider that we stand this day pleading for the violated majesty of the law, by the graves of a half million of martyred hero-patriots who made death beautiful by the sacrifice of themselves for their country, the Constitution, and the laws, and who by their sublime example have taught us that all must obey the law; that none are above the law; that no man lives for himself alone, but each for all; that some must die that the state may live; that the citizen is at best but for to-day, while the Commonwealth is for all time; and that position, however high, patronage, however powerful, cannot be permitted to shelter crime to the peril of the Republic.

"It only remains for me, sirs," said Bingham in conclusion, "to thank you as I do for the honor you have done me by your kind attention and to demand in the name of the House of Representatives and of the people of the United States judgment against the accused for high crimes and misdemeanors in office with which he stands impeached and of which before man and God he is guilty!" In a flash men and women rose to their feet cheering, clapping hands and waving handkerchiefs; a gallery which four years before gave three hearty cheers for the Union and for Andy Johnson of Tennessee now called for his blood, and would not be appeased. Such a scene, and yet one so natural in the rage and excitement of the day, rarely disgraced a court. "Order! Order!" the indignant Chief Justice called.

The Sergeant-at-Arms rushed to and fro. The crowd hissed and hooted. With difficulty the gallery was cleared and the mob driven from the chamber. Senator Cameron undertook to apologize for the disorder. The Chief Justice refused to hear him. There could be no apology. The matter was neither excusable nor debatable.

The Senate adjourned until May 11. The President, in the White House, during all this excitement, was dignified and silent. He had grown wonderfully in the estimation of his attorneys.[22] Stanton held his own in the War Office. Like a garrison in a besieged fort he and his friends kept watch by day and night against old General Thomas. Soldiers surrounded and filled the war building, lest "the rebels" should rise up and attempt to undo the work of the war. During the recess the Senate held a secret session and written opinions were filed by nearly all of the Senators. It leaked out that Grimes, Henderson and Fessenden were for acquittal and an indescribable gloom prevailed. On the eleventh the vote was to be taken and the excitement reached its highest pitch. On account of the illness of Senator Howard, however, the Senate adjourned to the sixteenth.[24] One day Groesbeck and McCulloch called on the President and canvassed the vote. Randall and Welles were already there. The vote will stand 22 to 32 all, except the doubtful Welles, declared. "I would rather see the votes," Welles cautioned.[25]

A few days previously Grimes had been confirmed in his desire to acquit the President by a ruse which S. S. Cox and Reverdy Johnson worked. Without the President's knowledge they arranged that he should "accidentally" meet Senator

22 DeWitt, p. 555.

23 Johnson MS. No. 27,299. In June 1878 Evarts wrote Mrs. Patterson as follows: "My intercourse with President Johnson gave me opportunities for service to the country, I ever enjoyed. President Johnson during the whole time of my acquaintance with him, impressed one with the dignity of his manners, the sincerity of his patriotism and his unfailing confidence in the spirit and purposes of the great body of the American people. I shared in the fullest degree in this estimate. Upon a just and candid estimate of President Johnson's public conduct in difficult times he will be surely placed by the general judgment of his countrymen, among those who have deserved the most and the best of the Republic."

24 Julian, *Recollections*, p. 215.

25 Welles, Vol. III, p. 352.

Grimes at Senator Johnson's rooms, at the Arlington Hotel. Early one evening Warden, the President's domestic, who was in the plot to arrange the conference, entered the President's office. He announced that Senator Johnson would like to see him at nine o'clock. As the President entered Johnson's room that evening, Senator Grimes and the Maryland Senator were engaged in conversation. A pleasant half hour was passed by the four. Reverdy Johnson then began to denounce the street rumors that the President would "do rash things and go on in excesses." "They have no warrant for such charges," the President retorted. "My whole life refutes it." Expressing the deepest love for the Union, he satisfied Grimes there was no danger from his acquittal. Next day the conservative Senators were reassured by Senator Grimes. "From the best authority," he stated to them, there would be no danger in voting not guilty.

But the Radicals were not idle. Heaven and earth were moved to whip weak-kneed Republicans into line. Grimes, Fessenden, Trumbull, and other Senators were denounced as "recreants, apostates and Judases." A Union, congressional committee was raised. It sent out appeals for help. "A fearful avalanche" from all parts of the Union came back. Loyal, but misguided men hastened to Washington to badger and coerce. If seven Republicans joined the Democrats the President would be acquitted. Six of the seven were known to be "wrong." Ross of Kansas had not committed himself. Trumbull, Fessenden, Grimes and General Henderson were subjected to threats and insults.[26] Republican Senators who had filed opinions that the President was not guilty were denounced by the press as apostates.[27] There was a general rumor that Sprague, a son-in-law of the Chief Justice, would be favorable to Johnson. Anthony, Frelinghuysen and others were doubtful. In order to counteract the influence of such rumors, Washburne sent a wire to the New Hampshire Republican Convention, "The recreant will be out of the White

[26] Cox, *Three Decades*, p. 593; Oberholtzer, Vol. II, p. 127; Rhodes, Vol. VI, p. 151.
[27] New York *Tribune*, March 12, 1868.

House in a week;" Butler followed, wiring, "Wade and prosperity are sure to come with the apple blossoms." [28]

The fateful day arrived, May 16. The court convened with Chief Justice Chase in the chair. Crowds filled the Senate chamber, the galleries and the corridors. "Indescribable anxiety was written on every face." [29] Senator Sherman asks that policemen be stationed throughout the building to prevent the repetition of the disgraceful scene recently witnessed. The Chief Justice so orders, though the situation is now well in hand. In a body the House files into the Senate chamber. The final scene has come. Manager Williams moves that the articles be voted on not in their numerical order, as theretofore agreed, but beginning with article eleven. Reverdy Johnson desires to know the reason for this change. Conness objects to debate. He is sustained by the Chief Justice. The motion to vote on the eleventh article first is put and carried—34 ayes, 19 nos. At this forecasting of the close result excitement increases. Senator Edmunds moves that the Senate "do now proceed to vote." Senator William Pitt Fessenden of Maine, with emotion in every lineament of his face, rises in his place. He asks a postponement of half an hour as "the Senator from Michigan, Mr. Grimes, is absent." "I saw Mr. Grimes last evening," Senator Fessenden announces, "and he told me that he should certainly be here this morning." "It was his intention—" Reverdy Johnson rises from his place. "Will the honorable member permit me to interrupt him for a moment?" he asks. "He is here." *Mr. Fessenden:* "I thought he was not." *Mr. Johnson:* "I have sent for him, he is downstairs. He will be in the chamber in a moment. Here he is." Senator Grimes is brought in, faint and sick. Every Senator is now in his seat—fifty-four of them.

The Chief Justice admonishes that silence and order must be preserved. He directs the Clerk to read the eleventh article. The Clerk reads the article. "The Clerk will now call the roll," the Chief Justice directs. The Clerk calls, "Mr. Senator Anthony!" Mr. Anthony rises in his place. "Mr. Sen-

[28] DeWitt, p. 575.
[29] Julian, p. 316.

ator Anthony, how say you?" the Chief Justice asks. "Is the respondent, Andrew Johnson, President of the United States, guilty or not guilty of a high misdemeanor as charged in this article?" Mr. Senator Anthony answers, "Guilty." The roll call proceeds, Bayard, Buckalew, Cameron, Cattell, Chandler! Such stillness prevails the breathing in the gallery can be heard at the announcement of each Senator's vote. Members grow sick and pale. "Mr. Senator Fessenden," the Clerk calls. The Chief Justice asks the usual question. "Not guilty," is Fessenden's response. The old guard of the Republican party is broken.

The Clerk proceeds, "Fowler, Grimes, Henderson." They vote not guilty. How will Senator Ross vote? So far he is understood to be non-committal, though he may have filed an opinion in the secret session. "Mr. Senator Ross?" the Clerk calls. "Not guilty," is the response. "Mr. Senator Van-Winkle?" "Not guilty." The roll call is finished and the Clerk announces the result. Thirty-five Senators have voted for conviction and nineteen for acquittal. The President is acquitted by one vote, thirty-six being a necessary two-thirds. The news is rushed to the White House. The President receives it with composure. Butler and Boutwell are beside themselves. They charge fraud and corruption. A committee is appointed to investigate but they enter upon a fruitless quest. "Radicals are wild with rage."[30] The Senate as a court of impeachment adjourns to May 26 to allow Congressmen to attend the Republican National Convention at Chicago. There, it is hoped, enough pressure can be exerted on the traitorous Republicans to cause them to change their vote.[31] On the heels of Senator Ross's vote to acquit, a telegram from his Kansas constituents comes:

Leavenworth, Kansas, May 16, 1868
Honorable E. G. Ross, United States Senator,
Washington, D. C.
Your telegram received. Your vote is dictated by Tom Ewing, not by your oath. Your motives are Indian contracts and green-

[30] Rhodes, Vol. VI, p. 151.
[31] *Ibid.*, p. 147.

backs.   Kansas repudiates you as she does all perjurers and skunks.

D. R. Anthony and Others.

On May 26 the vote was again taken.   The second and third articles were submitted to the Senate.   The same result followed as on the eleventh article, 35 Senators voting "guilty" and 19 voting "not guilty."   Thus came to an end the great Impeachment Trial.   On motion of Mr. Manager Williams, the Senate sitting as a court of impeachment did then "adjourn without day." [32]   The country heaved a sigh of relief, Europe applauded the verdict, the stock market rallied, Old Thad Stevens, broken-hearted, issued his valedictory to the American people.   "No Chief Executive will be again removed by peaceful means," he sorrowfully asserted, and went home to die.[33]

As a result of his connection with this case, Chief Justice Chase was insulted, even charged with corruption.   No doubt, the impeachment trial cost him the presidency.   The seven Republican Senators voting "not guilty" never held another office.   They were hounded to their political death.   "When I voted not guilty," said Ross, "I felt that I was literally looking into my open grave."   And yet will not the names of Fessenden, Fowler, Grimes, Henderson, Ross, Trumbull and Van-Winkle live when their detractors are forgotten?

It is interesting to speculate on what might have been the result if some one like Garfield had been the chief manager instead of Ben Butler.   Doubtless the case would have been managed quite differently.   No sharp practices would have been indulged in.   No request for time would have been denied; no evidence of the defense would have been excluded.   No appeals to passion would have been tolerated.   Doubtless the case would have been tried on the one technical point: The President willfully, deliberately, and with malice aforethought, disobeyed a statute.   By his conduct, he admitted this in the summer of 1867.   This was a crime.   In the excitement of the day, might

---

[32] *Globe*, p. 415.

[33] DeWitt, p. 598; Mr. Blaine records that "the Republicans never counted impeachment proceedings among their accomplishments;" Senator Edmunds, however, maintains that "but for distrust of Wade by the Senate, Johnson would have been convicted."—*Century*, Vol. LXXXV, p. 863.

not a verdict of guilty have resulted? Because of unfair play, on the managers' part, three Senators are understood to have voted "not guilty." Grimes, Henderson and Ross are understood to have voted not guilty because the President's cabinet were not allowed to testify. How would they have voted if there had been no unfair play?

The skill with which the President's case was managed is above praise. Scores of pitfalls were in the way of the lawyers for the defense. These were avoided. There was no abuse, no attack on Grant or Stanton. Seward was not put on the stand to belittle Stanton by showing he wrote the veto of the Tenure of Office bill. No party issue was raised. On the contrary, a lawyer-like appeal was made to American fair play; on this issue the President won. To the cool head and clear judgment of Evarts and Curtis and the diligence of Stanbery, it is due that the impeachment proceedings had so little effect on prices and business. The nation bore the strain easily and perfectly.[34] Stanton at once gave up his office. Schofield was appointed in his place and was confirmed. Stanbery, reappointed Attorney-General, was ungraciously rejected by the Senate. The position was tendered to Curtis, who refused it. Evarts accepted and was confirmed, adding great strength to the President's official family.[35]

[34] Rhodes, Vol. VI, p. 156.

[35] In 1870 Senator Sherman said to Senator Henderson, "You were right in your vote and I was wrong."—*Century*, December 1912, pp. 208-209. Sherman likewise wrote in his *Recollections*, "After this long lapse of time I am convinced that Mr. Johnson's scheme of reorganization was wise and judicious."—Burton, *Sherman*, p. 168.

CHAPTER VII

FOREIGN AND DOMESTIC POLICY

One of the most troublesome matters inherited by the Johnson administration related to Mexico. When the Civil War began that turbulent country was in a chronic state of violence, and in forty years the republic had had no less than seventy-three presidents. There was not a dollar in the treasury, interest on the public debt was not paid, and the leading road, from Mexico City to Vera Cruz, was infested by bandits. During Lincoln's administration our state department was full of complaints that American citizens were murdered and their property destroyed. But during war times these evils had to be borne for fear of an alliance between Mexico and the Southern Confederacy. While war was raging the Rio Grande had been kept open for rebel cruisers, and when the war ended Mexico became the refugee home of southern rebels.

But America was not the only nation that suffered at the hands of the Mexicans. British citizens had been foully murdered, the British legation at Mexico City attacked, and funds which Mexico had paid to be forwarded to British bond holders stolen. The French Foreign Office was also fired into and a bullet imbedded in the gallery of the legation. Spain fared no better than England or France, everywhere the cry being, "Death to foreigners." [1] These conditions induced England, France and Spain to combine for mutual protection. In October 1861, at a conference in London, they agreed on a joint military operation against Mexico, "not for the acquisition of territory or to prevent Mexico conducting its government as it chose," but to protect the person and the property of their citizens. America was invited to join in the expedition but declined. The first nation to arrive in Mexico was Spain, landing six thousand troops from fourteen transports

[1] Oberholtzer, Vol. I, p. 497.

and twelve warships at Vera Cruz in December 1861. The English squadron of ten ships and the French squadron followed in January 1862. These movements, destructive of the Monroe Doctrine, caused deep concern in Washington and Adams, our ambassador at London, notified the British authorities that the United States was looking on with disfavor.

At this time Benito Juárez, a full-blooded Indian and a man of character, was president of Mexico and M. Romero his Chargé at Washington; Thomas Corwin was Mr. Lincoln's representative at Mexico City. Lincoln proposed a settlement on the terms of a payment by the United States of interest at three per cent. on a debt of about sixty millions of dollars for five years. But drafts for the payment of interest were protested in Washington, the Senate declining to ratify the treaty. In this state of disorder the Mexicans themselves were divided. Ex-Presidents began to arrive from Europe. Chiefest of these was Miramón, a desperate character. Almonte, backed by Napoleon the Third, also put in an appearance. He was a Mexican monarchist who had been living abroad and communicating with Louis Napoleon. Dissensions also broke out among the allies. It became known that Napoleon was contemplating an empire in Mexico and that France had increased her demands by including fifteen millions of bonds incurred by the Miramón government. Thereupon English and Spanish forces were withdrawn in disgust by their governments.

President Juárez gathered his scattered forces together for the conflict, and Napoleon the Third, called by Hugo "Napoleon, the Little," showed his real intentions. "It is not to my interest," he declared, "that the United States shall grasp the whole Gulf of Mexico and rule the Antilles and South America." This bald statement came in the fall of 1862 when the United States was engaged in a fight for bare existence. Napoleon dispatched General Forney to command the French forces; Secretary Seward still protested "against anti-Republican or anti-American government in Mexico." In May 1863 General Forney captured Puebla and in June entered Mexico City in triumph. Many Mexican monarchists then crossed over to Paris and asked Napoleon to name an emperor for

Mexico.   Archduke Ferdinand Maximilian, brother of the Emperor of Austria, was suggested.   But Napoleon, with a show of fairness, demanded a vote by the Mexicans.   A plebiscite was held, though only about one-thirtieth of the territory and a small proportion of the population were under French control.   Though the election was a farce, it was certified to Napoleon that the people endorsed an empire and demanded Maximilian as emperor.   Mexican monarchists surrounded their new emperor at Trieste, shouting, "God save the Emperor Maximilian the First, and God save the Empress Carlotta." On June 12, 1864, while Lee in the Wilderness was mowing down Grant's veterans by the tens of thousands, while Lincoln was more fearful of the Republic than at any other time, expecting certain defeat for himself and the election of a copperhead president, Maximilian and Carlotta entered Mexico City in all their grandeur.

Secretary Seward protested more vigorously than before, and but for the American Civil War doubtless France and the United States would have fought out the issue at that time. In April 1865 Lee surrendered and the war was over.   War with France then seemed sure and war talk was in the air. General Grant could hardly be held in leash; in June 1865 he expressed the opinion to President Johnson that Napoleon's conduct was "an act of hostility to the United States."   General Grant arranged for Schofield to go down and coöperate with Juárez.   Johnson, Seward and the cabinet, however, regarded war as unnecessary and foolish.   Seward declared "Maximilian was caught like a rat in a trap" and would soon leave the country.   Nevertheless, Seward sent Schofield to Paris "to put his legs under Napoleon's mahogany" and tell Napoleon to take his troops home.   President Johnson requested Grant to go to Mexico and handle the situation, but the General declined, and Campbell of Ohio was appointed Envoy Extraordinary.[1a]   General Sherman and Campbell thereupon went down in the warship *Susquehanna*.   After looking about a long time for Juárez and being unable to find him, Sherman

[1a] This conduct of Johnson was afterwards used against him, he was banishing Grant!

wrote his brother that he felt "like Japeth in search of a father." Nothing was accomplished by the mission.

But fighting Phil Sheridan, Grant's favorite General, would not be restrained. He circulated rumors that he intended crossing the border and backing Juárez, and he likewise furnished arms and munitions to the Mexicans and encouraged the Republicans. Meanwhile, affairs in France were turning against Napoleon. Prussia was moving against Austria, and the French Assembly was complaining that, "in order to collect a paltry sum of money from Mexico Napoleon has spent four hundred millions of francs." The end had come, Napoleon agreed to withdraw his troops, and by November 1867 practically all troops had departed. In the summer Carlotta set sail for Europe, but could not move Napoleon to come to the relief of her husband. Maximilian gallantly refused to desert his Mexican followers, declaring that a Hapsburg never deserted. Seward continued to indulge the situation. By this time Maximilian and the French had ceased to be friendly. At length, with fifteen hundred troops, Maximilian left Mexico City to join Miramón at Querétaro. On the morning of May 14, 1867, the hapless emperor was betrayed, captured, and, after a court-martial trial, shot. Carlotta, her reason all gone, was sent to an asylum, there to remain as the "mad Queen" till her recent death—nearly sixty years afterwards.

During the war Secretary Seward observed that the United States navy suffered from the lack of coaling stations in the West Indies and in the Northern Pacific. As soon as peace came, and during Johnson's administration, Seward was resolved to acquire the necessary outposts for American ships. One day, in the late winter of 1866, there was a great buzz in the House of Representatives. Secretary Seward, a member of Andy Johnson's hated family, was seen to walk down the aisle and to go to Thad Stevens's desk and cordially greet him. When it leaked out that Stevens dined that evening with the Secretary of State, at his home, the House was more shocked than ever. A day or two afterwards Stevens rose to propose an extra appropriation for special service on a secret diplomatic mission to be expended under the Secretary of State.

Whatever the Old Commoner asked, Congress granted, of course. The appropriation was therefore voted. Seward had his eye on the Island of St. Thomas, a splendid land-locked harbor in the Caribbean, and was determined to get it as a United States port. Fred Seward, son of the Secretary, and Admiral Porter were sent to the island by the President. They discovered that it would be useless as a fort without the right to control the heights of San Domingo. In due time these rights were acquired and the Island of St. Thomas and appurtenances were the United States' for the asking—to the great delight of the President and the Secretary of State. Soon Señor Pujol arrived in Washington, clothed with authority to cede not only St. Thomas but the strategic position commanding the whole Antilles. A treaty, approved by naval experts, was duly signed, sealed and delivered and sent to the Senate, but was rejected by it. No southern territory was wanted, and nothing that Johnson or his cabinet might propose. It may not be amiss to inquire, had this treaty been ratified and the guns of the United States mounted so as to cover the entire Antilles, would the Spanish-American War have occurred?

About this time Seward was writing some interesting words in his diary. "Hot denunciation and defense of Andrew Johnson," he wrote, "through leafy June and dusty dog days, and press and public give cursory attention to foreign affairs which engross the Secretary of State." And those were busy days indeed for Secretary Seward. One evening in the spring of 1867, while the Secretary and his family were having a game of whist, at the Seward home just across from Lafayette Park, a visitor was announced, Baron Edward de Stoeckl, the Czar's minister at Washington. "I'm just in receipt of authority from my government to close with you for our colonies in America," the Baron said, "and if agreeable I will call at your office to-morrow." "Why not to-night?" the alert Seward asked, knowing the Senate would soon adjourn. In two hours the Secretary's official force was called together and by four o'clock next morning the treaty was drawn and executed.

That day it was presented to the Senate by Sumner, Chairman of the committee on foreign affairs.[2]

By this treaty there were ceded to the United States five hundred thousand miles of territory, with a coast line of four thousand statute miles, and with splendid bays and good harbors. This vast territory belonged to Russia by right of discovery. Early in the eighteenth century, Peter the Great, a lover of ships and navigation, wishing to ascertain if Asia and North America were one contiguous tract or were separated by water, set to work to ascertain the fact, but died before making the discovery. Empress Catherine, however, in 1728 fitted out an expedition and Vitus Behring, a Dane, sailed across and discovered the narrow neck of water separating Asia from America and now known as Behring Strait. There was much discussion about the name for the new purchase. Yukon was suggested, this being the name of the largest river. Alaska was finally selected, this being the name of the great peninsula. The price was not troublesome. Based on the price paid for French, Spanish and Mexican purchases, Stoeckl suggested ten million dollars. Seward proposed five million. The Baron was willing to split the difference. Seward suggested that five hundred thousand be knocked off. This was acceptable to the Baron, with two hundred thousand additional to liquidate claims of the Russian Fur Company. The total price therefore was $7,200,000. But a serious question arose. Though the Senate ratified the treaty on April 9, 1867, the House refused to vote the money. Nothing good could come out of the White House while Johnson was President![3]

Congress and the Radical press ridiculed the scheme, calling the purchase "Johnson's polar bear garden." On April 30 Nast had a screaming cartoon. King Andy was sitting viewing himself, in regal state, his crown on his head. Secretary Seward was rubbing on Russian oil. "The products of Alaska," said opponents of the Johnson administration, "are polar bears and icebergs; the vegetation is mosses; the ground freezes there six feet deep and the streams are glaciers."

[2] *Reminiscences of F. W. Seward,* p. 345.
[3] Oberholtzer, Vol. I, p. 542.

Mother Seward Rubs On Russian Salve

Johnson and the Constitution

The Supreme Court having held, in an early case, that the Senate could not ratify a treaty requiring the payment of money without the consent of the House, it seemed that the treaty was doomed to defeat. But Russia agreed to wait for her money. A sentiment favorable to Russia likewise grew, she having been the only foreign friend America had in the Civil War. Moreover, as Sumner put it, "A republican form of government in Alaska was worth more than quintals of fish, sands of gold, choicest fur or most beautiful ivory." . . . "This treaty," the philanthropic Sumner exclaimed, "dismisses one more monarch from this continent; one by one they have retired. First France, then Spain, then France again and now Russia, all giving way to that absorbing unity which is described in the national motto, *E Pluribus Unum*." Sir Frederick Bruce, the British ambassador, astounded at the action of America in this matter, telegraphed to London asking what should be done in the grave circumstances.

President Johnson did not wait for the House to appropriate the necessary funds. In October 1867 he took possession and unfurled the United States flag at Sitka. Russian and American soldiers paraded in front of the government house. The Russian colors were lowered and the Stars and Stripes hoisted in their stead, while artillery roared and troops took possession. Congress met and the House raged. General C. C. Washburne declared, "None but malefactors live in that country, where the skies rain three hundred days in the year. . . . As much right has the President to send an army to Canada or Mexico." At length, on July 14, 1868, the appropriation passed the House by a vote of 113 to 43. A scandal grew out of the treaty. Fraud and corruption were charged and an investigation was held. It was claimed that only five million of the treaty money ever found its way to Russia. Though this statement was proved false, several petty lobbyists were besmirched. By the irony of fate, Forney, President Johnson's "dead duck," was among the number. Forney admitted that his paper got three thousand dollars in gold for advocating the Russian treaty, but insisted that he declined to receive the money. It developed, however, that "this gold found its way into the pockets of D. C. Forney, his brother." [4]

Secretary Seward's task now and at all times was more trying than that of any of his associates. The thorough-going Welles delighted to denounce and to fight the Radicals; McCulloch, Secretary of the Treasury, went about his duties without much thought of politics, though he was bitterly denounced by the Radicals for appointing revenue officers in the South who were unable to take the ironclad oath. Randall had risen to the cabinet from an assistant's place and was content to fill his position faithfully. Stanbery, the Attorney-General and the President's personal friend, was engrossed in law duties. Stanton let himself be used as a spy and became a scapegoat to the Radical Congress. But Seward, a man of national and international fame, serving as a member of Johnson's official family, occupied an uncomfortable position. He had been the foremost Republican in America. In 1860 he had barely missed being President. He had likewise been the great Foreign Secretary under Lincoln. Now his friends charged that he was pulling the chestnuts out of the fire for Andy Johnson.

Nevertheless, cheerfully and nobly Seward went about his task, serving his country at home and abroad, "furnishing an example of calm judgment, unfailing patience and the largest charity." [5] In 1868 he resigned, but withdrew the resignation at the President's request. As has been said of him, "He betrayed no trust, he deserted no duty, quailed before no danger, he recoiled from no labor, he broke no friendship, he rose on no man's fall, he fed no grievances nor raised his own repute by defamation of others."

In 1868 Charles Francis Adams had partially negotiated with Lord Clarendon a treaty for the settlement of American claims against England, known as the Alabama claims, and growing out of the war. Adams then resigned and President Johnson appointed his old friend Reverdy Johnson in his place. This Maryland patriot, whom Sumner pronounced the greatest constitutional lawyer ever at the British court, with the possible

[4] *Oberholtzer*, Vol. I, p. 556.
[5] *Seward at Washington*, Evarts's Address, p. 532.

exception of William Pinkney, took up Adams's work and the result was the Johnson-Clarendon treaty.

Though this treaty gave to the United States all it got by the treaty with Washington, it was rejected by the Senate. The Senate claimed that the treaty belittled by its form the work to be done, ignored the greater national grievances, and contained no word of regret for the fact that American commerce had been swept from the sea by rebel cruisers. Yet much was gained by the Johnson administration through the Johnson-Clarendon Treaty. Theretofore Lord Russell had emphatically refused to admit any liability on England's part on account of depredations by Confederate privateers, but by this treaty there was an admission of the principle of arbitration for our damages from rebel cruisers and a satisfactory settlement soon followed.[6]

Complications with England because of the Fenian uprising early engaged the attention of the Johnson government. James Stephens was at the head of a movement in America called the Fenian Movement, based on the chronic hate of Irishmen for England. Meetings were held and much money raised. In October 1865 Fenians, from all parts of the country, gathered in Philadelphia. A Republic with a President, a Congress, a Secretary of War and of the Treasury, and having its bounds wholly within the United States, was organized. O. Mahoney, known as "The O. Mahoney," was reëlected president. The Moffatt house off Union Square in New York was leased for headquarters. Harps were displayed, the shamrock was on every coat, and the Goddess of Liberty smiled down on enthusiastic Irishmen. Bonds were issued and sold. But a quarrel arose as to the funds and also as to how to proceed. W. R. Roberts, vice-president, and General Sweeney insisted that the lion's tail be twisted and that Canada be captured. The brotherhood split between the O. Mahoneyites and the followers of Roberts. On account of these transactions relations between England and the United States were strained. In April 1866 about sixty agitators, claiming to be Americans, were in jail in Ireland and Lord Clarendon hoped "the United

6 Lothrop, *Seward*, p. 428.

States would not protect these conspirators." The British cabinet protested, and insisted that troops should not be drilled and money raised to invade Canada.

In order to harmonize the differences, James Stephens called C.O.I.R., Chief Organizer of the Irish Republic, came to America, but failed in his mission. The O. Mahoney agreed to disband his forces, but Roberts was not so complacent. At length the O. Mahoney yielded so far as to coöperate in the invasion of Canada, and backed up one Killian, who was to attack Canada from Maine. An iron steamer was purchased, and in April 1866 an expedition was to sail from Eastport to Campobello over the line, but British warships broke up the expedition. More fatal results followed in May and June. About fifteen hundred men crossed the Niagara River and raised the green flag over Fort Erie. On June 2 a collision occurred between Canadian regulars and volunteers and the Fenians. Several were killed and wounded on each side. This collision is called the battle of Limestone Ridge. The Irish in America espoused the cause of the Fenians and endeavored to deter President Johnson from opposing the Irish invasion. In this, however, they were unsuccessful, and the President issued a proclamation calling upon the Fenians to disband and cease operations.[7]

In matters of a domestic character, the financial situation was next in importance to reconstruction. During the war the currency had passed from a specie to a paper or greenback basis, and various acts authorizing the issue of legal tender notes had passed Congress. In October 1865 these notes amounted to about four hundred and thirty-three million dollars in all. As they were thought to be unconstitutional, they were of doubtful legal tender value.[7a] The public debt was two billion, eight hundred million dollars. Taxes were enormously high and were levied upon every species of property and franchise.[8] The questions confronting Secretary

[7] Johnson MS.; I have made free use of Oberholtzer's account of the Fenian uprising.

[7a] At first the Supreme Court held that they were unconstitutional but afterwards in the Legal Tender Cases—decided by a five to four vote on February 7, 1870,—their constitutionality was sustained.

[8] Rhodes, Vol. VI, p. 222.

McCulloch were, Should the United States go to a specie basis or remain on a greenback basis, and further, Was it possible to reduce taxes?   Fortunately, the Secretary of the Treasury was a man of sound financial views.   In 1863, under Lincoln, he had been Comptroller of the Currency and had succeeded Chase as Secretary of the Treasury.   After Lincoln's death he remained in President Johnson's Cabinet and the relationship between him and the President was at all times cordial and intimate.[9]

Secretary McCulloch advocated an early return to a specie basis, tax reduction and a brave confronting of the situation by the practice of thrift and economy.   In these views the President fully concurred.   At first Congress approved McCulloch's plan and on April 12, 1866, passed an act authorizing him to sell bonds and retire greenbacks.   Forty-four millions were sold under this act before McCulloch's policy was reversed by Congress.   In less than three years internal revenue taxes were reduced from three hundred and eleven millions to one hundred and sixty millions.   On February 4, 1868, however, the act authorizing the retirement of greenbacks was repealed.   The reason for this repeal is manifest.   Hard times had come upon the country, a reaction had set in, and the debtor was in a bad way.   Farmers and producers awoke to the fact that they were receiving for corn, wheat and cattle a paper dollar worth but little above fifty cents, while bond holders were paid in gold worth about one hundred and fifty.

Secretary McCulloch contended that these conditions would soon pass away if his plan was pursued, and that prosperity would come with a little fortitude on the part of the people.[10] He pointed to the fact that in 1866 and 1867 the wheat and corn crops were good, and in 1867 the cotton crop was also good and was bringing a fine price, that immigration was flowing our way, a million immigrants having arrived since July 1, 1865; that cotton spindles had increased and the production of pig-iron had greatly improved.   At that time also

---

[9] McCulloch, *Men and Measures*, p. 406.

[10] Rhodes maintains that if McCulloch's plan had been followed specie payments would have been resumed in 1873, six years before they were.—Rhodes, Vol. VI, p. 266.

tonnage on the great inland lakes had increased and nearly eight thousand miles of new railroad had been completed—thirty thousand Irish were working on the Union Pacific and perhaps as many Chinamen on the Central Pacific, and each road running a race to reach the ocean. Of course the Secretary called attention to the evils of a disordered currency. But he pleaded in vain. Complications arose which soon reversed his policy and caused him to be severely criticized.

In May 1866 a financial panic struck London and spread over Europe, reaching America in 1867. The United States was beginning to feel the effect of vast destruction of property during the war and of over-speculation. A speculating and gambling fever had pervaded America. Oil in Pennsylvania and in the Rockies had made and unmade fortunes. Young men of the Buck Fanshaw kind had rushed to the mines of Montana and Idaho. In these flush times the public conscience was deadened, adding to the demoralization. Thus the Central Pacific and the Union Pacific railroads were asking land grants and special privileges of various kinds from Congress and pursuing devious and doubtful methods. The Credit Mobiliér was very active. It was a fiscal corporation and an adjunct of the Union Pacific, and Oakes Ames, a Congressman from Massachusetts, was its backer. This corporation twined its tentacles around members of Congress, giving them stock for less than market value; it blasted the reputation of not a few public men. Congressmen and Senators who were daily denouncing Andrew Johnson as corrupt and profligate were, at that moment, pocketing Ames's Credit Mobiliér stock, which he had delivered to them "with intent to influence legislation." "Smiling" Schuyler Colfax, who as Speaker in December 1865 delivered Congress over to Thad Stevens and the Directory of Fifteen, was besmirched beyond recovery.[11] Brooks, the Democratic leader, along with Ames, was censured, though not expelled.

This orgy of speculation and corruption and disregard of

[11] For a list of Senators and Congressmen, likewise implicated in the Crédit Mobiliér Scandal, consult Oberholtzer's interesting account.—*History of the United States*, Vol. II, p. 602.

the principles of business was well understood to be the beginning of a panic. In December 1868, in his annual message, President Johnson admonished Congress accordingly. The Tenure of Office Act had tied his hands, he insisted, and "opened the doors to extravagance and corruption." The Government was "plunged into debt, eight hundred and fifty millions of dollars being due to foreign bond holders. . . . Usurpation of power and profligacy had made the bond holders masters of forty millions of American people. . . . Bond holders are to be paid in gold at the rate of six per cent., which equals nine per cent. in currency, adding two per cent., because of exemption of taxation, and it will be seen that the bond holders are getting seventeen per cent. in gold upon their investment." "What is the laborer receiving?" he asked. "He is to be paid in depreciated currency, in greenbacks."

"A system that produces such results," the President declared, "is justly regarded as favoring a few (at the expense of the many, and has led to the further inquiry whether our bondholders, in view of the large profits which they have enjoyed, would themselves be averse to a settlement of our indebtedness upon a plan which would yield them a fair remuneration and at the same time be just to the taxpayers of the nation. Our national credit should be sacredly observed, but in making provision for our creditors we should not forget what is due to the masses of the people." In his message the President also recommended that the President and Vice-president and Senators should be elected by a direct vote of the people and that in the event of a vacancy in the presidential office some one should be specifically designated to act as President. Further, that the terms of federal judges should be limited. Previous to 1868 the President stood with Secretary McCulloch in his recommendations to Congress. When the issue, however, was drawn between the capitalist and the laborer in financial matters, the President leaned to the latter. In this course it must be remembered the President was true to type. In Tennessee he had been known as the mechanic governor, in Washington he would be the mechanic president.

Yet the President would not remove McCulloch as Secretary

of the Treasury. Greenbackers and inflationists urged him to do so, but he would not. In fact, the President seemed to agree with McCulloch. The best thing, as he saw it, was to go to a specie basis, though, as we shall presently see, he was in favor of doing this at the expense of the bondholders and in a way peculiar to himself. The war had now been over nearly four years, and it was feared the public debt could never be paid in gold. There was not enough coin in the world to pay the debt, it was thought. How therefore should the debt be paid? Especially, how should the 5-20 issue of nearly six hundred millions of bonds be paid? On their face these bonds, bearing five per cent. interest and payable in twenty years, provided that *interest* should be paid in coin. But, as to the payment of the *principal*, the word coin was not mentioned.

By every rule of construction, therefore, the principal of these bonds was payable in the currency of the day, greenbacks. This was the opinion of some of the most distinguished lawyers, Allan G. Thurman being one of the number. The "Ohio idea" was the term used to express the greenback sentiment. John Sherman, General Logan, Governor Morton and other leading Republicans, "while not joining the inflationists, made pretense of doing so." Sherman was in favor of a compromise and the issue of new bonds at a lower rate; "in other words of modified repudiation." [12] Old Thad Stevens was enraged at the injustice of paying the laborer in rag money and the bondholder in gold. "I'll vote for no such swindle of the taxpayers of this country," he declared; "I'll vote for Frank Blair and the wicked Democrats first." Ben Butler afterwards rode into the governorship of Massachusetts on this issue; Hendricks endorsed the President's message; Garrett Davis and Bayard denounced the payment of the bonds in gold as "iniquity and robbery."

In 1868 the Republican platform avoided the use of the word "coin" or "gold," and straddled the issue, declaring, "The Republican party will soundly maintain the credit of the United States and pay the bonds according to the letter and

---

[12] Oberholtzer, Vol. II, p. 162: Here it is hastily charged that Sherman was "ignorant or dishonest."—*Cf. Nation*, December 28, 1871.

the spirit." [13]   The Republican party in Indiana and in other Western States advocated the payment of the public debt in greenbacks.   In the West and South the Democratic party, bag and baggage, went over to the "Ohio Idea."   In opposition to this policy of dealing with foreign creditors it was urged that Chase, the Secretary of the Treasury, had advertised that the bonds would be paid in coin and Garfield stated that the Committee on Finance so understood it.   Undoubtedly, the controlling reason for paying the bonds in gold and not in greenbacks, as the courts would no doubt have decreed, was "to maintain the credit of the United States and enable it to borrow more money." [14]

Unfortunately, Johnson went beyond Sherman or Thurman or the "Ohio Idea."   In 1868, in his message to Congress, he used language which might suggest the attitude of France and Italy in 1920 after the World War, in relation to their indebtedness to the United States.   In a word, Johnson advocated a scaling of the national debt due to England, just as England in 1923 requested America to scale its debt against her.   "It must be assumed," said the President, "that the holders of our securities have already received upon their bonds a larger amount than their original investment, measured by a gold standard.   Upon this statement of facts it would seem but just and equitable that the six per cent. interest now paid by the Government should be applied to the reduction of the principal in semi-annual installments, which in sixteen years and eight months would liquidate the entire national debt.   Six per cent. in gold would at present rates be equal to nine per cent. in currency, and equivalent to the payment of the debt one and a half times in a fraction less than seventeen years.   This, in connection with all the other advantages derived from their investment, would afford to the public creditors a fair and liberal compensation for the use of their capital, and with this they should be satisfied.   The lessons of the past admonish the lender that it is not well to be over-anxious in exacting from the borrower rigid compliance with the letter of the bond."

[13] *Life of Stevens*, p. 348.
[14] Dewey, *Financial History of the United States*, p. 347.

This idea of the President, the candid Welles calls "inexcusably weak and erroneous." [15] And he is undoubtedly correct. But as we have seen both political parties were at first badly off color on the currency question and the payment of the national debt. The President, though grievously wrong, was not standing alone. This must also be said: If he had written nothing else he would have called attention to a system "favoring the few at the expense of the many, and to the oppression of the people by the capitalists." That a day laborer must receive only a dollar a day in greenbacks, worth fifty cents, while the capitalist was to get on his dollar a gold dollar, worth twice a greenback dollar, was a condition Johnson would not endorse. In the House and in the Senate his message when it was read was heard with indignation and wrath. It was a "tirade against Congress, an offensive document." The Senate refused to hear it through, and by a vote of 26 to 20 adjourned during its reading. The House tabled it by a large vote. Next day it was read in the Senate "for the benefit of the country to show what sort of an official was at the head of the Government."

Great was the President's disappointment at the unfavorable reception of his message. Confidently he believed that the bondholders would agree to adjust their holdings, and scale their debts, and that specie payments could be resumed at once. This was his plan for protecting the laboring class, and this was not his plan alone. The year previous Thad Stevens, in tears, we are told, had submitted "to the stock jobbers, declaring they would cost the Government thousands of millions of dollars." [16]

[15] Welles, Vol. III, p. 478.
[16] Stewart, *Reminiscences*, p. 204.

CHAPTER VIII

LEAVING THE WHITE HOUSE

Soon after his acquittal, the President received a touching letter from his daughter Mary, down on the Stover farm in Tennessee. "Washington is ever dear to me," she wrote her father; "the happiest days of my life were spent there. We have been very uneasy but thank God you have come out victorious and we can say with Miriam:

> " 'Sound the loud symbols o'er Egypt's dark sea
> Jehovah has triumphed, his people are free.' " [1]

The Harvard Law School likewise sent congratulatory resolutions on the failure to convict. But neither words of praise nor of censure affected Johnson's outward appearance. One visiting the White House would discover no change in him. "God's will be done," he piously ejaculated.

"It is a victory not for myself," said he, "but for the Constitution and the country, and I look with perfect confidence to my ultimate vindication and to the justice of that future which I am convinced will not be long delayed. . . . A day of wiser thought and wiser estimates is near." [2] In truth, life to Johnson was but a fierce struggle and he knew how to take punishment. Hence he cherished no malice for opponents. Thad Stevens and Charles Sumner had fought him in the open, and, though fierce and terrible, they were never double-faced. Therefore, he bore them no resentment. Only the treacherous fellow excited his contempt, and even upon him Johnson wasted no anger. When the fight ended feeling subsided and he was content to bury the past.

"A heart full of kindness," said his secretary, "and a generous spirit of helpfulness to those in need or struggling

---

[1] Johnson MS. No. 21,068.

[2] *Harper's Weekly*, March 23, 1872; McPherson, *History of Reconstruction*, p. 143.

upward now characterized him." [3] "A nearer view of the man through five momentous years," the secretary continues, "has taught his opponents that they had not understood nor appreciated him." Or as N. G. Taylor, his old Whig opponent with pardonable pride asserted, "Standing between Radical fanaticism and the Constitution, he towered above contemporary politicians like the watch tower about the billows." [4] His loyalty to friendship and his kindness to Unionists and Confederates were everywhere manifest. Sam Milligan, companion of his early days, he kept by his side. In 1864 he made Milligan his secretary at Nashville; in 1865 he caused him to be put upon the Supreme Bench of the State, and in 1868, when a vacancy occurred in the Court of Claims at Washington, he elevated his wise old friend to that high place. Blackstone McDaniel, as we have seen, had been appointed United States Marshal; Return J. Meigs was made clerk to one of the courts of the District; N. G. Taylor was sent as Commissioner to the Indians. In 1863 and 1864 Taylor had gone to the cities of the North, and pleaded the cause of southern Unionists. He raised thousands of dollars, collected food and clothing and assisted in saving the mountaineers of East Tennessee from starvation. Lewis Self and William Lowry were put in charge of post offices. Even the Knoxville postmaster, and other postmasters who in 1861 had rifled Governor Johnson's mail and spied on him, were pardoned. And the patriotic preacher, J. P. Holtsinger, was not neglected.

His affection for those of his own household was well known. "He was noted for his devotion to his invalid wife," said a neighbor, "and to his children he was kind to indulgence." [5] "From personal experience and contact with Andrew Johnson," said Judge Barton, whose family had been next-door neighbors in Greeneville before the war, "I found him kind and helpful, specially to poor young men, and he was entirely without condescension." One day, when Barton was a mere lad of twenty

[3] Col. E. C. Reeves, Johnson's private secretary, in Knoxville *Sentinel*, May 30, 1923.
[4] Col. N. G. Taylor's pamphlet, *The Political Situation*, August 1866.
[5] Judge Barton, *Commercial-Appeal*, January 23, 1927; McCulloch, *Men and Measures*, p. 406.

and on his way to college, he met President Johnson on the train. "The President made me forget I was a timid boy and he a great figure," Barton wrote. "He spoke of my opportunities and drew out my own ideas, . . . for an hour he talked, but not an unkind word did he say of his opponents. In a few moments I felt as free and untrammeled as if I were talking to a boy companion." These friendly traits of character sat well on a President who, as his intimates boastfully asserted, had "the polish of a Chesterfield, was the personification of dignity, and admitted no familiarity." [6]

Many a southern home was gladdened by the President's acts of kindness. "With all his worries and burdens," as an old rebel said, "while the jackals were at his heels, and hell raged in East Tennessee, he did not forget his old friends and neighbors who had stood in the southern battle-lines, arrayed against him and his gallant sons who were in the Union army for four years. Without request from them he extended his protecting hand in their hour of need." . . . "Can I ever forget," said this southern judge, "when my own father was in danger and defenseless, and charged with treason, coming one dark day from our village postoffice with anxious heart, as I bore a letter in a large envelope with the White House address on it, and what was the joy at home when it was opened to find a pardon—an unasked pardon from Andrew Johnson, President of the United States—for his own sins in serving and aiding the rebellion." Or as Governor Vance put the case: "Through Andrew Johnson, and such as he, we begin to see how it is possible to love our whole country once more."

One day a letter came to the President from Mrs. General Donalson of Nashville. It told of the seizure of her home by the Freedmen's Bureau and of the operations of a sawmill, destroying her timber. Mrs. Donalson was a daughter of Governor Branch, formerly Governor of North Carolina. The President sent a wire to stop depredations and to restore the unlawfully confiscated estates. "Once when I was a lad," said the President to his secretary, holding the letter of Mrs. Donalson in his hand, "this woman's father came in the tailor shop at

[6] Col. E. C. Reeves, *supra.*

Raleigh, where I was an apprentice boy, and I held his horse. When he went out he gave me a half dollar and said, 'That's right, my son, be honest and industrious and you will make a great man.' I have kept that silver piece ever since," the President added.[7] One day Charles Dickens was a caller at the White House and was greatly impressed with the President. To this interpreter of human nature Johnson appeared as "a man with a remarkable face, indomitable courage and watchfulness and a certain strength of purpose." "I would have picked him out anywhere," wrote Dickens, "as a character of mark."

In the concluding days of his term President Johnson needed every ounce of patience. On July 7, 1868, Thad Stevens offered five additional articles of impeachment, supporting his resolution with bitter words. "No president," said Stevens biting himself with rage, "can be removed by the processes of the law. . . . If tyranny becomes intolerable the only recourse will be found in the dagger of a Brutus." In a few days Stevens, America's foremost parliamentary leader, was dead. When his will was opened it was found that the paradoxical man had used the tenderest words with reference to his mother and others. After providing an ample sum to care for his mother's grave, he requested the sexton "to keep the grave in good order and plant roses and other cheerful flowers at each of the four corners every spring."

General Grant was likewise unrelenting in his hatred of Johnson. It rankled in Grant's bosom that his conduct in surrendering the office of Secretary of War to Stanton smacked of treachery. In the impeachment trial it had been made plain that President Johnson was not endeavoring to involve the country in civil war, but just the opposite. He had, in good faith, asked General Grant to coöperate in testing the law through the courts. The General, after promising to do so, had failed to live up to his promise. No doubt the General thought the good of the country demanded that he pursue the course he did, and keep out of the controversy. At all events, thoughtful people regarded Johnson as the injured party. General Grant was implacable, nothing could induce him to

[7] Governor Peay, at Johnson tailor shop dedication, May 30, 1923.

forgive Andrew Johnson. In 1868, even during the Impeachment trial, he importuned Senator Henderson to vote to convict the President. Not so the President, however. True to that trait which McCulloch discovered of "never cherishing animosity after a contest was over," [8] Johnson time and again extended the olive branch to Grant.

Towards the end of his administration President Johnson appointed Grant's brother-in-law, Judge Louis Dent, to the Chilean Mission. During the Christmas holidays in 1868 he invited the Grant grandchildren to a birthday party which they did not attend. The President likewise extended an invitation to the General to New Year and other receptions, but the stern old warrior left town rather than shake the hand of one who had placed him in a bad light before the country. Now this pacific conduct of President Johnson's did not please his thorough-going Secretary of the Navy. Welles called it "temporizing." "No good can come of such temporizing," said he, "and as to Grant I want not his favors and I shun not his wrath." [9]

At this time, as always, Johnson continued to place implicit faith in the people. No matter what they did the people were right—his confidence in them was absolute and without reserve. If they fell short it was because they were misinformed or misled. In the impeachment troubles the people were not against him, he felt, they were deluded by the politicians. "I cannot complain," he wrote in the summer of 1868, "if the people while witnessing recent scenes have not been able to make my cause thoroughly their own, the defense of the laws their own battle." [10]

Try as he would, however, Andrew Johnson could not get on workable terms with the religion of the day. It seemed to him that the preachers and pulpits were fomenting strife and had substituted revenge and hate for love and charity. When the Northern Methodist Church took an active part in the impeachment trial, actually petitioning Congress to turn him out,

8 McCulloch, *Men and Measures*, p. 405.
9 Welles, *Diary*, Vol. III, p. 527. Welles charges Grant with falsehood.
10 DeWitt, *Impeachment*, p. 601.

Johnson thought of a new church. He began to attend St. Patrick's cathedral. Father Maguire suited him exactly. The Father cut out politics, preached neither hate nor malice and went back to the fundamental virtues—lowly-mindedness and charity. "I don't know anything more depressing," said the President one morning, after listening to a sermon by Father Maguire on the subject of slander and back-biting, "than for a man to labor for the people and not be understood. It is enough to sour his soil." [11] The Catholic Church appealed to him because of its treatment of rich and poor alike. In the cathedral there were no high priced pews and no reserved seats, the old woman with calico dress and poke bonnet sitting up high and being as welcome as the richest. And this was Andrew Johnson's touchstone. He would forgive a great deal if the principle of universal democracy was preserved.

In matters political the President was at sea, almost without the semblance of a party. The old Democratic party had lost favor with him, its platform of 1864 being damnable. While the Union was in danger it had denounced the war as a failure, a declaration which stultified the very name of Democracy. Only to the conservatives could he turn and to liberal Republicans. McCulloch, he would not dismiss, though the Blairs and other Democrats urged him to do so. McCulloch was treacherous, they insisted, and must go and Johnson must reconstruct his Cabinet and build up a strictly Democratic party. But this he would not do.

In May, at Chicago, the Republicans nominated General Grant for President and Schuyler Colfax for Vice-president. The platform declared for negro suffrage in the South but not in the North. It lauded the "Man on Horseback" and approved of the impeachment of Andrew Johnson. On July 4 the Democratic Convention met in New York. Here and there lovers of the old Constitution had been urging Johnson to stand for President, but he must first reconstruct his cabinet, he must have a party behind him. To these appeals he replied "that he was not ambitious for further service unless the call was so general and unequivocal that it would be an

[11] Moore, *Diary*, March 29, 1868. Oberholtzer, Vol. II, p. 127.

endorsement by the people of his endeavors to defend the Constitution and the reserved rights of the several commonwealths composing what was once in fact the Federal Union." . . . "Of such approval, in the present temper of parties," he said, "I can perhaps have no reasonable expectations. . . . In the midst of these embarrassments I have not been discouraged, when from the public prints, or from some unusually frank and outspoken friend I have heard that 'I have no party.' This suggestion has only served to remind me of a memorable remark, uttered when faction ruled high in Rome, that 'Cæsar had a party and Pompey and Crassus each a party, but that the Commonwealth had none.' " [12]

Johnson's name was presented to the New York Convention and on the first ballot he received the second highest vote, sixty-five; George H. Pendleton of Ohio receiving one hundred and five. The South, as a whole, did not stand by him and on the fifth day and the twenty-second ballot, Governor Seymour of New York was nominated. Ohio, the home of Salmon P. Chase, ostensibly his friend and backer, had deserted the Chief Justice, suddenly springing the name of Seymour on the convention. General F. P. Blair was the nominee for Vice-president. The platform adopted the "Ohio Idea." Thus the West got the platform and the East the candidate. [13] In this convention the southern people again misinterpreted the northern temper, sending as delegates such outspoken Secessionists as General Forrest, R. B. Rhett and ex-Senator Chestnut. The North, equally unwise, had sent Copperheads such as Vallandigham. The impulsive Blair, candidate for Vice-president, was a good general but a poor politician; in fact, he had killed the Democratic party before he became its candidate. On June 30, 1868, he had written the famous "Brodhead letter." "The only way to restore the government and the Constitution," he wrote, is to "elect a President who will declare Radical reconstruction null and void and with an army undo usurpations in the South and disperse carpet-bag

12 DeWitt, *op. cit.*, p. 601.
13 Oberholtzer, Vol. II, p. 171.

governments, superseding them with white governments." [14]
This meant civil war again. As Andrew Johnson with bitterness said to Welles, "it overturned everything." Despite
these handicaps Seymour and Blair came near carrying the
country in the fall. But for the South, indeed, they would
have done so. "It was a startling fact," says Blaine, "that if
Seymour had received the solid vote of the South he would,
in connection with the northern vote, have been elected." [15]
And Blaine was right. New York, New Jersey and Oregon
went Democratic. Ohio and Indiana were very close. North
Carolina, South Carolina, Tennessee, Alabama, Arkansas and
Florida, now Africanized, went Republican and elected Grant.

Congress continued to bedevil and harass the President.
Impeachment was held over his head. The reconstructed State
of Arkansas was to be admitted, in order to add two Radical
Senators to sit in another impeachment trial, though they had
not heard the evidence.[16] Prior to the adoption of the Fourteenth Amendment, Congress also voted to admit North Carolina, South Carolina, Georgia, Louisiana and Alabama, recently Africanized states. Their votes were needed to dispose
of the President at some later date if necessary, and to carry
the fall elections.[17] Reverdy Johnson insisted that no one
"with a sense of justice or any, the least sense of propriety"
would bring in new Senators, "who had not heard the evidence
to take part in the decision." Senator Sumner retorted, "Of
course they shall come in and vote."

But the President was not to be intimidated. On June 20,
1868, he vetoed the bill admitting Arkansas into the Union.
This bill provided "That the Constitution of Arkansas shall
never be so amended or changed as to deprive any citizen or
class of citizens of the United States of the right to vote who
are entitled to vote by the Constitution herein recognized." In
his blandest manner the President, commenting on this provision, declared, "I am unable to find in the Constitution of
the United States any warrant for the exercise of the authority

[14] *Annual Encyclopædia*, 1868, p. 746.
[15] Blaine, *Twenty Years*, p. 408.
[16] *Globe, Fortieth Congress, Second Session*, pp. 2437 and 2516.
[17] Oberholtzer, Vol. II, pp. 57 and 147.

thus claimed by Congress." . . . "In assuming the power to impose a 'fundamental condition' upon a state, which has been duly admitted into the Union upon an equal footing with the original states in all respects whatever," the President argued, "Congress asserts a right to enter a state as it may a territory and to regulate the highest prerogative of a free people—the elective franchise. . . . This question is reserved by the Constitution to the states themselves and to concede to Congress the power to regulate the subject would be—to place in the hands of the Federal government, which is the creature of the states, the sovereignty which justly belongs to the states or the people." [18]

In dispassionate language, he also vetoed the bills admitting North Carolina and other states and also a bill refusing to count the electoral vote of those states, and another, relating to the Fourth Freedmen's Bureau. The bills to admit the Southern States, he vetoed for the same reason he vetoed the Arkansas bill. On July 4, the nation's birthday, the President extended full pardon and amnesty, unconditionally and without reserve, to all rebels, except those under indictment. This he did though Congress had not adjourned but was in recess watching over him and denouncing his vetoes and pardons.

Through his Secretary of State, in July 1868, the President made proclamation that the southern states had been re-admitted into the Union. He did this in obedience to law, though he had vetoed the action of Congress in admitting them. On December 9 the President sent his last annual message to Congress, to portions of which I have already referred. A more exasperating and yet a more smoothly written document he had not issued. Reconstruction he declared to be a failure and the attempt "to put the white population of the South under the domination of persons of color had broken up the kindly relations subsisting between the races, creating animosity which had disturbed the entire nation." Party passion and sectional prejudice, he insisted, had frustrated the work of reconstruction which he had about accomplished in 1865; the

[18] Macdonald, *Documentary Source Book*, p. 532.

Constitution had been violated at every step and Congress should hasten to undo its illegal work.

The year 1868, full of worry and disappointment, was now drawing to a close and the old warrior in the White House began to sniff the political battle afar. He was going back to Tennessee and "swing round the circle" again. Already his enemies were at war with each other. Stanton, sour because Johnson had not been convicted, refused to recognize his old friend Fessenden. Soon the great War Secretary was to pass away, "mysterious secrecy enshrouding his last hours." [19] In August Stevens also died, his faith in popular government shattered. In the fall Ben Wade lost his seat in the Senate. The corrupt Ashley dropped out of sight. The blatant Boutwell was shortly repudiated. Sumner was to be disgraced by his party—deposed from the chairmanship of the Committee on Foreign Relations. He and Carl Schurz and Julian were bitterly to assail the Radicals. Grant and Sumner were shortly to become deadly enemies and Ben Butler and other charlatans to be reduced to ranks. The country was beginning to see its narrow escape when the unscrupulous Wade came so near entering the White House.

Christmas Day Andrew Johnson celebrated in splendid fashion. He extended pardon, absolutely and without restriction, "to all who directly or indirectly participated in the late rebellion," Jefferson Davis included. Eccentric and big-hearted old Horace Greeley went into ecstasy. "We seldom find of late a decent excuse for praising Andrew Johnson," said Greeley. "But we thank him for putting an end, even thus tardily, to the legal farce enacted every few months under the deceitful title of 'Trial of Jeff Davis.' [20] A swindle by which nobody is duped, a farce at which nobody thinks of laughing, must have outlived its day. . . . It is the most sweeping amnesty ever pronounced by man." Democrats, except the "Brigadiers," now claimed Johnson as their own. His example of honesty, economy, and simplicity they placed in contrast to the grow-

[19] DeWitt, *Impeachment*, p. 596; *Second Session Forty-second Congress*, Appendix 560.

[20] This utterance and the signing of Davis' appearance bond, probably made Greeley Democratic candidate for President in 1872.

ing extravagance and dishonesty of the times.   Before the southern whites were disfranchised, legislatures had passed endorsements of him and the southern press had forgiven his desertion of the South in 1861 and his "cruelties" while military-governor.   He was, now more than ever, the "protector of the Union and the defender of the Constitution."

These manifestations of approval were not lost on President Johnson, and he would respond and let the people understand he was still alive, and not as Parson Brownlow intimated, "the dead dog in the White House."   Accordingly, assisted by Mrs. Patterson, he arranged to throw open the Mansion to the public—to give a series of entertainments.   On Easter occasions the egg rollings of the Johnsons had become famous.   "Down the long slopes near the White House, children by the hundreds rolled and tumbled.   They would invade the grounds and indulge in Easter sports and games."   Now there was to be a genuine children's party, a "juvenile soirée, . . . the first ever seen in the White House." [21]   The President's birthday, December 29, was selected as the time.   "The White House was beautifully decorated with flowers, great chandeliers were ablaze with lights, the music was the best, and the refreshments all that could be desired or digested."   Hundreds of children were in attendance, fourteen dances were on the cards.   The Lancers, of course, and the Schottische; the Galop, the Varsovienne, Esmeralda, Quadrille Plain, Quadrille Backet, Quadrille Social; the Polka Plain and the Polka Redowa; of waltzes there was only one. [22]

Scarcely was this gay occasion ended before the White House was again "a scene of splendor."   Five thousand people, mostly what Mr. Lincoln called the plain people, sought admission to the New Year reception, "submitting the host to the inevitable handshaking."   Several thousand more were unable to gain admittance because of the crowd. [23]   Though President-elect Grant and leading Republicans were absent, some Radicals, of the Ben Butler type, were there.   "And what are you

[21] Colonel Crook, *Through Five Administrations.*
[22] Johnson MS.
[23] New York *Express*, January 1, 1869; *Journal* and *Tribune*, July 10, 1901.

doing here?" one of them would laughingly ask another. "I was about to put the same question to you," would be the rejoinder. None but personal friends were honored. Judge Samuel Milligan was at the head of the receiving line; then came General Thomas Ewing, Attorney-General Stanbery, Senator Fowler, and Senator Patterson. Mrs. Patterson and Mrs. Stover were dressed alike, in black silk, beaded and braided, with white lace collars.[24] "The girls wore tarleton of different colors, though silks and satins and silver and gold llama was also worn by many." "A scene of mortal grandeur," the enthusiastic reporters wrote, "magnificent to behold and never to be forgotten." The occasion was "one of sincere pleasure to the President who relaxed from his duties." . . . "The first affair of the season—the best Presidential reception ever seen." It was "the town talk, the street talk, and the talk of the capitol for twenty-four hours. Every one wished to shake hands with the great men." The President likewise entertained the foreign embassies, officials of the army and navy, the cabinet, and the seven Republican Senators voting "not guilty." Fessenden and Grimes, however, failed to appear on that festive occasion.

The last day of the year was cold and stormy. Gideon Welles remained indoors and had a free hand with his beloved diary. "An amiable, forebearing and honest President," he wrote, "striving to uphold the Government, has been impeached in party haste and barely escaped conviction. . . . The Radical Congress in the excess of party, have trampled the organic law under foot, when party ends were to be subserved, and assaulted and broken down the distinctive departments of the Government." In the opinion of the courageous Welles, "Senators and Representatives had conspired against the President and committed perjury in obedience to the dictates of party leaders, who found him an obstacle to their revolutionary schemes."

Abuse of the President produced the ordinary fruits. Cranks were lying in wait to assail or murder him. "A somewhat alarming incident occurred on February 10, 1869, when a

[24] Singleton, *Story of the White House,* Vol. II, p. 114.

woman named Annie O'Neil was found lurking in the corridor. She said: 'I am sent by God Almighty to kill Andrew Johnson.' Her old-fashioned, double-barreled pistol was, however, unloaded; and she was spirited away." [25]

As the fourth of March drew near a serious domestic question confronted the President and his cabinet. "Are we to participate in President Grant's inauguration or stay away?" they were asking. Welles was for staying away, as John Adams did when Jefferson was inaugurated and as John Quincy Adams and Henry Clay absented themselves when Jackson came in. But Seward and Evarts, McCulloch and Browning urged the President "to yield for appearance' sake." Undoubtedly the President would have yielded had General Grant met his peace offerings half way. The pacific Seward and his friend Evarts insisted that matters could be arranged by having two processions, President Grant leading one line of carriages and President Johnson the other. This enraged Welles no little. He wrote in his diary of March 2 that Seward was garrulous and "told over several egotistical and stale stories, claiming that President Johnson and his suite had the post of honor, on the right—appealed to custom, etc." . . . "Whenever before," wrote the indomitable Welles, "was such a thing as two processions heard of?" . . . "I disclaim any neglect or want of courtesy," he records, "but I would submit to none." Randall backed Welles in his opinion, "but McCulloch itching to go," as Welles affirms, remarked that "it would be small, and would be considered small, not to go."

On the evening of this conversation, March 2, the President gave a farewell reception, and an immense gathering was seen at the White House.[26] "Hundreds of friends and officials who wished to pay their respects to the President could not get near him; women with bonnets and shawls filled the reception room and rough fellows with overcoats and wool hats" were there; and "not a few fanatical politicians who had busied themselves in slandering and defaming the retiring President." But it

25 *Ibid.*, p. 116.
26 Welles, Vol. III, pp. 537 and 539.

was a glorious evening for Andrew Johnson. He could read his triumph in every honest handshake.

At nine o'clock on March 4, 1869, Secretary Welles, the truest friend of Johnson's official family, was the first to arrive at the White House, uncertain whether the President would follow his advice or Seward's. The President, at the time, was busy at his work. The two old friends shook hands. The President then quietly said, "I think, Mr. Secretary, we will finish our work here without going to the capitol." Presently the other cabinet officers came in, "Seward confident and smoking his inevitable cigar." . . . "Ought we not start immediately?" he briskly said. The President replied, "I am inclined to think we will finish our work here." "Well, you've carried your point," McCulloch whispered to Welles.

"After the silly, arrogant and insolent declarations of Grant," as Welles wrote in his diary, "that he would not speak to his official superior and predecessor, nor ride nor associate with him, the President could not compose a part in the pageant to glorify Grant without a feeling of abasement." [27] At a few minutes past twelve the President said to the members of the cabinet that they would then part. Feelingly, he shook hands with all and they with each other, and the turbulent administration of Andrew Johnson came to an end. From the White House he drove to the home of the editor of the *Intelligencer*, Jno. F. Coyne, where Mrs. Johnson had gone a few days before. There he remained as a guest until departing for Tennessee. That morning Mrs. Patterson and her children, having accepted an invitation from Secretary Welles, had gone to his home. First, however, Mrs. Patterson had put the White House "in spotless condition against the arrival of the Grants." When she and her mother quitted the White House the servants of the mansion gathered about them, "weeping and begging for photographs of their kind employers." The Washington papers were filled with accounts of "the simplicity and geniality of the Johnson family." "Of these plain people from Tennessee," the press declared, "it must be said they leave Washington with spotless reputations, they have received no ex-

[27] Welles, Vol. III, p. 542.

pensive presents, no carriages, no costly plate, they have dispensed a liberal hospitality . . . no old friends have been cut, no new ones turned away." [28] In his diary Welles feelingly wrote, "Socially and personally I part with them with regret; no better persons have occupied the executive mansion." [29]

It is now one o'clock, March 4, 1869, and President Grant is riding in triumph to his inaugural. Cannon are booming, bands playing, and the military resplendent. But what of Andrew Johnson as he goes out of office, is he discouraged and downcast? Far from it. Unconquered and unconquerable, at that moment, he is issuing a Farewell Address to the people of the United States as George Washington and Andrew Jackson had done. First he calls attention to the illegal and unconstitutional methods of Congress—"conscription, confiscation, loss of personal liberty," "subjection of states to military rule," "disfranchisement of whites," "enfranchisement of blacks for party ends." Next, he proceeds to say, "While public attention has been carefully and constantly turned to the past and expiated sins of the South, the servants of the people, in high places, have boldly betrayed their trust, broken their oaths of obedience to the Constitution, and undermined the very foundation of liberty, justice and good government. When the rebellion was being suppressed by the volunteered services of patriot soldiers amid the dangers of the battlefield, these men crept, without question, into place and power in the national councils. After all danger had passed, when no armed foe remained, when a punished and repentant people bowed their heads to the flag and renewed their allegiance to the Government of the United States, then it was that pretended patriots appeared before the nation, and began to prate about the thousands of lives and millions of treasure sacrificed in the suppression of the rebellion.

"They have since persistently sought to inflame the prejudices engendered between the sections, to retard the restoration of peace and harmony, and, by every means, to keep open and exposed to the poisonous breath of party passion the ter-

[28] Senator Doolittle, *Address*, 1869; Jones, *Life*, p. 333.
[29] Welles, Vol. III, p. 556.

rible wounds of a four years' war. They have prevented the return of peace and the restoration of the Union, in every way rendered delusive the purposes, promises, and pledges by which the army was marshaled, treason rebuked, and rebellion crushed, and made the liberties of the people and the rights and powers of the President objects of constant attack. They have wrested from the President his constitutional power of supreme command of the army and navy. They have destroyed the strength and efficiency of the Executive Department, by making subordinate officers independent of and able to defy their chief. They have attempted to place the President under the power of a bold, defiant, and treacherous Cabinet officer. They have robbed the Executive of the prerogative of pardon, rendered null and void acts of clemency granted to thousands of persons under the provisions of the Constitution, and committed gross usurpations by legislative attempts to exercise this power in favor of party adherents. They have conspired to change the system of our Government by preferring charges against the President in the form of articles of impeachment, and contemplating, before hearing or trial, that he should be placed in arrest, held in durance, and, when it became their pleasure to pronounce his sentence, driven from place and power in disgrace.

"They have in time of peace increased the national debt by a reckless expenditure of the public moneys, and thus added to the burdens which already weigh upon the people. They have permitted the nation to suffer the evils of a deranged currency, to the enhancement in price of all the necessaries of life. They have maintained a large standing army, for the enforcement of their measures of oppression. They have engaged in class legislation, and built up and encouraged monopolies, that the few might be enriched at the expense of the many. They have failed to act upon important treaties, thereby endangering our present peaceful relations with foreign powers."

The "Old Man's" boldness, in issuing this Farewell Address, caught the press. Some applauded him. Others ridiculed his pretensions. The Democratic dailies of March 5 were filled with stories of Andy Johnson. They played him up as the

Tennessee tailor, the runaway apprentice boy, the man who had "swung round the circle" and held every office from village alderman to President, and they predicted his early return to the Senate. On the other hand, the Radical papers were bitter in their denunciations. *Harper's Weekly* cartooned him as a fat and beefy Jew clothier, selling cheap and second-hand clothing from a Tennessee tailor shop.

Invitations came to President Johnson to visit friends and also to be the guest of English, French and German steamships.[30] These invitations were declined, except one to visit Baltimore. On March 12 President Johnson and his friends, in special cars, went over and attended a reception and banquet in that city. The reception was held in the rotunda of the post-office. Crowds from one o'clock until three passed through the building and grasped the hand of the old patriot. At night a banquet was given at Barnum's Hotel and patriotic toasts were responded to. The first toast presented, "Our guest, the patriot and statesman, Andrew Johnson, the bulwark of equal rights, the champion of the only true and permanent Union of these states and the defender and martyr of the Constitution." "History will vindicate his fame," was the next toast, and "record an impeachment of his impeachers, and a verdict of guilty by future generations of American freemen." "Baltimore bids you welcome to a place in the hearts of a great people," said a streaming banner, "for whose protection and happiness you bared your breast to the shafts of calumny, and for their sakes hazarded all that was dear to the man and the citizen." Altogether it was a great occasion for Andrew Johnson.

In a few days the ex-President and his family, having laid in a supply of furniture and other household goods, set out for the mountains of Tennessee. And surely the old Greeneville home needed refurnishing and renovating. It had had rough treatment. First occupied by Confederate armies, it had been a hospital for wounded soldiers. Taken over by the Union armies, it was afterwards a residence for officers. Later camp followers and "bummers" had captured it and converted it into

30 Oberholtzer, Vol. II, p. 208.

a negro brothel. Andrew Johnson had not laid eyes on this home for eight long years. In 1868 a correspondent of the New York *Herald* had visited the place. "The fences of the lot and windows of the house show evident signs of delapidation," he wrote, "the consequences of rebellion and rebel rule; a number of panes of glass are broken out and their places supplied with paper, glass not being obtainable in the Confederacy. Looking into the lot you see several young apple trees and in the space between potatoes are growing; in the rear of the kitchen a small aspen shade tree, and down in the lower end of the lot a grape vine trained upon a trellis, forming a pleasant bower; scattered around are a number of rows of currant and gooseberry bushes; at the lower end of the lot are two large weeping willows and under the shade is a very beautiful spring."

Andrew Johnson's home-going was memorable. At Lynchburg where, in 1861 he had been shot at and later burnt in effigy, he met a generous welcome. At Bristol, on the Tennessee border, he was met by a delegation from his home town. As the train passed along over the familiar mountains and down the Watauga and Nolichucky valleys, through Johnson City, Jonesboro, Carter Station near the Stover farm, and then on to Greeneville, people by the thousands gathered along the way to pay homage to a brave man. For forty odd years East Tennessee had been the apple of Andrew Johnson's eye, her mountains, her streams, and her brave sons were as the ruddy drops that visited his heart. And now he was home again.

The old tailor shop bade him welcome, and the Gum Spring, where he had camped that first September night forty-three years before, and the little mill not far away. Blackstone McDaniel and other old friends were there to greet him, but most of them had gone to their reward. Eight years before, when he fled from Greeneville to the mountain fastnesses, a banner had been stretched across Main Street, and on it was written, "Andrew Johnson, Traitor." Now another banner was stretched across the same street but it was quite a different

one, "Welcome Home, Andrew Johnson, Patriot." [31]   Fifteen
thousand mountaineers crowded the streets of Greeneville that
March day.   Mr. Brittain welcomed the exile home and to the
mountains of Tennessee, putting in his mouth the words of
Napoleon returning to Corsica.   "Blindfold, my native hills
I would have known."   Andrew Johnson, mechanic-governor
and tailor-president, ascends the platform, overlooking the old
Court House, where in days gone he had fought the people's
battles, and bared his breast to the storm, for the Union and
the Old Flag.   He tells of the dark days since he left them
eight years ago, of the sufferings he has undergone and the
sufferings they had undergone, and of the love he has ever
borne them.   With hands raised aloft he concludes in the
words of Cardinal Wolsey:

> "An old man broken with the storms of state
>   Is come to lay his weary bones among ye,
>   Give him a little earth for charity."

The Volunteer State is at attention.   From Cumberland Gap,
in the Virginia and Kentucky mountains, to Memphis, on the
Father of Waters, Andy Johnson's words have been heard.

[31] A few steps from this spot is a monument erected to the memory of
the Union soldiers of Greene County, Tennessee.   On it is written, "In time
of their country's peril they were loyal and true."

CHAPTER IX

THE COME-BACK

Andrew Johnson had passed his sixty-second birthday when he retired from the Presidency. His consuming thought, at that time, was that he had been misunderstood and his administration misrepresented. He was not satisfied with a mere verdict of acquittal. He wished an endorsement, and a vindication. Therefore, after a short rest he set out to feel the pulse of the people, visiting Knoxville, Chattanooga, Murfreesboro, Memphis and Nashville. In the western and middle sections the response to his appeal was cordial. He had become an object of curiosity—his career had been so checkered and so full of danger he was classed with Sam Houston, Dave Crockett and Andy Jackson. In his speeches he was careful to say that he was a candidate for no office. He intended to devote "the remainder of his life to a vindication of his character and that of his State." "I will indulge in no set speeches," he would say, "but I will have a few simple conversations with the people here and there." At Knoxville, after his first "conversation" of two hours or more, it was plain, however, that Napoleon was back from Elba; that Andrew Johnson had to be reckoned with. The masses crowded around him, as in former days, and the Radicals became thoroughly alarmed.[1] His voice rang out clear and strong, he was "as robust and vigorous, as positive and self-reliant" and his facts and figures as full and convincing as when first heard on the hustings, thirty years before. At Memphis his reception was significant. Near the spot where eight years before "the blackest negro slave in town" had set fire to a figure of "the traitor," great crowds gathered to honor the returned "patriot" and "hero." It soon became plain that Johnson was out for a purpose, that he was after the United States Senate and would

[1] Jones, *Life*, p. 343.

stand for election by the very next legislature to be chosen in August.

Never, however, had he encountered a more complex situation than he was now facing. Tennessee, the last State to secede from the Union, and the first to be re-admitted, had escaped military reconstruction and carpet-bag rule, nevertheless the battle for political supremacy between native whites was as fierce as in the reconstructed states of the Black-Belt. Democrats of the mountains, who had always idealized Johnson, had now quit him and joined the Radicals. He was too conservative for them. These Union men had suffered much at the hands of their Confederate neighbors and were unwilling to forgive or forget. Proscription, disfranchisement and punishment of the rebels they demanded and nothing less.[2] Like Dave Potter, the noted Union scout, they had followed Andy Johnson blindfolded into the Union ranks, but they were not going to fellowship with rebels, as he was doing.

"Dave," said Captain Polk, of Company F, Eighth Indiana Regiment, one night by the campfires, "how does it happen, you, a southern man, are in the Union army?" "Well, you see, Capt., it was this way," Dave replied. "My brother Ish is er eddicated man and he tried to get me to go along with him and jine the Secesh. Then I says to Ish, says I, 'Ish, how does Andy Johnson stand on this particular question?' Then Ish he says to me, 'Dave, Andy Johnson, damn him, is for the Union.' Says I to Ish, 'Well, if Andy Johnson's for the Union then by God I'm for the Union too, and I reckin' you and me will have to part company.' "[3] It was men like Dave Potter who had quit the Democratic party and become Republicans.[4]

Johnson had not only lost mountain followers like Dave Potter but also the old secession Democrats in the west and middle sections. That is to say, both extremes were against him. Rank Secessionists despised the man who in 1861 had

2 Fertig, p. 12.
3 Wabash *Courier*, November 8, 1900.
4 The old mountain district represented by Andy Johnson, which before the war usually gave him a Democratic majority of one or two thousand, after the war went Republican by 10,000 votes, electing W. G. Brownlow to Congress for many years.—Congressman Brownlow's *Address* in Congress, June 5, 1906.

deserted the South and taken part with the North, and as Military Governor, in 1862, '63 and '64, had "tyrannized" over Tennessee. Unionists were equally bitter because of his leniency to the Confederates. Though these extremes were opposed to Johnson, they were equally opposed to each other. Neither side recognized nor associated with the other. When a young Unionist, and a native of Tennessee, asked a Confederate damsel, who had had two brothers killed in the war, to give him a waltz, she grew highly indignant at the idea of dancing with a "yankeeized southerner." Her kinspeople then took up the matter and three men were slain before the affront was avenged. In such conditions, the economic, political and social affairs of the State were almost chaotic. Tennessee had been readmitted into the Union in July 1866 but under the Fourteenth Amendment, which it had adopted, leading whites were deprived of the ballot and by a combination of the liberated negroes and the Radicals the affairs of state passed into the hands of a corrupt and unprincipled gang.

Governor Brownlow—radical of the Radicals—though honest himself, was unable to control his "black and tan" followers. The worst element of the state rose to the surface. The legislature looted the treasury, issued millions of fraudulent bonds, wasted and stole public funds, and terrorized the state. White women and children in west and middle Tennessee, especially on the Mississippi River where the negroes were in a majority, were in daily fear of their lives. Offices were filled with negroes and confusion and discord prevailed. The powerless white man stood by witnessing the destruction of his country and the degradation of his race. Finally the whites determined to fight the devil with fire. They were going to save the state from Radical and negro rule or die in the attempt.[5] The plan adopted was revolutionary. The whites organized a secret oath-bound society, calling themselves the Ku Klux Klan. The entire South constituted the Invisible Empire, and the ruler was known as "the Grand Wizard." General Forrest, the noted Confederate, was the first to hold this office. Organized in Pulaski, Tennessee, in

5 Oberholtzer, Vol. II, p. 349.

1866, in less than two years it numbered its members by the hundreds of thousands. In New Orleans alone there were 17,000 members of the order. Corruption, crime and lawlessness were to be overcome with force; "miscegenation, to be prevented and the inferior race held down." Thoroughly the Ku Klux did its work.

The result was a reign of terror. By October 1868 it was reported that organized companies of men mounted, armed and disguised were spreading terror through the State. Though the Conservatives claimed that the conditions were not so bad as reported, in which view President Johnson concurred, they were bad enough, in all conscience.[6] The white man with a heritage of freedom of a thousand years was unwilling to abdicate in favor of his former slaves. "One hundred and sixty-two persons were murdered during the year ending June 1, 1868," General Thomas, Military Commander, reported. "Murders, robberies and outrages of all kinds are taking place in the country districts with no attempt of the civil authorities to arrest the offenders." [7] Memphis, with its immense negro population, was the Sodom of the South." "Absence of a daily account from that place of a riot, murder or some other outrage is conclusive evidence that the telegraph wires are down." President Johnson was charged with being a Ku Klux. This was a false charge, however. Such was the condition of affairs before Johnson's return home. In the summer of 1868 Governor Brownlow had determined to suppress the Klan and to overcome force by force. The legislature in special session enacted drastic laws against the Ku Klux. The members were declared outlaws. "Wherever found they were to be punished with death"—an open season for hunting and killing Ku Kluxers was provided. Soon the original klan disbanded and went out of business; and a hybrid affair operated under the same name, committing outrages, without the semblance of excuse.

The Republican party held its state convention in May 1869 and split into two factions, the radicals and the con-

[6] *Ibid.,* p. 371.
[7] *Reports of Secretary of War,* 1868-1869, Vol. I, pp. 717-724.

servatives. Colonel W. S. Stokes was nominated for Governor by the radical element and Governor Senter by the conservatives. Brownlow, just elected United States Senator, and opposed to negro domination, espoused the cause of Senter. The Democratic party as a political organization was practically extinct. The issue, therefore, was between the two wings of the Republican party, Stokes favoring further proscription of the whites and Senter advocating a milder course.

In the summer of 1869 Johnson, just recovering from an attack of bilious fever, took the stump for Governor Senter. Soon, however, he was called home on account of the sudden death of his son, Robert Johnson. This lovable man, "his own worst enemy," succumbed to the hardships of a strenuous life, a strenuous age, dying by his own hand. Eight years of proscription and war, of exile and ostracism had worn him out, the stimulants he indulged in but augmenting his troubles. Lawyer, legislator, Colonel of a Union regiment, patriot and assistant secretary to the President, the Colonel passed away esteemed and regretted, at the early age of thirty-three.[8] But neither life nor death, principalities nor powers, could stay the tough, fibrous father. Returning to the canvass, he laid his cause before the people, as he had done in the past. In the '40's and '50's he appealed to the people and never failed to win; in 1861 he went to the people of East Tennessee pleading the cause of the Union and won again. In 1866 he went to the people of the North in behalf of the outraged Constitution but they did not heed his message. They were deceived by politicians and demagogues, he maintained. So again to the people, the source of all power, he would go. Wherever he spoke great interest was aroused.

At Marysville, Tennessee, on August 3, he spoke to 1,500 voters, estimated to be one-third conservatives, and for Governor Senter and two-thirds radicals, and for Colonel Stokes. The crowd was turbulent and menacing; "three times they howled Johnson down," with yells for Stokes and with personal

[8] Dr. Charles Johnson had died at the age of thirty-three, and Andy Johnson, Jr., shortly afterwards passed away at the age of twenty-six.

abuse.[9] The Stokes men were determined "to prevent the speaking if possible, or failing in that to break it up in a row." Singleton, a conservative, and Phelps, a strong radical, "had a personal reconter." . . . "The crowd swayed and surged like forest trees in a gale . . . pistols were attempted to be drawn." . . . "Take him down," the crowd yelled. "Shoot the damn traitor." But Johnson held his own—"A man of marble," save that his eyes flashed fire; he went right on with his speech. "Why call me traitor?" he said. "I am no traitor. Secessionists and Radicals are traitors; these are the men who would break up our Union. Look at Grant, your President, appointing the rebel General Longstreet to office. Was it not Longstreet, who devastated your fields and villages while I was fighting for your homes and for the Union? I say to you that 'yankee-rebels and rebel-Radicals' are equally odious to me. The Radical party would take the devil himself to its bosom or even Jeff Davis, 'unwashed and unrepentant to-morrow, if he would join them.' " . . . "The fraudulent Tennessee bonds issued by the Radicals should be wiped out—the State got nothing from them and should pay nothing in return." [10] After speaking three and a half hours and submitting endless facts and figures, Johnson retired and "all who listened to him, including his enemies, went away with food for thought, sufficient for many a day."

At Abingdon, Virginia, Johnson assailed the Radical Congress; four years they waged war to keep the southern states in the Union, he declared, and four years to keep them out. President Grant's cabinet was "a sort of lottery," he asserted, "those getting the best places that paid the most." . . . "Stewart bought the Treasury Secretaryship with a check for $65,000.00, and Borie purchased his fat place with a fine house and furniture, and so on; offices were disposed of at various prices, from $65,000.00 down to a box of segars." [11] At a

[9] Daily *Whig*, August 3, 1866.

[10] The Democratic party under the leadership of its patriotic and worthy Governor, Isham G. Harris, afterwards settled its bonded indebtedness somewhat along the line advocated by Andy Johnson, though the best element of the Republicans called this repudiation.

[11] The *Virginian*, August 6, 1869.

speaking at Greeneville Johnson took high ground for universal education. "The poor boy and girl are entitled to be educated free," he declared. "The state owes something to the people, the toiling masses have been too long neglected and I—" Before he could finish the sentence some one yelled, "Oh, that's damn yankee talk!" Calmly and quietly Johnson resumed his speech, declaring that "the poor man's boy should be given an even chance with the rich man's." "Shoot him, damn him, kill the damn yankee," was hurled back. "Shoot away," said the speaker. "Here's a good target." And placing his right hand over his left breast, he invited the attack.[12] Thus day after day, the tireless man spoke, winning votes wherever he went. Occupying the middle ground between radicalism and secession-Democracy, his position was the safe and patriotic one. At the August election the radicals were defeated by 50,000 votes, the legislature was largely conservative, and Senter became Governor again.

The new legislature met in October and it was expected that Andrew Johnson would be chosen Senator without opposition. The Tennessee people, that is the masses, wished him to return to Washington at once and confront his enemies. But the fates were against him. President Grant had put the resources of the Government in Brownlow's hands and federal patronage as well. Johnson was defeated for the Senate by one or two votes. The vote of Edmund Cooper, Johnson's confidential friend and secretary at Washington, turned the trick.[13] Senator Brownlow, secretly dickering with the secessionists, had arranged to throw the Radical vote to Henry Cooper, brother to Edmund, if he would consent to run. The bargain was struck and Henry Cooper received the necessary vote. This political trick wounded Johnson but in the end helped him, as the people did not approve of it. Time and again Johnson was on the eve of getting the one necessary vote, but never did, Radical and Secessionist alike despising the man. A native of Virginia, residing in Chattanooga at the time, and serving

12 This incident was furnished me by H. G. Brown, a youth, in 1869, not in his teens.
13 Johnson MS. at Greeneville.

in the legislature, "was anxious to vindicate Johnson for recent services to the South," but dared not vote for him. "Time and again," he declared, "I was on the eve of voting for Mr. Johnson because of his recent services to the South, but then I would think of how he had treated the southern leaders, and the 'old Confederate snake' would rise in my throat and I just could not do it." [14] Thus the exquisite piece of retributive justice which was near completion and would have put Andrew Johnson back into the Senate, the same year he left the Presidency, failed.

Again in 1872 he was doomed to failure. Entering the race for Congressman-at-large, he was beaten by Horace Maynard. This was a three-handed race. Confederate General Cheatham was the Democratic nominee, Horace Maynard the Republican, and Andrew Johnson the Independent. As the canvass proceeded it became plain that Johnson would kill off the "Brigadiers" but would elect the Republicans. As Judge Milligan wrote his old friend Johnson, "The lion is killing the prey for the jackals to devour." The Republican party standing solid and Johnson's candidacy dividing the Democrats, Maynard's election was made sure. In the canvass Maynard threw up to Johnson the execution of Mrs. Surratt, charging him with her murder. Johnson's reply was open and bold. "In 1865," said he, "the city of Washington was an armed camp; Lincoln was our Commander-in-Chief; he was foully murdered and a court duly organized sat upon the case and convicted his murderers, a woman included; I was unwilling to pardon her and that is all there is to it."

In the western counties crowds of negroes attended the speaking, some evidently anxious to make good citizens. Addressing these colored people, Andrew Johnson explained his position. "If fit and qualified by character and education, no one should deny you the ballot," he said. "I have been ridiculed for saying I would be your Moses," he continued. "Yet I say again, I will be your Moses; and if you have a certificate to vote you should be allowed to vote." He called to an elderly colored man in the crowd and bade him come to the

[14] *Ibid.*

stand. Placing his hands on the snow-white, woolly head of this old slave, the ex-President extended his blessing and bade him go forth to labor for the upbuilding of his race. "The Radical Congress made a serious blunder," he went on, "when they enfranchised the negro race, as a whole, and before they were qualified to vote. This matter should have been left to the individual states. But let bygones be bygones and let us live together in peace and good fellowship; after an honest trial, if it is found that we can't live in peace, let it be arranged by voluntary colonization or otherwise, so that we may part in peace."

In 1873 an epidemic of Asiatic cholera swept over Tennessee. In Greeneville and Greene county there were nearly a hundred victims of the scourge. Andrew Johnson and his family had the means to flee and avoid the disaster but they chose to remain at home assisting the destitute and sick and sharing the afflictions of others. Shortly Johnson succumbed to the dread disease and for a while his life was despaired of. In fact, his recovery was not complete, he was never afterwards so strong and vigorous as he had been.

Before the next campaign, some one asked Johnson if he would again be a candidate for the Senate. "Of course I will," he jocularly remarked. "The damned Confederate Brigadiers having been destroyed, what hinders me from going to the Senate?" And in this surmise he was correct. In 1874, though opposed by Confederate General W. C. Bates and John C. Brown, leading Democrats, he made a wonderful canvass and comeback. His experience as President having taught the lesson of moderation, he spoke without bitterness and as a father to his children. Though the issue was largely personal he likewise advocated his old doctrines, retrenchment, honesty in public affairs and the preservation of local self-governments. Perhaps this campaign was the most gratifying of his long career. He saw his triumph in every shout of the people.

The speaking at Memphis, May 16, 1874, illustrates his wonderful comeback. On that occasion the Memphis theater was "crowded from pit to dome," there was standing room neither on the floor nor in the galleries. "The crowd was composed of every class,—laborers, artisans, merchants, manufacturers, bankers, lawyers, doctors and divines," . . . "nor was it stint in its plaudits." Mayor Loague introduced the speaker. "One whom the entire world has seen fit to honor," he declared, "as the defender of civil and religious liberty." From beginning to end "the Old Commoner" carried the crowd. Alternately "they laughed, applauded and shouted approval." For three hours he gave an account of his stewardship: How he had, in that very spot, twelve years before warned against Secession; how he had served the Union all his life, how as President he had endeavored to stand between the South and Radical oppression.[15]

"During all these years as Military Governor and as President," he said, "I have directed the spending of millions of your money, and thank God I can stand before the people of my State and lift up both my hands and say in the language of Samuel 'whose ox have I taken or whose ass have I taken? At whose hands have I ever received bribes to blind mine eyes therewith?' If there is any let them answer and I will return it." . . . "I know that when a man gets a little old," he said in conclusion, "he is regarded as a cinder, something that won't generate any more heat, and he is accordingly thrown out in the ash pile; you know there is always a heap of these cinders around a shop. But, thank God, there is a little of the fire of my youth running through my veins and in my heart yet and as time at last sets all things even, I look to the future to judge me. . . . I feel that my State was wronged, I feel that I was wronged in 1869, I feel that the legislature in that year was untrue to the people and I am free to say that the deepest wound inflicted upon me, yes, I may say, was by a member of my own household. . . . I would not be worthy to be called a man unless I was ambitious. I am ambitious, ambitious of acquiring a name in the minds of the people that I have been a faithful representative; that I have stood upon the watchtowers of my country, and defended and vindicated and guarded their rights when they were not in a condition to do it themselves. . . . I have lived and toiled for the people because I wanted their

[15] Johnson MS. at Greeneville.

approbation and esteem, and when the time shall come that my connection is to be severed with this people and all things that are mortal, and when the lamp of life is flickering the last, the most pleasant thoughts that can pass through my mind will be to feel and to know that I occupied a place in the respect and hearts of my countrymen."

A joint meeting of the two houses of the Legislature was held on January 26, 1875, to elect a United States Senator, to succeed Brownlow. On the fifty-fifth ballot Andrew Johnson, ex-President of the United States, was returned to the Senate, by a vote of fifty-two against the field—the only ex-President ever thus honored. Many conditions brought about this result. In the first place, the Republican party, in nation and state, had played its cards very badly. Early in 1869 Congress had been forced to admit its error in enacting the Tenure-of-Office Act. Neither Grant nor any other self-respecting man would serve as President with his hands tied by such a measure. Congress was therefore compelled to take the back track. The House voted to repeal the act, but the Senate, more timid if not more decent, refused thus to stultify itself. Again President Grant's hobby, seeking to take over the island of San Domingo, had offended the Abolitionists. Sumner likened Grant to "Franklin Pierce, John Buchanan and Andrew Johnson." The enraged Grant bitterly resented Sumner's insult. Frequently he would pass Sumner's residence by "shaking his fist at the closed windows" and threatening to fight him a duel. National politics had become thoroughly rotten, "it was controlled by hacks and flunkies." President Grant's appointments, said the *Nation*, "are the worst ever made by a civilized, Christian government; the parasites of the party are its masters." [16] "Office holders as scoundrels are allowed to loot the South under cover of loyalty and to help save the country from traitors, i.e., from anti-Grant Republicans and Democrats." . . . "The treasury is a hotbed of low jobbery. There is a mad whirl of office brokerage, and patriotism has become mere political lucre."

In 1872, so far did these troubles extend, liberals and con-

16 Oberholtzer, Vol. II, p. 308.

servatives in the Republican party, Sumner included, split off and set up a new organization which they called the Liberal Party. Uniting with the Democrats, this new party might have won in the ensuing election but for the nomination of the erratic Greeley for President. In a word, by the year 1875, when Johnson was elected to the Senate, the Republican party was in disfavor. It was plain that the people were going to repudiate it and restore the Democrats to power. Grant, the soldier, had been without a superior; Grant, the President, deceived by henchmen, was a failure. By this time also the South had begun to pull itself together and the North was beginning to see the difficulties in the way of southern rehabilitation, with the burden of the negro. In 1869 the Ku Klux were disbanded and, under wiser leadership, whites and blacks were getting along with less friction. Soon the negro was content to quit politics and go to work in the fields again. The "franchise," which the Radicals were going to give him had proved a delusion. The poor fellow imagined it was "a side of bacon"! And when he went to the polls with his haversack and found it wasn't "somethin' t' eat," he was disgusted. All these things were water on Andrew Johnson's wheel. Thoughtful people were beginning to contrast the simplicity, honesty, and ruggedness of the Johnson administration with the nepotism, extravagance and corruption of its successor.

Analyzing Johnson's great triumph in 1875, one will see that it was brought about by a union of the Conservatives and a handful of Republicans. Yet that is not half the story. Clean and honest and without the use of money or bribes undoubtedly it was, but his triumph was more personal than political. It was a tribute to bravery, to loyalty and to conviction. The legislature was made up of men whose rebel fathers had been pardoned by him; others whose estates had been saved from confiscation by him; not a few who had been assisted with money or advice by him; and of many friends and neighbors, mostly laboring men, men who naturally loved "Old Andy Johnson" and "gloried in his spunk." In 1875 it was recalled that Johnson, in his 1869 contest for the Senate, had fought fair and clean; that, at that session, a railroad magnate had come to Johnson's rooms and assured him that next day would witness his election, as the necessary votes would be forthcoming, and that Johnson had inquired, "How did you get them?" "I am to pay $2,000.00 for them," was the reply. "You will do no such thing," said the ex-President. "But, Mr. President," said the man, "it will not be your money, it will cost you nothing." "It will cost me my honor," Johnson retorted; "and if elected in that way I will go before the Legislature, expose the fraud and decline the office." [17]

Had it not been for the masses of the people, however, the legislature of 1875 might have turned Johnson down as it had done in 1869. But the plain people were not to be twice deceived. They kept the mails and the wires "hot" for Andy Johnson. Many came to Nashville to back him up. On the other hand the old "Secessionists" were splendidly organized. They were led by the Brigadiers and backed by President Grant and the power of his administration. Senator Brownlow, in Washington, was determined to put down Andy Johnson and Andy Johnsonism. Extremes had met. Now, however unpopular Grant may have become in the North, he had not lost the good will and esteem of the South. His generous treatment of Lee at Appomattox, and when it was proposed to arrest the beloved Southern Chieftain and try him for treason, had won southern hearts. His noble words, "Let us have peace," had given him a secure place in southern affection, despite his recent radicalism. But "the Old Commoner" was too much for President Grant and the Confederate Brigadiers combined. He effectually spiked their guns. One day during the session he met General Forrest on the streets of Nashville and asked the General to accompany him to his rooms, at the Maxwell House. General Forrest and Johnson had been old Democrats and states-rights men, and, besides, Forrest was as simple and plain in his taste as Andrew Johnson himself. "General," said Johnson to Forrest, "these damn fellows are just using you and your influence against me; if they want a sure enough General for Senator why don't they bring you

[17] Colonel Reeves in Knoxville *Sentinel*, May 30, 1923.

out?" The General, seeing the point, quit Nashville, a Johnson man, it was said, leaving the field to the ex-President.

Starting with thirty-six votes on the first ballot, going down to thirty-two, then up to thirty-three, thence to forty-four, and finally to fifty-two, Andy Johnson was once again a United States Senator with a safe majority of one.[18] When the news that "the Old Commoner" had "whipped out the crowd" spread over Nashville, "the shouts of many thousands were answered by shouts from Edgefield until it seemed that Nashville and its suburbs were almost unanimously for him." Alf Taylor, the member from Carter, wished to be the first to break the news to his father's old friend. Rushing down the street to the hotel, and crying out as he entered, "Mr. Johnson you are elected, you are elected," he fainted dead away and was not revived till a bucket of ice water was dashed in his face.[19]

No sooner had Speaker Payne announced that Andrew Johnson was elected to the Senate than the crowd rushed from the capitol to the Maxwell House, cheering and shouting. That night ten thousand people gathered in the public square to listen to the voice of the Tennessee patriot. A splendid speech he delivered—devoid of partisanship or bitterness. "I will go to the Senate," he said, "with no personal hostility toward any one, but with a large affection for, and a more intensified devotion to, the ancient landmarks. . . . My few remaining years shall be devoted to the weal and prosperity of my country which I love more than my own life." [20]

On Friday, March 5, 1875, the United States Senate met in extra session. The desk of Senator Andrew Johnson, which Senator Brownlow was reluctantly quitting, was covered with flowers. The galleries were filled with admiring friends. Shortly after twelve o'clock the sturdy ex-President, clothed in broadcloth, with standing collar and stock cravat, was seen slowly to enter the chamber—so full of memories for him. A group of Democratic Senators formed about him. Edmunds of Vermont was addressing the chair. Observing the group,

18 DeWitt, p. 622.
19 Knoxville *Sentinel*, May 30, 1923; article by Col. E. C. Reeves.
20 Jones, *Life*, p. 350.

he ceased to speak. In the excitement of coming face to face with the ex-President, whom he had voted to expel from office, he "kicked over a lot of old books on his desk and abruptly sat down." Many Senators rose to their feet "to honor Johnson's former greatness." Carl Schurz, now a liberal Democrat, and Henry Wilson, Vice-president, respectfully stood.[21] Senator Roscoe Conkling, whose "turkey-gobbler strut" Blaine had immortalized, was "pretending to read a letter and peering at the ex-President from the corner of his eye"; Senator Frelinghuysen "went down on his knees seeking either a book—or hatchet"; Senator John Sherman first stared about and was puzzled, then, recalling war days, when he and Johnson had canvassed Ohio for the Union, came forward and shook hands. Senator Oliver P. Morton was in the greatest quandary of all. He had been President Johnson's friend and supporter, then had changed and voted to impeach him. He, therefore, stood aloof. Magnanimously Johnson offered his hand; Morton gladly grasped it.[22] The clerk proceeded to call the roll of newly elected Senators. "Hannibal Hamlin!" he called. The Senator from Maine answered to his name. "Andrew Johnson!" he called. The ex-President answered "present." Henry Cooper, Johnson's colleague, came down the aisle. Bowing stiffly, he and Senator McCreery of Kentucky escorted the new Senator to the clerk's desk. The Vice-president, rising and respectfully standing, contrary to custom, administered the oath. And he, whom Morton had pronounced a "violator of the Constitution and a violator of his oath," was again a Senator of the United States.[23]

Tears were noticed in the ex-President's eyes as he went back to his place. "I miss my old friends," he said to Senator McCreery. "Bayard, Buckalew, Reverdy Johnson, Fessenden, Fowler, Trumbull, Grimes, Henderson, Ross, all are gone, all but yourself, Senator McCreery." But if many of Senator Johnson's friends were gone, many more of his enemies were likewise gone. Of the thirty-nine Senators voting to convict,

21 *Harper's Weekly*, Vol. XLVIII, p. 1356.
22 Morton, *Address*, Memorial Exercises of Andrew Johnson.
23 *Harper's Weekly*, Vol. XLVIII, p. 1356.

The Era of Disgrace

twenty-six had been decapitated, and only thirteen remained. "Bluff" Ben Wade, and Radicals of his kind had been swept out of Congress like chaff before the raging storm. In Ohio, the political revolution of 1869 was "as remarkable in character as it was sudden in time"; [24] . . . "a revolution of public sentiment without premonition and visible cause." In the House there was a majority of sixty-three against the Republican party. *Harper's Weekly*, which, a short while before, had heaped no end of ridicule on Johnson, had a fine picture, in which he was conspicuous. As he held in his hands a flagstaff, from which Old Glory was waving, Andrew Johnson's sturdy, honest face was good to look upon. In a few months the New York *Nation* declared of Johnson's administration that "it was in the main unexceptionable." Of Andrew Johnson it said, "His personal integrity is beyond question and his respect for the laws and the Constitution made his administration a remarkable contrast to that which succeeded it." [25]

On March 22, 1875, a resolution of the Senate to approve the action of President Grant, in protecting Governor Kellogg in Louisiana affairs, was under debate. Throughout Washington it had become known that Andrew Johnson was to speak, that he was to launch an attack on Grant's administration. Many spectators came to witness the onslaught. At that time the Republican party, as we have seen, was at a low ebb and Johnson was going to give it a parting kick. From 1870 to 1874, so far had fraud, peculation and corruption advanced, the period is called "the disgraceful period of American history." [26] During Grant's administration, indeed, "the orgy reached its limits," and Gould's corrupt corner on gold, culminating in "Black Friday," September 24, 1869, will never be forgotten. To these unhappy conditions Senator Johnson addressed himself in a speech of some power. This speech, it must be admitted, came as an anti-climax, after other and more exciting episodes. There were the "same peculiarities of style and diction," however, the same repeti-

[24] Blaine, Vol. II, p. 441.
[25] *Nation*, August 5, 1875.
[26] Dunning, *Reconstruction*, p. 290. Oberholtzer, Vol. II, p. 548.

tions and elaborations, and "the same habit of keeping the people ever in his eye," that had marked his whole career. He was severe on President Grant; President Grant's acceptance of gifts and his ambition for a third term were condemned. The speech was evidently a reply to Grant's assaults in the last Tennessee campaign, and not nationally significant. On the second day after, the Senate adjourned and Senator Johnson returned to Tennessee.

During the spring and early summer Senator Johnson devoted himself to private affairs and to a study of the currency question. Since his prostration by cholera, two years before, his health "had not been all that could be desired. Sometimes his heart had troubled him"; and after the campaign of 1874, "his powers did not obey his volition as promptly as before." Yet he continued active and alert, going to his office every day. Occasionally he visited towns nearby, and was always the center of admiring groups. Late in July he expressed a desire to run over to the Stover place and visit his daughter Mary, Mrs. Johnson having gone over a little while before.[27]

That July morning, on the train from Greeneville to Carter Station, there were a lot of friends and admirers of the ex-President. Alf Taylor, who happened to be on board, and others drew the old man out on his amazing career. He "was never more interesting." Alf Taylor's home, Happy Valley, adjoined the Stover place; and Taylor asked to call next day. Every one was struck with Johnson's vigor and vivacity.[28] They asked him about the execution of Mrs. Surratt, which had cut quite a figure in the recent fight. The ex-President assured them that he did not see the recommendation for mercy until two years after Mrs. Surratt was put to death. At Carter Station "the boys" accompanied their old friend to the car door and bade him adieu. He was met by a carriage from the plantation and driven six miles, to his daughter's home. There he arrived about eleven o'clock in the forenoon.

At the noon meal his spirits were buoyant, his conversation being of home affairs and general topics. Shortly afterwards

27 Johnson MS. at Greeneville.
28 Greeneville *Democrat Sun*, May 29, 1923.

he went to his room; Lillie Stover his granddaughter, once the joy of White House days, accompanied him. Seated in an arm chair, the old Patriot talked a few moments to his grandchild. She then turned and started to the door. Suddenly she heard something fall heavily to the floor. It was her grandfather. He had fallen forward on the carpet and was lying helpless. His left side was paralyzed, he feared. The family, in confusion, hastened to get a physician. But no! The indomitable man forbade it. He needed no doctor, he would overcome his troubles. It was then three o'clock Wednesday, July 27. During the next twenty-four hours he lay in bed and talked of things of long ago—his tailor shop days, his struggles upward. Next day at the same hour there came another stroke, extending through his whole frame. This attack extinguished every energy of mind and body. Physicians were summoned. In an hour or two, however, "the Old Commoner" was dead. Dead at the Stover place, he loved so well. The family called in no minister. They knew the dead man's wishes. But all day Friday and Saturday Masons from adjoining towns and neighbors, men from hill and dale, gathered. The Stover home was filled with mourners—plain people from mountain and cove, men who loved Johnson and whom he loved. During the silent night they watched by his bedside. Early Sunday morning they placed the dead in blankets, filled with ice. Depositing his mortal remains in a plain pine box they set out for Greeneville.

By Monday noon "every store, office and public building in town was put in the dressings of sorrow and mourning." "The Court House, where he had so often pleaded the cause of the Union, was hidden with festoons of white and black." The old tailor shop, "hung around with loops and knots of mourning, seemed to take unto itself an air of living gloom at the vanishing of a spirit which years before had gone from its portals to enduring fame." Telegrams and messages came from every portion of the Union; representatives of the metropolitan press arrived.[29] At length arrangements were completed. A suitable casket was secured, and the body transferred to it.

[29] Johnson MS. at Greeneville.

The simple words, "Andrew Johnson, Seventeenth President of the United States," were engraved on the silver plate. In a new, silken flag, the flag of his country, all bright and glorious with thirty-seven stars, not one omitted, they wrapped him. His lifeless fingers grasped its silken folds. Under his head they placed the Constitution of the United States, the first he ever owned. It bore the date 1835 and was marked and written over, from cover to cover. His wishes they had carried out to the letter: "Pillow my head on the Constitution of my country," he had asked. "Let the flag of the Nation be my winding sheet."

Tuesday morning the mother lodge No. 119, where both Andrew Jackson and Andrew Johnson first became Masons, requested that the body be removed from the residence and rest in the Masonic assembly room. The request was granted and the casket was placed on a catafalque, covered with flowers, in the Temple. It was then removed to the Court House. Special trains pulled into the little station. The great and powerful came—Governors, Judges, Congressmen, Legislators—forming a procession half a mile long. These great ones were welcome —these Captains and Kings. All were welcome. But not more so than the plain people, the mechanic, the laborer, the artisan, the farmer, "the mudsills of society." By the thousands they had come. One last look at him who had faced ostracism and obloquy for their sakes, they must have. W. D. Williams and Mrs. Williams, son and daughter of Dr. Alex Williams, laid flowers on the bier. Blackstone McDaniel was the chief mourner; other old cronies were all gone, all but "old Mac." Milligan, Self, Park, Mordecai Lincoln, John Jones, were no more. Passing through a line of Knights Templars, with crossed swords, McDaniel and seventeen others bore the dead to the carriage. The Dickenson Light Guards' Band played Webster's Funeral March. The Johnson Guards followed behind the line of marshals. Then came the family. Slowly ascending the conical-shaped hill, half a mile from the town, the procession halted—halted at the spot Johnson had selected for his resting place.[30]

30 Johnson MS. at Greeneville.

At this point the Knight Templar Masons took charge. Priest or prelate there was none. The Masonic official, U. A. Rouser,—the most skillful mechanic in the city of Knoxville,— spoke the final words. From the ritual he read a prayer. Softly the Masonic choir chanted their sad farewell.

"Christian warriors at the pealing
Of the solemn vesper bell,
Round the triform altar kneeling
Whisper each 'Immanuel.' "

The bugler sounded taps. In the bosom of the mountains they left the Old Commoner. Shortly afterwards on this spot, with its wonderful view of mountain and valley, his children put up a monument: a marble shaft surmounted by the American eagle, "Old Glory" draping the upper half. Cut into the side of the shaft is a copy of the Constitution; underneath, the words, "His faith in the people never wavered." [31]

[31] Among the Johnson papers was found a pencil memorandum written by him during the cholera scourge on June 9, 1873. "All seems glocm and despair," it reads. "Approaching death to me is the mere shadow of God's protecting wing. Here I know can no evil come; here I will rest in quiet and peace beyond the reach of calumny's poisoned shaft; the influence of envy and jealous enemies, where treason and traitors in State, backsliders and hypocrites in the church, can have no place; where the great fact will be realized that God is truth and gratitude the highest attribute of man."

CHAPTER X

SIXTY YEARS AFTER

In October 1926 the legal world was given a surprise. The Supreme Court struck down the old act of March 1867—the Tenure of Office Act—under which Andrew Johnson had been impeached and tried. "This act is invalid as an attempt to interfere with the constitutional rights of the President," the court said. The court also intimates that the act was monstrous and vicious. How could a President perform the duties of his office with an adverse cabinet? As we have seen, the court had previously held that President Johnson was within his rights when he vetoed the Civil Rights Act, when he vetoed the Freedmen's Bureau Act and the Reconstruction Acts.[1] And now, after more than sixty years, the court holds that the President was also right in his veto of the Tenure of Office Act and of the Command of the Army Act.[2]

In short, it is to-day held by the courts, and generally agreed by historians, that nearly every particle of reconstruction legislation after peace was restored was null and void and that Andrew Johnson was correct in his veto messages. It follows that the Fourteenth and Fifteenth Amendments, so far as the southern states are concerned, were adopted under compulsion and by means of illegal statutes disfranchising whites and enfranchising blacks. In other words, the courts lay down two principles, apparently contradictory, but really not so at all. During actual warfare, and in 1865 till order was restored, the Southern States had no civil government and martial law was necessary and proper. In 1867, however, after the war had ended and civil governments were functioning, Congress could

[1] *Wall.*, Vol. VII, p. 597; *United States Rep.*, Vol. CVI, p. 629; *United States Rep.*, Vol. CIX, p. 1; Lothrop, *Seward*, p. 420.

[2] *Myers vs. United States*, October 25, 1926; Warren's *Supreme Court*, Vol. III, pp. 300 and 331; *Atlantic*, Vol. CVI, p. 548.

not provide and enforce martial law. This was for the civil courts.[3]

Now the opinion in this Myers case is noteworthy. It was delivered by a Republican, Chief Justice Taft, formerly President. It was concurred in by Republican members of the court, while two of the three dissenting judges, McReynolds and Brandeis, are Democrats. The case is also full of historical interest. In July 1917 Myers was appointed by the President, by and with the consent of the Senate, first-class Postmaster at Portland, Oregon, for a four years' term ending in July 1921. Eighteen months before his term expired, he was removed by the President without the consent of the Senate. His suit was to recover from the Government the remainder of his salary for eighteen months. Now Myers came in under the Act of 1876, which provides that first-class postmasters shall be appointed by the President, but shall not be removable except by the consent of the Senate.

In construing this act of 1876, it became necessary also to construe the act of March 1867, the Tenure of Office Act. This the court did without flinching. "The power to appoint," says the court, analyzing the Tenure of Office Act, "carries with it the power to remove." As the Constitution gives the President power to appoint members of his cabinet he has the inherent power to remove any member, regardless of the Senate. "In 1867 when Congress passed reconstruction legislation," says the court, "it was attempting to redistribute the powers of the Government and to minimize the President;" that is, a Radical Congress "was paralyzing the executive arm." "These were extreme measures," and so were the other acts known as the Command of the Army Act and the act abolishing appeals in *habeas corpus* matters, to oust the jurisdiction of the Supreme Court in the McCardle case. "Therefore," says the court, "the Tenure of Office Act, insofar as it attempted to prevent the President from removing a member of his cabinet, was invalid." Thus does the Supreme Court wipe off the statute books the Tenure of Office Act, so far as it relates to the cabinet. Thereby the impeachment of President Johnson

[3] *Ex Parte Milligan;* Dunning, *Essays on Reconstruction,* p. 95.

is rendered ridiculous and absurd! In truth it was but a moot affair.

Were I dramatizing Andrew Johnson's life, I might avail myself of the playwright's privilege and utilize this final word as an epilogue. In the center of the stage Andrew Johnson would be discovered. Not "King Andy," with crown and scepter, with sable coat and ermine-edging, as the Radical cartoonists used to portray him, but a plain, rugged, two-fisted American President, striving to do the right thing as best he could. Grouped about him would be Seward and Stanbery, Welles and McCulloch, Randall and Browning. Warden, the doorkeeper of the White House, would enter and announce, "The Senate of the United States and the managers in the impeachment trial." The door would open and the Senate would approach, the President and his cabinet rising to their feet. John Sherman, on behalf of the Senate, would say, "Mr. President, in the light of the past sixty years and of the recent decision of our highest court, the Senate is here to extend an apology and to assure you that sixty years ago, when we questioned your patriotism, impugned your motives, and sought to impeach and expel you from the presidency, we were wrong. The Senate offers no excuses except the passions and bitterness engendered by war." While the President bows and Senators come forward and grasp his hand the voice of Thad Stevens would be heard in the ante-room. "Damn the Myers case, it is worse than Dred Scott or Milligan. It will damn the Chief Justice to an everlasting infamy and, I fear, to an everlasting fire."

But let us not set too much store by the courts and their rulings. It may be that Thad Stevens was correct and the courts wrong. In December 1865, though the South had grounded arms and accepted the situation, it may be the Constitution did not yet protect her. Perhaps necessity warranted Congress in acting regardless of the Constitution. Waving the constitutional aspects of the matter, therefore, let us inquire, Which was right, the President or Congress? Ought the Southern States to have been admitted in December 1865 or ought they to have been excluded till thoroughly reconstructed as in 1867 and 1868? Congress concluded that they should be reconstructed and had Johnson been a weak executive he would probably have coöperated with them. But would not such a course have turned southern state governments upside down, and produced a war of races or probably some new spasm of disunion? In 1865 was not the wiser course pursued by Andrew Johnson? He had to meet an emergency; there were no civil governments in the South and discord prevailed. He must act at once, and it was his job. He found Lincoln's plan of restoring the Southern States ready to hand. He adopted this plan, the whole of Lincoln's Cabinet holding office under him and composing a harmonious and united administration, approving his course.[4] Congress then overturned these governments, put the South under military rule again, and eventually under the negro.

But it is said that the Lincoln and Johnson plan of immediate restoration, if adopted, would have been worse for the country than this Congressional plan and that it would have been unjust to the negro, that the Fourteenth and Fifteenth Amendments were necessary to protect his rights. In the light of sixty years have the amendments protected the negro? Is the southern negro to-day any nearer political and social rights than in 1865? Is he not, in the expressive word of Dunning, "nil"? And will not this condition remain for a greater length of time than if Congress had entrusted the matter to the southern people themselves? [4a]

Had the South been readmitted to the Union in 1865, what might have resulted? At that time bad blood between the North and South had not been stirred up. Civil war did not anger or wound the pride of the South. In the main, the American civil war was the cleanest and fairest ever fought. Reconstruction and the attempt to put the negroes above the whites, created bad blood and the "Solid South." Had Congress approved Johnson's reconstruction measures in 1865, it is reasonable to predict that the Secession element in the South would never have been heard of more. The old Secession

[4] Schouler, Vol. VII, p. 45.
[4a] Burgess, p. 298

Democratic party would have been buried out of sight. At the end of the war it was anathema. In Tennessee specially, had Congress admitted Horace Maynard and other Unionists, there would have been no split in the Union ranks; Andrew Johnson, Horace Maynard and Parson Brownlow would have pulled together, controlling the State in favor of Union and conservative principles. In other Border States, and particularly in North Carolina, as Professor Hamilton points out, in the summer of 1865 the leading men were dead opposed to the old Secession Democratic party.[5]

It must be admitted that just after the war the South, undoubtedly the upper South, was ripe for a fraternal, forward movement and that the Radicals destroyed the opportunity. It is not too much, I trust, to predict further that if Lincoln's "Louisiana Plan" had prevailed in 1865, the southern states, one by one, would have enfranchised worthy negroes, those worth two hundred and fifty dollars and up or who could read and write. Self-interest, if not philanthropy, would have brought this to pass. In truth, prior to 1832 the "Free negro" voted in the State of North Carolina. The Louisiana Plan, being voluntary, would have caused no ill-will. There would have been no persecutions and no such terrible organizations as the Ku Klux Klan. The kindly feeling between the whites and blacks, existing during slavery days, would have been maintained.[6] Then again, a systematic movement to scatter the southern negro would undoubtedly have followed. Also voluntary colonization, as Mr. Lincoln had urged with all his might.[7] In the South as elsewhere the negro is the white man's burden; and no section should bear more than its pro-rata share of it. As we have seen, long before the Civil War, Johnson had discovered this fact. He had come to realize that the old southern idea, that negro slavery had created a great and a

5 In North Carolina Colonel Waddell, Colonel Carter, Judge Fowle, Lewis Thompson, B. F. Moore, the Settles, Dockerys, and practically all of the leading men were eager to cut loose from the old Democratic party, to organize a national party to be called the Conservatives, and to coöperate with the North. —Hamilton, *Reconstruction in North Carolina*, p. 187.

6 The course above indicated was urged by General Lee and General Wade Hampton, two men the South never failed to follow.—Rhodes, Vol. V, pp. 564, 604; Oberholtzer, Vol. I, p. 71.

7 *Ibid.*, pp. 75, 80.

prosperous South, and that manual labor was degrading, was both ridiculous and false. In the early days of the nation, as Johnson learned from Helper's *Impending Crisis*, the South was in advance of the North; South Carolina and Charleston excelled Massachusetts and Boston. In that early day, in the matter of shipping, of exports and of imports, Charleston was far ahead of Boston. Southern plow lands were more valuable than northern. But the blight of slavery had reversed these conditions and the South was lagging far in the rear.[8] As Uncle Joe Cannon, the Quaker, born in North Carolina, often remarked, "Into the southern Eden came the serpent slavery and in the '40's white families by the thousands left the South and trekked it to the Free States." Johnson was the only southern statesman to discover and act upon this fact.

Again, sixty years ago it was urged that the freedmen must be protected. They had fought for their freedom and should not be left naked to their enemies. But, as I shall presently attempt to show, the rights of the freedman could not be protected by coercive and alien laws. This was possible by natural processes only. Moreover, it must be said that the southern white man is not the enemy of the negro but is his friend;[8a] and that the suggestion that the negro, as a whole, fought for his freedom is a fallacy. The negro fought, not for the Union but against it and for the Confederacy and for his old master. About two hundred thousand negroes, bond and free, from North and South and from elsewhere, were on the Union side, mostly in fortification and similar work; whereas perhaps six or eight times that number were on southern plantations fighting for the Confederacy. But for negroes at home, raising hog and hominy for Confederate soldiers, the Rebellion might have collapsed in twelve months. Certainly, if one general negro uprising, as the Nat Turner Insurrection, had taken place Lee would not have had a soldier in his ranks. Every mother's son would have hastened back to protect his Dixie home.

---

[8] Helper, *Impending Crisis*.
[8a] Each southern state to-day and private philanthropy—not the general government—are caring for the negro.

Much was said in 1866, in opposition to the Louisiana Plan, about the condition of the black man. In him "Christ lay concealed," it was urged; he was God's image in ebony, a superior being, in fact. Now it must be said that the person who wishes ill of the negro is a bad citizen. The white man brought the negro to America and the latter is not at fault. Yet the likable race cannot be absorbed by the white race. Social equality is impracticable, and the negroes are "a people within a people." "We know of the existence of the negro race," says Agassiz, "with all its physical peculiarities, from the Egyptian monuments several thousand years before the Christian era." [9] During all these years, Agassiz continues, "in natural propensities and mental abilities, negroes were pretty much what we find them at the present day,—indolent, playful, sensual, imitative, subservient, good-natured, versatile, unsteady in their purpose, devoted and affectionate." Everywhere "the negro is the same. In Africa where he was originally found; in upper Egypt; along the borders of the Carthaginian and Roman settlements in Africa; in Senegal, in juxtaposition with the French; in the Congo, in juxtaposition with the Portuguese; about the Cape; and on the eastern coast of Africa, in juxtaposition with the Dutch and the English." And yet, as Agassiz goes on to say, "While Egypt and Carthage, Babylon, Syria, and Greece were developing the highest culture of antiquity, the negro race groped in barbarism and *never originated a regular organization among themselves*." [9a]

Overlooking these ethnological facts, Congress insisted that a race, just out of slavery, ignorant and untrained for citizenship, should be put in control and that their late masters should be disfranchised. And this monstrous thing, over the veto of President Johnson, was accomplished and, for six or eight years, the South was prostrate. It was easy enough, as Beecher warned, for one living in New England, where there were no negroes, to philosophize about the rights of the colored man. In South Carolina and Mississippi, however, with a fifty-five per cent. negro population and only a forty-

---

[9] Rhodes, Vol. VI, p. 37.
[9a] *Ibid.*, the italics are Rhodes'.

five per cent. white, it was a very different thing. In the South it was a fight for existence. This Johnson, even while in Congress, foresaw and predicted. Mr. Blaine, in Maine, could write of "justice to the negro, of the negro's patriotism, of full political and social rights;" he might insist that "the South should accept the justice of this principle and that, whether the South accepted it or not, the North was resolved that it should become a part of the organic law of the Republic;" he might even boast that "Republican legislation wiped out two hundred years of caste and put the races on an equality and that thereby the wrath of man was made to praise the righteous works of God." But unfortunately Blaine forgot that men are not angels—that racial antipathies exist the world over.[10] In 1865, had Congress adopted Lincoln's Louisiana Plan they would have admitted the South into the Union. Slavery had been abolished, Confederate debts wiped out and ordinances of Secession repealed. Lincoln and Johnson required no more. This matter, indeed, as Mr. Blaine declares, was the thought which "wholly engrossed the mind of Lincoln" on April 11, 1865, when he delivered his last address, "speaking like an oracle."

In the light of recent years and of racial conflicts, the world over, it must be recognized that racial instincts and antipathies are ineradicable. Lincoln and Johnson appreciated this fact. Congress overlooked it. Lincoln and Johnson knew that a civilization could not be uprooted over-night; that it must grow and develop. The customs and manners of a people, a people's *mores*, may be gradually modified by agitation and by time, but it is a gradual process. The hasty re-organizer of society often does more harm than good. Having "found out the truth" this reformer wants "to get a law passed" to realize it right away and is only a mischief maker. "The *mores* of the South," as Professor Sumner declares, "were those of slavery in full and satisfactory operation, including social, religious, and philosophical notions adapted to slavery. . . . In the North the abolition of slavery had been brought about by changes in conditions and interests, but in the South emanci-

10 Blaine, *Twenty Years*, Vol. II, p. 267.

pation and franchise were produced by outside forces, against the *mores* of the whites; the consequence has been forty years of economic, social and political discord." [11]   It is often said that Mr. Lincoln set free millions of slaves "by a stroke of the pen." "Such references," says Sumner, "are only flights of rhetoric." [12]   "They entirely miss the apprehension of what it is to set men free, or to tear out of a society *mores* of long growth and wide reach."   Slavery, as Lincoln often declared, was dealt with, during the war, as a war measure, not for the sake of freedom, and not ethically.

It may be objected that if the Louisiana Plan had been adopted there would have been neither a Fourteenth nor a Fifteenth Amendment.   It may be asked: Would there have been a need for them?   "Trust the southern people," said Mr. Lincoln.   And if this had been done gradual enfranchisement might have taken place and gradual dispersion of the negro from the South.   Also gradual, voluntary, and peaceful colonization.   In a word, the negro might have been provided with a *Fatherland*.   Besides, may it not be asked, Is the Fourteenth Amendment, after all, an unmixed blessing?   Transcendent and epoch-making, it is.   Undoubtedly it nationalized the United States, making them the wonder among Nations; and it gives protection to great financial enterprises.   But are nationalization, centralization and bigness wholly desirable? From the viewpoint of the World War can it be said that civilization had been advanced by that national, dominating spirit, which took possession of the nations between 1860 and 1870? Would it not have been wiser to leave the United States unnationalized?   So Thomas Jefferson and Madison designed, and so Andrew Jackson and Andrew Johnson insisted.   In Webster's phrase, would not "an indissoluble union of indissoluble states" have been just as efficient and less complicated than a huge nation?   With prohibition on America's hands, with child labor laws unsettled, with an urge for uniform divorce and election laws and for Mann acts and other criss-cross legislation, regulating the private, intimate affairs of the citi-

[11] Sumner, *Folkways*, p. 113.
[12] *Ibid.*, p. 90.

zen, what trouble has America in store? At all events, Andrew Johnson was of opinion that a homogeneous state could more wisely function and legislate, in local and domestic matters, even in the matter of adjudging citizenship, than a heterogeneous nation. Time only can tell whether he was right. This much we do know, however: If the Secession Democracy of 1860 was silly, wicked, criminal, the Radicalism of 1865-69 was more wicked and more criminal.

I have pointed out that courts and historians are beginning to find something of interest in Andrew Johnson. If I were disposed to dwell on the subject, I could point to a revival of popular interest as well. The National Government has acquired the hill, where he lies buried, and converted it into a national cemetery, and a United States soldier nightly guards the spot. Tennessee has constructed a boulevard, stretching five hundred and odd miles from Bristol to Memphis, passing the door of the old tailor shop. It is called the "Andrew Johnson Highway." Tennessee has likewise purchased the tailor shop itself, encased it in brick, and provided a caretaker. Each year fifteen thousand pilgrims drive over the Andrew Johnson Highway and sit on the bench, where the tailor-president once sat and plied his trade. They rest under the trees he planted, wander to the spot where Morgan was killed or go down by the old ruined mill site. They climb High Hill and look off toward the blue peaks so dear to Johnson's heart. They imbibe the spirit of the tailor-president, they visualize one who met the supreme test of physical courage and daring. Perhaps they bend their way to Nashville, the capital of Tennessee, and, ascending to the cupola of the State House—in the days of civil war called Fort Andrew Johnson—behold a fair land, a land saved from slavery and disunion, largely by one whose name is written in the book of National Heroes.

APPENDIX A

Johnson Papers, vol. 13; 2870

> State of Maryland
> Executive Chamber
> Annapolis
> Sep^t 2. 1861.

Hon. Andrew Johnson of Tenn
    Dr Sir

Please accept my thanks for your Excellent speech delivered in the U.S.S. on the 27th July 1861.

Especially do I thank you for your Patriotic and Country loving course. You have shared the abuse of the disorganizers and Country distroyers, but it can do you no injury. Time will put *you* right and *them* in the shade.

God grant yourself and Other Patriots success in your manly effort to save Tennessee by bringing her back to the Union Fold. With great respect I have the Honor to be your ob^t

> Servt & fellow sufferer
> Tho H Hicks

APPENDIX B

Fellow-Citizens: Tennessee assumed the form of a body politic, as one of the United States of America, in the year seventeen hundred and ninety-six, at once entitled to all the privileges of the Federal Constitution, and bound by all its obligations. For nearly sixty-five years she continued in the enjoyment of all her rights, and in the performance of all her duties, one of the most loyal and devoted of the sisterhood of States. She had been honored by the elevation of two of her citizens to the highest place in the gift of the American people, and a third had been nominated for the same high office, who received a liberal though ineffective support. Her population had rapidly and largely increased, and their moral and material interests correspondingly advanced. Never was a people more prosperous, contented and happy than the people of Tennessee under the Government of the United States, and none less burdened for the support of the authority by which they were protected. They felt their Government only in the conscious enjoyment of the benefits it conferred and the blessings it bestowed.

Such was our enviable condition until within the year just past, when, under what baneful influences, it is not my purpose now to inquire, the authority of the Government was set at defiance, and the Constitution and Laws condemned, by a rebellious, armed force. Men who, in addition to the ordinary privileges and duties of the citizens, had enjoyed largely the bounty and official patronage of the Government, and had, by repeated oaths, obligated themselves to its support, with sudden ingratitude for the bounty and disregard of their solemn obligation, engaged, deliberately and ostentatiously, in the accomplishment of its overthrow. Many, accustomed to defer to their opinions and to accept their guidance, and others, carried away by excitement or over-awed by seditious clamor, arrayed themselves under their banners, thus organizing a treasonable power, which, for the time being, stifled and suppressed the authority of the Federal Government.

In this condition of affairs it devolved upon the President, bound by his official oath to preserve, protect and defend the Constitution, and charged by the law with the duty of suppressing insurrection and domestic violence, to resist and repel this rebellious force by the military arm of the government, and thus to reëstablish the Federal authority. Congress, assembling at an early day, found him engaged in the active discharge of this momentous and responsible trust. That body came promptly to his aid, and while supplying him with treasure and arms to an extent that would previously have been considered fabulous, they, at the same time, with almost absolute unanimity declared "that this war is not waged on their part in any spirit of oppression, nor for any purpose of conquest or subjugation, nor purpose of overthrowing or interfering with the rights or established institutions of these States, but to defend and maintain the supremacy of the Constitution and to preserve the Union with all the dignity, equality and rights of the several States unimpaired; and that as soon as these objects are accomplished, the war ought to cease." In this spirit and by such coöperation, has the President conducted this mighty contest, until, as Commander-in-chief of the Army, he has caused the national flag again to float undisputed over the capitol of our State. Meanwhile the State government has disappeared. The Executive has abdicated; the Legislature has dissolved; the Judiciary is in abeyance. The great ship of state, freighted with its precious cargo of human interests and human hopes, its sails all set, and its glorious old flag unfurled, has been suddenly abandoned by its officers and mutinous crew, and left to float at the mercy of the winds, and to be plundered by every rover upon the deep. Indeed the work of plunder has already commenced. The archives have been desecrated; the public property stolen and destroyed; the vaults of the State Bank violated, and its treasures robbed, including the funds carefully gathered and consecrated for all time to the instruction of our children.

In such a lamentable crisis, the Government of the United States could not be unmindful of its high constitutional obligations to guarantee to every State in this Union a republican form of government, an obligation which every State has a direct and immediate interest in having observed towards every other State; and from which, by no action on the part of the people in any State, can the Federal Government be absolved. A republican form of government, in consonance with the Constitution of the United States, is one of the fundamental conditions of our political existence, by which every part of the country is alike bound, and from which no part can escape. This obligation the national government is now attempting to discharge. I have been appointed, in the absence of the regular and established State authorities, as Military Governor for the time being, to preserve the public property of the State, to give the protection of law actively enforced to her citizens, and, as speedily as may be, to restore her government to the same condition as before the existing rebellion.

In this grateful but arduous undertaking, I shall avail myself of all the aid that may be afforded by my fellow-citizens. And for this purpose, I respectfully, but earnestly invite all the people of Tennessee, desirous or willing to see a restoration of her ancient government, without distinction of party-affiliations or past political opinions or action to unite with me, by counsel and coöperative agency, to accomplish this great end. I find most, if not all of the offices both States and Federal vacated either by actual abandonment, or by the action of the incumbents in attempting to subordinate their functions to a power in hostility to the fundamental law of the State, and subversive of her National allegiance. These offices must be filled temporarily, until the State shall be restored so far to its accustomed quiet, that the people can peaceably assemble at the ballot box and select agents of their own choice. Otherwise anarchy would prevail, and no man's life or property would be safe from the desperate and unprincipled.

I shall, therefore, as early as practicable, designate for various positions under the State and county governments, from among my fellow citizens, persons of probity and intelligence, and bearing true allegiance to the Constitution and Government of the United States, who will execute the functions of their respective offices, until their places can be filled by the action of the people. Their authority, when their appointments shall have been made, will be accordingly respected and observed.

To the people themselves, the protection of the Government is extended. All their rights will be duly respected, and their wrongs redressed when made known. Those who through the dark and weary night of the rebellion have maintained their allegiance to the Federal Government will be honored. The erring and misguided will be welcomed on their return. And while it may become necessary, in vindicating the violated majesty of the law, and in re-asserting its imperial sway, to punish intelligent and conscious treason in high places, no merely retaliatory or vindictive policy will be adopted. To those, especially, who in a private, unofficial capacity have assumed an attitude of hostility to the Government, a full and complete amnesty for all past acts and declarations is offered, upon the one condition of their again yielding themselves peaceful citizens to the just supremacy of the laws. This I advise them to do for their own good, and for the peace and welfare of our beloved State, endeared to me by the associations of long and active years, and by the enjoyment of her highest honors.

And appealing to my fellow-citizens of Tennessee, I point you to my long public life, as a pledge for the sincerity of my motives, and an earnest for the performance of my present and future duties.

ANDREW JOHNSON.

APPENDIX C

"For nearly three years, in the midst of dangers and difficulties the most complicated and perplexing, I have earnestly labored to restore the state to its former proud position in the Union. My constant effort has been to save it, not to destroy it; but the rebellious sentiment of the people often interposed obstacles which had to be overcome by military power. The task was painful, but the duty has been performed, and the result has passed into history. Time, I am happy to say, has greatly calmed the passions of the people, and experience restored them to reason. The folly of destroying their government and sacrificing their sons to gratify the mad ambition of political leaders needs no longer to be told to the laboring masses. The wasted estates, ruined and dilapidated farms, vacant seats around the hearthstone, prostrate business, and even life itself, everywhere proclaim it in language not to be misunderstood.

"But all is not lost. A new era dawns upon the people of Tennessee. They enter upon a career guided by reason, law, order, and reverence. The reign of brute force and personal violence has passed away forever. By their own solemn act at the ballot-box, the shackles have been formally stricken from the limbs of more than 275,000 slaves in the State. The unjust distinctions in society, fostered by an arrogant aristocracy, based upon human bondage, have been overthrown, and our whole social system reconstructed on the basis of honest industry and personal worth. Labor shall now receive its merited reward, and honesty, energy, and enterprise their just appreciation. Capital, heretofore timid and distrustful of success, may now confidently seek remunerative and profitable investments in the State. Public schools and colleges begin anew their work of instruction upon a broader and more enduring basis. The foundations of society, under the change in the constitution, are in harmony with the principles of free government and National Union; and if the people are true to themselves, true to the State, and loyal to the Federal Government, they will rapidly overcome the calamities of the war, and raise the State to a power and grandeur not heretofore even anticipated. Many of its vast resources lie undiscovered, and it requires intelligent enterprise and free labor alone to develop them and clothe the State with a richness and beauty surpassed by none of her sisters."

BIBLIOGRAPHY

MANUSCRIPT COLLECTIONS OF SOURCES

Johnson Manuscripts, in the Library of Congress; covering the years 1831-1875. Purchased in 1904; 15,000 separate pieces in more than 225 bound volumes. A storehouse of events and opinions as presented by all classes. Johnson's rehabilitation is no doubt due to this unexpurgated collection. Consult the Report of the Librarian of Congress for the year ending June 30, 1904, for further information.
——In the Library of the Pennsylvania Historical Society.
——In the Hall of History, Raleigh, N. C. These include material relating to Johnson's parentage, early years, and apprenticeship.
——In the Library of The Tennessee Historical Society and in the Carnegie Library at Nashville.
——A private collection of Andrew Johnson Patterson at Greeneville, Tenn., consisting of old scrap books, clippings, newspaper files, and personal memoranda relating to politics.
Black, J. S., Manuscripts; in the Library of Congress. Deal largely with the Impeachment and the Crédit Mobilier affair.
Chase, S. P., Diaries and Correspondence; in the Library of Congress, 141 bound volumes.
Holt, Joseph, Manuscripts; in the Library of Congress. These relate to the trial of Mrs. Surratt and the labors of Judge Advocate Holt.
Nelson, T. A. R., Manuscripts; in the Lawson McGhee Library, Knoxville, Tenn.
Sumner, Charles, Manuscripts; in the Library of Harvard University.
Young, John Russell, Manuscripts; in the Library of Congress.

PRINTED COLLECTIONS OF SOURCES

American Annual Cyclopedia. N. Y. 1861-1875. Important public events, not otherwise available for the ordinary reader, recorded.
Fleming, W. L. *Documentary History of Reconstruction.* New Haven, Conn. 1907. A useful publication.

Hart, A. B. *American History Told by Contemporaries.* N. Y.
    1897-1901. Contains numerous excerpts from public and
    private papers, throwing light on this period.
MacDonald, William. *Documentary Source Book of American
    History.* N. Y. 1912. Contains copious notes referring
    to Congressional proceedings and to Supreme Court de-
    cisions.
McPherson, Edward. *The Political History of the United States
    During Reconstruction.* Wash. 1875. A reprint of Mc-
    Pherson's Political Manuals from 1866 to 1870.
Moore, Frank. *Rebellion Record.* N. Y. 1861-1868. 11 vols.
Political Textbook for 1860. N. Y. 1860.
Stanwood, Edward. *A History of the Presidency.* Bost. 1898.
    Contains party platforms and popular and electoral vote.

PUBLIC DOCUMENTS

Congressional Globe, after March 4, 1873, Congressional Record.
    Congressman Johnson's record in the 28th, 29th, 30th, 31st
    and 32nd Congresses (1843-1853), and Senator Johnson's
    in the 35th, 36th, and 37th Congresses (1857-1862), and in
    the 40th Congress (1875), are here set out.
Executive Documents, Reports of Committees, and *Miscellaneous
    Documents of Senate and House.* In the order named, these
    contain information submitted to the houses by the Presi-
    dent, the reports made to the various committees, and a
    wide range of matters investigated, including testimony
    taken by investigating committees on the affairs of the South
    and on President Johnson's management of the government.
Richardson, J. W. *Messages and Papers of the Presidents.*
    House Miscellaneous Documents, 53rd Congress, 22nd Sess.
    210. Wash. 1897. The messages, proclamations, and ex-
    ecutive orders of Johnson and Grant are here compiled.
Trial of Andrew Johnson, President of the United States. Wash.
    Government Printing Office. 1868.
Supreme Court Reports of the United States. Our period is
    covered by the reports from the 3rd Wallace to 4th Otto,
    inclusive; or, according to numbers, from the 60th volume
    of the reports to the 94th. Myers vs. United States, U. S. R.
    272, 52 (decided in 1926) is the most important case in
    our study of the impeachment and trial of the President.
Tennessee Senate Journals and House Journals. Sessions
    1835-36, 1839-40, 1841-42, 1853-54, 1855-56. While John-
    son was Military Governor in 1862, 1863, and 1864, there
    was no Union Legislature in Tennessee.

United States Statutes at Large, XIV to XIX, and the abridgement, *Revised Statutes of the United States* (2nd ed. 1878). These laws and the public documents connected with them are indispensable to an understanding of Johnson's administration.

United States War Department. *Rebellion Records of the Union and Confederate Armies*. Wash. 1880-1901.

CONTEMPORARY PAMPHLETS AND NEWSPAPERS

Pamphlets: Addresses, National Johnson Club, Documents 1 and 2, 1866.

An Account of a Mass Meeting of the Citizens of New York approving Johnson's policy. 1866.

Andrew, John A. Address to the Massachusetts Legislature, 1866.

Beecher, H. W. Two Letters on Reconstruction, 1866.

Comitatus, Zedekiah. Reconstruction on My Policy. 1866.

Crosby, A. Phi Beta Kappa Address at Dartmouth, 1865.

Curtis, G. W. Ad Interim and Ad Outerim. 1868.

Forney, J. W. Biographical Sketch of Andrew Johnson. 1864.

Gasparin, Count de. Loyal Publication Society, No. 87. 1865.

Hallett, B. F. A Speech before the Baltimore Convention. 1860.

Holt, Joseph. Vindication. 1872; Reply, 1873; and Johnson's Reply to Holt's Vindication in Washington newspapers of Sept. 8, 1872. A vast quantity of material on the Surratt trial is in the Library of Congress.

Ingersoll, E. C. Reconstruction and Andrew Johnson. 1866.

Johnson, Andrew. Letter to Constituents, October 15, 1845.

——Inaugural Addresses, 1853-55. In the Public Library at Nashville, Tenn.

——Address to the Tennessee Agricultural Society. Nashville, 1875.

——Address on the Political Issues. Nashville, 1859.

McCutcheon, E. Swinging Round the Circle. 1868.

National Union Convention at Philadelphia. 1866.

"Old Andy," "My Policy," "Saint Andy, the Apostate," "R. I. P.: Hic Jacet Impeachment, Requiescat in Pace," "George Washington's Lost Birthday," and other ridiculous pamphlets are in the Library of Congress.

Poole, John. A Political Address. March, 1867.

Schieffelin, S. B. The President and Congress. 1867.

Sumner, Charles. The One Man Power vs. Congress. Oct. 1866.

The Great Impeachment Trial, a popular account. 1866.

The Tailor Boy. 1865.

Newspapers: Jonesboro Whig, later *Knoxville Whig*, W. G.
  Brownlow, editor. Opposed Johnson from 1843 to Dec.
  1860. Congress has just acquired the *Jonesboro Whig*
  from May 6, 1840, to April 19, 1849 (9 vols.), and the
  Knoxville Whig from 1849 to 1862.
Memphis Daily Eagle, Whig, also assailed him. See issues of
  July 13 and 22, 1853.
Republican Banner, Whig, likewise opposed Johnson (Oct. 10,
  1853). The campaigns of 1853, 1855, 1857, and 1859, conducted in June, July, and the early part of August, largely
  centered around Governor Johnson and his anti-Southern,
  plebeian, and labor record.
The *True Whig*, also assailed Johnson. See July 7, 8, 20, 1853.
Nashville Union and American, Democrat, sustained Johnson's
  policies (April 29 and May 5, 1853). In 1860 when Johnson threw in his fortunes with the Union, the Democratic
  papers of Tennessee and the South deserted him, and the
  Whig papers endorsed him. When the Civil War began,
  the press of Tennessee and the South, both Whig and Democrat, assailed him.
National Intelligencer, Washington, was President Johnson's
  organ.
Philadelphia Press, J. W. Forney, editor, was favorable to Johnson until the spring or summer of 1865, when it opposed him.
The *Ledger* was also in opposition.
Henry J. Raymond, Editor of the *New York Times*, advocated
  Johnson's reconstruction policy and thereby lost ground to
  Horace Greeley's *Tribune*. The *Evening Post* was friendly
  at first, but was afterwards hostile. The *Herald* stood by
  the President until he went down in defeat. The *World*,
  charged with being a "copperhead," denounced Johnson till
  the summer of 1865, when it embarrassed him by its support.
  The *Nation*, E. L. Godkin, was critical of President Johnson
  almost from the first, and so was *Harper's Weekly*, edited
  by George W. Curtis. Godkin, Curtis, and Theodore Tilton
  of the Washington *Independent* used their influence to nullify Johnson's policy. Thomas Nast in *Harper's Weekly*
  caricatured him without mercy. In 1866 and 1867 James
  Russell Lowell, in the the *North American Review*, by ridicule, sought to make Johnson obnoxious.
The *Tribune*, the *Springfield Republican*, and many other papers
  deserted the Republicans, organized a new party, and supported Horace Greeley for the Presidency in 1872. On
  Sept. 8, 1872, the *American*, of Nashville, gave an account
  of Johnson's connection with the execution of Mrs. Surratt.

In the spring of 1875, Johnson was elected to the Senate; in July, he died; in 1877, his monument was unveiled; and in 1922, the tailor shop was purchased by the state; at these times the newspapers of Memphis, Nashville, Knoxville, and Greeneville carried columns about the runaway apprentice boy, the mechanic governor, and the tailor president. The Greeneville *Intelligencer,* at the time of Johnson's death was edited by his son, Andrew. It collected many personal incidents. (The *Intelligencer* file is in the Patterson collection.)

DIARIES, MEMOIRS, AND REMINISCENCES

Andrews, Sidney. *South Since the War.* Bost. 1866.

Blaine, J. G. *Twenty Years of Congress.* Norwich, Conn. 1886. Interesting, but untrustworthy.

Boutwell, G. S. *Reminiscences of Sixty Years in Public Affairs.* N. Y. 1902. A partisan publication.

Brownlow, W. G. *Parson Brownlow's Book.* Phila. 1862.

Butler, B. F. *Ben Butler's Book.* Bost. 1892.

——*Private and Official Correspondence.* Norwood, Mass. 1917.

Clingman, T. L. *Speeches and Writings.* Raleigh. 1877.

Cox, S. S. *Three Decades of Federal Legislation.* Providence. 1885. A plea for the Democratic Party.

Craven, J. J. *Prison Life of Jefferson Davis.* N. Y. 1905.

Crooke, W. H. *Through Five Administrations.* N. Y. 1910.

Grant, U. S. *Personal Memoirs.* N. Y. 1885.

Halstead, Murat. *Caucuses of 1860.* 1860.

Julian, George W. *Political Recollections.* Chicago. 1884.

Lamon, W. H. *Recollections of Abraham Lincoln.* Wash. 1911.

Locke, D. R. (Petroleum V. Nasby) *Ekkoes from Kentucky: A Perfect Reminder uv the Dimocricy Doorin the Eventful Year 1867.* Bost. 1899.

——*Swinging Round the Circle.* N. Y. 1866.

McCulloch, Hugh. *Men and Measures of Half a Century.* N. Y. 1889.

Morgan, J. M. *Recollections of a Rebel Reefer.* Bost. 1917.

Olmsted, F. L. *A Journey to the Seaboard Slave States.* N. Y. 1857.

Polk, J. K. *Diary.* Chicago. 1910.

Poore, Ben Perley. *Perley's Reminiscences.* Phila. 1866.

Russell, W. H. *My Diary North and South.* Bost. 1863.

Schofield, J. McA. *Forty-six Years in the Army.* N. Y. 1897.

Schurz, Carl. *Reminiscences.* N. Y. 1908.

Seward, Fred W. *Autobiography of W. H. Seward*, with Memoir. N. Y. 1877.

Sheridan, P. H. *Personal Memoirs.* N. Y. 1888. A soldier's bluff record.

Sherman, John. *Recollections of Forty Years.* N. Y. 1895. Interesting and generally impartial.

Sherman, W. T. *Memoirs.* N. Y. 1891.

Stephens, A. H. *Recollections* and Diary. N. Y. 1910.

Stewart, W. A. *Reminiscences.* N. Y. 1908. Unreliable.

Watterson, Henry. "*Marse Henry.*" N. Y. 1919.

Welles, Gideon. *Diary.* Bost. 1911. Though biased in the President's favor, the most valuable single publication in a study of Andrew Johnson. 3 vols.

White, A. D. *Autobiography.* N. Y. 1907.

Wise, J. S. *Recollections of Thirteen Presidents.* N. Y. 1906.

ARTICLES IN PERIODICALS

Early Love Affair. (G. Rouquie) *Nat. Mag.* (Bost.), 6:63.

Personal Incidents. (H. S. Turner) *Harper's*, 120:168; (W. H. Crook) *Century*, 76:653, 863; (E. V. Smalley) *Indep.*, 52:2152; (J. M. Scovel) *Nat. Mag.* (Bost.), 18:111; (C. K. Tuckerman) *M. Am. H.*, XX:41; (B. C. Truman) *Century*, 85:435; (M. Gardner) *Norm. Instr. and Prim. Plans*, 32:48; (W. M. Stewart) *Saturday Evening Post*, about 1908 (vide *Stewart's Reminiscences*, supra, p. 195); (Carl Schurz) *McClure's*, 29:494; (George Creel) *Collier's*, 78:23; (C. Nettles) *So. Atl. Quart.*, 25:55. The foregoing are popular and generally sensational. Some are not without error. Cf. (W. G. Brownlow) *Taylor-Trotwood Magazine*, Sept., 1908; (R. M. Barton) *Memphis Com. Appeal*, Nov., 1926; (J. H. Malone) *Current Hist.*, 26:7; (J. Chambers) *Harper's Weekly*, 48:1356; (W. E. Horner) *Carolina Mag.*, 51:17; (W. G. Moore) "Notes," *Am. Hist. Rev.*, XIX:103.

The Homestead. (T. J. Middleton) *Sewanee Review*, 15:316; (St. George L. Sioussat) *Miss. Val. Hist. Rev.* 5, No. 3:253. This article is of great historical value.

Execution of Mrs. Surratt. (Joseph Holt) *No. Am. Rev.*, July, 1888, and April, 1890.

Impeachment. (E. I. Sears) *Indep.*, 117:545; *Nat. Quar.*, 16:373; 17:144; (E. L. Godkin) *Nation*, 3:310; 4:170; 175, 214; 6:184, 404; (W. F. Allen) *Nation*, 6:490; F. A. Burr) *Lippincott's*, 63:512; (G. S. Boutwell) *McClure's*, 14:171; (E. G. Ross) *Forum*, 19:595; (E. G. Ross) *Scrib-*

ner's, 11:519; (F. T. Hill) *Harper's,* 113:827; (Carl
Schurz) *McClure's,* 31:145; (D. M. DeWitt) *Indep.*
55:1812; (DeWitt's magazine articles are now in book form,
supra); (W. W. Boyce) *DeBow,* 1:16; (G. F. Edmunds)
Cent., 85:863; (D. Y. Thomas) *Am. Hist. Rev.,* 9:188
(very interesting); (L. H. Gipson) *Miss. Val. Hist. Rev.,*
2:263; (W. C. Wilkinson) *Indep.,* 63:146; Specially (W. A.
Dunning) in *Am. Hist. Assn. Papers,* Vol. IV, Pt. 4, p. 469.
N. Y. 1890.

Charges of Plagiarism, Bombast, etc. (J. R. Lowell) *N. Am.
Rev.,* 102:530 (Cf. Parrington, V. L., *Main Currents,* vol. 2,
pp. 460-470, N. Y., 1927, for criticism of Lowell); (E. L.
Godkin) *Nation,* 82:91; (W. A. Dunning) *Am. Hist. Rev.*
XI, No. 3:574. *Contra:* (C. R. Fish) *Am. Hist. Rev.,*
11:951; (M. D. Conway) *Fortn. Rev.,* 5:98; and specially
(C. Aldrich) *M. Am. Hist.,* 25:47.

Defense of Johnson. (D. M. DeWitt) *Pub. So. Hist. Asso.,*
8:437; 9:1, 71, 151, 213; (James Schouler) *Bookman,*
34:498; *Outlook,* 82:69, 266; (Gaillard Hunt) *Cent.,*
85:421; (Gideon Welles) *Atl.,* 105:697, 815; 106:78, 238,
388, 537, 680, 818; (George Baber) *N. Am. Rev.,* 145:69;
(J. M. Schofield) *Cent.,* 32:576; (John B. Henderson)
Cent., 85:199; and specially the three following: (St.
George L. Sioussat) *An. Report of Am. Hist. Asso.,* 1914,
vol. i, 245; (J. G. deRoulhac Hamilton) *Proc. State Lit. and
Hist. Asso. of N. C.,* 1915:65; and *Dearborn Independent,*
Feb. and Mch., 1927; (M. S. Gerry) *Cent.,* Nov. and Dec.,
1927.

Policy of Andrew Johnson. (E. P. Whipple) *Atl.,* 18:375; (C.
Mackay) *Fortn. Rev.,* 4:477; *New England,* 25:711;
Frazer, 75:243; *Nation,* 2:422; (C. E. Norton) *N. Am.
Rev.,* 102:250; (W. G. Moore) *Am. Hist. Rev.,* 19:98; (G.
S. Boutwell) *N. Am. Rev.,* 141:570 (a fierce attack); (L.
H. Gipson) *Miss. Val. Hist. Rev.,* 2:363; (C. Nettles) *So.
Atl. Quar.,* 25:55; (B. J. Ramage) *So. Atl. Quar.,* 1:2;
(M. H. Albjerg) *So. Atl. Quar.,* Oct., 1927.

BIOGRAPHIES AND BIOGRAPHICAL SKETCHES OF JOHNSON

Bacon, George W. *Life and Speeches of Andrew Johnson.* London. 1865. An Englishman's concise estimate, together
with Johnson's earlier speeches.

Cowan, Frank. *Andrew Johnson; Reminiscences of His Private
Life and Character.* Greensburg, Pa. 1894. An account of
President Johnson's life in the White House by an official.

Foster, Lillian. *Andrew Johnson, President of the United States.*
N. Y. 1866. Introductory chapter of some fifty pages with
speeches and addresses.

Hall, Clifton R. *Andrew Johnson, Military Governor of Tennessee.* Princeton. 1916. An interesting and accurate
account of Military Governor Johnson's record.

Jones, J. S. *Life of Andrew Johnson.* Greeneville, Tenn. 1901.
The only *Life* since Johnson was President, poorly written
by an unpracticed hand.

Life and Character of Andrew Johnson, Memorial Addresses.
Wash. 1876.

Life, Speeches, and Services of Andrew Johnson. Phila. 1865.
This anonymous publication appeared when Johnson was a
popular favorite.

Moore, Frank. *Life and Speeches of Andrew Johnson.* Bost.
1865. The introductory chapter is useful and the addresses
well selected.

Rayner, Kenneth. *Life and Times of Andrew Johnson.* N. Y.
1866. The bombastic and laudatory work of a Southern
Union Whig.

Savage, John. *Life and Public Services of Andrew Johnson.*
N. Y. 1866. Partial and lacking in historical value;
serviceable, however, because the author conferred with the
President.

BIOGRAPHICAL SKETCHES

Appleton's Cyclopedia, III: 436, article "Andrew Johnson," illustrated.

Ashe, S. A. *Biographical History of North Carolina,* article
"Andrew Johnson," IV: 228. Greensboro, N. C. 1895:
Ashe is a North Carolina historian.

Battle, K. P. *The Early History of Raleigh.* Raleigh, N. C.
1893. Battle was President of the University of North
Carolina.

Battle, R. H. *Library of Southern Literature,* VI: 2719. New
Orleans, 1907. R. H. Battle was President of the North
Carolina Literary and Historical Association.

Clark, Champ. Richardson's *Messages and Papers of the Presidents.* Introductory chapter, "Andrew Johnson."

New International Encyclopedia, "Andrew Johnson," XII: 736.

Sioussat, George St. L. "Andrew Johnson and Early Phases of
the Homestead." *Miss. Val. Hist. Rev.,* V. No. 3: 253. An
excellent study by a practiced hand, covering much of Johnson's career, besides his homestead record.

Swain, D. L. "Early Times in Raleigh," and "A Memorial Address on Jacob Johnson," Raleigh, N. C. 1867. Swain's addresses are by a contemporary of Johnson and furnish the best understanding of the lad before leaving North Carolina and of his father, Jacob Johnson. Swain was President of the University and also an antiquarian.

The National Cyclopedia of American Biography. II, 454. "Andrew Johnson." This article (1921) is fair and discriminating, as are nearly all modern estimates of Johnson. Cf. *Enc. Brit.*, *Enc. Amer.*, and *Studies in History, Economics, and Public Law*, edited by the faculty of Political Science of Columbia University covering the reconstruction period.

Wheeler, J. H. *Reminiscences.* Columbus, O. 1884.

GENERAL BIOGRAPHICAL AND HISTORICAL WORKS

Barnes, W. H. *History of the Thirty-ninth Congress.* N. Y. 1868.

Beard, C. A. and M. R. *The Rise of American Civilization.* N. Y. 1927.

Bowers, Claude G. *The Party Battles of the Jackson Period.* Bost. 1925.

Burgess, John W. *Reconstruction and the Constitution.* N. Y. 1902.

Chadsey, C. E. *The Struggle between President Johnson and Congress over Reconstruction.* N. Y. 1896.

Cole, A. C. *Whig Party in the South.* Wash. 1913.

Curtis, W. E. *Life of Zachariah Chandler.* N. Y. 1879.

Davis, Jefferson. *The Rise and Fall of the Confederate Government.* N. Y. 1881. Controversial and disappointing.

DeWitt, David Miller. *Impeachment and Trial of Andrew Johnson.* N. Y. 1903. Despite its restricted title, deals interestingly and dramatically with many other phases of Johnson's life.

——*The Assassination of Abraham Lincoln and Its Expiation.* N. Y. 1909.

Dodd, W. E. *The Cotton Kingdom.* New Haven, 1921.

Dunning, W. A. *Reconstruction: Political and Economic.* N. Y. 1907.

——*Essays on the Civil War and Reconstruction.* N. Y. 1908. Dunning is favorable to Johnson, though often critical and semi-humorous.

Fertig, J. W. *The Secession and Reconstruction of Tennessee.* Chicago. 1898.

Fessenden, Francis. *Life and Public Service of William Pitt Fessenden.* Bost. 1907.

Flack, H. E. *Adoption of the Fourteenth Amendment.* Balt. 1908.

Ficklen, J. R. *History of Reconstruction in Louisiana.* Balt. 1910.

Fleming, W. L. *Reconstruction of the Seceded States.* Albany. 1905.

——*The Sequel of Appomattox.* New Haven. 1919. Professor Fleming's works are of high value.

Foulke, W. D. *Life and Public Service of Oliver P. Morton.* Indianapolis, 1899.

Garner, J. W. *Reconstruction in Mississippi.* N. Y. 1901.

Garrett, W. R. and Goodpasture, A. V. *History of Tennessee.* Nashville. 1900.

Gorham, G. C. *Life and Public Services of Edwin M. Stanton.* Bost. 1899.

Greeley, Horace. *The American Conflict.* Hartford. 1866.

Guild, Jo. C. *Old Times in Tennessee.* Nashville. 1878.

Hale, W. T., and Merritt, D. L. *Hist. of Tenn.* Nashville. 1913.

Hamilton, J. G. deR. *Reconstruction in North Carolina.* N. Y. 1914.

Hamlin, C. E. *Life and Times of Hannibal Hamlin.* Cambridge. 1898.

Hart, A. B. *Salmon Portland Chase.* Bost. 1899.

Helper, H. R. *The Impending Crisis.* N. Y. 1857. An epoch-making book, more statistical and political than historical.

Herbert, H. A. *Why the Solid South?* Balt. 1890. A partisan, but graphic, picture of reconstruction days.

Hill, F. T. *Decisive Battles of the Law.* "The Impeachment of Andrew Johnson, a Historical Moot Court." N. Y. 1917.

Hodgson, J. *The Cradle of the Confederacy.* Mobile. 1876.

Hollister, O. J. *Life of Schuyler Colfax.* N. Y. 1887.

Holst, Hermann E. von. *Constitutional History of the United States.* Chicago. 1876.

Hosmer, J. K. *The Outcome of the Civil War.* N. Y. 1907.

Howe, D. W. *Political History of Secession.* N. Y. 1914.

Humes, T. W. *Loyal Mountaineers of Tennessee.* Knoxville, 1888.

Ingle, Edward. *Southern Side Lights.* Bost. 1896.

Kendrick, B. B. *The Journal of the Joint Committee of Fifteen on Reconstruction.* N. Y. 1914.

Lamon, Ward H. *Recollections of Abraham Lincoln.* Wash. 1911.

Linn, W. A. *Horace Greeley.* N. Y. 1903.

Logan, J. A. *The Great Conspiracy.* N. Y. 1886. A partisan plea.

Mason, E. C. *The Veto Power.* Bost. 1891.

McCarthy, C. H. *Lincoln's Plan of Reconstruction.* N. Y. 1901.

McClure, A. K. *Abraham Lincoln and Men of War Times.* 3rd ed. Phila. 1892.

McDonald, William. *Jacksonian Democracy.* N. Y. 1906.

McGee, G. R. *A History of Tennessee.* Bost. 1900. Elementary but useful.

Moore, John Trotwood, and Foster, A. P. *Tennessee.* Chicago. 1923.

Nicolay, J. J., and Hay, John. *Abraham Lincoln.* N. Y. 1890.

Oberholtzer, E. P. *A History of the United States Since the Civil War.* N. Y. 1917. Copious footnotes.

Payne, A. B. *Thomas Nast, His Period and His Pictures.* N. Y. 1904.

Pierce, E. L. *Memoir and Letters of Charles Sumner.* Bost. 1894.

Pierce, P. S. *The Freedman's Bureau.* Iowa City. 1904.

Pike, J. S. *The Prostrate State.* N. Y. 1874.

Proudfit, S. V. *Public Land System of the United States.* Wash. 1923

Reeve, F. A. *East Tennessee and the War of the Rebellion.* 1902.

Riddle, A. G. *Life of Benjamin F. Wade.* Cleveland. 1888.

Rhodes, James Ford. *History of the United States and the Compromise of 1850.* N. Y. 1893. Footnote references are excellent.

Robertson, W. J. *The Changing South.* N. Y. 1927.

Schouler, James. *History of the Reconstruction Period.* (In History of the United States, Vol. 7.) N. Y. 1913. Schouler is Johnson's defender and has delved into the Johnson manuscripts.

Seward, F. W. *Story of the Life of W. H. Seward.* N. Y. 1891.

Singleton, Esther. *The Story of the White House.* N. Y. 1907.

Smith, T. C. *Life and Letters of James Abram Garfield.* New Haven. 1925.

Stephens, A. H. *War between the States.* Wash. 1867. Partisan and prolix. (*Reviewers Reviewed,* N. Y., 1872, is a supplement.)

Stephenson, G. M. *Political History of the Public Lands from 1840 to 1862.* Bost. 1917.

Stoddard, W. O. *Lincoln and Johnson.* N. Y. 1888.

Storey, Moorfield. *Charles Sumner.* Boston. 1900.

Stovall, P. A. *Robert Toombs.* N. Y. 1892.

Tarbell, Ida. *The Life of Abraham Lincoln.* N. Y. 1917.

Temple, O. P. *East Tennessee and the Civil War.* Cincin. 1899.

——*Notable Men of Tennessee.* N. Y. 1912.

Warren, Charles. *Supreme Court in United States History.* Bost. 1925.

Weed, Thurlow. *Life.* Bost. 1884.

White, Horace. *Life of Lyman Trumbull.* Bost. 1913.

Wilson, Henry. *History of the Rise and Fall of the Slave Power.* Bost. 1872.

Wilson, Woodrow. *Division and Reunion.* N. Y. 1893.

Woodburn, J. A. *The Life of Thaddeus Stephens.* Indianapolis. 1913.

INDEX